CADOGAN
GUIDES

S0-BDA-478

GERMANY

Cadogan Books plc
Letts House, Parkgate Road, London SW11 4NQ

The Globe Pequot Press
6 Business Park Road, PO Box 833, Old Saybrook, Connecticut 06475–0833

Copyright © Rolt Bolt 1994
Illustrations © Brian Hoskin 1994

Book design by Animage
Cover design by Ralph King
Cover illustration by Povl Webb
Maps © Cadogan Guides, drawn by Thames Cartographic Ltd

Proof Reading: Chris Schüler and Geraldine Beattie
Indexing: Ann Hall
Production: Book Production Services
Mac Help: Jacqueline Lewin

Editing: Rachel Fielding, Antony Mason and Chris Schüler
Series Editors: Rachel Fielding and Vicki Ingle

A catalogue record for this book is available from the British Library
ISBN 0–947754–520

Library of Congress Cataloging-in-Publication-Data
Bolt, Rod
    Germany/ Rod Bolt.   p. cm. -- (Cadogan guides)
    "A Voyager book."
    ISBN 1–56440–179-0
    1. Germany--Guidebooks.   I. Title. II. Series.
    DD16.B65 1993
    914.304 879--dc20   93--11605
                                    CIP

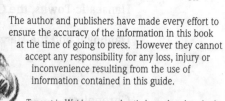

The author and publishers have made every effort to ensure the accuracy of the information in this book at the time of going to press. However they cannot accept any responsibility for any loss, injury or inconvenience resulting from the use of information contained in this guide.

Typeset in Weidemann and entirely produced on Apple Macintosh with Quark XPress, Photoshop, Freehand and Word software.

Printed and bound in Great Britain by Staples Printers Rochester Ltd, Rochester, Kent on Selkirk Opaque supplied by McNaughton Publishing Papers Ltd. CRC by Cooling Brown.

Acknowledgements

I would like to thank the many tourist offices whose advice was a great help in writing this book—some of them offering assistance and hospitality way beyond the call of duty. Particular thanks go to Claudio Montani Adams for taking me under his wing. I am also indebted to German Rail, Scandinavian Seaways, Queens Hotels and the Kempinski Hotel group for their assistance with the project. Jutta Gräbner of the Bremen Tourist Office was especially helpful and supportive, and my very deepest gratitude goes to her and her family for their friendship and extended hospitality.

Heartfelt thanks, too, to my editors Antony Mason and Rachel Fielding for their good cheer, understanding and support, and for welcome advice. Vicki Ingle and the staff at Cadogan were also a great help in times of need. An enormous thankyou goes to Jacqueline Lewin for her DTP skills, and for keeping an eagle eye on the corrections.

This book has been a massive undertaking that could never have been completed without the loving support (and, in some instances, financial intervention) of my friends. Special thanks go to my parents, Les and June Bolt, and to my aunt Muriel Bydawel, Jo Beall, Lorna Marshall, Silvie Brauns and Anna Arthur. Without the practical help and nurturing care of Annelies Basie and Iris Korfker, I—and the book—would never have made it through the final stages. Thanks also to Steve Caldicott, David Hines and Frank Oorthuys for fishing me out of sticky situations, to Patrick Beerepoot for still being there, to Jörn Langrehr for refuge in Berlin and to Henner Harders and Ursula Wächter for helping to keep me sane in Bremen.

One last nod of respect to Roula, the ancient van that was home and wheels for over 20,000km and who has not yet wheezed her last—and to the honest mechanics and men from the ADAC who rescued me along the way.

About the Author

Rodney Bolt grew up in Africa, was educated at Cambridge University where he read English, and now lives in Amsterdam. He has travelled throughout Europe and has lived and worked in Greece, the Netherlands and Germany. He also writes and directs for the stage, and for some years ran a London pub theatre. In 1992 he set off in a battered Volkswagen van on a two year-long journey through newly-united Germany to research this book.

Please help us to keep this guide up to date

We have done our best to ensure that the information in this guide is correct at the time of going to press, but places and facilities are constantly changing, and standards and prices in hotels and restaurants fluctuate. We would be delighted to receive comments concerning existing entries or omissions, as well as suggestions for new features. All contributors will be acknowledged in the next edition, and will receive a copy of the Cadogan Guide of their choice.

Contents

The Rhine: Cologne to Mainz   117–174

Frankfurt and the Mosel   175–232

Baden-Württemberg   233–306

Bavaria   307–424

Thuringia and Saxony 425–466

Berlin and the Spree 467–514

Hanseatic Towns, the Coasts and Islands 515–572

Hannover and the Harz Region 573–603

Directory 604–622

Chronology 623–624

Glossary and Language 625–632

Further Reading 633–634

Introduction

I confess, all travellers are not of alike Temper, some delight them-selves in Contemplation of the Curiosities of Arts, some are taken with the Varieties of Works of Nature, others speculate, with a kind of Reverence, the Decays and Ruins of Antiquity; others studiously inform themselves with the Transactions of Modern Times; others with the Government and Polity; others speculate the strange Customs and Fashions of the Places they pass through; to be short every one labours to entertain the Reader with those Objects and Rarities of Foreign Parts his Genius and Inclination is most affected with.

William Carr, British diplomat, 1691

The popular, stereotypical image of Germany obscures the astonishing variety this country has to offer. Whatever your Temper, and whatever most affects your Genius and Inclination, this guide is sure to reveal something that delights you. Nature offers the Alps, huge forests, Europe's mightiest rivers, limpid lakes, bird-rich fens and sandy, windswept islands. The Romans left behind some of the most impressive ruins outside of Italy. You'll also find dumpy Romanesque chapels, soaring Gothic cathedrals, unassailable stone castles, whole avenues of Baroque mansions, and fairytale villages of crooked, half-timbered houses. There are splendid palaces and scores of world-class museums—the legacy of myriad independent dukes and princelings of yore. You can watch good burghers prance about in medieval garb at touristy pageants, or raise your mug with the locals at authenti-cally raucous village beanos. Those who prefer to grapple with the Transactions of Modern Times, can go to cafés where barside philosophers sound forth on the pains and glories of reunification; or visit the sombre sites that recall Germany's heavy historical baggage.

1

The outsiders' image of a country full of fat men in *Lederhosen*, munching sausages and rocking their foaming tankards to the beat of an oompah band is one of the first to crumble when you actually arrive in Germany (unless you alight in southern Bavaria, where such things do go on). For a long time the French for 'Germany' was a plural word: *Les Allemagnes*: too many warring tribes, clashing styles and conflicting temperaments raged in these central European states to refer to the inhabitants as a single nation. Modern Germans can reel off a list of tribal traits: dour northerners; jovial Rhinelanders; coarse Bavarians; stingy, hard-working Swabians; stiff, obsessive Prussians. Clichés all, but each retaining that grain of truth that has made it a cliché. The atmosphere does change markedly as you journey through the country. Join strangers at a table in a Cologne café, and you'll be chatting away in no time. Do the same in Bremen and your overtures will be met with shocked discomfort. Jump on a train in a northern, Protestant town, prim and deathly quiet on a religious holiday, and head south to a Roman Catholic stronghold: there you'll find jolly festivities, gaudy processions and decorated Madonnas in wall-niches on the street.

The true borders in Germany are not the lines drawn between the states or *Länder* (often artificial boundaries created by politicians), but older frontiers beyond which loaves of bread change shape, wine replaces beer as the local tipple, or people greet each other with *Grüß Gott* rather than *Guten Tag*.

Guide to the Guide

Because cultural and geographical boundaries do not conform to the political ones, this guide is not divided into chapters devoted to each of the various *Länder*, but is structured around regions that have a common outlook or historical traditions, or which visitors are likely to tackle as a single piece. A trip down the most attractive stretch of the Rhine, for instance, takes you through three different *Länder*.

For convenience's sake the chapters follow a roughly circular path, working anti-clockwise from the northwest of the country, along the Rhine to the Alps in the south, then back through Bavaria and what was East Germany to the Baltic and North Sea Coasts, before dipping south again into the centre of the country.

In the flat, northwestern regions of the **Lower Rhineland** are Roman ruins, Emperor Charlemagne's magnificent capital of Aachen (Aix-la-Chapelle), and the infamous Ruhrgebiet—not entirely a hell-hole of dark satanic mills, but patched with green and offering first-class museums and the odd forgotten town of half-timbered houses.

To the south lies the **River Rhine** and Cologne, with its gigantic Gothic cathedral and scattering of Romanesque churches; the sleepy ex-capital of Bonn; and the most dramatic and castle-encrusted part of the Rhine, where the vines on the steep riverside slopes produce the famous wines and villages erupt in a year-round cycle of festivals.

Next we go to high-powered **Frankfurt** and more excellent museums, up through the gentle countryside of Hessen to Marburg, Germany's most atmospheric university town, and back east to the **River Mosel**. The route follows the tightly twisting river through the vineyards to Trier, where there are spectacular Roman ruins. Along the way there are diversions into the rolling countryside and castles of the Eifel.

The route through **Baden-Württemberg** runs parallel to the Rhine again, into the shady depths of the Black Forest, and covers the towns east of the river—Heidelberg, steeped in tradition and swarming with tourists; flashy, materialistic Stuttgart; Baden-Baden, which just manages to keep up its image as a genteel spa; Freiburg in the Black Forest, one of the most attractive cities in Germany; and the famously picturesque Lake Constance. The region can also boast stunning Baroque churches and the country's most subtle cuisine.

The first part of the section on **Bavaria** follows the route of the Romantic Road from the lively town of Würzburg in the heart of excellent winelands, past quaint medieval (though overcrowded) villages, to the fantasy castles of the dreamy King Ludwig II. Then it moves eastwards, through Alpine scenery to elegant, vibrant Munich. From here we move north to the Italianate cities of Regensburg and Passau on the Danube, into the less accessible (but delightful) regions of the East Bavarian Forest, and on to rather stuffy Bayreuth, home to the Wagner Festival.

Next come the gentle woodlands of **Thuringia** and a string of towns once hidden behind the Iron Curtain: Weimar, long-time home to Goethe and other luminaries and now Germany's cultural mecca; Leipzig, an underrated gem; and Dresden, with some of the most impressive art collections in the country. Close at hand are the bizarre rocky gorges of Saxon Switzerland, best viewed from a paddle steamer on the River Elbe.

The next section focusses almost entirely on **Berlin**, Germany's seamy, exciting and still very much divided capital; but it also takes in palaces at Potsdam and the curious, marshy regions of the Spreewald, where people punt about the forest in flat-bottomed boats.

The section on the **Hanseatic Towns and the northern coasts** begins with glitzy Hamburg and its more *gemütlich* neighbour, Bremen. It follows the shoreline, first through East Frisia with its sandy islands, then up into the lonely reaches of Schleswig-Holstein and back past the long beaches of the Baltic coast to the low-key brick architecture of the Hanseatic towns of Lübeck, Rostock and Stralsund, and the faded turn-of-the-century resorts on the island of Rügen. Inland lie the Mecklenburg lakes, not yet overrun with tourists, and the wide Lüneburg Heath populated by little else besides its wildlife and its heather-munching sheep.

Hannover and the Harz Mountains lie in the central region of northern Germany, stamping ground of the Grimm brothers and the old Welf monarch Henry the Lion. The Harz Mountains are really just stubby hills, but are dotted with villages that have escaped the ravages of industry, the Second World War and mass tourism.

Cities: Munich, Leipzig, Freiburg, Berlin.

Altstadt: Quedlinburg, Regensburg, Bamberg.

Student towns: Marburg.

Cathedrals: Paderborn, Cologne, Freiburg.

Roman ruins: Porta Nigra, amphitheatre and baths in Trier.

Castles: Burg Eltz; Neuschwanstein.

Palaces: Schloß Augustburg, Brühl; Residenz, Würzburg; Residenz, Munich.

Theatres: Cuvilliéstheater, Munich; Markgräfliches Opernhaus, Bayreuth.

Domestic architecture: Bremen.

Jugendstil: Darmstadt.

Musical instrument museums: Leipzig, Bruchsal.

Museum cafés: Museum für Kunst und Gewerbe, Hamburg; Karl Valentin Museum, Munich.

Stone carving: Statues by the Master of Naumberg, Naumberg cathedral.

Wood carving: Erasmus Grasser's Morris Dancers in the Munich Stadtmuseum; work by Tilman Riemenschneider in Würzburg and around Bavaria.

Scenery: Saxon Switzerland, Bavarian Alps, Rhine between Koblenz and Mainz.

Forest: East Bavarian Forest.

Lakes: Lower part of Lake Constance.

Island: Rügen.

Quiet beaches: Zingst Peninsula.

Luxury hotel: Vier Jahreszeiten Kempinski, Munich.

Local food: Bavaria, Franconia and Baden-Württemberg.

Rathaus: Bremen, Lüneburg.

Park: Englischer Garten, Munich; Nymphenburg Park, Munich; Burgerpark, Bremen.

Treasure: Grünes Gewölbe, Dresden.

Monastery: Maulbronn.

Markets: Viktualienmarkt, Munich; fleamarket, Frankfurt; daily market, Freiburg.

Christmas markets: Rothenburg ob der Tauber, Bremen, Düsseldorf, Nuremberg, Augsburg.

Pageants: *Drachenstich*, Furth in Wald.

Towns for Carnival: Rottweil, Mainz, Cologne.

Spa baths: Friedrichsbad, Baden-Baden; Stadtbad, Leipzig.

Travel

By Air

For travellers from outside mainland Europe, flying is often the most economical way to get to Germany. Flights from Britain are fast and frequent and sometimes cheaper than long, sticky train journeys. The presence of US military bases in Germany has meant that the country is well served by American airlines. Despite military cutbacks, Germany is still one of the cheapest of trans-Atlantic destinations. Australians and New Zealanders, however, may find that it makes more sense to fly to London and buy a further ticket to Germany.

Germany's main international airports are at Frankfurt (the largest), Munich, Berlin, Hamburg, Stuttgart and Düsseldorf. There are also flights to Britain and other European capitals from smaller cities.

From the UK and the Republic of Ireland

The lowest fares are usually to Düsseldorf or Frankfurt. A look through *Time Out* or the Sunday papers is sure to uncover something for under £100 return, on a scheduled flight. British Airways and Lufthansa both offer special deals in the £100 region provided you stay for five days, one of which must be a Saturday. Student and youth fares are unlikely to better any of the special deals you can find elsewhere. Berlin flights are the priciest of the lot—sometimes double the cost of a ticket to Frankfurt. If you intend to travel around Germany, then a flight to Frankfurt in conjunction with a rail pass is the best bet.

Fares from Dublin work out at nearly double those from London, so it may well be worthwhile crossing to the UK for a cheaper flight.

There are flights to Germany from Heathrow, Gatwick and Stanstead. (When comparing prices remember that trains to Gatwick and Stanstead add another £16 or so to the cost.) The chief regional airports with connections to Germany are Manchester and Birmingham.

> **British Airways**: 156 Regent St, London W1R 5TA, reservations ✆ (0345) 222 111.
> **Lufthansa**: 10 Old Bond St, London W1, ✆ (081) 750 350?.
> **German Travel Centre**: 8 Earlham St, London WC2, ✆ (071) 836 4444.
> Good air ticket bargains.
> **STA Travel**: 86 Old Brompton Rd, London SW7, ✆ (071) 938 4711.
> Specializes in student and youth travel.

From the US and Canada

By far the cheapest flights are on the New York–Frankfurt route. Off season you can pick up flights for under $400 return. Even in summer you can fly for around $500. Prices increase for flights from cities other than New York, but Delta offers off-season round-trips from any major US city to any of the main German airports for just on $500 (though prices more than double in season). West Coast fares—from Los Angeles or San Francisco to Frankfurt—are about the same as East Coast ones off-season, but rise a bit at peak periods. The best deals are available through seat consolidators (scour the Sunday papers), with APEX rates on the major carriers coming a sorry second. All US fares are subject to airport taxes and surcharges.

Canadians can expect APEX fares of around CDN$800 from Toronto or Montreal, and pushing on CDN$1000 from Vancouver. Budget options are limited; your most economical alternative may be to fly to London and pick up a cheap connection.

Air Canada: 26th floor, Place Air Canada, 500 Dorchester Blvd W, Montreal PQ H2Z 1X5, ✆ (0514) 879 7000.

British Airways: 530 Fifth Ave, New York, NY 10017, ✆ toll-free 800 247 9297; 1001 Bd de Maisonneuve O, Montreal, PQ H3A 3C8, ✆ toll-free 800 668 1059; 1 Dundas St W, Toronto, ON M5G 2B2, ✆ (426) 250 0880.

Delta Airlines: Hartsfield Atlanta International Airport, Atlanta, GA 30320, ✆ (404) 765 5000.

Lufthansa: 680 Fifth Ave, New York, NY 10017, ✆ 800 645 3880.

TWA: 100 South Bedford Rd, Mount Kisco, NY 10549, ✆ toll-free 800-892 4141.

Virgin Atlantic Airways: 96 Horton St, New York, NY 10014, ✆ toll-free 800-862 8621.

By Train

Travelling by train to Germany is time-consuming and (unless you're over 60 or under 26) usually more expensive than flying. Trains from London leave from Victoria Station (1hr 40min channel crossing to Ostend) or Liverpool Street Station (6½hr crossing to Hook of Holland). Total journey times: London–Berlin 20 hours, London–Cologne 9 hours.

The only **budget** option is the European Saver return/round trip fare (Hamburg £140, Cologne £86, Dortmund £92) which limits your stay to four days. Normal return tickets are valid for two months (Hamburg £172, Berlin £185, Cologne £108, Munich £180). Students, and people aged under 26 or over 60, qualify for various discount schemes (details from any British Rail station). A small surcharge of £21 will convert the ordinary Senior Citizen Railcard into a **Rail Europ Senior** card, which gives you 30 per cent discount on rail and sea travel throughout Western Europe. An **InterRail Pass** (£249), not valid in France, Spain, Italy, Switzerland or Belgium, gives free travel on the continent and half-price travel on British trains, as well as discounts on some channel crossings, to European residents under 26, for one month. The senior version of this pass offers the same deal to older travellers, minus the half-price British travel (£269). German Rail also offer travel passes (*see* p. 11) which will cut your costs substantially.

By Coach

Journeys to Germany by coach don't compare favourably with cheap air travel either. At best the trip will be long and uncomfortable, at worst nightmarish, with stops every few hours, just as you are finally getting off to sleep. The main carrier from London is National Express/Eurolines, 52 Grosvenor Gardens, London SW1 0AG, ✆ (071) 730 0202). Coaches leave two to five times a week for Berlin (26 hours, single £58, return £99), Frankfurt (18 hours, single £49, return £83), Munich (24 hours, single £60, return £99) and other major German cities. Discounts of around 10 per cent are available for travellers between the ages of 13 and 25.

By far the most pleasant way to arrive in Germany is on a Scandinavian Seaways overnight ferry from Harwich to Hamburg. You can while away the evening at the smorgasbord or in the bars, disco or casino, have a good night's sleep in a luxury cabin (at a price), then wake up to find yourself sailing gently up the Elbe past Hamburg's most luxurious villas. Prices start at £55 (one way), which includes the use of a couchette. Cabins cost £123. Add a further £58 if you want to take your car. Fares rise at weekends and at peak periods, but students get a whacking 50 per cent discount. If you are aiming to drive around southern Germany you will find it quicker to make a shorter ferry crossing to France or Belgium, and then to head for the border (*see* below).

Ferries plying the Channel from Dover, Folkestone or Ramsgate to Boulogne, Calais or Dunkerque in France or Ostend or Zeebrugge in Belgium—or from Harwich to the Hook of Holland—all deposit you within 2–3 hours' drive of the German border. From then on the journey (in Holland and Belgium at least) can proceed entirely by motorway. There is little difference in price between the main ferry operators, and your choice of destination will depend largely on where you are heading for in Germany. Crossings cost around £250 for a car and up to five people in high season, dropping to around £130 in low season. There are special prices for stays of less than 5 days.

British drivers using their own car need to take a valid driver's licence, insurance certificate (a Green Card is recommended), MOT and the vehicle's registration documents. You should fit small stickers that deflect the beam of your headlights. It is compulsory to carry a warning triangle in Germany, and your car (if British-registered) should have a GB label on the back. All of these accessories are available at British garages and motor shops.

> **Scandinavian Seaways**: Parkeston Quay, Harwich, Essex CO2 4QG, ✆ (0255) 241 234; 15 Hanover St, London W1, ✆ (071) 409 6060.
>
> **Sealink**: Charter House, Park St, Ashford, Kent TN24 8EX, ✆ (0233) 64707.
>
> **P&O**: Channel House, Channel View Rd, Dover, Kent CT17 9TJ, ✆ (0304) 203 388.
>
> **Sally Lines**: 81 Piccadilly, London W1V 0JH, ✆ (071) 409 2240.

Entry and Residence Requirements

European Community citizens, Americans, Canadians, Australians and New Zealanders do not need **visas** to visit Germany. A valid **passport** or British visitor's card will do. If you are arriving by road from another EC country you are likely to find border posts unstaffed, or (unless you appear deeply suspect) to be waved through without a second glance.

If you intend to stay for longer than 90 days, you should visit the local *Meldestelle* (registration office) to register your address (*see* p. 27).

Since the dissolution of internal borders in the EC there are no restrictions on the quantities of alcohol, tobacco and perfume that can be taken across EC borders, provided it has been bought duty-paid (i.e. not in a duty-free shop) for personal use only. You would have to have a good excuse—such as an imminent wedding reception—if you were found transporting a vanload of Liebfraumilch over the border.

American citizens may take up to 100 cigars and 200 cigarettes back into the USA. You may also take in one litre of alcoholic beverages. Most states restrict the import of alcohol and the laws of the state in which you arrive override Federal law—so it's worth checking up on this before you leave.

No currency restrictions are in operation. You can bring any amount of money into the country, and take as much as you want out.

Special Interest Holidays

From the UK

Andante Travels (cultural coach tours, staying in castles and historic inns), Grange Cottage, Winterbourne Dauntsey, Salisbury SP4 6ER, ✆ (0908) 610555.

Bent's Bicycle Tours (cycling and walking in Bavaria), The Priory, High Street, Redbourne, Herts AL3 7IZ, ✆ (0582) 7793768.

Groups International (wine tours of the Mosel), Little Felden House, Felden Lane, Hemel Hempstead, Herts HP3 0BB, ✆ (0422) 213213.

Inscape Fine Arts Tours (Berlin tours), Austins Farm, High Street, Stonesfield, Oxon OX8 9PU, ✆ (0993) 891726.

Major and Mrs Holt's Battlefield Tours (military history tours of the Rhine Crossing, Munich, Nuremberg and Berchtesgaden), 15 Market Street, Sandwich, Kent CT13 9DA, ✆ (0304) 612248.

Moswin Tours Ltd (wide range of independent and escorted holidays—themes include winter sports, cycling and rambling tours, language, music, history, aarchaeology, steam railways, river cruises, Christmas markets, wine and beer festivals), Moswin House, 21 Church Street, Oadby, Leicester LE2 5DB, ✆ (0533) 719922.

Martin Randall Travel (art, music and Christmas tours), 10 Barley Mow Passage, Chiswick, London W4 4PH, ✆ (081) 742 3355.

Travel for the Arts (opera and music tours, including Bayreuth Festival), 117 Regents Park Road, London NW1 8UR, ✆ (071) 483 4466.

From the Republic of Ireland

John Galligan Travel (castle holidays, Rhine cruises, Munich Oktoberfest), 29 Fitzwilliam Place, Dublin 2, ✆ (01) 619466.

From the USA

DER Tours (Christmas tours and Munich Oktoberfest), 11933 Wilshire Blvd, Los Angeles, CA 90025, ✆ (310) 479 41440.

Gerhard's Bicycle Odysseys (cycle tours), PO Box 757, Portland, OR 977207, ✆ (503) 223 2402.

KD Line (river cruises), 323 Geary Street, Suite 603, San Francisco, CA 94102–18860, ✆ (415) 392 8817.

Travcoa (medieval castles and towns), PO Box 2630, Newport Beach, CA 92658 2630, ✆ (714) 476 2800.

Viva Tours (Bayreuth), 12 Station Road, Bellport, NY 11713, ✆ (516) 286 2626.

For a complete list of US tour operators to Germany, contact **The German National Tourist Office**, 122 East 42nd Street, 52nd Floor, New York, NY 10168–0072, ✆ (212) 661 7200, fax 212 661 7174.

German Embassies Abroad

Australia: 119 Empire Circuit, Yarralumia AC, Canberra 2600, ✆ (062) 701 911.

Canada: PO Box 379, Post Station A, Ottawa, Ontario K1N 8V4, ✆ (0613) 232 1011.

Great Britain: 23 Belgrave Square, London SW1X 8PZ, ✆ (071) 235 5033.

Republic of Ireland: 31 Trimelston Avenue, Booterstown, Blackrock, Co. Dublin, ✆ (01) 693 011.

New Zealand: 90–92 Hobson St, Wellington, ✆ (04) 736 063.

USA: 4645 Reservoir Rd NW, Washington 20007, ✆ (0202) 298 4000.

Getting Around in Germany

By Train

Germany's eastern and western rail networks are now fully integrated, and **German Rail** (*Deustche Bahn*) can whizz you around the country—even to remote corners—with speed and awesome efficiency. Travel from west to east does, though, still involve slower trains, and more difficult connections.

The **InterCityExpress** (**ICE**, Germany's answer to France's TGV) shoots about at 250kph, while passengers recline in sleek, air-conditioned carriages. The main ICE line connects Hamburg to Frankfurt and Munich, and there is another via Würzburg and Nuremberg. Unless you are travelling on a German Rail Pass (*see* below) you will need to pay a surcharge for this speed and comfort. You also need to pay a supplement (DM9) for the next notch down, the **InterCity** (IC) and **EuroCity** (EC) (international) express trains. Unless you are in a real hurry, you'll find these just as good a means of city-hopping as ICE. For journeys between smaller centres there are the **InterRegio** trains, or you can meander about on the local D-Zug (normal service) or E-Zug (slow) trains.

Thomas Cook publish an indispensable **Timetable Summary** (£3), which you can buy from local agencies in Britain. (It comes free with a German Rail Pass.) Over weekends and during the holiday periods trains can get very crowded, and it is advisable to book a seat (for which there is a small extra fee). If you are travelling long distances overnight you can bite the bullet and sit the whole way, or share a couchette (4-berth, 6-berth, not sex-segregated), or lord it in a sleeper. Prices vary according to distance travelled, for example: Ostend–Munich 4-berth couchette £16.70, 6 berth £11.90, double sleeper £50.20, single sleeper £107.80.

Ticket (*Fahrkarte*) prices are based on the distance travelled, so a return journey is no cheaper than two singles. This does mean, however, that you can break your journey along the way. Tickets are valid for two months. Children under 4 travel free, those from 4–11 travel at half price.

If you are thinking of doing any amount of rail travel at all, it is worth considering a **Euro Domino Pass** (adult pass for 3 days £138, 5 days £154, 10 days £229; youth pass (under 26) for 3 days £103, 5 days £114, 10 days £171). These are available only to non-residents of Germany, and should be bought before you leave. (German Rail offices and some travel agents can supply you.) With a rail pass you can travel on everything from the humblest E-Zug to the ICE, without surcharge. It also allows you to travel up the Rhine and the Mosel on boats of the Köln-Düsseldorfer Line, on bus services run by German Rail (to places not served by trains and along tourist routes such as the Romantic Road) and on local **S-Bahn** (suburban railway) trains.

UK: German Rail Services Suite 4, The Sanctuary, 23 Oakhill Grove, Surbiton, Surrey KT6 6DU, ✆ (081) 390 0066.

USA: German Rail DER Tours Inc., 9501 W. Devon Avenue, Rosemont, LI 60018–4832, ✆ (708) 692 6300.

By Car

During the 1930s Germany built the world's first **motorways**. Today's Autobahn network is still one of the most extensive and best maintained on the continent, and there are no charges for using them. Regional roads ('B' roads) and country routes (in the west) are also impressive. There is no speed limit on open stretches of motorway and driving on them requires nerves of steel. If you do not have the mechnical means or the psychological mettle to overtake at supersonic speeds, then stick to the slow lane. Otherwise a giant Mercedes or BMW will bear down on you out of nowhere, lights flashing furiously, and travel within inches of your rear bumper until you get back to where you belong. On B roads outside of built-up areas there are **speed limits** of 80–100kph. In towns the limit is 50kph, and these rules are dutifully adhered to. (In some places in eastern Germany limits are set a little lower, and there are still some motorways with a 100kph limit.)

Motor travel in **eastern Germany** is no longer the bumpy and nerve-wracking experience it once was. Roads have been widened, surfaces are much improved and you no longer have to carry about spare cans of fuel because of the paucity of petrol stations. There is a price to pay for all of this. Construction is still very much in progress, so be prepared for tortuous detours. (Sometimes the road you want is simply closed, and you are left to work out your own alternative.) Most of the Federal budget has been funnelled into improving main routes, so if you opt for scenic country roads you are likely to be juddered to a jelly, or to end up creeping along behind an ancient, clapped-out piece of farm machinery. Even on main routes signposts are liable suddenly to dry up on you (especially if you are trying to follow a national road through the middle of a town); and though new petrol stations have sprouted all over the place, they are still nowhere near as thick on the ground as in the west, so you should not allow your tank to run too low. East Germany has gone car crazy since reunification, and the roads in many towns are simply not big enough to cope. Be prepared for frustrating traffic jams and parking difficulties.

If you have an **accident** in Germany you must wait until the police arrive. Failure to do this can result in prosecution. It is not enough simply to swap insurance details. If your car **breaks down**, then you should move it to the side of the road and place a warning triangle a few metres behind it. The German motoring organization, the **ADAC**, will give you free help (and sometimes even repair your car) if you break down on a main road. However, you will have to pay for parts and towing. You can call the ADAC on orange emergency telephones by asking for *Strassenwachthilfe*, or by telephoning direct on 19211. If you are a member of the AA or RAC in Britain you should make enquiries about reciprocal deals before you leave. If you take your car to a garage to be repaired, you are legally required to leave the registration documents with it.

In Germany you **drive on the right** and overtake on the left. As in Britain, cars already travelling around a roundabout have right of way. Be especially careful in cities with trams. **Trams** always have right of way, even crossing roundabouts or junctions. Often they travel up and down the centre of wide roads, but the stops are on the pavement, so tram-users have to cross the flow of traffic to reach the tram. When a tram stops in such places, cars are not allowed to overtake, and must leave access to the doors clear. Often there is a line on the street coincident with the back of the tram to show you where to stop, but sometimes there is no marking at all.

In many of the larger cities and historical resorts, the centre of town is closed to motor traffic. There are usually ample garages and **car parks** around the periphery. These are invariably well sign-posted, sometimes even with electronic signs telling you how many spaces are left. Park-and-Ride facilities (marked P+R) are usually further out, but with direct public transport connections to the centre. Parking here is cheaper, and may be free. Street parking is either metered or works on the 'pay and display' system (you put your money in a central machine and leave the ticket it prints out on the inside of your windscreen). Sometimes parking is free, but subject to a time limit. This is indicated by a blue P sign with a dial underneath. Here you should leave an indication on the dashboard of when you arrived (you can buy cardboard clocks that do this at petrol stations).

The major **car hire** firms—Avis, Budget and Herz—have branches all over Germany. It is cheaper to book a car in advance from an office in your home country than to rent it in Germany, though local firms may offer rates that undercut the big names.

Perhaps the cheapest way of all to get around Germany is by making use of the **Mitfahrzentralen**—lift agencies. For a small fee the agency will put you in touch with a motorist driving to your destination. After that all you pay is a contribution to the petrol costs. (This is also a way of cutting costs for the motorist.) Usually the *Mitfahrzentrale* recommends a price—a fraction of the cost of any other means of travel. Drivers have to leave their address and registration number at the *Mitfahrzentrale*, and you usually meet at the agency itself, so the system is quite safe.

By Bus

There is no national German bus network—there is little need for one with such an efficient rail service. German Rail itself runs buses to many areas not served by trains (train tickets and rail passes are valid on these routes). Otherwise local buses can be useful for visiting more out-of-the-way sights and travelling between villages. Such long distance coaches that do exist are usually privately run and aimed at the tourist market (such as the one from Frankfurt to Munich, which travels along the Romantic Road with sightseeing stops along the way, *see* p. 311).

By Air

Lufthansa offers a good internal service between major German cities, but flights are expensive (for example Berlin–Munich one way £162.40, return £212.00). Student discounts apply only to people living and studying in Germany. If you buy all your tickets before you leave, you can often get a cheaper rate, but have to stick with the dates you have chosen.

By Boat

If you had the time, you could visit virtually all of Germany by boat, taking in some of Europe's most romantic rivers on the way. Local cruise liners and ferries make a slow but delightful travel alternative, and sometimes afford the best views of all. Particularly recommended are the routes along the Rhine (especially between Bonn and Mainz, *see* p. 152, 161), along the Mosel (p. 210), on Lake Constance (p. 300), along the easternmost stretch of the Danube (p. 381) and along the Elbe beyond Dresden (p. 464). In the Spreewald (p. 512) you can travel about on punts in what the tourist brochures call a 'rural Venice'.

Bicycling and Hiking

The Germans are enthusiastic walkers and cyclists, and both activities are well catered for. Often a bike is by far the most sensible, convenient and economical means of transport in a town. Most towns, especially in the west, have well-laid-out **cycle paths**, which makes getting around easy and safe. You will also find cycle paths alongside regional roads and criss-crossing the countryside between villages. In cities the pavement is often divided into two, with the cyclists' part marked by paving stones of a different shape or colour. Pedestrians should remain on their half, or risk being mowed down by a mountain bike.

If you have a valid train ticket, you can **hire bicycles** from most rail stations for only DM10 a day (ask at the left luggage counter). German Rail Pass holders get a further 50 per cent discount. In rural areas you are sometimes even allowed to take the bike on to the next station and leave it there. Commercial bicycle hire firms are listed under the separate Getting Around sections for each city—or you'll find them in the phone book under *Fahrradverleih*. (Most of these require your passport or around DM50 as a deposit.) To take your **bicycle on a train** you will have to buy a ticket for it (*Fahrradkarte*) and put it in the luggage van yourself. (InterCity and EuroCity trains and some local trains don't allow bicycles, so it is always a good idea to check first.) A number of firms offer **organized bicycling holidays** (transporting your luggage to the next inn for you). One of the friendliest and best organized of these is the British-based Bents Bicycle Tours (The Priory, High Street, Redbourn, Herts AL3 7LZ, ☏ (0582) 793 249), which specializes in Bavarian tours.

Country areas are webbed with well-marked **hiking trails**. Few of them are very arduous, and over weekends and holidays they swarm with healthy marchers (many of whom really *do* wear knee-breeches and bright woollen socks). Even the longer trails are liberally punctuated by shelters, villages and inns, so there is rarely any danger of starving, or of dying a lonely death on a mountainside. Nevertheless it is a good idea to carry an adequate **map** (the local tourist office can generally oblige), as signposting sometimes isn't clear.

Urban Transport

Trams and **buses** make up the backbone of public transport in many German cities. When you have the choice, you'll find trams the quicker and more frequent of the two. Larger cities may have an **U-Bahn** (Untergrundbahn, underground railway). An U-Bahn tends to be an inner-city metro system which may also run overground, while an **S-Bahn** (Stadtbahn, town railway) is a suburban railway, which sometimes runs underground.

Tickets are usually dispensed by automatic machines at stations and stops and are valid on all forms of public transport (subject to zone restrictions). Rail Passes and Deutsche Bahn (DB) tickets are valid on the S-Bahn but on none of the others. In some cities tobacconists and newsagents also sell tickets. Single journeys can be expensive, but a day pass (*Tagekarte* or *24-stunde-karte*), which offers unlimited travel on whatever the city has to offer, is always good value. Keep an eye open also for special deals over weekends and for families. Whatever form of ticket you buy, you must validate it, before or as you board, by sticking it in the franking machines on trams and buses and at the entrance to station platforms.

Travellers with Disabilities

Travellers with disabilities will find themselves well-catered for in most of western Germany. Buses can be a problem, but many of the newer trams have low steps to assist people of limited mobility. Rail stations that are not fully converted for wheelchairs have eagle-eyed attendants waiting to help. (If you find you do need assistance, look out for someone with a *Bahnhofsmission* armband.)

In Germany the **Touristik Union International** (TUI, Postfach 610280, Hannover, ☏ (0511) 5670) has a list of hotels with facilities that cater for special needs. The list ranges from the humblest pensions to the poshest Grand Hotels. The organization also provides advice and assistance on travelling in Germany. When cities offer special facilities for the disabled they have been listed here under the relevant Tourist Information or Getting Around sections. Otherwise look in the phone book under *Behinderter* (Disabled). In Britain you can get advice, and information on specialized holidays, from RADAR (25 Mortimer St, London W1M 8AB, ☏ (071) 637 5400).

Practical A–Z

Addresses

In Germany the street name is written before the number. *Straße* (street, abbreviated to Str.) is joined on to it, unless the name is an adjective (usually a town name ending in *er*), hence Fauststraße, but Berliner Straße. Other common terms are Platz (square), Gasse (alley), Ufer (quay/bank) and Ring (ring road). Politicians, dead or alive, make favourite street names, as do other towns (don't be surprised to find a Münchener Straße tucked away in some corner of northeast Germany, or a Hamburger Straße in the south). Most streets named after discredited leaders and events in former East Germany have now reverted to their pre-war names or been given new ones. This guide uses the new names wherever possible, but the process is still going on.

Children

The Germans are the first to talk anxiously about the nation's supposed *Kinderfeindlichkeit* (antipathy to children). In public, children are generally well-disciplined—all part of civic duty, reinforced by public notices addressed to parents to remind them of their responsibilities. A rabble of noisy foreign brats will be looked on very coolly indeed.

Before unification West Germany had the lowest birthrate in Europe and was in many respects a very adult-orientated society. (The situation was always rather different in the East, where people married young, had large families and access to free crèche facilities.)

That said, it is easier to find somewhere to eat and drink as a family in Germany than it is, for example, in Britain, where attitudes to children are supposed to be more sympathetic. Children, accompanied by adults, are welcome in inns and cafés. Many city museums (especially scientific or technological ones) are especially aimed at younger visitors, with lots of hands-on exhibits and displays.

Climate and Packing

Germany is in the Central European Temperate Zone, but that does not mean that it has a uniform climate. In fact there is a marked climatic difference between regions. The south tends to be warmer and sunnier, with cold but bracing winters. In the north the winters are damp and soggy, and around Berlin and the plains of northeastern Germany winter can be particularly bitter and depressing. Freiburg in the Black Forest boasts that it is the sunniest city in Germany. The weathermen, however, give the palm to the Rhineland. Certainly a good summer in the Rhineland-Palatinate, Baden-Württemberg or Bavaria can seem positively Mediterranean, with long scorching days and sultry nights. Even in northern cities there will be periods where you can wear shorts and a T-shirt all day.

Spring comes to Freiburg at the beginning of April, a good six weeks earlier than to the heart of the Black Forest, just a few kilometres away. Around this time you can still ski in the Alps, then nip down to Lake Constance for an invigorating first swim of the season. In the north people are probably still wrapped up in coats and jumpers. Misty autumn is the perfect time to visit forest areas, which dissolve into shades of gold, and wine-growing regions, where you can soak in the infectious energy of the harvest, then sit in warm taverns drinking the cloudy, newly fermented grape juice.

		Temperature Chart in °C		
		Berlin	Hamburg	Munich
January	max	9	2	2
	min	−12	−2	−5
April	max	22	13	13
	min	−2	3	3
July	max	32	22	23
	min	9	13	2
October	max	21	13	17
	min	−1	6	9

If you are travelling around the country it is a good idea to pack your winter woollies as well as your summer cottons and silks at most times of the year. Take an umbrella, too. Rain falls throughout the year. In summer especially there may be sudden storms.

Business **dress codes**, especially at a senior level, tend to be conservative, with dark suits the norm for men and neatly tailored clothes preferred by women. Some very exclusive restaurants demand a collar and tie, but otherwise dress in restaurants tends to be informal, but smart. New clothes are one of the ways in which west Germans in particular display their wealth and your favourite old coat or faded cotton shirt may leave you feeling distinctly out of place.

It is also a good idea to pack a few **books**. German bookshops in larger cities do carry a range of English titles, but they tend to be very expensive. You may also need adaptors or **special plugs** for electrical equipment (*see* Electricity below). Throw in a box of **aspirins**, too. In Germany you can only buy them in pharmacies, at about four times what they would cost at home.

Crime and the Police

See also Emergency Numbers below.

Germany does not have a particularly bad crime problem. Unemployment in the east and drug problems in Berlin and Frankfurt lead to high incidences of theft, especially from cars, but provided you take the normal precautions (hang on to your handbag, don't keep your wallet in your back pocket, and avoid dodgy areas at night), you shouldn't be troubled.

If you are robbed, then report the incident to the **police** immediately. This will plummet you into the usual morass of bureaucracy, but is essential if you are going to make any insurance claims.

You are required to have some form of **identification** with you at all times (preferably a passport). If you are found to be without one, you may be subject to prosecution.

If you end up on the wrong side of the law, get in touch with your consulate at once— though you are unlikely to receive much sympathy in drug-related offences. The possession of any **illegal drugs** is a punishable offence, for which the penalty is a prison sentence or deportation.

Electricity

The supply in Germany is 220 volts, so all UK appliances (which require 240 volts) will work. American equipment will need a transformer. The plugs are the two-pronged kind, standard in much of continental Europe. Adaptors are available from electrical suppliers in Germany and can also be found in travel and specialist electrical shops outside Germany.

Embassies and Consulates

Bonn

Australian: Godesberger Allee 119, Bad Godesberg, ✆ (0228) 81030

British: Friedrich-Ebert-Allee 51, ✆ (0228) 234 061

Canadian: Friedrich-Wilhelm-Str. 18, ✆ (0228) 231 061

New Zealand: Bonn-Center, ✆ (0228) 214 021

USA: Deichmanns Ave 29, Bad Godesberg, ✆ (0228) 3391

Berlin

UK: Unter den Linden 32–4, ✆ (030) 10117

USA: Clayallee 170, ✆ (030) 819 7465

Australia: Berlin Hilton, Mohrenstr. 30, ✆ (030) 23 82 2041

Emergency Numbers

Throughout the country you can reach the **police** by dialling 110; for an **ambulance**, or the **fire brigade**, call 112. Other emergency numbers are listed under the separate city entries.

Germany is still a very formal society, especially in the world of business. Work colleagues—even of the younger generation—still tend to use *Herr* (Mr) and *Frau* (Mrs/Ms) instead of first names, and often use the formal *Sie* rather than *du* form of 'you'. This can be the case even among people who have worked in the same office for decades. Leaping the chasm between *Sie* and *du* is a tricky exercise, even for Germans themselves. Generally the rule is always to use *Sie* with a stranger or new acquaintance, until you mutually agree not to. The older or more senior person will suggest this first. The transition is often made quite formally—and is sometimes even marked with a toast. Younger people meeting in informal situations—such as bars or discos—usually use *du*, but the borders can be hazy.

If someone has a title, use it when addressing him or her: *Herr Professor*, *Frau Doktor*, for example. Women get lumbered with their husband's title as well. Gone are the days when you would even call your baker *Herr Bäcker*—though you will still hear older people summoning a waiter with *Herr Ober!* ('Mr waiter').

Festivals and Events

The German calendar is crammed with festivals, from the formal national and religious holidays to riotous local romps, usually with pagan roots. Local festivals are listed under the towns where they occur, but here is an overview.

Date	Place	Event
February (lead-up to Shrove Tues)	Countrywide mainly Cologne, Mainz and Rhineland	Carnival
30 April/1 May	Marburg	Town and Gown Festival
Sundays between Easter and September	Rothenburg	Shepherds' Dance
Whit weekend	Rothenburg	Mayor's wine-quaffing and fancy-dress
Sundays from Whit to September	Hamelin	Performance of Pied-Piper legend
Corpus Christi	Bavaria	Street processions
May/June	Countrywide, especially Rhineland	Spring/summer festivals
June/July (1996, 1999)	Landshut	Landshut Wedding
August	Rhine towns	Rhine in Flames

Aug/Sept/Oct	Wine-growing regions	Summer and harvest festivals
Sept/Oct	Munich	*Oktoberfest*
	Bad Canstatt	*Cannstatter Volkfest*
October	Bremen	*Freimarkt*
November	Düsseldorf	St Martin's procession
Advent	Countrywide (especially Nuremberg, Bremen, Rothenburg)	Christmas markets

The most important festival across the country is **Christmas**, a time of candlelight and gingerbread, relaxed chats over *Glühwein* around the fire and magical Christmas markets. Christmas decorations are less tacky, and festivities less forced, than in most parts of the English-speaking world. **Carnival** (*see* p. 127) is essentially a southern, Roman Catholic tradition, but is beginning to catch on in the Protestant north as well.

Food and Drink

Eating is a serious business in Germany. There are strong local culinary traditions and tremendous variation between regions. (Swabian, Bavarian and Franconian food has the best reputation). People eat out frequently and plentifully. Even supermarkets may reserve a corner where hefty hubbies can gather to demolish knuckles of pork and grilled halves of chicken. Feeding is the focal activity of most fairs; drinking the *raison d'être* of many festivals.

Basic German cookery is a meat-and-one-veg affair. Potatoes and cabbage (the latter boiled, pickled as *Sauerkraut*, or cooked with apples to make *Apfelrotkohl*) are the favourite vegetables. 'Meat' almost invariably means pork. The Germans get through 50kg of it per head each year, and eat every conceivable part of the pig, cooked in all imaginable ways. Nowadays, especially in newer restaurants, the heavy, fatty meat dishes are offered together with a contrasting array of well-prepared fresh salads and a more imaginative selection of vegetables.

Vegetarians will have a difficult time. Pork appears quite without warning—a sausage floating in bean soup, or bacon mixed in with a side-dish of potatoes. Often the only 'vegetarian meal' on the menu involves fish. Until recently 'salads' meant pickles, or meat and tinned vegetables smothered in mayonnaise. (This is still true in some traditional eateries.) In the larger cities you will find specialist vegetarian restaurants, while the mainstream ones will also offer more of a choice to vegetarians. Keep an eye open also for *Reformladen* (**health food shops**, and *Naturcafés*, which sell wholefood (but again not necessarily purely vegetarian fare).

The prospect of such hearty, meat-based grub might be daunting, but German dishes are often subtle and delicious. Standards are high, and proportions generous. ('It looked an infamous mess,' remarked one 18th-century traveller of the meal set before him in Nuremberg, 'but tasted better than passable'.)

Soups range from clear broths populated by plump dumplings to purée-thick mixtures of potatoes or beans. An ideal autumnal tummy-warmer is an *Eintopf* (literally: 'one pot'), a cross between a soup and a stew, containing anything the cooks could lay their hands on. (*Eintopf* on the main part of the menu means casserole). You can have extra sausages chopped into it if you wish. Another favourite, adapted from the Hungarian original, is a thick, peppery *Gulaschsuppe*.

Sausages come in all colours and thicknesses. Most are made with pork. White ones (*Weißwurst*) are popular south of Frankfurt (the river Main is nicknamed the *Weißwurst* equator), and contain veal and brains. Black ones are made with blood. The most popular of all is the *Bratwurst* (literally; 'grilled sausage', though often it is deep fried), which is served with a bread roll and a dollop of mild mustard. The best sausages come from Nuremburg, Thuringia, Leipzig and the Münsterland and are cooked over wood grills. You'll find sausages at fast-food stalls, in beer halls and taverns. In Bavaria there are even specialized *Wurstküchen* (sausage kitchens) which can boast Michelin ratings.

Apart from sausages, the most ubiquitous pork dishes are *Schweinhaxen* (huge knuckles of pork that look as if they belong on a medieval banqueting table), *Eisbein* (trotters—popular in the east), and *Schweinbraten* (roast pork, often sprinkled with ground coriander). **Veal**, **chicken** and **game** (especially venison, boar and hare) make their way onto many menus. Venison is often cooked in fruity sauces and served with wild mushrooms, or simmered in a mouthwatering stew. **Goose** and **turkey** are common, even out of the festive season. **Beef** makes its appearance mainly as steak, though along the Rhine you often find *Sauerbraten* on the menu—a sort of pickled pot roast. **Lamb** is more of a rarity, confined mainly to Turkish and Middle-Eastern restaurants, though in Lower Saxony you can eat *Heidschnucken* (an aromatic mutton from the sheep that graze on the heather and juniper berries on the Lüneberg Heath). The coastal regions along the North Sea and the Baltic serve an abundance of fresh salt-water **fish**. Inland the favourites are carp, salmon, trout and perch. In north-eastern Germany, especially, you'll find tasty **eel** dishes. Fish is cooked with delicacy and flair, though it is usually more expensive than other items on the menu.

In the south, potato **dumplings** (Knödel) or light, crinkly **noodles** (*Spätzle*) come with almost everything. Dumplings may also be made from stale bread (*Semmelknödel*) or with liver (*Leberknödel*). A variation on the stringy noodles is the Swabian *Maultasch*, a sort of giant ravioli.

Desserts are fairly run-of-the-mill, though *Rote Grütze* (a tangy mush of various red fruits and berries, with lashings of cream) makes an invigorating palate cleanser. The Bavarian *Dampfnudel* (steamed dumpling, smothered in sweet, fruity sauce) is a meal in itself. You can also indulge your sweet tooth by joining in the great pastime of **Kaffee und Kuchen** (coffee and cake)—the German equivalent of English afternoon tea. *Kaffee und Kuchen* can be the end-point of a Sunday afternoon excursion, the excuse for a good gossip in the local café, or a genteel means of whiling away the morning. *Apfelkuche* (apple pie) is a reliable standard and *Schwarzwalderkirschtorte* (Black Forest cherry cake) can be found all over the country—but you are more likely to be tempted by the splendid, calorie-charged creations of a local baker supremo.

Meals

Breakfast, in all but the stingiest of hotels, involves coffee and fruit juice, cold meats, cheeses (including *Quark*—curd cheese a little like yoghurt), jams, fruit and a bewildering variety of **breads**. German bread is one of the great plusses of the cuisine. Even small local bakeries are cornucopias of thirty or so different varieties—ranging from damp, heavy *Schwarzbrot* (black bread) and healthy granary loaves to crusty white rolls. The famous *Pumpernickel*—a rich, black rye bread—is by no means the only *Schwarzbrot*. You can get variations with hazelnuts and all sorts of other additions. Brown breads can be made with combinations of three, four or six different types of grain, and are often pepped up by the addition of sunflower seeds, onion or spices. A sandwich made with a good, grainy brown loaf can keep you going all day.

Lunch is still the main meal of the day for most German families (though this doesn't preclude eating out in restaurants at night). The **evening meal** usually takes the form of a light supper (*Abendbrot*), similar in style to breakfast but with the addition of salads and sometimes a soup. Late afternoon or evening entertaining may take place over cakes and wine.

Eating Out

For a quick snack or take-away there is the ubiquitous **Imbiß**. There are two main categories of Imbiß: traditional (mainly sausages), and foreign (mainly Turkish doner kebabs or Italian pizzas)—though sometimes there are inspired regional variations, such as stalls serving fried forest mushrooms or delicate noodle dishes. In an Imbiß you usually order at the counter, pay on delivery and eat standing up, or at one of a scattering of plastic tables. Sausages, hamburgers and meatballs are the usual fare, though some Imbißes are more sophisticated and offer modest meals. *Halbes Hähnchen* (spit-roast chicken, unceremoniously hacked in two) is usually good value at around DM4.

Another place for a quick lunch or snack is the **Stehcafé** (literally: standing café). These are usually attached to bakeries or butchers, or found in stations or busy shopping areas. You buy your food at the counter then devour it standing up at elbow-high tables nearby. It is perfectly acceptable behaviour to get your bread roll at one shop, your cream cake at another and polish them off in a third which sells coffee. Often a number of establishments will share a group of tables so you can do just that.

At the other end of the scale are classy **restaurants**, good enough to rival any in the world. Often, though, you end up paying well over the odds for food that isn't particularly special. Germans seem best at cooking variations of their own cuisine, rather than imitating others. Recently, though, a **New German Cuisine** has emerged. This blends traditional ingredients and techniques with a lighter, French-influenced approach—subtle sauces and imaginative combinations of flavours—with delicious results.

For a tasty, good-value meal by far the best option is to head for a *Gaststätte*, *Gasthaus*, *Brauhaus* or *Wirtschaft*—inns that serve *gutbürgerliche Küche* ('good solid cooking'). Standards are higher than you would expect in similar establishments in Britain or the USA: food is often simple, proportions are generous and you will rarely eat a bad meal.

You can join in the ritual of *Kaffee und Kuchen* in a **café** or **Konditorei** (cake shop)—some are quite trendy, others the realm of redoubtable old ladies in severe hats. A *Konditorei* will usually have a better selection of cakes, and often hand-made chocolates too. The usual practice is to choose your cake at the counter, tell the attendant, then order your coffee from the waitress at your table. She will then bring everything together.

Restaurant and bistro prices given in this guide are for a three-course meal for one with a glass of wine.

expensive	over DM65
moderate	DM20–65
inexpensive	under DM20

In cafés and inns most main dishes (often with vegetables or salad) are around DM10. In general, prices are reasonable by European standards.

Drinking

The distinction between restaurants and bars is less rigidly drawn in Germany than in most English-speaking countries. At a **café**, **Weinstube** (wine bar) or **Bierstube**, you can also usually get good, freshly cooked food. Nobody complains, though, if you want only a beer or a cup of tea.

Bars that are mainly for drinking are called **Kneipe**. Even here, people seldom stand and drink, as they do in an English pub. If there is no table free, in southern Germany it is perfectly acceptable to join a table of strangers. You might even end up chatting to each other for the rest of the evening. In the more dour north this practice is looked upon with horror and disapproval. Regulars will have a private table—a *Stammtisch*—in one corner of the pub. Sometimes this is marked by a small sign. Even if it isn't, you'll soon be told if you sit at the *Stammtisch* by mistake.

Beer

Germany's annual beer consumption averages 150 litres a head for every man, woman and child in the country (more than their consumption of milk, wine and soft drinks together). Tourists do their bit to add to the statistics, but there can be little doubt that beer is Germany's favourite drink. The nation has over a third of the world's breweries (more than half of them in Bavaria). Even in the wine-producing western part of the country beer is seen not as just a drink, but as part of the German way of life—with all the associated tradition. Beer and *Abendbrot* (snacks) is a countrywide evening pastime. It is still common to see colourful horse-drawn dray-carts delivering wooden barrels of beer to pubs around town. The Munich Oktoberfest is by no means the only big beer-drinking beano. Spring and autumn beer festivals abound (virtually every town in Bavaria has one).

There is a distinct genre of German painting devoted entirely to portraying people drinking beer—from impressionist studies of ladies sipping out of small glasses under chestnut trees, through jolly tavern scenes to the pictures of fat, greedy-eyed monks with foaming tankards by the painter Eduard Grützner (1846–1925). Beer-drinking paraphernalia, such as the carved and painted stone beermugs with pewter lids, make valued collectors' items.

Controversies centred on beer can incite fervent passion. In the 19th century rioters stormed and sacked breweries in Munich when the government tried to raise a tax on beer. Today even the most devoted European federalist will bridle if you mention the *Reinheitsgebot* (Purity Law), legislation which dates back to 1516. Its strict regulation of standards of beer production (which preclude the use of any chemicals) were rigidly adhered to for centuries, but recently EC bureaucrats ruled that the law amounted to an illegal restriction on trade. Beer from other countries is full of preservatives—foam stabilizers, enzymes, and additives such as formalin and tannin—and so could not be imported to Germany. The German government was forced to back down, but feeling still runs high. Over 95 per cent of the populace believed that the *Reinheitsgebot* should have been maintained—and most German breweries still obey its strictures.

Much of the beer brewed in Germany is aimed primarily at the home market. Sampling a region's, or a town's, beer is as crucial a part of a visit as tasting the local cuisine. Many towns have excellent local breweries, with a **Brauhaus** (drinking tavern) on the premises—often a good place for a hearty meal and rousing evening. Bamberg is known for a smoky beer that gets its taste from beechwood burned during the brewing process. In Neustadt (near Coburg) the beer also gets a fine, smoky flavour after hot stones are plunged into the brew to caramelize the malt. Cologne is famous for its *Kölsch*, a light bitter beer. Berlin is best known for *Berliner Weiße*, made from wheat. Düsseldorf has a particularly distinctive dark *Alt* ('Old') barley malt beer, still made according to an ancient recipe. Munich and Dortmund vie for the position of top European beer-producing city. Both offer a wide range of brews from light lagers to various *Bocks*, the strongest beer type. Kulmbach (near Bayreuth) comes up with the strongest beer on the world, at 28 per cent proof. Though most German beer production takes place in the south of the country, it is two northern beers that are perhaps the most popular exports—*Becks* from Bremen and *Holstein* from Hamburg. (The term *Export*, originally referred to beers made to be exported, but now denotes a stronger variety of lager.)

Beer in Germany is either bottom-fermented (the process most common in other countries, whereby beer is made with yeast that has sunk to the bottom of the fermentation tank) or top-fermented (an age old process, recently revived, made with yeast from the top of the tank). Top-fermented beer tends to have more body, and be more characterful than beer made by the easier, more modern method—though *Pils*, a bottom-fermented beer high in hop content, is nationally the most popular brew.

Beer is served in a variety of glasses—wide bowls for *Berliner Weiße*, thin flutes for *Kölsch*, tall glasses and squat tankards. In Bavaria you can get it in a *Maß*—a challenging litre-tankard. Whether you are gulping down a *Maß* in a rowdy beer tent, or sipping a bowl of *Weiße* in a smoky cellar, or drinking alongside the huge copper vats in a local *Brauerei*, or sailing down the River Isar propped up against your own barrel (a popular Bavarian spring-time activity), your encounters with beer in Germany may well number among the most memorable moments of your visit.

Wine

Don't be put off by the sickly sweet *Liebfraumilch* that is often the foreigner's first experience of German wine. Many German wines are dry and delicious. Whites feature more strongly than reds because red-wine grapes don't ripen easily so far north. The greatest grape is unquestionably the Riesling, which produces fragrant, fruity wines which age well in the bottle. Gewürztraminer makes a tangy, spicy wine and Silvaner is milder and more full-bodied. Kerner (if it isn't too sweet) is another variety worth looking out for. The grape used for most house wines in bars and restaurants, however, is the ubiquitous Müller-Thurgau. The result is all too often the wine drinker's equivalent of easy listening—bland and quite forgettable.

Tafelwein is basic plonk, **Landwein** is just a step up from that (like the French *vin du pays*). Better quality wines are labelled **Qualitätswein**, and *really* good wines will have an additional *mit Prädikat* or *Kabinett* (grower's reserve) on the label. Better quality wines may also be labelled according to the timing and manner of the harvest. *Spätlese* ('late-picked') wines are full and juicy, while for *Auslese* ('specially selected') brands the grapes are picked separately to produce a rich, ripe, honey-sweet nectar. Wines from Franconia (in dumpy, flask-shaped bottles), Mosel Rieslings and wines from the Johannisberg area of the Rheingau are the ones to look out for. (Wines are discussed in more detail in the chapters on the Rhine, the Mosel and in the section on Franconia.)

In addition to bottled wine, restaurants often sell half and quarter litre carafes of a wide selection of wines—not just the house plonk. It is also acceptable practice for people eating together to order their own glasses or mini-carafes to go with a meal. In summer many prefer a refreshing *Schorle*—wine with mineral water or soda.

Warmth and Spirit

Even in the humblest Imbiß **coffee** is likely to be freshly brewed and filtered. Cafés and restaurants will also offer espresso and capuccino. **Tea** is usually taken black, except in Friesland, where it comes with enormous sugar crystals and cream (*see* p. 549). Herb and fruit teas are becoming popular, and some cafés have long tea 'menus'.

In the winter, street-side stalls pop up selling **Glühwein** (hot, spicy mulled wine) and **Feuerbohle** (a similar brew that has had a rum-soaked sugar cone melted over it). Common **spirits** include **Schnapps** (often drunk with beer as a chaser) and **Korn** (a fiery northern favourite, traditionally drunk from a long tin spoon). There is also a wide range of sticky, fruity liqueurs.

The Gay Scene

Germany has a relaxed, tolerant and thriving gay scene (in German the word for gay is *schwul*). The main centres of gay and lesbian life are Berlin, Hamburg, Cologne, Frankfurt and Munich. In Berlin and Munich especially the scene is busy and friendly (though elsewhere in the more conservative Roman Catholic south public attitudes can be intolerant—a recent law in Bavaria introduced mandatory AIDS testing for people 'suspected of being HIV positive'). The international publication *Spartacus* (available in gay bookstores) lists clubs and discos around the country, or you could buy the glossy local magazine *Männer* (available in pubs and some bookstores). In Berlin the cheekily named *Berlin von hintern* (Berlin from behind) tells you what is on around town. Some of the other large cities publish similarly named equivalents. All of these publications are aimed mainly at gay men, though they contain information relevant to lesbians too. Germany's main lesbian magazine is the *UKZ-Unsere Zeitung*.

Addresses

Bundesverband Homosexualiteit PO Box 120 630, Bonn (central gay organization)

Deutsche AIDS-Hilfe, Nestorstr. 8–9, Berlin, ✆ (030) 896 9060

Geography

The Federal Republic of Germany comprises 16 states: Bavaria (*Bayern*), Baden-Württemberg, Brandenburg, Hessen, Mecklenburg-Lower Pomerania (*Mecklenburg-Vorpommern*), Lower Saxony (*Niedersachsen*), North Rhine-Westphalia (*Nordrhein-Westphalen*), Rhineland-Palatinate (*Rheinland-Pfalz*), Saarland, Saxony (*Sachsen*), Saxony-Anhalt (*Sachsen-Anhalt*), Schleswig-Holstein, Thuringia (*Thüringen*) and the city-states of Berlin, Hamburg and Bremen. Together they spread over 357,000sq km.

There are two coastlines—one on the Baltic (*Ostsee*) and one on the North Sea (*Nordsee*). The land in the northern part of the country is flat—very often fenland or lakeland—but begins to rise from a line drawn between Dortmund and Dresden, until it reaches the giddy heights of the Alps on the southern border. There are some notable mountain ranges along the way, such as the Erzgebirge in the east, the Hunsrück and Taunus mountains in the west and the Harz, Vogelsberg and Rhön in central Germany. Mighty rivers criss-cross the countryside. The Rhine flows northwards from the Alps, for almost the entire length of the land. The Danube flows from west to east across the southern part of the country, and the Weser and Elbe wind their way through the middle.

Berlin is the biggest city, with a population of 3.4 million. Then come Hamburg (1.6 million), Munich (1.2 million), Cologne (1 million) and a host of other cities with populations of 500,000–600,000—79 million people in all, of which 5.6 million are foreigners.

Insurance and Medical Matters

EC nationals are entitled to free medical care in Germany—but you must carry a form E111 (fill in application form SA30, available from DSS branches or post offices). Theoretically you should organize this two weeks before you leave, though you can usually do it over the counter in one visit. Citizens of other countries have no such privileges, and the E111 does not insure personal belongings. For these reasons, all travellers are advised to take out some form of **travel insurance**. Consult your insurance broker or travel agent, and shop around for a good deal. Also check out any existing policies you have, as you might already be covered for holidays abroad.

Many travel insurance packages include not only medical cover, but lost luggage, theft and ticket cancellation. If you do suffer any of these misfortunes, check the small print for what documentation—police reports, medical forms or receipts—you require to make a claim.

You get prescription drugs from an *Apotheke*. A list of duty emergency pharmacies, which stay open after normal working hours, is posted on the door of all *Apotheken*. Even emergency pharmacies may look closed; ring the doorbell and the pharmacist will emerge from an inner recess and serve you through a hatch in the glass.

The Germans are a litigious bunch, and losers in court have to pay the opponent's **legal costs** as well. If you are involved in a motor accident, scratch somebody's car with your shopping trolley, or knock over something in a shop, you could find yourself involved in a costly court action. If you are staying in Germany for any length of time, or doing much bicycling, it is a good idea to take out **personal liability insurance** (*Haftsversicherung*). In Germany nearly everybody does this, and policies are correspondingly cheap (around DM70 a year). Most travel insurance also includes cover for third-party liabilities.

Laundry

Most hotels provide efficient, if pricey, laundry services. Launderettes/laundromats (*Wascherei*), however, are a rarity, even in the biggest cities. Over 80 per cent of Germans have their own washing machine. Those that don't take their laundry back to mummy. When you do find a launderette (try the yellow pages under *Wascherei*), a single load will cost you around DM7. Dryers will cost at least another DM4. **Drycleaners** are more plentiful, but also expensive. Look out for signs advertising *Reinigung* (literally, 'cleaning').

Living and Working in Germany

If you intend to stay for longer than 90 days, you should visit the local *Meldestelle* (registration office) to register your address. You will also need to show proof of some income (non-EC nationals must have a job *before* they come into the country) in order to get a **residence permit** and a **work permit**. Set aside a good two days and take some valium. You are likely to be shuffled between at least three different offices at opposite ends of town, and will experience grinding German bureaucracy at its most Kafkaesque. Be prepared to wait for hours in a queue simply to be handed a form to fill in (three minutes' work), then shunted to the back of the queue in order to hand your form in again. Anything slightly out of the ordinary in your story will have you tangled up in this process indefinitely. Come with every possible personal document you can lay your hands on. The only way to survive the ordeal is to beat them at their own game.

Accommodation in Germany is at a premium, especially in lower rent-brackets. Even in provincial towns apartments can be very hard to come by. A **Mitwohnzentrale** can arrange medium-term lets, or find you room in shared accommodation until you find your feet, but be prepared to pay over the odds.

The **Goethe Institute**, which exists to promote German culture, offers reasonably priced language courses, usually of a high standard. There are branches throughout Germany and in major cities around the world.

Maps

The ADAC offer excellent route maps (free to members and at a minimal charge to others). There is a simplified tourist map which divides Germany into three parts (north, middle and south). This shows only motorways and main roads, but gives information (in German) on the interesting towns. Far more useful is the detailed 37-part **Generalkarte** series— clear, individual maps printed in great detail. The handiest and most up-to-date city maps are published by Falk.

If you want to buy a map before you leave, look for one published by Falk, RV, or Kümmerly und Frey. In Britain, Stanfords (12–14 Long Acre, London WC2 9LP, ✆ (071) 836 1321) has the best selection. In the US try the Complete Traveler (199 Madison Ave, New York, NY10016, ✆ (0212) 685 9007). The best source of **specialist hiking and cycling maps** is the tourist office in the relevant region.

Media

Newspapers in Germany tend to be regional rather than national, in focus and distribution. The main, respectable exceptions are the *Frankfurte Allgemeine Zeitung* (popular with the business community) and its liberal counterpart the *Frankfurter Rundschau*, both of which are read all over Germany. The Munich-based *Süddeutsche Zeitung* also has a country-wide circulation, as does the left-wing Berlin paper, the *Tageszeitung*, known as the *Taz*. The best-selling papers are the right-wing *Die Welt* and the notorious, sleazy, sensationalist *Bild Zeitung*—both products of the publishing empire of the late Axel Springer (*see* p. 488). The two most prominent **magazines** are the leftish *Der Spiegel* and the right-of-centre *Die Zeit*, both serious and informative publications. The once fairly respectable *Stern* has never recovered from the humiliation of publishing (as genuine) the forged Hitler diaries a few years ago, and has now joined the ranks of the populist press. In most cities and larger towns, leading **British and American newspapers** are on sale on the day of publication. Railway station newsagents are the surest places to find them.

There are two main national **television** channels—*ARD* and *ZDF*—as well as a host of regional stations and satellite channels, but there is little on any of them to warrant staying in at night. A more informative alternative is **BBC Radio**. You can get the World Service on 604 kHz MW and on 90.2 FM in the Berlin area, and Radio 4 on 198 longwave.

Money and Banks

> *The Reichs Doller of Germany is worth foure shillings foure pence, and the silver Gulden is accounted three shillings and foure pence English. Twenty Misen silver Groshes, 32 Lubecke shillings, 45 Embden stivers, foure Copstocks and a halfe, 55 groates, 36 Maria grosh, 18 spitz-grosh, 18 Batz, make a Reichs Doller. Two seslings make a Lubecke shilling: foure Drier a silver grosh: two dreyhellers a Drier: two schwerd grosh a schneberger: foure creitzers a batz: foure pfennig a creitzer.*

(A travel guide of 1617).

Today things are a touch simpler. There are 100 pfennigs to a deutschmark (DM), and the currency is valid over the whole country, east and west. At the time of writing there are about 2.5 DM to the pound and roughly 1.6 DM to the US dollar.

Germany is very much a cash society. **Eurocheques** are sometimes used in place of cash and some hotels only accept Eurocheques and cash. You cannot take it for granted that restaurants and shops (especially those not on the tourist circuit) will accept **credit cards**: many don't. However, petrol stations, larger hotels and upmarket restaurants will take plastic. **Travellers' Cheques** in dollars, sterling or marks are the safest way to carry around your money; banks will give you the best rates for changing them into cash.

Banks are generally open Mon–Fri 9–12.30 and 1.30–3.30. On Thursdays some remain open until 6pm, but all are shut on Saturdays and Sundays. Banks with extended hours and commercial **Bureaux de Change** can be found near railway stations and airports. 'Hole-in-the-wall' money changing machines are also beginning to make an appearance. EC card holders can also draw money from machines at banks, provided they know their personal number.

Museums

Germany has an extraordinary array of high-quality museums. For centuries Germany was a constellation of independent states. Each ruler built up an art collection, and most collections have stayed put, so that even provincial towns can have museums of a surprisingly high standard.

Opening hours vary across the country, though you will frequently find museums closed on a Monday. Smaller museums may close for lunch; opening hours in winter may be shorter. In some towns museums stay open until 8pm on a Wednesday or a Thursday night.

Alte Pinakothek (Munich, p. 353): one of the world's great art galleries, with an outstanding collection of German masters.

Dahlem Museum (Berlin, p. 497): close runner-up to the Alte Pinakothek, with an excellent Dutch and Flemish collection, and an ethnological museum thrown in.

Wallraf-Richartz/Ludwig Museum (Cologne, p. 130): good on early German painting and superb on modern art.

Grünes Gewölbe (Dresden, p. 461): jewels and exquisitely wrought treasures that are hard to beat.

Pergamonmuseum (Berlin, p. 490): great chunks of cities from classical and ancient civilizations.

Germanisches Museum (Nuremberg, p. 409): a shrine to the artefacts of German civilization throughout the ages.

Gemäldegalerie (Dresden, p. 459): Old Masters—not a vast collection, but each one a gem.

Kunstsammlung Nordrhein-Westfalen (Düsseldorf, p. 95): a notch above the other superb galleries of contemporary art, narrowly beating those at Bremen (p. 543), Aachen (p. 89) and Frankfurt (p.184).

Deutsches Museum (Munich, p. 357): the country's top technological museum.

Staatsgalerie (Stuttgart, p. 256): excellent collection of old and modern painting in Germany's most stylish new museum building.

(*see* also Best of Germany, p. 4).

Opening Hours: Business and Shopping

Germany has the most irritating and inconvenient shopping hours in Europe. Shops close at 5.30 or 6pm on weekdays and between 12.30 and 1pm on Saturdays. After that you can buy *nothing*, not even in major cities, unless you are prepared to trek to the main railway station or airport where there will be a poorly stocked and over-priced supermarket. Petrol stations also sell a few meagre provisions, though by law they should only serve passing motorists. To make matters worse, staff begin to wind down a full hour before closing time. Meat and fresh produce are packed away early and (just as office workers are tearing into the store for the brief 30 minutes they are allotted to stock up on provisions) the check-out staff pack up and go home, leaving one or two brave souls to cope with queues that snake back through the entire shop.

Saturday mornings are hell. This is the only time that anyone with an office job can do the weekly shopping. You have to fight for a supermarket trolley, bakeries run out by 11am, fruit and vegetables disappear by 12-noon and the same rule of diminishing checkout attendants applies. Saturday afternoons in Germany have a depressing, eerie stillness.

Everywhere is closed and the populace creeps home to sleep off the horrors of the day. This is not all. Except in the very centre of the largest cities, all shops and businesses take a **lunch hour**. (This includes banks, post offices and even most tourist offices.) Lunch hour is a misnomer. Businesses are closed for 1½–2 hours, sometimes longer. This lunch break may begin at 12, 12.30 or 1pm—so unless you know the exact idiosyncracies of all the shops want to go to, you might as well write off the hours of 12–3. You'll find very few shops open before 9 or 9.30 in the morning.

Once a month (usually the first or last Saturday) shopworkers will steel themselves for a *Lange Samstag* (literally, 'Long Saturday') and bravely work on until around 4pm. Some businesses do this on a Thursday too (*Lange Donnerstag*, when they stay open until 6 or 7pm), but you can never be sure.

Many office workers (especially in the public services) quite officially go home at lunchtime on Fridays. The suggestion of a business appointment for a Friday afternoon is likely to be met with stunned silence. If one of the numerous public holidays falls a day's gap away from the weekend, it is taken as read that the intervening day will be taken off, and that you will go home at lunchtime of the day before this newly created long weekend.

Post and Telephones

Post Offices are open Mon–Fri 8–6 and Sat 8/9–12-noon. Some cities have extended or 24-hour services—usually at the post office nearest the station. You can send **telegrams** from a post office or by phoning 1131. Different counters have different functions (look at the sign above the clerk's head), though most sell stamps (*Briefmarken*) and accept parcels (*Pakete*). You can also change money at a post office. Larger post offices operate a **Poste Restante** service—letters should be clearly marked *Postlagernde Sendungen*.

Germany's **telephone** system is at last fully integrated: for months after reunification dialling codes were changing on an almost weekly basis, making communications between east and west unreliable and frustrating. Telephones, especially public call boxes, are still much scarcer in the east than in the west: sometimes restaurants, people letting private rooms, and even small hotels will not have a phone.

Most **public telephones** now operate on the **phonecard** system. You can buy a card (*Telefonkarte*) from a post office for DM12 or DM50, and it is a good idea to carry one. Coin-operated phones require a minimum of 30 pfennigs. **Hotels** charge well over the odds for use of room telephones, but have to advertise the rate on the same card as the room rate (usually pasted on the back of the door). You can **call abroad** from most public telephones, and **receive calls** on those that display a picture of a bell on the booth. If you can't find a call box, try a café—many have telephones with meters for public use, but may charge a little more than the going rate.

Operator 03

Directory enquiries 1188

International enquiries 00118

International dialling codes

Britain: 00 44

USA and Canada: 00 1

Australia: 00 61

New Zealand 00 64

Public Holidays

New Year's Day (*Neujahr*, 1 Jan)

Epiphany (*Heilige Drei Könige*, 6 Jan)

Good Friday (*Karfreitag*, changes annually)

Easter Monday (*Ostermontag*, changes annually)

May Day (*Maifeiertag*, 1 May)

Ascension Day (*Christi Himmelfahrt*, changes annually)

Whit Monday (*Pfingstmontag*, changes annually)

Corpus Christi (*Fronleichnahm*, changes annually, only in Baden-Württemberg, Bavaria, Hessen, Rhineland-Palatinate, North Rhine-Westphalia and Saarland)

Feast of the Assumption (*Mariä Himmelfahrt*, 15 Aug; only in Bavaria and Saarland)

Day of German Unity (*Tag der Deutschen Einheit*, 3 Oct)

All Saints Day (*Allerheiligen*, 1 Nov; only in Bavaria, Baden-Württemberg, Rhineland-Palatinate, North Rhine-Westphalia and Saarland)

Day of Prayer and National Repentance (*Buß- und Bettag*, variable date in Nov)

Christmas Day (*Erster Weihnachtstag*, 25 Dec)

Boxing Day (*Zweiter Weihnachtstag*, 26 Dec)

Religious Affairs

There is no state religion in the Federal Republic. At the latest census 72 per cent of the population registered as Christian, almost precisely half each Roman Catholic and Protestant. The south of Germany is predominantly Roman Catholic, and the north mainly Protestant. Eastern Germany was also traditionally a Protestant Lutheran stronghold, though since reunification, new charismatic denominations are proving popular.

As you are entering a city you will see the times of church services posted on boards beside the road. Germans are not particularly avid churchgoers, though in Roman Catholic regions the religious festivals are very much part of a town's cultural life, and are celebrated by everyone. Most Germans pay a church tax (an additional 5 per cent of their normal tax bill). This money is used to support various church charities. Payment is not compulsory, but you have to go down to the town hall and 'de-register' yourself if you don't want to pay it, and most people don't bother.

Before the holocaust there were over 530,000 Jews living in Germany. Today there are just on 30,000, mostly in Berlin and Frankfurt. There are about 65 Jewish congregations scattered throughout the country. You can get further information from the Zentralrat der Juden in Deutschland, Fischerstr. 49, Düsseldorf.

Despite the large Turkish population in Germany, there is little evidence of **Muslim** places of worship. Mosques tend to be makeshift affairs in private homes or obscure buildings.

Sports and Activities

There is an old local joke that when two Germans meet they shake hands, when three meet they form a society. This certainly holds true in the world of sport. Every third inhabitant of Germany is a member of a **sports club**. Public sports facilities are good and well maintained—but even here you are likely to find courts, fields or lanes reserved for organized club activities.

Soccer is by far the most popular sport, with over 4.5 million registered members in clubs around the country. The most famous team is Bayern München, though recently Werder Bremen have been making a mark. Thousands attend matches in season (Germany isn't plagued by hooliganism to the extent that the UK is). League matches are held on Saturday afternoons, while European cup games usually take place on Wednesday evenings.

Gymnastics and **tennis** are fairly distant runners-up to soccer in the popularity stakes. But local champions Boris Becker and Steffi Graf are the focus of pop-star-like adulation and have made tennis a very popular spectator sport.

The Germans are an outdoor folk. Most towns, even in colder parts of the country, will have a *Freibad* (open-air swimming pool) that opens for the summer months. Many of the rivers, and most of the lakes, are clean enough to swim in and **watersports**—especially windsurfing—are becoming increasingly popular.

Hiking and **cycling** are two great national enthusiasms and are practised with vigour. Marked hiking trails abound, especially in mountain resorts. Many Germans take a winter **skiing** holiday. The Bavarian Alps offer the best resorts (*see* p. 374 and 377), but smaller ranges such as the Harz Mountains are also popular (and generally cheaper).

Students

Germany has 54 universities, and a significant percentage of its youth in higher education. Most museums, and some theatres and concert halls offer reduced prices on production of a student card. In addition, some universities will allow you to eat in the *Mensa* (student cafeteria)—though it is best to check with the cashier first. (For reduced fares, *see* pp. 7, 11.)

Time

In essence Germany's time is GMT plus one hour. However, clocks go an hour forward at the end of March to GMT plus two hours, and back an hour at the end of September.

Tipping

Tips are included in restaurant bills, but it is customary to round up the amount to the nearest mark, or to the nearest five if the bill is large. Additional tips for exceptionally good service never go amiss. Taxi drivers and hairdressers also expect an extra mark or two.

Toilets

The availability of public loos varies tremendously from town to town. Some will have just one or two (usually on the market place), others seem to have one on practically every corner. Look out for signs reading WC. *Herren* means Gents, and *Damen* is the Ladies. You are usually expected to pay for the privilege of use—anything from 25 to 80 Pfennigs. It is also possible to use the lavatories in cafés—though in touristy areas the propietors are sometimes not too keen on this, and it is wise to ask first.

Tourist Information

There is a comprehensive network of Tourist Offices in Germany—even small villages are likely to have one. The most usual locations are in or near the main railway station or on the market square. Ask for the *Verkehrsamt* or simply Tourist Information. Most offer **room reservation** services with local hotels (for a booking fee of around DM3), and can also help you find accommodation in private homes (*see* **Where to Stay**, below). The offices are also well-stocked with brochures and maps, and staff can give you information about local events and guided tours.

For information about Germany before you leave, contact one of the branches of the German National Tourist Office:

> **Australia**: Lufthansa House, 12th floor, 143 Macquarie Street, Sydney,
> ✆ (02) 221 1008

> **Britain**: Nightingale House, 65 Curzon Street, London W1Y 7PE,
> ✆ (071) 495 3990

> **Canada**: Place Bonaventure, Montreal, Quebec, H5A 1B8,
> ✆ (0514) 8778 9885

> **USA**: 747 Third Avenue West, New York, NY 10017,
> ✆ (0212) 308 3300

After yet another uncomfortable night Mark Twain wrote of the beds in one Rhineland hostelry: 'They were fully as narrow as the usual German bed... and had the German bed's ineradicable habit of spilling the blankets on the floor every time you forgot yourself and went to sleep.' Eighteenth-century travellers complained of having to undress in front of the landlord and share their quarters with cows and hogs. A travel guide of the time advised visitors to push furniture against the door at night and to make an extravagant display of their firearms before retiring.

Today, life in Germany's inns and hotels could hardly be more different. In western Germany standards are uniformly high. You are unlikely to have to share your room with even the most harmless of local fauna, the beds will be spotless and comfortable, and the only accusation you are likely to level would be one of dullness. In the east, however, the question is one of finding, rather than choosing, somewhere to stay. Under the DDR there were only about 60 hotels open to foreigners in the entire country. Many new hotels have since been built, but it is still difficult to find a room, the new buildings are bland and functional and prices are high.

German hotels are graded on a scale of nearly 80 classifications, which is ironic as (apart from the luxury end of the market), standards are pretty even. Certainly this makes any corresponding star system out of the question. In the broad bracket of moderate-priced hotels, you will find rustic ones (with wooden beams and folksy knick-knacks), others stuck in a 1970s time warp (decorated in purple, brown and orange) and smart new ones with plastic-coated furniture chosen from a catalogue. An *en suite* bathroom or shower is standard, except at the lower end of the market. You are also likely to find a TV and phone in the room. Service is usually efficient and often friendly.

Most of the hotels mentioned in this book have been chosen because they offer something exceptional—in atmosphere, location or service. (However, in the chapters on eastern Germany, the hotels listed are occasionally the only ones there are.) Prices are for one night in a double room with bathroom or shower *en suite*, including breakfast. For single rooms, reduce the price by 30 to 40 per cent. It is worth bearing in mind that festivals and trade fairs can double prices and devour available accommodation.

Inexpensive alternatives to hotels are **pensions** (which also keep high standards) and **private rooms**. The latter are a good bet in country areas. Look out for signs advertising *Fremdenzimmer* or *Zimmer frei*. Here you can simply walk up and knock on the door. Local tourist offices carry lists of private landlords and landladies offering rooms, and the staff can often make a reservation for you. In eastern Germany private rooms are by far the cheapest (and often the only) option—with the bonus of a chance to hear a first-hand account of life since reunification.

The first **youth hostel** (*Jugendherberge*) in the world was in Germany, and youth hostels still provide cheap and reliable dormitory accommodation to people of all ages (except in Bavaria, where there is an age limit of 27). Most hostels are members of the International Youth Hostel Association, and to use them it is necessary to become a member. You can sign up at the first hostel you visit (you'll need a passport photograph), but it is cheaper to join at a branch of your own national association before leaving home. Many hostels close for the winter months.

History

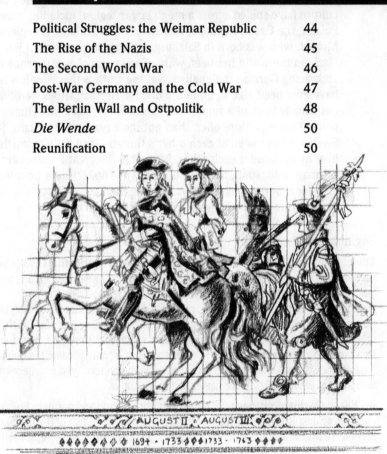

AUGUST II · AUGUST III

1694 - 1733   1733 - 1763

This country is open to all the winds of the continent.

André François-Poncet,
French Ambassador to Germany before and after the Second World War

Apart from the sea in the north and the Alps in the south, Germany has no natural frontiers. Over the centuries it has been a conduit for wandering tribes, a crucible for conflicting invaders and a refuge for those fleeing battles elsewhere in Europe. The Rhine, the Danube, the Main and other big rivers might have checked the human ebb and flow from time to time, but were more often the channels that carried the tide.

If Germany's physical frontiers seldom seem to have stayed in one place for more than a few decades at a time, ethnographic borders are even harder to pin down. Who *are* the Germans? Historically their borders and culture have spilled across a much larger region, including parts of Poland, the Czech Republic, Austria and Switzerland. (People happily call Mozart, who was born in Salzburg, a 'German composer'.) Ever since the Nazi era the world has been wary of any signs of a resurgence of an all-embracing German nationalism, yet the truth is that very few leaders have ever been able to unite the diverse German tribes. National feeling has usually been of a superficial, sentimental (albeit sometimes dangerous) variety. More often than not the Bavarians, Prussians, Saxons and Swabians have been at each other's throats—and even today they have a healthy disdain for each other. Bismarck, the great Prussian architect of German unification, noted in his diary in 1862: 'I have no mind whatsoever for a German nationality. Fighting the King of Bavaria or Hannover is like fighting against France. It is all the same to me.'

Beginnings

The first humans we know of in Germany were the **Neanderthals**. They were, in fact, named after the Neander Valley (German: Neandertal) near Düsseldorf, where 50,000 year-old fossil remains were found in 1856. (Later, Neanderthal bones and skulls were found all over Europe, and in western Asia and northern Africa.) The Neanderthals died out in 30,000 BC. The next significant record of inhabitation is of the **Celtic tribes** who originated in southwest Germany and Switzerland in *c.* 800 BC and spread knowledge of iron working throughout much of Europe, though they only became the dominant culture here after *c.* 400 BC. They left behind a wealth of fine pottery, gold jewellery and decorated weapons, as well as a few place names still in use today.

By 200 BC **Germanic tribes** migrating south from Jutland and northern Polish regions had come up against **Roman armies** marching north. In 113 BC two of these tribes, the Cimbri and the Teutones, had the effrontery to defeat a Roman army in the Alps. In turn, they and their kind were very nearly annihilated by the great Roman general Marius.

The Romans

From 58 to 50 BC **Julius Caesar** not only conquered Gaul, but also subjugated all the Germanic tribes living west of the Rhine. The Roman armies then moved northwards up the Rhine, successfully colonizing territory along the way. However, they ran into trouble when they tried to move eastwards to the Elbe (which runs through Dresden to Hamburg). Roman soldiers, used to marching in glittering formation and fighting in open spaces, were flummoxed by thick German forests and hand-to-hand combat not governed by strict rules of engagement. The leader of the Germanic tribes was **Hermann**, chieftain of the Cherusci (sometimes known by his Latin name, Arminius). As a young hostage in Rome he had picked up some handy tips on Roman military strategy. In AD 9 he led an uprising which completely vanquished three Roman legions (about 15,000 men) in the Teutoburg Forest, becoming Germany's first national hero in the process. After this defeat the Romans decided to confine themselves to the lands along the Rhine and the Danube. The fortified settlements that they built along the banks of both rivers became the basis of many a present-day German town. Trier, Regensburg, Augsburg and Cologne were important outposts of the empire, and you can find Roman ruins throughout western and southern Germany.

For the next two hundred years the Romans kept an uneasy peace with the tribes across the rivers. It was at this time that the Roman historian Tacitus wrote his *Treatise on the Situation and the People of Germania*, establishing for posterity the label *Germani*. (The Latin *Germani* probably comes from a Celtic word meaning 'the shouters'—and indeed Tacitus noted that the men went into battle uttering blood-curdling cries, encouraged by a chorus of wailing children and shrieking women 'thrusting forward their bared bosoms' close behind.) Tacitus found the Germans a fearsome lot who 'have no taste for peace', who loved to 'count and compare cuts and gashes' after a battle, and who 'cannot be kept together except by means of violence and war'.

The Romans never penetrated the Germanic lands beyond their provinces on the Rhine and Danube. Non-Roman Germania was a vague and unchartered territory that covered much of eastern Europe. After about AD 300 the scattered German clans began to group together into aggressive tribes whose names have a more familiar ring—the Goths, Vandals, Franks, Lombards, Burgundians and Alemanni. After decades of constant battering, the Roman defences finally gave in, and the Germanic tribes swept across the waters to establish lands for themselves south of the Danube and west of the Rhine.

Charlemagne and the Holy Roman Empire

In the chaos of the collapsing Roman Empire the **Franks** under King Clovis (*c.* 466–511) emerged as the most powerful tribe in northern Europe. Clovis established the Christian **Merovingian** dynasty, which ruled over nearly all of France and the Low Countries, as well as most of western and southern Germany, for two and a half centuries. Gradually, however, successive Merovingian kings began to lose power to a court official known as the 'Mayor of the Palace'. By the time the last of the line, King Childeric III, was on the throne, the king was just a figurehead and Mayor of the Palace had become an hereditary title. Childeric had no wealth, little authority and his Mayor of the Palace, Pepin (son of the celebrated and powerful Charles Martel), used to send him about in an ox cart. It was but a short step for Pepin to become king, and one that he took easily in AD 743. The line that he founded was later called the **Carolingian** dynasty after his son, the great **Emperor Charlemagne** (c. AD 742–814), known to the Germans as **Karl der Grosse**.

Charlemagne conquered the Lombards (in present-day Italy) in AD 774, set about Christianizing and taming the wild north-German Saxons (AD 772–804), and subjugated the other German tribes. He was a fearless warrior, but also an astute statesman and wise ruler, establishing a loyal court and building a great cathedral at his capital, Aachen. In Rome on Christmas Day AD 800, the Pope crowned Charlemagne 'Roman Emperor'—ruler over an empire comprising most of present-day Germany, the Czech Republic and Slovakia, northern Italy and virtually all of France and the Low Countries. Charlemagne saw himself as the legitimate heir to the Roman Empire—or rather the 'Empire of the West' that existed after the split of the Roman Empire in the 4th century AD. (The powerful Byzantine Empire was the direct heir to the Eastern Roman Empire.)

After the death of Charlemagne's son, **Louis the Pious**, in AD 840 his empire split up into three separate kingdoms. The German kings continued to call themselves 'Roman Emperors', ruling over what was later referred to as the **Holy Roman Empire of the German Nation** (although their empire, or *Reich*, comprised only Germany and northern Italy). They revived the practice of going to Rome to be crowned by the Pope, and saw themselves as the direct descendants of the Caesars and defenders of the universal Church, deriving their authority from God. They dispensed knighthoods, granted cities their 'freedom' and invested princes. But while these emperors created for themselves an illusion of a great and united *Reich*, their underlings often paid them lip-service only, and beneath them Germany crumbled into a fragmentary cluster of separate states.

Hohenstaufens and Hapsburgs

Initially, the title of Holy Roman Emperor was taken up by the leader of whichever feuding dynasty was dominant at the time. Later the Emperor came to be chosen by a body of seven Electors—powerful local princes or bishops. (This process was formalized by the **Golden Bull** in 1356.) In practice, though, the title became almost hereditary, falling to one dominant princely family for long periods at a stretch. One of the earliest of these was the **Hohenstaufen** dynasty, who provided rulers of the empire from 1138 to 1254. The most brilliant of the Hohenstaufens was **Frederick I** (1123–90), known as **Barbarossa** because of his fiery red beard. Under Barbarossa the empire expanded and flourished. He invigorated trade in towns like Hamburg, Bremen and Lübeck, paving the way for the **Hanseatic League** (*see* p. 517), one of Europe's most powerful and wealthy trading alliances. The languages we now know as Old High German and Middle High German emerged from the Babel of local dialects. In courts around the empire ladies were wooed by poets rather than warriors, and entertained by epics that are now classics of the language—such as Wolfram von Eschenbach's *Parzifal* (c. 1200) and Gottfried von Strassbourg's *Tristan und Isolde* (c. 1210).

But Barbarossa overreached himself. His attempts to extend the empire further into Italy led to bloody conflicts with papal forces, while in Germany the rival princes became more powerful and more quarrelsome in his absence. He drowned accidentally on a crusade in

Turkey, and his body was never found. Legend has it that he is asleep in the bowels of the Kyffhaüser mountain in Thuringia, waiting for the moment when a united Germany will call on him to take up the throne again.

As the power of the Hohenstaufens waned, bickering between the German princes turned into bitter conflict and, by the second half of the 13th century, into civil war. But while the nobles were at each other's throats, the new merchant class was steadily building up its wealth and power—both in the Hanseatic towns in the north, and in towns such as Augsburg and Regensburg on the busy southern trade routes. The most powerful trading towns became **Free Imperial Cities**, responsible only to the emperor. Outside of the strongholds of the towns, however, Germany was backward, chaotic and violent. Over 300 separate princes, dukes, counts, bishops and burgomasters ruled over independent patches of land where warfare was considered the normal state of affairs.

By the time the first of the **Hapsburg** family came to power in 1440 the Holy Roman Empire was already well on the way to fitting Voltaire's memorable definition of its being 'neither holy, nor Roman, nor an empire'. The Hapsburgs failed hopelessly to impose any authority over the warring German factions, and ended up with direct control over an empire that, in practice, included only Austria, Bohemia and Hungary. Astute match-making did, however, make the Hapsburg family the most powerful in Europe, which led to controlling interests in the Netherlands, Spain and part of France as well. In Germany the rulers of the more powerful states—Bavaria, Brandenburg and Saxony—sometimes fought the Hapsburgs and sometimes sided with them. The governing families and prince-bishops also fought each other, and the Free Imperial Cities took on the lot. In this way the Holy Roman Empire limped on until 1806, when it was disbanded by Napoleon.

The Reformation

In 1517 a hitherto obscure Augustinian monk, **Martin Luther**, calmly walked up to the chapel at Wittenberg castle and nailed his **95 Theses** to the door. The theses were concerned mainly with papal indulgences and superstition in the Church, but this quiet act of defiance against all-powerful Roman Catholicism made theologians across Europe braver and more audible in their criticism, and sparked off the Protestant Reformation. At the **Diet of Worms** in 1520 Luther was excommunicated and banished to Wartburg castle in Thuringia, but the momentum for change was unstoppable.

In Germany the Reformation took on a social and political significance. The Hapsburgs were fervent Catholics, so by espousing Protestantism princes armed themselves with a ready excuse to oppose them. The merchants in wealthy trading cities (especially those in the north) who had been doing battle with local prince-bishops for decades, eagerly took up the new faith. Southern states tended to remain more conservatively Catholic (a division still roughly true today). When Emperor Maximilian I died in 1519 there was a scrabble for the crown, during which the princely families, usually trumpeting one or the other of the faiths, took the opportunity to extend their independence even further.

In the countryside the peasants, suffering appalling feudal oppression, and fired by Luther's plea for the 'liberty of Christian men', took up clubs and pitchforks and challenged their local nobles. In 1524 the **Peasants' Revolt** broke out in the Black Forest, and soon spread through Swabia, Hessen, Thuringia and Saxony. The poorly equipped and disorganized peasant bands were cruelly quashed by princes' armies, and those who were not put to death found themselves even more heavily oppressed and taxed than before.

After Luther's death in 1546 the Catholic Church's fortunes rose again as the **Counter-Reformation** got underway. But despite the 1555 **Peace of Augsburg**, which preached religious tolerance and *cuius regio, eius religio* (that subjects assumed their monarch's faith), bad feeling deepened. By 1609 Germany had split into a **Protestant Union** led by the Palatinate—the Rhineland, Baden-Württemberg and Hessen—and a **Catholic League** centred on Bavaria. Bigotry and persecution were rife, and by 1618 the situation erupted into one of the most pointless and destructive conflicts Europe has known—the **Thirty Years' War**. France, Spain, Denmark and Sweden were sucked into the fray. For three decades armies plundered and pillaged the land, swapping sides at will and losing any sense of what they were fighting for (apart from self-gain). Whole towns and villages were destroyed, vast areas of land were devastated, millions were slaughtered, trade and agriculture collapsed and famine reduced some people to cannibalism. (Sweden, though, achieved a brief moment of glory when her armies defeated the notoriously cruel **Johann Tilly**, commander of the Catholic League forces, and for a while dominated Germany.)

The **Treaty of Westphalia**, which ended the war in 1648, took four years to negotiate. By the time it was signed the population of Germany had been reduced from 21 million to 13.5 million, and some towns and cities were in such a state of collapse that it took centuries for them to recover. The treaty recognized the sovereignty of over 1300 separate states, so by the mid-17th century there was still not the slightest glimmer of German unity.

Rebirth

Religious strife in the early 17th century, and the Thirty Years' War, consumed all the oxygen of the German Renaissance. When the great painters—Dürer, Cranach and Altdorfer—died, no-one of much calibre took their place. The only literary work of any great impact to emerge from this time was Luther's German translation of the Bible which, like the King James version in England, established the language as a literary one.

After the Thirty Years' War the German states set about the massive task of rebuilding their battered towns and castles. Dynamic local rulers poured whatever funds they could generate into stylish new Baroque buildings, the sciences and arts. The head of the Wettin family, **Augustus the Strong** (1670–1733, *see* p. 453), King of Poland and Elector of Saxony, built up a treasure-house in Dresden (much of it jewellery he had made for his mistresses), commissioned music from the composer J.S. Bach, and locked up an alchemist until he had discovered the way to produce **Dresden porcelain** (*see* p. 460). In 1714 the **Hanoverian** branch of the Welf family from Lower Saxony managed to wheedle their way onto the British throne when George, Elector of Hannover and great grandson of James I, was identified as the closest heir to Queen Anne. Later the **Hohenzollern** ruler **Frederick the Great** (1712–86, *see* p. 268), King of Prussia, emerged as a warrior-king with a philosophical bent. He wrote poetry and music, befriended Voltaire and held a glittering and cultured court in Berlin.

Frederick the Great also built up a strong army with which he seized Silesia from the Austrians in 1748. The Hapsburgs responded with force to check Prussian ascendancy, but in the **Seven Years' War** (1756–63) Frederick subjugated Saxony and began to transform Prussia into a major European power. Berlin became an important world capital, and one that was to play a leading role in European history over the next 150 years.

Napoleon and Bismarck

In 1806 Napoleon led his Revolutionary army across the border into Germany. The Catholic southern states—Bavaria, Baden and Württemberg—succumbed to French rule with scant resistance. Prussia and Austria put up more of a fight. Both were defeated, and Napoleon dissolved the all-but-defunct Holy Roman Empire. (The Hapsburgs had to settle for the title of 'Emperor of Austria'.) In 1813 Napoleon was defeated in Russia. Prussia cleverly joined the Anglo-Russian forces in a 'war of liberation', trounced the French in the Battle of Leipzig, intervened decisively at the Battle of Waterloo, and reaped rich territorial rewards when the spoils were divided up at the **Congress of Vienna** in 1815.

The Congress left Austria and Prussia as the two main regional powers. The 200 or so other German states were reduced to just 39, a move that was intended to defuse revolutionary demands for more democratic government by curbing the power of local princes. These states were loosely grouped into the **German Confederation**, under the leadership of Austria. Later, in 1834, a customs union, the **Zollverein**, was formed with Prussia at its centre.

The new Confederation led to a blossoming of German nationalism and liberal thought—which was not welcome to its authoritarian rulers. The Berlin government and the Austrian chancellor **Metternich** (1773–1859) responded with a programme of repression, setting up a ruthless police state. Only after a wave of popular **revolts** in 1848 did the Prussians allow even a modicum of democratic representation, setting up a largely ineffective **National Assembly** in Frankfurt.

In 1862 the wily **Prince Otto von Bismarck** (1815–98), a member of the **Junker** class of almost feudal Prussian landed gentry, became Prime Minister of Prussia. He set about equipping the army with the latest military technology, building it into a slick, muscular, murderous fighting force. In 1864, together with the Austrians, Prussia invaded Denmark and annexed the duchies of Schleswig and Holstein. But then Bismarck picked a fight with the Austrian government over who should control the new territories. In the swift **Seven Weeks' War** (1866) the crack Prussian troops trounced their former allies, leaving Bismarck free to set up the **North German Federation of States** (comprising all the states north of the Main), with himself as chancellor. Then, in 1870, he teased the French into a **Franco-Prussian War** and, after beating them soundly, engineered a gathering of German leaders at the Palace of Versailles. With some coaxing (especially in the case of Bavaria) he persuaded the other rulers to accept King Wilhelm I of Prussia as *Deutsche Kaiser* (German Emperor) of the **Second Reich**. For the first time since Charlemagne, Germany (including the former French territories of Alsace and Lorraine) was united in a single state, and was now independent of Austria.

German Imperialism and the First World War

The late 19th century was a boom time for the Second Reich. The Industrial Revolution had got off to a late start, but Germany soon rivalled Britain and the USA as an industrialized world power and began to itch for a few mineral-rich colonies—'a place in the sun'. Unfortunately, by the time she began to cast her imperial eyes about, it was too late. Other European countries, Britain in particular, had already conquered the natives and raised the flag in most of the territory up for grabs. Then in 1888 Kaiser Wilhelm II—Kaiser Bill— came to the throne. A believer in the divine right of kings, he was by all accounts every bit as puffed up, vicious and autocratic as later British propaganda would paint him. He sacked the ancient Bismarck in 1890, built up a formidable battle fleet and aggressively set about acquiring an overseas empire for his nation. This dream of a noble imperial Germany inspired the wealthy middle classes and muted the grumbles of the working classes, most of whom lived in appalling conditions in the rapidly expanding industrial cities. But the rest of Europe bristled at the Kaiser's hawkish militarism and expansionist spirit. An **arms race**, served amply by the Krupp family armaments factory, exacerbated the situation (*see* p. 101).

There were whisperings in diplomatic corridors, telegrams and warnings flew between courts. Unease tightened into tension. Relations between states became increasingly brittle and the major powers drew themselves into two **alliances**. Germany, Austria and Turkey were ranged against France and Russia, with Britain (whose royal family had links with Germany) attempting to hold the balance of power. On 28 June 1914, a Serbian conspirator assassinated Archduke Franz Ferdinand of Austria in Sarajevo. Austria immediately threatened retaliation against Serbia. This was the only spark needed to ignite the powder keg. The Russians mobilized to protect their fellow Slavs. On 1 August Germany declared war on Russia and then on France. The quickest route to France was through Belgium, whose neutrality was guaranteed by Britain. Over the next few days Britain declared war on Germany and Austria-Hungary declared war on Russia. The Kaiser, with fond recollection of the ease of Bismarck's 1870 campaign, thought that the French would be defeated in six weeks and the Russians in a few months, but this time the battle dragged on for four years, with losses on all sides that have never been equalled. It was only after the USA (harrassed by German U-boats) brought fresh energy to the war in 1917 that the German Western Front finally collapsed. Kaiser Wilhelm abdicated on 9 November 1918, and the Social Democratic Party declared a German republic. An armistice was signed, and firing ceased at 11am on 11 November.

Political Struggles in Germany: the Weimar Republic

Towards the end of the war, as it became clear that the Kaiser's days were numbered, a new set of political alliances and conflicts came into play. The **Social Democrats** wanted a parliamentary democracy. Aligned against them was a growing **Communist** movement, inspired by the success of the Russian Revolution of 1917. In 1918 and 1919 riots broke out in cities around Germany. In Munich and Hildesheim breakaway republics were formed. The Social Democrats, however, had done a deal with the army and with the major industrialists. In return for the military hierarchy being left intact, the generals gave the new government their support in quelling unrest. The industrialists backed the formation of the **Freikorps**, volunteer units comprising mainly ex-officers and right-wing extremists who gleefully and violently stamped out any opposition to the government.

In January 1919 there was a major uprising in Berlin, led by the **Spartacus League**, the forerunner of Germany's Communist Party, named after the leader of a slave revolt in ancient Rome. The rebels were shot down in the streets, and by 12 January the revolt had collapsed. On 15 January members of the Freikorps sought out and murdered the leaders of the Spartacus League, **Karl Liebknecht** and **Rosa Luxemburg**. Elections for a National Assembly were held, and on 6 February the Assembly met at Weimar to draft a constitution and elect a president. (The conservative city of Weimar was chosen as it was a safe distance from radical, eruptive Berlin—but Berlin remained the capital and the true cultural centre of Germany.) Predictably the office of president went to **Friedrich Ebert** (1871–1925), leader of the Social Democrats.

The **Weimar Republic** was to last for just 14 years. It seemed doomed from the start. Real power in Germany was still held by a small group of wealthy industrialists, and by a lumbering civil service, neither of which really accepted the new regime. The **Treaty of Versailles**, signed on 28 June 1919, officially ended the First World War, and landed Germany with a crippling reparations bill—132,000 million gold marks to be paid off over 59 years. The treaty also ceded Alsace-Lorraine to France, northern Schleswig to Denmark and West Prussia to Poland. Germany thereby lost 10 per cent of its population and 13.5 per cent of its former territory. The unequal struggle to meet reparations payments pushed inflation to dizzying heights: in 1914 a US dollar was worth 4.2 German marks; by 1923 it was worth 6600 billion marks. Those who had work brought their wages home in sacks. 'Before the War,' the saying went, 'you went to market with your money in your pocket and came back with your purchase in a basket. Now it is the other way around.'

The Rise of the Nazis

'Hitler was a naturalised German subject,' (wrote the humorist George Mikes). 'He was the worst bargain in history. No other naturalised person has ever caused half as much trouble to his new fatherland.' In 1919 the ex-Austrian Adolf Hitler (1889–1945)—one-time corporal and failed postcard painter—joined the Munich-based **German Workers' Party**. At the time the party's assets amounted to a resounding 7.50 marks (about £2) and membership didn't even reach three figures. But Hitler went to work immediately. In 1920 he renamed the party the **National Socialist German Workers' Party** soon to be referred to in its shortened form, the **Nazis**. He adopted the ancient good-luck symbol the swastika, and established the brown-shirted *Sturmabteilung* (SA; **Stormtroopers**), a group of armed heavies that lined the walls at meetings and beat up opponents.

In 1923 Hitler had enough confidence in his private army to make a grab at power. Backed by some 600 followers he staged the **Munich Beerhall Putsch**, storming into a beerhall, firing into the air and capturing the Bavarian state leaders. (He wanted to persuade them to lead a march on Berlin.) The next day he held a mass demonstration, but the police turned out in force and opened fire. Sixteen Nazis and three policeman were killed, and Hitler and his cronies were arrested. He was tried for high treason and sentenced to five years' imprisonment—though he was released after only nine months (an indication of prevailing right-wing sympathies). He used his time in prison to write his manifesto *Mein Kampf* ('My Struggle'), in which he outlined his strategy for world domination and set out his anti-semitism.

Hitler had demonstrated his dramatic powers of oratory at his trial. After his release he began to whip up nationalistic fervour, to preach revenge against the perpetrators of the Treaty of Versailles, and to blame the rest of Germany's woes on the Jews. Germany began to make a slow economic recovery in the late 1920s, but the 1929 Wall Street Crash sent her spiralling downward once more. Hitler appealed to the people suffering the most in the crisis, and offered easy solutions to their problems—and the dream of a glorious **Third Reich**. In the 1929 and 1932 elections, support for the Nazis burgeoned. In 1928 the party had held 12 of the 608 seats in the Reichstag (the national parliament). By 1932 they had 230 seats and were by far the biggest party in the country, but just short of holding complete majority. In 1933 the ageing president of the Weimar Republic, **Field Marshal von Hindenburg**, was persuaded to appoint Hitler as chancellor of a coalition govern-ment. This marked the end of the Nazi's democratic rise to power. From this point on Hitler quickly established himself as **Führer** (Leader), an absolute dictator. The Reichstag voted itself out of existence by the **Enabling Bill**—Hitler had previously arrested enough Communist and SPD deputies to ensure a two-thirds majority for the Nazis. The black-shirted **SS** (*Schutzstaffel*) led by **Heinrich Himmler** (1900–45) assumed power over the Stormtroopers, and began their reign of terror. Opponents were imprisoned, exiled, or simply killed. The notorious **concentration camps** began to swallow up Communists and other dissenters, gypsies, homosexuals and—scapegoats for all of Germany's ills—the Jews.

With power now firmly in his grasp, the new *Führer* promised a *Reich* that was to last 1000 years. He began to gear up Germany for war in order to recapture territory ceded in the Treaty of Versailles and more, so as to offer the German people increased *Lebensraum* ('living space').

The Second World War

Initially Britain, France and the USSR followed a policy of appeasement. On 30 September 1938 **Neville Chamberlain**, the British Prime Minister, flew to Germany to meet Hitler and returned waving a piece of paper and declaring that there would be 'peace in our time'. ('He seemed a nice old man,' Hitler quipped after the interview, 'so I thought I would give him my autograph'.) Then Hitler signed a **non-aggression pact** with Russia in August 1939. In September Germany invaded Poland, overrunning the country in just 18 days and sparking off the Second World War.

At first things went swimmingly for the Nazis. By June 1940 Germany had occupied Belgium, Holland, Denmark, Norway and France. Hitler now prepared **Operation Sea Lion**—the invasion of Britain. Meanwhile Italy joined in the war on the side of the Germans, attacking Greece and Egypt. By June 1941, however, Hitler had lost the air **Battle of Britain**. Lacking air supremacy he decided to postpone Operation Sea Lion, and concentrated instead on **Operation Barbarossa**—the invasion of his former allies, the Soviet Union, and his first big mistake. The German armies got to within 24km of Moscow when Hitler (remembering Napoleon's disastrous campaign) ordered the troops not to take the capital. This gave the Russians time to regroup and bring in reinforcements. The German battalions were trapped in a bitter Soviet winter, and though casualties mounted catastrophically, Hitler refused to sanction a retreat. Eventually, of the 1.5 million men who went into Russia with the Sixth Army, only 220,000 returned.

Hitler's reverse in fortunes was compounded by his second blunder. After the Japanese attack on **Pearl Harbor** in December 1941, he declared war on the USA—drastically underestimating the States' ability to wage war in Europe. Meanwhile, Allied forces were advancing steadily in the **North African campaign** and, in May 1942, Britain began serious **bombing raids** on German cities with a 1000-plane attack on Cologne. The tide had begun to turn. In 1943, with the bombing of German cities at fever-pitch, the Allies invaded Italy and began to win the **Battle of the Atlantic** at sea. The Soviets managed to retake lost territory and on 6 June 1944 the Allies invaded Normandy, creating a second front. Soon France and Belgium were liberated, but the German forces held on tenaciously and it was some months later (on 7 March 1945) that the Allies finally flooded over the Rhine at **Remagen**. On 30 April, with Soviet troops already on the outskirts of Berlin, Hitler and his bride, Eva Braun, committed suicide together in his bunker in the heart of the city. A week later German forces surrendered unconditionally and the Second World War was over. It had cost an estimated 50 million lives, six million of them in concentration camps and gas chambers, in a horrifying programme of extermination and genocide with which the German nation is still struggling to come to terms.

Post-war Germany and the Cold War

In his last days Hitler had been given to half-crazed monologues, many of them faithfully recorded by his side-kick Martin Bormann. On 2 April the *Führer* predicted with uncanny accuracy that: 'With the defeat of the Reich, there will remain in the world only two Great Powers capable of confronting each other—the United States and Soviet Russia. The laws of both history and geography will compel these two powers to a trial of strength, either military, or in the fields of economics and ideology.'

At **Potsdam** in August 1945 Germany was divided into four **zones** among the occupying Allies: Britain, France, the USA and the Soviet Union, who took the the eastern sector. Berlin, in the east of the eastern sector, was similarily divided into four. Silesia, most of Pomerania and East Prussia were given to Poland. Nazi leaders were tried for war crimes at **Nuremberg** and the Allies began a desperate search for leaders untainted by Nazi affiliations to take control of a new Germany and put the country back on its feet. There were some notorious compromises during this era—industrial magnates who had been Nazi sympathizers, such as Thyssen and Krupp, were soon released to run their businesses, scientists of the Nazi war machine were sent to work in the USA, and war criminals in possession of vital intelligence were syphoned off into obscurity in South America.

Initially the Allies seemed to be getting along rather well, but gradually ideological cracks began to show. In the eastern zone the Russians nationalized industries, enforced collectivization and introduced Soviet-style government centred on a Politburo. The other Allies set about drawing up a new democratic parliamentary constitution and stimulating private enterprise. The crunch came in 1948 when the western Allies introduced a currency reform in their zones (and later in West Berlin). In order to assist recovery, the old Reichsmark was replaced by the Deutschmark, effectively reducing its value by 93 per cent, and wiping out the national debt. The Russians responded to this rallying of capitalist power by closing all land and water routes to the former capital. The **Berlin Blockade** lasted for 10 months. Supplies were **air-lifted** to the isolated West-Berliners, until the Russians finally relented, but by this time it was already clear that Germany was being split into two separate states. In May 1949 the three western zones joined to form the **German Federal Republic** (German: Bundesrepublik Deutschland or BRD, known informally as West Germany). Four months later the Russian zone became the **German Democratic Republic** (German: Deutsche Demokratische Republik or DDR, or East Germany).

In West Germany the Social Democratic Party continued as the party of the left, while the new **Christian Democrats** (CDU) emerged as the party of the moderate right. The Federation was presided over by a figurehead president, but power lay with the *Bundestag* headed by a Chancellor. After the first elections the CDU emerged as the largest party, and their leader, the 73-year-old **Konrad Adenauer** (1876–1967), erstwhile mayor of Cologne, took up the reins. He was to remain in power for another 14 years, and takes much of the credit for Germany's dramatic recovery—though the chief architect of this **Wirtschaftswunder** (Economic Miracle) was the statesman Ludwig Erhard. Bomb-devastated Germany was at **Stunde Null** (Hour Zero), and began with a clean slate. With new factories, the latest equipment, progressive management structures and sheer hard work West Germany achieved an average annual growth rate of 8 per cent. By the 1960s the Gross National Product had increased threefold, exports were up 500 per cent and Germany had the strongest economy in Europe. In 1955 West Germany became fully accepted as a member of NATO, and two years later signed the **Rome Treaty** which established the **European Economic Community** (EEC).

Meanwhile, East Germany had become a one-party state under the **Socialist Unity Party** (SED) with power in the hands of **Walter Ulbricht** (1893–1973), the party secretary. Apart from keeping it subordinate, demanding reparations and stripping it of artworks and machinery, Stalin seemed to have little interest in this new German satellite state. Many East Germans fled to the west, and in 1953 a rebellion was successfully crushed by Soviet tanks. In 1957 East Germany became a member of the **Warsaw Pact**, a defence union of USSR-dominated East-European states. In the second half of the decade, a programme of heavy industrialization began and East Germany experienced its own Economic Miracle. In 1958 Ulbricht even boasted that the DDR would overtake West Germany in per capita income.

The Berlin Wall and Ostpolitik

Ulbricht's confidence was premature. In the late 1950s the West German economy boomed as never before. To meet the demand for labour the Federal government invited in *Gastarbeiter* (literally 'guest workers')—unskilled labourers who were given long-term residence and work permits, but no other rights of citizenship. The first *Gastarbeiter* came from Italy, Greece and Spain, but later vast numbers came from Turkey. Good salaries and the high standard of living also began to lure professional and skilled staff from East

Germany. Ulbricht grew alarmed at the brain drain. The main borders could to some extent be controlled, but West Berlin provided a conduit through which large numbers of East German workers were now flowing. Ulbricht persuaded his Russian superiors to seal the city off. On 13 August 1961—literally overnight—the graders and concrete mixers moved in and threw up the **Berlin Wall**. From the start this 'Anti-Fascist Protection Wall' was patrolled by guards with orders to shoot to kill. Other borders were strengthened and East Germany withdrew behind the longest fortification in the world after the Great Wall of China, to become one of the most impenetrable (and inescapable) of all the eastern bloc countries.

Soon after Adenauer's retirement in 1963, the parties in the Bundestag realigned themselves in a **Grand Coalition**, with the SDP playing a part in government for the first time since the 1930s. The new foreign minister was the dynamic **Willi Brandt** (1913–1992), who had been mayor of West Berlin in the period leading up to the building of the Wall. By 1969 Brandt was Chancellor. He took advantage of a thaw in Cold War relations to implement his conciliatory **Ostpolitik**. In 1972 the two Germanies signed a **Basic Treaty** in which, for the first time, West Germany officially recognized the existence of its neighbour (though it stopped short of full diplomatic relations). West Germans were allowed to visit their relatives in the east, and pensioners and the disabled (both a drain on State funds) could travel in the other direction. Ulbricht, who had not been in favour of many of the terms of the treaty, was ousted in 1971 by his Soviet overlords and replaced by **Erich Honecker** (b.1912). The signing of the treaty seemed to put paid to any hope of German unification. The neighbouring Germanies stood back-to-back, facing in different directions. In 1974 East Germany got a new constitution which 'for ever and irrevocably' allied it with the USSR and committed it to a socialist economy. In a 1980 opinion poll 70 per cent of the West Germans polled said that they thought German reunification was no longer possible.

Brandt resigned in 1974 following a scandal, when a friend and close aide, Günter Guillaume, was exposed as an East German spy. His successor **Helmut Schmidt** (b.1918) immediately had to steer the country through the tricky waters of the OPEC **oil crisis**. (The quadrupling of oil prices hit Germany especially hard because of its export-orientated economy and car manufacturing industries.) Further oil price increases in the early 1980s redoubled the Chancellor's problems. Unemployment went up to 2 million (the worst figures since the 1930s) and the budget deficit soared. In 1983, after a vote of no confidence, the government collapsed. A new coalition, headed by the CDU under **Helmut Kohl** (b.1930) called for an election and came through it in pretty much the same shape as before. Kohl gave Ostpolitik new impetus by paying an official visit to East Germany in 1987. He also bribed East Germany with interest-free loans, in return for their allowing more emigration. Emigration, however, was difficult and risky; if your application wasn't successful, you risked ruining what chances you had of a comfortable life in East Germany. Honecker did his utmost to exclude the reforming winds of *glasnost* and *perestroika* blowing in from Gorbachev's Russia, and continued to pursue a shoot-to-kill policy against people trying to jump the border. The last person to die in this way, a young East Berliner called Chris Gueffroy, was shot just nine months before the Wall came down.

Die Wende

The year 1989 saw one of the biggest changes of gear in European history this century, and was the most significant moment in German history since the Second World War. Germans call it simply *Die Wende* ('the turn' or 'the change').

On 2 May a hole appeared in the Iron Curtain—Hungary opened its borders into Austria. Thousands of East Germans flocked south, ostensibly to holiday in Hungary. By August they were jumping the border from Hungary into Austria at a rate of 200 a night, and there were 20,000 East Germans in refugee camps around Hungary awaiting official permission to leave for the West (which the Hungarian government granted on 10 September). When Honecker stopped travel to Hungary, the refugees headed for Prague. Meanwhile, opposition groups in East Germany were becoming more vociferous. The fortieth anniversary celebrations of the German Democratic Republic, on 7 October, erupted into massive **demonstrations** all around the country. Honecker was replaced by the right-wing hard-liner **Egon Krenz**. He lasted barely three weeks. Following a demonstration of over one million people in East Berlin on 4 November the old government toppled, and a liberal prime minister **Hans Modrow** took control. On Thursday 9 November, almost as an aside towards the end of a press conference, the East Berlin party chief Günter Schabowski announced that citizens of East Germany were free to travel to the West (they still needed visas, but these would be issued automatically). That weekend there was a spontaneous and emotionally charged **street party** at the Brandenburg Gate, on the border between East and West Berlin, and over 2.5 million East Germans visited the West.

Reunification

On 1 December 1989 the new East German government promised **free elections**, but the offer was upstaged a few weeks later by Helmut Kohl's declaration that his aim was a united Germany. From then on things went at breakneck speed. An **economic union** came into effect on 1 July 1990 and (after a summit with Gorbachev in the Caucasus) full **unification** took place on 3 October. In December Kohl's CDU party swept to victory in the first united German elections, forming a coalition with the small FDP (Liberal Party) and right-wing CSU to force the SDP into opposition.

Suddenly the new Germany began to feel sharp and uncomfortable **morning-after pains**, following this hectic *Wende*. To rescue the East from the economic and industrial doldrums into which it had drifted, and to pay the other costs of reunification, Kohl introduced a **special tax** in western Germany, which is proving very unpopular. Unemployment has rocketed, the economy has slid into recession and, most worrying of all, sections of the society are blaming the *Ausländer* (foreigners) for all their problems. Racist attacks, particularly against Turks, have been increasing alarmingly. A reform of Germany's liberal **asylum laws** put a squeeze on the flow of refugees from former Eastern Bloc countries (to much opposition from the Left), but at the time of writing Kohl's government still refuses to grant *Gastarbeiter*, or children born in Germany to *Gastarbeiter*, German citizenship. The fledgling united Germany is an uneasy place. The ideal of national unity has once again been stripped of its romance. On both sides of the country you'll hear people mutter that they wish someone would put the wall back up again.

The Arts and Culture

The princelings, archbishops, kings, dukes and electors who parcelled up Germany into states, then ran their domains with all the pomp and splendour they could muster, left a trail of grand palaces, beautiful churches and rich art collections right across the country. Wealthy burghers in the merchant towns joined in with competitive zeal, and the result is a prodigious, widespread artistic heritage. Local princes kept a tight hold on their collections, so Germany's treasures haven't all filtered down to one capital city, or been carried off to foreign museums. (This is one of the reasons that German art is so little known abroad.) The fierce sense of *Heimat* and (in the 19th century) a growing Romantic nationalism meant that local works of art stayed put, so small-town museums still come up with big-time surprises. Post-war prosperity, the federal system and fat arts subsidies have helped to maintain this tradition, and German children seem to grow up with a more deeply developed sense of *Kultur*, and more first-hand experience of great art and architecture than their English or American counterparts.

The petty rulers and their protegés were conservative, however, and took a while to get to grips with new ideas. Artists kept a self-effacing anonymity long after their colleagues in other countries were signing works, and are known to us by the names of their major achievements (such as the Master of the Bartholomew Altar). The Gothic style arrived later and stayed on longer than elsewhere in Europe, and the first shoots of the Renaissance in Germany appeared nearly a century after Italy was already blossoming. Of course you can see French, Italian and Netherlandish influences at work, especially in border regions, but schools and movements usually centred on one or two of the tiny states, developing a distinctive style, though often with little international recognition or impact. In their own day, many of Germany's greatest artists were local heroes only.

German art has, however, had at least two Golden Ages—one in the 16th century, with Cranach, Dürer, Grünewald and Holbein as the stars, and another early this century, when the German Expressionists developed a powerful individual style, and the Bauhaus group (quite literally) changed the shape of 20th-century architecture.

Early Days

Apart from a few **Roman** buildings such as the superb remains at Trier, Germany's earliest surviving architecture dates back to the **Carolingian Period** (9th century). Charlemagne saw himself as a direct successor to the Caesars, and energetically set about imitating things Roman. He imported southern building techniques and design for his huge palace chapel at

Aachen, and established the prototype for what was later to develop into the Romanesque style (*see* below). The secluded upper floor—from which the emperor could watch the goings-on at the high altar without being seen by the masses below—became the basis for later *Doppelkirchen* ('double churches') throughout Germany.

Although he could barely read himself, Charlemagne was an enthusiastic collector of books, and imported whole libraries from Italy and Byzantium. The lavish illustrations in these tomes must have astonished the hitherto rather inept northern painters, who were stimulated into a frenzy of **manuscript illumination**—much of it deft, vibrant and extraordinarily sophisticated. Germany's first acknowledged great painter, known as the **Master of the Registrum Gregorii**, was an illuminator—you can see his *Codex Egberti* in Trier. Charlemagne also commissioned the renowned scholar, Alcuin of York, to renovate the alphabet, which had collapsed into an illegible scrawl through centuries of semi-literate scribes copying out the pages of the Bible. The letters on this page are descended from the alphabet worked out by Alcuin and his followers at Tours in France.

Charlemagne's empire survived him by a mere 30 years. Plundering Vikings and Magyars plunged the land into desolation and confusion. But a new dynasty of German emperors, the **Ottonians**, emerged in the mid-10th century and managed to salvage Carolingian culture. During the Ottonian period there were even greater advances in manuscript illumination and architecture. The massive St Michael's in Hildesheim is the finest of surviving Ottonian churches.

Romanesque Art

Between the 10th and the 12th centuries medieval Europe stopped looking back over its shoulder at imperial Rome, and began to explore new directions for itself. Church building became an obsession, even (wrote Raoul Glaber, an 11th-century monk) when congregations were 'not in the least need... It was as if the whole earth, having cast off the old... were clothing itself in the white robe of the church.' Nineteenth-century historians called the style that emerged 'Romanesque', in the mistaken belief that it was an imitation of Roman monumental building, and just a flawed step on the way to Gothic perfection. They were wrong—Romanesque architecture has a spirit all of its own.

The new generation was determined to build in stone. They could still remember the earlier wooden-roofed buildings going up in smoke as barbarians had burned their way through the land. Enterprising masons came up with groin vaults that supported daringly large stone ceilings. The churches they put up were solid, blocky masses of geometric shapes—rectangles, cubes, cylinders and semi-circular arches. Less successful Romanesque churches are heavy and ponderous, but the best ones are sublime. The rhythmic patterns of rounded arches and columns have a soothing, meditative effect—a purity and simplicity closer to Islamic than to later Christian architecture.

Decorative elements are confined to repetitive carving on the columns and around portals, some chunky relief work and sculpture, and **frescoes**. Fresco cycles—picture-bibles for an illiterate congregation—developed into a major art form in Romanesque churches. Good examples can be found in the church of St Georg on the island of Reichenau and St Gereon in Cologne—though heavy-handed 19th-century restoration often spoils the effect.

The Romanesque cathedrals at Mainz, Worms and Speyer, smaller churches dotted around Cologne, and the magnificent abbey at Maria Laach are milestones of the period. A distinctive Rhineland style developed, marked by clusters of towers, some with roofs shaped like bishops' mitres, rows of blind arcading and a *Zwerggalerie* (dwarf gallery) looping along at roof height. These decorative effects possibly originated in Lombardy (art critics bicker over it in volumes), but the trefoil floor plan and adventurous groin vaulting are definitely local. The achievements of the 11th and early 12th centuries were Germany's first and (until the Bauhaus in the 20th century) last major contributions to international architectural design.

The Gothic Period

Renaissance critics, who revered classical antiquity, first used the term 'Gothic' as a derisive label for a style they thought violated the standards of Greece and Rome, and so simply must have come from the nasty, barbaric Goths. 'May he who invented it be cursed,' wrote one outraged historian. The exuberant, decorative style does seem cheerfully to ignore most good and true classical norms, but it has its roots in a change of mood that was permeating Europe. 'The air of the city is the breath of freedom' went the slogan. The insecurities of rural, feudal life were disappearing. A middle class of wealthy merchants and professionals, safe in their walled towns, could keep the aristocracy in check. Soaring Gothic cathedrals expressed this new confidence. They were real images on Earth of the Heavenly Jerusalem, often (in Germany at least) paid for by public subscription rather than aristocratic largesse. Burghers proudly called these new churches that towered over their towns *opus modernum* (modern work).

The attitude to women was changing too. The heroes of earlier ballads waxed rhapsodic about their swords, those of the Gothic minnesingers (lyric poets and musicians) swoon over their ladies. This was the time of gallant knights and courtly love. The church eased its restrictions on representing women in art, and the cult of the Virgin Mary burgeoned all over Europe. Romanesque painting and carving had dwelt on severe themes such as the Last Judgement. Gothic work favours gentler subjects, often centering on the Madonna.

Architecture

The pointed arches, flying buttresses, high towers and delicate tracery that characterize Gothic architecture are not merely decorative but the result of complicated new building ideas. Pointed arches led to a lighter and far more flexible system of vaulting, opening up possibilities for a more varied ground plan and much bigger windows. Buttresses helped carry the weight of the supporting masonry, so cathedrals could shoot up to impressive heights. Filigreed stonework gave support, yet also helped architects to realize their ambitions of building almost diaphanous structures. **Stained glass** flourished as an art form.

New Gothic styles had begun to appear in France around 1140, but nearly a century passed before they took hold in Germany. Early Gothic churches, like the Elizabethskirche in Marburg can seem prosaic in comparison to contemporary French achievements. But soon

German builders were imitating the Gallic flair, and by 1250 had embarked on their supreme achievement, the cathedral at Cologne. Many German builders, though, favoured the more sober **Hallenkirche** (hall church—a church with nave and aisles of the same height, sometimes with a flat roof), which had its origins in the design of monasteries for the austere Cistercian order. The Liebfrauenkirche in Munich is one of the most famous.

Sculpture

Early Gothic stone-carving, especially in Thuringia and Saxony, was in the aptly named **Zackenstil** ('jagged style'). Hard, angular lines of cloth covered the scarcely perceptible anatomy of the figures. Soon French influence was felt here, too. In around 1300 masons began to carve in the so-called **Soft Style**—soft, flowing robes, draped over perfectly moulded limbs and bodies: they were obviously working from live models. Along with this move towards naturalism came far more subtle characterization. Intense, anguished facial expressions became a speciality, and the *Man of Sorrows* was a favourite subject. Christ's face on crucifixes began to show real suffering—such as the one from St Maria im Kapitol in Cologne. **Portraiture** began to emerge as an art form, and patrons often appeared in works they had commissioned.

Some of the best carving in the Soft Style is by the **Master of Naumburg** (*see* p. 171 and 451), a German who studied in France, and introduced new ideas way ahead of his time. Other notable carvers include **Master Hartmann** and **Hans Multscher**, whose main works can be seen around Swabia, and **Heinrich Brabender**, who worked in Westphalia. The work of the **Parlér** family became famous throughout Europe during the 14th century. The father, Heinrich, came from Cologne, but moved to Swabia, where he built the Heigkreuzmünster in Gmünd. Peter, one of his sons, perfected the brilliantly realistic Parlér style of carving and achieved celebrity status when he was commissioned by Charles IV to build St Vitus's in Prague.

Tilman Riemenschneider (1460–1531), arguably the greatest sculptor of the late-Gothic period, worked mainly in wood. His restless, flamboyant carvings crop up all over Germany, but especially in and around his native Würzburg. The other great wood-carver of the period was **Veit Stoss** (*c.* 1447–1533), a talented old rascal (*see* p. 409) who spent most of his working life in Nuremberg turning out exquisite, realistic masterpieces. Of the late-Gothic stone-sculptors the Mainz artist **Hans Backoffen** stands out. His monumental works represent a transitional stage between the Gothic period and the Renaissance.

Panel Painting

When artists began to paint on wooden panels (in Germany around 1300), art became portable and saleable, and styles began to spread more quickly. Painting had evolved out of manuscript illumination. Early painters were seen as craftsmen, trained and controlled by powerful guilds. The guild got them commissions, and made sure that the work was well-paid. It was only later, during the Gothic period and early Renaissance, that artists began to emerge as individuals and personally sign their work. In Germany this took a long time, as the guilds were more powerful than elsewhere in Europe.

Most early panel paintings were intended as altarpieces. Initially, the pictures were quite static. Backgrounds were of gold leaf or covered in ornament, and figures related to each other with stylized gestures. Later, the Soft Style (which is also known as the International Style) took over here too. Painters created little scenes; people talk to each other, there is far more realism and a stronger narrative element than before. **Master Bertram** (c. 1345–1415), a Hamburg painter and the first German artist we know by name, liked to paint narrative cycles on small panels that he would group around a sculpture. **Conrad von Soest** (active c. 1394–1422) did appealing, brightly coloured pieces with fine attention to detail. **Conrad Witz** (c. 1400–46) did much to move German painting towards a greater sense of realism, though his work is very much in a blunt, sculptural 'hard' style. It was **Jan Joest** of Kalkar (c. 1455–1519) and **Hans Pleydenwurff** (c. 1420–72) who were most influenced by Netherlandish naturalism. Pleydendurff's panels especially show a richness of colour and careful composition reminiscent of the Flemish painter Dirk Bouts. Pleydendurff was the first German to paint landscapes (rather than patterns or cities) into the background of his works. Painters of the **Danube School** based in Passau and Salzburg refined this technique towards the end of the 15th century, filling out their panels with lush Danube country scenes.

Artists working in the south, such as Conrad Witz (who spent much of his life in Switzerland) and the Tyrolean **Michael Pacher** (c. 1435–98) came under Italian influence. Pacher painted with hard, bright colours. A harsh light shines on his subjects, casting strong, clear shadows. (You can see examples in the Alte Pinakothek in Munich.) Painters in Cologne, on the other hand, followed the trends in the neighbouring Netherlands. In the 15th century they developed such a distinctive style that later art historians have grouped them together as the Cologne School.

The Cologne School

The first to paint in this softer, more realistic Cologne style was the **Master of St Veronica** (c. 1420). He is named after a painting (now in the Alte Pinakothek in Munich) of St Veronica holding up the Sudarium (a cloth she had offered to Christ on the road to Golgotha to wipe the sweat from his brow, and which was handed back with the Lord's face miraculously imprinted on it). The large-scale image of Christ's countenance, and Veronica's gentle features are said to have sent Goethe into raptures.

The supreme artist of the school, if not of the entire German Soft Style, was **Stephen Lochner** (c. 1410–51). He paints with loving detail, and his works are subtly shaded, often with a glowing ethereal quality. (You can see many of his paintings in the Alte Pinakothek or in Cologne, where his masterpiece, the *Epiphany Triptych*, is in the cathedral.) Later artists of the Cologne School, such as the **Master of the Life of the Virgin** (active c. 1460–85) and the **Master of the St Ursula Legend** (active c. 1490–1505), developed a more narrative style and filled their panels with anecdotal detail. The School's last great practitioner was also its most idiosyncratic. The **Master of the St Bartholomew Altarpiece** (active c. 1470–1510) handles colour in a more sophisticated way than even Lochner, but includes quirky details. In the St Bartholomew altarpiece his fashionably dressed, bejewelled women look like anything but the saints they are meant to depict. Strung behind them, a brocade backdrop recalls the gold backgrounds of earlier paintings; over the top of it, you can see a more modern dreamy landscape.

The Renaissance

Architecturally, Germany was immersed in the Gothic until well into the 16th century, though in sculpture and painting new forces were already stirring in the late 1400s. At the turn of the century this new energy burst into a brief but brilliant Golden Age of German painting. By 1528, with the death of the main exponents, Dürer and Grünewald, the force seemed spent and the Golden Age fizzled out just as quickly as it had begun. The exact reason for the sudden decline is not clear—though the religious wars that racked the land and the rise of Protestantism no doubt played a part.

Painting and Graphics

The new movement was triggered by a conscious desire to copy what was going on in Italy at the time. Wealthy merchants in south Germany had close contact with Venice, and Germany's humanists were in touch with scholars in Florence. Italian engravings circulated throughout northern Europe, and led to a corresponding German interest in **graphic arts** (i.e. line drawing, illustration and printmaking). The most skilled and adventurous German engraver was **Martin Schongauer** (c. 1450–91). His subtle metal-engraving technique became a standard for German graphic artists, and his blending of realism with delightful innovation, and choice of exotic (even demonic) subjects, have led art-historians to call him the father of the German Renaissance.

The name that overshadows all others of the period is that of the Nuremberg artist **Albrecht Dürer** (1471–1528). He is Germany's complete Renaissance Man—an artist, scientist, mathematician and thinker—the 'Leonardo of the North'. Dürer was the first northerner to travel to Italy expressly to study art. He worked with tremendous energy and was the first artist outside of Italy to become internationally famous in his own time. His engravings—many of them of popular subjects at a price ordinary people could afford— spread his renown, and made him a rich man. Many say that he is at his best as an engraver—the versatility, luminosity and dramatic power of his woodcuts have never been surpassed. He could also show a sensitive and delicate touch, and is equally celebrated for beautiful watercolour nature studies (though the fading originals of these are rarely exhibited). His later paintings, such as the *Four Apostles* (1526) in the Alte Pinakothek in Munich, show a subtlety of touch and extraordinarily strong characterization. Dürer's paintings and woodcuts surface in museums all over Germany, but his best work can be seen in Munich, Nuremberg and Berlin.

Matthias Gothardt-Niethardt, known as **Grünewald** (c. 1480–1528), another artist of highly original genius, worked for the archbishops of Mainz as court painter, architect and hydraulic engineer before fleeing Germany in 1525, having been on the wrong side in the ill-fated Peasants' Revolt. Unlike Dürer, he was largely forgotten until recent years. His reputation rests mainly on an enormous polyptych, the *Isenheim Altarpiece* (1510–15), which many regard as the supreme achievement of German art. The original altar is in

Colmar (now in France), but there is a gruelling version of the *Crucifixion* panel in Karlsruhe—perhaps the most memorable interpretation of the subject ever. It is a taut, agonized picture, painted in dissonant colours and angular shapes. **Jerg Ratgeb** (*c.* 1480–1526), a fiery painter who was also involved in the Peasants' Revolt (and ended up cut in quarters), painted expressive works that show Grünewald's influence. You can see his frescoes in Frankfurt and Maulbron, and an altarpiece in Stuttgart.

Albrecht Altdorfer (*c.* 1480–1538) was the kingpin of the **Danube School** (*see* above), which continued to flourish into the Renaissance, and is credited with the first landscape in Western art painted for its own sake. He was a talented and unorthodox colourist, especially when it came to light and atmospheric effects, and had a penchant for depicting fantastic buildings (he was also an architect). His most important work, the enormous *Battle of Issus* (1529, in the Alte Pinakothek) swarms with insect-like soldiers, each finished with a miniature-painter's precision. At least half the canvas is taken up by a dramatic landscape that gives the onlooker a god's-eye view across the Alps to Cyprus and Egypt.

Lucas Cranach the Elder (1472–1553), another artist of the Danube School, is best known for his later works. These are usually on humanist rather than religious themes (mythology, history and portraits) and feature nudes, which Cranach paints with disarming, almost naive, charm. A strain of humorous, rather wicked eroticism runs through his paintings. In the latter part of his life, in answer to a summons from the Elector of Saxony, he settled in Wittenberg. Here he became a friend of Luther, and established a workshop that churned out paintings at an alarming rate. His son **Lucas Cranach the Younger** (1515–86) carried on the work, a worthy imitation of his father, but without much original flair.

The period's quirkiest painter was **Hans Baldung** (1484–1545), known as **Grien** because he always wore green clothes. He studied under Dürer, from whom he learnt his fine colouring technique. His choice of subject matter and even his treatment of conventional themes is delightfully (almost wilfully) bizarre. Baldung's works are scattered throughout Germany, but you can easily spot them. In the Early German galleries of a museum, if your eye is caught by an odd painting of an evil-looking cupid, a bewitched child or a weird woman, it is sure to be by Baldung.

Augsburg, as seat of the Hapsburg court and home to the powerful Fugger family (*see* p. 326), was an influential centre of the Renaissance in Germany, The most notable artists to rise from this milieu were **Hans Bugkmair** (1473–1531), a master of opulent Italianate decoration, and **Hans Holbein the Younger** (1497–1543), best known for his firm, faultless portraits. When Holbein upped sticks for England in 1531, he left the German Renaissance in its dying throes.

While it lasted, it was primarily a boom in painting and graphics. Developments in **architecture** came later and were more episodic. In Augsburg **Elias Holl** (1573–1646) took Italian models to heart, and put up buildings that have little of Germany about them at all. Most survivors of the period are civil or domestic buildings—ornate Rathäuser or high-gabled merchants' houses decorated with scrolls, obelisks and statues. The most charming architecture of the period is to be found along the river Weser in the north, around

Hamelin and Hannover. Here Dutch and Flemish styles exerted an influence, and a **Weser Renaissance** style developed. Multi-storeyed, gabled houses with large bay windows are richly ornamented with spiky projections, scrollwork and *Neidköpfe* (grotesque carvings of jealous neighbours' heads).

Baroque and Rococo

There is no clear dividing line between Renaissance and Baroque. The Renaissance was an age of innovation and discovery, but its images were relatively static. Baroque art moves. Artists tested the new ground their predecessors had laid out, took a few shaky steps, then ran riot. Art historian Helen Gardner described the era as 'spacious and dynamic, brilliant and colorful, theatrical and passionate, sensual and ecstatic, opulent and extravagant, versatile and *virtuoso*.' Façades are sinuous and irregular. Interiors writhe with twisted pillars, horseshoe vaulting and stucco. The dome, oval and circle are the underlying shapes of design. Bumps are gilded, and flat surfaces covered in bright painting. Witty *trompe l'oeil* abounds, often combined with clever 3-D stucco trickery. Stained glass is banished and churches are flooded with light—often from hidden sources that throw up contrasting patterns of shade. Enthusiasm for the Virgin and the saints was redoubled, and altarpieces became monumental. Later, as Baroque broke into the lighter, airier and even more fantastic Rococo, stucco-work became less intense, but even more irregular. Asymmetrical cartouches and cake-icing licks of dazzling white plaster are spread with happy abandon.

Early Baroque painting in Germany is fairly unremarkable: the glory days were in the latter part of the 17th and early 18th centuries, as late Baroque became Rococo. After about 1660 abbots and bishops in the south of the country—back in place after the Counter-Reformation—set about rebuilding their churches with exuberance. Most couldn't resist a show of triumph and commissioned top, fashionable architects who came up with the most ambitious plans their patrons could afford. Today Germany's most spectacular Baroque and Rococo art is to be seen in the frescoes, decoration and design of these southern churches and palaces. The responsibility for most of the best work lies with a brilliant few who seldom restricted themselves to one skill but designed, painted frescoes and often did the stucco work too.

The Big Names in Architecture

Balthasar Neumann (1687–1753) was the era's supremo. He started work in Würzburg as a bell-founder, took up architecture as a hobby and was soon snapped up by the powerful Schönborn family to build churches and palaces throughout Germany. His complicated designs have such energy and intricate detail, and there is such a flowing pulse between space and massive structure, that at least one art-critic likens them to a Bach fugue—as 'frozen music'. Neumann relished meetings with other architects and enriched his own style with what he learnt from great French, Viennese and Italian artists of the time. Grand, sweeping staircases were a speciality (you can see fine examples in Würzburg and Brühl), and his churches can be breathtaking—the Vierzehnheiligenkirche near Bamberg being one of the best.

The **Asam Brothers**—sculptor Egid Quirin Asam (1692–1750) and painter Cosmas Damien Asam (1686–1739)—formed a team, first to decorate existing churches, later to undertake entire projects of their own (such as the Asamkirche in Munich). The brothers studied in Rome and were never seduced from their stately, southern High Baroque style into the frivolities of Rococo. Cosmas Asam became particularly well-known for his tricks with perspective and vast dome paintings of the open heavens.

The Rococo period was dominated by two other siblings, architect **Dominikus Zimmerman** (1685–1766) and his fresco-painting brother **Johann Baptist Zimmerman** (1680–1785). Together they worked on the Wieskirche in 1750 (*see* p. 333), which many hold to be Germany's supreme achievement in the style. Johann Baptist also worked with another great architect of the time, the Belgian **François Cuvilliés** (1695–1767), on the Munich Residenz and Schloß Nymphenburg. The diminutive Cuvilliés was originally employed by Elector Max Emmanuel as a court jester, and only began working as an architect in his thirties. His theatre in the Munich Residenz and the Amalienburg in the Nymphenburg park are Rococo at its most delightful.

Neoclassicism

Frederick the Great's Berlin became the focus for growing moves towards a more restrained Neoclassicism, which later also became fashionable in Munich and around Mainz and Cologne. Neoclassicism was a more stringent and academic revival of Greek and Roman architecture. Buildings became plainer, with simple pediments and colonnaded porticoes in front of the entrances. Interiors were muted, with the odd Rococo flourish, or decorated in the styles of Greece and Rome. (Excavation of Pompeii, which began in 1748, fired enthusiasm for this, and threw new light on ancient design.) German architects favoured colder Doric styles, and the desire for symmetry became obsessive. In some churches a false pulpit was even erected to counterbalance the functional one. Leading architect of the day was **Karl-Friedrich Schinkel** (1781–1841). His long colonnades are a characteristic feature of central Berlin.

Neoclassical painting tended to be skilful, though cold—or subject to nationalistic fervour. One painter who did introduce some warmth into his canvases was **Johann Heinrich Wilhelm Tischbein** (1751–1829), the youngest of a dynasty of Neoclassical artists. His idyllic landscapes were a source of great inspiration to Goethe, whose portrait Tischbein painted, lounging in an Italian setting. **Januarius Zick** (1730–97), the most prominent member of another painter family, is best known for monumental frescoes (such as those at Bruchsal and Wiblingen).

The Nineteenth Century

We desire to surrender our whole being, that it may be filled with the perfect bliss of one glorious emotion.

Goethe's romantic hero, Werther

Eighteenth-century gallants thought it in bad taste to be 'original' or 'enthusiastic' (read 'eccentric' or 'sincere'). Stony, sober Neoclassicism vanquished the artifice and frivolity of Rococo, and banished emotion even further from polite society. Yet, almost at the same time, after 1750, another quite different mood was filtering through Europe. It became quite fashionable to swoon, languish in unrequited love and weep. All of this was done with gusto by the heroes and heroines of a new literary phenomonen that was sweeping the continent—the novel (German: *Roman*). German critics were the first to call this flowering of sensibility 'Romantic'—to distinguish what they saw as peculiarly 'modern' traits in the arts from the old values of Neoclassicism.

In Germany the Romantic movement, which reached its peak in the first half of the 19th century, was felt primarily in music and literature, and to a lesser extent in painting. In architecture Neoclassicism held out until around 1830, when it was routed by **Neo-Gothic**. For the Romantics the Gothic style epitomized their dreamy ideal of Old Germany, and many great Gothic cathedrals received their finishing touches in the 1800s, seven centuries after they had been started. (The famous spires on Cologne's cathedral were topped off only in 1880). Fake Gothic—and some classical—'ruins' popped up in the grounds of grand homes all over the country. In Bavaria King Ludwig II outdid everyone with his series of fairytale castles (*see* p. 338, 370 and 374).

The year 1850 saw the beginning of the **Gründerjahre** (Founders' Period), when wealthy industrialists put up showy mansions (design invariably coming second to size in their priorities) and filled the rooms with reproduction medieval furniture. The middle classes contented themselves with **Biedermeier**—lighter, comfortable, cushioned furniture characterized by simple, flowing lines, elegant wood veneers and glass-fronted cabinets.

Romantic Painting

In **Caspar David Friedrich** (1774–1840) you can see Romantic painting in its very essence. He is perhaps the one 19th-century German painter whose works are widely popular and familiar outside of his own country. His highly original pictures of mist-shrouded Gothic ruins, winter-blasted landscapes and violent, windswept seas, hauntingly reveal the Romantic obsession with death and isolation, and prints of these adorn the walls of sensitive and suicidal youth throughout the western world. Human figures (if they feature at all) are tiny, often seen from the back, and overwhelmed by powerful Nature. Friedrich's most dramatic and moving works can be seen in Hamburg and Berlin.

Few other German artists of the time can match Friedrich's stature. The architect **Karl-Friedrich Schinkel** (*see* above), who took to painting to earn extra money, managed to slip easily into a more Romantic style and came up with spectacular architectural fantasies. **Philipp Otto Runge** (1777–1810) is best known for his portraits of chubby-cheeked children (usually his own), but at the time of his early death was collaborating with Goethe on a project involving vast paintings, poetry and music with which he hoped to recover the lost harmony of the universe. Only studies of the paintings—*The Times of Day*—remain. **Anselm Feuerbach** (1829–80), an artist rather neglected outside of Germany, painted big, Italianate canvases and is at his best with powerful, brooding portraits of women. The

Swiss-born **Arnold Böcklin** painted delightful, fey pictures on mythological or fairytale themes. **Hans Thoma** (1839–1924), the erstwhile director of the Karlsruhe art museum, could come up with sensitive, moving paintings, but often lapsed into gooey sentimentality.

In an abandoned monastery in Rome **Johann Friedrich Overbeck** (1789–1869) founded the **Nazarene Brotherhood**—a group of German artists who painted detailed, idealistic, rather enchanted canvases in a style later taken up by the Pre-Raphaelites in England. Overbeck lived out his life in Italy, but other painters—including **Peter von Cornelius** (1783–1867) and **Wilhelm Schadow** (1788–1862)—returned to Germany, where their activity centred on the **Düsseldorf Academy**. Here the style of the school degenerated into vast, pompous historical paintings. The painters were popular, however, and their frescoes are emblazoned on the walls of public buildings across the country.

Other 19th-century Painters

During the 19th century Munich and Berlin became centres of the arts, each developing avant-garde groups that rebelled against powerful, conservative institutions such as the Düsseldorf Academy. In Berlin painters formed the **Secession movement**, headed by **Max Liebermann** (1847–1935), but it was in the Schwabing quarter of Munich that the most adventurous artists gathered (*see* p. 352–3). At the centre of the Munich movement was **Franz von Stuck** (1863–1928), a highly individual artist whose dark, mysterious paintings seem an odd mixture of Pre-Raphaelite style and Expressionist violence.

Portraiture was in popular demand and obliging artists such as **Franz von Lenbach** (1863–1904) moved in the highest society, making themselves very rich. (Lenbach painted Bismarck no fewer than 80 times.) **Realism** returned as a style later in the century. **Adolf Menzel** (1815–1905) was one of the first painters to capture scenes from the newly industrialized cities on canvas, while **Wilhelm Liebl** (1844–1900) is especially renowned for his studies of Bavarian peasants, painted from life. **Impressionism** made very little impact on Germany—perhaps the bright colours and light touch just didn't appeal to the national temperament. The only really exciting German impressionist was **Lovis Corinth** (1858–1925)—though his large, gentle pictures often seem rather cold.

Jugendstil

Towards the end of the 19th century a reaction set in against the blunt, hard shapes that were the aesthetic by-product of industrialization. Influenced by the flowing lines of Japanese prints, and by William Morris's intricate, interwoven designs and radical views which put handicraft back on its medieval pedestal, a new style emerged, centred mainly in Paris and Vienna. The French called this ornamental style of graceful, serpentine lines and organic forms Art Nouveau. In Germany it was known as Jugendstil—the style named after the journal which promoted it, *Jugend* ('Youth'). Architecture, sculpture, painting and especially the applied arts (furniture, ceramics, glassware and even jewellery) were swept up into an enormously popular movement that lasted until the First World War. Early Jugendstil architecture in Germany shows its Neoclassical ancestry. Houses are symmetrically and solidly built, but graced with flowing decoration—often with fruit and flower motifs or wistful women's faces. (There are charming pockets of domestic Jugendstil in

Bonn and Bremen.) Later, lines became stronger and more dramatic and seem to prefigure Expressionist and Bauhaus styles. (The main buildings at Mathildenhöhe in Darmstadt are a case in point, *see* p. 197). German furniture makers and glass-blowers excelled themselves, and exquisite examples of their work crop up in museums all over the country. Look out for jewellery by Patriz Huber, glassware by Peter Behrens and stylish household goods by Joseph M. Olbrich. (The Landesmuseum in Karlsruhe, the Museum für Angewandte Kunst in Cologne, the Glasmuseum in Passau and the Künstlerkolonie Museum in Darmstadt all have superb collections of Jugendstil.)

The Twentieth Century

It was France that led European painting into the 20th century. Germany lagged rather sorrowfully behind. Impressionism hardly made a mark east of the Rhine, but when the Fauves (French for 'wild beasts') under the leadership of Henri Matisse hit Paris in 1905, German artists began to stir again. The Fauves' shocking colours and bold patterns were far more appealing. The Germans began to turn out intense, savage canvases, lashed with vigorous brushwork, blazing with clashing colours and strongly expressive of personal feeling. The movement, which became known as **Expressionism**, also affected literature (especially drama) and film, and produced the first German art for centuries to make an impact on the outside world. German Expressionism was still going strong in the 1930s when Hitler labelled the movement 'degenerate'. Works were banned, a lot was destroyed, and many of the artists fled the country. Some of the painters who come under the expressionist umbrella were also part of simultaneous movements—such as the anarchic **Berlin Dadaists** and **Neue Sachlichkeit** (*see* below), a 'post-expressionist trend' which began years before Expressionism was exhausted. The **Bauhaus** school—which grew out of Jugendstil and the British-inspired Arts and Crafts movement—attracted some major Expressionist artists, but developed an individual style that was to set the pace for 20th-century architecture and design.

The German Expressionist Painters

Although the expressionist movement was ignited by the Fauves it burned on solid German fuel. The strong colour, hard line, emotional subject matter and even the otherworldly overtones are direct descendants of earlier German painting and engraving. The expressionists organized themselves into two schools: **Die Brücke** ('The Bridge'—uniting nature and emotion) and **Der Blaue Reiter** ('The Blue Rider'—after a picture by Kandinsky).

Die Brücke was founded in Dresden in 1905 by three disgruntled architecture students who had taken to painting—**Ernst Ludwig Kirchner** (1880–1938), **Erich Heckel** (1883–1970) and **Karl Schmidt-Rottluff** (1884–1976). They revived the woodcut as an art form and put such emphasis on colour that it became as much a component of their paintings as the subject itself. Soon after it was founded the group (with some new members tagging along behind them) moved from Dresden to Berlin, left off painting gaudy landscapes and turned to scenes from city life. They broke up to follow their individual careers in 1913, Kirchner having the most sustained success.

Der Blaue Reiter was formed in 1911 by two artists scorned by the powerful Munich establishment—**Wassily Kandinsky** (1866–1944) and **Franz Marc** (1880–1916). Later they were joined by (amongst others) **August Macke** (1887–1914) and the Swiss painter **Paul Klee** (1879–1940), and *Der Blaue Reiter* became a more loosely-knit group, aimed at promoting Modernism in all the arts. Colour, line and shape became more important than subject matter—a brave and imaginative step that set painting well on the way to pure abstraction. Kandinsky was already being called an 'abstract expressionist' in 1919. He divided his work into *Compositions* (consciously planned and ordered geometrical shapes) and *Improvisations* (spontaneous arrangements of colour). Marc's work was more representational; he loved painting animals. He was beginning to move towards a more abstract, geometrical style when he was killed in the First World War. Macke (who also died in the war) painted gentle scenes—often of slender, brightly dressed figures floating through parks or down quiet streets. Before he died his work began to show a Cubist influence. Klee was the oddest of the four. His paintings and drawings are usually small—subtle, whimsical figures of men, animals and fantastical creatures drawn with child-like brevity. They seem to lift the lid on a sensitive, very personal view of a mysterious universe.

Many of Germany's most renowned Expressionists, however, belonged to neither school. The most individualistic of these (though he was for a time a member of *Die Brücke*) was **Emil Hansen** (1867–1956), known as **Nolde** after his birthplace. His distorted, violent canvases are very much reminiscent of Grünewald, or the Flemish painter Hieronymus Bosch. **George Grosz** (1893–1959) was a prominent member of the anarchic Berlin Dadaists (*see* below), and is best known for the savage, indignant caricature-like drawings with which he lambasted capitalist society, and the decadent Weimar Republic in particular. **Käthe Kollwitz** (1867–1945), one of the leading women artists of the 20th century, took the woodcut and engraving to heights not reached since Dürer. Her wrenching black and white images are usually powerful, poignant cries against the horrors of war. After her son was killed in the First World War she became preoccupied with a Mother and Child theme, and when her grandson was killed in the Second World War her woodcuts and sculptures became howls of the deepest tragedy. **Ernst Barlach** (1870–1938) produced haunting sculptures with sharp, smoothly-planed lines that show medieval influence. He is best known for his *Memorial Angel* (1927)—a war memorial depicting the dying soul at the moment it is about to awake into everlasting life (now in the Antoniterkirche in Cologne). **Max Beckmann** (1884–1950) was an independently minded painter who bridged the gap to *Neue Sachlichkeit* (*see* below). His bitter paintings of distorted figures accentuated by hard, black lines reflect the horrors of the First World War and of Nazi oppression. Often he paints himself as a clown, king or convict—the artist buffeted by his times.

Bauhaus

In 1906 the Belgian Jugendstil designer Henry van de Velde (1863–1957) started a School of Arts and Crafts in Weimar. When he left Germany at the outbreak of the First World War he recommended an ambitious young architect, **Walter Gropius** (1883–1969), as his successor. In 1919 Gropius took over the directorship, changed the name of the school to Das Staatliche Bauhaus Weimar, redesigned the curriculum and eventually (in 1925) moved the whole caboodle to a sparkling new building in Dessau. The new Bauhaus, which immediately attracted artists such as Kandinsky and Klee as teachers, was rooted in the Arts and Crafts tradition of the previous century in that it offered a broad range of disciplines from architecture to drama and basket weaving. However, it set itself squarely in post-war Germany and, unlike the Arts and Crafts movement in Britain, it was prepared to exploit modern mass-production techniques to solve problems in areas such as housing and urban planning. Bauhaus wanted to unite art and technology and had two main aims—to work '*am Bau*' (in connection with a real building, rather than just theoretically), and to come up with inventive, but practical prototypes for industry.

In 1911 the American architect Frank Lloyd Wright (1867–1959) held a tremendously influential exhibition in Berlin. Around the same time the Swiss architect Charles Edouard Jeanneret-Gris (1887–1965, known as Le Corbusier) was designing rectilinear 'functional' houses—'machines for living'. Both men used the new invention of prestressed concrete to revolutionize building design, and became leading exponents of the **International Style**—a 'machine-age' architecture of clean, straight lines, open-plan interiors and no decoration at all. (One architect went so far as to call decoration a 'crime'.) The Dessau Bauhaus not only fitted into this climate, but firmly established the principles of the International Style. Indeed Gropius designed the skeleton of concrete slabs held up by steel pillars that was to be the heart of Le Corbusier's buildings and which still forms the basic structure of much of 20th-century architecture. Buildings designed by Gropius and other Bauhaus architects, such as the superbly imaginative **Ludwig Mies van der Rohe** (1886–1969, designer of New York's Seagram Building), became touchstones of modern architecture. A number of Bauhaus architects went to the USA in the 1930s. Their enormous influence on the design world there helped to make the USA the leader of architectural and design style in the immediate post-war era.

Neue Sachlichkeit

Neue Sachlichkeit is usually translated into English as 'New Objectivity'—a loose term which is really only right when you take objectivity to mean neutrality or 'matter-of-factness'. The name describes a small trend that grew up in opposition to Expressionism around 1923. *Neue Sachlichkeit* artists painted with a ruthless realism, often with a harsh almost sadistic touch and an acid left-wing political comment. Though many of the painters in this new movement had come through a period of Expressionism, they now renounced what they regarded as Expressionism's emotional excess and lack of control. The *Neue Sachlichkeit* painters, as had many of the Expressionists, used the city as subject matter, but their focus was hard and (they believed) without sentiment. 'Man is good' had been the Expressionist dictum. 'Man is a beast' retorted George Grosz at the beginning of the 1920s. George Grosz and Max Beckmann were both associated with the style for a time, but its most famous practitioner was **Otto Dix** (1891–1969). His meticulous, at times rather vicious pictures show grotesque, larger-than-life characters and dwell on human suffering and the decadence of city life. The Galerie der Stadt Stuttgart has by far the most comprehensive collection of his work.

Oddly, *Neue Sachlichkeit* and Bauhaus had little to do with each other, though the no-frills, tidy approach characteristic of both schools has led to the work of some later Bauhaus artists being given a *Neue Sachlichkeit* label. Later *Neue Sachlicheit* work spills over into complete abstraction with the work of **Willi Baumeister** (1889–1955) and **Oskar Schlemmer** (1888–1943), a mercurial artist who flits between styles and schools. He is perhaps most famous for the ballets he designed for students at the Bauhaus.

The Dadaists

The zany, irreverent, nihilistic Dada movement (which was based mainly in Zurich, Barcelona and New York) had its followers in Berlin and Dresden too. Dada art was intentionally disruptive and ephemeral. **Kurt Schwitters** (1887–1948), however, did contribute some more lasting works. He made collages from rubbish and scrap paper, which he called *Merz Pictures*. (*Merz* is a syllable from the German word for 'commercial', and caught Schwitters' attention one day when he was cutting up newspapers). **Max Ernst** (1891–1976) began as a Dadaist, also making collages, but in the 1920s he left Germany for America and France, where he turned more towards Surrealism.

After the War

In 1937 the Nazis had held an exhibition of *Entartete Kunst* ('Degenerate Art') in Munich. Most of the prominent artists of the day were featured, and their work was later banned or destroyed. It is not surprising that after this, and the horrors of the Second World War, German artists wanted to start afresh. In 1957 Heinz Mack (b.1931), Günther Uecker (b.1930) and Otto Piene (b.1928) formed **ZERO**. Their aim was to strip away all the elements by which art was traditionally defined and reduce it to pure absolutes—space and colour. Their anti-individualist manifesto had an influence all over Europe, and in the 1960s artists began to come up with completely blank monochrome canvases.

Other German artists, working in more individual ways, have also made a mark on the international scene. **Georg Baselitz** (b.1938) is the most easily recognizable, as he hangs his bright, energetic, rather primitive paintings upside down in an attempt to make you redefine the way you see things. **Sigmar Polke** (b.1941) began by painting abstract designs onto boards, blankets and odd bits of cloth, but has recently become intrigued by colour, producing thinly coated pastel-shaded panels. **Anselm Kiefer** (b.1945) wants to counter the power of American culture by appealing to the traditions of Old Europe. He works on a monumental scale employing good, old-fashioned painterly skills in new ways. His vast paintings would seem to hark back to the styles of the Renaissance, but are filled with modern surprises such as tacked on bits of paper and the odd hole in the canvas. **A.R. Penck** (b.1939) paints giant stick figures interspersed with symbols from different epochs—from mythological signs to technical designs.

The movement of art over the past few decades—away from painting and towards installation, performance and constructed sculpture—is seen by many to have its origins in the work of **Joseph Beuys** (1921–85, see p. 95). Beuys has been called the father of the European avant-garde. His piles of fat and felt and esoteric statements on man and nature are to be found all over Germany, and are imitated in art colleges around the world. His 'action art'—walks or water journeys, planting oak trees in Kassel (*see* p. 207)—have become the core of much recent ecologically focussed work.

The work of **Gerhard Richter** (b.1932) is more accessible and is becoming increasingly popular. He begins with photographs (often of animals, the sky, or family snaps), blows them up and lightly stylizes them, frequently in shades of grey and blue paint. **Jörg Immendorf** (b.1945) is best known for his grotesque carvings, and nightmarish paintings that would seem to owe a debt to Otto Dix. Like Dix, he takes his politics seriously and his works often carry an overt political message.

The destruction wrought by Allied bombers led to a building boom in the 1950s and 1960s. Much of the work was hurried, functional and ugly. The trend towards **Brutalism**—an austere style that had its origins in the Bauhaus and is characterized by its emphasis on the building materials (especially bare concrete) and unconcealed service pipes—did little to improve the situation. The one area where there was interesting innovation was in **church architecture**. The most exciting designs are by **Gottfried Böhm**, who also has a flair for shiny glass hotels and office blocks. Healthy federal budgets, and imaginative planning, have resulted in a number of spectacular, though sometimes controversial, museum buildings and concert halls such as Frankfurt's Museum für Moderne Kunst and the Philharmonie in Berlin. Big Business has added a few spectacular landmarks such as the Thyssen Steel headquarters in Düsseldorf, or the Frankfurt Messe Tower.

Today Cologne and Düsseldorf are the main centres of the German art trade, and Munich and Stuttgart universities seem to attract the more exciting art students.

Literature: A Concise Chronology of German Writing

See also **Further Reading** p. 634 for more detail on some of the works mentioned below.

Middle Ages

With the exception of some clerical writings, the ancient Germans had no literature. Closer contact with French culture during long marches to the Holy Land in the 12th century fired crusaders with an enthusiasm for ballads and narrative poems and led to the evolution of the *Minnesang* (*see* **German Music** below). At the same time writers began to record sagas from Germany's rich oral tradition.

c. 1200: The Nibelungenlied. An epic poem that embroiders true historical events surrounding the fall of the Burgundian nation. Part one relates how Siegfried (the dragon-slayer) defeats the supposedly invincible Brunhild, thus winning her hand for King Gunther of the Burgundians. In return Siegfried is allowed to marry Kriemhild, Gunther's sister. Jealousy between the two women leads to Siegfried's murder. The second part of the poem deals with Kriemhild's revenge, as she brings about the fall of the Burgundian dynasty.

1200–1210: Parzifal. An Arthurian legend about a knight in quest of the Holy Grail, by Wolfram von Eschenbach (*c.* 1170–1210). The epic poem is full of prescriptions for correct courtly behaviour.

1170–1228: Walther von der Vogelweide, greatest of the minnesingers (*see* p. 430).

c. **1510:** First publication of the anecdotes about **Til Eulenspiegel**, a prankster and practical joker who had lived near Brunswick at the beginning of the 14th century. (Later the subject of an orchestral piece by Richard Strauss and an epic poem by the 19th-century writer Gerhart Hauptmann.)

The Reformation

1534: Luther finishes his translation of the Bible—the point taken as the foundation of modern German as a literary language.

1618–48: The Thirty Years' War devastates the country and wrecks any chance of cultural advance for decades afterwards.

1669: Johann von Grimmelhausen publishes **Simplicissmus**, a picaresque novel set against the backdrop of the Thirty Years' War, and considered a highpoint of 17th-century European literature.

The Enlightenment

The Age of Reason, during which philosophical, rather than literary, writing predominates. Germany begins to earn its reputation as a nation of *Dichter und Denker* (poets and thinkers).

1646–1716: Gottfried Wilhelm Leibnitz. Historian, linguist and philosopher. He wrote *Théodicée* (in French; 1710) and invented differential calculus independently of Newton.

1729–81: Gotthold Ephraim Lessing. His rationalist plays and critical writings are considered to be the basis of modern German drama.

1724–1803: Friedrich Gottlieb Klopstock. Considered one of the forefathers of German Classicism. He saw himself as a Christian Homer and devoted most of his life to the epic *Der Messiade* (The Messiah).

1724–1804: Immanuel Kant. An idealist philosopher. His main works, *Critique of Pure Reason* (1781) and *Critique of Practical Reason* (1788), examine the balance between liberty and morality.

Sturm und Drang and Classicism

Sturm und Drang, in reaction to the rationalism of the previous age, exalted nature, sentiment and personal liberty. Goethe, the greatest writer of the time, later tempered the exuberance of *Sturm und Drang* with the vision of a harmonious classical ideal.

1749–1832: Johann Wolfgang von Goethe. A wide-ranging genius whose output ranged from scientific theses to drama, poetry and novels. He was also a painter, musician, naturalist and politician. He spent much of his adult life in Weimar, at the centre of the cultural circle that developed there.

1759–1805: Friedrich von Schiller. A poet and playwright known mainly for historical dramas extolling liberty, such as *William Tell* (1802). He settled in Weimar after 1787 and was a close associate of Goethe.

1774: The Sorrows of Young Werther. The early epistolary novel that earned the young Goethe his reputation, and caused a sensation by dealing frankly with the subject of suicide.

1788: Goethe, after a long stay in Italy, returns to write his great classical dramas: *Iphigenia in Tauris*, *Egmont* and *Torquato Tasso*.

1808 and 1832: Faust Part One and Part Two. A dramatic poem by Goethe, considered by many to be the supreme achievement of German literature. In Goethe's version Dr Faust is essentially good. His scholastic zeal drives him to make a pact with the devil, but also in the end leads to his salvation.

The Romantic Movement

The Romantic Movement lasted roughly from 1790 to 1850 and affected music and painting as well as literature. It emphasized feeling and content rather than order and form.

1770–1831: Georg Wilhelm Friedrich Hegel. The philosopher who expounded his theories on historical conscience and dialectic in *The Phenomenology of Mind*.

1805: The Child with the Enchanted Horn. An anthology of poems inspired by popular tradition that was part of a revival of interest in the medieval period and Germany's mythological heritage.

1777–1811: Heinrich von Kleist. A soldier turned writer, he is known for his forceful dramas, disturbing short stories set in exotic locations, and the lyric intensity of his prose.

1812: First edition of **Grimms' Fairy Tales**, stories from the oral tradition of central Germany collected by the brothers Grimm.

1776–1822: E.T.A. Hoffmann. A civil servant and failed painter who also worked as a composer and theatre director. His stories formed the basis of Tchaikovsky's ballet *The Nutcracker* and Delibes' *Coppelia*. The tales are often the extremely bizarre products of his schizophrenic mind. (Hoffmann's own life is the subject of Offenbach's opera *The Tales of Hoffmann*.)

Realism and Naturalism

Later in the 19th century there was a trend towards more naturalistic styles, in reaction to the idealism of the Romantic era. The social changes and problems which resulted from the Industrial Revolution led to a growth in political writing—both in theory and fiction.

1797–1856: Heinrich Heine. The author of the *Lorelei* poem later renounced Romanticism and embarked upon a series of brilliantly evocative travelogues. Poems from his *Buch der Lieder* (1827) have been set to music by Schubert, Schumann and Brahms.

1788–1860: Arthur Schopenhauer. Philosopher noted for his pessimistic theories on the will to live and the urge to pity.

1848: Karl Marx (1818–83) and **Friedrich Engels** (1820–95) publish the *Communist Manifesto*. Marx's *Das Kapital* followed in 1867.

1862–1946: Gerhart Hauptmann. The Nobel Prize-winning writer is known chiefly for his realistic, socially aware work for the theatre, notably *Die Weber* (The Weavers, 1892).

1844–1900: Friedrich Nietzsche. The philosopher who wrote in lyrical prose on the decadence of humankind, the death of God and the moral freedom of the *Übermensch* who would rise above good and evil as the pinnacle of human evolution.

The Early Twentieth Century

1875–1926: Rainer Maria Rilke. Impressionistic Austrian poet, author of *Sonnets to Orpheus* (1926).

1875–1955: Thomas Mann. The leading member of a literary family, Mann's most popular works include the epic *Buddenbrooks* (1901) which charts the decline of a merchant family similar to his own; the short story *Death in Venice* (1913); *The Magic Mountain* (1924), a weighty critique of European society; and a reworking of the Faust legend (1947). He won the 1929 Nobel Prize for Literature. Mann's brother **Heinrich** (1871–1950) wrote *Professor Unrat* (1905) later filmed as *The Blue Angel* with Marlene Dietrich.

1877–1962: Hermann Hesse. Hesse wrote dense and complex books such as *Steppenwolf* (1927) and *The Glass Bead Game* (1943). He won the Nobel Prize for Literature in 1946.

1883–1924: Franz Kafka. Kafka—the son of German Jewish parents—lived in Prague, but wrote in German. His nightmarish, absurd novels include *The Trial* (1925) and *The Castle* (1926).

1898–1956: Bertolt Brecht. His politically engaged work and writings on the theory of performance revolutionized modern theatre practice. Among his most frequently performed works are *The Threepenny Opera* (1928) and *Mother Courage and her Children* (1941).

After the Second World War

After the horrors of the war there was much talk of *Stunde Nul* (hour zero)—the need for a 'clean sweep' and a search for new values. There was a feeling that the German language had been debased—by Nazi propaganda, and by its inadequacy to describe the experiences people had been through. This was followed by a period of writing with a strong left-wing commitment, which had its high points in the 1960s. The 1970s saw a re-emergence of *Innerlichkeit* (inwardness) and a focus on personal feelings.

1947–67: Gruppe 47 (Group 47). This informal association of artists and writers, which met annually and awarded a prize to a young writer, was the driving force behind a German literary revival. Leading lights included **Heinrich Böll** (1917–85), author of *The Clown* (1963), *The Lost Honour of Katharina Blum* (1974), and winner of the 1972 Nobel prize; and **Günter Grass** (b.1927), famed for his novel *The Tin Drum* (1959).

Since 1970: Böll and Grass continued to rank as Germany's leading authors. **Peter Handke** (b.1942) is perhaps the country's most successful experimental writer—especially in the field of theatre. Playwright and novelist **Botho Strauss** (b.1944) is building a good reputation for works that concentrate on the lack of human communication and the purposelessness of society. Of East German authors, more widely available since the *Wende*, Christa Wolf (b.1929), 'the GDR's Virginia Woolf', is making most impact.

Music

Germany has produced some of the world's greatest composers. (Many—such as Mozart—were, in fact, Austrian, but this is a pedantic quibble.) For centuries Vienna and Leipzig were the twin vortices of European music, and in each major period German musicians have been among the great movers and shakers in their field. Even the briefest of overviews of the development of German music leaves you wondering if there was anyone of note left who *wasn't* German.

Beginnings

Discounting ancient military horns whose chief function was to make a stirring racket, we can trace the beginnings of German music back to the early Middle Ages, and to two main sources—the church and the court. The first manuscripts of **ecclesiastical music** (such as the *Carmina Burana*) date back to the 12th century, and as early as the 11th century courtiers were entertained by wandering troubadours. These minstrels developed a form of lyrical ballad known as the **Minnesang** (from the German for love song). Most famous of all minnesingers was **Walther von der Vogelweide** (1170–1228)—some of his songs have survived, and devotees still decorate his grave in Würzburg with flowers (*see* p. 430). By the 15th and 16th centuries the minnesingers had organized themselves into guilds, and were recognized as master craftsmen—local supremos being granted the title of *Meistersinger* (master-singer). The inventiveness and spontaneity that had characterized the *Minnesang*, however, was strangled by rigid and complicated rules enforced by the guilds. Top-ranking Meistersinger of all time was Hans Sachs (1494–1576), a Nuremberg cobbler who produced some 6000 works. In the 19th century Richard Wagner—who, like his Romantic contemporaries, was fascinated by Germany's medieval past—celebrated Sachs and his colleagues in the opera *The Mastersingers of Nuremberg*.

Early Music and the Baroque Period

For a long time court and church music developed alongside each other. In the churches the **part-song** flourished, and led to the growth of motets and masses. The earthier, more popular hymns that came into fashion in Protestant churches during the Reformation had repercussions in Roman Catholic church music too, developing into chorales and cantatas. After the banquet and around the hearth the movement was more towards instrumental and dance music. The main domestic instrument was the lute, though later small orchestras were formed and from the 15th century onwards independent instrumental forms—

such as the sonata and the concerto—began to emerge. Also at around this time the organ began to be used as a solo instrument in churches.

The Thirty Years' War put a stop to most cultural activity across the whole country. The Germany that emerged after the war was a very different place. Old feudal structures had been severely shaken, and local merchants were becoming more powerful. When a musical revival came, it happened in town orchestras, choirs, student *Collegia Musica* and opera houses. (Germany's first opera-houses opened in the second part of the 17th century in Dresden, Munich and Hamburg.)

Two rival musicians emerged during this period—Georg Philipp **Telemann** (1681–1767) and Johann Sebastian **Bach** (1685–1750). At the time Telemann was considered the superior of the two. Bach's work as a composer was all but forgotten after his death (*see* p. 431). Even though he had given new depth and impetus to forms such as the cantata and oratorio, and propelled chamber music to new heights, this was only acknowledged in the 19th century when his great works—such as the *Brandenburg Concertos* and the **St Matthew Passion**—were rediscovered. Another innovative composer of the time, an early master of opera and oratorio, was Georg Friedrich **Händel** (1685–1759). Händel eventually settled in England, where he changed his name to Handel and composed the famous *Messiah* (1741).

The Classical Period

The second half of the 18th century saw the blossoming of new musical genres, most notably the symphony. Many of these new forms, as well as older ones such as the sonata and concerto, were given their classical shape by composers Joseph **Haydn** (1732–1809) and the man many consider to be the greatest musical genius of all time, Wolfgang Amadeus **Mozart** (1756–91). Mozart also took German opera to a new summit, while Ludwig van **Beethoven** (1770–1827) is usually considered to be the most powerful exponent of the symphony. He gave the three dominant forms of the classical period—the symphony, the string quartet and the piano sonata—dramatic new expression; his tremendous, moody, later symphonies set the tone for the Romantic movement of the 19th century.

Romantic and 19th-century Music

The success of the French Revolution seemed to inspire artists to a celebration of humankind's freedom and power, which was accompanied by a loosening of classical restraints on form. Early 19th-century instrumental music—such as that by Felix **Mendelssohn-Bartholdy** (1809–47) and Robert **Schumann** (1810–56)—is still bound by classical structure, but the final operas of Carl Maria von **Weber** (1786–1826), and music by Anton **Bruckner** (1824–96) and Johannes **Brahms** (1833–97) align German music with the Romantic movement that was sweeping the country.

The grand master of the Romantic opera is undoubtedly Richard **Wagner** (1813–83). Wagner drew on heroic tales from German mythology, wrote his own libretti and involved himself in all aspects of staging. He wanted his 'musical dramas' to be spiritually uplifting

Gesamtkunstwerke (total works of art), and brought a new psychological density to opera. Musically, his approach was also revolutionary—especially in his use of the *Leitmotiv*, a recurring theme used to depict a character, or evoke an idea or change in psychological state.

Two further developments occurred in the 19th century that are still felt today. The German **Lied**, which had had its foundations in song-cycles by Franz **Schubert** (1797–1828), became an independent form that was to keep its popularity with composers into the 20th century. Also, people began to make a clearer distinction between serious and light music, though the latter had perfectly respectable champions in German-born Jacques **Offenbach** (1819–80)—best known as the composer of *Orpheus in the Underworld*, the music used for the can-can—and in the father and son whose name is synonymous with the waltz: Johann **Strauss** Senior (1804–49) and Junior (1825–99).

Into the 20th Century

Gustav **Mahler** (1860–1911), who carried the torch for the symphonic form, and Richard **Strauss** (1873–1946), whose operas such as *Salome* and *Der Rosenkavalier* are very much constructed on groundwork laid out by Wagner, move German music into contemporary times. In the 20th century Germany has had its share of inventive, though traditionally orientated, composers—such as Paul **Hindemith** (1895–1963) and Carl **Orff** (1895–1982), whose energetic *Carmina Burana* is one of the most widely listened to of all modern 'serious' compositions. More adventurous experimenters include Arnold **Schönberg** (1874–1951), whose **twelve-tone system** completely redefined musical frontiers, and the Cologne-based Karlheinz **Stockhausen** (b.1928) whose performances continue to delight and perplex.

Cinema

The Great German Cinema Revival

In the 1920s and early 1930s German films enjoyed world renown. These were the 'golden years' of the Weimar Republic, when Berlin was one of the cultural centres of Europe. Directors such as Joseph von **Sternberg** (1894–1969), Erich von **Stroheim** (1885–1957) and Fritz **Lang** (1890–1976)—all of them, in fact, born in Austria—were beginning to make a name for themselves. Classics of the silent screen such as Robert Wiene's *The Cabinet of Dr Caligari* (1919) and Fritz Lang's *Metropolis* (1927) were being made; Marlene Dietrich shot to fame after starring in *The Blue Angel* (1928). But Nazi oppression and the lure of Hollywood led to a massive exodus of talent from Germany.

After the Second World War it was more difficult for cinema to make a new start than it was for theatre or the other arts. The expertise was simply not there, cinema wasn't taken seriously by Germany's intellectuals, and the films that were made tended (with some exceptions) to be superficial and aimed entirely at the commercial market.

Then in 1962, at a festival of short films held in the Ruhr town of Oberhausen, 26 angry young directors came up with the *Oberhausen Manifesto*. They proclaimed the old cinema dead and demanded the freedom to create the new German feature film. Only two of the group, Alexander **Kluge** (b.1932) and Edgar **Reitz** (b.1932), went on to make a name for themselves, but the manifesto drew attention to the sorry state of German cinema and was instrumental in prompting Federal funding for the industry. This paved the way for the more adventurous directors who were to come.

Soon young German directors were making a mark on the international circuit. The first breakthrough came with Kluge's *Yesterday Girl*, which won the Silver Lion at the 1966 Venice Film Festival. In the same year Volker **Schlöndorff's** film *Young Törless* showed to critical acclaim at Cannes. Schlöndorff (b.1939) went on to make the box-office hits *The Lost Honour of Katharina Blum* (1975) and *The Tin Drum* in 1979. Other successes followed—films by directors who came to rank with the top names in art cinema: Fassbinder, Herzog and Wenders.

The centre of the revival was Munich. Munich is a small city and many of the leading participants knew each other, although they never made up a formal movement. Directors tended to work as *auteurs*, often producing the film and writing the screenplay as well, giving the work a distinctive personal imprint. But the films also had much in common— they were essentially German, not imitative of art-cinema styles in other countries but creating a distinct mood and grappling directly with the moral and philosophical problems that Germans faced after the war. The 1970s were the heyday of this new German cinema, with the big three directors (Fassbinder, Wenders and Herzog) producing a string of award-winning films and commercial successes.

Wim **Wenders** (b.1945)—despite a later fascination with America evident in his 1984 film *Paris, Texas*—can be seen very much in the tradition of brooding German romanticism, especially in 'road movies' such as *Alice in the Cities* (1973). Werner **Herzog** (b.1942) is the most eccentric and fantastical of the three. He likes to work in exotic locations, and his films often deal with visionaries and fanatics such as the crazed hero of *Fitzcarraldo* (1982), who hauls his steamship over a hill in the Amazon. Rainer Werner **Fassbinder** (1946–82) made pessimistic—some say self-pitying—films about people victimized by society or exploited in relationships. *The Bitter Tears of Petra von Kant* (1972), about a lesbian fashion designer who is used then deserted by a younger woman, and *The Marriage of Maria Braun* (1978), the story of a woman's fight for survival in tough, materialistic post-war Germany, are his two greatest successes.

By the mid-1980s, however, the new movement had lost impetus. Fassbinder was dead and Herzog, Wenders and Schlöndorff had left Germany. In 1984 Edgar Reitz made the brilliant TV series *Heimat*—a critical, but affectionate saga of three rural German families between 1919 and 1982—but there has been little else in recent years to equal the quality of films made during the 1960s and 1970s.

The Lower Rhineland and around the Ruhr

The Lower Rhineland and the Ruhr

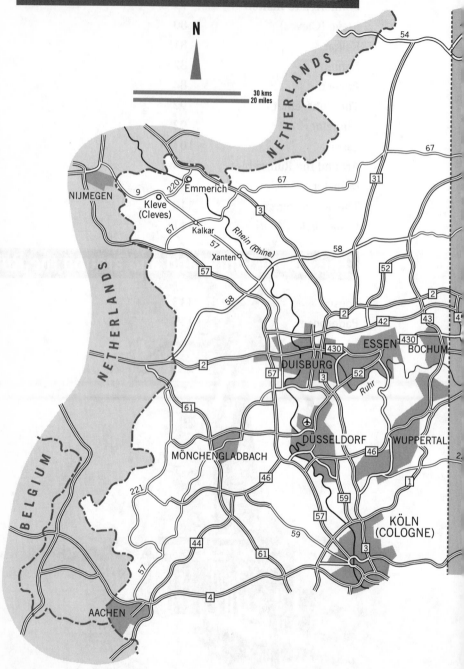

The Lower Rhineland and around the Ruhr

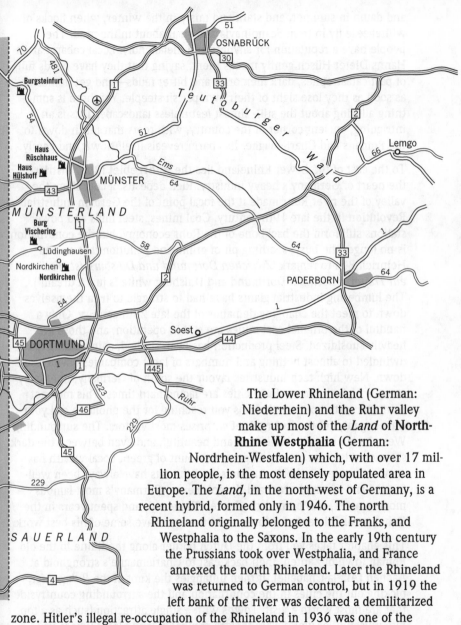

The Lower Rhineland (German: Niederrhein) and the Ruhr valley make up most of the *Land* of **North-Rhine Westphalia** (German: Nordrhein-Westfalen) which, with over 17 million people, is the most densely populated area in Europe. The *Land*, in the north-west of Germany, is a recent hybrid, formed only in 1946. The north Rhineland originally belonged to the Franks, and Westphalia to the Saxons. In the early 19th century the Prussians took over Westphalia, and France annexed the north Rhineland. Later the Rhineland was returned to German control, but in 1919 the left bank of the river was declared a demilitarized zone. Hitler's illegal re-occupation of the Rhineland in 1936 was one of the events that led up to the Second World War.

Like the neighbouring Netherlands, the Lower Rhineland presents a prospect of dykes, water and grassland so flat that windmills, thin lines of poplars, and even the black and white cows stand silhouetted against the skyline. Here it is green and damp in summer, and stark and misty in the winter, when flocks of whitegeese fly in from Scandinavia and strut about in the mud. The people have a reputation for shyness and melancholy. Local cabaret artist Hanns Dieter Hüsch gently mocks them, saying that they have heads full of past catastrophes, dark memories and bitter feuds—and get homesick as soon as they lose sight of their own parish steeple. Yet there is something alluring about the still, almost featureless landscape. This is an intriguing, ancient corner of the country, with roots that reach down to the Romans and Charlemagne. Its charm reveals itself slowly and gently.

To the east of the Lower Rhineland lies the **Ruhrgebiet** (Ruhr district), the heart of Germany's heavy industry. Rich deposits of coal along the valley of the river Ruhr made it the focal point of the German Industrial Revolution in the late 19th century. Coal mines, steel mills and power stations still form the backbone of the Ruhr economy, but the conurbation is no longer the busy, seething pit of grime and pollution that caused Heinrich Böll to remark '*Zwischen Dortmund und Duisburg ist Weiß nur ein Traum'* ('Between Dortmund and Duisburg white is just a dream'). The lumbering industrial giants have had to struggle to trim themselves down to meet the changing demands of the late 20th century. Only a handful of the original coal mines are still in operation, and those are heavily subsidized. Steel production has been slashed, shipbuilding has dwindled to almost nothing and numbers of large companies have closed down. New high-tech industries favour the south of Germany, unemployment is high and many Ruhr cities are facing hard times. This may not paint the sort of picture that has you reaching for the phone to call your travel agent, but the **Ruhrgebiet** surprises most visitors. The surrounding Westphalian countryside is lush and beautiful, and even between the dark satanic mills there is an unexpected amount of green. Local wealth has spawned some excellent museums, and the arts have always been well-funded and of a high standard. Joseph Beuys, Germany's most famous modern artist, was born in the Lower Rhineland, and spent years in the Ruhr city of Düsseldorf. Museums in the area have some of his best work.

This chapter takes you from the Dutch border along the Rhine to the old Roman town of Xanten, then back east to Charlemagne's stronghold at Aachen (Aix-la-Chapelle). It then untangles the knot of the *Ruhrgebiet*, picking out the cities in the conurbation and the surrounding countryside that are most worth a visit. Towns with a single attraction (such as a top-rate museum, or world-class theatre company), and places where you might end up on business, are dealt with in the Directory.

Despite the proximity of the *Ruhrgebiet*, this is the most attractive stretch of the Lower Rhine in Germany. The countryside offers good opportunities for walking and cycling, and the historic towns have well-stocked museums and pretty, Dutch-style brick architecture.

See also Directory entry for Mönchengladbach.

Getting Around

By car: Emmerich is just 7km from the Dutch border on Autobahn 3 (which becomes Dutch motorway A12 to Arnhem and Utrecht). Autobahn 3 takes you a further 70km into the heart of the Ruhr conurbation. A more scenic route, whichever way you're heading, is the B57 which crosses the border near the Dutch town of Nijmegen and goes on to Duisburg on the western edge of the Ruhrgebiet. The B57 also links Cleves, Kalkar and Xanten.

By train: There is no rail connection between Emmerich, Cleves and Xanten. Local trains between Emmerich and Duisburg take 1 hour, but Emmerich is also a stop on the Cologne–Amsterdam express line (seven times daily: Cologne 1hr 15min, Duisburg ½hr, Amsterdam 1½hr). A separate train travels from Cologne to Cleves (1hr 50min), and there is yet another line between Duisburg and Xanten (hourly, 50min).

By bus: If you are using public transport you will probably find it easier to hop between Lower Rhineland towns using buses. The local bus network is extensive, and buses are fairly regular. Buses leave from the Bahnhof at Xanten and Cleves, and from the Markt at Kalkar.

River cruises: H. Hell Schiffahrt, Waldweg 5, Emmerich, ✆ (02822) 68306, offer trips up and down the Lower Rhine as far as Arnhem in the Netherlands (DM5–20).

By bicycle: This is an excellent and popular way to get around. You can hire a bike from **Fahrradhandel Peter Messink**, Wassenbergstr. 49, Emmerich, ✆ (0282) 51956, or **Jugendwerkstatt**, Thaerstraße, Cleves, ✆ (02821) 18270. Most German Rail stations in the area also hire out bicycles at the bargain price of DM10 a day (DM5 if you have a rail ticket). Apply at the parcels office. Cleves and Xanten tourist offices sell cycling maps of the area. Good places to head for are the Reichswald near Cleves and the protected area east of Xanten, where there are also **nature trails** for walkers.

Tourist Information

Emmerich: Martinikirchgang 2, ✆ (02822) 75400.

Kalkar: Markt 20, ✆ (02824) 13120.

Cleves: Rathaus, ✆ (02821) 84254.

Xanten: Rathaus, Karthaus 2, ✆ (02801) 37238.

Emmerich

The small town of Emmerich is an odd sight. Its smokestacks and elegant Neoclassical houses crowd together on the east bank of the Rhine. From their midst an enormous red suspension bridge (the longest in Germany) seems to float gracefully out across the river—and end in a field of cows, with not another building in sight. Emmerich's main attraction is the **Schatzkammer** (Treasury) *(no fixed opening hours; adm DM1)* of the collegiate church of **St Martini**. The church itself is an odd marriage of separate Gothic and Romanesque buildings, but the treasury—built up since the 11th century—rivals that of many of Germany's leading cathedrals. Pride of place goes to the **Ark of St Willibrord**, an ancient reliquary supposedly holding the remains of the Anglo-Saxon missionary Willibrord (AD 658–739) who founded the church. The simple original container has been embellished over the centuries, and is today a splendid bejewelled box of embossed and filigreed gold. Other treasures include finely made goblets, candlesticks, statues and more reliquaries—including a very peculiar one made out of glass and shaped like a fish on legs. The **Rheinmuseum**, opposite St Martini *(Mon–Wed 10–12.30 and 2–5, Thurs 10–12.30 and 2–6, Fri and Sun 10–12.30; adm DM1)* is a not very inspiring shipping museum that contains mostly models, old instruments and charts.

Kleve (Cleves)

Cleves, 9km west of Emmerich, is most known to English speakers for supplying King Henry VIII's fourth wife, **Anne of Cleves**, daughter of the local duke. In 1539, after the death of Jane Seymour (his third queen), Henry sent his court painter, Hans Holbein the Younger, around Europe to dash off likenesses of prospective brides. This was a tricky task as the portraits also had to meet the approval of ambitious parents. King Henry agreed to marry Anne on the basis of Holbein's portrait (now in the Louvre in Paris), but when they met he took an instant dislike to her, nicknaming her the 'Flanders Mare'. He dismissed Holbein, and six months later sent the unfortunate Anne packing too.

Cleves is dominated by a towering cliff (hence its name). Perched on top is **Schwanenburg** (Swan Castle), the Kleve family seat. It gets its name because of the association with **Lohengrin**, the mysterious knight who, legend has it, came floating up the Rhine in a boat drawn by swans to rescue the Duchess of Cleves from the hands of a lecherous usurper. (The story later inspired Wagner's opera *Lohengrin*.) The present castle was built in an odd hotch-potch of styles between the 11th and 17th centuries. Today it is occupied by law courts and government offices, but you can climb the **tower** *(Apr–Sept daily 11–5; Nov–Mar Sat and Sun 11–5; adm DM2)*. The tower also houses a rather good photography gallery (changing exhibitions), as well as a natural history museum displaying bits of mammoth, fossils and rocks. Its main attraction is the view it offers for miles over the surrounding flat countryside.

Cleves was badly bombed during the Second World War, and few of the old buildings survived. There is not much to see in the rest of the town, although the 15th-century brick church **St Mariä Himmelfahrt** (just below the Schwanenburg) is worth a visit to see the

high altar by the Kalkar woodcarver Heinrich Douvermann. The altar is sculpted in intense detail, and features a jolly, beaming Madonna and child. West of the town centre is the **Tiergarten**, a vast park laid out between 1653 and 1657, which served as the model for later gardens in Berlin and Versailles.

Kalkar

Kalkar, 12km south of Cleves on the B57, is a pretty little town of stocky brick buildings with bright shutters and Dutch gables. The town seems to belong more in the Netherlands than in Germany, and the local dialect is very similar to Dutch. At one time Kalkar was right on the Rhine, but river banks silt up easily in this flat countryside, and now Kalkar lies well inland.

Kalkar boomed as a medieval cloth centre, but the Netherlands' 80-year war of independence and the Thirty Years' War destroyed trade. The town lay poor and all but forgotten until King Friedrich Wilhelm IV passed through in 1833 and rediscovered the extraordinary art treasures in the church of **St Nicolai** *(Apr–Oct Mon–Fri 10–12 and 2–6, Sat 10–12 and 2–5, Sun 2–5; Nov–Mar daily 2–5; adm DM1)* alongside the Markt. In

the mid-15th century the rich local burghers founded a school of woodcarving, and the cream of its output fills the church. The main *Passion altar* was begun in 1488 by **Master Arnt von Zwolle**, the founder of the school, and finished by his pupils. Crowded with over 200 exquisitely carved figures, each individually and sensitively characterized, the composition is perfect, and the overall effect quite breathtaking. There are further stunning pieces by **Heinrich Douvermann**, a leading late-Gothic carver. His *Altar of the Seven Sorrows of the Virgin* in the south apse soars heavenwards in a series of giddy loops and spires. Below, in the predella, Jesse (the father of King David) sleeps in a tangle of roots, his head resting on his hand and a gentle smile on his lips.

The focal point of the Markt itself is a stately brick **Rathaus** (1431–45) with an octagonal tower. Behind it is the oldest house in town, a step-gabled brick building that now contains the **Stadtmuseum** *(Tues–Sun 10–1 and 2–5; adm DM1)*. This consists of a small but inviting display of old furniture, manuscripts and paintings, as well as temporary exhibitions of modern art.

Xanten

Xanten, 17km further south along the B57, is one of the oldest towns in Germany. The Romans established a camp here in 15 BC, and by AD 100 the settlement had become *Colonia Ulpia Traiana*, or CUT, a town with full colonial status—the only one in the Rhineland besides Cologne. The Romans originally came to control the disruptive local German tribes, but withdrew in the middle of the 4th century as the empire disintegrated under the pressure of the barbarian invasions. Two legends grew out of the ruins of CUT. The graves of 363 Christian martyrs led to the (mistaken) belief that **St Victor** and the Theban Legion *(see p.146)* had met their end here. The town's present name is a contraction of the Latin *Ad Sanctos* ('to the Holy Ones'). The great German epic, the *Nibelungenlied (see* p. 67), cites Xanten as the birthplace of an even more glamorous hero, the handsome and invincible **Siegfried**. (Wagner later used a version of Siegfried's adventures among the Nibelungen as the basis for his Ring cycle.)

Although badly bombed in the Second World War, Xanten has been carefully rebuilt. Some streets such as Brückstraße manage successfully to recapture a medieval atmosphere, and the modern town is pretty much the same shape as it was five centuries ago. Old **towers** pop up along the lines of the original fortifications. The most impressive is the grand **Klever Tor**, a double gateway at the northwestern entrance to the town; another has been converted into a windmill. Xanten's main attraction, however, is the **Dom**, just off the Markt, snug in its own close or 'Immunity'. The land within the Immunity walls belonged to the church and was not subject to secular law—so it became a tax haven to those who lived there and a refuge to anyone fleeing the city justices (though the latter would find themselves subject to ecclesiastical law, which could be even nastier). The striking west towers give the impression that St Victor is a Romanesque church, but most of the building is subdued early Gothic. The towers were built between 1180 and 1213, and made higher in the 16th century, but the Romanesque nave was replaced by a Gothic construction from 1263 onwards. Around the back of the church is a brightly painted, but rather glum-looking, 15th-century statue of St Victor. The five aisles of the gloomy **interior** create a catacomb of nooks and crannies, cluttered with religious painting and carving—including more superb work by the Kalkar carver **Heinrich Douvermann**. He is responsible for the splendid High Altar, as well an altar to the Virgin in the south aisle, with a *Tree of Jesse* in the predella even more finely rendered than the one at Kalkar.

The **Regionalmuseum** *(Tues, Thurs and Fri 10–5, Wed 10–8, Sat and Sun 11–6; adm DM3)* in the southwest corner of the Immunity, is a fairly dry collection of Roman paraphernalia and cathedral cast-offs—though it does have a good **café**. To the northwest of the centre (about 10 minutes' walk down Rheinstraße and across the main road) is the site of the old Roman settlement of CUT. Later builders of Xanten pillaged CUT for stone, but didn't build on top of the city itself. Today reconstructions of the old Roman buildings rise out of the foundations to create an **Archäologischer Park** *(daily 9–6; adm DM3)*, a cross between an archaeological site and a theme park. As well as a freshly built ruined temple there is a massive amphitheatre (sometimes used for staging Roman pageants), a bath-house, villa, city wall and much more. There is even a restaurant where the waiters wear togas (over jeans in nippy weather) and serve 'Roman' food, and a playground for children which offers some genuine Roman games. Everything is unashamedly new, but you do get an idea of the enormous size of the old Roman settlement.

Where to Stay

Inexpensive and comfortable accommodation is to be had in **private rooms** around the Lower Rhinelands. Look out for *Zimmer frei* signs, or enquire at the local tourist office.

Kalkar

Hotel Siekman, Kesselstr. 32, © (02824) 2305 (DM76–90). Modern, bland, but efficiently run. Somewhere to fall back on if you're stuck.

Hotel Nern, Markt 6, © (02824) 2252 (DM70–80). Small, traditional, family-run hotel in one of the oldest buildings in town.

Xanten

Hotel van Bebber, Klever Str. 10, © (02801) 6623, fax 5914 (from DM175). An 18th-century building in the shadow of the cathedral, and the best address in the region. A classic grand hotel with a touch of rural folksiness. Charming service, and rooms dotted with antiques.

Hotel Galerie an de Marspoort, Marsstraße 78, © (02801) 1057 (DM70–90). Dinky, lovingly run hotel with lots of individual touches—including changing art exhibitions (usually local landscapes). The rooms are small, but individually decorated and comfortable.

Klever Tor and **Rundturm am Westwal**. The old city gates have been converted into top-class self-catering apartments. The Klever Tor has three floors, each with a minimum of a double bed, cooking facilities and bathroom (DM55 per apartment per night, minimum 3 nights, bedding/towels extra). The Rundturm sleeps four (one double, one bunk) and has a separate living room and kitchen (DM65 per night, same conditions as above). Reservations can be made through the tourist office.

Youth Hostel: Villa Kunterbunt, Xanten-Wardt, © (02801) 5806.

Eating and Drinking

Emmerich

Oude de Poort, Rheinpromenade 23, © (02822) 45265 (DM20–40). Traditional inn on the Rhine promenade. Soups thick enough to stand your spoon up in.

Cleves

Bacco, Stechbahn 1–3, ✆ (02821) 17648 (DM20–60). Snug Italian restaurant that serves pastas, homemade pizzas and more substantial dishes.

Conditorei Wanders, Kavarinerstr. 6, ✆ (02821) 20744. Airy café with a terrace and a wickedly wide selection of cream cakes.

Kalkar

De Gildenkamer, Kirchplatz 2, ✆ (02824) 4221 (DM45–70). A 15th-century building that still has an original painted ceiling and the remains of frescoes. The chef, on the other hand, is influenced by *Neuen Deutsche Küche* (German *nouvelle cuisine*). All too often this means mingy portions in garish colours. Here it means fresh produce and even some vegetarian options (asparagus dishes are a speciality).

Ratskeller Kalkar, Rathaus, ✆ (02824) 2460 (DM40–60). Reputedly the best food in town—succulent fillets with creamy sauces; mussels and asparagus in season.

Restaurant Nern, Markt 6, ✆ (02824) 2252 (DM25–45). Good home-cooking in atmospheric old inn. Steaming goulashes, fat joints and good game dishes.

Xanten

Restaurant van Bebber, Klever Str. 12, ✆ (02801) 6623 (DM40–70). Classy restaurant in the town's best hotel. Local cuisine with an individual flourish.

Alte Kornbrennerei, Marsstraße 56, ✆ (02801) 9449 (DM20–30). Down-to-earth brewery with solid cooking. Try the beer soup or Kasseler steaks with sauerkraut.

Aachen

Aachen is a vibrant city with a rich history. If you have time for just one stopover in the region, this should be it. The town's French name—Aix-la-Chapelle ('spa with a chapel')—gives a clue to its appeal. The sizzling natural spring waters (up to 74°C—the hottest north of the Alps) attracted the great man-of-action, empire-builder and all-round hero **Charlemagne** (German: Karl der Grosse). He loved to bathe in the waters, and could outswim everyone in his court. Such was the attraction of these bracing morning dips that in AD 794, after 26 years of vigorous campaigning around Europe, Charlemagne chose Aachen as his permanent base. From here he ruled over an empire that covered most of modern Germany and France, the Benelux, Austria and Switzerland, as well as much of Italy and parts of Spain (*see* **History** p. 40). Even before he settled here, the devout emperor had set about building a church and amassing treasures that still surpass nearly any other collection you'll see in Germany.

After Charlemagne's death the empire broke up and Aachen declined in importance—though German kings continued to be crowned here until 1531 (some 32 in all). The town remained a popular and fashionable spa up until the early 19th century. Today local college and university students (some 45,000 out of a population of 250,000) give the town youthful verve. There's a buzzing international atmosphere too, as Aachen is just a few minutes' drive from both the Belgian and Dutch borders.

Getting Around

By car: If you are travelling from Britain, you can get to Aachen along the Dutch motorway A76 or the Belgian A3 (from Brussels). Aachen is just 50km west of Cologne and about 70km south-west of Düsseldorf. If you have been visiting the Lower Rhineland, keep travelling on the B57, which skirts the western edge of the *Ruhrgebiet* and takes you all the way to Aachen. Most of the Altstadt is pedestrianized, but there is ample parking around the Grabenring.

Mitfahrzentrale: Roerminder Str. 4, ✆ (0241) 155 087.

By train: The **Hauptbahnhof** (information ✆ (0241) 19419) is 10 minutes' walk south of the city centre (along Theaterstraße). There are frequent connections to Cologne (approx. 50min) and Düsseldorf (approx. 1½hr).

Public transport: With the exception of the Ludwig Forum, all the sights are within easy walking distance of each other in the centre. If you think you will be using local buses, invest in a **Tagesnetzkart** (day ticket, DM4.60).

Taxis: ✆ 34441.

Tourist Information

Tourist information office: There are two branches, one at the Hauptbahnhof, Bahnhofplatz 4, ✆ (0241) 180 2965 *(Mon–Fri 9–6.30, Sat 9–1)* and one nearer the centre at the Elisenbrunnen, ✆ (0241) 180 2960 *(same hours)*. They offer a variety of city tours with well-informed guides, and can help with brochures, maps and hotel reservations.

Post office: The main post office is on Kapunizergraben, a few minutes walk from the Elisenbrunnen.

Bank: The Kreissparkasse at the Elisenbrunnen offers exchange facilities during normal banking hours and on Saturdays from 9–12. For an after-hours service you'll have to travel to one of the border posts on the Autobahn.

Police: ✆ 110.

Festivals

The town's main bash is the **Karlsfest** in honour of Charlemagne. This consists of the usual fairs and revelry, and is hardly over when the city celebrates **carnival** with Rhenish abandon. Rhineland bonhomie again bursts out during the summer **wine festival**, when you can sample wines from around the country. As with most German towns Aachen has a **Christmas Market** during advent. During this time the city becomes hellishly busy with visitors from across the borders.

The Dom

Charlemagne was quite sure of his place in the world: 'Under the everlasting reign of our Lord Jesus Christ, I, Charles am by the grace of God and the gift of His mercy King and Ruler of the Frankish Empire and the devoted protector and humble helper of holy Christendom'. As the divinely appointed successor to the great Roman emperors, and the champion of Christianity on Earth, he needed an appropriate church. In AD 785 he had started to transform the Frankish kings' temporary camp in Aachen into a more permanent residence. A few years later work on the **Pfalzkapelle** (Palace Chapel) began.

Einhard, Charlemagne's close friend and adviser, and a later biographer, Notker the Stammerer, marvel at the wealth and expertise that went into the construction. Craftsmen were called in from around the empire, and only the best materials were used—gold, silver, bronze, and marble imported from Ravenna. The marble columns were considered valuable even when Napoleon's army invaded in 1794. They were hacked out and taken to Paris, where you can still see six in the Louvre. A few were later returned to Aachen.

Part of the Pfalzkapelle's consecrational inscription reads: 'Once the living stones have all been joined together in peaceful union, and all measurements and numbers are in agreement throughout, the works of the lord who created this great hall shall shine forth brightly'. The 'measurements and numbers' of the chapel are in most rigorous agreement. The church takes the shape of an octagonal dome (the number eight represented perfection), surrounded by a 16-sided ambulatory on which rests a two-tiered gallery with eight arcades. The proportions of the building are based on an arithmetical system inspired by the seventh vision of St John's *Revelation*, which describes the New Jerusalem, as measured by an angel's 'golden reed', to be 144 cubits in length, breadth and height. Cubits were translated into Carolingian feet, and the shape and dimensions of the entire church are determined by the numbers 7, 12 and 144. The length, breadth and height of the central building are all 7 times 12 Carolingian feet, the perimeter of the octagon is 144 feet; that of the outer polygon is twice 144 feet, and so on. Even the small chancel that projects to the east fits into the system, jutting out precisely 24 feet. This immensely complicated design was realized by one **Odo von Metz**, and gives the Pfalzkapelle, from inside and out, an air of perfect harmony. (The sense of divine symmetry seems to have been extended to the emperor himself. Einhard records that Charlemagne's height 'was just seven times the length of his own feet'.)

Around the beginning of the 13th century the Pfalzkapelle got hold of some top-flight relics—supposedly the swaddling clothes and loin cloth of Christ, the gown Mary wore on the night of Christ's birth and the bloody cloth used to wrap John the Baptist's severed head. The relics, as well as the cult of Charlemagne which grew up in the 12th century, brought floods of pilgrims to Aachen. The small chapel had to be expanded, so a **Gothic chancel** modelled on the Sainte-Chapelle in Paris was added in the latter half of the 14th century. The extension was nicknamed the 'Glass House of Aachen', because of the soaring windows that seem to make up most of the building. The original stained glass has not survived, but new windows installed in the 1950s fit tastefully into the design.

At the entrance to the cathedral you can see the bronze **Wolf Door** which dates back to the Carolingian period. An anachronistic legend tells how the local city council, hard up for funds to complete the cathedral, made a pact with the devil. If Satan gave them the money they needed, then the first soul through the doors would be his. The council tricked the Prince of Darkness by smuggling a wolf into the church just before the consecration ceremony and (goes the legend) you can still see the cracks in the door made by the devil's enraged hammering.

Successors to Charlemagne poured treasures into the Pfalzkapelle, giving it one of the most ravishing **interiors** in Christendom. An altar panel of embossed gold—the **Pala d'Oro**—covers the front face of the main altar. It was probably made from gold found when Emperor Otto III exhumed Charlemagne's grave in the 11th century. In the choir you can see the **ambo**, a gold-plated copper pulpit encrusted with ivory carvings, precious stones, large chunks of agate and even bits of crockery—anything, in fact, that the donor, Emperor Henry II (1002–24) could spare from his treasury. The cupola is covered in a splendid 19th-century **mosaic**. This is a reconstruction of the 9th-century original, which cracked under the weight of the enormous wheel-shaped **chandelier** (donated by in 1156 by Frederick Barbarossa) that hangs from the centre of the dome. At the end of the chancel is the heavily decorated and gilded **shrine of Charlemagne**. Charlemagne had originally been buried in a marble sarcophagus. In 1165, largely due to the efforts of Frederick Barbarossa, he was canonized and interred in the present tomb. This shrine took over 50 years to make, and depicts not the Apostles (as was usually the case), but Charlemagne's successors. The face of Barbarossa himself was used to portray Charlemagne, the blended portraits suggesting that he was the great emperor's true replacement.

When he attended masses, Charlemagne used to sit out of sight in the gallery, but with a personal grandstand view of the high altar. Today in the gallery you can see the marble **imperial throne**, now thought to have been made not for Charlemagne, but for Otto I a century later. This was the coronation throne for German kings for six centuries. The marble for its construction came from paving stones on the Greek island of Paros—you can still see the marks of a children's street game scratched on the side. Access to the gallery is by **guided tour** only *(times posted at Schatzkammer; adm DM2)*.

The Schatzkammer

Entrance on Klostergasse; Tues–Sat 10–5, Sun 10.30–5, Mon 10–2; adm DM3.

The cathedral's Schatzkammer (Treasury) is packed with booty accumulated over centuries, and outshines any other in northern Europe. The most precious pieces are kept in the basement. Here you'll find the **Lothair Cross**, a 10th-century gold processional cross that drips with jewels, filigree and pearls. A hefty cameo of the Emperor Augustus sits at the intersection of the beams, and there's a smaller engraved crystal portrait of King Lothair (855–869) at the base of the cross. The crucified Christ is relegated to a sketchy engraving on the reverse side. The **Golden Bookcover** (*c.* 1020) is made in very much the same style as the Pala d'Oro, and probably comes from the same workshop. In the centre is an ivory panel of the Madonna and child in a style much favoured by the Orthodox Church.

Pick of the other exhibits in the basement includes a heavy **holy water vessel** (*c.* 1000) carved from ivory, the **Roman sarcophagus** believed to have been used as Charlemagne's original tomb, and the ornate **Shrine of the Virgin** which contains all four Great Aachen Relics.

On the ground floor you'll find further impressive reliquaries, treasures from the 14th–16th centuries and hosts of donations from foreign monarchs, including a crown given in 1474 by Margaret of York, sister of the English king, Edward IV. Look out for the gold and silver **Bust of Charlemagne** (*c.* 1349). It contains a piece of Charlemagne's skull, and was borne towards German kings during the coronation ceremony, as though Charlemagne himself was receiving his successor. A charming **Coronation Robe** (*c.* 1414) has small white blossoms on the reddish velvet, surrounded by squares of gold thread. The hood is edged with littte three-dimensional embroidered birds and there are 100 silver bells along the hem that tinkle as they knock each other.

Around the Markt

Aachen's old market place is still the social hub of the town. Most of the medieval houses lining the edges have been converted into restaurants or cafés. On summer nights people spill out all over the square, sitting on chairs or benches, or just plonked down on the ground around the fountain. Then the Markt echoes with conversation, like a huge hall before a concert. The **Rathaus** *(Mon–Fri 8–1 and 2–5, Sat and Sun 10–1 and 2–7; adm DM1)*, on the northern edge of the square, is on the site of Charlemagne's original palace. Two towers of the old *Pfalz* remain, giving the present Rathaus (built in the 14th century) more of the appearance of a fairy-tale castle than a town hall. Inside are a number of sumptuous Baroque rooms, and the **Kaisersaal**, renovated and restored beyond any claim to authenticity. Here you can see enormous murals by local painter **Alfred Rethel** (1818–59) depicting scenes from the life of Charlemagne, and copies of the Carolingian crown jewels. (The originals were whisked off to Vienna by the Hapsburgs in the early 19th century to adorn the new Emperors of Austria.)

On Pontstraße, which runs northwards off the Markt, is the **Internationales Zeitungsmuseum** (International Newspaper Museum) *(Tues–Fri 9.30–1 and 2.30–5, Sat 9.30–1; adm free)*, just a few yards from the house where **Paul Julius von Reuter** established his news agency—with carrier pigeons to transport the reports. The museum shows an intriguing collection of original editions from around the world, selected to show parallel responses to important events.

On its southeast edge the Markt blends into the Hühner Markt where you'll find the **Couven-Museum** *(Tues–Fri and Sun 10–5, Sat 10–1; adm DM2)*. Here there is some stylish 18th- and 19th-century furniture, a decorative collection of four centuries of Dutch tiles and a reconstructed apothecary. If you follow Krämerstraße, south off the Hühner Markt, you'll pass the **Puppenbrunnen** (Dolls' Fountain). With its quirky moving figures, this is the favourite among Aachen's 17 fountains. At the end of Krämerstraße and across Munsterplatz you come to the small park and Neoclassical pavilions of the **Elisenbrunnen**, a public drinking fountain designed by Schinkel. Marble tablets on the rotunda list famous visitors to the Aachen spa—from selected Medicis to Peter the Great and Albrecht Dürer. The water is a steaming, sulphurous brew that seems to come from Hell itself. Still, there are elderly residents of Aachen who swear by its healing powers and totter down every day for a drink.

East of the Centre

If you follow Peterstraße east from the Elisenbrunnen, you soon come to Komphausbad-straße. Here the 18th-century **Altes Kurhaus** is a temporary home to part of the collection of the **Suermondt-Ludwig-Museum** *(Tues–Sat 10–5, Sun 10–1; adm DM2)* while its own premises at Wilhelmstr. 18 undergo restoration indefinitely. Until work is completed you will be treated to a small selection of the excellent collection of religious sculpture, extravagant fantasies by the local goldsmith Dieter von Rath and a core of Old Masters that includes work by Cranach and Rembrandt.

Peterstraße leads across Hanseman Platz to Jülicher-Straße. Here, in an old Bauhaus umbrella factory, you'll find the **Ludwig Forum für Internationale Kunst** *(Tues–Sun 11–7, Thurs to 9; adm DM4; Bus 1, 11, 21)*, an exciting multi-media visual arts centre. It is based on the collection of local chocolate manufacturer **Peter Ludwig**. In the 1950s and 1960s he and his wife Irene began collecting contemporary art and have built up a stash of work that now not only forms the backbone of the Ludwig Museum in Cologne *(see* p. 131), but feeds galleries around the world. Exhibitions in the large white-painted factory space change, but the Ludwig collection is one of the best in the world and you can be sure to catch many of the greatest names in post 1945 art, as well as top-notch work by contemporary artists.

Shopping

The main shopping precinct is pedestrianized. In Adalbertstraße, Holzgraben and Damengraben you'll find department stores and shops to meet your every need.

Entertainment and Activities

If you want to ease aching joints, or discover just what it was that gave Charlemagne such a kick, you can swim about in the spa waters at the Jugendstil **Römerbad**, Buchkremerstr. 1 *(Mon–Fri 7–7, Wed to 9pm, Sat and Sun 7–1)*. You'll need a bathing costume and swim cap (the latter is available from the baths). The water hisses as you float about, and is kept at a steady 33°C. From time to time someone in a white uniform barks instructions and everyone forms rows and goes through a series of water gymnastics. If you're more serious about taking a cure, head for the **Kurbad Quellenhof** *(Mon–Fri 7–7, Wed to 9, Sat 7–6, Sun 7–1)* in the spa quarter around Monheimsallee, just east of the centre. Here the waters are 36°C, and there are massage facilities and solariums. Next door is the **casino** *(daily 3pm–2am, Fri and Sat to 3am; minimum stake DM5, formal dress preferred)*, though if you really want to savour the atmosphere of a spa casino, you'd best go to Baden-Baden *(see* p. 277).

The **Stadttheater**, Theaterplatz, ✆ (0241) 478 4244, keeps up a high standard of **drama** and **opera** (Herbert von Karajan first made his name here). The tourist office runs a **ticket booking service** for these and other events around town. Aachen's most popular **disco** is the Metropol, Blondelstr. 9, which plays anything from heavy metal to jazz.

Aachen ✆ (0241–)

Where to Stay

expensive

Steigenberger Quellenhof, Monheimsallee 52, ✆ 152 081, fax 154 504 (DM270–390). Stately pile in the heart of Aachen's spa quarter. You live in pampered luxury, and have access to the hotel's own indoor pool and thermal spring.

moderate

Aquisgrana City Hotel, Büchel 32, ✆ 4430, fax 443 137 (DM 195–215). Modern, very central and smart—if a little soulless. It also has its own swimming pool and thermal baths.

Hotel Arcade, Zollernstr. 2, ✆ 51840, fax 518 4199 (DM148–208). Convenient for the Bahnhof and the Altstadt. Pleasant rooms and efficient service.

Hotel Brülls am Dom, Hühnermarkt, ✆ 31704 (DM135–155). Small hotel, plum in the centre of the Altstadt, and one of the few with any atmosphere. Service has a personal touch and the rooms are simple, but welcoming.

Hotel Rütten, Krefelder Str. 86, ✆ 157 345, Bus 51 (DM100–110). Plain but friendly family-run hotel a little way north-east of the centre, but convenient for the spa quarter and Ludwig Forum.

inexpensive

Hotel Klenkes, Heinrichsallee 46, ✆ 509 034, fax 532 470 (DM85 without private bathroom–DM115). Old-style hotel convenient for the Altstadt and the spa.

Karls-Hotel, Leydelstr. 10, ✆ 35449 (DM80 without private bathroom). Clean hotel within spitting distance of the Bahnhof. No restaurant.

Youth Hostel: Maria-Theresia Allee 260, Bus 2 to Ronheide.

Eating and Drinking: Restaurants and Taverns

Elisenbrunnen, Freidrich-Wilhelm-Platz 13, ✆ 29772 (DM45–65). Sedate restaurant overlooking the fountains of the small Elisenbrunnen park. A hushed haven of clinking glasses, silently gliding waiters and *nouvelle cuisine*.

Aachener Ratskeller and Postwagen, Am Markt, ✆ 35001 (DM35–55). Rustic tavern that clings barnacle-like to the side of the Rathaus. Inside it is all wood panelling and intimate snugs. Outside on the terrace you're subject to bursts of impromptu music as buskers serenade newly-weds emerging from the Registry Office. Daily specials according to season, and good solid German soups and stews.

Zum Schiffgen, Hühnermarkt 23, ✆ 33529 (DM20–35). Charming inn, a little touristy, but with good value set menus that change daily.

Degraa, Fischmarkt 6 (DM20–25). Big communal wooden tables, hearty local fare such as hunks of boiled pork and gallons of *Degraa*, Aachen's only local brew.

Bars and Cafés

The liveliest bars and cafés are in the **student quarter**, which centres on the Markt and Pontstraße. At the top end of Pontstraße you'll also find a cluster of good-value **pizzerias**.

Zum Goldenen Einhorn, Markt 33 (DM25). Elegant old inn on the Markt, where you can people-watch and have a drink set back a little from the sweaty student throngs. Also serves food (veal and Greek dishes a speciality). If you feel like more boisterous company in a similar setting try the **Goldener Schwann** further along. **Zum Goldner Kette**, just off the Markt towards Jakobstraße, is quiet, has a beer garden and serves cheap vegetarian food.

Café Kittel, Pontstraße. Good, noisy student fun that spills out onto the terrace.

Tangente, Pontstraße. Friendly, relaxed daytime café that ups the music volume and becomes more animated after sunset.

Labyrinth, Pontstraße. Simple wooden tables and quieter atmosphere. Less serious drinking and more serious conversation.

Hauptquartier, Promenadenstr. 46. Aachens's most intensely trendy café, with plaster chipped off the walls to expose the bricks, painted fabrics draped from the ceiling, and gaudy youth posing at the bar.

Café Schnabeltasse, Alexanderstraße, off Monheimsallee. Arty watering-hole. Good for late-night live music and lingering breakfasts.

Domkeller, Hof 1, ✆ 34265 (DM20). Old-style café with sunny terrace in an attractive nook just off the market. Also serves cheap light meals.

Leo van den Daele, Büchel 18. Try Aachen's speciality, *Printen*—a spicy gingerbread that looks as if it has failed to rise—hard-going on the teeth and jaw muscles.

The Ruhrgebiet

The Ruhrgebiet's reputation as an industrial hell-hole puts off many foreign visitors. It is true that many of the towns in the conurbation meld seamlessly and are indistinguishable in style, but the Ruhr valley and the surrounding Westphalian countryside are well-stocked with pleasant surprises.

See also Directory entries for Bochum, Dortmund, Duisburg and Wuppertal.

Düsseldorf

Even in the Ruhrgebiet's belching, smoggy heyday, Düsseldorf was a haven of green. It was known as the *Schreibtisch* (writing desk) of the Ruhr—the clean-aired administrative centre of the industrial zone, with more millionaires and jewellers to the square mile than anywhere else in Germany. The city still drips with luxury, yet it wears its wealth well. The trouble with Düsseldorf millionaires, remarked the humorist George Mikes, 'is that they seem to have taste, which is rather annoying'. Königsallee, the main shopping boulevard, is the one street in Germany that could match Paris's *Champs Elysées*—bracingly cosmopolitan, chic and vibrant without being brash. Ruhr industry might be on the decline, but Düsseldorf has become Germany's leading centre of international banking and finance after Frankfurt. Thousands of foreign firms have offices here—there are more Japanese residents in Düsseldorf than in any other city outside Japan.

Nearly 80 per cent of the centre of Düsseldorf was destroyed during the last war, and, like many other German cities, it suffered even further from insensitive subsequent rebuilding. But there are large parks (with more in the pipeline), a lively Altstadt and enough bravura modern architecture to excuse the earlier mistakes. What is more, you'll find some excellent museums, as Düsseldorf has a history of channelling much of its wealth into culture. The 17th-century Prince Elector Johann Wilhelm was a keen patron of the arts and learning. He set up court in Düssledorf, and his reign (1679–1716) was a Golden Age for the town. Nineteenth-century industrialists continued the tradition, and during the first part of this century the local art academy built up a world-wide reputation. Düsseldorf became a centre of the visual arts, attracting painters such as Max Ernst, Otto Dix and Paul Klee. Joseph Beuys, arguably the most influential artist in post-war Germany—some say the father of the European avant-garde—was a professor at the Academy for many years. Today Düsseldorf, as an art market, is second only to its arch-rival Cologne.

Getting Around

By Air

Düsseldorf Airport, © (0211) 4211, is the second busiest in Germany and the destination of most charter flights. It is connected directly to the national rail system (*see* below) and is only 13 minutes journey from the centre of town by S-Bahn (trains every 20 minutes to and from the Hauptbahnhof). Taxis take around 20 minutes.

By Car

The A3 links Düsseldorf with the Dutch border via Emmerich (110km), the nearest Belgian border crossing is at Aachen (85km). Cologne is just 45km away on the A57 or A59. Parking in the city centre is virtually impossible during office hours, and a foreign number-plate won't save your car from being towed away. The multi-storey car parks between the Hauptbahnhof and Berliner Allee are your best bet.

Mitfahrzentrale: Lölnerstr. 212, © (0211) 774 011.

By Rail

The **Hauptbahnhof**, information © (0211) 19419, is a few minutes walk south-east of the centre. Düsseldorf is at the intersection of a number of Intercity routes, including Frankfurt (3hr), Cologne (½hr), Hamburg (3½hr). There are also frequent connections to other cities in the Ruhrgebiet and around the Lower Rhineland.

Public Transport

Düsseldorf has an extensive and efficient system of U-Bahn trains, trams and buses and an S-Bahn that inter-connects with other Ruhr towns. Tickets are sold on board and from automats at the stops. If you're travelling for under 2km you will save money by asking for a **Kurzstrecken-Fahrausweis** (short hop ticket). A **Tageskarte** (day ticket, DM8.50) gives you unrestricted travel on all public transport for 24 hours. Some hotels dish out a free 2-day pass to guests.

Taxis: © 33 333. If you're a driver and have been pole-axed by Altbier, you can ask for a **Rettungsring** (literally: 'life-belt')—a second taxidriver will drive your own car home (for three times the normal fare).

River Cruises

This is not the most beautiful spot along the Rhine for a cruise, but the local **White Fleet**, © (0211) 375 020, offers a variety of party-cruises. The famed **Köln–Dusseldorfer Line** (Rathausufer, © (0211) 498 0370) can take you further afield to more scenic sections of the river.

Tourist Information

Tourist information office: Konrad-Adenauer-Platz (opp. Hauptbahnhof), © (0211) 350 505 *(Mon–Sat 8am–10pm, Sun 4–10)*.

Post office: The main post office is at Charlottenstr. 61 *(open daily 8–8)*.

Exchange: After-hour exchange facilities are available at the airport and Hauptbahnhof.

Police: © 110.

Medical emergencies: © 19292.

Market days: There are two daily fruit and vegetable markets—a modest one in front of the Alte Rathaus and a bigger one on Karlsplatz.

Festivals

In the second half of July the **Sankt-Sebastian-Schützenverein** (St Sebastian Rifleman's Club) holds its annual parade and there is a huge 9-day fun fair on the Oberkasseler Rheinwiesen (the meadows beside the Rhine just across from the Altstadt). This is the biggest festival in the region, and has less to do with shooting than with dressing up, feasting and knocking back vast quantities of beer and wine.

If you're wandering down Königsallee around 10 November watch out for **Radschläger**—cartwheeling boys who tumble past, then ask for '*eene Penning*' (one penny) for their prowess. (Too literal an interpretation of this request won't go down at all well.) Later in the day there is a cartwheel competition on Königsplatz. All this is part of the **St Martin's Eve** festival, which includes processions of around 50,000 children carrying home-made lanterns, singing and exacting sweets from their audience. Grown-ups content themselves with roast goose (the traditional upper-class meal) followed by buckwheat pancakes with sliced apple (the working-class fare).

The next day is the official first day of **Carnival**. The 'fifth season' is celebrated here with just as much gusto as elsewhere along the Rhine, and has an interesting local twist. On 11 November 'Hoppeditz', a clown who speaks in rhyming couplets, hops out of a 'grave' in the market square in a thick cloud of dry-ice. He spouts witty doggerel satirizing events of the past year, and is welcomed by the Lord Mayor. The main Carnival celebration, however, is in the lead-up to Ash Wednesday, culminating in a parade of colourful floats on Rose Monday (late Feb–early March).

The Northern Altstadt

Düsseldorf's Altstadt is a pulsating collection of pubs, restaurants and traditional taverns that keeps going day and night. In the summer tables are set out under the trees and the whole quarter seems to teeter on the brink of becoming one big street party. The tiny **Markt** is tucked away at the western edge of this frenzy, almost on the banks of the Rhine. Here you can see the courtly Renaissance **Rathaus**, and a podgy equestrian statue of the city's great benefactor **Elector Johann Wilhelm II** ('Jan Wellem' in Rhenish dialect). The statue is by his court sculptor, the Italian Gabriel de Grupello. Legend has it that Jan Wellem was so popular that locals donated their kitchen cutlery when the artist ran out of metal—this despite the fact that Jan Wellem had bankrupted the city by his generous sponsorship of the arts and reputedly sold off local children as mercenaries to foreign rulers.

North of the Rathaus, on Burgplatz, is the **Schloßturm**, the last remnant of the elector's castle. These days it is a small **Schiffahrt-Museum** (Navigation Museum) *(Tues–Sun 11–5; adm DM2)*—a missable collection of models, documents and pictures portraying 2000 years of navigation history. The square itself, on the banks of the Rhine, is one of the most pleasant in the city, and has a cheeky *Radschläger* statue.

Just off the northern edge of Burgplatz is the 13th-century **St Lambertus**, with its curiously twisted spire. Inside there is a delicate late-Gothic tabernacle. A few minutes' walk to the east (up Mühlerstraße) brings you to **St Andreas** (1629), former court church of the electors. The grand, galleried interior contains their mausoleum. A little further on you come to the **Städtische Kunsthalle**, guarded by a bird-like statue by Max Ernst and host to many excellent travelling art exhibitions.

Across the way, in a striking new building, is the **Kunstsammlung Nordrhein-Westfalen** *(Tues–Sun 10–6; adm DM5)*, devoted entirely to 20th-century art. Here you'll recognize not only great names, but familiar images—such as **Picasso's** blue *Woman in an Armchair* and *Two Sitting Women*, **Léger's** *Adam and Eve*, or **Chagall's** *The Fiddler*. There is also outstanding work by Miró, Max Beckmann, Modigliani, Ernst Kirchner and many other 20th-century greats. The backbone of the display is a collection of nearly 90 of the delicate, rather magical paintings of **Paul Klee**, professor at the Academy from 1930 until the Nazi purges of 1933. Another ex-professor, **Joseph Beuys**, also gets an exceptionally good showing. There's a much wider range of his work here than you usually see on permanent exhibition—sketches and paintings as well as the customary installations with lumps of felt and fat. These two substances were a personal symbol of rebirth for Beuys. He had been a fighter pilot during the war, and after crashing in the Crimea his life was saved by Tartars who wrapped him in felt and rubbed him with fat. Beuys was also a founder member of the Greens, and much of his work concerns the way we relate to nature and the environment. (Locals used to call him 'bath-tub Beuys' because of his exploratory paddlings on the Rhine). On the upper floor of the museum there is an ethereally trendy **café**.

The Southern Altstadt

A walk south down the busy Heinrich-Heine-Allee and right into Kasernenstraße brings you to Wilhelm-Marx-Haus, built in 1922 and hailed as **Germany's first skyscraper**—all of 12 storeys high. Back westwards along Flingerstraße you come to Schneider-Wibbel-Gasse, where there is a glockenspiel (11am, 1, 3, 6, 9) depicting **Schneider Wibbel**. This wily local tailor sent a journeyman in his stead to debtors' prison. The journeyman died, and Wibbel had to stand by and watch his own funeral. (In the 1920s, during a play based on the story, the famous local actor Paul Henkels came up with the now classic ad-lib: 'God, I'm a beautiful corpse'.)

To the south of the Markt, in Schulstraße, is the **Hetjens-Museum** *(Tues–Sun 10–5; adm DM3)*, with an impressive collection of 8000 years of ceramics from all over the world. A little further south, on Bergerallee, a sweeping glass-walled modern building and an old patrician palace are home to the **Stadtmuseum** *(Tues, Thurs, Fri Sun 11–5; Sat 1–5, Wed 11–8; adm DM3)*. As you wander around the museum you come across original fittings of the 17th-century mansion, while the vast windows of the new wing open out onto a row of well-preserved Jugendstil houses, seeming to include them in the collection. Dynamic directorship has put Düsseldorf's Stadtmuseum a notch above most others. Lively and imaginative displays on city history mix the old photographs, documents and memorablia with work by contemporary artists, passing a telling commentery. Artists are also invited to create installations using museum stock. The collection of sculpture is especially good—look out for the endearing *Schreitender Jude* by **Otto Pankok** and powerful work by **Eberhard Linke**. There is much on Düsseldorf as an art centre, including some portraits of the ample **Mutter Ey**.

Johanna Ey ('Mutter Ey')

 Peering out from behind thick, round spectacles in a number of portraits painted just after the First World War are the black, glinting eyes of Johanna Ey. She is a big woman, usually draped in volumes of dark fabric, and she looks as if she would stand no nonsense from anyone; but there is an upward twist at the corners of her mouth, and a good-natured softening around her eyes belies her stern expression.

Mutter Ey (Mother Ey) had run a small gallery in Düsseldorf before the First World War, dealing mainly in works by painters of the conservative Düsseldorf School. After the war, however, she became interested in the work of Otto Dix, Otto Pankok, Max Ernst and numbers of other young artists who were hovering around the local art academy. She took them in hand, gave them exhibition space, lent them money, dispensed copious amounts of beer, cake and coffee and gave sound and intelligent advice. She used the gallery windows to introduce the general public to the new art (whether they wanted it or not), and fiercely promoted the work around the country. Mother Ey's cosy shop on Ratinger Straße became a meeting place for some of the most progressive artists of the day—the womb for a renaissance in German painting.

A little to the east of the Stadtmuseum (on Bilker Straße, off Karlplatz) is the **Heinrich-Heine-Institut** *(Tues–Sun 10–5; adm DM2)*, a research institute and small museum (with manuscripts, first editions, letters and a death mask) commemorating one of Germany's leading 19th-century men of letters *(see* p. 69). (There's also a quaint, but moving, tribute to Heine in the centre of town—an installation in the Mata Hari Passage, off Hunsrücken-straße, inspired by a letter he wrote to his sister.) Much of the land to the south-west of the Stadtmuseum is being converted into a riverside park. Here you can see the imaginative new amphitheare-shaped **Landtag** (parliamant building) and the **Rheinturm** (radio tower, 234m), the highest building in Düsseldorf. A lift *(daily 10am-midnight, DM4)* whisks you up to the revolving café/restaurant for a view over the city and way down the Rhine.

The Königsallee and the Museum Quarter

Running from north to south up the eastern side of the Altstadt is Dusseldorf's—if not Germany's—swishest shopping street, the **Königsallee** (known locally as the Kö). A grand 19th-century boulevard, it is thick with chestnut trees and lined by international banks on one side and top designer shops on the other. What remains of the river Düssel flows through a moat down the middle, traversed by elegant bridges. A strong and rather frightening Triton leers at the swans from the midst of his fountain, putti cavort on bridge-ends and ornate wrought iron street lamps are dotted along the way. Even the modern telephone boxes are different here—a special dispensation from central government permitted a more appropriate design than the usual brash yellow booths. The Kö is peopled with all the chic that money can buy, and even if your budget restricts you to window-shopping is worth a stroll *(see **Shopping** below)*. The northern end of the Allee leads into the **Hofgarten**, one of the large parks laid out around the city by the 18th-century electors. To the right you can see the three tall silvery slivers of the **Thyssen-Haus**, the steel company's headquarters built in 1959. Locals call it the *Dreischeibenhochhaus* ('Three-slice skyscraper'). Despite its size it looks fragile and temporary. The eastern part of the park sweeps up to the Baroque **Schloß Jägerhof** which now houses the **Goethe-Museum** *(Tues–Fri and Sun 11–5, Sat 1–5; adm DM3)*, a large but run-of-the-mill collection of manuscripts and memorabilia.

A walk through the northern arm of the park, past the **Ratinger Tor**, a heavy Neoclassical gatehouse, brings you to the **Ehrenhof**, a complex of heroic brick buildings put up for a fair in the 1920s, and now used mainly as museums. The most important of these is the **Kunstmuseum** *(Tues–Sun 11–6; DM5, Tram 701, U-Bahn to Nordstraße)*. The **Glass Collection** on the ground floor, based on a private collection of the Düsseldorf architect Helmut Hentrich, is one of the most comprehensive in the world, with pieces ranging from 1555 BC to present times. The Art Nouveau collection is unsurpassed, with a glittering display of works by Tiffany and Gallé.

There is also a good stock of Islamic arts and crafts, with some particularly fine textiles (first floor), but most of the museum is given over to painting. Elector Jan Wellem had an enormous collection of Flemish and Dutch Old Masters. These were whisked off to Munich for safe-keeping during the Napoleonic invasion and, as with so much that the greedy Wittelsbachs got their hands on, that is where they stayed. Two hefty paintings by Rubens, *The Assumption* and a magnificent *Venus and Adonis* were too big to cart away, and so remain in Düsseldorf. The 19th-century **Düsseldorf Academy** painters—notable for their monumental historical paintings—dominate the second floor, but are joined by less bombastic contemporaries such as Böcklin and Feuerbach. There is also work by the 20th-century Young Rhinelanders, including more portraits of their beloved Mutter Ey.

Post-war art at the Düsseldorf Academy set trends in Germany. Here you can see a *Passion* by **Otto Pankok** that seems charged with the horrors of the Holocaust; abstract work by the influential 1950s ZERO group and by Beuys. There is a modest sprinkling of works by other late 20th-century artists such as Gerhard Richter and Nam June Paik.

Opposite the Kunstmuseum is the **Kunstpalast**, used for travelling exhibitions and performances, and next door is the **Landesmuseum Volk und Wirtschaft** (State Museum of Society and Economy) *(Mon–Fri 9–5, Wed to 8, Sun 10–6; DM1)*, a crushingly dry collection of maps, graphs and diagrams on the world and its economy.

Further Afield

North of the museum quarter (U-Bahn Line 78 or 79 to Nordpark/Aquazoo) is the new **Löbbecke Museum and Aquazoo** at Kaiserwerther Str. 380 *(daily 10–6; adm DM6)*, an aquarium, terrarium and insectarium that goes down a treat with children. In the adjoining Nordpark, Düsseldorf's Japanese community have installed an attractive **Japanese Garden**.

The vast **Südpark** in the south of the city (S-Bahn from Hauptbahnhof) was laid out in 1987 for the National Garden Show, and is still famed for its spring flowers. Further down the line you'll find **Schloß Benrath** *(Tues–Sun 10–5; adm DM2)*, a pretty pink late-Baroque palace commissioned in 1755 by Elector Carl Theodor. The architect, Nicholas de Pigage, was also a landscape gardener (he designed the Hofgarten too). His castle fits snugly beside a large ornamental pond in a beautifully laid out park. The interior has recently been restored—the grand reception rooms, rich with stucco-work, are especially worth a look.

Shopping

Düsseldorf is the **fashion** capital of Germany, and *the* spot for big name designers is along the eastern stretch of the Königsallee. The boulevard has much else to offer too, such as the Auktionshaus at No. 76. There are surprising bargains to be had—or you can just pop in for the excitement of the bidding. The glass-domed **Kö Galerie** is the zenith of Mall shopping. Bakers and fruitsellers rub shoulders with achingly exclusive boutiques and jewellers. A live pianist tinkles away in the heart of the atrium (no piped music here). Top **department stores** are the Kaufhof, in a splendid Jugendstil building on the Kö and the Carsch Haus on Heinrich-Heine-Platz. The Carsch Haus (also a Jugendstil building, taken down a few years ago and reconstructed 30m to the west of its original position) has a superb **food hall**. **Schadowstraße** (off Schadowplatz at the top of Königsallee) is a descent from the stratosphere of the Kö. Here you'll find the more ordinary shops and department stores, though it too has its fair share of boutiques. The shoe shops alone gross over DM20 billion a year.

Düsseldorf © (0211–)

Where to Stay

expensive

Steigenberger Park-Hotel, Corneliusplatz 1, © 13810, fax 131 679 (DM430–560). Classic, elegant hotel on the edge of the Hofgarten—the best address in town.

Schnellenberg, Rotterdamer Str. 120, © 434 133, fax 437 0976 (DM200–300). Smart, pleasantly situated hotel on the banks of the Rhine, near the Japanese Garden and exhibition grounds.

moderate

Hotel Cristallo, Schadowplatz 7, © 84525, fax 322 632 (DM198). Delightfully eccentric hotel in the centre of town, full of gilt mirrors, cherubs and vines. No restaurant.

Domo, Schreurenstr. 4, © 374 001, fax 370 921 (DM109–229). Cheap and cheerful hotel near the station. There are a few even cheaper rooms without private bathroom (from DM79). No restaurant.

Astor, Kufürstenstr. 23, © 360 661, fax 162 597 (DM110–185). Friendly management, simple but comfortable rooms and centrally situated. No restaurant.

CVJM-Hotel, Graf-Adolf-Straße 102, ℂ 360 764 (DM90 without private bathroom–DM131). The old YMCA hitched a few notches upmarket, with dorms converted to private rooms. Functional but comfortable.

Youth Hostel: Düsseldorfer Str. 1, ℂ 574 041.

Eating and Drinking

Düsseldorf's speciality is **Altbier**, a bitter, strong, dark brown top-fermented beer that needs to be drunk young (it is called 'Alt' because it was around long before the 'new' Pilsner). The best place to drink Altbier is in one of the 'house-taverns' of a local brewery. Here *Köbes*—skilled waiters in long aprons and blue shirts—whisk around with large trays of beer and plates of fulsome nosh. The best of these taverns fill up quickly in the evenings, so it's a good idea to book a table if you are going to eat.

Restaurants

Zum Schiffchen, Hafenstr. 5, ℂ 132 421 (DM20–35). Lively inn in the southern Altstadt that dates back to 1628. Napoleon quaffed beer here after his victory parade. (On one wall there's a picture of Boney arriving in the city through a cardboard and *papier-mâché* Triumphal Arch, hastily erected for the purpose). The food here is excellent—try the juicy *Sauerbraten*, or beef 'Jan Wellem' with tangy mustard sauce—another Düsseldorf speciality.

Meuser, Alt Niederkassel 75, ℂ 51272 (DM20–30). Old family beerhall on the other side of the Rhine, in the same hands since 1853. Famed for its bacon pancakes—hearty creations more like an omelette.

Tante Anna, Andreasstr. 2, ℂ 131 163 (DM50–60). Romantic 17th-century wine tavern, with over 150 varieties to choose from, and good cooking too.

Im Füchschen, Ratinger St. 28, ℂ 84062 (DM20–45). One of the town's most popular breweries, producing an Alt more bitter than most. Also serves good traditional fare such as *Flönz met Ölk* (black pudding with onion rings and Düsseldorf mustard).

Im Goldenen Ring, Burgplatz 21, ℂ 133 161 (DM25–50). Good, solid family restaurant with a shady terrace. Serves tasty German food, steaks, good salads and (in season) huge dishes of mussels that have been boiled with pepper and onions.

Confetti's Trattoria, Düsseldorfer Str. 2, ℂ 572 666 (DM20–50). A new generation of artists and budding hopefuls knock back plates of pasta and filling Italian fare.

Nippon-Kan, Immermannstraße 35, ℂ 353 135 (DM40–70). Traditional Japanese restaurant, one of the best of many around town.

Tuka, Immermanstr. 18 (DM15–30). Simple but authentic pop-in sushi bar.

Bars and Cafés

Zum Schlüssel, Bolkerstr. 43, © 326 155. Cavernous beerhall, popular with after-work drinkers.

Zum Uerige, Bergerstr. 1 (DM10). Simple but atmospheric watering hole with concrete floors, upturned barrels as tables and lots of smoke-filled nooks. Chalk marks on the wall show your drinking score. Its beer is famous throughout Germany—but all you can get to eat is sausages.

NT Pub, Königsallee 27, © 132 311. Media pub filled with the aroma of freshly brewed coffee. Inside a kiosk sells newspapers from around the world, a telex clatters away with the latest news and headlines flash across an an electronic screen on the wall. Locals nickname it the 'Ente' ('Duck', from NT).

Entertainment and Nightlife

Both Mendelssohn and Schumann were at one time Directors of Music in Düsseldorf, though the latter failed dismally here—the cello concerto he wrote in his Düsseldorf days is suitably melancholic. Standards these days are not quite as high, but **opera** and **classical music** still enjoy a good regional reputation. The main opera and ballet companies perform at Deutsche Oper am Rhein, Heinrich-Heine-Allee 16a, © 890 82110. The city orchestra is the *Düsseldorfer Symphoniker* which usually plays at the Tonhalle, Ehrenhof 1, © 899 6123. Blockbuster **pop concerts** are held in the Philipshalle, Siegburger Str. 15, © 775 057. Werkstatt Bühne Düsseldorf, Börnestr. 10, © 360 391, present exciting **contemporary dance** from all over the world. The Düsseldorfer Schauspielhaus, Gustaf-Gründgens-Platz 1, © 162 200, offers mainstream drama. ZAKK (Zentrum fur Alternative Kunst und Kultur), Fichtenstr. 40, © 973 0010, tram 705/6/7, is a vibrant arts centre that puts on a wide programme of dance, theatre, jazz, art exhibitions and video work. Children might enjoy the **puppets** at the Düsseldorfer Marionettentheater, Bilkerstr. 7, © 328 432, and if your German is up to it you could visit the Komödchen, Kunsthalle, © 325 428, a long-established **satirical cabaret** venue. The **cinema** most likely to be showing interesting films in the original language is the Black Box Kino, Heinrich-Heine-Platz, © 899 3766. **Jazz** fans should head for Miles Smiles, Akadamiestr. 6, or Dr Jazz, Rheinstraße, two popular jazz bars in the southern Altstadt.

The poshest **nightclub** in town is Sam's West, Königsallee 27. A younger and more relaxed crowd fill **discos** such as Soul Centre (Bolkerstraße), or the cavernous Tor 3, Ronsdorfer Str. 143.

The best way to find your way through the above maze is to get hold of *Biograph*, a clearly laid out free **what's on magazine** available in cafés, venues and from the tourist office.

Essen is the biggest city in the Ruhrgebiet, and the fifth largest in Germany (beating even Frankfurt and Stuttgart). At first glimpse it seems to offer little more than the grey mixture of 1960s concrete architecture and grimy older buildings that characterize so much of the Ruhrgebiet. Yet the city has an ancient cathedral stocked with remarkable treasures, and one of the best museums of 19th- and 20th-century art in the country. It also boasts Europe's biggest synagogue, oldest parish church and tallest town hall—though these are less likely to prove an attraction.

In AD 852 the Bishop of Hildesheim founded a convent here for daughters of royalty and the aristocracy, and for centuries Essen pottered along quite happily as an unimportant little town, very much under the control of its local abbesses. Then, in the 19th century, **Alfred Krupp** (1812–87) turned what was already a thriving family hammerworks into an industrial empire, and founded a dynasty whose wealth, triumphs and intrigues would put most soap operas in the shade. The wily magnate provided good housing, kindergartens and pensioners' homes for his workers, largely in the hope of defusing the power of the growing Trades Union movement. Essen expanded enormously—at one time nearly a third of the town was in Krupp's direct employ. Alfred Krupp plunged enthusiastically into the arms trade. Each wave of defensive weapons that flowed from a Krupp factory was made obsolete by one of even more powerful offensive weapons—which then set up a market for more effective defensive weapons. The Krupps sold to all comers, creating an arms race which culminated in the First World War. During the Second World War the Krupp industries poured money into the Nazi cause and manufactured ever more sophisticated weapons, not hesitating to use slave labour from the concentration camps. At the Nuremberg trials the heads of the family, Gustav Krupp von Bolen and his son Alfried, were given heavy prison sentences. However, Alfried was released after only three years—the Allies realized they needed his expertise to get the German steel industry back on its feet. Alfried Krupp built up a massive fortune for himself (estimates hover around 1000 million dollars), but later lost his grip and the firm fell into decline. In 1967 the company went public and the family lost its controlling interest.

By car: Essen is at the heart of the Ruhrgebiet, with easy motorway connections to Düsseldorf (40km), Dortmund (40km) and Cologne (80km).

Mitfahrzentrale: Heinickestr. 33, ℰ (0201) 221 031.

By train: The **Hauptbahnhof** is plum in the city centre. Frequent trains connect with Frankfurt (2hr), Cologne (50min), Düsseldorf (½hr) and Aachen (2hr).

Public transport: An S-Bahn network connects all the main towns in the Ruhr. Within Essen itself there is a comprehensive system of buses and trams. A 24-hour ticket (*Tageskarte*, DM8.50) is a good investment.

Tourist information office: Hauptbahnhof (south-west side), ℰ (0201) 235 427 *(Mon–Fri 9–8, Sat 10–8, Sun 10–12).*

Around the Münster

Essen's solemn, almost eerie **Münster** (cathedral), founded in AD 852, is the only building in the city centre really worth a visit. You enter the church through a quiet Romanesque atrium, and walk on into the meditative gloom of the **west chancel**. Erected in the 11th century, the chancel is supposedly based on the octagon of the Pfalzkappele at Aachen, and is all that was left after a fire swept through the church in 1275. The intimate, low-ceilinged Gothic hall church that was built after the fire makes up most of today's cathedral. At the entrance to the nave is an enormous (2.26m tall) seven-armed **candelabra** (*c.* 1000), but the prime attraction of the Münster is the **Goldene Madonna**, in a special chapel at the end of the north aisle. This simple, chunky Madonna and Child—carved out of limewood and covered with gold-leaf—dates back to AD 990, and is the oldest statue of its kind in the world. There are further ancient treasures in the **Schatzkammer** *(Tues–Sun 10–5, DM2)*. Here you can see the splendid **crown of Otto III** (983), encrusted with sapphires and pearls; superb 11th-century processional crosses (most notably the **heophanu-Kreuz** with a shadowy Christ visible beneath its large pink central gem); an intricately carved ivory gospel book-cover and much else.

Joined to the Münster (via the atrium) is the tiny Gothic **Johanniskirche**, where you can see a double-sided altarpiece by the Cologne painter **Bartholomew Bruyn** (1492–1555). You will see either the Easter or the Christmas face—according to the time of year.

Most of the rest of the centre is a bland modern shopping precinct, built mainly in the 1960s and 1970s. Between the Münster and the Hauptbahnhof, at Steeler Str. 29, you can see Europe's biggest **Synagogue** *(Tues–Sun 10–6; adm free)*, an ugly turn-of-the-century building that now houses photographs and mementos of the Holocaust. The lofty **Rathaus** (106m), a 1970s monstrosity, is further along in Porscheplatz.

South of the Centre

Essen's two main museums are located in Goethestraße, 15 minutes' walk south of the Hauptbahnhof (from the Hauptbahnhof follow Kruppstraße, cross Bismarckplatz, then left along Bismarckstraße; Tram 101, 107 or 127). **Museum Folkwang** *(Tues–Sun 10–6; DM5)* is a top-ranking museum of 19th- and 20th-century art. The 19th-century German section is particularly strong. Look out especially for the Romantic Caspar David Friedrich's stormy *Landscape with a Rainbow* (1809) and later gems by Arnold Böcklin and Lovis Corinth. There are two rooms of French Impressionists and Neo-Impressionists, with familiar works by Renoir and Monet (including a version of *Rouen Cathedral* and *Water Lilies*). The bridge to modernism is made with a good selection of Van Gogh (*The Harvest*), Cézanne, Gaugin and Matisse. Twentieth-century German movements—such as the Brücke, Blaue Reiter, Bauhaus and Expressionism are amply represented. There is also a sound collection of Cubists and 1960s Op Art, as well as work by some leading post-1970 artists such as Mario Merz, Gerhard Richter and Anselm Kiefer. Be careful not to miss the *Shadow Orchestra*, an installation by Peter Vogels in a room of its own on the ground floor. A wave of your hand sets the hammers, wheels, strings and bells of a sprawling Heath-Robinson contraption in motion. To the accompaniment of the tinkles, groans and drones (which you can to some extent control), you watch the moving silhouette on the wall.

The **Ruhrland Museum** (same times, included in ticket price) is part of the same complex as the Folkwang. It houses a large, but not especially remarkable, collection of exhibits on local history and folklore. The most interesting sections are those depicting the grim life of miners and factory workers in the 19th century.

Further to the south is the **Gruga Park** *(Apr–Sept 8–midnight, Oct–Mar 9–dusk; adm DM3)*, the beginning of a green belt that stretches as far east as Dortmund. Beyond the park is the **Baldeneysee**, a narrow lake popular in the summer for watersports. Beside the lake is the old Krupp family residence, **Villa Hügel** *(Tues–Sun 10–6; adm DM1.50; S-Bahn from Hauptbahnhof)*. The home is a palatial affair, built between 1868 and 1872 and, with the pictures of Kaisers alongside family portraits, obviously meant to put the Krupps on a par with the noble families of Europe. Nowadays you can wander about admiring the fine furniture and art, and visit an exhibition on the history of the firm which glosses glibly over the more sinister bits.

Essen © (0201–)   **Where to Stay**

Central Essen offers little besides a range of bland modern hotels, catering mainly for the business visitor, but there are some atmospheric hotels in the suburbs.

expensive

Schloß Hugenpoet, August-Thyssen-Str. 51, © 12040, fax 120 450 (DM265–425). Luxury hotel in converted 16th-century castle in the southwestern suburb of Kettwig (S-Bahn Line 6 or Bus 142, 152). Stylish, sedate, with friendly management.

moderate

Parkhaus Hügel, Freiherr-von-Stein-Str. 209, ℃ 471 091, fax 444 207 (DM175). Lakeside hotel in the parkland around Villa Hügel (S-Bahn Line 6). Charm, comfort and good value.

inexpensive

Zum Deutschen Haus, Kastanienallee 16, ℃ 232 989, fax 231 173 (DM75). Clean and centrally situated.

Eating and Drinking

Interesting restaurants are similarly thin on the ground in the centre.

Le Bistro, Am Hauptbahnhof 2, ℃ 17080 (DM30–55). Hotel restaurant in the Mövenpick chain—reliable for good food and tasty salads, though with a fairly run-of-the-mill menu.

Franziskus Keller, I. Weber-Str. 6. Café with young crowd and inexpensive daily specials of hearty German dishes.

Folkwang Museum Café, Goethestraße (DM15–25). Serves light meals as well as the usual run of coffee and cakes; the *Gulaschsuppe*, served in a baked crust of bread rather than a plate, is delicious.

Around the Ruhrgebiet

The region north, east and south of the Ruhrgebiet is known as **Westphalia**—named after one of the three main Saxon tribes. Administrative borders have shifted over the years, but the Westphalians see themselves as inhabiting the land between the Netherlands in the west and the river Weser in the east—whatever successive governments might think. Westphalia can be divided into three main areas. To the north is the **Münsterland**—flat, fertile land dotted with **Wasserburgen** (waterside castles). To the south and east is the more rugged **Sauerland**, a land of deep valleys, artificial lakes, tough little mountains and scrubby forests. (The name literally means 'sour land', but nobody knows whether this refers to the stroppy Saxons who gave Charlemagne such a hard time, or to the hostile unfertile terrain.) Along the eastern edge of Westphalia runs the lush **Teutoburg Forest**.

The Teutoburg Forest (German: Teutoburger Wald) to the east of Osnabrück is renowned for two curiosities, both of which have nationalist associations. The **Hermannsdenkmal** *(Apr–Oct daily 9–6.30, Nov–Mar 9–4.30; adm free)*, a few kilometres southwest of the town of Detmold, is a 53m-high statue of Arminius (Hermann:*see* p. 39), the Germanic chieftain who vanquished the Romans and who is seen as the country's first national hero. The figure was erected in the 19th century in a wave of enthusiasm over German unification—though funds kept running out and it took some 35 years to complete. About 5km further south you come to the **Externsteine**, craggy rocks around an artificial lake. Carved into one of the rocks is a 12th-century Romanesque relief of the descent from the cross, and also a pulpit, two chapels and a tomb. It is thought that this was a centre of pagan worship long before the 12th century, and it is still the focus of celebrations at the summer solstice. The Nazis took over this ritual, endowing it with a mystical nationalism; as a result the ceremony has been tainted and is not so keenly followed today.

Below the Hermannsdenkmal is a large **Vogelpark** (Bird Park) *(Apr–Oct daily 9–6; adm DM5)* full of remarkable birds from all over the world. A footpath leads up to the **Adlerwarte** *(daily 8.30–6 or until dusk in winter; adm DM3)* where there is a fearsome array of eagles and other birds of prey. On the outskirts of Detmold is the **Westfälisches Freilichtmuseum** *(Apr–Oct Tues–Sun 9–6; adm DM5)*, an open-air museum with a spectacular collection of Westphalian rural buildings dating from the 15th to the 19th centuries.

Locals pride themselves on enjoying the simple things in life and are famous for their hams, schnapps and rye bread. Fellow Germans flock from the Ruhrgebiet and elsewhere to join the feast, fish in the lakes and march about the landscape on the numerous marked trails. Foreign tourists seem more reticent. This section picks out a few towns in the area that are interesting in themselves, but could also serve as bases for ventures into the countryside.

See also Directory entry for Lemgo.

Getting Around

By air: Osnabrück and Münster share an airport (halfway between them on the A1). There are daily flights to all the main German cities as well as to Paris, Zürich and London. A bus runs from the airport to Münster Hauptbahnhof (hourly, duration 30min, DM10.80). The cheapest way to get to Osnabrück is to join a communal taxi bus (© (02571) 4525 at least 2 hours in advance, journey time 40min, DM10.80)

By car: Autobahn 1 runs through the centre of the area linking Osnabrück, Münster and the eastern edge of the Ruhr conurbation. From here Route B1 runs east to Soest and Paderborn. It is about 100km from Osnabrück to the heart of the conurbation, and 60km from Dortmund to Paderborn.

Car hire: Avis, Bohlweg 10, Münster, © (0251) 43143; Heinrich Brehe, Kamp 72, Osnabrück, © (0541) 586 299.

Mitfahrzentrale: Aegidiistr. 20a, Münster, © (0251) 40961.

By train: Münster and Osnabrück are on the main Hamburg–Frankfurt line (Münster–Osnabrück 25min, Münster–Frankfurt 4hr, Münster–Hamburg 2½hr, Münster–Düsseldorf 1½hr, Münster–Dortmund ½hr). Soest and Paderborn are on the Dortmund–Fulda line (Dortmund–Soest 50min, Dortmund–Paderborn 1¼hr). Another train connects Paderborn with Hannover (2hr).

Bicycle hire: Cycling is a popular and sensible way to get about—especially in the flat Münsterland. Most major Railway stations hire out bicycles (ask at the parcels section—*Gepäckabfertigung*). You can rent a bike for as little as DM10 a day, sometimes for less if you have a valid rail ticket.

Münster: Bahnhofstraße, opp. the Bahnhof, ℂ (0251) 510 180 *(Mon–Fri 9–8, Sat 9–1, Sun 10.30–12.30)*.

Osnabrück: Markt 22, ℂ (0541) 323 2202 *(Mon–Fri 8.30–6, Sat 8.30–1)*.

Paderborn: Marienplatz, ℂ (05251) 26461 *(Mon–Fri 9–6, Sat 9–1)*.

Soest: Am Seel 5, ℂ (02921) 103 323 *(Mon–Fri 8.30–12.30 and 2–4.30, Sat 9.30–12)*.

Festivals

The region's most famous fair is the **Allerheiligenkermis** (All-Saints Fair) held for the five days following All Saints' Day in Soest. The huge funfair, beer-tents and well-stocked food stalls attract over a million visitors a year. Just as jolly, but not quite as hectic is the **Send**, held three times a year (March, June, October), for five days at a stretch on the Hindenbergplatz in Münster. Paderborn's answer to all this is the **Libori Festival** (last week of July), during which the relics of the town's patron saint are paraded around the cathedral. The town then erupts in five days of festivities which include concerts, circuses, a flea-market and the inevitable funfair. Münster and Osnabrück both have strong Roman Catholic communities and celebrate **Carnival** with fervour. Both towns also have good **Christmas Markets** with all the traditional trappings of Glühwein, gingerbread and wooden toys. Soest also has a small *Weihnachtsmarkt*, and a long tradition of Christmas oratorios and nativity plays in its various churches.

Münster

Münster is a cheery university town that swarms with bicycles, their baskets stuffed with books, cheap fruit from the market or pot plants for digs. Students play soccer in front of the Schloß, or have loud conversations across the street in the comfortable assurance that the town is theirs. Much of Münster had to be rebuilt after Allied bombing raids, but on the whole this has been well done. Today you can see whole streets of elegant period architecture, and outcrops of every style from Romanesque to Baroque amongst the concrete and glass of the 1960s shopping precincts.

The town gets its name ('Minster') from the monastery of the missionary St Liudger, who was sent here in 792 by Charlemagne to tame the fierce Saxons and convert them to Christianity. Since then Münster has been fervently Roman Catholic—apart from a short spell in 1534 when the Anabaptists held sway under Jan van Leyden, self-styled 'King of Münster'. He convinced his followers that the Second Coming was imminent and that Münster was to be the New Jerusalem. But the new 'Reich' was shortlived; after just a few months of rule the prophet and his followers met a sticky end at the hands of the local bishop's troops.

The Dom

Münster's Dom is a low-slung colossus that wavers between Gothic and Romanesque. It was built in the first part of the 13th century—the point of transition between the two styles. The body of the building and the two stocky towers are solidly Romanesque, but there are flutters of Gothic decoration about the transepts and the **Paradise** (entrance porch). The Paradise was supposed to represent the Gate of Heaven, but most of the original carving was smashed by the Anabaptists. Statues of Christ and some of the apostles from the 13th century survived, and a figure of St Paul was added in 1540. Inside the cathedral, at the beginning of the ambulatory, you can see a decorative **astronomical clock** (1540–43). It not only tells the time but gives the position of the sun, shows the movement of the planets and has a calendar of moveable feasts. The face is decorated with delicate paintings by the leading Münster painter **Ludger tom Ring**, and the upper part of the clock is adorned with moving figures. Death strikes the quarter while Chronos meaningfully twists his hour-glass, a chubby trumpeter marks the hour, and at noon the Three Magi appear and, accompanied by the faint tune of a carillon, pay homage to the Christ child . Next to the clock is the tomb of **Clemens August von Galen** (1878–1946), an outspoken and courageous opponent of the Nazis, and a candidate for canonization.

The **Domkammer** *(Tues–Sat 10–12 and 2–6; adm DM1)* has some rich treasures, including a 13th-century gold Madonna, some heavily bejewelled processional crosses and a reliquary made out of a coconut. Star of the show, however, is the 11th-century **Head Reliquary of St Paul**, finely worked in gold, and thought to be the first of its kind.

Around the Dom

The sprawling Domplatz hosts the best **market** in the region *(Mon–Sat, mornings only)*. Here you'll find racks of Westphalian hams and fat sausages, piles of produce from the surrounding farms as well as foreign fare—barrels of olives, fragrant herbs and spices and bottles of flavoured vinegar. Just across from the cathedral is the **Landesmuseum** *(Tues–Sun 10–6; adm free)*. Confusingly, you'll find exhibits from the 10th–17th centuries in the Neubau (new building) and works from the 18th century onwards in the Altbau (old building). On the ground floor of the Altbau you can see the delicate **Überwasser sculptures**, which once graced the Überwasserkirche just west of the cathedral. Anabaptists smashed and buried the figures in the 16th century, but they were dug up and put back together over 300 years later. There is also work by early 16th-century sculptor **Heinrich Brabender** (much of it taken from the cathedral). He was a master of individual characterization, and sensitive to the finest detail, down to a carefully knotted drawstring on the thief's knickers at Calvary. His son **Johann Brabender** excelled at smaller-scale work: look out for his lively *Adam and Eve*.

Upstairs you'll find work from the late-Gothic, Renaissance and Baroque periods. You can trace the history of Westphalian painting from the Soft Style of **Conrad von Soest** to later Mannerist pieces. There is a large collection of paintings by the local **tom Ring** family. Especially worth a look are Ludger the Younger's almost cuddly animal studies. Keep an eye open also for work by Derick Baegerts (active 1476–1515 in nearby Wesel). His exuberant paintings are full of quirky wit and detail. There are also one or two pieces by German greats, such as Cranach, Grien and Bruyn, but the Dutch and Flemish collection is mediocre—except for some extraordinary *pronkstilleven*, ostentatious still lifes involving dead peacocks and lobsters.

The post 17th-century art in the Altbau is not nearly as impressive as the earlier work, but there are two rooms devoted to Expressionism, with a number of good paintings by **August Macke**. The Landesmuseum interconnects with the **Museum für Archeologie** *(same times; adm free)*, an uninspiring world of broken pottery, models of Saxon houses and bits of mammoth.

East of the Cathedral

A walk down one of the alleys leading east off the Domplatz brings you to the **Prinzipalmarkt**, a long street of beautifully restored pale stone buildings with trim gables. At the top end of the street is **St Lamberti**, a Gothic hall church with a tall filigreed spire. High up on the tower hang the three **wrought iron baskets** that were used to display the bodies of the Anabaptist leaders once their 'Kingdom of Mümster' had been crushed. Halfway down the street you come to the Gothic **Rathaus**, famed for its airy, soaring gable. Here in 1648 the signing of the **Peace of Westphalia** brought the Thirty Years' War to an end (see p. 42). Inside you can visit the council chamber where the treaty was negotiated, known as the **Friedensaal** (Hall of Peace) *(Mon–Fri 9–5, Sat 9–4, Sun 10–1; adm DM1.50)*. The chamber is lined with carved Renaissance wood-panelling. In a little cabinet in one corner is an odd collection of objects: a golden cockerel (*c.* 1600) used as a wine decanter for special guests; a withered human hand of unknown origin (maybe from one of the Anabaptists); and a slipper that once belonged to the Duchess of Orleans, a famous beauty who accompanied her husband to Münster for the peace negotiations.

Salzstraße, which leads off the Prinzipalmarkt, takes you to the **Erbdrostenhof** a stately 18th-century patrician mansion with especially decorative Rococo frescoes. At the time of writing the Erbdrostenhof is being restored as a museum. Across the way is the new **Stadtmuseum** *(Tues–Sun 10–6; adm free)*. The most interesting exhibits are a reconstructed grocer's shop (1911) and an original Volkswagen Beetle.

Outside the Centre

The **university** is housed in an 18th-century **Schloß**, a few minutes walk west of the Domplatz. The Schloß, a sober Baroque building, opens out at the back into the **Botanical Gardens** *(daily 7.30–5; adm free)*—a pleasant place for a stroll in the summer, but otherwise not worth the detour. South of the University is the **Aasee**, a lake that seems to attract the entire population of the city on fine days. On the furthest bank is the **Mühlemhof** *(Apr–Oct daily 10–5, Nov–Mar Mon–Sat 1.30–4, Sun 11–4; adm DM4, Bus 14)*, a small but enlightening collection of reconstructed old mills and agricultural buildings from around Westphalia.

Schloß Wilkinghege, Steinfurter Str. 374, © 213 045, fax 212 898 (DM210–260). Dreamy 16th-century *Wasserschloß* in lush parkland in the northwest of the city, converted with taste and flair. It must be one of the few hotels in the world with its own chapel.

Romantik-Hotel Hof zur Linde, Handorfer Werseufer 1, © 325 002, fax 328 209 (DM185–200). A 17th-century farm building in the northeast of town, enchantingly stuck in a time-warp with heavy antiques, crackling log fires in winter, deeply soporific four-poster beds and charming management.

Hotel Überwasserhof, Überwasserstr. 3, © 41770, fax 417 7100 (DM140–180). Smart, glossy hotel on the edge of the Kuhviertel—a trendy nightlife quarter. All rooms have cable TV; there's a Westphalian breakfast buffet of banquet proportions.

Hotel Busche am Dom, Bogenstr. 10, © 46444 (DM90–145). Very friendly, intimate hotel right near the cathedral. Rooms vary a lot in size, but they are all spotless and comfortable, and the cosy breakfast room tempts you to linger over endless cups of coffee. No restaurant.

Zum Schwan, Schillerstr. 27, © 661 166, fax 67681 (DM88 without private facilities–DM106). Just behind the station. Simple but clean and one of the most reasonably priced hotels in town.

Youth Hostel: Bismarck Allee 31, © 43765.

Eating and Drinking

The highest concentration of good pubs and restaurants is in the **Kuhviertel** near the Überwasserkirche.

Drübbelken, Buddenstr. 14, © 42115 (DM30–60). Old wooden inn with atmospheric interior and excellent cooking. The menu is wide-ranging, but fish dishes are a speciality. Try the enormous Drübbelken platter, with four different types of fish, salad and potatoes. For the more adventurous there is eel with apple rings.

Restaurant Wielers Kleiner Kiepenkerl, Spiekerhof 47, © 43416 (DM25–45). Odd copper pots hang from the low beams, and the friendly owner/chefs serve up hearty Münsterland fare, such as the filling *Bauernschmans*, a farmer's dish of potatoes, ham, sausage and bacon.

Fischbrathalle, Schlaunstr. 8 (DM20–30). Big scrubbed tables, minimal decor and plain, delicious fish. Open during the day only.

Pinkus Müller, Kreuzsstr. 4–10, © 45151 (DM40–60). Adjoining pub and restaurant of local brewery. Cluttered, crowded and convivial. The food is excellent, but pricey—try the pork stuffed with herbs and served with a beer and cream sauce. The Alt beer is much favoured by locals. In the summer you can drink it as a punch mixed with fresh raspberries and peaches.

Altes Gasthaus Leve, Alter Steinweg 37 (DM20–30). Huge, old-fashioned Gasthaus with superb cooking. Game dishes are especially good—try the roast venison and pears stuffed with wild mushrooms.

Ricos, Rosenplatz 7, © 45979 (DM10). *Stehcafé* serving salads and wholemeal *Auflauf* (baked dishes).

Café Malik, Frauenstr. 14. Popular student pub full of nooks and tiny rooms. Down-to-earth beer drinking and earnest conversation.

Grotemeyer, Salzstr. 24. Shades of old Vienna—plush seats, strong coffee and enormous cream cakes.

The Wasserburgen

In the Münsterland around Münster there are over 50 Wasserburgen—modest castles surrounded by moats or lakes (water being the most sensible deterrent against attackers bowling across the relentlessly flat countryside). The castles were first built in the 16th century. Later, splendid Baroque country houses replaced the more practical fortified homes. Sadly, the best views you'll get of most castles are in coffee-table books—aerial photography providing a perspective that the flatlands simply can't. Also, most Wasserburgen are still in private ownership, and the hoi polloi are kept well at bay. All too often the only reward for your journey is a glimpse through a hedge or over a wall. Local buses can get you from castle to castle, but progress is slow and erratic. By far the better idea is to go by car or hire a bike (*see* **Getting Around** above). There is seldom much to detain you inside the castles, and you could happily see three or four in a day. The Münster tourist office stocks maps of the area and brochures on the castles. Pick of the bunch are:

Haus Rüschhaus *(Apr–mid-Dec Tues–Sun 10–12.30 and 2.30–5; adm DM3.50; Bus 5)*. Closest Wasserburg to Münster, on the north-western edge of the city. More cottage than castle, a quirky Baroque building that was home to Germany's most prominent 19th-century poetess **Annette von Droste-Hülshoff** from 1826–46. Some of her best work evokes the mood of the surrounding fenlands.

Haus Hülshoff *(Mar–Oct daily 9.30–6; adm DM4 for park and house; Bus 563)*. The somewhat grander Hülshoff family seat, Annette's birth-place and just half an hour's walk along a footpath from Haus Rüschhaus. A classic Renaissance Wasserburg with a stocky fortified outer ring (the *Vorburg*) and a residential inner building (*Hauptburg*). Inside you can see just six rooms, all decorated in a 19th-century style in homage to the poetess.

Burgsteinfurt *(by appointment only, © (02551) 1231; train from Münster)*. Haphazard, romantically rambling building with Romanesque, Renaissance and Baroque bits. Begrudgingly admits individual travellers.

Burg Vischering *(Mar–Oct Tues–Sun 8.30–12.30 and 2–5.50; Nov–Feb Tues–Sun 10–12.30, 2–3.30; adm DM2; bus or train from Münster to Lüdinghausen)*. Small, mainly Renaissance, castle 30km southwest of Münster. It is built from a jumble of different stones, with bright shutters and a perky octagonal tower. One of the prettiest and most touristy of the castles, it now houses the **Münsterland Museum**, a fairly uninspiring collection of folkloric knick-knacks and displays on life in the Wasserburgen.

Nordkirchen *(free open access to exterior, tours of interior Sat and Sun only 2–5, on the hour, or © (02596) 1001; adm DM2; very restricted bus and train service on weekends).* Just 8km south of Lüdinghausen, this is the grandest of all the Wasserburgen, nicknamed the 'Westphalian Versailles'. A large, but restrained, symmetrical building finished in 1734, with Baroque statues placed strategically around the formal lawns. A tight rein was also kept on the interior décor. All the elements of Baroque splendour are there—stucco, carved panelling and ceiling paintings—but kept under firm control.

Osnabrück

Although now technically part of the *Land* of Lower Saxony, Osnabrück is historically and culturally very much allied to Westphalia, and has close connections with Münster, just 50km to the south. The town was founded as a bishopric by Charlemagne in 780 and, like Münster, hosted negotiations for the **Peace of Westphalia** which ended the Thirty Years' War. Osnabrück also suffered badly from bombing during the Second World War. Here the restoration has not been quite so successful, but the churches and old buildings that remain do warrant a visit. Osnabrück has two latter-day claims to fame. The *Osnabrücker Nachrichten*—one of Germany's most go-ahead daily newspapers—is published here, and the city was the birthplace of Erich Maria Remarque, author of *All Quiet on the Western Front*, one of the best novels to emerge from the First World War.

The Dom

Osnabrück's cathedral grew up gradually, sprouting odd spires along the way. Three of these remain: a pretty octagonal tower from the early 12th century over the transept, a slender Romanesque tower on the west side and a neighbouring Gothic one, twice its width. Inside the church is a large, polychrome **Triumphal Cross** (1230). The figure of Christ has open eyes (not usually the case), and this gives him a resigned, agonized expression. The **Master of Osnabrück**, an unknown artist who continued to carve in the Gothic style well into the 16th century, contributes two sensitive carvings—the *Margarethenaltar* in the ambulatory, and the *Madonna with a Rosary* on the wall of the north transept.

There is a small **Diözesanmuseum** *(Tues–Fri 10–1 and 3–5, Sat and Sun 10–1; adm DM1.50)* above the cloister. Here you'll find more work by the Master of Osnabrück, an 11th-century cross encrusted with gems and cameos, and carved figures from the rood screen that once stood in the church.

Around the Markt

The triangular market square is just west of the cathedral. Up one side is a row of dapper orange and ochre medieval houses, modelled on the step-gabled architecture of the wealthy Hanseatic ports. At the far end of the square is the **Rathaus**, originally built between 1487 and 1512 but almost entirely reconstructed after the Second World War. An ornamental row of various emperors across the façade looks clumsy and out of place. The Rathaus was a venue for the long negotiations that led to the Peace of Westphalia, though the wood-panelled **Friedenasaal** (Hall of Peace) *(Mon–Fri 8.30–6, Sat and Sun 10–1; adm DM1.50)* is not nearly as impressive as its Münster counterpart. However, your ticket does also give you access to the **Schatzkammer** (ask for a key at the porter's desk if closed) where you can see the gargantuan **Kaiserpokal** (Emperor's Goblet) which dates from the 13th century, and some valuable charters and documents. Next to the Rathaus is the old **Stadtwaage** (Weigh-house, 1532) an attractive step-gabled stone building with red and white Dutch-style shutters. The northern edge of the square is taken up by the **Marienkirche**, a Gothic hall church with an eccentric, spindly spire. The *Passion Altar*, made in Antwerp in 1510, is worth a look for its skilful carving and finely painted wings.

The only other part of Osnabrück really worth exploring is the little quarter of old houses, now greatly gentrified, bounded by Bierstraße and Marienstraße. Heger Straße, with its rows of half-timbered buildings, is the most attractive.

Osnabrück ✆ (0541–)   ***Where to Stay***

Hotel Walhalla, Bierstr. 24, ✆ 27206, fax 23751 (DM150–160). Half-timbered hotel in one of the more atmospheric streets in town. The décor is catalogue-repro, but there's a sauna, jacuzzi and solarium for the guests. Management is friendly in a Westphalian sort of way. (The saying goes that you would get through a bag of salt with a Westphalian before you got to know him.)

Hotel Meyer am Neumarkt, Johannisstr. 58, ✆ 24771 (DM128–135). Ordinary, centrally situated hotel for use in emergencies. The rooms lurk behind heavy net curtains—but at least they're not grimy.

Haus Vennemann, Johannisstr. 144, ✆ 572 589 (DM60 without bathroom). Small, simple but well-run hotel convenient for the tourist sights and station.

Youth Hostel: Iburger Str. 183a, ✆ 54284.

Eating and Drinking

Café Wintergarten, Lohstr. 22, ✆ 24440 (DM10–30). An alternative crowd relaxes over breakfast until 5pm—sipping coffee out of pudding-bowl-sized cups. Also serves pastas, steaks and salads.

Walhalla, Bierstr. 24, ✆ 27206 (DM25–45). *Gemütlich* hotel restaurant with a frequently changing menu. The chef comes up with such delights as fresh mussels baked with cheese and herb butter.

Weinkrüger, Marienstr. 18, ✆ 23353 (DM15–45). Heavy low beams, Delft-tiled walls, hearty Westphalian cooking and a wide range of wines. Traditional dishes such as *Grünkohl* (cale), with generous helpings of sausages, pork loin and neck of beef.

Just to the east of the Ruhr conurbation, along the B1, lies the comparatively sleepy town of Soest. Like many other towns in Westphalia, Soest was founded by Charlemagne during his campaigns to Christianize Saxony. For 500 years successive Archbishops of Cologne took Soest under their wing, making sure that it was rich, powerful and grateful—and so a good base for extending their control over Westphalia. Trade flourished, Soest became an influential member of the Hanseatic League and the first town in Germany to have its own municipal law. (This was drawn up in 1130. A century later the same system had been adopted by over 60 German towns, including Hamburg, Bremen and Lübeck). But in 1444 the people of Soest decided they could fend for themselves, and with characteristic forthrightness wrote to the Archbishop of Cologne: 'Know ye, high-born prince, lord Dietrich of Mörs, Archbishop of Cologne etc, that we, mayor, council, guilds, offices, brotherhoods and the whole municipality of the town of Soest want to be your enemy'.

This did not prove to be a very good idea. Although the archbishop's armies lost the ensuing battle (they arrived with ladders too short to scale the ramparts), everything went downhill for the town after that. Trade with America weakened the power of the Hanseatic League, Soest's new ally, the Duke of Cleve involved the town in a crippling war of succession and, finally, the Thirty Years' War put paid to any last vestige of prosperity.

Soest ticked over quietly for centuries, hardly expanding beyond the medieval city walls. Second World War bombs destroyed much of the town, but the handsome churches, half-timbered houses and cobbled alleys lined with six-foot-high garden walls, have been painstakingly rebuilt. Soest may be only 40km from Dortmund, but it has an endearing village atmosphere, and is certainly worth a day's visit.

The Centre

The stately Romanesque church of **St Patrokli** (inaccurately, though understandably, called the Dom), stands bang in the middle of town, its square tower dominating the skyline. The church is built of an oddly coloured local sandstone, giving it a feverish green hue. The interior is even more colourful—thanks to a series of bold, bright anachronistic but splendid stained glass windows installed in the 1980s. Remnants of the precious original 12th-century glass can be seen in the **Dommuseum** *(Sat 10.30–12.30 and 2–4, Sun 11.30–12.30 and 2–4; adm DM1.50)* which occupies the upper gallery. A few yards to the west of St Patrokli is the diminutive **Petrikirche**. The foundations date back to the 8th century, but the church is Romanesque with a Gothic chancel. The tower is topped with a rather frivolous three-tiered Baroque spire. In the nave you can see two frescoes of the Crucifixion (*c.* 1400) reputedly by local painter **Conrad von Soest**, one of the few medieval artists known by name. Around the east side of St Patrokli is another tiny Romanesque church, the **Nicolaikapelle** *(Tues, Wed, Fri and Sun 11am–12, or key from Wilhelm-Morgner-Haus opposite)*. In the dim, rich **interior** you can see an altarpiece that definitely *is* by Conrad von Soest.

Adjoining St Patrokli on the north side is the red, arcaded **Rathaus** (1713), one of the few important buildings to go up after Soest's decline. Further north down Rathausstraße you come to the expansive Markt, where you'll find *Wilhelm Haverland*, a celebrated **pumpernickel bakery** which has been in operation since 1799. The sticky, black bread originated in Soest, and is one of the foods that foreigners most associate with Germany. A simple shop in the side-street behind the bakery sells several varieties of the bread.

To the south of St Patrokli, down Ulricherstraße and along Burghofstraße, is the **Burghof** *(Tues–Sat 10–12 and 3 –5, Sun 11–1; adm DM1)*, a pretty 16th-century patrician mansion in a high-walled garden. The Burghof now houses a local history museum, but the exhibits are less interesting than the elaborate stucco biblical scenes in the **interior**. Tucked away behind the mansion is a rare **Romanesque house** (1200) built out of the peculiar local green sandstone.

The Wiesenkirche and the Hohnekirche

A walk northwards from the Rathaus, along Am Seel, past an old water mill and up Wiesenstraße, brings you to the **Wiesenkirche** *(summer daily 10–12.30 and 2.30–6; winter daily 10–12 and 2–4)*, the most beautiful church in town and one of the finest examples of a Gothic hall church in Germany. From the outside the Wiesenkirche looks fairly ordinary, but the **interior** is breathtaking. You are surrounded by soaring spear-shaped panes of **stained glass** (dating from 14th–16th centuries), delicately painted so as to let in floods of coloured light. As if not to intrude, the stonework in between rises swiftly to the vault in slender, graceful columns. One of the windows (over the north portal) shows a *Last Supper* with Christ and the apostles sitting down to a good Westphalian meal of ham, roast boar's head and (if you look carefully) rye bread and beer. Behind the Wiesenkirche (up Hohengasse off Wiesenstraße) is the dumpy Romanesque **Hohenkirche** *(summer daily 9.30–12 and 2–4; winter daily 1–4)*, an earlier and clumsier attempt at building a hall church. Inside you can see some of the original 13th-century frescoes, a late 15th-century *Passion Altar* by the Westphalian Master of Liesborn, and the **Scheibenkreuz** (1200), a unique triumphal cross carved in relief on a disc and decorated with scenes from the life of Christ.

Soest ✆ (02921–) **Where to Stay**

Im Wilden Mann, Markt 11, ✆ 15071 (DM80–180). Half-timbered building on the Markt with well-appointed rooms and a good Westphalian breakfast.

Hotel Stadt Soest, Brüderstr 50, ✆ 1811 (from DM120). Fake Persian rugs, stripes, checks and flower prints galore—but efficiently run and centrally situated.

Hotel Drei Kronen, Jakobistr. 39, ✆ 13665 (DM84–94 without private bathroom). Dinky half-timbered building with six tiny rooms (each with cable TV) and a big warm welcome.

Youth Hostel: Kaiser-Friedrich-Platz 2, ✆ 16283.

Zwiebel, Ulricher Str. 24, ✆ 4424 (DM20–40). Old half-timbered tavern with a pleasant roof-garden. Tasty but standard fare—schnitzels, steaks and sausages.

Im Wilden Mann, Am Markt 2, ✆ 15071 (DM20–60). Traditional inn on the Markt, justifiably popular with tourists for its Westphalian cuisine. Try the *Pfefferpotthast*, a peppery beef and onion stew served in a bowl made of toast.

Im Osterkamp, Walburger Str. 10, ✆ 15402 (DM10–25). Secluded *Gaststätte* with a large shady beer garden, and a fine line in smoked meats.

Paderborn

Paderborn is 55km east of Soest along the B1. The jewels of its architecture are set in a cardboard crown; over 80 per cent of the town was destroyed during the Second World War, and most of what was rebuilt is relentlessly bland. But, plum in the centre of town, is a magnificent and ancient cathedral and the ruins of Ottonian and Carolingian palaces—alone quite enough to make a visit well worthwhile. Beside the cathedral flows what must be the most top-heavy river in Europe. Two hundred hot springs spurt to the surface at a rate of 9000 litres per second. Together they form the river Pader which flows just 4km from its source, joining the River Lippe before it's even had a chance to leave town.

Charlemagne—who had a failing for hot springs—set up base here in AD 777, during his campaigns against the Saxons. In 799 Paderborn was a temporary haven to Pope Leo III, who had just escaped assassination. He and Charlemagne formed an alliance that led directly to the establishment of the Holy Roman Empire (Charlemagne was crowned a year later in Rome), thus governing the shape of German politics for the next 1000 years.

The Cathedral and the Palaces

When Charlemagne heard of Pope Leo III's impending visit he set about building a new church 'of remarkable size'. The Pope returned the compliment by immediately conferring upon it the status of cathedral. The present church, built in the 13th century in the so-called transitional style (between Romanesque and Gothic), is stately, all sweeps and curls of golden sandstone. Odd carvings (part of a blocked portal) grace the south transept: a fox dressed up in a gown receives a diploma, a hare plays the fiddle and there's a boar blowing a horn. Inside, the church is cavernous, but bright and cheerful, lined with rows of 17th-century monumental sculpture—including the rather pompous **tomb of Prince-bishop Dietrich von Fürstenburg** by the Mannerist Heinrich Gröniger. The High Altar seems enormously distant; on it a golden urn glows mysteriously, picked out by hidden light. More animal fun lies at the end of the trail, marked by signs reading **Hasenfenster** (Hare Window). In the tracery of a window in the cloister is a bit of visual trickery that has become Paderborn's symbol. Three hares run in a circle. Each has two ears—but the mason has carved only one per animal. (Something to puzzle over on your journey to Paderborn.)

In the 1960s, during rebuilding work to repair war damage, workers uncovered the remains of the original **Carolingian Palace** and the **Ottonian Palace** that replaced it after a fire in 1000 razed it to the ground. Today you can see some of the excavated ruins to the north of the cathedral. Under the stairs to the north portal (covered by glass) is the **open-air throne** used by Charlemagne. The later Ottonian Palace has been reconstructed by Gottfried Böhm, Germany's leading modern architect. It is now a small museum *(Tues–Sun 10–5; adm DM1)*, containing photographs of, and fragments from, the 1960s digs—though it is really only worth a visit to savour the way in which Böhm has managed to capture the atmosphere of the old building. Outside the entrance to the museum is the **Bartholomäuskapelle** (1017), the only original survivor of the Ottonian Palace and the oldest hall church in Germany. It is a tiny building with an extraordinary acoustic.

Around the Cathedral

Paderborn holds a few other delights. West of the cathedral lies the source of the Pader, set in a lush park. It is a good place for a cooling summer stroll, as the breeze circulating above the warm waters acts as a natural air-conditioner. To the north (on Thisaut, follow the signs from the cathedral) is the **Adam-und-Eva Haus**; this prettily carved and painted 16th-century half-timbered house is Paderborn's oldest. Today it is the local history **museum** *(Tues–Sun 10–6; adm free)*, yet again more interesting for the interiors than the collection itself. On the **Markt**, off the south side of the cathedral, is the **Diözesanmuseum** (at the time of writing closed for renovations), a sombre building by Gottfried Böhm, made up of layers of lead plates and glass. When the museum re-opens you will see the **Imad Madonna**, a serene, detached virgin carved in wood around 1056, and other treasures from the cathedral. The high-gabled **Rathaus** (on Schildern, just off the Markt) is in the 17th-century Weser Renaissance style more common in cities west of Westphalia (*see* p. 59).

(*see* p. 59)

Paderborn © (05251–)   ***Where to Stay***

Hotel Ibis, Paderwall 1–5, © 25031, fax 27179 (DM163). Functional hotel with pleasant service and light, comfortable rooms.

Hotel Abdinghof, Bachstr. 1a, © 12240, fax 122 419 (DM110-120). The only really atmospheric hotel in town, set on the edge of the park right at the source of the Pader. The owner is an artist, and rooms are individually decorated.

Haus Irma, Bachstr. 9, © 23342 (DM70–80). Pleasant, quiet little Pension on the edge of the park. No restaurant.

Youth Hostel: Meinwerkstr. 16, © 22055.

Eating and Drinking

Weinkrüger, next to Adam-und-Eva-Haus (DM20–40). An old half-timbered house—one of the few restaurants in Paderborn with any atmosphere. The food is good too, with dishes cooked with local fruit and Rhine wines.

Jeans Baguetterie, Mühlerstr. 24 (DM10–20). Osnabrück's trendies sip beer and knock back lengthy, well-stuffed baguettes.

The Rhine: Cologne to Mainz

The Rhine:
Cologne to Mainz

The map shows the Rhine region from Köln (Cologne) to Mainz, including: Köln (Cologne), Schloß Augustusburg, Brühl, Phantasialand, Bonn, Bad Godesberg, Königswinter, Rolandseck, Remagen, Ahr, Bad Breisig, Leutesdorf, Andernach, Laacher See, Schwarzrheindorf, Heisterbach (ruins), Schloß Drachenburg, Bad Honnef, Unkel, Linz, Rhein (Rhine), Agger, Sieg, Siebengebirge.

*There was
a Roman
centurion—
swarthy bloke,
brown as a ripe
olive—he taught a
blonde girl Latin. And
then a Jewish spice-dealer
joined the family, a serious
fellow who had turned
Christian before the marriage
and founded the family's Catholic
tradition. And then came a Greek
doctor or a Celtic legionnaire, a mercenary
from Graubünden, a Swedish knight, one of
Napoleon's soldiers, a Cossack deserter, a
raftsman from the Black Forest, a wandering Alsatian
miller, a fat seaman from Holland, a Magyar, a
Pandour, a Viennese officer, a French actor, a Bohemian
musician—all these people lived on the Rhine, brawled
and boozed, sang and spawned children there—and Goethe
came out of the same pot, and Beethoven, and Gutenberg and
Matthias Grünewald. They were the best, dear boy! The best in
the world! And why? Because they came from a mixture of races.
The Rhine—that's what western civilization means.*

Carl Zuckmayer in The Devil's General

The Rhine (German: Rhein) begins as a brook in a bleak part of
Switzerland, flows into Lake Constance, then gushes out at a walloping
365 cubic metres per second and heads for the North Sea. On the way it
squeezes through gorges four times taller than the river is wide, surges by
precipitous terraces of vineyards, and courses through valleys of
cornfields and fruit trees. Finally it skulks past some of the most densely
populated industrial cities in the world and widens out across placid, flat
grazing land, before meandering to a rather ignoble end in the waterways
of Holland.

This chapter focusses on that part of the river which people usually think of as 'the Rhine', working upstream (the way most tourists do it) across the Rhine plain from Cologne to Bonn, past the stunted outcrops of the Siebengebirge (Seven Mountains), and on through a gentle valley to the confluence with the Mosel at Koblenz. From here on the landscape changes dramatically. The sides of the valley heave up to form a jagged gorge, at times towering over 400m above the water level. This is the Rhine of treacherous currents, the Lorelei, romantic castles, misty sunsets and vertical vineyards. It's the Rhine celebrated by Goethe, Wagner and Heinrich Böll, subject of countless fairy-stories and legends. It is also the Rhine of relentlessly chugging diesel barges, thundering goods trains and swarms of tourists.

The river is navigable up to Basle (with the assistance of various canals to straighten out its meandering course) and remains a major European waterway—as anyone who spends the night in a waterfront hotel will testify. Tourists have poured into the gorge ever since Karl Baedekker made it the subject of his first guidebook 150 years ago, but millions of staring eyes cannot wear out the scenery. If you avoid the Summer high season and find a hotel set back from the river, you can give yourself a chance of enjoying some of the most spectacular vistas Germany has to offer. Though you won't find anywhere innocent of tourism, you *can* find precious sanctuaries away from the crowds—particularly in the Siebengebirge, where there are long marked walks through protected land. In the cities you'll find superb

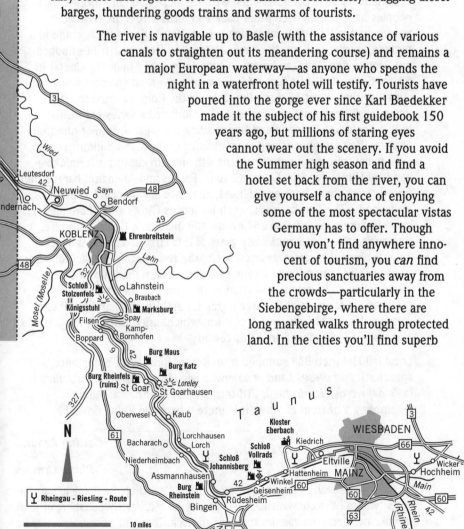

Romanesque and Gothic architecture, excellent museums and a convivial atmosphere. The food is lavish, if not particularily subtle, and the wines are among the best in the land. The Rhinelanders really do live up to their reputation as cheery, slightly zany *bons vivants*, and extroverts will find the period of Carnival festivities (in the weeks preceding Lent) a cathartic time to visit.

The earliest inhabitants of the Rhinelands date back 600,000 years—the oldest signs of human settlement in the area were unearthed near Andernach. Since then, in the words of a 19th-century traveller, the Rhinelanders have been 'fattened with the best blood of Europe'. Various peoples have chased each other back and forth across the river and numerous armies, while sweeping across the continent, have come to a momentary standstill on the banks. Migrating Germanic tribes nudged out Bronze Age Celts, and were in turn vanquished by Julius Caesar in 58 BC. Caesar built the first bridge over the river, an apologetic wooden structure that lasted 18 days. But later, as the Romans retreated from unsuccessful campaigns in the east, they founded a series of fortified towns (including Cologne and Bonn) along the west bank. For hundreds of years the permanence and magnificence of the stone buildings struck local tribes with awe, but during the 4th and 5th centuries formidable bands of Huns, Vandals, Goths, Saxons, Franks and Alemanni barged their way through these frontier defences, and once again occupied the Rhinelands. The Franks, under such leaders as Clovis and Charlemagne, came to dominate the area and eventually the whole German empire. It was during the prosperous early years of this First Reich that wily local knights along the narrower stretches of the river began to exact tolls from passing ships, and to build strong castles to ensure that they got them. There followed invasions and counter-invasions by the Prussians (responsible for most of the area's grander architecture) and the French (responsible for blowing much of it up) which lasted through the Napoleonic era and well into this century.

Local lad Heinrich Böll summed it up in his Nobel Prize acceptance speech: '*Wenn dieses Land je so etwas wie Herz gehabt haben sollte, lag's da, wo der Rhein fließt*'. (If this country ever had anything resembling a heart at all, then it is there where the Rhine flows.)

Getting Around

Rhine Cruises

As early as the 18th century tourists were being floated up the Rhine in wooden boats 'with all the conveniences of a palace', and delicately partaking of local salmon, asparagus, strawberries and Rhenish Hock. Today Rhine cruises tend to be less lavish affairs, though local companies do still offer feast and party cruises. A boat trip on the Rhine is one of the best ways of getting an overall impression of the river—but it is slow going (especially upstream), and not such a good idea if you want to explore towns and castles in detail. The riverscape really only becomes interesting to the south of Bonn, and it is the stretch between Koblenz and Mainz that offers the most romantic views. So the best idea is to do most of your travelling by land and save the cruise for a trip past the scenic bits of the river.

Small companies based along the river offer short hop and speciality cruises (*see* **Getting Around** for Bonn and Koblenz, pp. 145 and 157), but the main carrier is the **Köln-Düsseldorfer Line**, which plies the river between Cologne and Mainz. Cruises operate from the beginning of April to the end of October, stopping at towns and villages all along the way. The company has a deal with German Rail, so Rail Passes are also valid on the boats. This means that you can hop on and off at will—the Rail Pass proves a particularly good investment here (*see* p. 11). Even if you don't have a Pass you can speed up your journey by transferring onto a train for a small extra charge—a useful move if you want to visit a town—then catch up the boat later on. Larger boats have restaurants and cafés, where the leisurely can while away the hours, sipping Rhine wine and looking at the view. If time is short, however, you can zip about at 60kph on a hydrofoil.

Landing stages are clearly marked with a bright KD. Here you'll find timetables (also available from most tourist offices) and ticket offices. The company's Head Office is at Frankenwerft 15, 5000 Köln 1 (information © (0221) 20 88 318/319; booking © (0221) 20 88 288).

It's not usually necessary to book in advance (except for the hydrofoil), and generally more fun to make up your journey as you go along. An unbroken cruise between Cologne and Mainz takes 10 hours downstream and 12 hours upstream, and a ticket will set you back DM143 (daily services downstream only). Unless you really are addicted to river travel it is best to save your time and money and go on a shorter jaunt between Koblenz and Mainz. The full trip from Koblenz to Mainz takes nearly 8 hours (5 hours downstream) and costs DM72.50. (The hydrofoil cuts journeys by more than half, but there is a surcharge). Short hops cost around DM20, and there is a reduction on round trips.

Rhine Crossings

There are bridges across the Rhine at Cologne, Bonn, Neuwied, Bendorf, Koblenz and Mainz. Car ferries cross the river from Bad Godesberg to Königswinter, from Bad Honnef to Remagen, from Linz to Remagen, from Andernach to Leutesdorf, from Boppard to Filsen, from St Goar to St Goarhausen, from Kaub to Bacharach/Oberwesel, from Niederheimbach to Lorch and from Bingen to Rüdesheim.

Köln (Cologne)

Cologne is the city of cheap scent and exalted churches, a focus for painters and art-dealers—and the front line of the Rhineland's wild pre-Lenten revels. Architecturally, it wears its motley all year round. The streets are a patchwork of soaring Gothic, cosy Romanesque, Prussian pomp, concrete and glass boxes and provocative post-modern extravaganzas. Motor traffic roars around medieval towers and trains rumble up almost to the cathedral door. As you pick your way through a maze of pavement art in one of the ubiquitous pedestrian zones, you might suddenly come across a bit of Roman wall, or a tomb or half-buried tabernacle.

At night, Cologne lights up from top to toe. You can rollick about the city centre or wander off with the locals into one of the outlying pockets of trendy cafés. Dark-haired, latinate, Kölners speak with a bouncing dialect, specialize in sharp repartee and incomprehensible in-jokes and tirelessly (if not exhaustingly) affirm their reputation as jolly carousers. There's a strong dash of arrogant city pride, too. A Kölner is a Kölner before being a German, or even a Rhinelander—outsiders are called '*Imis*' (imitation Kölners). Sometimes it all gets a bit much. But if you weary of the gusto and cronyism, you can withdraw to enjoy the more sedate pleasures of Cologne's brimming museums, the magnificent cathedral, or the smaller churches—many of them touchstones of German ecclesiastical architecture.

History

Cologne began life in 33 BC as an obscure Roman fortress town. Germanicus was stationed here in AD 15 when his daughter, Julia Agrippina, was born. Having schemed her way to becoming the wife of the emperor Claudius, Agrippina persuaded him to up the status of her obscure Rhineland birthplace to that of an official Roman colony. It was known as *Colonia Claudia Ara Agrippinensium* (or CCAA, Claudian colony of the imperial altar of the Agrippinensi)—a mouthful which, understandably, locals shortened to Colonia. Her immortality thus assured, Agrippina poisoned her husband, only to be dispatched in turn by her son Nero.

In AD 313 Maternus (later to rise from the dead bearing St Peter's staff) became the first Bishop of Cologne. Church power burgeoned under the Frankish occupation and Charlemagne created an archbishopric here in AD 795. The archbishops of Cologne wielded considerable secular power until 1288, when wealthy and disgruntled citizens' guilds seized control at the battle of Worringen, and set themselves up as a Free Imperial City. Cologne flourished both as a trading city (it became an important member of the Hanseatic League) and religious centre nicknamed Hillige (holy) Köln. The Reformation passed Cologne by. The city was always fiercely Roman Catholic—as late as 1790 citizens were threatening 'uproar, murder and fireraising' should Protestants be granted civil rights and freedom of worship.

The invasion of the French revolutionary army in 1794 put an end to the Free Imperial City. French occupation lasted until the 1815 Congress of Vienna, when Cologne reluctantly became part of the Kingdom of Prussia. Nineteenth-century industrial development and prosperity were so solid that the city managed by and large to ride out the economic depressions of the early 20th century. Under Lord Mayor Konrad Adenauer the city administration made a brave stand against Nazi control in 1933—a move that earned Adenauer the job of West German Chancellor after the war. In the meantime, however, up to 95 per cent of Cologne's town centre had been reduced to charred rubble by Allied bombers. Rebuilt in the 1950s and 1960s, Cologne is today the fourth largest city in Germany: a busy Rhine port with thriving motor and pharmaceutical industries, host to numerous trade fairs, the cultural capital of the Rhineland and, of course, beloved of Eau-de-Cologne-using grannies everywhere.

Getting Around

By Air

The **airport**, © (02203) 40 4001, to the southeast of the city, serves both Cologne and Bonn. There are connections to all major European capitals and to Washington and New York. The **airport bus** (Line 170) will whisk you into town in 20 minutes for a mere DM3.60, while a **taxi** will knock you back DM33. **British Airways** is at Marzellenstraße 1, © (0221) 13 5081 and Lufthansa is at Bechergasse 2–8, © (0221) 20824.

By Train

The **Hauptbahnhof** (information © (0221) 141 3281)—right next door to the cathedral and trying desperately to upstage it—is on a main German north–south rail route and also offers direct lines into Italy, France, Belgium, Britain and the Netherlands. Main German connections include Berlin (7hr), Dresden (12hr), Frankfurt (2½hr), Heidelberg (4hr) and Munich (5½hr).

By Car

Car Hire: Hertz, Airport, © (02203) 61085, and Bismarckstr. 19–21, © (0221) 51 5084; Sixt Budget, Airport, © (02203) 40 2142; Avis, Clemensstr. 29, © (0221) 24 1699. **Carparks** are plentiful in the city centre. They're well signposted—and the boards even indicate how many empty spaces are left.

Mitfahrzentrale: Beethovenstraße 16–18, © (0221) 21 9067; Saarstraße 22, © (0221) 21 9991; and Maximinenstraße 2, © (0221) 12 2021.

Public Transport

Most of Cologne's museums and tourist sights are in a compact area around the cathedral. Some of the Romanesque churches lie further afield, but even these are within reasonable walking distance. If you'd prefer to use the **U-bahn** or **trams** (information © (0221) 547 3333), it's best to get a day ticket (DM8) or 3-day ticket (DM14) for unlimited travel.

Taxis: © 2882.

Dampfschiffahrt Colonia, Lintgasse 18–20, ℂ (0221) 21 1325, offer hour-long round trips on the Rhine and panoramic evening cruises. The K-D Line, Frankenwerft 15, ℂ (0221) 208 8288, can take you further afield (*see* **Rhine Cruises** above).

Tourist Information

The main **tourist information office** is opposite the cathedral, at Unter Fettenhennen 19, ℂ (0221) 221 3345. Its staff can arrange private sightseeing tours, book you on the guided city tour and make hotel reservations on the day. They have shelves of information on the city's attractions and can give advice on walks and Rhine cruises.

Post office: The main post office is at An den Dominikanern *(24-hour service)*. Parcel depot on Marzellenstraße.

Police: ℂ 110.

Medical emergencies: ℂ 72 0772.

Market days: Friday in the Alter Markt. There is also a fleamarket every third Saturday in Alter Markt.

Festivals and Fairs

Carnival (*see* below) or **Corpus Christi** (with processions in late May or early June) are the most festive times to visit this Catholic stronghold. Although Carnival officially starts on 11 November of the preceding year, the climax is the *Drei Tollen Tage* (three crazy days) just prior to Lent. Cologne is packed—especially around the cathedral area—and all shops and museums are closed. With true German thoroughness, all pole positions along the routes for the *Schullun Veedlezög* (Sunday Parade) and *Rosenmontagzug* (Rose Monday Parade) are booked in advance. Transgress at your peril. (The tourist office supplies maps of routes and can help with booking space.) The Rose Monday Parade has become very slick and professional; the Sunday parade has a more folksy, neighbourhood feel. It is not as spectacular, but can be more enjoyable—and you're less likely to be squeezed to a pulp.

There's a world-renowned **art fair** in the Messe (exhibition centre) each March, and two attractive **Christmas markets** during Advent. The better of these is held on the Alter Markt. Here you will find not only mulled wine, roast chestnuts and gingerbread, but also Christmas fare from south Germany (such as *Zwetschgen-manderl*—plums filled with almond paste). Colourful booths are laden with gifts and carved wooden Christmas decorations. On 6 December Santa Claus drives his sleigh down the Hohe Straße, followed by the *Hillige Mann* (Holy Man) who manages to distribute 2000 *Weckmänner* (doll-shaped dough cakes) along the way.

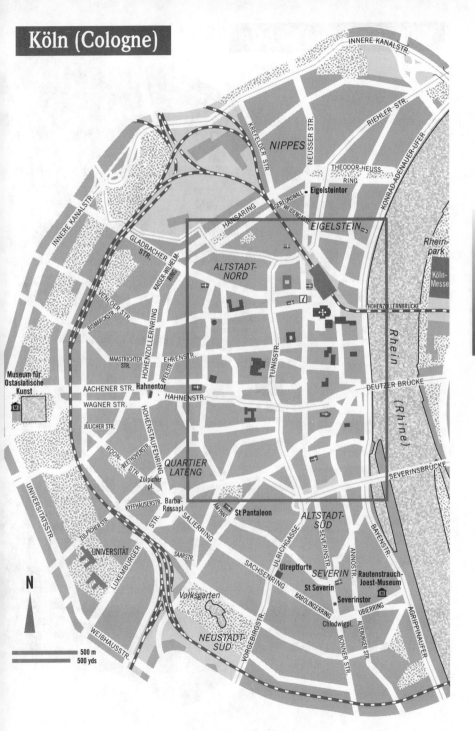

Köln (Cologne)

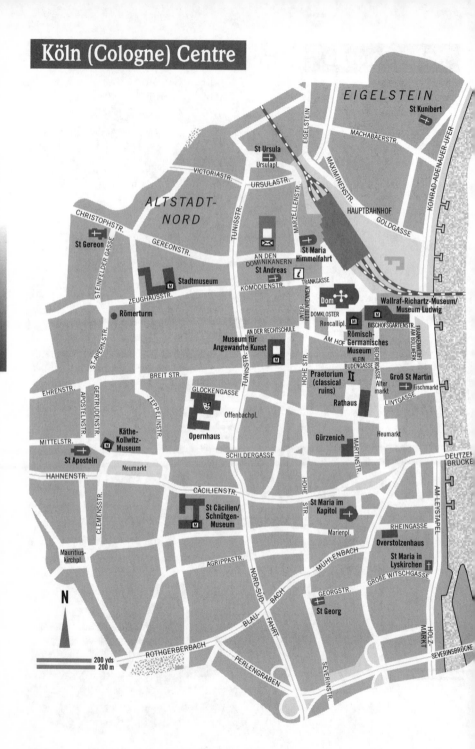

Köln (Cologne) Centre

Carnival

 Rio de Janeiro and the idea of Carnival are almost insepa- rable; mysterious masked figures on their way to balls seem appropriate in wintry Venice—but the picture of cities erupting in colourful anarchy is one that few people readily associate with Germany. Yet all over the Roman Catholic south (and these days even in the Protestant north) good, respectable German burghers annually launch themselves into a season of sub- versive revelry.

The origins of Carnival are probably pagan (this shows in the grotesque masks and strange dances that take place in some towns), but officially the festival is a sustained final fling before Lent. The 'fifth season' begins on 11 November (officially on the 11th minute of the 11th hour of the 11th day of the 11th month) and builds up to a three-day bash before Ash Wednesday. The word carnival comes from the Old Italian for 'removal of meat'. Local dialect words for *Karneval—Fasteleer* or *Fastelavond* in Cologne; *Fastnet, Fastnacht* or *Fasching* further south and in Bavaria—also refer to the same idea.

Subverting natural order, tweaking at social taboos, and simply letting your hair down and drinking too much are all part of the fun. Parties, processions of floats, and songs or speeches lampooning anyone in authority are the basic ingredients of Carnival everywhere in Germany, but there are any number of regional variations to the final recipe. The city of Mainz specializes in clever satire (its celebrations are televized and transmitted all over the country). The small Baden- Württemberg town of Rottweil stages a *Narrensprung*—a 'Parade of Fools' wearing extraordinary carved wooden masks and including such characters as *Gschell* (who represents the coming summer) and an evil-looking *Federahannes* (a personification of winter). In some towns gaudily dressed figures charge through the streets beating people with inflated pig's bladders. Often a local legendary character will feature in the festivities—as does the drunken jester, Perkeo, in Heidelberg, or the cheeky Schambes in Mainz. Many of the seemingly ancient traditions, however, date back only to the early years of the last century when there was a revival of interest in medieval customs, and when the presence of French, and later Prussian, invaders stimulated the Rhinelanders into finding a safe way of expressing opposition to their foreign rulers. (In Mainz the carnival flag is an inverted Tricolour and the 'council' that runs the show parodies the structure of the one that governed the city during the French occupation in 1806.)

The most famous *Karneval* city of all is Cologne. The pattern of events here mirrors what is going on in towns all over southern Germany. On 11 November the Lord Mayor kicks off with a speech from the Rathaus, and selected singers and poets try out their works on the assembled crowds (at this early stage the songs are mostly a rehash of the previous year's material). Confusingly, successful singers and speakers are rewarded with hissing and a slow handclap—and the carnival cry of 'Alaaf!' ('Helau!' elsewhere in the country).

Long before the 11 November a Festival Committee (as well as a score of local societies) will have been gearing themselves up to organize costume balls, *Sitzungen* ('sessions' of feasting and speeches) and the big parades. To be head of the main committee, 'Prince' of the carnival, is a prestigious—and expensive—role that usually falls to a local magnate. The Prince plays host at innumerable Carnival functions, for which he has to foot the bill—an honour that in Cologne can cost him around DM100,000. In Cologne the Prince is assisted by a *Jungfrau* (virgin—always a man in drag) and a *Bauer* (peasant), though in other towns his sidekick is usually a (non-transvestite) Princess.

The *Sitzungen* range from local sports association booze-ups to black-tie affairs, and are a means of raising funds for the final Carnival procession. (Cologne's parade costs over a million deutschmarks each year.) The balls, too, include everything from the skittle club's annual dance to glittering high-society events. Between New Year's Eve (when the season gets underway in earnest) and Ash Wednesday, Cologne has over 400 *Sitzungen* and costume balls. New Year's Eve also sees the first appearance of the *Blaue Funken* (Blue Sparks) and *Rote Funken* (Red Sparks), comical military corps in bright dress uniform who wilfully disobey all orders. (Their original function was to send up the Prussians, who were obsessed with military drill.)

The climax of the activity in Cologne comes in the last days before Lent. At 11am on *Weiberfastnacht* (women's carnival), the Thursday before Ash Wednesday, the Lord Mayor hands over the keys of the city to the Carnival Prince, and *Drei Tollen Tage* (three crazy days) of revelry ensue. From now on pubs have no official closing time and there are parties all over town (the Prince and his Carnival Court visit as many as they can in succession). Things quieten down a little during working hours—though you will still see people wandering about in fancy-dress. *Weiberfastnacht* is a day of defiance for women. This they express symbolically by cutting off men's ties. In the days that follow there are pageants and processions all over town (some 50 in all), notably the *Schullun Veedlezög* (Sunday Parade). People dress up in costume just to go to the pub, and you are likely to get your fair share of *Bützchen*—pecks on the cheek from complete strangers. Rhinelanders say that 'Anyone who is not foolish at carnival is foolish for the rest of the year', and maintain that adultery during carnival cannot be cited as grounds for divorce. If you don't dress up and join in the fun you are branded a *Karnevalsmuffel*, a 'sourpuss'.

The highlight of the festivities is the Rosenmontagzug (Rose Monday Parade) on the Monday before Lent. Hundreds of thousands of people line the streets for hours on end to watch the procession of brass bands, brightly decorated floats and bizarrely dressed people. First comes a pageant on the history of the city, then a parade that makes fun of politicians, then the Carnival Prince and his retinue and lines of extravagantly decorated floats. Revellers throw sweets, chocolates, flowers and little bottles of Eau de Cologne into the crowd and pour out warming tots of Schnapps. '*Wer am Zug war und hat den Zug gesehen, der war nicht am Zug*', goes the local saying ('If you were at the procession and saw the procession, then you weren't at the procession'.) The burghers of Cologne get through some 40 tons of sweets, and hundreds of thousands of chocolates and flowers every year. Similar parades happen all over southern Germany—though none is quite so extravagant as the one in Cologne.

Shrove Tuesday sees the final, and most prestigious, ball of the season, where the Prince hands back power to the Lord Mayor. At midnight straw dolls that have been hanging up outside pubs are solemnly cremated, and Carnival is at an end. On Ash Wednesday there is one final party as all the waiters, chefs, cab drivers and others who have been hard at work over the 'crazy days' hold their own celebration. For others a simple fish supper marks the beginning of Lent.

The Dom

The twin spires of Cologne's Gothic cathedral (German: *Dom*) seem to touch the very heavens and can be seen from miles away, divine emanations from the surrounding squat buildings and flat countryside. The railway station deposits awed travellers right on the doorstep. Stately and solitary, the cathedral stands in the middle of a square that echoes with platform announcements and seethes with people walking backwards, glued to their cameras, trying to fit it all in.

Work began on the cathedral in 1248, but by 1560 had run out of steam with the building only half-finished. For 500 years voyagers up the Rhine recognized Cologne from the distinctive landmark of a dumpy half-tower and an enormous crane. Construction was completed during the 19th-century Gothic revival, the Prussians having decided that such a grand building would make an impressive national monument for the new Reich. Heinrich Böll preferred the homelier medieval church, and harrumphed '*Die Preusen haben ja den Dom dann gebaut und diesen ganzen vaterländischen Scheiß drum gemacht.*' ('Sure, the Prussians then built the cathedral—and added all this patriotic crap').

The generations of builders never wavered from Master Gerhard's original plan and, rare for Germany, the cathedral is high Gothic from the cornerstone to the tips of its filigreed spires. However, nothing can prepare you for the impact of the **interior**. The lofty vaulted ceilings reduce the tourist hordes to scuttles of insignificant dwarves and the theatrical gloom—dappled by coloured light from the magnificent windows—is spellbinding. Look out especially for the 13th-century **Bible windows** in the ambulatory and two sets of **windows of the Three Magi**—a busy and delicate 16th-century version in the northern side-aisle opposite the bolder **Bavarian windows** donated by Ludwig I in 1842.

The focal point of the **high altar** is a three-tiered gold sarcophagus, the **Shrine of the Three Magi**, said to contain the bones of the Three Wise Men. It was designed by goldsmith Nicholas of Verdun in 1183 and is plastered with gems and cameos donated by the pious wealthy. The powerful Archbishop Reinald von Dassel ('Barbarossa's helper and horror') snatched the relics of the three Magi from a ravaged Milan in 1164. Pursued by agents of Pope Alexander III, he passed off his booty as the bodies of dead comrades and hotfooted it over the Alps and up the Rhine to the safety of his own city walls. (All along the Rhine, at points where he stopped, you can find pubs and inns named after the Three Wise Men).

Other artistic highlights include the **Agilofusaltar**, a virtuoso piece of 16th-century Flemish woodcarving; the Gero Crucifix (c. 970), the oldest life-sized carving of Christ, and Stephan Lochner's lucidly painted **Dombild** (c. 1400). The Magi once again make an appearance in the central section; St Gereon stands rather belligerently on the right panel, and on the left St Ursula gracefully leads her 11,000 virgins to their deaths (see p. 135).

The **Treasury** (Mon–Sat 9–5, Sun 1–5; adm DM2) contains the usual array of outrageous ornament, as well as a fragment of St Peter's staff (see **History** above) and assorted bits of other saints. You can climb up the tower (95m high) to the viewing platform (Mon–Sat 9–5; adm DM2) for a fine view of Cologne and the Rhine plain.

South of the Dom: the Main Museum Complex and the Altstadt

Cologne's best museums are conveniently lumped together right next door to the Dom. The museums are pricey by German standards, but the tourist office can sell you a **Museum Pass** (DM10), which allows admission to all municipal museums on any three days within a week.

The **Wallraf-Richartz-Museum/Museum Ludwig** at Bischofsgartenstr. 1 (Tues–Thurs 10–8, Fri–Sun 10–6; adm DM8 to both) share the enormous, scalloped modern arts centre between the cathedral and the Rhine with the city's new concert hall. Together these museums offer one of the best collections of art in the country. You could spend a happy two to three hours looking at pictures, occasionally glimpsing out of the windows at the Rhine, or at stonemasons chipping away on the cathedral.

The Wallraf-Richartz-Museum occupies the middle floor. It is based on two 19th-century donations, one from a cleric, Canon Franz-Ferdinand Wallraf, the other from a local merchant, Johann-Heinrich Richartz. The heart of the collection is the section of medieval Cologne painting (in all rooms labelled B). For the entire 15th century Cologne shone out as a centre of supremely fine painting. Artists of what is now known as the **Cologne School** (see p. 56) were (like their German predecessors) mostly anonymous, and have been named after their most important works. However, unlike earlier artists, they began to develop very distinctive personal styles. One of the first to do this was the **Master of St Veronica** (active c. 1400–20), noted for his fine attention to miniature figures, and for an equally assured touch with large faces. Look out especially for his pensive *Madonna of the Sweet Pea Flower* (1410).

One artist dominates the period, and was so famous in his time that his name has survived. **Stefan Lochner** (c. 1400–51, see p. 56), adopted the Master of St Veronica's gentle 'Soft Style', and is renowned for his painstaking attention to detail. In his *Last Judgement*, complacent purple angels flit about while a fearsomely lurid devil dispatches terrified hordes of the damned.

Later painters of the Cologne school were strongly influenced by Dutch artists. The leading light of this period is the **Master of the Life of the Virgin** (active 1460–85), who painted lively narrative panels peopled with sumptuously clad figures and filled with exquisite background detail. The bright, quirky, hard-edged works of the **Master of the Bartholomew Altar** (active 1470–1510) round off the period with a flourish.

Later German painting fills rooms marked with a C or D, most importantly some fine works by Cranach the Elder and Dürer. Dutch and Flemish Masters are well represented (Rooms G to L), with self-portraits by **Rubens** and **Rembrandt** and a nastily gloating Delilah by the **Jan Steen**. Other periods and countries are less comprehensively featured, but there are good pieces by Canaletto, Titian, Tintoretto and Murillo. There is a healthy collection of French Impressionists, as well as intensely dramatic landscapes by the German Romantic painter **Caspar David Friedrich**.

The Museum Ludwig on the top floor is named after the Aachen collector Peter Ludwig (*see* p. 89), and is devoted entirely to 20th-century art. In room after airy room, up and down stairs, in little nooks and large halls you pass by a grand parade of brand-name 20th-century art. The museum has an excellent **Picasso** collection and some well-chosen pop art, including works by **Roy Lichtenstein** and rows of **Andy Warhol's** tins of Campbell's Tomato Soup; an interesting section on early 20th-century Russian avant-garde (with some intriguing early landscapes by Malevitch), and corresponding displays by Bauhaus artists (*see* p. 64). German painters are particularly well represented, with some much-reproduced work by artists of *Die Brücke* (*see* p. 63) and Expressionist schools. There is some suitably disturbing **Otto Dix**—especially his nightmarish *Portrait of Dr Hans Koch*—and unexpectedly calm, almost airless landscapes by **Max Beckmann** (usually a portayer of 'savage, cruel, magnificent' life). You're brought more up to date with Rothko's moody blobs of colour, Beuys's felt and fat, upside-down Baselitz, Cy Twombly's manic scratchings and Penck's stick figures. All in all it's likely to knock you reeling, especially if you have just spent a quiet hour or two with the gold leaf and gentle Madonnas downstairs.

On the ground floor you'll find the **Agfa Foto-Historama** (hours as above; admission included in the ticket), a small museum of photographic history built up from two private collections and the Agfa archives from Munich. There are photographs, old cameras and viewing equipment on show.

The **Römisch-Germanisches Museum** (Roman-Germanic Museum), Roncalliplatz 4 *(Tues–Sun 10–5, first Thurs in month to 8pm; adm DM5)* is right next door. The museum was built over the remains of a Roman villa, found during the building of an air raid shelter in 1941. The centrepiece is the floor of the dining hall, the glittering **Dionysian Mosaic** (*c.* AD 200). A boozy Bacchus is surrounded by tripping maenads and groping satyrs, and the whole picture is edged with festive symbols—grapes, oysters, a peacock, even a dog waiting for left-overs. It is made from over a million pieces of ceramic and glass, and is one of the finest intact mosaics north of the Alps. The museum also houses the 15m-high **Tomb of Poblicius** (*c.* AD 40); the original arch of the north gate of the Roman city, bearing the inscription CCAA (*see* **History** above); and a surprisingly comfortable and modern-looking reconstructed carriage. Smaller artefacts are displayed according to type rather than chronologically, so the visitor has to deal with over 1000 clay lamps, then case upon case of cooking implements, and on and on. Some of the jewellery, however, is breathtaking, and the collection of glass is unrivalled. Before Venice led the market, Cologne glass—with its twirling threads of colour—was coveted throughout Europe. The **diatreta** (cage cups)—delicate networks of glass resting on the flimsiest of struts, dating from *c.* AD 330—were especially popular.

The Altstadt

The **Altstadt** lies to the south of the cathedral and the museums. Here, despite some crass modern development, you'll still find cobblestones, crooked alleys and the occasional quiet square with a fringe of period façades and pavement cafés. A walk down Bechergasse brings you to the **Alter Markt** (Old Market). Normally you would expect this to be the centre of the city, but here it seems a little neglected (the Dom is the real heart of Cologne, and Neumarkt its commercial centre). However, the square brightens up with fruit and flower vendors on market day (Friday) and hosts the better of Cologne's two Christmas fairs. In a tiny square behind the only two surviving 16th-century houses on Alter Markt (Nos. 20 and 22), you can see a statue of tubby Tünnes and lanky bowler-hatted Schäl. These two fictitious comic characters crop up in various forms all over Cologne, and are the subjects of a stream of luke-warm jokes. Here is one of the better ones:

> TÜNNES: Why do we have to pay the church tax?
> SCHÄL: Why not?
> TÜNNES: I thought the Good Lord gave us everything for free.
> SCHÄL: Via a middleman, Tünnes, via a middleman.

The rather solid Romanesque tower of **Groß St Martin** *(Mon–Sat 10-12, Mon–Fri and Sun 3–5)* pokes up its turrets between Alter Markt and the Rhine. From the 10th to the 13th centuries Cologne was at its zenith. Glitterati with a concern for their well-being in the after-life would top up church coffers in exchange for a few intercessory prayers. The result is a garland of Romanesque churches, only recently restored after the devastation of the Second World War. Their round arches and cosy proportions make a soothing antidote to the cathedral's soaring Gothic. Groß St Martin (built between 1150 and 1240) is one of the biggest, and was Cologne's prime landmark, before it was usurped by the new cathedral towers in 1880. The large building lacks the intimate atmosphere of the city's other Romanesque churches, but in the eerily lit crypt you can see the ruins of the Roman warehouse that 10th-century monks converted into the first church on the site.

Wedged between Groß St Martin and the Rhine is the **Fischmarkt**, a touristy but pretty riverside square with brightly painted houses, burgeoning window boxes and packed outdoor cafés. Opposite the church, on the other side of the Alter Markt, a flight of stairs leads off to the old **Rathaus** *(Mon–Fri 9–4.30; tours in German Mon, Wed, Fri 3pm)*. The textbook Renaissance portico sprouts a late Gothic tower to the left and an 8m-long decorative bronze panel from the 1970s to the right—an architectural potpourri that befits the city. Under the glass pyramid across from the city hall, you can see a medieval **Mikvah** (Jewish ritual bath). If you want a closer look, the keys are available from the Rathaus custodian. Around the corner in Klein Budengasse is the entrance to the **Praetorium** *(Tues–Sun 10–5; adm DM2)*, the remarkably intact foundations of the Roman governor's palace (ranging over four building periods from the 1st to the 4th centuries). Children seem to prefer the 100m-long **Roman sewers** (entered through the ruins)—dim, echoing and quite high enough to run about in.

South of the Rathaus, in Martinstraße, is the stolidly bourgeois **Gürzenich** built by the citizenry between 1437 and 1444 as a banqueting hall. The interior is hideous 1950s, and is still used for receptions and carnival balls. Next door is the bombed-out shell of the 10th-century **St Alban's** church, now a desolate war memorial with a replica of Käthe Kollwitz's statue *The Mourning Parents*.

From here you can cut through to Cologne's **main shopping street**, the **Hohe Straße**, which runs south from the cathedral along the route of the original Roman Rhine road. Today, troops of avid consumers relentlessly plunder its length.

As you battle your way back up towards the cathedral, take time to duck down An der Rechtschule to the **Museum für Angewandte Kunst** (Museum for Applied Art) *(Wed–Sun 10–5, first Thurs of month to 8pm; adm DM5)*. It is a gem. Visitors are led clockwise through three-quarters of a millenium of European culture. Everything is beautifully presented, there's no overkill and the selection is exquisite. One floor ranges from the Middle Ages to Jugendstil, and the rest of the museum is devoted to the 20th century. Here you'll find the best the Western world has to offer in jewellery, tapestry, fashion, furniture, marquetry, kitchenware, china, glass, engravings and posters.

West of the Dom

Almost opposite the Dom, on Komödienstraße, is **St Andreas'** *(Mon–Fri 10–12, Mon–Sat and Sun 3–5)*, a Romanesque church which grew up unevenly between the 10th and 15th centuries. The low, flat 11th-century ceiling still determines the shape of the building, despite Late Gothic rebuilding of the choir and nave. (The capitals of the pillars in the nave remain untouched—showpieces of Romanesque carving.) The church contains the tomb of Thomas Aquinas's mentor, Albertus Magnus, and the 16th-century Shrine of the Maccabees—ornately carved in the spirit of the cathedral's Shrine of the Magi.

Komödienstraße leads into Zeughausstraße, where (at Nos. 1–3) you'll find the **Stadtmuseum** *(Tues–Sun 10–5, Thurs 10–8; adm DM5)*, which houses historical city bric-a-brac, taking up where the Römisch-Germanisches Museum leaves off. Carnival trappings, batteries of Eau de Cologne bottles, suits of armour and an early model Ford feature in a varied display, which is especially appreciated by children.

West of the museum, up Gereonstraße, is the Romanesque church of **St Gereon** *(Mon–Fri 9–12, Mon–Sat and Sun 3–6)*, built (*c.* 1227) on the oval base of a 4th-century Roman church. You can see the remains of a 12th-century gilt mosaic floor and some wonderfully gaudy ceiling painting. The unusual 13th-century decagon tower soars up four storeys to a ribbed dome—the world's third largest in Christian architecture (after Hagia Sofia in Istanbul and Florence cathedral).

If you walk south down Steinfelder Gasse, you come to the **Römerturm**, a corner tower of the Roman city wall built in AD 50. Because of its medieval function as a lavatory for the nearby St Clara Nunnery, it has survived intact (other ruins were plundered for stone). The beautiful rosettes, triangles and zigzags of its multi-coloured brickwork are quite atypical of Roman fortification architecture—there are even hints of temple design in the carving.

Continuing south along St-Apern-Straße and Gertrudenstraße, you come to **St Aposteln** *(Mon–Fri 10–12, Mon–Sat and Sun 3–5)*, an early Romanesque church, begun in 1021. The church presumptuously claims the patronage of all the Apostles, which is usually reserved for important churches in Constantinople or Rome. The interior stands whitewashed and expectant while various committees bicker on about how it should be decorated.

St Aposteln faces onto **Neumarkt**, Cologne's commercial heart. The vast square is skirted by shops and department stores (*see* p. 137) and thunders with traffic. The barren paved central island is populated by small bands of alcoholics. A few sorry flower stalls are unsuccessful in brightening things up. The **Käthe-Kollwitz-Museum**, housed in a bank at Neumarkt 18–24 *(Mon–Wed 9–4.30, Thurs 9–6, Fri 9–3.30; adm free)* has a large collection of graphics, and also some sculptures, from one of Germany's greatest Expressionist artists. Her black-and-white pacifist lithographs and horrific war scenes are especially moving.

The flat-roofed **St Cäcilien** (*c.* 1250), off the other end of Neumarkt on the site of the old Roman Baths, was once an institution for gentlewomen and now contains the **Schnütgen-Museum** *(Tues–Sun 10–5, first Thurs in the month to 8pm; adm DM5)*. This is a rewarding little museum of ecclesiastical art, containing such treasures as St George's sword (a flimsy affair with a butterfly on the hilt), fine Rhineland carvings and some of the best bits out of the other Romanesque churches in Cologne. In the sacristy, well worth a look, are slide-out panels containing glitzy liturgical robes and secular embroidery from as early as AD 600. The spray-painted skeleton on the blocked-up western portal is not the work of vandals, but of the Swiss artist Harald Nägeli, commissioned at great expense.

A walk back north up Tunisstraße brings you to Glockengasse, and the house of **Eau de Cologne 4711**.

Eau de Cologne

 In 1709 Paolo Feminis and Johann Maria Farina arrived in Cologne from Italy with a recipe for dissolving the essences of flower blossoms in alcohol to produce a fragrant water. They named their concoction L'Eau Admirable. This water, they claimed, was a panacea of 'exceeding strength' and 'penetrating effect', especially good for curing strokes, coughs, gout, impotence and even the plague. Half a century later, when Napoleonic legislation demanded that makers of medicines register the recipes, the Farina family downgraded their product to 'toilet water' rather than reveal the secret. Customers began to use the euphemism 'Eau de Cologne', and the name stuck. Today the word 'cologne' is common usage for many kinds of perfumed liquid, and local manufacturers have taken to labelling their bottles *Echt Kölnisch Wasser* (real Eau de Cologne).

The Farina firm still exists, but by the end of the 18th century a rival distilling dynasty—the Mühlens family—had set up shop in Glockengasse. In 1794 the French army of occupation did away with street addresses and assigned all the houses in the city a number. The number of the Mühlens' house gave the name to what was to become the most famous of all Cologne waters—4711. Today there are over 20 manufacturers of Eau de Cologne in the city, but the two original dynasties have kept their recipes a close secret, passed down from generation to generation. Even today outsiders have only a rough idea of the ingredients—80 per cent alcohol mixed mostly with orange and lavender oils, and matured in wooden casks for from six to twelve months. The actual proportions and methods of mixing, however, are known to only one family member at a time, and are kept locked away in a safe. When new essences are needed he withdraws with the crucial formula to a private laboratory to concoct a new supply.

Much further to the west of the centre, at Universitätsstr. 100, is the **Museum für Ostasiatische Kunst** (Museum of East Asian Art) *(Tues–Sun 10–5, first Thurs in the month to 8pm; adm DM5, Tram 1 and 2 from Neumarkt)* which contains art and artefacts from Japan, China and Korea. Here you'll find one of the most important collections of Korean ceramics outside of that country, hundreds of fine Japanese woodcuts and some exquisite lacquer work and screen-painting. The museum specializes in Buddhist painting and sculpture and has an exceptional collection of Japanese religious woodcarvings. The modern building (designed by Tokyo architect Kunio Mayekawa) opens out onto a peaceful riverside Japanese garden.

North of the Centre

Just to the north of the Dom is the strikingly pink **St Mariä Himmelfahrt** (built 1618–78), the only Baroque church of any note in Cologne. Inside, it is a fricasee of stucco, coloured marble and flying cherubs. If you follow Marzellenstraße up past the church, you come to the Romanesque church of **St Ursula** (*c.* 1110) *(Mon–Sat 10–12, Mon–Fri and Sun 3–5)*—easily recognized by the crown atop its steeple, a reminder that Ursula was an English princess. In about AD 400 she reputedly led 11,000 virgins to total massacre by the Huns—the church was later built over their graves. The remains of this hapless army, dug up during the construction of the church, were made into a splendidly gruesome mosaic. Neat patterns of assorted bones, overlaid with Latin inscriptions spelled out in femurs, make up the walls of the church's Goldene Kammer *(Mon and Thurs 11–12, Wed and Fri 3–4, Sat 4–5; adm DM1.50)*. Ornate Baroque gilding added a few centuries later only serves to heighten the macabre effect.

Duck under the railway line east of Ursulaplatz, and you come to the **Eigelstein** district— scruffier and noisier than the centre, but jostling with a faintly oriental feel. Exotic smells and Turkish music fill the air, shops spill out onto the pavements and side-streets are lined with gently decaying Jugendstil buildings. It is a good area for inexpensive restaurants and authentic local taverns (*see* **Eating and Drinking** below), and in Weidengasse you'll find some bargain junk shops.

Down Machabäerstraße, off the main street, is **St Kunibert's** (1247) which, at the time of writing, is being restored to a disconcertingly pristine state. Consecrated the year before building began on the cathedral, it was the last of the Romanesque churches to be built, and already shows signs of capitulation to the new Gothic ideas.

North of Eigelstein, beyond the medieval **Eigelsteintor** (an old city gate) lies **Nippes**, another rewarding spot if you are looking for good, non-touristy places to eat (*see* below). A walk back along Gereonswall offers further glimpses of the old **city wall**, and gets you back to the western edge of the city centre.

South of the Centre

Cologne's most attractive Romanesque churches lie south of the city centre. On Marienplatz, just beyond Heumarkt you'll find **St Maria im Kapitol** (*c.* 1065) *(Mon–Sat 10–12, Mon–Fri and Sun 3–5)*. In the 8th century Plectrudis, wife of Pippin the Major-Domo, founded a nunnery for the *crème de la crème* of the local nobility. Two centuries later Abbess Ida, trying to outdo her sister Theophanu in Essen, and keep up with the imperial Salians in Speyer (*see* p. 230), decided to build a showcase church. By cribbing the clover-leaf design of the choir of the Church of the Nativity in Bethlehem, she succeeded in setting the pattern for later churches throughout the Rhinelands (St Aposteln and Groß St Martin in Cologne being among the first to follow suit). The highlight of the church is a pair of vividly carved door panels (1065) depicting scenes from the life of Christ.

A walk down to the Rhine, along Rheingasse, takes you past the the **Overstolzenhaus**, a Romanesque patrician townhouse with an impressive step-gable. (Only the facade remains.) Turn upstream along the river bank and you come to the comparatively tiny **St Maria in Lyskirchen** (*c.* 1210) *(Mon–Sat 10–12, Mon–Fri and Sun 3–5)* which began life as a parish church for sailors. Inside, it has a jollier atmosphere than the other churches (sermons are sometimes even given in *Kölsch* dialect). A Madonna holds a ship's wheel, saints dangle anchors and the ceiling blazes with gaily coloured painting. The church escaped relatively unscathed from the Second World War, and in the crypt you can see perfectly detailed 13th-century murals with scenes from the Old and New Testaments.

Walk down the side of the church, along Große Witschgasse and up Georgstraße, to find the soothingly calm **St Georg** (*c.* 1060–1150) *(Mon–Sat 10–12, Mon–Fri and Sun 3–5)*, with the only remaining columned basilica in the Rhineland. The elegant carved crucifix in the nave is a replica; the original (1156) is in the Schnütgen-Museum. Across in the western choir hangs a blood-splattered Christ (14th-century). The windows by Dutch artist Jan Thorn-Prikker (1930) surpass all other modern glass in Cologne.

Further west, on Am Pantaleonsberg, the fortress-like **St Pantaleon** (begun AD 980) is the oldest church in Cologne. It is still very much a working cloister, with nuns flitting through the arches and gliding out across the garden. Highlights are a delicate Gothic rood screen and a stone head of Christ from the Middle Ages. **St Severin** (1237) *(Mon–Sat 10–12, Mon–Fri and Sun 3–5)* isn't really worth the extra walk south, unless you're already heading for the trendy Severin quarter, with its vibrant daily street market and outdoor grills. Much of the original building has been superseded by late Gothic construction, though there are patches of 14th-century ceiling painting, and the 13th-century choir stalls and mosaics are worth a look. A Roman-Frankish graveyard was recently discovered underneath and can be visited by guided tour *(Mon and Fri 4.30pm; adm free)*.

On the eastern edge of the Severin quarter, near the river at Ubierring 45, is the **Rautenstrauch-Joest-Museum** *(Tues–Sun 10–5, first Thurs in the month to 8pm; adm DM5, Tram 15 and 16)*, a large ethnological museum with a particularly good Indonesian exhibition and collection of toys. Among the thousands of exhibits you can see a splendid coat of multi-coloured feathers once owned by a 19th-century Hawaiian prince, gold figures from ancient Peru, awesome African masks and an well-designed display on Native American life.

Shopping

In 1988 the insurance company Colonia built an enormous glass-domed shopping arcade on Neumarkt, the Olivandenhof. Hertie, the upmarket department store, linked itself to the mall by means of glass walkways. So did the rival store, Karstadt. Then Hertie extended glass bridges over to Richmod's, the posh shopping mall next door. Soon everyone was linking up and glassing over. The result is an enormous indoor shopping complex that now covers some 50,000 square metres and stretches between Neumarkt in the south, Breite Straße in the north, Gertruden-straße to the west and Zeppelinstraße to the east. Here you'll find the chicest boutiques, Gonski (Cologne's biggest bookshop), specialist shops selling everything from exotic teas to kites, and scores of restaurants and cafés. The Bazaar de Cologne (a world of palm trees, water curtains and glazed courtyards) which had the idea long before the mall mania even began, still lies quietly across the square next to St Aposteln.

For less upmarket, everyday shopping head for the Hohe Straße, and for trendy fashion shops try the area between Pfeilstraße, Mittelstraße and Ehrenstraße (north-west of Neumarkt). The leading art galleries and antique shops are in St Apern Straße, off Breite Straße.

For a DM3 booking fee, the tourist office can help find accommodation on the day you arrive. Even during Carnival, this shouldn't be too much of a problem.

expensive

Dom-Hotel, Domkloster 2a, © 20240, fax 202 4260 (DM514–594). Cologne's grandest hotel. An old-fashioned haven of crystal, chintz and deference overlooking the cathedral.

Maritim, Heumarkt 20, © 20270, fax 202 7826 (DM264–464). A flash glass and marble palace with transparent fairy-lit lifts, designed by Gottfried Böhm, Germany's leading modern architect. You can eat, party, shop, swim, steam, suntan or work out without ever having to venture into the outside world.

moderate

Chelsea, Jülicher Str. 1, © 234 755, fax 239 137 (DM139–240). A comfortable modern hotel which sponsors artists, and gives studio space to some. Consequently the rooms are adorned with contemporary paintings, sketches and sculpture.

Rheinhotel St Martin, Frankenwerft 31–33, © 23 4031/2/3, fax 240 2020 (DM85–195). The cosiest of the little cluster of hotels along the Rhine behind the cathedral—the prettiest place to stay in the Altstadt. The touristy situation doesn't detract from its allure, or result in shoddy service.

Römerhafen, Am Bollwerk 9–11, © 210 325, fax 210 326 (DM115–220). Smart hotel with friendly management near the Fischmarkt. The rooms are comfortable, and many overlook a small park and the Rhine.

inexpensive

Lindenhof, Lintgasse 7, © 231 242 (DM80). A charming small hotel, with a family-run atmosphere and airy rooms overlooking one of the Alstadt's quieter squares. Excellent value.

Drei Könige, Marzellenstr. 58–60, © 132 088, fax 132 462 (DM60–90). Central, clean and cheap, if a little spartan.

Youth Hostel: Siegesstr. 21, © 814 711 (DM15.50).

Eating and Drinking: Restaurants and Taverns

Although Cologne is so close to the Rhine winelands, its most famous drink is *Kölsch*—a light, dry, top-fermented beer served in thin, stemless glasses. The best place to try *Kölsch* is in one of the *Weetschaften*—traditional taverns that usually brew their own. The waiters (*Köbes*), dressed in long blue aprons and blue cardigans are employed as much for their cheeky backchat as for the ability to spin about between the tables balancing a dozen or so glasses on a tray. *Weetschaften* serve up such delights as jellied pigshead and whopping great knuckles of pork. Rhineland cuisine has few fine points. Be warned: *Halver Hahn* is not half a chicken; but pongy cheese on bread and *Kölscher Kaviar* is raw onions and blood pudding on rye—understandably cheaper than its Black Sea namesake.

expensive

Em Krützche, Am Frankenturm 1–3, ✆ 21 1432 (DM60). Elegant but pricey riverside restaurant on the tourist strip behind the Dom. Calf's brains and sweetbreads for connoisseurs—the place to go if you'd like to sample local delicacies that *are* a bit more delicate. The less adventurous can settle for venison or fish.

Chez Alex, In der Mühlengasse 1, ✆ 230 560 (DM120). Classic French cuisine in elegant surroundings. One of three Cologne restaurants with a Michelin star.

Bastei, Konrad-Adenauer-Ufer 80, ✆ 122 825 (DM70). Tasty Franco-German cuisine in a converted fortress on the Rhine.

Soufflé, Hohenstaufenring 53, ✆ 212 022 (DM45–65). Top-bracket French restaurant in the Quartier Lateng. The menu changes daily.

moderate

Altstadt

Früh am Dom, Am Hof 12–14, ✆ 236 618 (DM20–50). Busy tavern, which can get a bit touristy in the outer room, but is jollier and more local in the inner recesses. A good place to launch into *Hämchen* (cured knuckle of pork served with sauerkraut and mashed potatoes).

Alt Köln, Trankgasse 7–9, ✆ 134 678 (DM20–50). Cosy old tavern with a garden for fine nights and good *Soorbrode* (or *Sauerbraten*—spicy marinated beef served up with dumplings and apple purée).

Haus Töller, Weyerstr. 96 (DM20–50). A little further out (south of Neumarkt, U-Bahn to Barbarossaplatz) but more authentic than city-centre taverns. Locals still call it 'Zum reinlichen Döres' (Tidy Döres' Place) after an obsessively clean (even for Germany) turn-of-the-century landlord. You might try Himmel un Äd ('Heaven and Earth', mashed apple (heaven) and potato (earth), served with blood sausage and hot cooking fat).

Eigelsteintor and Nippes

The lively district across the railway track, north of the cathedral, is dotted with good, inexpensive restaurants and old *Weetschaften*. Along the main street (Eigelstein) you'll find:

Chez Mario, Eigelstein 36, ✆ 121 548 (DM20–50). A cheery and wholesome Italian restaurant with tasty homemade pizzas and pastas, as well as fresh fish dishes.

Em Kölsche Boor, Eigelstein 120, ✆ 135 227 (DM20–50). Big-bellied locals get through gallons of *Kölsch* and plates piled high with pork and potatoes.

Vogel, Eigelstein   (DM20–50). A narrow, tunnel-like establishment which serves good beer, and lighter meals (such as the ubiquitous *Halver Hahn* and *Bratwurst*).

Past the Eigelsteintor you come to **Nippes** (Tram 6, 9, 10, 12 or U-Bahn to Florastraße), far beyond the tourist tentacles.

Em golde Kappes, Neusser Str. 295, ✆ 734 932 (DM20–50). One of the best taverns in town, resplendent with original Jugendstil decor. Thirsty office workers pack the small front room in the early evening, while in the spacious eating hall you can tuck into deliciously prepared Hämchen, smoked bacon pancakes or *Decke Bunne* (herby broad beans with bacon).

Tafelspitz, Einheitsstr. 15, ✆ 779 552 (DM20–50). Cherubs, tarnished chandeliers, flea-market furniture and an inspired chef. The French-influenced menu changes frequently, but is sure to contain delicately cooked meats and fish, with subtle sauces concocted from fruit, fresh herbs or wild mushrooms.

inexpensive

Quicksnack, Hohestraße. Has more atmosphere than the name leads you to expect. At lunchtime it gets packed out with portly locals solemnly munching their way through *Schlachplatte* (various bits of pork and a blood sausage piled onto sauerkraut and mashed potato).

Päffgen, Heumarkt 62. Rollicking beer tavern which also serves up tasty and inexpensive local standards.

Bars and Cafés

Altstadt

Kännchen, Am Bollwerk 13. Smokey, poky traditional pub.

Päffgen, Heumarkt 62. Boisterous local watering hole.

Café Bar Heute, Apostelnstraße. Pleasant café full of trendies who have been haunting the nearby boutiques, and are too tired to make the journey to Severinstor.

Gertrudenhof, Apostelnstr. 85. Popular with shoppers for coffee or a drink.

Café Limelight, Bismarckstr. 44. Busiest and best of the arty cafés situated around Brüssler Straße, to the west of town. **Alcazar**, Bismarckstr. 39. A retreat for customers of the Limelight once they've passed the age of 30.

Quartier Lateng

South-west of the centre, around Zülpicher Platz, is the **Quartier Lateng**, erstwhile 'in' area, now in the 'discovered' category.

Peppermint Lounge, Zülpicher Platz 17. Attracts a relaxed studenty crowd, but only really gets going after midnight.

Oskars, next door is all cheek-bones and haircuts and would appeal only to the intensely fashionable.

Kyffhäuser Keller, Kyffhäuserstr. 47. A well-stocked wine bar, where grey hair would go unnoticed.

Vanille, Zülpicher Str. 25. Good traditional café with a wide selection of newspapers and scrumptious salads.

Filmdose, Zülpicher Str. 39. 'A place to be' says a sozzled duck on the sign outside the bar, and so it is. Here you'll find cabaret, films in English and bands of hearty, arty drinkers.

Severinstor

The vicinity of the pixie-capped Severinstor, south of the centre, is currently the trendiest part of town. Most of the activity centres on the patch around Chlodwigplatz.

Linus, Ubierring 22. A pulsating live-music pub.

Schröders, Altenburger Str. 11. Chichi café with self-aware smart-dressers. Soft lights and loud conversations.

Chlodwig-Eck, Annostr. 1. Smoky back-street bar with an arty clientele.

Entertainment and Nightlife

The Cologne listings magazine, available from newsagents, is *Stadt Revue* (DM3.50).

The new underground **Philharmonie** (✆ 204 2100), in the same complex as the Wallraf-Richartz-Museum, hosts visiting musicians as well as the local Gürzenich Orchestra, and the rather better Westdeutsche Rundfunk Orchestra (the WDR, one of Germany's best broadcasting stations, is based in Cologne). The **avant-garde music** scene is strong, with WDR studios, the controversial Karlheinz Stockhausen and the Cologne Ensemble still blazing the trail. The **Opera House**, Offenbachplatz, ✆ 221 8400, also shines best with contemporary work, while many of the Romanesque churches stage chamber music recitals. **Jazz**, too, is not always as mainstream here as in other German cities—try Em Streckstrump, Buttermarkt 37, ✆ 21 7950, for more traditional bands, or Stadtgarten, Venloerstr. 40, ✆ 51 6037, home of the innovative *Kölner Jazzhaus Initiative*. The venues most on the ball with **live music** are Petit Prince, Hohenzollernring 90, ✆ 574 0725, and the Live Music Hall, Lichtstr. 30, ✆ 54 3172. For a **sweaty bop** try the Rose Club, Luxemburger Str. 37, ✆ 23 7495, or the more conventional Luxor, Luxemburger Str. 40, ✆ 21 9506. There's **political cabaret** at Die Machtwächter, Gertrudenstr. 24, ✆ 24 2101, and Kölsch-speaking **marionettes** at Puppenspiele, Eisenmarkt

2–4, ✆ 21 2095. In the summer a younger crowd head for the Volksgarten, where there are waterside pubs and **open-air theatre and music**. The local **talent shows** (Fridays in the summer) in the Rheinpark are a riot: arrive around 7pm for an 8pm start. The only rules are no alcohol and no weapons. For an even odder experience, try the Hotel Timp (Heumarkt 73), a crumbly, red-painted hotel run and inhabited by **transvestites**. As the witching hour approaches they totter downstairs in 10-inch heels and half-an-inch of make-up and let rip with divinely tacky cabaret.

Around Cologne

Tourist Information

Brühl: Rathaus, ✆ (02232) 79345 *(Mon–Wed 8–12noon and 2–4, Thurs to 6pm, Fri 8–12noon)*.

Archaeology buffs might like to head out to **Weiden**, 10km west of the city centre and just off the A4 (take buses heading for Brauweiler). Right on the main road running through the town, at Aachenerstr. 1328, there's a well-preserved **Roman family tomb** (*c.* AD 200) *(Tues–Thurs 10–1, Fri 10–5, Sat 10–1; adm DM1)*—look out for the sign reading 'Graben'. You usually have to ring a bell to be let in—but then you're left alone to descend the stairs and see the family busts and a sarcophagus covered in dancing allegories of the seasons. If no one is looking, you can even sit on a real marble Roman chair. Eight kilometres further along the road at **Brauweiler**, a 12th-century Benedictine monastery church with no fewer than six towers pokes up between the trees. It has one of the best Romanesque interiors in the area, with original pink and green stripes around the arches, bright decorative patterning and clear murals. The simple stone retable in the southern apse—portraying St Nicholas with a Madonna and Child— is acknowledged as a highpoint of Romanesque sculpture for the quality of its carving and its graceful composition.

Fifteen kilometres south of Cologne, at **Brühl** on the B51 (U-Bahn Line 19, Tram 18 and regular rail services), is the lavish 18th-century **Schloß Augustusburg** *(Feb–Nov Tues–Sun 9–12 and 1.30–4; adm DM2—guided tour only (1hr))*. This sumptuous Baroque and Rococo palace, one of the Rhineland's architectural gems, was built by Archbishop-Elector Clemens August, one-time Archbishop of Cologne and a pampered son of the powerful Bavarian Wittlesbachs. Proximity to the cathedral plagued his conscience, and he preferred to live here, where he could fly falcons, seduce women and eat anything put before him. He died after a particularly strenuous dance. Clemens August imported his favourite Bavarian architects, François Cuvilliés (designer of the Munich Residenz Theatre, *see* p. 352) to realize the interiors, and the renowned Balthasar Neumann (*see* p. 59) to come up with the outrageous centrepiece—a great sweeping staircase laden with brightly coloured stucco decoration. (The stucco was dyed with wine, beer, milk and blood.) You can also see some magnificent 18th-century Bavarian tiled stoves, kept hot by servants who scuttled unseen through passages concealed in the thickness of the walls, and a pink dining-room with a balcony from which local worthies would watch Clemens eat. It was a great honour to be invited, and the favoured had to run a gauntlet of guards who inspected their attire, and even their fingernails. In the elegant formal gardens you'll find the somewhat milder **Jagdschloß** (also by Cuvilliés) and the **chapel** (with an altar by Neumann). There's a **café** in the Orangery adjoining the Schloß.

Also in Brühl is **Phantasialand** *(BAB 553 Exit Brühl-Süd, © (02232) 44061; adm; regular bus service from Brühl Bahnhof)*, Germany's biggest theme park. There are performing dolphins and albino tigers, watershoots, a monorail and vintage buses. You can take a boat through lush tropical jungle, walk about a mock-up of a pre-war street in Berlin, or watch live magicians and ostrich-feathered dancing girls. Four restaurants offer French, German, Mexican or Chinese fare.

Bonn

There would be nothing wrong with Bonn as long as it remained a university town. But as soon as it tries to pose as a capital city, its dreary provinciality and its parochial puniness cry aloud.

George Mikes

Bonn has been dubbed 'the Federal Village', 'a tedious little place' and (by one visiting American journalist) 'half as big as the central cemetery in Chicago and twice as dead'. If you come expecting zip, tang and pzazz you'll be similarly disappointed, for Bonn is a country girl, unconvincingly got up in city gladrags, and very much looking forward to the day, any time now, when she can stop pretending. And what is beneath the sham? A charming Rhineland town, with a lick of Rococo, a dash of Jugendstil, more than a dollop of culture and laced with more greenery than nearly any other city in Europe. If you can excuse Bonn for not being a flashy capital city, you'll find her simpler guise quite beguiling. Nobody realizes this more than the politicians themselves, who are displaying great reluctance in packing their despatch boxes, and show every sign of creeping rather unwillingly to Berlin.

Accusations of sleepiness have some foundation—literally. It was the Ministry of Finance that first complained that its employees kept falling asleep. They had simply tumbled to something that the dozy locals had known all along. Bonn is said to have the worst climate in Germany. It's low-lying, wet, oppressive and soporific. That's not all. There is a local grumble that '*Entwede es rähnt, oder man ist müde, oder der Schranken sind herunter*' ('Either it's raining, or you're tired, or the barriers are down'). The Federal Railway cuts the city in half. There are few bridges, but numerous level-crossings—and the barriers are guaranteed to come down (for up to 10 minutes at a time) just when you're in a hurry. '*Sechs Semester in Bonn studiert, drei Semester vor den Schranken gestanden*' ('Six semesters studying in Bonn, three semesters waiting at the barriers') observes one graffitist in the University library loos.

History

Apart from the remains of the world's earliest recorded pet (a 14,000-year-old dog dug up with its owners near Oberkassel), there is little evidence of settlement in Bonn until 30 BC, when the Ubii built a ford over the River Rhine. Then the Romans marched in, built a bridge and in AD 69 established a camp which they called **Castra Bonensia**, picking up on the existing Celtic name. When the Franks took over the fort in around AD 450, they named it Bonnburg. A little to the south of the city a small stone altar marked the spot where some martyrs of the Theban Legion (*see* below) had been killed. This grew into a church, and later a minster, all the time drawing the focus away from the military encampment. By the end of the millenium 'villa Basilica' had become the true centre of town, with the name 'Bonn'.

At first the nascent city had a rough time. It was burnt down by Normans in AD 881 and 892, by the Staufens in 1198 and by the Duke of Brabant in 1239. Finally, in 1244, Archbishop Konrad von Hochstaden allowed the beleaguered citizens to build a defensive wall. This officially confirmed Bonn's status as a town.

In 1583 an affair between the Elector Gebhard Truchsess von Waldburg and a local canoness, Agnes von Mansfeld, became too indiscreet and her brothers demanded that the elector marry her. He did (converting to Protestanism to do so)—but refused to give up the spiritual electorate of Cologne. He was excommunicated and an army of the Bavarian Wittelsbach dynasty (who had been promised the archbishopric) stormed north, laid siege to Bonn, and blew nearby Godesburg sky-high with 1500 pounds of gunpowder. Two centuries of Bavarian rule under the Wittlesbach family followed, ending only with the French invasion in 1794.

The superstitious Napoleon decided not to make Bonn a fortress after his horse stumbled on the cobbles. The town escaped heavy bombardment in subsequent battles and, under Prussian rule following 1815, became increasingly prosperous. For over a century the rest of the world paid Bonn little attention. Then, in 1938, Hitler and Chamberlain held a series of meetings in Bad Godesburg in the lead-up to the Munich Conference. Ten years later, on 5 July 1948, a charred and defeated city hosted the meeting of a preliminary constituent assembly for the new Germany and on 3 November 1949 the new Bundestag confirmed Bonn as (provisional) capital of the Federal Republic. The official city records abandon their usual formality to report that Bonners '*hätten recht feucht gefeiert*' (celebrated with a really good binge).

Why Bonn? It was central (south Germans would never accept being governed from Hamburg, nor north Germans from Munich) and it was obscure. In 1949 politicians looked forward to eventual reunification, and didn't want a real capital for only half a country. Whispers have it that the reason Bonn was preferred over the more rational choice of Frankfurt was that Chancellor Adenauer lived nearby and had his finger on the scales.

On Unification Day (3 October 1990), Berlin once again became the capital and on 20 June 1991, the Bundestag (Lower House) voted to move. The Bundesrat (Upper House), on the other hand, wants to stay in Bonn. The relocation is supposed to take four to eight years, but mutterings in the corridors of power would indicate that few people really want to go. The official excuse is the expense, but the real reason is that Berlin is big, dirty and difficult, whereas Bonn is convenient, spacious and leisurely. The result will probably be that heavy-weight ministries like Foreign and Internal Affairs, Commerce and Justice will make the jump, while the others will stick tight.

Getting Around

By Air

Bonn shares an **airport** with Cologne (*see* p. 123). There are bus transfers to Bonn Hauptbahnhof every 20 minutes (Line 670, journey time 30min, DM7.20). Taxis take 20 minutes and charge around DM50.

By Train

The **Hauptbahnhof** (© (0228) 19419) is on main Euro city and Inter city routes to Munich, Hamburg, Hannover, Frankfurt and Dortmund. In front of it junkies and alcoholics bicker and sprawl around the gaping 'Bonner Loch' (Bonn Hole), the entrance to the U-bahn.

By Car

Car hire: Avis, Adenauerallee 4–6, © (0228) 223 047; Hertz, Adenauerallee 216, © (0228) 217 041. (For details of car hire at Cologne airport, *see* p. 123.)

Parking garages are indicated by signs that also inform you of the number of available spaces, but note that in Bonn unwary drivers can easily find themselves sucked into a one-way system and end up driving in circles.

Mitfahrzentrale: Herwarth Str. 11, © (0288) 19444.

Public Transport

Most of what you'll want to see is within easy walking distance, but should you want to travel a bit further afield **trams** and the **U-bahn** are brisk and efficient. Buy a *3-Tage-Karte Bonn und Umland* ('Bonn and District' card valid for three days; DM25). A *3-Tage-Karte Bonn* (three-day ticket for Bonn only) costs DM14, and a *24-Stunden-Karte* (24-hour ticket) is DM8. For information telephone (0228) 711 817.

Taxis: © 555 555 or 650 055.

River Cruises

Personenschiffahrt Siebengebirge, Rheinallee 59, © (0228) 363 737, offer Rhine and Mosel cruises and a floating discotheque. Daytrips (dep. Bad Godesburg to Linz, Boppard or St Goarhausen and back) cost between DM25 and DM30. There are substantial reductions on *Familiefahrschein* (family tickets for two adults and two children under 14). Bonner Personen Schiffahrt, Brassertufer, Am Alten Zoll,

© (0228) 636 542, offer similar services but are marginally more expensive. Köln-Düsseldorfer, the main river carriers (*see* p. 121), are also on the Brassertufer (© (0228) 66542).

(*see* p. 121)

Tourist Information

The **tourist information office** is at Cassius-Bastei, Münsterstr. 20, © (0228) 773 466 *(Apr–Oct Mon–Sat 8am–9pm, Sun 9.30–12.30; Nov–Mar Mon–Sat 8–7, Sun 9.30–12.30)*. The staff can help with finding accommodation, have a wide range of information on the city and distribute the *Kulturkalender*, which will tell you what's on in town.

Post office: The main post office is at Münsterplatz 17.

Police: © 110.

Ambulance: © 110.

Market days: Daily on the Markt. Fleamarket every third Saturday on Rheinaue.

Festivals

Despite getting off to a wobbly start in 1845, when Liszt snubbed Berlioz and caused a riot, and Lola Montez, mistress of the King of Bavaria, scandalously danced on the table, the **Beethoven Festival** has become a Bonn's cultural highpoint. It is held every three years in September (next one 1995) and attracts musicians of world renown. The **Bonner Sommer** is a spirited annual festival of open air events between May and September. **Pützchens Markt** (second weekend in September) is the Rhineland's answer to the Oktoberfest; and during **Rhein in Flammen** ('Rhine in Flames', first weekend in May) over 50 decorated boats sail past, while fireworks and Bengal lights are set off along the banks.

The Altstadt

Around the Münster

Bonn's Altstadt is a busy jumble of modern architectural offences, pedestrian shopping precincts and rows of unscathed 17th- and 18th-century façades. The modest, but rather graceful **Münsterbasilica**, just north of the Bahnhof, makes a good starting point for your exploration. It was completed around the same time as the foundation stone was laid for Cologne's cathedral, but is more cautiously Romanesque than go-ahead Gothic. The serene **cloister** is one of the most perfectly preserved in Germany. The church grew out of an earlier one, built to honour two Thebaean martyrs. The Thebaean Legion consisted of Christians who refused to persecute their brethren or worship the emperor. For this obstinacy their commander Mauritius was executed (at St Moritz) and, subsequently, every tenth man in the legion. The two who met their end in Bonn were SS Cassius and Florentius.

North of the Münster you'll find the triangular **Markt**, with a smattering of fruit stalls and a stern obelisk—once the site of furious witch-burning, now a punk totem pole. The **Rathaus**, a Rococo confection in blue, pink, white and gold, was built under the auspices of the sybaritic Archbishop-Elector Clemens August in 1737. Visiting heads of state will pause on the perron, behind gold-plated banisters, to wave at the crowds in the square. Then they're whisked inside, or off to the Schloß at Brühl—another Clemens August extravaganza, and the government's favourite venue for state functions (*see* p. 142).

Off the western corner of the market, at Bonngasse 20, you'll find the **Beethovenhaus** *(1 Apr–30 Sept Mon–Sat 10–5, Sun 10–1; Winter Mon–Sat 10.30–4, Sun 10–1; adm DM5)*. The great composer's parents lived in a humbler rear extension of this grand Baroque town house, and it was here, in a slanting attic room, that Ludwig was born in 1770. He was already dashing off sonatas by the age of 12, was second court organist at 14 and headed off for Vienna and immortality at 22. Inside the museum you can see life and death masks, some of Beethoven's own instruments and, most poignant of all, a selection of ear trumpets. These were made by a friend, J.N. Mälzel, and became larger and more Heath-Robinson as the composer's deafness progressed. A sign at the ticket office, rather disarmingly, but nonetheless accurately, offers 'Guided Tours (gratuitous)'.

If you follow Sterngasse (also from the western end of the market) to the outskirts of the Altstadt, you come to the **Alter Friedhof** (Old Cemetery). A walk in the cemetery is a favourite Bonn pastime—not as macabre as it sounds, for the leafy *Friedhof* was God's acre for wealthy 19th-century residents and abounds in marvellously extravagant tombstones. Robert and Clara Schumann and Beethoven's mum are buried there.

East of the Münster

Between the Münster and the Rhine lies a park called the **Hofgarten**, a vast, flat expanse of grass once beloved of political demonstrators. In a move that seems quaintly German, rallies are now discouraged because they make too much mess. Completely dominating the city end of the park (and looking a little like an elegant upturned bedstead) is the one-time residence of the Archbishop-Electors of Cologne, who lived in Bonn after the Kölners had made them feel unwanted during the Battle of Worringen (*see* p. 122). Since 1818 this sturdy, yellow Baroque fortress has housed the **University**. Students lounge about on the grass in good weather, or wander over to nearby **Kaizersplatz** for a coffee. The paths are lined with second-hand book waggons—portable kiosks that unflap, unfold and disgorge retractable tome-laden shelves.

Across the lawns, opposite the university at Am Hofgarten 21, is the **Akademisches Kunstmuseum** *(Sun and Tues 10–1, Thurs 4–6; adm 50 pfennigs)*, which has a rather tedious collection of classical castings, and some original sculpture.

A wander through the park towards the Rhine will bring you to the **Alter Zoll** (Old Customs Point), a sturdy stone bastion on the river's bank, which offers one of the best views possible of the Siebengebirge (*see* p. 152).

Just behind the Hauptbahnhof, at Colmantstr. 14–16, is the only museum in Bonn really worth a detour, the **Rheinisches Landesmuseum** (Rhineland Museum) *(Tues and Thurs 9–5, Wed 9–8, Fri 9–4, Sat and Sun 10–5; adm DM4)*. The prize exhibit is the **skull of a Neanderthal Man**, around 60,000 years old, found near Düsseldorf in 1856. There is also an intriguing array of German helmets, dating from 5 BC, in which you can trace the sprouting of the spike made famous by Kaiser Bill and Hollywood. Paintings to look out for (in an otherwise fairly bland collection) include richly textured work by the 15th-century **Master of the Bonn Diptych**, and five panels by the **Master of the St Ursula Legend**—scenes from a much longer series of the life of St Ursula painted in delicate golden browns, pinks and sepia, like pages from an old book. Both Masters were painters of the Cologne School (*see* p. 56).

A walk down Baumschulallee brings you to the Poppelsdorfer Allee, a long avenue of chestnut trees (Bonn's abundant trademark). At the end of the avenue is **Schloß Poppelsdorf** (completed 1753), a second electoral palace that now houses the university's natural science collections. The palace was designed by the Frenchman Robert de Cotte, who played an architectural trick—the stolid, square exterior is built around a neatly circular courtyard. The palace grounds are now the **Municipal Botanical Garden** *(summer Mon–Fri 9–7, Sun 9–1; winter Mon–Fri 9–4.30; adm DM1)*.

West of the Botanical Gardens (down August Straße, at Sebastianstraße 182) is the **Schumannhaus** *(Mon–Fri 10–12, Mon and Fri 4–7, Wed and Thurs 3–6, Sun 10–1, closed Tues; admission free—to those who can work out the opening hours)*. This was the asylum where the composer Robert Schumann spent his last two distracted years. (He had lived in the house next door.) Now it houses pictures, letters and other memorabilia, but is of interest really only to Schumann fans.

However, the suburb to the east of the Botanical Gardens, the **Südstadt**, is a gem of *fin de siècle* architecture. During the 19th century Bonn became an extremely prosperous residential town—by 1910 no fewer than 200 millionaires lived here. They erected piles along the river, but the upper-middle classes built grand showhouses in the Südstadt, which have survived the ravages of the Second World War. The houses got more and more spectacular as neighbours worked themselves up into a frenzy of one-upmanship. Today you can still see entire streets of their three and four-storey homes, painted white, ochre or in pastel shades of pink, blue and green. Oriental minarets and Dutch-style gables poke up through the chestnut trees and the houses are adorned with garlands of stucco foliage; delicately vacant female faces; cherubim and seraphim; winking, grinning suns; noble busts; peacocks and sea monsters. A stroll through the Südstadt on a summer's evening is a heavenly pursuit. (Schloßstraße, Weberstraße and Argelanderstraße are the best.) The fading sun picks out the colours, the day's noise is reduced to the odd dog bark or strain of a Beethoven sonata, and under the thick tunnel of chestnut leaves, the gaslamps light up one by one.

The Government Quarter

By contrast to the Südstadt, the **government offices** are a collection of thoroughly unremarkable buildings situated out along Adenauerallee on the banks of the Rhine. The main parliament building is a converted teachers' training college, the Federal Chancellery is an anonymous 1970s building that looks like a teachers' training college. As the 29-storey MPs' administration block doesn't even have a name, locals have nicknamed it 'Langer Eugen' (Big Eugen) after a former Parliamentary President. Only **Villa Hammerschmidt**, the president's residence and **Palais Schaumburg**, official home of the Chancellor—both 19th-century mansions—might justify a closer look, but you're not allowed near them.

Kunst Museum Bonn

A little further down Adenauerallee you come to the new Bonn Art Museum *(Tues–Fri 10–5; adm DM4)*, which houses modern German art, and has a particularly good collection of Expressionist paintings. Augustus Macke (*see* p. 64) is especially well represented, as is the school of Rhineland Expressionists that he gathered around him during his stay in Bonn (1910–13). The healthy post-war collection includes the dark, monumental paintings of Anselm Kiefer; brighter, quirkier work by Sigmar Polke and A.R. Penck and the inevitable Baselitz and Beuys. There is also a good range of video work.

Around Bonn

From **Kreuzberg**, a wooded hill that rises high above Bonn to the southwest of the centre (Bus 624, 625 or 626), you can see as far as Cologne cathedral. The pretty **Kreuzbergkirche** *(summer daily 9–6.30; winter daily 9–5)*, perched right on top, is another Baroque fantasy funded by Clemens August. Inside the porch a magnificent marble 'Holy Stairway' (designed by Balthasar Neumann) ascends abruptly through 28 steps. The devout climb up on their knees, stopping for a prayer (and a breather) on each step. The second, eleventh and top steps are said to conceal fragments of the cross.

The quiet village of **Schwarzrheindorf** (Bus 550, 640), 4km up the right bank of the Rhine, has a rare **Doppelkirche** *(see* p. 86) *(summer daily 9–6.30, Sun from 12; winter daily 9–5)*. The diminutive Romanesque church (consecrated 1151) is encircled by a delicate dwarf gallery. Inside, a button to the left of the door will light up a masterful cycle of Romanesque murals on the Old Testament.

Bad Godesberg (U-Bahn to Rheinallee), 8km south of the city, once a prosperous spa town, is now effectively part of Bonn. It is leafy, sedate and encrusted with ambassadorial mansions. The neo-classical ball room **La Redoute**, last of the electoral commissions, is mild by comparison with earlier Baroque and Rococo creations, and the **Schloß**, crowning a knob above the town, has never quiet recovered from the impact of 1500 pounds of gunpowder in 1583 (*see* **Bonn History** above). These days it's a hotel and restaurant.

expensive

Steigenberger Venusberg, An der Casselsruhe 1, © 2880, fax 288288 (DM320–360). Set in a nature reserve on a hill overlooking Bonn and the Rhine, with spectacular views of the city and across to the Siebengebirge. The hotel is modern and luxurious, but also small and intimate, with the air of a private château in lush surroundings.

Rheinhotel Dreesen, Rheinstr. 45–49, © 82020, fax 8202153 (DM198–260). A genteel 19th-century hotel that was the venue of the meetings between Chamberlain and Hitler in 1938. You can sip champagne on your bedroom balcony with nothing but a footpath between you and the Rhine.

moderate

Eden, Am Hofgarten 6, © 225075, fax 225070 (DM146–188). A plain hotel overlooking the Hofgarten. It is central and has heel-clickingly efficient service and quiet, spotless rooms.

Beethoven, Rheingasse 26, © 63141, fax 691629 (DM145–165). A little bland, but clean and comfortable. Convenient for the opera and good views of the Rhine.

Bonn Aigner, Dorotheenstr. 12, © 631 037, fax 630 017 (DM105–135). Good value modern hotel with all mod cons—including cable TV and lock-up garages. Most rooms open out onto a quiet inner courtyard, and you also get a hearty breakfast buffet.

inexpensive

Haus Hofgarten, Fritz-Tillmanstr. 7, © 223482, fax 213902 (DM75–160). Away from the bustle of town, but quite near enough to walk. Family management gives it a friendly, homely feel.

Mertens, Rheindorferstr. 134, © 474 451 (DM95–110). Cheap 'n' cheery hotel across the river. The rooms are comfortable, and the management friendly.

Bergmann, Kasernenstr. 13, © 633 891 (DM75 without private bath). Tiny, well-run boarding house right in the centre.

Youth Hostels: Haagerweg 42, © 3281200 (DM26.20), and Horionstr. 60, Bad Godesburg, © 919290 (DM26.20)

Eating and Drinking: Restaurants and Taverns

Central Bonn does not overflow with exciting restaurants. People tend to head out to the surrounding suburbs for a top-class meal.

Le Marron, Provinzialstr. 35, Lengsdorf, ✆ 253 261 (DM80). *Nouvelle cuisine* in an elegant setting, west of the Kreuzberg.

Maternus, Löbestr. 3, Bad Godesburg, ✆ 362 851 (DM60). Renowned more for its top brass customers than its kitchen.

Da Bruno, Hotel Cäcilienhöhe, Goldbergweg 17, ✆ 321 001 (DM60). Way up above Bad Godesburg—has spectacular views and fine Italian cooking.

moderate

Em Höttche, Markt 4, ✆ 658 596 (DM20–50). One of the few Altstadt taverns with an authentic atmosphere, and tasty Rhenish food too—try the spicy *Sauerbraten* (marinated beef).

Salvator, In der Sürst 5–7, ✆ 635 528 (DM20–50). Cheery Bavarian establishment serving good beer and Bavarian cuisine. The delicate *Krautspatzen* (fine noodles with bacon and sauerkraut) and the pork roasted with caraway seeds are both delicious.

Im Bären, Acherstr. 1-3, ✆ 633 200 (DM20–50). A simple tavern with a very good cook. The soups are excellent, and if you are lucky there will be *Speckpfannekuchen* (fluffy fried pancakes with smoked bacon). Excellent value.

inexpensive

Im Stiefel, Bonngasse 30, ✆ 634 806 (DM15–25). Busy Altstadt pub where you can get basic but tasty local cuisine.

Südstadt-Kniepe, Königstr. (DM20–30). Studenty bar which serves reasonably priced light meals.

Bars and Cafés

Café am Kaiserplatz, Kaiserplatz 18, ✆ 634 644. The most popular of the daytime student hangouts on bustling Kaiserplatz. A place to eavesdrop on undergraduate discussions and watch personal dramas unfold.

'aktuel' Nachrichten Treff, Gerhard-von-Are-Str. 8, ✆ 653 077. Watering-hole for journalists and (other) serious drinkers.

Zur Kerze, Königstr. 25, ✆ 210 769. Arty Bonners sit in candle-lit alcoves and chat away until 5am.

Bahnhöfchen, Rheinaustr. 116, ✆ 463 436. A converted station overlooking the Rhine, across the river in Beuel. It also serves cheap food. (As you cross the Kennedybrücke look out for the little statue of a man baring his bum at the good citizens of Beuel, who wouldn't contribute a pfennig to the bridge's construction.)

In order to put on a good show as capital city, and now to compensate for not being so, Bonn has poured money into the arts. The *Kulturkalender*, issued fortnightly by the tourist office, will let you know what's on. **Opera**, in the spanking new Opernhaus (Am Boeselagerhof 1, ✆ 773 666) is of a particularly high standard. **Symphony concerts** are held in the Beethovenhalle, Wachsbleiche 26, ✆ 774 508. Advance bookings for both (and indeed all municipal events) can be made at the Theaterkasse, Mülheimer Platz 1 *(Mon–Fri 9–1 and 2–6, Sat 9–12)*, ✆ 773 666/7; telephone bookings Mon–Fri 1–3.30 only. Recitals are held at the Beethoven-Haus, Bonngasse 24–26, ✆ 658 245, and in churches around town. Advance reservation for these can usually be made in music shops such as Buchhandlung Bouvier (Am Hof 28; no phone bookings). Alternative theatre and dance can be seen at **Pantheon**, Bundeskanzlerplatz, ✆ 212 521, in the heart of the Government Quarter. They also hold a disco after 11pm over weekends—one of the best spots for dancing in Bonn. Otherwise the city's rather limp nightlife tends to revolve around student activity, which centres on clubs and bars around Berliner Platz.

The Rhine from Bonn to Koblenz

See also Directory entries for Rolandseck, Remagen, Benndorf.

The Siebengebirge

Outside Bonn, stretching for 15km along the right bank of the Rhine and reaching 5km inland, lie the **Siebengebirge** (Seven Mountains). This is a bit of a misnomer as there are nearly forty of them, and even the locals admit that they're just *Hubbeln* (bumps), but there are seven main peaks (six of which can be seen from Bonn). Legend has it that Snow White and the Seven Dwarves lived here, and that the mountains were shovelled into place by kindly giants to dam the flooding of the Rhine. Byron enthused that the rolling hills were 'rich with blossom'd trees', and as Germany's oldest nature reserve, they still are. It is a perfect place for walks, and makes an easy day trip from Bonn. The going is never too strenuous, you can escape the Rhine-faring throngs, and from time to time you'll pop up through the trees on a hilltop to find a splendid view—sometimes as far as Cologne.

Grosser Ölberg (461m) is the highest of the mountains and affords vistas east over the Taunus as well as over the Rhine; **Petersberg** has a very exclusive hotel; and on **Löwenburg** you could be chased by the ghost of a cruel huntsman. In the valley below Grosser Ölberg you'll find the ruins of the 13th-century cloister of **Heisterbach**—lonely, decaying and overgrown, it is truly the stuff of the early 19th-century Romantics. There is even an appropriate legend. In the Middle Ages Heisterbach was renowned as a seat of learning, but Brother Maurus, one of the cleverest monks, began to be gnawed with doubt. He spent a whole day contemplating the text 'A thousand years are but as a day in Thy sight', but simply could not believe it. In despair Brother Maurus went for a walk in the cloister garden, sat under a tree and fell asleep murmuring a prayer to the Lord to help him in his unbelief. The bell for Vespers broke his nap, but when he got back to the chapel he didn't recognize a soul—three hundred years had passed while he was asleep. His face turned ashen at the discovery, the little circle of his hair went white, and he died on the spot, muttering the words of the text. Today there is a convent of nuns at Heisterbach. They run a café, and have a fine line in gooey cakes.

The most famous of the Siebengebirge is **Drachenfels**, itself the source of many legends. This is where Siegfried did battle with the dragon and where the same beast was reduced to a quivering wreck by a maid flashing a crucifix. Siegfried is said to have given himself an invincibly tough skin by bathing in the dragon's blood (save for a fatally vulnerable spot caused by a falling leaf)—hence the inappropriate name of the light, fruity red wine grown on the hillside: *Drachenblut* (Dragon's blood).

With its towering volcanic cliffs, Drachenfels looks the most exciting of the Siebengebirge. On top are the ruins of a 12th-century fortress, and halfway up is the gloriously kitsch **Schloß Drachenburg** *(guided tours only Tues–Sun 10–6; adm DM3)*, a 19th-century Neo-Gothic fantasy of towers and buttresses, painted walls and mysterious staircases. The terrace **café** offers one of the best views. All this contributes to making Drachenfels Germany's most climbed mountain. Over 3 million people a year tramp up the steep paths or hitch a ride on the 19th-century **rack and pinion railway** (*see* **Getting Around** below). The route up is lined with souvenir stalls and cafés. Prices inflate with altitude— it's best to hold out until the Schloß, where at least you get your money's worth. Don't let all this commercialism put you off, the rewards are ample—though the **Drachenhöhle** (Dragon's Cave) *(Feb–Nov daily 10–6, weekends only in winter; adm DM5)* with its model dragon, live snakes and crocodiles and piped Wagner, is a horror best avoided.

Getting Around

By car: Drachenfels, the lowest (and most interesting) of the main peaks is just behind the town of Königswinter, 12km from Bonn on the B42 (rail connections from Bonn, U-Bahn 64 or 66 to Königswinter). Clearly marked **walking routes** will guide you from here to the other mountains. Noticeboards showing the routes can be found in the car parks and at the tourist office.

By train: The Drachenfels **rack railway** (German: Zahnradbahn) departs from Königswinter (Drachenfelsstraße), ascent DM8, descent DM7, return DM10.

Carriages and donkey rides: Also leave from Drachenfelsstraße and ascend the Drachenfels (donkeys from DM10, carriages from DM50).

Waggon trips: M. Kaspers, Ölbergringweg 86c, Königswinter, © (02223) 3863 (price by arrangement) offers tailor-made trips in open carriages through the Siebengebirge, and can even throw in suckling pig and a barrel or two of beer.

Bicycle hire: Firma Gambino, Grabenstr. 62, Königswinter, © (02223) 1265 (DM8 per day). For the fit.

Königswinter: Drachenfelstr. 7, ✆ (02244) 889 325.

Bad Honnef: Hauptstr. 28, ✆ (02224) 184 170.

The Bonn tourist office can also help with detailed information on the area.

Where to Stay

Königswinter (*see* Directory) makes a good base for exploring the Siebengebirge, but the mountains are quite close enough to Bonn to visit on a day trip.

expensive

Gasthaus Petersberg, Petersberg, ✆ (02223) 740, fax 24313 (DM400–500). Stratospheric position, luxury and prices. A rambling turn-of-the-century health resort high atop Petersberg, tastefully converted into a swish hotel that has accommodated the likes of Queen Elizabeth, Brezhnev and the last Shah of Iran.

moderate

Hotel im Hagen, Ölbergringweg 45, ✆ (02223) 23072 (DM130–150). Cosy, family-run hotel on the edge of town. The rooms have Alpine-style wooden balconies with views over the valley, and the breakfast buffet is prepared with ravenous hikers in mind.

Jesuiterhof, Hauptstr. 458, ✆ (02223) 22650 (DM130). Creaky, romantic old half-timbered house in the town centre. The owner has his own vineyards and dispenses the products generously.

Hotel and Restaurant Siebengebirge, Hauptstr. 342, ✆ (02223) 21359 (from DM100). Well-run, comfortable hotel in the high street, with an excellent restaurant attached.

inexpensive

Pension Käthe Krebs, Meerkatzstr. 10, ✆ (02223) 22951 (DM60 without private bath). Lovingly decorated and caringly run *Pension* set in its own lush garden near the Rhine.

Gasthaus Schwippert, Grabenstr. 20, ✆ (02223) 22948 (DM80). Centrally situated guest house that has been run by the same family for three generations. Recently spruced up.

Eating and Drinking

Café Dix, Hauptstr. 427, ✆ (02223) 21963. Comfortable spot for coffee and cakes with rooms for non-smokers and a roof garden in the summer.

Milchhäschen, Elsiger Feld, ✆ (02223) 24446 (DM15–25). Nestles in the heart of the forest and serves up delicious waffles and a variety of teas. There are also grills and casseroles for hungry walkers.

Bauernschenke, Heisterbacher Str. 123, © (02223) 21282 (DM25–35). Rustic restaurant with a good, seasonally changing menu. The venison stews are usually delicious, and there is a discerning selection of local wines.

Andernach

Andernach, on the west bank of the Rhine, about 40km south of Bonn, is a town that invites aimless wandering. Side streets draw you in, you're lured this way and that into inviting alleys of crumbling houses, past a mish-mash of *fachwerk*, Jugendstil and pastel-coloured Rhenish villas. Even the tourist strips seem jolly rather than tacky.

Andernach claims to be the oldest town on the Rhine—if not in Germany—dating back to a Roman base camp over 2000 years ago. A 13th-century **fortified wall** follows the line of the original Roman foundations, and is still largely intact. Shops and houses pop out of it like barnacles, and it has grown a few eccentric towers—odd patchworks of different period styles. The most striking of these is the 15th-century **Runder Turm** on the river's edge at the northern end of town. It is an imposing cylinder of stone topped with a frivolous little octagonal tower. In 1688 the invading French, who blew up nearly everything else along the Rhine, managed only a dent on the Runder Turm (you can still see it). On the river bank nearby is a remarkably intact **16th-century crane**. The huge wooden cogs, which you can see if you peep through a hole in the side, only ground to a halt in 1911. The water-levels of some of the more dramatic Rhine floods are marked on the walls—some of them way above your head.

Midway along the stretch of riverfront hotels is the **Rheintor**, a medieval city gate with two little statues of the **Andernacher Bäckerjungen**. These 'bakers' boys of Andernach' were two early risers who in 1475 spotted an army from Linz creeping up on the city. There was no time to ring the alarm bells, so they tipped their beehives on the invaders, whose cries then woke up the guards. A little further south you come to the remains of **Electors' Palace**, once the most important town castle in the Rhineland. Here the French invaders were more successful. All that is left is the 15th-century **Pulverturm** (powder magazine) and parts of an earlier residential wing, with pretty wooden walkways.

Andernach's main street, the Hochstraße, runs north from the palace. The **Haus von der Leyen**, halfway up the street, is a gaudy Renaissance town house with some impressively moustached beam-ends. It now houses the city **museum** *(Tues–Fri 10–12, 2–5, Sat and Sun 2–4; DM2)* which is devoted mainly to temporary exhibitions. A little further on is the stately **Pfarrkirche Mariä Himmelfahrt**—rightly nicknamed 'the Andernach Dom'—a good example of Rhenish Romanesque, with towers shaped like bishop's mitres and a dwarf gallery running along the outside. The finely carved alabaster **Marienaltar** (1622) in the northern side aisle is especially worth a look.

Getting Around

By car: Andernach is about half-an-hour's drive south of Bonn on the B9.

By train: There are hourly **rail connections** from Bonn Hauptbahnhof (30min).

By boat: The **K-D Line** boats stop off on the Rhine Promenade.

Tourist Information

The **tourist information office** is in Läufstraße, near the Rathaus, ✆ (0263) 406 224 *(Mon–Fri 8–12.30 and 1.30–5, Sat 9–12)*.

Where to Stay

You could see Andernach in a couple of hours. If you do decide to stay over, bear in mind that most hotels are prone to invasions of coach parties and charge individual travellers well over the odds. The tourist office can help with **private rooms**, often the best alternative. One point in Andernach's favour is that it's one of the few towns on this stretch of the Rhine that doesn't have trains thundering between it and the river.

Hotel Meder, Konrad-Adenauer-Allee 17, ✆ (02632) 42632 (DM150). A family-run hotel which, though a bit pricey, is comfortable, friendly and right on the Rhine promenade.

Rhein Hotel Andernach, Konrad-Adenauer-Allee 20, ✆ (02632) 42240 (DM100). Tacky décor, a faint smell of burnt cooking oil and middle-aged waiters with dyed hair. Tremendous potential for a TV sitcom, but friendly and one of the cheapest hotels on the promenade.

Eating and Drinking

Cafés abound along the promenade, but you'll get better value in town.

Zum Franciskamer, Hochstraße (DM15–20). A plain eaterie favoured by tubby locals. You can get good wholesome versions of Rhineland standards such as *Kasseler Rippchen* (smoked pickled loin of pork) and sauerkraut.

Puth's, Am Helmwartsturm 4–6, ✆ (02632) 492047 (DM50–70). Near the market square. One of the few really good restaurants in the area, with Franco-German food cooked by the owner.

Koblenz

Koblenz has one of the most dramatic city skylines anywhere on the Rhine. The rambling Ehrenbreistein Fortress tumbles downhill to the monolithic lump of a monument at Deutsches Eck, where the Mosel joins the Rhine. From here a prickling of church spires and faintly oriental minarets dance off to meet gaunt chimneys in the haze. The best way to arrive is by boat in the late afternoon. Failing that, stand on one of the bridges, or nip across to the west bank at sunset to take in the whole panorama.

Koblenz celebrated its 2000th birthday in 1992. From the original Roman *Castrum apud Confluentes* it passed through the usual Rhine-town succession of occupations by the French and Prussians, becoming *Confluence* and finally Koblenz in the process. It flourished as the residence of the powerful Electors of Trier (from the 11th to the 19th centuries), but from then on had wavering political importance. For 20 years it was the capital of a French *département*, then, until 1950, the capital of Rheinland-Pfalz. Nowadays it is an administrative centre for the wine trade, and attracts its share of Rhine-trippers.

Getting Around

By car: Koblenz is 60km south of Bonn on the B9 and 100km from Frankfurt (Autobahn 3 then 48, or 60 and 61 via Mainz). Most of the Altstadt is pedestrianized, but there are car parks around the edges and along the banks of the Rhine.

Mitfahrzentrale: Rheinstr. 34, ✆ (0261) 18505.

By train: There are frequent rail connections to Bonn (½hr) and Frankfurt (1¼hr). The Hauptbahnhof is on the eastern edge of the Altstadt (✆ (0261) 19419).

Taxis: ✆ 33055 or 18119.

Rhine cruises: Rhein- und Moselschiffahrt Gerhard Collée-Hölzenbein, Rheinzollstr. 4, ✆ (0261) 37744, offer cruises down the Mosel (round trips from DM12–28) and day trips on the Rhine (DM22 to the Lorelei, DM34 to Rüdesheim). The K-D Line jetties are along Konrad-Adenauer-Ufer near Deutsches Eck, and further down the promenade at Kaiserin-Augusta-Anlage.

Bicycle hire: Fahrrad Franz, Hohenfelder Str. 7, ✆ (0261) 18478 (DM12 per day).

Tourist Information

The **tourist information office**, ✆ (0261) 31304, is in the pavilion opposite the Hauptbahnhof *(Mon–Fri 8.30–6, Sat 9–2)*. The staff can supply a city map and organize guided tours.

Post office: The main post office (with a bureau de change) is near the Hauptbahnhof on Bahnhofplatz *(Mon–Fri 6 am–9 pm, Sat 6–6, Sun 10–6)*.

Banks: Deutsche Bank, Löhrstr. 66d, ✆ (0261) 3951. Other banks on Bahnhofplatz and Bahnhofstraße.

Police: ✆ 110.

Medical emergencies: ✆ 41933.

The Altstadt and Deutsches Eck

Until the 19th-century Koblenz was hemmed in by a fortress. The railway was built outside the walls—so if you turn right out of the Bahnhof you'll miss the city completely. From the tourist office, a walk up Löhrstraße will take you into the **Altstadt**. The streets still reflect the curves of the old city wall and can be disorientating, but as the entire Altstadt is squeezed onto the peninsula between the Mosel and the Rhine, you'll always pop out somewhere recognizable. Above the succession of everyday shopfronts, Koblenz is a city of exquisite detail. Madonnas smile down from first floor niches, joined occasionally by Jugendstil maidens or Baroque putti. On each of the houses at the end of Löhrstraße is an ornate **17th-century oriel turret**.

Up to the right is **Am Plan**, a vast square with a gory history. Once a meat market, then a duelling arena and place of execution, it now encloses a bland sea of day-trippers. A little to the east of Am Plan is the rather plain **Rathaus** (1694), formerly a Jesuit college. A passage leads you through into a small courtyard where, if you're not wary, the jokey **Schängenbrunnen** (ragamuffin fountain) will douse you with one of his periodic long-range spits. Behind the Rathaus is the peaceful **Jesuitenplatz**. Here life is altogether more leisurely than in the other squares. On sunny mornings well-coiffured ladies in perfectly tailored suits sit bolt upright, nibbling elaborate ices, sipping champagne and rubbing shoulders with Koblenz's younger arty set. On one side of the square is all that remains of the early 17th-century **Jesuitenkirche** (Jesuit church)—a splendidly carved **portal**. Inside you'll find one of the most beautiful modern **apses** in Germany. Boldly coloured stained glass soars from floor to ceiling and, instead of being nailed to a cross, Christ's arms are carved to represent God the Father and the Holy Ghost, and curve upwards to form a circle. After this the 12th-century **Liebfrauenkirche**, (across Entenpfuhl, east of Jesuitenplatz), is a bit of an anti-climax, though its onion domes (added in 1693–4) form a quirky part of the city's skyline.

If you carry on across Marktstraße you come to Münzplatz, where you can see the house (No. 8) where the 19th-century Austrian statesman **Prince Metternich** was born, and the **Alte Münze**, the handsome yellow Mint Master's House built in 1733 (under the Electors of Trier, Koblenz was allowed to mint its own coins). Duck through a door marked 'Kunstgasse', just behind the Münz, and you'll find yourself in another world—a recently restored alley and courtyard of half-timbered houses, now converted into shops and a small jazz cellar.

From Münzplatz it is a short walk to the Mosel. Here, off Floriansmarkt, is the fine **Alte Kaufhaus** (Old Department Store, 1419). The face on the turret, said to be that of a robber knight wrongly hanged in 1536, rolls its eyes and pulls a tongue at you as the clock strikes. Having served some time as the Rathaus, the Alte Kaufhaus is now the **Mittelrhein-Museum** *(Tues–Sun 10–4.30; adm free)*. Here you can trace the history of the middle Rhine from earliest times to the present day. It isn't a riveting collection, but there are olympian Rococo paintings by Januaris Zick (*see* p. 60) and beautifully carved Middle-Rhine Madonnas, with their characteristic enigmatic smiles and cauliflower-eared babes.

The promenade along the Mosel at this point is a tour de force of good architecture. The pink **Schöffenhaus** (1528) with its delicate oriel and perky corner towers, the sturdy 13th-century castle, the **Alte Burg** (now the Municipal Library) and the **Deutscher Kaiser**, a 16th-century inn with a fringe of battlements, exist quite happily alongside bits of Roman wall and an unabashedly modern residential development.

Following the Mosel down towards the Rhine you come to **St Kastorskirche** (*c.* 1208), recently granted cathedral status. In 1812 the toadying Mayor of Koblenz erected a great plinth in front of the church, in anticipation of a victory statue, and had it inscribed *Mémorable par la Campagne contre les Russes sous la Préfecture de Jules Doazan* (To Commemorate the Russian Campaign, during the Prefecture of Jules Doazan). Unfortunately his boss Napoleon was trounced during the campaign. The commander of the Russian regiment that then occupied Koblenz was an exiled Frenchman—with a sense of humour. He had inscribed, in bigger letters, the standard phrase used by senior civil servants to approve a junior's correspondence: *Vu et approuvé par nous Comdt. Russe de la Ville de Coblenz le 1er Janvier 1814.*

Beyond St Kastor's lies the **Deutsches Eck**, the point of land where the Rhine meets the Mosel. Here there is an even bigger statueless plinth. This 23m-high pedestal used to have another 14m of equestrian statue on top—an incarnation of Prussian pomposity erected in 1897 by Kaiser Wilhelm II to honour the rampantly imperialistic Wilhelm I. The statue became a symbol of German nationalism and the focal point of enormous rallies. (Deutsches Eck is also supposedly the spot where the Teutonic Knights, fathers of the German nation, first settled.) Allied soldiers blew up the copper Kaiser towards the end of the war. His head is in the Mittelrhein-Museum, but the rest was melted down and made into overhead tram wires—making him the longest monument in the world, quip the locals. Recently, much to the embarrassment of the *Land* administration, a wealthy businessman donated 3 million DM to recast the statue. Rather in the manner of an unwanted wedding present, the government accepted the gift, but didn't put the statue up—so the new Wilhelm I floats rather sullenly in a barge moored nearby. These days the plinth is a monument to German reunification.

The **Promenade** back along the Rhine is one of the most beautiful on the river, a long stretch of trees and blossoms running beside some rather grand government buildings.

Ehrenbreitstein

To see the Ehrenbreitstein fortress on the opposite bank of the river you'll have to take a ferry (DM1.20) or cross on the bridge—unlike St Riza who used to walk across the water to Mass (her relics are in St Kastor's). Once on the other side you can follow a path, or take the Sesselbahn (chairlift, DM4.50) up the hill. Bus 8, 9 or 10 (from the Bahnhof) will also get you to the top.

Ehrenbreitstein is the only fortress along the Rhine never to have been taken by force. Its inspired strokes of defence architecture intrigue military buffs and the casual visitor alike. Although Ehrenbreitstein has grown up haphazardly since the year 1000 (counting Albrecht Dürer and Balthasar Neumann in its pedigree of designers), most of the present structure dates from Prussian times. It is an ingenious construction of impact-dissipating brickwork, bullet deflecting angles, siege-foiling cisterns and tunnels, and the world's first bulwarks. You can wander around at will—a guide to the fortifications is available from the shop/café. Ehrenbreitstein also houses the Youth Hostel and the **Landesmuseum** *(mid-Mar to first Sun in Nov, daily 9–12.30 and 1–5; adm free)*. Here among the generations of

Rhine boats, wine presses and industrial knick-knacks you'll find an old car called a Horch, after its maker. He went bankrupt, managed to start over again, but wasn't allowed to use the old trading name. So he changed it to the Latin equivalent: *Audi* (*horch* is the imperative of the German verb *hören*, to hear).

The imposing red and white Baroque buildings at the foot of the hill were also designed by Neumann as the Royal Stables and *Dikasterialgebaüde* (administrative buildings, 1762), and are nowadays used as offices.

Koblenz ✆ (0261–)   ***Where to Stay***

Koblenz is a cheaper place to stay than either Bonn or Cologne.

moderate

Hotel am Schänge, Jesuitenplatz 1, ✆ 38648 (DM105). Tiny hotel with snug rooms and a congenial atmosphere, run by a warm young couple. It is tucked away in one of the least touristy bits of the Altstadt.

Hotel Kleiner Riesen, Kaiserin-Augusta-Anlagen 18, ✆ 32077, fax 160 725 (DM150). Smart hotel with snappy service and spotless rooms. It overlooks the trees and flowers of the most attractive promenade on the Rhine.

Zum Schwarzen Bären, Koblenzerstr. 35, ✆ 44074, fax 403 834 (DM120). A jolly wine-house near the Mosel, with homely rooms and matey management.

inexpensive

Christ, Schützenstr. 32, ✆ 37702 (DM60) will come to the rescue if money is tight. Simple, but wholesome.

Hotel Weinand, Weißernonnengasse 4–6, ✆ 32492, fax 38110 (DM56). Good-value guesthouse, but a little close to the main railway line and Autobahn.

Youth Hostel: Ehrenbreitstein, ✆ 73737 (DM16.90).

Eating and Drinking: Restaurants and Taverns

Weindorf, Rheinanlagen, just past Pfaffendorfer Brücke, ✆ 31680 (DM10–35). An ersatz wine village popular with tourists and locals alike. You can carouse in the courtyard, or eat a tasty meal inside—anything from Bratwurst to venison stew with wild mushrooms. The Weindorf has its own tiny vineyard which, despite growing on builders' rubble and producing just 1000 bottles a year, still manages to pick up the odd medal. The wines (Schnorbach-Brückstück label) are certainly worth a try.

Hubertus, Florinsmarkt 6, ✆ 31177 (DM25–35). The oldest tavern in town, dating back to 1689. Rather reminiscent of a pirates' tavern, but with respectable bourgeois clientele. Here you can get Rhine specialities—such as chicken soup with egg or a hearty bean gulasch—and good local wines. Try the the Deinhard

Deutsches Eck Riesling Spätlese which, despite the touristy name and label, will make a fine, fresh accompaniment to a meal.

Robert's, Jesuitenplatz, ✆ 37985 (DM15–20). Bright *Weinkeller* with an attractive terrace. Serves mammoth lunchtime salads.

Rüüan, Florinspfaffengasse 7, ✆ 37710 (DM20–30). Plainly decorated restaurant that serves delicate and delicious Thai food.

Bars and Cafés

Café Miljöö, Gemüßegasse, off Florinsmarkt. Haircuts and fashion from the pages of *Elle*—and conversation from the previous night's TV. For serious trendies only.

Café Grössenwahn, Altenhof, off Marktstraße. Candlelit nook off the tourist track, better for a quiet drink than a meal.

Weinkontor, Mehlgasse 16, ✆ 14626. Historic vaulted Weinkeller below a Baroque town house. Touristy, but with a good list of local wines.

The Rhine from Koblenz to Mainz

When most people think of the Rhine, this is the part they imagine: the Rhine of ancient castles, heroic legends, treacherous waters—and sparkling glasses filled with Germany's finest wines. It is a busy, working river, and in season battalions of tourists join the procession of barges, lorries, boats and trains. What follows is an unashamedly personal selection of what to see.

See also Directory entries for St Goarhausen, Kaub, Rüdesheim.

Getting Around

The most appropriate way to see this part of the Rhine is by boat (*see* **Getting Around** p. 121), though if you want to stop off at castles or visit wine estates, this can be a little time-consuming and a car is a better idea. Roads *and* railway tracks wind along both sides of the gorge.

Tourist Information Offices

Bacharach: Rathaus, ✆ (06743) 1297.

Boppard: Oberstr 118 (pedestrian zone), ✆ (06742) 38 88.

St Goar: Heerstr 120, ✆ (06741) 383.

Wine Routes and Estates

For further information on special wine routes and estates in the Middle Rhine region (Bingen to Koblenz) contact Mittelrhein-Burgen und Wein, Am Hafen 2, St Goar, ✆ (06741) 7644.

The **German Wine Academy**, PO Box 1705, 6500 Mainz, offer a six-day study trip with lectures in English and tastings through seven wine regions, including the Middle Rhine and the Rheingau.

There are two **Rhein in Flammen** (Rhine in Flames) festivals—boat processions with fireworks. One takes place around Koblenz at the beginning of August, the other at the Lorelei in September. May brings a rash of **Spring festivals** which usually involve lots of eating and drinking and a fair amount of dressing up and dancing for tourists. The best one is in Boppard. Local **wine festivals** tend to be more authentic—with lots of Rhenish food and wine, a village party atmosphere and often the election of a local 'Wine Princess'. Most of these take place in the late summer or around harvest time (September). Look out for signs advertising Weinfest or Winzerfest. The **Glorreiche Rheingau Tage** (Kloster Eberbach, second weekend in November, see **Rheingau Wines** below) is a three-day celebration of Rheingau wine and culture and the **Rheingauer Weinwoche** (Wiesbaden city centre, mid-August) is a nine-day extravaganza where over 100 growers show their wines.

From Koblenz, you don't get off to a particularly good start. The unmistakably yellow **Schloß Stolzenfels**, on the west bank just outside the city, is a 19th-century imitation, and on a mound above **Rhens** the **Köningsstuhl**, ('Seat of Kings', the spot where the German electors met to choose the king) is now crowned with an uninspiring 19th-century Gothic viewing platform. You do, however, get an inkling of what is to come.

Marksburg

The Marksburg *(guided tours only, hourly mid-Mar–mid-Nov 9.30–5, winter 11–4; adm DM5)*, 25 minutes' walk above the dull village of **Braubach**, on the opposite bank, is the only castle on the Rhine never to have been blown up and rebuilt. It has grown in spurts since the 12th century, was continuously inhabited for 700 years and, unlike any other castle on the river, really feels lived in. In the Gothic *Rittersaal* (knights' hall) you feel that you've stumbled in just after the troubadours have packed up and left, the ladies retired to their tapestry in one of the alcoves and the men gone to drink around the fire. The kitchen evokes centuries of rollicking servants' parties. There are rows of giant wooden jugs for the daily wine ration (five litres—the average medieval knight must have been permanently tiddled), and even a 19th-century refrigerator. Above the main entrance, a pretty little bay window has a false floor that enabled inhabitants to drop hot oil and tar on unwanted visitors (the loo is of the same design, and opens out onto the herb garden). In the armoury, the well selected and chronologically arranged suits of armour make far more sense than the usual higgedly-piggedly displays, and from the top of the slender keep you get a stunning view as well as a clear idea why the castle was so impregnable.

Boppard

From Braubach the Rhine makes a tight loop to Boppard, a pretty old Celtic town where you can see well-preserved remains of a 4th-century **Roman wall**, some medieval fortifications, and the castle, the **Alte Burg**, built by the Electors of Trier to help keep a thumb on the locals. In the **Karmelitenkirche**, there are some clear 14th-century murals and a **Traubenmadonna**, at whose feet the first grapes of the harvest are left each to wither and rot. The town is dominated by the twin steeples of the **St Severuskirche**, which also sports some fine 13th-century ceiling paintings. The vineyards on the south-facing slopes of the loop in the river here are among the region's best, so Boppard is a good place to seek out a few *Weingüter* or try to catch a wine festival. The **promenade** is the venue for cheery revelling throughout the year.

Around St Goar

After Boppard the valley narrows and rises sharply on both sides. Fifteen minutes walk above the pretty, but touristy St Goar are the ruins of **Burg Rheinfels** *(Apr–Sept daily 9–6, Oct 9–5; adm DM3)*. This 13th-century castle was extended in the 16th and 17th centuries, blown up by the French in 1796, and was partially rebuilt in 1925. It is much more fun than many a stuffily over-restored castle so common along the Rhine. You can clamber among the ruins, walk along high battlements, climb towers and disappear down tunnels. In the process you'll get a far better insight into the construction of Rhineland fortresses than most other castles can offer. Part of Burg Rheinfels has been converted into a hotel and **café**, and there's a small **museum** with a model that shows just how magnificent and sprawling this castle once was.

If you look across to the other bank you can see the imposing 14th-century stronghold of the Counts of Katzenelnbogen, **Burg Katz** (Cat Castle). This so upstaged the castle of the Archbishops of Trier just to the north, that locals nicknamed it **Burg Maus** (Mouse Castle).

Back down in St Goar, head straight for the **Deutsches Puppen und Bären Museum** (Doll and Teddy Museum) at Sonnengasse 8 *(Apr–Dec daily 10–6; adm DM5, children 4–11 DM2.50)*. It is magical. Antique dolls, dolls in national dress, posh Barbies and nappy-wetting babies are shown off in cosy, domestic settings. Hundreds of teddies—a couple of centimetres to a couple of metres high—are piled on sofas, pop out of desk drawers and ride carts across the carpet. There's even a rather macabre doll in a coffin and an opium-puffing bear. Downstairs is a richly nostalgic toyshop.

From the Lorelei to Rüdesheim

At the bend after St Goar, the gorge shrinks to a mere 112m wide, and shoots up to a lofty 400m high. Here, on the east bank is the famous **Lorelei**, treasure-house of the Nibelungen and perch of Alte blonde, hair-combing siren whose voice would lure sailors to their deaths—spun by the currents and smashed up against the rocks. Best take the advice given to the sailors and pass by quickly with averted eyes, for the Lorelei is nothing but a rocky bluff with a tacky tourist café on top and a statue that looks better in the postcards.

Burg Katz

The appropriately named **Bacharach** (Bacchus's Altar), on the other hand, is a fairytale hamlet of wonky half-timbered houses and taverns. Don't be put off by the dull row of riverfront houses: behind them lies the best village in the gorge to spend the night, and on the slopes above, the top Riesling vineyards in the area. Even the highstreet taverns are unspoiled, and although it's busy during the day, the seething hordes of visitors dissipate at sunset. In the **St Peterskirche** recent restoration work uncovered some bright 12th-century murals, and behind the village is the **Wernerkapelle**, the romantic skeleton of a never-completed Gothic chapel.

Around the next twist of the river, on the west bank, you'll find **Burg Rheinstein** *(daily 9.30–6.30; adm DM4.50)*. The owner himself, Hermann Hecher, a retired opera singer, will sell you a ticket. His son Marcus will serve you in the panoramic terrace café. They bought the derelict Burg in 1975, and have been restoring it themselves. Inside it's a quirky mixture of Rhineland antiquity and great-aunt's attic. Up a flight of perilously narrow steps you'll find a crow's nest with superb views and a *Strafkrone*—a metal basket (with a nasty-looking spike) in which offenders were dangled way, way above the rocks. Herr Hecher combines his passions and holds opera seminars and stages pageants in his castle.

The ghastly **Rüdesheim**, though famous for its wines, is a tourist hell-hole with wall-to-wall souvenir shops and shoulder-to-shoulder day-trippers, many of whom seem bent on obliterating themselves in the nearest 'fun pub'. This is, however, the beginning of the **Rheingau**, which stretches down the Rhine and across the surrounding hills to Wiesbaden and Mainz and is one of the great wine-growing regions of the world (*see* **Rheingau Wines** below).

This stretch of the Rhine is one of the most tourist-infested parts of Germany, and it is well nigh impossible to find an unaffected spot. One of the few places to retain any vestige of romance is Bacharach—and this is the only really recommendable village for an overnight stay. Alternatively, some of the better castle hotels capture the old Rhenish atmosphere, but are usually quite pricey. The cheapest hotels are in St Goar.

Castle Hotels

Schloß Hotel Rheinfels, St Goar, ✆ (06741) 8020, fax 7652 (DM180–225). Heady luxury and dizzy views—as well as a sauna, swimming pool and gym.

Burg Schönberg, Oberwesel, near Bacharach, ✆ (06744) 7027 (DM200). A cosier alternative. Family-owned, stuffed with old furniture (including pamperingly soft four-poster beds), intimate and achingly romantic.

Klostergut Jakobsberg, Geisenheim, ✆ (06742) 3062 (DM200). A tastefully converted 12th-century monastery in the forests 12km north of Boppard. It teeters way above the river and has its own swimming pool and sports centre.

Burg Stahleck, Bacharach, ✆ (06743) 1266 (around DM20 per person). If your budget doesn't allow much extravagance, here is a castle that has been converted into a **youth hostel**.

Boppard

Bellevue Rheinhotel, Rheinallee 41–42, ✆ (06742) 1020, fax 102 602 (DM170–300). Spacious establishment with the air of a beachfront Grand Hotel.

Rheinvilla, Rheinallee 51, ✆ (06742) 2582 (DM98–110). A converted 19th-century villa, all stucco ceilings and parquet floors, which knocks the other hotels on the promenade into a cocked hat.

Hotel Rebstock, Rheinallee 31, ✆ (06742) 4876, fax 4877 (DM90–160). The best of a rather humdrum lot if everywhere else is booked up. It is clean and the management is friendly.

St Goar

Hotel Traube, Heerstr. 75, ✆ (06741) 7511 (DM70). Simple, pretty, family-run hotel with a view of the river. The owner occasionally organizes wine-tastings.

Hotel Zur Post, Bahnhofstr. 3, ✆ (06741) 339 (DM60–90). Functional and set back from the river, but clean and cheap.

You can get even better deals in **private rooms**. Try Frau Wolters, Schloßberg 24, ✆ (06741) 1695 (DM28 per person) on the way up to Burg Rheinfels; or Frau Kurz, Ulmenhof 11, ✆ (06741) 459 (DM28) on the road behind the Bahnhof.

Bacharach

Altkölnischer Hof, Oberstraße, ✆ (06743) 1339, fax 27 93 (DM85–120). Central, family-run hotel with an old world atmosphere and a good restaurant.

Hotel Gelber Hof, Blücherstr. 26, ✆ (06743) 1017 (DM90–100). Backing onto vineyards at the edge of town and owned by the same family since 1768, though rather tackily modernized. Nevertheless clean, quiet and comfortable.

Pension Im Malerwinkel, Blücherstr. 41–45, ✆ (06743) 1239 (DM50–80). A gem at the edge of the village with vineyards beyond it, a little stream in front and a ruined tower next door—and at a suprisingly low price too.

Eating and Drinking

Boppard

There are a number of restaurants and cafés around the Markt. **Ratstube**, tucked away in the corner is the best. It attracts a local clientele, serves tasty snacks and giant sandwiches for around DM10. **Petit Restaurant** across the square is cosy and friendly, and serves reliable Rhine standards such as *Azezupp* (thick pea soup) and various Schnitzels for under DM20.

Klostergut Jakobsberg, ✆ (06742) 3061 (DM80). A converted 12th century monastery about 12km north of Boppard. Top-class Franco-German cuisine.

St Goar

Gasthaus Zur Krone, opposite the Stiftskirche. A lovely old traditional wine tavern which also serves light meals.

Silberne Rose, Heerstr. 63, ✆ (06741) 7040 (DM35–55). Restaurant overlooking the river. Specializes in Balkan food.

Bacharach

Altes Haus, Oberstraße. Mouth-watering dishes, such as loin of pork in a Riesling and shallot sauce (DM18). In one corner there's a piano that tempts customers into spontaneous outbreaks of music-making.

Weingut Fritz Bastion, Oberstraße. Promises an even jollier time—groups of musicians hold informal get-togethers, lubricated by local wine.

Kurpfälzische Münze, Oberstraße. Here the boss plays the music, while chubby locals dance cheek-to-cheek.

Posthof, Oberstraße. A converted post office that attracts trendies from miles around. There is a good buffet bar (DM30) and a smart wine bar.

Winkel

Graues Haus, Graugasse 10; ✆ (06723) 26 19 (DM80–100). Intimate restaurant in a stone house built in AD 850. It serves gourmet food (and charges appropriately). The wine list could keep you reading till dawn.

Eltville

Altes Holztor, Schwalbacherstr. 18. Traditional old wine pub with a good selection of Rheingau wines. Also serves light meals.

Rheingau Wine

Between Mainz and Rüdesheim the Rhine veers round to flow from east to west. The sunny south-facing slopes along the right bank produce some world-famous wines. Viticulture in the Rheingau can be traced back to Roman times, and much of German wine terminology originated here. *Kabinett* (indicating wines of top quality) was first used in the 18th century at Schloß Vollrads, where superior vintages were stored separately in a special 'Cabinet' cellar. The neighbouring estate, Schloß Johannisberg, was the first to harvest grapes at various stages of ripeness, coining terms such as *Spätlese* (late harvest) and *Auslese* (very ripe), now in general use.

Over 80 per cent of the grapes grown here are of the Riesling variety, which yields fruity white wines with explosive bouquets—in fact the Riesling grape probably originated here. The other great grape of the region is Spätburgunder (Pinot Noir), imported from Burgundy in France. From this vine come rich, velvety red wines with a bitter, nutty tang. A speciality of the region is the honey-sweet Beerenauslesen, made from grapes that stay on the vines way beyond their sell-by date and form a 'noble rot'. The berries are then selected and picked individually, which explains why these wines are so outrageously expensive. Although they are white, Beerenauslesen wines age forever and make a good investment.

The western vineyards are steep cliffs of quartzite and slate that produce robust, piquant wines. Further east (beyond Hattenheim), gentler slopes and richer soils make for a softer, fruity, mild taste.

The best wines in the area come from the private growers rather than large co-operatives, and don't always make it onto the international market. Look out for the 'Weingut' signs which indicate the cellars and tasting rooms (usually in villages rather than in the vineyards themselves). In early April and late September many estates hold a *Tag der offenen Weinkeller* (open day), when you can visit without an appointment, taste wine and chat with the owner.

Wine Routes

You can potter about the area at will, or follow the **Rheingau Riesling Route**, a 70km-long marked motor route along the B42, from one extremity of the region to the other (Lorchhausen, north of Rüdesheim to Wicker, east of Mainz). Eager walkers can follow the **Rheingauer Riesling Pfad**—a hiking trail that winds for 100km through forests and vineyards and past some very welcome tasting stands.

For **information** about estates, wines and special wine routes in the Rheingau contact Der Weingau, Im Alten Rathaus, Johannisberg, 6222 Geisenheim, ✆ (06722) 8117.

Assmannhausen, one of the northernmost towns in the Rheingau, is home of the best Spätburgunder—soft, fruity reds that are lighter and less tannic than their Burgundy counterparts. Weingut Krone (Rheinuferstraße) is a renowned producer. A few minutes further south on the B42, just where the Rhine bends, is **Rüdesheim**, the most famous (and most horribly touristy) wine village in the area. Rüdesheim produces flavoursome Rieslings with flowery bouquets, fine Sekt (sparkling wine), and brandy. Its *Berg* vineyard is world-renowned for ripe, up-front flavours, and supplies a number of producers (look out for labels with *Berg* in the name, such as Berg Schloßberg, Berg Rottland or Klosterberg).

Just outside the village of **Winkel** (8km past Rüdesheim) are the two best-known estates in the region, **Schloß Vollrads** and **Schloß Johannisberg**. The former produces elegant, tangy Rieslings, while the wines of the latter are rich and spicy with a distinctive acidity. Both have a restaurant and wine shop in the grounds. You can visit Schloß Johannisberg (by appointment only, write to Schloß Johannisberg, 6222 Geisenheim Johannisberg) or catch one of the periodic wine tastings in the old palace at Schloß Vollrads (write to Gutsverwaltung Schloß Vollrads, 6227 Oestrich–Winkel). The impressive cellars at Schloß Johannisberg also house the **Bibliotheca Subterranea**, an 18th-century underground library of rare books.

The sloping vineyards outside Hattenheim (another 10km down the B42) produce **Marcobrunn**, a sultry Riesling also of world repute. A few kilometres inland, and most certainly worth a visit, is **Kloster Eberbach** *(Apr–Sept daily 10–6; Oct–Mar Mon–Fri 10–4, Sat and Sun 11–4; adm DM1.50, DM2.50 with tour)*, a rambling old monastery that has been producing powerful, fruity wines since the 12th century. You can wander through the gardens, taste the wine or visit the monastery itself—well-preserved with cavernous, bare Gothic and Romanesque buildings.

The road past Kloster Eberbach takes you back to **Eltville** (home of Thomas Mann's fictional hero Felix Krull) on the B42. Here the gentle slopes and rich loess soil yield excellent *Sekt*. Eltville is also headquarters to the *Staatliche Weinbaudomäne* (State Wine Domain) which produces wines of high quality (unlike many French State Domaines). From here you can take a short cut on the motorway (A66/A671) past Wiesbaden and Mainz to **Hochheimer**, whose full-bodied, earthy Rieslings were much favoured by Queen Victoria. Their English nickname 'Hock' became a generic name for all Rhenish wines.

Mainz

'*Mainz liebt auf seinen Platzen*' ('Mainz lives on its squares') goes the local saying and, indeed, this is the most carefree and Mediterranean of all the Rhine towns. The hometown of Gutenburg (the father of printing) also has a world-famous series of Chagall stained-glass windows and a cathedral that is a peak of Rhineland Romanesque, but seems happiest in its traditional pursuit of *Weck, Worscht und Woi* (bread, sausages and wine).

Mainz bubbles with a Carnival atmosphere all year round, and would be anarchic were it not so laid back.

History

Mainz gets its name from the Celtic god Mogo, who was worshipped here before the Romans set up camp in 2 BC. They honoured the old deity by calling their settlement Mogontiacum, and lived happily for 400 years until bands of Alemanni, Vandals and Goths sacked the town. It took an Englishman, St Boniface, to restore order. In 742 he created an archbishopric, and made Mainz into the most important centre of the Christian church in Germany. Its Archbishops were powerful Prince-Electors of the Holy Roman Empire (*see* p. 40). Bibles churned out by Gutenberg's presses, at what seemed an almost devilish rate, made the city even more famous. But Napoleon reduced it all to rubble again. For two decades Mainz limped along as *Mayence*, never quite recovered under Prussian rule, and was again laid flat—this time by the British—on 27 February 1945. In 20 minutes bombers destroyed 85 per cent of the inner city. In an heroic frenzy of reconstruction the people of Mainz lovingly rebuilt many of the old landmarks, put up some rather sorry new ones, and finally found the courage and money to invest in some bravura modern architecture. Today Mainz is *Land* capital of Rheinland-Pfalz, home to ZDF (the second German television station), IBM and Nestlé—but, more evidently, it is Germany's premier wine market and its second Carnival city.

Getting Around

By air: Mainz is only 30 minutes away (on the S-Bahn) from **Frankfurt Airport** (trains every half-hour to and from Mainz Hauptbahnhof, information from Lufthansa, © (06131) 674 021).

By train: The mainline **Hauptbahnhof** is to the west of the Altstadt. There are trains to Frankfurt (½hr), Munich (4hr), Bonn (1½hr), Hamburg (6hr) and Freiburg (2¼hr).

Car hire: Becker, Bonifaziusplatz 1, © (06131) 60066; InterRent, Rheinstr. 107, © (06131) 677 073.

Public transport: © 60011 or 676 000.

All the tourist sights are within easy walking distance. Orientation is easy: red street names on streets running to the Rhine, blue for those running parallel. Should you need a local **bus** or **tram**, the main depot is outside the Hauptbahnhof (information © (06131) 124 758). Trams run all the way to Wiesbaden. Machines at the stops dispense single tickets and passes.

Taxis: © 60011 or 676 000.

Bicycle hire: Fahrrad-Laden, Albinistr. 15, © (06131) 225 013.

Rhine cruises: The kiosk for the **Köln-Düsseldorfer line** (© (06131) 224 511) is on Adenauerufer in front of the Rathaus.

Tourist information office: Bahnhofstr. 15, ✆ (06131) 233 741 *(Mon–Fri 9–6, Sat 9–1)*.

Post office: Bahnhofstr. 2 *(Mon–Fri 8am–9pm, Sat and Sun 8–8)*.

Police: ✆ 110.

Medical emergencies: ✆ 232 323.

Market days: Tues, Fri and Sat on the Domplatz. Fleamarket every third Saturday near Theodor-Heuss-Brücke.

Mainz has three main festivals. The **Carnival** celebrations (at the onset of Lent) are rivalled only by those in Cologne. Unlike the more commercial festivities in Cologne, Mainz's Carnival has always had a political edge (*see* p. 127). Since recent organizing committees have been in the hands of the Right, and all the festive satire is broadcast throughout Germany, the city has been slurred unjustly with a reactionary reputation. **Johannesnacht**, a cultural festival to commemorate Gutenberg, is held on the penultimate weekend in June. On the last weekend in August and the first in September there is a bibulous **Wine Market**, with wines on sale from scores of local producers, mounds of food and a fair in the Volkspark.

The Cathedral Square

The Mainz cathedral, dominating the centre of the city, is a megalithic jumble of red sandstone, trimmed with pretty Romanesque galleries and blind arcades, and topped with a compendium of different towers. It was built between the 12th and 16th centuries, after overzealous adornment with candles had put paid to an earlier cathedral on its inauguration day. The Archbishop of Mainz was considered the representative of the Pope north of the Alps, so, as in St Peter's in Rome, the main altar is in the west part of the church. The huge **bronze doors** (AD 988) at the main entrance are the oldest in Germany after those in Aachen, though the heavy lions' heads are a 14th-century addition. The rings through their mouths were 'immunity rings': if you managed to evade your pursuers and grab the rings, you couldn't be taken to justice. Inside is a cavalcade of sumptuous monuments to past bishops of Mainz, ranging from the 13th to the 19th century. Napoleon sold off most of the paintings from the cathedral, and those you see today are rather sensitive 19th-century replacements.

After the commodious gloom of the cathedral, its sidekick, the tiny grey stone **St Gotthard's** (1137), seems positively cosy. This Romanesque *Doppelkirche* was the bishops' palace chapel. Through a meditative **Gothic cloister** (*c.* 1400) you come to the **Diocesan Museum** *(Mon–Sat 9–12, Mon–Wed and Fri also 2–5; adm free)*, worth a visit primarily for the *Kopf mit der Binde* (Head with a Bandage, *c.* 1240)—a sublimely expressive carving by the **Master of Naumburg**, an inspired medieval sculptor, way ahead of his time, who was named for his later work in Naumburg cathedral near Weimar.

The cathedral opens out onto the **Markt**, edged with bright 16th, 17th and 18th century façades (all post-Second World War reconstructions). The cheerfully painted Renaissance **Marktbrunnen** (Market Fountain) is surmounted by a Madonna and adorned with putti and stern bishops, but on the pillars fat naked farmers and jolly drunkards cavort, oblivious to their impending doom. The 5.7m-high **Heunensäule** (Giant's column) is a 1000-year-old pillar with a modern bronze base that allegorically tells the story of Mainz. Mice represent today's political parties. Three nestle inside a medieval helmet, whilst a fourth—the Green Party—has escaped.

Abutting the eastern side of the cathedral is Liebfrauenplatz, where your eye is immediately caught by the pink Rennaissance façade of the **Haus zum Römischer Kaiser**, once a hotel frequented by Goethe, Voltaire and Mozart. Emperor Franz Joseph *nearly* stayed there, but as he travelled incognito with only two horses, he didn't look important enough, and had to put up in the inn next door—an experience he so enjoyed that on future visits to Mainz, he would stay nowhere else.

Behind these buildings is the **Gutenberg-Museum** *(Tues–Sat 10–6, Sun 10–1; adm free)*. Johannes Gutenberg (1398–1468) is known as the inventor of printing. In fact, what he invented was *movable type*—block-printing was already well-known. He borrowed heavily to set up his printshop, and was later bankrupted by short-sighted creditors who confiscated his equipment, and even took the credit for the invention. Gutenberg died destitute. Today we are not even sure what he looked like, hence the confusingly dissimilar busts, statues and portraits all over town. Pride of place in the museum is given to the famous **42-line Bible**. Only the black lettering was printed, red letters and the elaborate illuminations were still done by hand. This Bible shares a special strong room with a number of other precious volumes, including a 1459 Psalter with enormous print; books were expensive, so the whole choir had to be able to read from just one copy. Downstairs there's a reconstruction of Gutenberg's workshop, complete with dogskin inking balls and a working printing press—the staff give demonstrations and sometimes let visitors have a go. The rest of the museum is given over to the history of printing, with some exceptionally beautiful tomes, the world's smallest book (which looks as if it belongs on a Swiss Army knife) and all manner of equipment.

The Altstadt

South of the nearby Gutenbergerplatz, the Alstadt begins. Mainz's old town is a lively jumble of brightly painted walls, Madonnas in niches, impeccably restored half-timbered buildings (brown wood for artisans and merchants, red wood for the judiciary) and romantic alleys of crumbling, very much lived-in old houses, with washing strung between the balconies and noisy children in the courtyards. Weihergarten 5 is the home of Schott Music Verlag, Wagner's long-suffering publishers. In Augustinerstraße, inside the grandiose Baroque **Augustiner-Kirche** (*c.* 1770) you can see the serene **Lindenholz Madonna** (1420) and a little further south is the **Holzturm** (Wood Tower, *c.* 1300) once part of the city wall and a prison. Nearby in Kapuzinerstraße is the **Ignazkirche** (*c.* 1774), relatively plain for the period, but with a luminous Baroque interior. Outside (over his own tomb) is a crucifixion group by local sculptor **Hans Backoffen** (1440–1519), one of the leading lights of his time, and genitor of many of the monuments in the cathedral.

If you follow Holzstraße and Weißliliengasse around to the western edge of the Altstadt, you'll see the Gothic **Stephanskirche** (1269–1340), *(daily 10–12 and 2–5)* perched on a nobby hill. The church is most famous for its **Chagall windows**, installed between 1978 and 1989. The Jewish artist Marc Chagall was initially chary about a commission for a Christian church in Germany. His solution was to create a work that emphasized reconciliation and Jewish-Christian unity. Christ's loincloth is a Jewish prayer shawl; the glass is predominantly blue, for Chagall the colour of peace and divinity.

A steep descent down Stefansberg brings you to Balplatz, flirting ground for local lads and girls from the prestigious Maria Ward school, and then to Schiller Square and the **Fastsnachtsbrunnen** (Carnival Fountain, 1967) a busy 200-figure allegory of different carnival events and traditions, with water spraying everywhere. The whole composition inverts the shape of the main cathedral tower.

At the end of Schillerstraße and right along Große Bleichestraße, you'll find the **Landesmuseum** *(Tues–Sun 10–5; adm free)*, the only other museum really worth a visit. Highlights include the Jupitersäule (a Roman triumphal column), paintings by Baldung, Cranach and the Master of St Bartholemew and a good collection of Jugendstil glass.

Mainz ℂ (06131–)   ***Where to Stay***

Hotels in central Mainz are not cheap, and are run-of-the-mill. The **Grüngürtel** (Green Belt) of parks around the edge of town offers more attractive possibilities.

expensive

Mainz Hilton, Rheinstr. 68, ℂ 2450, fax 245 589 (DM310–490). Service and trappings to the usual high standards, but in a brash modern building. The hotel is in two parts—make sure to get a room in the bit that overlooks the Rhine.

Hotel Kurmainz, Flugplatzstr. 44, Mainz-Finthen, ℂ 4910, fax 491 128 (DM180–280). Modern, family-run hotel nestling in orchards in a green-belt suburb 7km east of the centre (Tram 10 and 11). If you tire of sight-seeing you can play tennis, work out, swim in the indoor pool or lounge in the sauna or steam room.

moderate

Am Römerwal, Am Römerwal 51–55, ℂ 232 135, fax 237 517 (DM160–200). Pleasant hotel in the green hills behind the Bahnhof (15 minutes' walk into town; trams or buses to Universitätsklinik). Airy, comfortable rooms and friendly service.

Central Hotel Eden, Bahnhofplatz 8, ℂ 674 001, fax 672 806 (DM156–230). Warmly elegant, traditional hotel; well-modernized and efficient. Just as convenient (though maybe not quite as idyllic) as the name suggests.

Hotel Hammer, Bahnhofplatz 6, ✆ 611 061, fax 611 065 (DM150–180). The brightest and most modern of the hotels around the station. It has friendly, enthusiastic owners, double-glazing against the traffic noise and a sauna to collapse in after tramping around the Altstadt.

Hotel Hof Ehrenfels, Grebenstr. 5–7, ✆ 224 334 (DM145). Cosy old hotel and wine tavern in the heart of the Altstadt.

inexpensive

Richter's Eisenbahn Hotel, Alicestr. 6, ✆ 234 077 (DM89 without private bath–115). Clean and functional central hotel.

Zum Schildknecht, Heiliggrabgasse 6, ✆ 225 755 (DM70 without private bath–98). Delicately seedy guesthouse in the middle of the Altstadt.

Youth Hostel: Am Fort Weisenau, ✆ 85332.

Eating and Drinking: Restaurants and Taverns

Weinstube Schinderhannes, Augustinerstraße (DM20). Good, *bürgerlich* couples munch *nacksche* (literally, 'naked'—skinless sausages) and other local delicacies.

Dr. Flotte, Kirschgarten 1, ✆ 234 170 (DM20–30). Atmospheric wine tavern on one of the prettiest squares in the Altstadt. It serves healthy salads as well as the usual heavy fare, and is ideal for lunch (except in season, when it is overrun with tourists).

Gebert's Weinstube, Frauenlobstr. 94, ✆ 611 619 (DM20–35). Cosy old wine tavern with a wide selection of Rhine wines and local snacks such as *Määnzer Handkäs mit Musik* (bread and cheese smothered in onions, oil, vinegar and pepper), delicious asparagus dishes in season and meaty Rhenish meals.

Heilig Geist, Rentengasse 2, ✆ 225 757 (DM45–65). Part of a 13th-century hospital. It serves excellent German food, and the beautiful original interior is romantically decorated with draped fabric.

Goldene Schipp, Fischtorstraße (DM45–65). Popular glass-fronted restaurant which serves excellent fish dishes, and has its own fish shop attached.

Bars and Cafés

Serious wine-drinking goes on in Mainz. At one time tavern landlords charged by the hour, rather than by the bottle. In Scönborner Hof you can see one of the city's favourite statues—a boozy little man holding what appears to be a pint beer glass. In fact he's drinking wine, which traditionally in Mainz comes in half-litre tumblers called *Schoppen*. Thankfully for the timid at heart, these are served half full— which is why, when you order wine, you ask for a *halbe* (a half). These days (sadly, for some) many establishments use more conventional glassware.

Augustinerstraße is a vibrant, jovially hectic thoroughfare popular with tourists and locals alike. **Café Zum Schambes** (named after a carnival character, a bastardization of 'Jean-Baptiste') buzzes day and night at the top end of the street. **Schönner Brünnen**, halfway down Augustinerstraße is the showroom for Mainz's latest haircuts and fashion, but has a cheery atmosphere nonetheless.

Altstadt Café and **Weinhaus Bluhm** in Rochusstraße, around the corner from Wagner's publishers, are hangouts of musicians and men with beards. Both also serve baguettes and pub meals.

Quartier Mayence. Local young trendies loll about in a little court off Weihergarten, where there's often live jazz.

Weinhaus Zum Beichstuhl, Kapuzinerstraße. A tiny, smoky, wood-panelled bar where the entry of a stranger can stop the conversation.

Rote-Kopf, Rentengasse. A sedate wine bar around the corner from **Altenwein-stube** (the rollicking inn where Franz Joseph spent many a happy night).

After Mainz the Rhine becomes less interesting. Much of this stretch of the river was straightened out by engineers in the 19th century and so bypasses the centres of the towns along the route. The southernmost section of the river forms part of the border with France, but here it is the Black Forest to the east of the river that provides the most captivating scenery. It is only at Lake Constance (the Bodensee, *see* p. 299) on the Swiss border that the river again begins to feature on most visitors' itineraries.

Frankfurt and the Mosel

Frankfurt is a hard-edged, nervy city: one of the world's most important banking centres, with the biggest airport in continental Europe. As such it is many people's first (sometimes only) taste of Germany—one, like bitter cough mixture, that they are willing to take only in small, strictly necessary doses. This is unfair. Frankfurt has many saving graces: it has some excellent museums, odd nooks of almost rustic snugness, and far more cosmopolitan verve than most other German cities. Towns within easy reach are also enticing— **Marburg** surpasses Heidelberg for university-town atmosphere, and is far less touristy; while **Darmstadt** boasts gems of Jugendstil architecture.

The **Mosel** (French: Moselle) twists tortuously between Trier on the Luxembourg border and Koblenz, where it joins the Rhine. In many ways it is a daintier version of the Rhine, flowing past precipitously steep vineyards, edging around castles and through busy little villages. The Mosel siphons off its fair share of the tourists that pour up and down the larger river, but (apart from a seething high season) generally makes a quieter and more charming alternative to its bigger sister. To the north are the plains and rolling hills of the **Eifel**, to the south the forests of the **Hunsrück**. At **Trier**—the *Roma Secunda* (second Rome)—you can see some of the most impressive Roman ruins outside of Italy.

Frankfurt and the Mosel

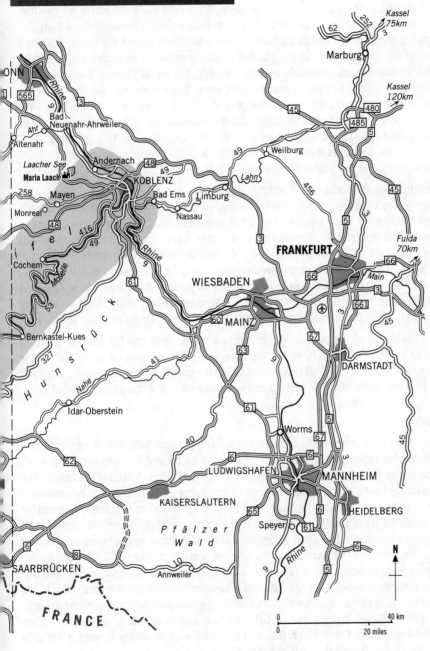

Frankfurt, which straddles the Main river some 30km from the point where it flows into the Rhine, is home to the all-powerful Deutsches Bundesbank (German Federal Bank), to Germany's main stock exchange and to 426 other banks from around the world. It is also a focus for Germany's advertising and publishing industries and its exhibition centre hosts a number of major international trade fairs, including the world's largest book fair every October. All this leads to a highly charged competitive atmosphere, and has resulted in the cluster of shiny show-off skyscrapers that give the city its nickname—'Mainhattan'. Yet running through the metropolitan maelstrom there is a current of friendly, cosmopolitan tolerance, and a thriving alternative culture. The city council is run by a left-wing SDP/ Green coalition, and gives 8 per cent of its annual budget to the arts (more than any other city in Europe), and the local university is known as the most hotly radical in the country.

Before the Second World War Frankfurt had a large and grand Altstadt. Little of that remains—two bombing raids in the last stages of the war flattened the alleys of half-timbered houses. In the 1950s and 1960s the go-ahead authorities made little attempt to restore the old buildings, but hastily put up new ones. These concrete and glass boxes can all too easily be your dominant impression of Frankfurt, but there are alluring pockets of the city that open up to the curious traveller—traditional markets and quiet shady squares, old apple-wine taverns in **Sachsenhausen** across the river, and lively bohemian haunts in the **Bockenheim** district. Added to that is a compendium of good museums offering quality and variety that is hard to surpass, and a dazzling programme of music and theatre.

With a population of just on 635,000, Frankfurt is not really all that big. Most of the main sights lie close to each other within the boundaries of the medieval town walls, now marked by a strand of parkland that loops through the city. It may seem tempting simply to walk from one to the next—but by the end of the day you'll find that you've covered miles.

History

Frankfurt has long wielded enough commercial and political influence to be Germany's capital, but has never quite made it. The Main forms an equator between north and south Germany, and Frankfurt's strategic position made it an obvious choice for settlement. The Romans traded here, and in the 8th century Charlemagne set up fort (though he eventually chose to settle near his favourite hot springs in Aachen). Frankfurt's markets prospered. In 1240 Emperor Frederick II granted the city the right to hold trade fairs—a privilege still vigorously exercised today. From 1356 the commercial centre began to acquire political clout—the election of German monarchs was held here, and from 1562 the Holy Roman Emperors were crowned in the cathedral. In 1585 Germany's first stock market and currency exchange was set up in the city, and a banking tradition grew up that was, in the 19th century, to lead to the emergence of banking giants such as the Rothschild dynasty. After the Napoleonic invasion had brought the Holy Roman Empire to an end, an ineffectual federation, the **Deutscher Bund** (1816–66), was established, with a virtually powerless Diet in Frankfurt (*see* **History** p. 43).

Later, after the 1848 Revolution, the city hosted the first freely elected (but rather short-lived) German parliament. Under subsequent Prussian rule, Frankfurt was reduced to a provincial capital. Its importance as a banking centre, however, continued to grow and in 1949 Frankfurt was almost chosen as the new capital of West Germany. It was pipped at the post by the casting vote of Chancellor Konrad Adenauer (who chose Bonn, many say, because it was closer to his home).

Getting Around

By Air

There are flights to Frankfurt airport from major cities around the world. The **information desk**, ✆ (069) 690 3051 *(6.45am–10.15pm)* is in Arrival Hall B, Level 1. The airport connects directly with the autobahn system. **Taxis** into the centre take about 20 minutes and cost around DM30. There is an **S-Bahn** service to and from the Hauptbahnhof every 10 minutes (duration 11min) and to the Hauptwache (town centre) every 20 minutes (duration 15min). The cost of the journey is DM5.20—so you may find it worthwhile to invest immediately in a *Tageskarte* (a Day Ticket, *see* below).

Lufthansa: Am Hauptbahnhof 2, ✆ (069) 25700.

British Airways: Düsseldorfer Str. 1, ✆ (069) 232 441/250 121.

TWA: Hamburger Allee 2–10, ✆ (069) 770 601.

Qantas: Bethmannstr. 56, ✆ (069) 230 041.

Air Canada: Friedensstr. 7, ✆ (069) 250 131.

Air New Zealand: Friedensstr. 7, ✆ (069) 230 277.

By Train

The **Hauptbahnhof** (information ✆ (069) 19419) is about 15 minutes' walk east of the centre (Tram 11 takes you right into the Altstadt). Frankfurt is at the nexus of a number of main rail routes. Trains (including the high-speed ICE) come in from all over Germany, and to other European capitals (around one train an hour to most major cities). Journey times: Paris (6¼hr), Amsterdam (5¼hr), Vienna (7hr 40min), Munich (4hr 20min ICE), Cologne (2hr 20min), Hamburg (3hr 40min ICE), Trier (2¾hr), Koblenz (1hr 40min), Darmstadt (¼hr), Marburg (1hr).

By Car

Frankfurt is also a hub of the motorway system, with Autobahns spoking out in all directions: Cologne (190km), Freiburg (270km), Hamburg (486km), Munich (392km), Amsterdam (457km), Paris (581km), Milan (731km). The rush hours can be hectic (7.30am–9am and 4.30pm–6pm), but there is ample parking in the city's 23 central parking garages (DM1–3 per hour).

Car hire: Avis (Airport Arrival Hall A), ℭ (069) 690 2777; Eurorent (Arrival Hall A), ℭ (069) 690 5250; Hertz (Arrival Hall A), ℭ (069) 690 5011; Europcar (Arrival Hall A), ℭ (069) 690 5464.

Mitfahrzentrale: Gutleutstr. 125, ℭ (069) 230 5113; Baseler Str. 7, ℭ (069) 236 444.

Public Transport

A highly efficient network of buses, trams, U-Bahn and S-Bahn trains covers the entire city. Tickets can be bought from automatic blue dispenser machines at stops (also from bus drivers). These must be validated when you begin your journey; simply push them into the franking machines on board buses and trams and at the entrance to station platforms. There is a DM2 flat rate for all single journeys (including transfers), so the **Tageskarte** (Day Ticket, DM6) which allows unlimited travel on the day of purchase, is good value.

Taxis: ℭ (069) 250 001 or 230 033.

Bicycle rental: Theo Intra (Westerbachstr. 273), ℭ (069) 342 780.

River Cruises

Frankfurter Personenschiffahrt (Mainkai 36), ℭ (069) 281 884, offer various pleasure cruises on the Main and Rhine. For information and reservations on the **Köln-Düsseldorfer Line** (the main Rhine cruise company) contact Deutsche Touring GmbH (Mannheimer Str. 4, ℭ (069) 230 735).

Tourist Information

There are two **tourist information offices**, one at the Hauptbahnhof (opposite Track 23), ℭ (069) 212 38849 *(Mon–Sat 8am–10pm, Sun 9.30–6; Nov–Mar Mon–Sat 8–9)* and one in the Altstadt, Römerberg 27, ℭ (069) 212 38708 *(Mon–Fri 9–7, Sun 9.30–6)*. Here you can pick up maps and all manner of leaflets on what to do in Frankfurt, day and night. The tourist office can also make room reservations and arrange city tours. The **Freundeskreis Liebenswertes Frankfurt e.V.** is a club whose members volunteer to guide visitors around the city. Tours are usually in English, and make an interesting and personalized way to see the town.

Disabled travellers: A city guide for the disabled is available free of charge by writing to Frankfurter Verein für Soziale Heimstatten e.V., Kennedyallee 80, 6000 Frankfurt 70. There's a taxi service for disabled people (ℭ (069) 230084), and the city municipality can also arrange special transport (ℭ (069) 748 090 for information and charges).

Banks: Deutsche Bank and the Commerzbank have branches at the airport that stay open until 10pm. The Deutsche Verkehrs-Kredit Bank has late-opening branches at the airport and at the Hauptbahnhof (south side).

Post office: The main post office is at Zeil 110, and there is a branch at the Hauptbahnhof open 24 hours a day.

Police: ✆ 110.

Medical emergencies: Doctor ✆ (069) 795 02200; Ambulance ✆ (069) 490 0001; Dentist ✆ (069) 660 7271; Pharmacy ✆ (069) 11500.

Markets: There is a daily fruit and vegetable market in the Markthalle (*see* below) and an excellent Fleamarket along the Museumsufer on Saturday mornings.

Festivals

The Spring and Autumn **Dippe** (three weeks in April and September respectively) began as stoneware markets in medieval times. Today they've developed into handicrafts fairs, though the chief attraction is the big funfair at the Festplatz on Ratsweg. On the first Tuesday after Whitsun, Frankfurters head out to the woods for the **Wäldchestag**. Long trestle tables are set up under the trees in the Stadtwald, the kegs are unstopped and celebrations last well into the night. More beer-drinking goes on at the **Main fest** (end of July/beginning of August), when the Römerberg is transformed into a throbbing beer garden.

Frankfurt holds a number of major trade fairs each year at the Messe-Gelände complex near the Hauptbahnhof. These include the International Automobile Show in September and the famous **Frankfurt Book Fair** (the largest and most important one in the world) in early October. Thousands of publishers from all over the word gather to set out their wares at the Book Fair. Their main interest is to sell foreign rights (the rights to publish editions either in translation or in the original language in foreign countries). Selling editions of books like this can be vital to the financial health of a publishing company: the atmosphere is intense, appointments diaries are often full months in advance. Hence this is not a place for the browsing public— indeed the general public are only allowed in on the last days of the fair. Unless you've come especially for the fair, this is generally a time to avoid the city.

Around the Römerberg

The Römerberg is a large square on a rather half-hearted mound in the middle of the city. This was the focal point for medieval markets, fairs and festivals, and is still the hub of tourist Frankfurt. Across the eastern end of the square runs a frieze of tall, straight-backed half-timbered houses, built in the early 1980s using original medieval plans and traditional methods. Opposite is the **Römer**, Frankfurt's Rathaus since 1405, with a cascading Gothic step-gable. (It stands on the site of a rich Roman merchant's warehouse—hence the name.) Inside you can visit the **Kaisersaal** *(guided tours only, daily on the hour 11–3; adm DM1)*, scene of the coronation banquets for the Holy Roman Emperors. Today it is easier to imagine the room as the venue for a town council sub-committee meeting or a Rotary Club lunch. The only hint of its distinguished past is a series of 19th-century portraits of emperors from Konrad I (911–18) to Franz II (1792–1806). The small **Nikolaikirche** on the south end of the square was once the court chapel. Inside its 15th-century Gothic husk

Frankfurt

500 metres
500 yards

N

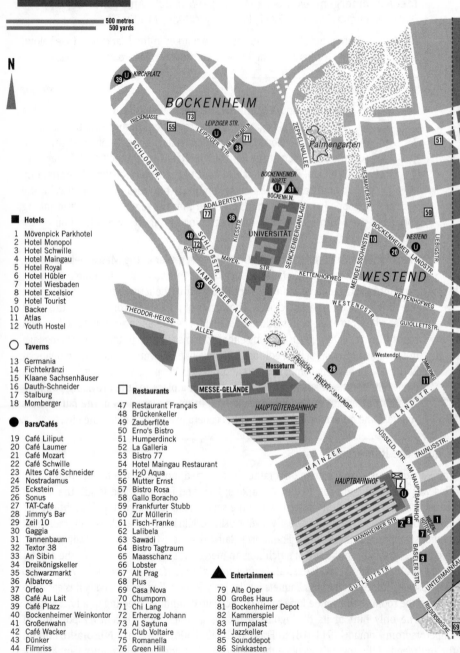

Hotels

1 Mövenpick Parkhotel
2 Hotel Monopol
3 Hotel Schwille
4 Hotel Maingau
5 Hotel Royal
6 Hotel Hübler
7 Hotel Wiesbaden
8 Hotel Excelsior
9 Hotel Tourist
10 Backer
11 Atlas
12 Youth Hostel

Taverns

13 Germania
14 Fichtekränzi
15 Klaane Sachsenhäuser
16 Dauth-Schneider
17 Stalburg
18 Momberger

Bars/Cafés

19 Café Liliput
20 Café Laumer
21 Café Mozart
22 Café Schwille
23 Altes Café Schneider
24 Nostradamus
25 Eckstein
26 Sonus
27 TAT-Café
28 Jimmy's Bar
29 Zeil 10
30 Gaggia
31 Tannenbaum
32 Textor 38
33 An Sibin
34 Dreikönigskeller
35 Schwarzmarkt
36 Albatros
37 Orfeo
38 Café Au Lait
39 Café Plazz
40 Bockenheimer Weinkontor
41 Großenwahn
42 Café Wacker
43 Dünker
44 Filmriss
45 Strandcafé
46 Earl's

Restaurants

47 Restaurant Français
48 Brückenkeller
49 Zauberflöte
50 Humperdinck
51 Humperdinck
52 La Galleria
53 Bistro 77
54 Hotel Maingau Restaurant
55 H2O Aqua
56 Mutter Ernst
57 Bistro Rosa
58 Gallo Boracho
59 Frankfurter Stubb
60 Zur Müllerin
61 Fisch-Franke
62 Lalibela
63 Sawadi
64 Bistro Tagtraum
65 Maasschanz
66 Lobster
67 Alt Prag
68 Plus
69 Casa Nova
70 Chumporn
71 Chi Lang
72 Erherzog Johann
73 Al Saytuna
74 Club Voltaire
75 Romanella
76 Green Hill
77 Da Cimino
78 Malepartus

Entertainment

79 Alte Oper
80 Großes Haus
81 Bockenheimer Depot
82 Kammerspiel
83 Turmpalast
84 Jazzkeller
85 Sounddepot
86 Sinkkasten
87 Batschkapp
88 Cooky's

it keeps much of its original quiet Romanesque charm. Beyond this lies the **Historisches Museum** *(Tues–Sun 10–5, Wed 10–8; adm free)*, an uninspiring museum where the only highpoints are replicas of the crown jewels of the Holy Roman Empire and an early 20th-century model of the city, which gives you an idea of how beautiful it was before Allied bombers and 1960s architects had a go at it. The museum building incorporates the **Saalhof** (a 12th-century chapel—all that is left of the old Imperial Palace) and the **Rententurm** (1455), an old defence tower. The café doubles as an *Apfelwein* museum, crammed with paraphernalia relating to the making and drinking of the local nectar (*see* **Eating and Drinking** below).

Off the eastern end of the Römerberg a walkway sweeps you up between the half-timbered houses and deposits you in front of one of Frankfurt's newest and most controversial public buildings, the **Schirn Kunsthalle** (1986) which, with its rotunda and long exhibition hall looks like a giant lollipop (or, say locals, a bowling alley). It takes top marks, though, for eye-catching magnificence, and houses first-rate temporary art exhibitions. Behind it, crumbly foundations of past Roman and Carolingian buildings poke up in the **Historisches Garten**, a little patch cleared in the concrete. Alongside is the red sandstone church of **St Batholomaüs**, built in the 13th and 14th centuries on the foundations of a Carolingian chapel. This is Frankfurt's most important church, the scene of the imperial coronations and so generally (though wrongly) referred to as the *Dom* (cathedral). The odd **tower** *(Apr–Oct daily 9–12.30 and 2.30–6; adm DM1)*, with its cluster of supporting pinnacles was thought daring and outrageous when it was added in the 15th century, and remains one of the most curious creations of German Gothic. Splendidly carved Gothic figures adorn the **Marienportal**, the northern portal at which the newly crowned emperor would make an appearance before processing across to the Kaisersaal. Inside the church is the simple **Wahlkapelle**, where the seven Electors would meet to battle out their final choice for a new ruler. At the time of writing St Bartholomaüs is undergoing extensive renovations, though parts of the **interior** are opened up from time to time. With luck you might catch the impressive Crucifixion group by the Mainz sculptor **Hans Backoffen** (on the west wall), and the touching 14th-century **Maria-Schlaf-Altar** in which grieving apostles crowd the bed of the dead Virgin, while putti gently close her eyes.

North of the Römerberg

Immediately to the north of the Römer, in a square of its own, stands the bulky Neoclassical **Paulskirche**, most famous as the venue for Germany's first freely elected parliament—the short-lived German National Assembly, which met here from 1848–9 (*see* **History** p. 43). Today the Paulskirche houses a cursory exhibition on the history of German democracy (in German) and a grotesque 20th-century mural commemorating the 1848 assembly.

A short walk east up Braubachstraße brings you to the **Museum für Moderne Kunst** (MMK, Museum of Modern Art) *(Tues–Sun 10–5, Wed 10–8; adm DM6)*. Opened in 1991, the museum is shaped like an enormous slice of cake, a companion to the post-modernist Schirn Kunsthalle nearby—like two bits of the same continent that have drifted apart.

Although the museum got off to a bit of a shaky start, massive funding from local government is helping it to build up a really meaty collection of modern and contemporary art. There are 20th-century classics by the likes of Andy Warhol, Roy Lichtenstein, Francis Bacon, Gerhard Richter and Josef Beuys, a good collection of work by the sculptor Claes Oldenburg (from his 1960s period of big, floppy 'soft sculptures' of household objects) and exciting work by some of the best artists of the past two decades—such as Mario Merz, Julian Schnabel and Bruce Nauman. The design of the building results in some odd wedge-shaped halls and peculiar nooks, especially well-suited to displaying installations. Look out for Nam June Paik's *One Candle* (in which a single flame is processed by a mass of hi-tech equipment) and the disorientating *The Stopping Mind* (1991) by Bill Viola. (Here you are surrounded by projections of a rocky landscape which lurch and shake to deafening and unpredictable earthquake rumbles.)

To the north of the MMK, up Hassengasse, you come to the **Kleinmarkthalle**. Duck through the doors between the bicycle shop and bookshop at Hassengasse 7, and you find yourself in a lively covered food market replete with shiny fruit, skinned sheep's heads and pig trotters, Japanese delicacies, teas, herbs and hot loaves of bread. Live fish swim about in a bath in the cellar, and one wall is lined with makers of homemade sausages. A fat, juicy Krakauer from the Schreiber family's stall—which has been going for nearly a century—will banish all thoughts of lunch, and possibly dinner too.

Leaving the market through the west entrance, you come to a quiet, shady square, the Liebfrauenberg. On one side is the **Liebfrauenkirche**, built in 1308 and enlarged in the 15th century, though rebuilt after the Second World War. Inside look out for the tympanum of the *Adoration of the Magi*—the original Gothic south doorway, intricately worked in terracotta with licks of gold. There is also some fine 15th- and 16th-century altar painting—and clusters of local down-and-outs who come in for the shelter and succour offered by the church's Capuchin monks.

Further west, down Bleidenstraße and Kleine Hirschgraben, you come to the **Goethehaus** at Große Hirschgraben 23 *(Apr–Sept Mon–Sat 9–6, Sun 10–1, Oct–Mar Mon–Sat 9–4, Sun 10–1; adm DM3)*, birthplace of Germany's most famous poet. Goethe was born into a wealthy patrician family in 1749, and wrote his early works in this house before upping sticks for Weimar at the age of 26. The house was destroyed during the Second World War, but the furniture was saved and later installed in the reconstructed mansion. You can see some original manuscripts in Goethe's neat, rather deliberate hand, paintings of the poet's contemporaries and four floors of sparsely furnished rooms—none of them particularly atmospheric.

North of here, up Roßmarkt, is the **Hauptwache**, a chunky Baroque police station built in 1729. Today it is a café that looks a little lost in the midst of rather nasty 1960s architecture. West and east of the Hauptwache lie Frankfurt's main shopping streets (*see* **Shopping** below). Further to the west, beyond the line of the old city wall, are the glass towers of Frankfurt's finance district. The most impressive is the shiny pencil-shaped **Messe**, by the doyen of high-rise mirror buildings **Helmut Jahn**. At 256.5m high it beats every other skyscraper in Europe.

West of the Römerberg

Walking westwards along the Main from the Historisches Museum, you come to the **Leonhardskirche**, a gloomy 13th-century church with five naves, a gaudy altar and heavily carved pews. Highlights include a well-preserved, elegant **Romanesque main portal** and intricate 16th-century **pendant vaulting** in a chapel on the north side, the *Salvatorchorlein*. Diagonally behind the church, in Karmelitergasse, is the **Karmeliten-kloster** *(Tues–Sun 11–6, Wed 11–8; adm free)*, a late Gothic monastery. In the cloister you can see some beautifully restored **frescoes** (1514–21) by the fiery Swabian artist Jerg Ratgreb. The paintings are vividly coloured, with delightful touches of realism—Joseph and Mary flee to Egypt laden with pots and pans, a short-sighted rabbi dons spectacles to perform Christ's circumcision. Part of the monastery is now given over to the **Museum für Vor- und Frühgeschichte** (Museum of Archaeology) *(Tues–Sun 10–5 , Wed 10–8; adm free)*. The Roman, Greek and prehistoric exhibits will only excite real devotees, but there are some interesting burial finds from post-Roman settlements around Frankfurt. Further west along Untermainkai is the **Judisches Museum** *(same times; adm free)*. Housed in the old Rothschild palais, the museum has interesting displays on Jewish culture and religion (aimed mainly at non-Jewish visitors), and exhibitions and short films tracing the history of Frankfurt's once influential Jewish population.

The Museumsufer

All the museums open Tues–Sun 10–5 and Wed 10–8.

Most of Frankfurt's best museums line up impressively along the south bank of the Main, roughly opposite the Altstadt. The stretch between the Friedensbrücke and Alte Brücke has become known as the Museumsufer ('Bank of Museums'). Hopping your way up the line is a perfectly feasible way to see them. There's enough variety here to dispel any possibility of museum fatigue, though it would be better to begin with the heavyweight collections in the west, and work your way eastwards.

On Saturday mornings a **fleamarket** adds to the attraction. It's one of the best in the country. Traffic is banned along the river bank and scores of stallholders spread out their antiques (from chipped teacups to Jugendstil wardrobes), Indian prints, Peruvian knits, dusty junk, suspect electrical equipment, and racks of flashy clothing. In true German tradition beer flows freely, there's Glühwein in winter and also coffee, cakes and a massive outdoor grill.

The first museum in the string is the **Liebieghaus** *(adm free)*, which gives you a superb overview of the development of European sculpture, from ancient Greek to neoclassical times. Look out for the tiny but graceful *Prudentia* made for a 12th-century altar, a delicate alabaster Crucifixion altar (1430) made in the Netherlands for a church in the Italian city of Rimini, and Matthias Steinl's rather voluptuous *Maria Immaculata*, carved in limewood at the end of the 17th century. Germany's golden age of carving—the late 15th and early 16th centuries—is well represented, with important works by masters such as Tilmann

Riemenschneider and Nikolaus Gerhaerts. Among the statues in the garden you can see a famous 18th-century statue of *Ariadne on the Panther*. The odd dappled marble did not impress one contemporary visitor to Frankfurt, who complained that 'The Goddess of Naxos looks as if she had been hewn from old Stilton cheese'.

A little further along you come to the **Städelsches Kunstinstitut**—known as the **Städel** *(adm DM6)*. This is the city's major gallery, with paintings from 14th–20th centuries. It was founded as an art college in the 19th century. Paintings were chosen to teach students about art, and the result is a tight, manageable selection, not nearly as overwhelming as the vast royal collections in Munich or Berlin.

The top floor contains paintings from the 14th to the 18th centuries. All the big German names are here, with choice pieces by Cranach, Dürer, the Holbeins and Altdorfer. There's a gorgeously detailed *Married Couple* by the 15th-century Rhenish Master WB, a mournful *Job on his Dungheap* by Dürer, a *Passion Altar* painted for Frankfurt's Dominican monastery (one of the elder Cranach's most beautiful works) and an odd, modernistic painting of *Two Weather Witches* by the eccentric 16th-century painter Hans Baldung Grien. For once the Dutch and Flemish collection outshines the German section. There's an especially good range of paintings from the early **Flemish Renaissance**: star of the show is the shimmering, meticulous *Lucca Madonna (c.* 1430) by Jan van Eyck, the artist credited with the invention of oil painting. Highlights from the 17th-century Dutch Golden Age include Rembrandt's *Blinding of Samson*, Vermeer's calm, luminous *Geographer* and the grimacing recipient of Adriaen Brouwer's *Bitter Drink*. You'll also find a healthy Italian collection, with paintings by Fra Angelico, Botticelli and Canaletto.

Works from the **19th and 20th centuries** occupy the lower floor. This is a good place to get a taste of the best German painting of the 19th century, such as the magical, rather fey work of Arnold Böcklin; Anselm Feuerbach's sultry, powerful portraits of women and the sometimes stickily sentimental paintings of Hans Thoma. There are familiar images from French painters Renoir, Degas and Monet, and later works of the German impressionist Lovis Corinth. The 20th-century collection includes a smattering of Matisse and Picasso, but is strongest on the German expressionists, with especially good works by Max Beckmann and a big range of Nolde and Kirchner. On the ground floor you'll find temporary exhibitions and selections from the graphics collection.

The next museum up the line is the **Deutsches Postmuseum** (German Postal Museum) *(adm free)*—a far more interesting prospect than it sounds, with vans and buggies, photographs and posters, all manner of telephones and hands-on displays. There are also changing exhibitions of stamps drawn from a vast collection. Right next-door is the award-winning **Deutsches Architekturmuseum** (Museum of Architecture) *(adm DM4)*, a 19th-century patrician mansion that has been gutted, given a sharp new interior and painted a blinding white. The permanent collection comprises drawings and models of interest mainly to aficionados, but the museum stages appealing temporary exhibitions—on themes ranging from doorhandles to Lego blocks. A passageway from the café leads to the **Deutsches Filmmuseum** *(adm free)*. This is a small museum, but great fun—with a romantic backstage atmosphere and sets that you can clamber about on and have yourself filmed in (including one where you can be pictured driving a car at top belt through city streets). You can visit a reconstruction of the Grand Café in Paris (where the Lumière brothers showed the first public movie), sneak a look at a few peep-shows, and see working models of screen monsters and all sorts of movie equipment. Film-buffs can engross themselves in a complete history of the German cinema, and there are interesting daily programmes of films at the in-house Kommunalkino.

A few minutes' walk along the riverbank brings you to the **Museum für Völkerkunde** (Ethnological Museum) *(adm free)* which has a good collection of masks, but otherwise serves chiefly as a home to travelling exhibitions. Next comes the excellent **Museum für Kunsthandwerk** (Museum of Applied Arts) *(adm free)*, a treasure-trove of good design and precious things. There are four sections: European (which starts with 12th-century ecclesiastical objects and progresses through eight centuries of beautifully crafted furniture and household ware, with some fine Jugendstil pieces); Far Eastern (mainly Chinese ceramics and lacquerware, but with a discriminating collection of Japanese work too); Islamic (with ceramics and glasswork as well as rich carpets and embroidery); and Books and Graphics (where you can see illuminations and emblematic books from the 16th to the 18th centuries, as well as illustrations, engravings and decorative bookcovers up to the present day). In a separate building just around the corner at Brückenstr. 3–7 is a fifth department, the **Ikonen-Museum** *(adm free)*, a collection of around 200 Russian icons, mostly from the 18th and 19th centuries.

South and east of the Ikonen-Museum is the district of **Sachsenhausen** a romantic, (though in spots touristy) quarter of the town famed for its *Apfelwein* taverns (*see* **Eating and Drinking** below). Just behind the museum (in Große Rittergasse) is the **Kuhhirtenturm** (Cowherds' Tower), part of the 15th-century Sachsenhausen fortifications. The composer Paul Hindemith (1895–1963) lived and worked in the tower for many years—today it forms part of a youth hostel complex.

Shopping

Frankfurt's main shopping street is the **Zeil**, to the north of the Altstadt, stretching between An der Hauptwache and Konstablerwache. Once the prettiest street in town, the Zeil must now rank as one of the most hideous thoroughfares in the country—a hard concrete corridor of featureless 1960s architecture, emblazoned with neon signs and gaudy advertising. Here you'll find all the major chain and department stores, and headlong consumerism—sales turnover on the Zeil is higher than anywhere else in Germany. Konstablerwache, at the end, is a focus for the dealers and broken products of Frankfurt's thriving drugs scene (worse here than in other German cities), and gets particularly unpleasant at night.

West of An der Hauptwache you enter a different world entirely. Here, along **Goethestraße**, are the city's most upmarket stores, starting at the eastern end of the street with the likes of Laura Ashley, and working upwards through Louis Vuitton to the giddy heights of Cartier and Tiffany. Roughly parallel to

Goethestraße is **Große Bockenheimer Straße**, a street of delectable, stylish and outrageously expensive foodshops, butchers, and delicatessens known to locals as the **Fressengasse** ('Guzzle Alley').

For better bargains and more **alternative shopping** it's best to head further west to **Bockenheim** (U-Bahn to Leipziger Straße), where Leipziger Straße is all that the Zeil isn't—with rows of brightly painted 3- or 4-storey 19th-century buildings housing pokey and interesting shops. South of the river, in the area around Wallstraße and Brückenstraße in **Sachsenhausen**, you'll find a delightful collection of bookshops, antique stores, shops selling ethnic art, and good local bakeries and wine stores.

Frankfurt © (069–)   ***Where to Stay***

Accommodation in Frankfurt is pricey at the best of times. During the Book Fair in early October, rates increase by at least 20 per cent. There are few hotels with any individual atmosphere—most were built after the war and are smart but dull, aimed largely at busy, expense-account clientele. There is a cluster of hotels around the Hauptbahnhof, convenient not only for transport, but also for the Messe (the trade fair centre), business district and the Altstadt. This is where you'll find many of the cheaper options, but you have to be careful—it is a seedy area, and standards are very uneven. Right next door to a smart chain hotel, you'll find a run-down flophouse with a wheezy manager and clientele who seem to have stepped out of a TV crime series.

expensive

outside Frankfurt **Hotel Gravenbuch Kempinski Frankfurt**, 6078 Frankfurt/Neu-Isenburg 2, © (06102) 5050, fax (06102) 505 445 (from DM350). Classic country hotel beside its own lake in 37 acres of lush parkland, only 15 minutes from Frankfurt's centre. An old manor, modernized and extended with style and restraint, it makes the perfect escape from hectic city life. In fact, most people seem reluctant to leave, what with indoor and outdoor pools, tennis courts, an in-house gym and beauty farm, and three excellent restaurants, including a drinking tavern that attracts locals. On the B459 off the Offenbacher Kreuz at the junction of Autobahns 3 and 663. If you're flying with Lufthansa you can check in at the hotel lobby.

Mövenpick Parkhotel, Wiesenhüttenplatz 28–38, © 26970, fax 2697 8849 (DM298–438). The jewel in the crown of the Mövenpick hotel group. Behind the imperious turn-of-the-century façade, the Parkhotel is all pastel shades and winning smiles. There's a catalogue of luxurious extras, from a steam bath to a private limousine service.

Hotel Monopol, Mannheimer Str. 11–13, © 227 370, fax 2560 8374 (DM275). Stately but not stuffy, with all the soft carpets, crystal chandeliers and careful deference of the Grand Hotel tradition. Just around the corner from the Hauptbahnhof.

Hotel Schwille, Große Bockenheimer Str. 50, © 920 100, fax 920 10 999 (DM200–260). Bright, elegant hotel on the 'Fressengasse', far more worth the whack than others in its price-range.

moderate

Hotel Maingau, Schifferstr. 38–40, © 617 001, fax 620 790 (DM160–195). Pleasantly situated Sachsenhausen hotel, overlooking a green square. A touch more upmarket than the Royal, though the sniffy staff have delusions of grandeur.

Hotel Royal, Wallstr. 17, © 623 026 (DM140–170). Simple hotel with small rooms verging on the spartan. But the management is friendly and the hotel is in a lively part of Sachsenhausen. No restaurant.

Hotel Hübler, Große Rittergasse 91–3, © 616 038, fax 613 132 (DM140). Harmlessly kitsch little nook in the heart of the Sachsenhausen publand. Privately owned and well-run. No restaurant.

Hotel Wiesbaden, Baseler Str. 52, © 232 347, fax 235 802 (DM135). Facing the Hauptbahnhof. Tired but well-meaning and (for Frankfurt) cheap. No restaurant.

Hotel Excelsior, Mannheimer Str. 7–9, © 256 080, fax 2560 8141 (DM150–230). Opposite the south entrance of the Hauptbahnhof. Smart and efficient (if a little soulless) business hotel that is good value for money.

inexpensive

Hotel Tourist, Baseler Str. 23–5, © 233 095 (from DM90 without private bathroom). Clean and comfortable—a safe bet in the Hauptbahnhof area. No restaurant.

Backer, Mendelssohnstr. 92, © 747 990 (DM45–60 without private bathroom, DM3 for use of shower). Down-to-earth establishment bristling with back-packers. Pleasant situation out near the university (U-Bahn to Westend). No restaurant.

Atlas, Zimmerweg 1, © 723946 (DM70–95 without private bathroom). Near the Hauptbahnhof, but out of the sleaze-zone. Clean and capably-run. No restaurant.

Youth Hostel: Deutschherrnufer 12, © 619 058, Bus 46 from Hauptbahnhof.

Eating Out: Restaurants and Bistros

expensive

Centre

Restaurant Français, Frankfurter Hof Hotel, Kaiserplatz 1, © 215 865 (DM150–200). Classic hotel restaurant with impeccable service and superb French cuisine (coming up with the odd surprise—such as lobster with kumquats).

Brückenkeller, Schützenstr. 6, © 284 238 (DM150–200). Some of the best food in Frankfurt, underneath the arches in a 300-year-old cellar, surrounded by antiques and mumuring diners. The six-course set menu changes daily; dishes such as roast turbot with baby artichokes, prepared with classic simplicity.

Zauberflöte, Opernplatz, ✆ 134 0386 (DM100–160). Tucked away in the superbly restored Alte Oper—with music piped in from the concert hall. Service is friendly, and the menu includes such adventures as *Matjes* (raw herring) under crusty potato, with apple and cucumber soup, and a heavenly hazlenut soufflé.

Erno's Bistro, Liebigstr. 15, ✆ 721 997 (DM80–120). Hardy Westend perennial with consistently high standards, and a legendary gooseliver with brioche. The set menus are excellent value, and there are over 350 wines to choose from.

Humperdinck, Grünebergweg 95, ✆ 722 122 (DM100–150). For the well-heeled and fastidious. Unusual combinations such as beef tartare and caviar, also delicious dessert soufflés.

La Galleria, Theaterplatz 2, ✆ 235 680 (DM100). Top-class Italian restaurant. Home-made pastas with mussels, mushrooms swimming in a variety of sauces, fresh fish and fine roast duck.

Sachsenhausen

Bistro 77, Ziegelhüttenweg 1–3, ✆ 614 040 (DM90–150). Lobsters, duck and lamb flown in from France for superb classic French cuisine. A good list of French and German Wines includes bottles from the family's own vineyard in Alsace.

Hotel Maingau Restaurant, Schifferstr. 38–40, ✆ 617 001 (DM70–100). Award-winning chef famed for his fish dishes, such as lobster au gratin with spinach and fettucini, or a mouthwatering monkfish covered in bacon, with spinach cooked in Chianti.

moderate

Centre

Mutter Ernst, Alte Rothofstr. 12, ✆ 283 822 (DM25–45). Solid, no-nonsense German cookery. Hefty portions of succulent chops and spareribs, meaty stews and all the local favourites.

Bistro Rosa, Grünebergweg 25, ✆ 721 380 (DM45–55). Carefully chosen wine list, good French Bistro food and pigs of all shapes and sizes adorning the walls. Jovial service.

El Gallo Boracho, Zeißelstr. 20, ✆ 557 433 (DM25–40). Good *tapas* bar with fine selection of Spanish wines.

Frankfurter Stubb, Bethmannstr. 33, ✆ 215 679 (DM25–45). Rustic restaurant that specializes in dishes from the Hesse region, but with subtle variations. Try the beef with *Grüner Sosse* (a rich mayonnaise with seven herbs including chives, sorrel, parsely and cress). You can also get home-made *Ebbelwoi* champagne.

Zur Müllerin, Weißfrauenstr. 18 (DM35–50). Faded photographs of obscure German actors on the walls, a patronne who seems to have been here forever and to know everyone, and simply delicious local food—such as *Sauerampfesuppe* (sorrel soup), doughy dumplings or wild mushroom ragout.

Fisch-Franke, Domstr. 9, ✆ 296 261 (DM20–30). Refuge from solid, meaty cookery. Simple fish restaurant selling grilled or baked fresh fish.

Lalibela, Klingerstr. 2, ✆ 293 831 (DM20–30). Scrumptious Ethiopian food, such as *Doro Wet* (chicken with a tangy cream sauce) served with *Injera*—unleavened bread that replaces cutlery. You eat from a communal platter, with your fingers (it is the height of bad manners to lick them).

Sawadi, Friedberger Str. 34, ✆ 281 563 (DM30–40). Heavenly Thai food but appalling service. You can *only* book a table for 6pm, 7.30 or 9, and daren't linger over your meal. The most irritating thing is that the food is so delicious that you are prepared to go back.

Sachsenhausen

Bistro Tagtraum, Altentorplatz 20 (DM20–30). Simple neighbourhood Bistro with well-prepared healthy food. The menu changes daily, and holds such delights as potato, orange and ginger soup, and spinach and sheep's cheese lasagne.

Maaschanz, Färberstr. 75, ✆ 622 886 (DM35–65). Unpretentious atmosphere and excellent French cuisine, with individual touches such as campari sauce and langoustine ravioli.

Lobster, Wallstr. 21 (DM30–50). Wood-panelled bistro/wine bar with a good cellar and daily changing menu of Italian and French dishes.

Alt Prag, Klappergasse 14, ✆ 614 434 (DM35–45). Czech beers and food in a comfy, friendly restaurant. Thick soups, meat smothered in cream sauces and fat fruit dumplings. Definitely not for weightwatchers.

Plus, Oppenheimer Landstr. 31, ✆ 615 999 (DM25–40). The current insider's tip. Trendy, packed bistro with a friendly atmosphere and well-prepared food—with ingredients brought fresh daily from local markets.

Casa Nova, Stresemannallee 59, ✆ 632 473 (DM40–60). Lively Italian restaurant, spread through a cluster of small rooms. Generous portions of pasta, pizza and other Italian fare, and quick, good-natured service.

Chumporn, Dreichstr. 7, ✆ 618 173 (DM20–40). Delicate and spicy Thai food amid bamboo panelling and tropical fish-tanks.

El Nil, Wallstr. 19 (DM20–40). Good couscous—and belly-dancers after 10pm (Wed, Fri and Sat).

Bockenheim

Chi Lang, Am Weingarten 14, Bockenheim, ✆ 772 483 (DM30–50). Chinese and Vietnamese standards (such as spring roll, duck and pineapple, chicken and ginger) in a room crammed with eastern antiques (which are also for sale).

Erherzog Johann, Schloß Str. 92, 573 800 (DM45–65). Waltzes, zither music and tasty Austrian food, such as *Rinderbeuschel* (beef, bacon, onions and dumplings).

Al Saytuna, Leipziger Str. 108, ✆ 772 257 (DM35–55). Friendly, family-run Lebanese restaurant where you can feast on a variety of starters and small dishes, and wash it all down with a powerful *arak*.

inexpensive

The best bet for cheap, hearty food is at one of the Apple Wine Taverns (*see* below), though you do need to be choosey. Other options include:

Club Voltaire, Kleine Hochstr. 5, City Centre, ✆ 292 408 (DM15–20). Casual, friendly atmosphere and a change from heavy *gutbürgerlich* cooking. The daily menu goes up on a blackboard—often offering paella, or prawns with garlic—and at low, low prices.

Romanella, Wolfsgangstr. 84, ✆ 596 1117 (DM20–30). Cheery halfway-house between restaurant and pizzeria. Seemingly endless menu that allows you to splash out on swordfish or make do with spaghetti. Either way the food is delicious.

Green Hill, Gutzkowstr. 43, Sachsenhausen (DM10–20). Good vegetarian restaurant with a big garden. There's a bright and various cold buffet, as well as delicious hot dishes (with a Turkish touch).

Da Cimino, Adalbertstr. 29, Bockenheim, ✆ 771 142 (DM5–12). The best of the fast-food pizza-and-pasta joints.

Malepartus, Bornheimer Landwehr 59, Bornheim, ✆ 447 910 (DM20–25). Wooden tables under the trees in the summer, cosy inside in winter and big helpings of solid German food. (Schnitzels and steaks come with piles of vegetables.)

Apple Wine Taverns

Frankfurt's favourite drink is *Apfelwein* (in dialect *Ebbelwei*, *Ebbelwoi*) or simply *das Stöffche*—'the stuff'), an apple wine that is similar to cider. It is served in a blue and grey stone jug called a *Bembel* and drunk out of a hefty diamond-patterned tumbler (*Schobbeglas*). *Ebbelwoi* comes in four main varieties. Novices stick with *Süsser*—sweet, harmless and fresh from the presses. To tackle the subtle but fierce *Rauscher* you need a streak of machismo (if not masochism). Somewhere in between is the mellow *Alte* and the mild, crystal-clear *Helle*. It is a good idea to have something to eat with your *Ebbelwoi*. *Handkäse mit Musik* (pungent, rubbery cheese and onions laced with vinegar) is popular, but heavier meaty meals also go down well. The best place to savour *Ebbelwoi* is shoulder-to-shoulder with the locals at one of the long wooden tables in an Apple Wine Tavern—recognizable by the *Fichtekränzi* (pine wreath) hanging outside. The most atmospheric taverns are in Sachsenhausen. Over the past few years Sachsenhausen has become the stomping ground of American G.I.s and backpacking tourists, but, with a little poking around, you can still find old taverns with a cheery village-like atmosphere. Here are some to start you along the way:

Germania, Textorstr. 16, ✆ 613 336. Very much the real thing—granny's sitting-room décor, long, packed tables and reputedly the best *Ebbelwoi* in town. There is a daily changing menu, but the food is pretty ordinary.

Fichtekränzi, Wallstr. 5, ✆ 612 778. Brown, basic and foggy with tobacco smoke. Men wanting the loo are directed out into the back yard.

Klaane Sachsenhäuser, Neuer Wall 11 (food around DM14). A shady, rustic courtyard and cosy rooms packed with families and respectable Frankfurters. Good simple food—*Rippchen mit Kraut* (spareribs and sauerkraut) is a speciality.

Dauth-Schneider, Neuer Wall 7 (food around DM12). Long tables, bright lights, barrels of *Ebbelwoi* and crowds of hearty youth tucking into large helpings of liver and roast pork.

Stalburg, Glauburgstr. 80 (U-Bahn Line 5 to Glauburgstraße). Down-to-earth tavern, not in Sachsenhausen but in the north of the city. Favoured by those in the know—though certainly not for the food.

Momberger, Alt Heddernheim 13, ✆ 576 666 (food DM7–25) (U-Bahn Line 1, 2 or 3 to Heddernheim). In an old north-western suburb. Another connoisseurs' favourite—this time with good food too. As well as the traditional *Ebbelwoi* side-dishes of *Handkäse mit Musik* and *Rippchen*, you can get grills and tasty steaks.

outside **Zum Goldenen Löwen**, Reginastr. 6, Harheim, ✆ (06101) 42982 (DM10–25) (S-Bahn Line 6 to Berkersheim). In summer cyclists flock north out of the city along the river Nidda, trail across the little bridge at Harheim, through the allotments and past the pigsty, to sit under the ancient willows and drink the *Ebbelwoi* pressed here by the Schaak family for over 150 years. There's a small menu of delicious home-made and home-grown food (the sausage and potato salad is a must).

Bars and Cafés

There are sedate cafés and trendy hot-spots dotted all about the centre and Sachsenhausen. For student life and Bohemian flair head west to **Bockenheim**, for neighbourhood charm try the older northern suburbs of **Nordend** and **Bornheim**.

Central

Café Liliput, Sandhofpassage, Neue Kräme 29, ✆ 285 727. Unexpected haven of green, a stone's throw from the Römerberg. Smart, on-the-ball clientèle and prices a touch below average for the city centre.

Café Laumer, Bockenheimer Landstr. 67, ✆ 727911. One of Frankfurt's oldest cafés. Good breakfasts and famous cakes (especially the chocolate *Herrentorte*). Favourite Book Fair retreat.

Café Mozart, Töngesgasse 23, ✆ 291 954. Period movie café with comfy chairs and chandeliers, old ladies in hats, cigar-puffing men reading the papers, nervous scribblers and excellent cakes.

Café Schwille, Große Bockenheimerstr. 50, ✆ 920 10910. Den of serious cake-eaters in the Fressengasse. There is another branch at the Hauptwache.

Altes Café Schneider, Kaiserstr. 12, ✆ 281 447. Cramped turn-of-the-century café with home-made cakes and chocolates, and the owner's dog firmly ensconced in its own corner chair.

Nostradamus, Heiligkreuzgasse 16–18, ✆ 294 428. Low cellar arches, chunky furniture, a darts club and a cheery crowd knocking back Irish beer.

Eckstein, Staufenmauer 7, ✆ 287 520. Perennial 'in' café that leads a conventional day-time life, but hots up at night when media and arty types crowd into the upstairs bar, or drift down to the basement to listen to avant-garde music.

Sonus, Bockenheimer Anlage 1a, ✆ 596 2525. On the edge of the financial district. The street number is 1a, the clientele are A1. Designer suits and spectacles against a backdrop of elegant colonnades and Egyptian tiles.

TAT-Café, Escherheimer Landstr. 2, ✆ 592 887. Obligatory *Szene-café* ('in' café), with all the accompanying evils—slow service, indifferent food and crowds of hangers-on. The name becomes more apt as the years draw on.

Jimmy's Bar, Friedrich-Ebert-Anlage 40, ✆ 75400. A classic—wood-panelling, leather upholstery, soft piano music and regular customers' names on the bottles.

Zeil 10, Zeil 10, ✆ 285 011. Late-night arty watering-hole with good menu for post-midnight munchies. Open until 4am over weekends.

Sachsenhausen

Gaggia, Schwanthaler Str. 16, ✆ 626 220. Lively café with a high customer turnover. Schoolboys pop in for their morning break, students come to avoid writing essays and others come in after work, or to meet up and plan the rest of their evening.

Tannenbaum, Brückenstr. 19, ✆ 611 304 (DM30–40). Long-standing haunt of the chattering classes, with a comfortable bar and imaginative menu (such as lamb in nut butter with lime slices).

Textor 38, Textorstr. 38, ✆ 627 413. Good down-to-earth pub with an assortment of wooden tables, cosy corner benches and a small menu of tasty food (especially the home-made pasta).

An Sibin, Wallstr. 9, ✆ 603 2159. Cellar bar for the homesick Irish and lovers of Guinness and Murphy's. There is often live music, and always a rousing atmosphere.

Dreikönigskeller, Färberstr. 71, ✆ 629 273. Sweaty, smoky, stuffy and swarming live-music pub.

Schwarzmarkt, Brückenstr. 37, ✆ 623 447. Chess players in one corner, a *Stammtisch* dominated by Baron Münchhausen's great-great-grandson (or so he claims) in the other, and lots of artists and tale-spinners in between.

Bockenheim

Albatros, Kiesstr. 27, ✆ 707 2769. Breakfast all day, a lush, quiet garden and stray straggles of students.

Orfeo, Hamburgerallee 45, ✆ 709 118. Afternoon breakfasts, good food all day and a chatty, friendly crowd of students, writers and advertising types.

Café Au Lait, Am Weingarten 12, ✆ 701 039. Walls in post-modern grey with odd-shaped mirrors, but a clientèle that ranges from local grannies to trendies who travel across the city to get here.

Café Plazz, Kirchplatz 8, ✆ 774 827 (DM20). Friendly family café that spills out onto the quiet square. Good daily changing menu.

Bockenheimer Weinkontor, Schloßstr. 92, ✆ 702 031. Thirty-and forty-something things sit about on wine boxes and garden chairs sipping wine and chatting till late.

Nordend/Bornheim

Großenwahn, Lenaustr. 79, ✆ 599 356 (DM30). Faded hippies, fresh students, the grocer from the corner—all squash in to drink beer, play pinball and savour the excellent pub food.

Café Wacker, Kantstr. 13, ✆ 446 437. One of the best cafés in town simply to sit in, sip good coffee, do the crossword and meet the neighbours—from punks to local housewives who've abandoned their shopping.

Dünker, Berger Str. 265, ✆ 451 993. Stand, or sit about on barrels in a vaulted wine cellar crammed with local students and OAPs sampling a superb range of German wines at under DM2 a throw.

Filmriss, Adlerflychstr. 6H, ✆ 597 0845. Foyer bar for earnest movie buffs that also attracts local wags, visually impaired people from the institution next door and bleary-eyed students who come in for the Low Budget and No Budget breakfasts which are served until 4pm.

Strandcafé, Koselstr. 46, ✆ 595 946. Perfect alternative café. Three rooms and a small garden filled with lively, chatty people consuming cheap food and coffee.

Earl's, Homburger Landstr. 3, ✆ 559 092. Small bar with a big, popular owner. Favoured by Black American ex-pats. Hot and cool.

Entertainment and Nightlife

Frankfurt's main **listings magazine** is the *Frankfurter Journal*, which comes out fortnightly and is sold at all newsagents. The tourist office brings out a free magazine *Frankfurter Woche*, and there are also comprehensive listings in *az (Andere Zeitung)* and *Frankfurter Stadt Illustrierte*. You can buy **tickets** for most events at the agency in Hertie department store (Zeil 90, ✆ 294 848) or at the Journal Ticket Shop (Hauptwach Allianz-Passage, ✆ 296 929).

Frankfurt's leading **orchestra** is the *Radio-Sinfonie Orchester Frankfurt*, which can often be heard at the **Alte Oper** (Opernplatz, ✆ 1340 400). The Alte Oper plays host to visiting orchestras and bands, but **ballet** and **opera** productions take place in the **Großes Haus** of the **Städtische Bühnen** (Theaterplatz, ✆ 236 061). The complex also contains two auditoriums for mainstream **theatre**. There are two other *Städtische Bühnen* stages: **Bockenheimer Depot** (Bockenheimer Warte, ✆ 212 37444) and the **Kammerspiel** (Neue Mainzer Str. 17, ✆ 212 37444). For more experimental work of all kinds head for the Künstlerhaus Mousonturm (Walsschmidtstr. 4, ✆ 405 8950). You can catch **English-language theatre** at the English Theatre (Kaiserstr. 52, ✆ 2423 1620). **Films in English** are shown at Harmonie (Dreieichstr. 54, ✆ 613 550) and at the Turmpalast (Eschenheimer Turm, ✆ 281 787). Films in their original language are marked OF, those with German subtitles have OmU—otherwise assume that the movie has been dubbed into German (most are).

The **Jazz** scene in Frankfurt is of a high standard and is centered on Kleine Bockenheimer Straße ('Jazzgasse') in the city centre. The most prestigious venue is the **Jazzkeller** (Kleine Bockenheimer Str. 18a, ✆ 288537), a tiny basement club that has hosted nearly all the big jazz names. The **Sound depot** (Ostendstr. 25, ✆ 447 018) has an innovative programme and sometimes runs jazz discos.

Good **live music** venues abound. At **Sinkkasten** (Brönnerstr. 9, ✆ 280 385) you can catch Reggae and R&B. The **Batschkapp** (Maybachstr. 24, ✆ 531 037) throbs with indie bands and rock, and is also a good place to **dance**. Visiting pop stars look in at **Cooky's** (Am Salzhaus 4, ✆ 287 662) for a bop, though on weekends the disco is invaded by the very young. **Dorian Gray** (✆ 690 2212), a disco in Hall C of Frankfurt Airport, attracts a very trendy crowd on Friday nights, but is more conventional on other days of the week. The admission charge to discos is usually around DM10.

Darmstadt

From 1567 to 1918 Darmstadt was the capital of the state (for a time the powerful Grand Duchy) of Hesse-Darmstadt. In September 1944 300,000 Allied incendiary bombs all but destroyed the city, killing 12,000 people in one night. Today's Darmstadt is an ugly sprawl, and there is little to detain you in the centre. Head for **Mathildenhöhe**, an erstwhile artists' colony east of the city, where you'll see some of the most spectacular Jugendstil architecture in Germany—certainly worth an afternoon's excursion from Frankfurt.

See also Directory entries for Wiesbaden and Fulda.

Getting Around

By car: Darmstadt is 20km south of Frankfurt on the B3.

By train: Darmstadt is only 15 minutes away by train or S-Bahn (Line 12) from Frankfurt Hauptbahnhof. Bus F will take you direct from Darmstadt Hauptbahnhof to Mathildenhöhe, and goes through the town centre and past the Hesse Landesmuseum (get off at Marktplatz). For Mathildenhöhe get off at the beginning of Dieburger Straße, then climb the hill up Stiftstraße and walk through the park. Alternatively you can wander up from the centre of town along the Erich-Ollenauer-Promenade (15min).

Tourist Information

There are two **tourist information points**, a pavilion at the Hauptbahnhof, ℭ (06151) 132 783 *(Mon–Fri 8.30–6, Sat 8.30–12)* and the main office in a shopping mall in the town centre, Luisenplatz 5, ℭ 132 781 *(Mon–Fri 9–6, Sat 9–12)*.

Mathildenhöhe

In the 19th century Grand Duke Ludwig II laid out the Mathildenhöhe park on a small hill to the east of the city. In 1899 the last Hessian Grand Duke, Ernst Ludwig, established an artists' colony here, and a series of great exhibitions (1901, 1904, 1908 and 1914) spawned a complex of trend-setting Jugendstil architecture—not just studios and exhibition halls, but a number of grand private residences too. These bold, striking buildings seem to be moving away from the organic curves of earlier Jugendstil towards harder lines, prefiguring styles which developed between the two World Wars.

Three structures crown the little hill. The 48m-high **Hochzeitsturm** (Wedding Tower), built in 1905 to celebrate the Grand Duke's marriage, pokes five finger-like loops skywards. You can take a **lift** to the top *(Tues–Sun 10–6; adm DM2)* to look out over Darmstadt, but this is not particularly helpful as the city's most attractive buildings are in the immediate vicinity. Behind the tower lies the monumental **Austellungsgebäude** (Exhibition Hall, 1908), still in use today. On the first floor is a café—the best place for tea or a light meal if you're here on a day trip. To the right of the tower are the glittering domes and mosaics of the diminutive **Russische Kapelle** (Russian Chapel) *(daily Apr–Sept 9–8; Oct–Mar 9.30–4; adm DM1.50)*, donated in 1899 by the last Czar of Russia, Nicholas II (the Czarina had been born in Hesse). Despite being the architectural odd man out, the chapel—with its oriental decoration and elaborate curls and curves—is quite at home against the Jugendstil backdrop.

Behind the chapel, around the south side of the Ausstellungsgebäde, is the **Ernst-Ludwig-Haus**, designed for the 1901 exhibition. The dazzling white building has a monumental portal in the shape of a Greek omega, flanked by a moody Adam and wanton Eve. The bronze figures in the door niches and gold ornaments on the wall could have been lifted from the Russian chapel next door. Inside is the new **Künstlerkolonie Museum** (Artists' Colony Museum) *(Tues–Sun 10–5; adm DM5)*, an exhibition of choice Jugendstil furniture, and also posters, jewellery and glassware. Most of the artists' houses on **Alexandraweg**, below the museum, were bombed and haven't been well restored, though a quick walk along the street will still reward you with glimpses of some beautifully designed gates and doorways. The two **Glückert** houses, roughly opposite the museum, are the most impressive.

The Town Centre and the Landesmuseum

The only buildings in the centre of any real interest are gathered around the triangular **Marktplatz**. There is a gabled Renaissance **Rathaus**, the **Weisse Turm**, a 15th-century defence tower with Baroque embellishments, and the **Schloß**—part Renaissance, part Baroque, but entirely rebuilt after the Second World War. Nowadays the Schloß houses the city library, a technical university and the **Schloßmuseum** *(Mon–Thurs 10–1 and 2–5, Sat and Sun 10–1, guided tours only; adm DM2.50)*, where the only real highlight is a fine *Madonna* by **Hans Holbein the Younger**, painted in 1526.

Behind the Schloß is the **Hessisches Landesmuseum** (Regional Museum) *(Tues, Thurs, Fri, Sat 10–7, Wed 10–1 and 2–9, Sun 11–5; adm free)*. Here the collection is more interesting. The ground floor has paintings from 1550 to 1800—a small display, but with notable work by **Cranach**, **Rubens** and **Brueghel**. Pick of the bunch is **Stephan Lochner's** rich *Presentation of Christ in the Temple*, one of the supreme works of the Cologne School *(see p. 56)*. There are good canvases by **Böcklin** and **Feuerbach** in the 19th-century section, but the 20th-century collection is less rewarding (though Beuys fans will find their enthusiasm tested by a horde of over 300 examples of the artist's work).

There is some notable religious sculpture, in particular a *Crucifixion* group by the medieval carver **Tilman Riemenschneider**—detailed down to the wrinkles on Christ's toes. The museum also contains some good **stained glass** (most of it medieval, but including work by William Morris and the Dutch expressionist Johan Thorn Prikker), as well as Jugendstil *objets d'art* and a vast natural history section.

Near the Hauptbahnhof, at Berliner Allee 65, the **Wella Museum** promises an extraordinary collection of everything imaginable to do with hair, from a Japanese wedding wig to tapestries woven in human hair by 19th-century apprentice hairdressers (though at the time of writing the museum is closed for renovation).

Marburg

Marburg rises steeply up from the River Lahn to a lofty Schloß, 102m above the banks. In 1527 **Landgrave Philipp the Magnanimous** founded Germany's first Protestant university here. Marauding armies over the centuries left the students pretty much alone, and today Marburg is the most delightful and atmospheric of all the old German university towns. Between lectures the population seems to double. The narrow stairways, which twist up the mountain and tumble down between tall stone walls and old half-timbered houses, fill with chatty youth. At night the stairs fill up again as the pubs and inns burst at the seams, and people carry their drinks outside.

One in four people in Marburg has something to do with the university, and out of term the town seems hushed, expectant and a little sad. There is enough here for a good day's sightseeing, but Marburg's real appeal lies in wandering about the streets, sitting in cafés or plunging into the cheer and bustle of its evening pub-life.

By car: Marburg is on the B3, midway between Frankfurt and Kassel (both about 90km away).

By train: The **Hauptbahnhof** is at the northern end of the lower town, and rail connections are good. There is a minimum of one train an hour to both Frankfurt and Kassel, and journey time in each case is 1 hour.

The main **tourist information office** is at the Hauptbahnhof, ✆ (06421) 201 262 *(Mon–Fri 8–12.30 and 2–5; Apr–Sept also Sat 9.30–12)*, but shops around town displaying an 'i' sign can also help.

Police: ✆ 110.

Medical and pharmaceutical emergencies: ✆ (06421) 35001.

Market days: There is a weekday fruit and vegetable market on the market square, and a flea market on Steinweg on the first Saturday of the month.

The Lower Town

The most important building in the lower town is the **Elizabethskirche** *(daily Apr–Sept 9–6, Oct 9–5, Nov–Mar 10–4, Sun from 11; adm DM2)*, a few minutes' walk from the Hauptbahnhof (up Bahnhofstraße and left into Elizabethstraße). This was Germany's first purely Gothic church, and its unadorned elegance has proven hard to beat. The church lacks all the flutter and frills of its French-influenced successors—it is a solid hall-church with austere twin towers that stretch heavenwards with Germanic vigour.

The Hard, Fast Route to Sainthood

St Elizabeth (1207–31) was the daughter of the King of Hungary. When she was 14 she was despatched to the Wartburg (near Eisenach in east Germany, see p. 428) to marry the high-living Ludwig IV, Landgrave of Thuringia. She riled the local nobility by spending more time with the sick and the poor than at court. When Ludwig died of the plague on a crusade, six years after they were married, Elizabeth and her children were expelled from the Wartburg, and came to Marburg. Here she entered a Franciscan nunnery, established a hospital and led a life of such hard work and ascetic rigour that she wore herself out, and died a few years later at the age of 24. The **Order of Teutonic Knights** (a powerful, rather ferocious, military and religious brotherhood who owned land on the right bank of the Lahn) saw to it that Elizabeth was canonized within four years of her death, and immediately set about building the **Elizabethskirche** on the site of her hospital.

Inside the church you can see, in astonishing contrast to Elizabeth's lifestyle, a worldly, alluring **statue** of her (commissioned by her descendants *c.* 1470) and a spectacularly extravagant **golden shrine** (*c.* 1235), which once held her remains. The Protestant Philipp the Magnaminous later had the body interred to put an end to her cult, and to stop the distribution of parts of the skeleton as relics. Each time the shrine has been sent away for safe-keeping, it has come back with fewer of its original 879 jewels—but it is still an awesome sight. The church also contains a number of fine **altars** and **murals** depicting scenes from Elizabeth's life.

Around the east end of the church is a group of buildings (ranging from the 13th to 16th centuries) that belonged to the Teutonic Knights. Nowadays they are used by the university. On a small hill to the west of the church is the Knights' funerary chapel, the **Michaelskapelle**, and the quiet cemetery where Landgrave Philipp had St Elizabeth buried. Most of the rest of the lower town is taken up by modern university and government buildings, but the **Universitätsmuseum für Bildende Kunst** (University Museum of Fine Art) at Biegenstraße 11 *(Wed–Mon 10–1 and 3–5; adm free)* is worth a visit. (Follow Deutschhausstraße down the side of the Elizabethskirche, then right into Biegenstraße, or cut through the Botanic Gardens.) This modest collection has some surprises—a charming Picasso, works by Cranach and Tischbein, and one or two interesting Moderns. Keep an eye open for paintings by local artist **Carl Bantzer** (1857–1941), especially his vibrant, swirling painting of a country festival, *Schwälmer Tanz* (1898).

The Upper Town and the Schloß

Biegenstraße leads past the University Museum into Pilgrimstein. From here you can climb the Mültreppe stairway to the Upper Town. (*'Zu Marburg muß man seine Beine rühren und treppauf, treppab steigen'* ('In Marburg you've got to get your legs going and climb up and down the stairs') complained one of the University's famous alumni, folktale collector Jakob Grimm). The Mühlentreppe deposit you on the Kornmarkt opposite the **Alte Universität** (Old University). Once it was a Gothic Dominican monastery, though all that remains of the original complex is a rather severe chapel *(daily except Wed, 9–6)*. Most of the rest of the building was built in the late 19th century. You can visit the grand **Aula** (Main Hall) *(Mon–Fri 11–5; adm 30 pfennig, key from porter)* which has monumental murals, rich panelling and rather delicate stained glass windows.

North of the Alte Universität is the **Marktplatz**, where the 16th-century **Rathaus** stands, an economical building with just two adornments—a relief depicting St Elizabeth above the portal, and a pretty Renaissance stairtower gable with an oversized clock and small Glockenspiel. On the first Sunday in July around 5000 Professors, students and ex-students (along with tourists) cram the small square for a traditional morning pint of ale—and stay on well into the afternoon.

Nikolaistraße leads off the Marktplatz to the 13th-century **Marienkirche**, an ornate church with deeply coloured windows. From here those with enough puff can climb the Bickell-Treppe up to the **Schloß** *(Tues–Sun 11–1 and 2–5; adm free)*. (Alternatively take Bus 16 from the Marktplatz.) In the mid-13th century St Elizabeth's daughter, Sophie of Brabant, decidedly more worldly than her mother, claimed her son to be the rightful heir to Thuringia. In the end she was placated with the new Landgraveship of Hesse, and set up headquarters for the future dynasty at Marburg. She immediately began rebuilding the old Schloß on the hill—though most of what you see today dates back to the early 16th century. In the pink **Schloßkapelle** (built in the 14th century, just before the Landgraves moved their capital to Kassel) are some of the original murals and floor mosaics. The **Saalbau** in the northern wing was the scene of the **Marburg Colloquy**, a series of religious debates organized by Philipp the Magnanimous. Martin Luther met with Huldrich Zwingli and other reformers for discussions that lasted three days. The Protestants agreed on all but one of 14 points—they were unable to reach a common interpretation of the Last Supper. In the **Wilhelmsbau**, on the eastern side of the castle, the **historical museum** *(Tues–Sun 10–1 and 2–5; adm free)* involves even more climbing—up and down spiral staircases—for a look at local folk costume, swords and armour and *bürgerliche* furniture.

Marburg © (06421–)   **Where to Stay**

Hotels are surprisingly thin on the ground in Marburg—especially in the more attractive Upper Town.

moderate

Europäischer Hof, Elizabethstr. 12, © 6960, fax 66404 (DM130–230). Smart, modern, though unexciting. The best of the cluster of hotels near the station.

Hostaria del Castello, Markt 19, © 25884, fax 13225 (DM160–180). Right on the market place. Heavy oak beams and traditional décor though some rooms are on the small side.

Hotel Zur Sonne, Markt 14, © 26036, fax 131648 (DM130). Tiny hotel in a half-timbered house, tucked away on the edge of market. (Look out for the dangling sign of the sun.) It has been a guesthouse since 1569 and is the cosiest and most atmospheric of the hotels in town.

inexpensive

Gästehaus Müller, Deutschhausstr. 29, © 65659 (DM50 without private facilities–DM90). Clean, comfortable and friendly guesthouse near the station.

Eating and Drinking

The traditional student rollicking grounds are along the streets leading off the Markt—such as Hirschberg and Steingasse. In **Weidenhäuser Straße**, just across the river, there are wonky half-timbered houses, quaint shops, and pubs and cafés that most tourists do not reach.

Zur Sonne, Markt 14, © 26036 (DM20–50). The charming little hotel also has the best restaurant in town. The delicious home-cooked food includes local dishes and imaginative specials, such as cheesy *Schnitzel* with peach and pineapple glaze.

Café Barfuß, Langasse. Trendy student café serving good salads and pastas.

Schamdan, Weidenhäuser Str. Busy bar that also sells tasty, cheap Turkish food.

Hinkelstein, Markt 18, ℂ 24210. Busy student cellar tavern that sometimes puts on live bands.

Café Bar De Gass, Weidenhäuser Str. Quiet, candlelit café. Hangout of the more earnest students.

Zum Krokodil, Weidenhäuser Str., ℂ 23234. Older students, university staff and townsfolk drink beer and shout above Rock classics.

From Marburg the river Lahn winds south-west to join the Rhine near Koblenz. The Lahn is a sleepy river that meanders through rugged little hills and at times near-deserted countryside. Tufts of natural forest sprout from the hillsides—the valley is at its most beautiful in the early autumn, when it slips into every imaginable shade of gold and brown. At Koblenz the Rhine is joined by an even more alluring river, the Mosel (French: Moselle).

For towns along the Lahn valley see Directory entries for Weilburg, Limburg, Bad Ems.

Kassel

Once a struggling provincial town only 35km west of the DDR border, Kassel suddenly finds itself plum in the centre of the new Germany, filled with eager shoppers and enjoying a building boom. Showy new 1990s architecture is livening up what was a bleak cityscape. As a major tank and locomotive manufacturing town, Kassel was relentlessly bombed during the Second World War, then hurriedly rebuilt during the 1950s. Some of the box-shaped, pastel-coloured Lego-like houses are such period classics that there are moves afoot to declare them historical monuments.

This is not Kassel's first boom. In the late 17th and 18th centuries, the town prospered magnificently, stimulated by the influx of the money and talent of the Huguenots (Protestants who were fleeing religious persecution in France). Then from 1806 to 1813 the town was the royal seat of the Kingdom of Westphalia, with Napoleon's brother Jérôme on the throne. Jérôme was a scurrilous and unpopular monarch who (according to a 19th-century commentator) 'laboured under such a want of head, such a horror of business and such a devotion to grovelling pleasures that it was only by mistake that he could stumble on anything good.' When their king absconded with much of the public treasury a few years later, the people of Kassel were surprised not so much at the baseness of the deed, but by his possessing so much forethought. Jérôme also contributed to the defeat of Napoleon at the Battle of Waterloo by turning what was intended as a diversionary tactic into an all-out assault. Kassel has, however, inherited a lustrous line-up of museums, some eccentric monuments and a public park the size of the Principality of Monaco.

Later in the 19th century the **Brothers Grimm** settled here to compile their German dictionary (they got as far as the letter 'F'). It was at this time that they set about collecting the folktales that were to make them world famous. Soon after the Second World War, Kassel once again made its mark on the international scene as the home to **documenta**, one of the world's major contemporary art shows. For decades zany and provoking artworks—

from a 12m-high pickaxe to 7000 especially planted oak trees—have been foisted upon the wary burghers. Gradually the locals have come to tolerate and even encourage the adventures, so that today Kassel has a curious mixture of bland architecture and bizarre public sculpture—together with a lively, go-ahead atmosphere.

Getting Around

By car: Kassel is on the A7 160km from Hannover and 220km from Frankfurt. The centre of town was the first in Germany to be pedestrianized, and there are numerous parking facilities around the perimeter.

Mitfahrzentrale: Citynetz, Friedrich-Ebert-Straße 107, ✆ (0561) 77 33 05.

By train: A spanking new Bahnhof has been built at **Wilhelmshöhe** featuring every high-tech gizmo imaginable but (until a hasty last minute adjustment) no public lavatories. This station has taken over from the Hauptbahnhof as Kassel's main rail station and superfast ICE trains converge on here from all over Germany. There are connections to Hannover (2hr ICE), Hamburg (2½hr ICE), Frankfurt (1½hr), Munich (3½hr ICE) and Göttingen (20min). Frequent mainline trains will transfer you onward to the **Hauptbahnhof,** which is more conveniently situated just a few minutes' walk north-east of the centre. Alternatively, you can catch Trams 1, 3, 4, 6 or 9 to Königsplatz.

Public transport: Most of the main sights are grouped around the city centre, but you'll need wheels to get out to Wilhelmshöhe. A **Tagesnetzkarte** (DM6.50) allows you onto buses and trams throughout the network for a 24-hr period.

Taxis: ✆ (0561) 770 066.

Tourist Information

The **tourist information office,** ✆ (0561) 34054 *(Mon–Fri 9–6 and Sat 9–1)* is at the new Kassel-Wilhelmshöhe Bahnhof. Here you can get maps of the city, reserve rooms and also find out more about the **Fairytale Road** (*see* p. 000).

Banks: High-street banks are around Königsplatz and along Königsstraße.

Post office: The main post office is at the northern end of Königsstraße.

Market days: Thursdays and Saturdays.

Festivals and Events

The good burghers of Kassel totter from one festival to the next, scarcely allowing themselves time to knock back an *Underberg* (a good hair-of-the-dog restorative). Despite Kassel's Protestant heritage there are lively **Carnival** celebrations, followed a few weeks later by an **Easter fair and market**. In early August there is the **Zissel**, a folk fair with processions, jousting competitions and plenty of feasting. Then in September Wilhelmshöhe explodes in a massive **display**

of fireworks, while down in the town there is a **wine market** centring on one particular region each year. In November things take a more sober turn with the **Kasseler Musiktage**, one of Germany's oldest festivals of classical music. The **Weihnachtsmarkt** leading up to Christmas always has a fairytale theme (a different tale each year, with displays from other countries too).

Kassel's most renowned event, however, is the **documenta**. After the Second World War, Arnold Bode, a local artist and academic, decided to stage an exhibition of new art to show the Germans what they had been missing during the years of Nazi suppression. He paced out the ruined Fridericanum, proclaimed it big enough, and set to work. The first documenta was held in 1955, and there has been one every five years since then. The exhibits now cover every medium from painting to performance art and video, and fill buildings all over town, even spilling out into the parks and streets. Documenta has grown into the art-world's acid-test of the avant-garde. Each time round, the selection of exhibits is very much the subjective choice of a different director (Jan Hoet, the hapless incumbent in the years leading up to documenta 9 in 1992 was besieged by nearly 4000 hopeful applicants). The result generally reads as a Who's Who of contemporary art. The next documenta is scheduled for June–Sept 1997.

Wilhelmshöhe

The Schloß

Kassel's main permanent attraction is some 6km west of the centre (Tram 1 or 9). Wilhelmshöhe, once the favourite residence of the landgraves of Hesse, is now a spacious public park complete with fantastical follies. First stop is the **Schloß**, a graceful Neoclassical pile built in three separate parts in the 1780s. When King Jérôme arrived in 1806, he joined the outer wings to the central building with wooden passages, renamed the palace 'Napoleonshöhe', and made it his home. The pure, unadorned lines of the Schloß held little appeal for the scratchy John Russell, an Englishman who came here in the 1820s and really didn't enjoy his visit. 'Simplicity,' he complained, 'is an excellent thing, but only in its proper place and within proper bounds.' He dismissed unfairly Schloß Wilhelmshöhe as 'mean and unfinished-looking' for a palace, and wondered who had had 'the barbarous idea of emblazoning the name of the building on the frieze of the portico'.

Today one wing is occupied by the **Schloßmuseum** *(Mar–Oct Tues–Sun 10–5, Nov–Feb Tues–Sun 10–4; adm DM2)*, where you can see a collection of furniture, porcelain and various *objets d'art* that once graced the palace. The central building now houses the far more exciting **Gemäldegalerie Alte Meister** *(Tues–Sun 10–5; adm free)*. Downstairs are antique sculptures, notably the **Kassel Apollo**, a Roman copy of a bronze Greek statue reputedly found on the Acropolis. Upstairs is the collection of Old Masters built up by Landgrave Wilhelm VIII in the early 18th century. There are some fine **Rembrandts**, including an early self-portait, a portrait of the heiress Saskia van Uylenburch done in 1633

(Rembrandt fell in love with her while she was sitting for it, and married her a few months later), and a gentle, moving depiction of *Joseph Blessing the Sons of Jacob*. There are sumptuous paintings of wanton godesses by **Rubens**, and good solid Dutch merchants and their wives by **Van Dyck**. **Jan Steen**, master of raucous inn scenes, contributes a bean-feast or two, there is a characteristically hushed church interior by **Saenredam**, and a host of good paintings by other Dutch and Flemish Masters. German painters are well represented, too, with works by Cranach, Dürer and Altdorfer, and a painting by Hans Baldung (the quirkiest of Old German painters) of Hercules and Antaeus locked in a below-the-belt wrestling clinch. The collection also includes notable works by Tintoretto, Murillo and other southern European painters.

The Park

Beyond the palace, the park stretches out in an informal English style, with copses, streams, 800 species of tree and over 300km of paths. Directly opposite the Schloß, at the top of a steep hill is an artificial castle, the **Oktagon** (1717), out of which protrudes a thin pyramid crowned with a really gigantic, supremely nonchalant **statue of Hercules** (height 8.25m, shoe-size 1.5m). ('I know not how many persons are said to be able to stand comfortably in his calf, dine in his belly and take their wine in his head', wrote the jaundiced John Russell.) Today any number of people can climb up inside the pyramid for a breathtaking **view** from the Harz to the Rhön *(Tues–Sun, 9–5; adm DM2)*. In the summer *(Wed, Sun and public holidays 2.30pm)* water hurtles from the foot of the monument down a 250m-long, 885-tier **cascade** before plunging underground and gushing up (entirely under its own pressure) as a 53m-high **fountain** just outside the Schloß. Another stream plummets over an artificial **waterfall**, under a bridge and through the fake ruins of a Roman **aqueduct**.

Just to the north of the Schloß you can see the **Ballhaus**, built as a theatre and 'fitted up with the most useless voluptuousness' (John Russell again) for King Jérôme. Later it was coverted into a ballroom, and is still used for dances and exhibitions today. Nearby is the capacious glass-walled **Gewächshaus** *(Jan–May daily 10–5; adm DM1)*, a 19th-century greenhouse stocked with palms and camellias. Hidden in the trees to the northwest is the score of broken turrets and spires of the **Löwenburg** *(Mar–Oct Tues–Sun 10–5, Nov–Feb Tues–Sun 10–4; adm DM2)*, built between 1793 and 1801 as a romantic hideaway for Landgrave Wilhelm IX's mistress. Löwenburg was based on medieval English and Scottish castles and was meant to look like a ruin, though Allied bombs have added to its haggard appearance. Inside you can see a collection of armour from the 16th to 18th centuries, and valuable medieval stained glass pillaged from surrounding chapels to satisfy Wilhelm IX's desire for authenticity.

There is a good café in one of the Schloß outhouses, and just opposite the tram terminus is an entirely modern delight, the **Kurhessen Therme**, Wilhelmshöher Allee 361, © (0561) 32761 (adm DM16), a paradise of mineral baths, saunas and steam rooms with log fires, banks of sunbeds, bars and restaurants and even a cinema.

The City Centre

Around Königsplatz

Kassel's main city square is, in fact, a circle. It was designed in the mid-18th century, though only one of the original buildings (now a bank) remains. Today **Königsplatz** is criss-crossed by sleek modern trams and busy pedestrians, but at one time it was the marketplace where **Dorothea Viehmann**—the woman who told the Brothers Grimm at least 18 of their tales—had her stall. Her Huguenot parents had owned an inn, and she had heard the stories as a child from passing soldiers and travellers. In the centre of the Platz is a wide, triumphal stairway that leads absolutely nowhere. From the landing you can can get a good idea of the city's layout.

Northeast, along Königsstraße, is the **Martinskirche**, which went up in fits and starts between the 14th and 19th centuries, but was completely destroyed in 1943. The church was rebuilt with a newly designed interior, but still contains the florid alabaster and black marble memorial to **Landgrave Philipp the Magnaminous**, patron of Luther and founder of Marburg University. A walk along the southwest branch of Königsstraße brings you to Friedrichsplatz, where you can see the **Museum Fridericianum** (1779), Germany's first Neoclassical building and the headquarters for documenta. (When documenta is not on, the gallery is used for visiting exhibitions.) In the middle of the square is one of the most popular of recent documenta left-overs, Jonathan Borofsky's *Man Walking to the Sky*: a long steel column sticks up out of the ground at a 45° angle. Two thirds of the way up a human figure strides confidently towards his unknown fate. Next to it is a more enigmatic offering—a 5cm-wide brass circle called the 'Kassel Hole', a vertical kilometre of brass sunk into the earth by the artist Walter de Maria. In front of the Fridericianum are the first and last of Joseph Beuys's *7000 oaks*. During documenta 7 in 1982 Beuys had 7000 basalt rocks dumped on Friedrichsplatz and demanded that the city council plant a new tree for each one. All over town you can see young oak trees with a basalt rock at the base. The square was only finally cleared in 1987, when Beuys's widow planted the last tree at the opening of documenta 8. Behind the Fridiricianum is the **Zwehrenturm**, part of the medieval fortifications. Since documenta 6 a laser beam has been projected nightly from here to the statue of Herkules in Wilhelmshöhe.

Further down Königsstraße, you come to the **Landesmuseum** *(Tues–Sun 10–5; adm free)*, an uninspiring collection of handicrafts and archaeological bric-a-brac. In the same building, however, is the fascinating **Deutsches Tapetenmuseum** (German Wallpaper Museum) *(Tues–Fri 10–5, Sat and Sun 10–1; adm free)*, a colourful and cleverly presented display of wall coverings from Spanish leather to Japanese silks including 19th-century panoramas, 1960s pop art and designs by famous painters.

Along Karlsaue

Along the eastern edge of the city is another vast park, the **Karlsaue**. At the north end is the early 18th-century **Orangerie**, which houses a superb **Museum für Astronomie**

und Technikgeschichte (Astronomy and Technology Museum) *(Tues–Sun 10–5; adm free)* with a model of Foucault's pendulum and a wealth of beautifully designed old clocks and instruments (many originally the property of star-struck landgraves). Alongside is the **Marmorbad**, a decorative bathroom built for Landgrave Carl in the 1720s ('merely a pretext for spending money and marble' according to John Russell). The original fittings are intact, but plumbing was never installed and the taps have never worked.

Further south, on a terrace overlooking the park, is the **Brüder Grimm-Museum** *(daily 10–5; adm free)*. The museum, sadly, is a bit of a disappointment, with displays illustrating the history of the brothers' lives and some interesting manuscripts (including their annotated manuscript of the anthology), but little on the tales themselves.

The Brothers Grimm

 The bitter misogynist **Jakob Grimm** (1785–1863) and his younger brother **Wilhelm** (1786–1859) were born in nearby Hanau, educated at Marburg University and worked for years as court librarians in Kassel before moving on to Göttingen University and Berlin. It was in Kassel that they began to collect folk tales such as Cinderella, Rumpelstiltskin and Snow White. Wilhelm was all for preserving the dark original versions (Sleeping Beauty, for instance is raped rather than kissed by the Prince, and only wakes up when she gives birth to twins nine months later). Jakob was of a more literary bent, and liked to embellish the tales. The anthology they compiled together, suitably cleaned up, is familiar to children all over the world.

Next door is the **Neue Galerie** *(Tues–Sun 10–5; adm free)* comprising mainly German art from the mid-18th century to the present day. There is plenty of documenta flotsam, including work by Beuys, Mario Merz, Penck and Baselitz—but the collection doesn't carry the weight you would expect. Just around the corner, on Weinbergstraße is the peculiar **Museum für Sepukralkultur** *(Tues–Sun 10–5; adm free)*, devoted to charting the development of cemeteries, graves and tombs in western culture and likely to be of interest only to fans of funerary practice.

Marburg © (0561–) **Where to Stay**

expensive

Hotel Gude, Frankfurter Str. 299, © 48050, fax 480 5101 (DM230). Modern hotel, some way south of the centre (Tram 5), comfortably fitted out and with its own sauna, gym, pool and bowling alley.

moderate

Hotel Mercure Hessenland, Obere Königstr. 2, © 91810, fax 918 1160 (DM190). Classic 1950s Art Deco hotel, in the running for national monument status. Efficient, pleasant staff and a good breakfast buffet. No restaurant.

Hotel Chassalla, Wilhelmshöher Allee 99, ℂ 92790, fax 927 9101 (DM190). Small, unpretentious hotel midway between the centre and Wilhelmshöhe. Personal, friendly service. No restaurant.

Hotel Neue Drusel, Im Druseltal 42, ℂ 32056, fax 313 321 (DM135). Peaceful hotel on the edge of the Wilhelmshohe park. Excellent retreat from documenta hype and earnest arty conversations.

inexpensive

Gasthaus Neue Holland, Hüttenbergstr. 6, ℂ 33229 (from DM90). Charming family-run guesthouse near the Wilhelmshöhe park.

Hotel Hamburger Hof, Werner-Hilpert-Str. 18 (entrance Erzberger Str.), ℂ 16002 (DM90). Clean hotel centrally situated near the Hauptbahnhof.

Youth Hostel: Schenkendorfstr. 18, ℂ 776 455.

Eating and Drinking: Restaurants and Taverns

Restaurant Pfeffermühle, Frankfurter Str. 299, ℂ 48050 (DM50–70). Best restaurant in town and favoured hangout of the local bigwigs. The sort of place where the chef flies back from a skiing holiday to prepare a valued customer's favourite sauce. Unelaborate, but superb dishes such as succulent venison and cranberries with wild mushrooms.

Ratskeller, Rathaus, Königstraße (DM20–30). Light meals and seasonal specials. Try the bass cooked in beer and wrapped in pastry.

Zum Postillion, Brüder-Grimm-Platz 4, ℂ 17831 (DM20–30). Comfy basket chairs and tasty food (mainly steaks and pastas).

Königskeller, Königsplatz (DM20–35). Good, central lunchtime stopover. Big salads, pastas and schnitzels.

Bars and Cafés

Eppos Bierhaus, Friedrich-Ebert-Str. 40, ℂ 773 227. Big, noisy, popular beerhall.

Duck Dich, Wilhelmshoüher Allee 296, ℂ 312 881. Friendly student beer and wine bar with beergarden.

Galerie im Hölkeschen Haus, Friedrichstr. 36, ℂ 773 464. Trendy but relaxed café in one of the few old buildings left standing. Serves snacks and soups as well as drinks.

Schloßcafé Wilhelmshöhe, Schloßpark 2, ℂ 32543. Stylish café with terrace view of the Schloß and tasty cream cakes.

The Mosel

The Mosel (French: Moselle) is a swift, sparkling river that twists through dramatic loops and tight hairpin bends. Locals say that it gets its name from the German word for moss, because of its odd green hue. Glistening forests come down to the banks and rows of stubby vines cover dizzily precipitous slopes, where you're surprised to see anything growing at all. You'll find villages with crooked half-timbered houses and crumbling stone-walled alleyways; *Weingüter* where you can sit in vine-covered courtyards sipping choice vintages; famously delicious cuisine, and one of the most breathtaking castles in Germany. The valley attracts its fair share of tourists, but in the villages folk get on with the daunting task of cultivating their vertical vineyards, and the cathartic merriment of their spring and harvest festivals in much the same way as they would do if the tourists were not there.

Getting Around

By Car

A car is by far the most convenient way of seeing the valley. The B49 and B53 criss-cross the river and take you through dozens of wine villages. (For most of the way these roads correspond with the **Mosel Wine Road** (*Mosel Weinstraße*—follow the green and orange signs depicting an M and a bunch of grapes). There are **bridges** at frequent intervals down the river, and often **car ferries** in between. For **car hire** see entries under Trier and Koblenz.

Public Transport

A non-stop **train** journey from Koblenz to Trier takes 90 minutes, but just as the river begins its more convoluted and dramatic twists, the track takes the easy way out and wanders off into far less interesting terrain. If you're relying on public transport, local **buses** between towns are a better option than the train. Services are good, but your progress is still likely to be slow.

By Boat

A sublime way to make the trip—if you have the time. A number of companies offer jaunts on the river. Most are based either at Trier, Cochem or Bernkastel-Kues and offer round-trips and pleasure cruises as well as trips between the towns (stopping off at smaller resorts along the way). To travel the full length of the river you would have to hop between different services, buying a new ticket for each trip—a time consuming and ultimately expensive business. The more attractive stretch of the river is between Cochem and Trier, especially around Bernkastel-Kues. Approximate travel times are: Koblenz–Cochem 4½hr, Cochem–Traben-Trarbach 5¼hr, Traben-Trarbach–Bernkastel-Kues 2hr, Bernkastel-Kues–Trier 5hr.

Köln-Düsseldorfer Lines, Rheinwerft Koblenz, © (0261) 31030: Koblenz–Cochem—also three-day luxury cruises from Frankfurt or Cologne to Trier (from DM416 incl. meals).

Gebrüder Kolb, Briedern, ✆ (02673) 1515; Cochem, ✆ (02671) 7387; Trier, ✆ (0651) 263170: Cochem–Trier.

Undine, Cochem, ✆ (02671) 7431: Pleasure cruises around Cochem.

Hans Michels, Goldbachstr. 52, Bernkastelkues, ✆ (06531) 8222: Bernkastel-Kues–Traben-Tarbach and pleasure cruises around Bernkastel-Kues.

Hiking

Many of the wine villages have a marked *Weinlehrpfad*—an **Educational Wine Trail**—that takes you on an educative route to different estates. There is a famous 350km-long hiking route, the **Moselhöhenweg** (Mosel High Road) between Koblenz and Trier—most of it quite easy going. You can get maps and information from any of the tourist offices along the way.

Tourist Information

Bernkastel-Kues: Gestade 5, ✆ (06531) 4023.

Cochem: Endertplatz, ✆ (02671) 3971.

A cheap alternative to hotels is to stay in private rooms. Tourist information offices carry lists and often have notice boards advertising rooms outside. Alternatively, look out for *Fremdenzimmer* or *Zimmer frei* signs in windows. Prices range from DM40 to DM50 for a double room with breakfast.

For more information on **wine** in this region, write to Weinwerbung Mosel-Saar-Ruwer, Gartenfeldstr. 12a, 5550 Trier, ✆ (0651) 76621.

Festivals

Nearly every village along the Mosel will have a **wine** festival to mark the arrival of the buds in spring or the harvest in autumn. Others have festivals in mid-summer just for the hell of it, and in the late autumn there are *Federweißen* festivals where you can drink the smoky cider-like newly fermented grape-juice. Celebrations often involve the crowning of a Wine Princess (these days usually selected for her knowledge of the trade) and, of course, lots to eat and a good chance to sample Mosel wines. Many locals dress up in *Tracht*, and the bigger festivals often include **folk-dancing competitions**. One of the most spectacular celebrations is at the end of May in **Winningen**, where the local spring festival has become a parade of international traditional dress. Winningen also holds Germany's oldest wine festival (at the end of August), when the town fountain gushes with wine instead of water. The biggest wine festival is in Bernkastel-Kues on the first weekend in September, and the most touristy is at **Cochem**, where, on the last weekend in August, thousands of people pack the streets. Cochem also hosts the **Mosel Wine Week** in mid-June, when vintners from all over the valley set up stall in the riverside carpark and sell samples of their best vintages. For folksier village festivals look out for signs advertising *Weinfest*, *Winzerfest* or *Weinkermis*.

Mosel Wines

A good Mosel Riesling is one of the best wines in the world. It is a tinge darker than water with a clean, hard, slaty taste and little explosions of apple and honey. The Romans first planted vines here over 2000 years ago, because nothing else would grow on the steep slopes. Later the vineyards were taken over by prince-bishops and monasteries, which explains the many religious-sounding labels, such as the awe-inspiring *Bischöfliches Priesterseminar*. The difficult terrain means that most cultivation is still done by hand. As in Roman times, each vine is trained up a stake rather than horizontally along a trellis—something you won't see often outside the Mosel. This enables the grapes to get a lot of fresh air and sun, especially on south-facing slopes, and is one reason that a region so far north can produce such excellent wine.

At one time only Riesling grapes were cultivated here, but many growers have succumbed to the ubiquitous, thoroughly inferior but high-yielding Müller-Thurgau variety (and who can blame them with land that is so hard to work). Not an exciting grape at the best of times, Müller-Thurgau from the Mosel tends to make sharp, curranty wines. Nowadays bottles that don't specify either Müller-Thurgau or Riesling are usually disappointing blends—but the true Riesling from a good vintage will be worth whatever you have to pay for it. Vintage is important in the Mosel. A wet summer can mean that the grapes don't ripen; cold weather can give the wine an acid taste. The best years are 1983, 1985 and—by all reports—1992. Good Rieslings age well in the bottle, and reach their peak after about five years.

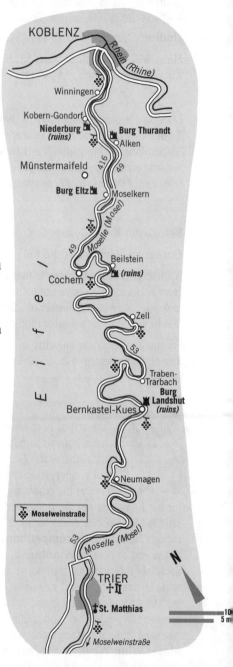

The region includes vineyards along the rivers Saar and Ruwer near Trier, and is divided into five **Bereiche** ('designated districts'). Moseltor and Obermosel, both near the French border, don't produce much of note. Most of the output is turned into party *Sekt*. *Bereich Zell* (stretching from Koblenz past Cochem to Zell) produces some good blended wine, but it is **Bereich Saar-Ruwer** and **Bereich Bernkastel** that come up with the really memorable flavours.

Bereich Bernkastel is a bit of a misnomer—the district takes in most of the middle Mosel, from Zell as far up as the Ruwer. The village of Bernkastel itself has the famous **Doktor** vineyard, which produces Germany's priciest and most renowned wine. (Legend has it that the vineyard was given its name after Bernkastel wines completely cured the fever of an ailing 14th-century bishop.) Rieslings from these slopes are strong, fragrant, deliciously acid wines reminiscent of flowers and honey. **Piesport**, a little further up the river has long south-facing slopes and produces gentler wines that have become popular the world over. As a result, growers who can claim any sort of proximity to the village put 'Piesporter' on their labels, and even the classic estates are under pressure to churn out as many bottles as they can—so standards have dropped. If you want a taste of the sort of wine that really made Piesport famous, you would be better off with a bottle from **Brauneberg**, a village just down the river which has similar south-facing vineyards to Piesport, but can take more care over the wines it produces. The *Bereich* has two curiosities: the 'Zeppelin' wine from the village of Mülheim (near Braunberg), once served on the great airships, and *Nacktarsch* ('Naked Arse'), a wine from the village of Kröv (the name possibly comes from 'nectar').

The best vineyards in *Bereich Saar-Ruwer* are owned by the state, the church, or old families that have worked them for generations. The wines they produce are often quite idiosyncratic—but world-class. Try the intense wines from Maximin Grunhaüser on the Ruwer, or one of the steely Kabinetts from the villages of Ayl or Ockfen, especially from Ockfen's Bockstein or Geisberg vineyards.

Most growers own patches of vineyard on various slopes in the area, but live and make their wine in the village itself. Small shops where you can buy (and often taste) wine are attached to many village *Weingüter*, and some have good restaurants too (*see* **Eating and Drinking** below). From time to time one will have an 'Open Day', when you can visit the cellars and chat with the owners about the wines. Look out for signs advertising *Tag der offenen Keller*—though if you ask nicely many will let you in at other times too. Good producers (other then those already mentioned) include: Lauerburg (Am Markt 27, Bernkastel), Zentralkellerei (Bernkastel, ℂ (06531) 570), Theo Loosen (Mittelstr. 12, Klotten, ℂ (02671) 7501), **Bischöflichen Weingüter** (Gervasiusstr. 1, Trier, ℂ (0651) 43441) and Friedrich-Wilhelm-Gymnasium (Weberbach 75, Trier).

First stop, just a few kilometres out of Koblenz, is **Winningen**, a pretty little village with creaky half-timbered houses, brightly painted murals and overflowing windowboxes. The village has a history of vehement witch-hunting. During the Thirty Years' War 21 women were burnt at the stake on the **Hexenhügel** (Witches' Hill)—now it is a picnic spot. About 5km further on you come to **Kobern-Gondorf**. In the village you can see Germany's oldest half-timbered houses (dating from 1320), but the main attractions here are just out of town. You can follow a path that winds up through the vineyards to the **Niederburg**, a collapsed castle with a neatly restored 14th-century **clock tower**. Higher up you come to the **Oberburg** and the dumpy Romanesque **Matthiaskapelle**, which once supposedly housed the relics of the Apostle Matthew.

Across the river and a kilometre or two down the B49 is the village of **Alken**, built largely out of stone brought down from the vineyards. Above the village is **Burg Thurandt** *(unpublished opening times; check with the regional tourist information office in Koblenz, Bahnhofstr. 9, © (0261) 14024)*. With its clutch of peaked roofs and odd turrets it looks a fitting residence for Count Dracula. There's even a gargoyle over the entrance and a resident howling dog, but inside it is a cosy, eccentric castle made up of odd bits from the 12th century onwards. There is a courtyard garden where you can have coffee, a tiny Baroque chapel cut into the rock and a cluttered *Jagdzimmer* (Hunting Den).

Back on the left bank of the river, about 10km upstream you come to Moselkern. From here you can follow signs to **Burg Eltz** *(Apr–Oct daily 9–5.30, Sun 10–5.30; adm DM6.50)*, a few kilometres inland. It is a long (and at times steep) walk from the **car parks** (adm DM2) to the castle (40min from the lower carparks, 20min from the upper one), but there is a **mini-bus** (DM1.50 per journey) if this seems too daunting. (To get to Burg Eltz by public transport you will need to catch Bus 6039 from Hatzenport (on the Mosel, just before Moselkern) to Münstermaifeld, where you  will be able to get a special bus all the way to the castle.) Burg Eltz lies completely isolated beside a river in a thickly forested gorge. Its strong, high stone walls thrust magnificently above the tree-tops and end in a flippant frill of pixie-capped turrets. The castle is usually filled with tourists and visitable only with a (German) guided tour, but worth every bit of the trouble. It is breathtaking, outside and in. The German art historian George Dehio called it simply '*The* Castle'.

Burg Eltz was probably begun in the 13th century, and for the next 500 years was simultaneously inhabited by three branches of the Eltz family—the Kempenichs, the

Rodendorfs and the Rübenachs. Through the centuries each family built a house of its own. From the inner courtyard you can see all three—the heavy stone Rübenach House along the north wall dates from the 15th century; the more decorative Rodendorf houses, which curve around the east side, were finished in the 16th century; and the white, gabled Kempenich house was built along the south side a hundred years later. Apart from a siege in the 14th century, Burg Eltz has never been attacked (even Napoleon's armies left it alone—a member of the family was a French officer). The castle remains in perfect nick, and is still owned by the Kempenich branch of the family.

The tour trails you through rooms in all three houses. Highlights are the gorgeous wall-paintings in the Rübenach bedchamber (restored in the 19th century), the **Hall of Banners** with spectacular late-Gothic star-vaulted ceilings, and the **Rübenach Untersaal** (living room) with 16th-century Flemish tapestries and a painting attributed to Cranach the Elder, *Madonna of the Grapes*. The **Schatzkammer** (adm DM2.50) is worth the extra entrance fee for the splendid collection of jewellery and precious tableware. There's a drinking vessel in the shape of a boar (1590), made out of a coconut, and another (in gold and silver) of Diana on horseback (1600), with a clockwork mechanism in the base to trundle it along the table.

Where to Stay

Winningen

Hotel Marktschenke, Am Markt 5, ✆ (02606) 355 (DM150). Family-run hotel with simple but comfortable rooms, and wines from its own vineyards.

Kobern-Gondorf

Hotel Simonis, Marktplatz 4, ✆ (02607) 203 (DM98–120). Smart, well-run hotel that has been going for over a century. Also known for its good restaurant.

Pension Kastorschänke, Bahnhofstr. 18, ✆ (02607) 1259 (DM70–80). Half-timbered guesthouse with friendly management and big rooms, though a little near the busy main road.

Eating and Drinking

Winningen

Gutschänke Höreth-Schaaf, Fährstr. 6, ✆ (02606) 597 (DM30). Birgitt Höreth-Schaaf, descendant of an old wine-growing family, runs a superb *Weinstube* in an old stone farm building with a rustic courtyard. Well-selected Moselle wines, and good food too.

Weinhaus Hoffnung, Fährstr. 37, ✆ (02606) 356 (DM30–60). Sedate restaurant with good classic fish dishes, and various cuts of pork in juicy sauces.

Goldene Traube, Herrenstr. 8, ✆ (02606) 2182. Despite its name (Golden Grapes), a speciality beer pub which attracts local boisterous youth.

Schänke beim Weinbauern Thomas Höreth, Im Mühlental 17, ✆ (02607) 6474 (DM30–60). Run by another of the Höreth clan, on the road out to the castle. (Within walking distance of the centre, but not clearly marked—look out for the hanging sign of an angel with a trumpet.) Twelfth-century mill, with snug niches inside and long wooden tables in a shady, secluded courtyard. Wines from the Höreth vineyards and delicious seasonally changing dishes thought up by the Austrian chef.

Hotel Simonis, address above (DM50–90). Top-class restaurant specializing in fish dishes. Baked pike-perch or trout is a good match for a light Mosel wine, though you need something a little tougher to hold its own against the creamy, flavoursome eel dishes.

Cochem to Trier

Cochem, 25km past Moselkern, is the most touristy town on the Mosel, with a brassy, rather jolly seaside atmosphere. It is a busy, noisy place, thronging with coach parties and day-trippers, but somehow keeping a tacky charm. Hemmed in between the river and mountain slopes, it has something of the reckless mood of a holiday island. There is a half-timbered **Marktplatz** with a Baroque **Rathaus**, a church with a 15th-century-style tower (entirely rebuilt after the Second World War) and three of the original **city gates**. From one of these, **Endertor**, a **chairlift** *(daily 9–6, DM5.50)* will brush you over the tops of the vines to the crown of the 255m-high **Pinnerkreuz**, from where you get good views of the town and Mosel valley. On a hill of its own just outside the town is **Reichsburg Cochem**, a multi-turreted 19th-century reconstruction of a medieval castle. The fake interiors are disappointing after Burg Eltz and Burg Thurant, though there are some interesting original 15th-century *Stollenschranke* (chests).

Beilstein, a few kilometres upstream on the right bank, is the complete antithesis of Cochem. A charming little cluster of stone and half-timbered buildings pushes up towards a Baroque church, perched halfway up a slope in the middle of vineyards. High above the village are the straggling ruins of a 13th-century castle. On the diminutive Marktplatz you can see the **Zehnthaus** (1577), a stone building with a pentagonal stairtower where villagers had to pay their taxes (10 per cent of the harvest). Pride of place in the convent church on the hill goes to the **Black Madonna**, an elegant 13th-century Moorish sculpture brought here by Spanish monks. Beilstein is an easy contender for the title of the most beautiful village on the Mosel and is a good place to spend the night.

The double town of **Bernkastel-Kues** straddles the river about 80km upstream from Cochem, nestling at the foot of famous vineyards. In Bernkastel (on the south side) cream and brown half-timbered houses prop each other up around the **Marktplatz**. Standing grandly in their midst is the gold and terracotta **Alte Rathaus** (built 1608, now a restaurant). Teetering precariously on its narrow base, in an alley off the Marktplatz, is the crooked **Spitzgiebelhaus**, built in the 16th century, and now housing a minute *Weinstube*.

Across the river in Kues is the **St Nikolaus-Hospital**, a tranquil building that has served as a home for 33 elderly men for over 500 years. It was founded in 1451 by a great German scholar, diplomat and philosopher, Nikolaus Krebs (known as **Cusanus**—the man from Kues). The **chapel** *(daily 11–5)* is open to the public and contains an altar painting of the *Crucifixion* by the **Master of the Life of the Virgin**, a leading painter of the Cologne School (*see* p. 56). At the foot of the cross Cusanus is pictured at three stages of his life, as rich merchant's son, young priest and cardinal. You can also visit the **Stiftsbibliothek**, an old library lined with huge leather volumes and containing some of Cusanus's astronomical instruments, but for this you need an appointment (information from the tourist office).

For a good view over the town climb up to **Burg Landshut**, in the 13th century a fortress of the Bishop of Trier but now a dramatic ruin.

From Bernkastel-Kues it is just 60km to the gem of the whole region, the city of **Trier**.

Where to Stay

Cochem

Hotel Alte Thorschenke, Brückenstr. 3, ✆ (02671) 7059, fax 4202 (DM65–205). Romantic old building dating back to 1332. Now a comfortable modern hotel, but scattered with heavy antique furniture. The cheaper rooms are a bit cramped.

Hotel Zenthof, Zenthausstr. 9–11, ✆ (02671) 3052, fax 7286 (DM80–140). Old communal bakery recently converted personally by the owner. Real wood rather than veneer, and a clutter of his antique bric-a-brac. The restaurant serves steaks sizzling on hot volcanic rocks.

Pension Hendriks, Jahnstr. 8, ✆ (02671) 7361 (DM50–70). Clean, comfortable pension on the way up to the castle, away from traffic noise and tourist knots.

Beilstein

Haus Lipman, Marktplatz 3, ✆ (02673) 1573 (DM90–120). Cosy old inn on the market place with good service and comfortable rooms.

Altes Zollhaus, 5591 Beilstein, ✆ (02673) 1574 (DM90–120). Quaint little half-timbered building. All the rooms have a view over the Mosel.

Hotel Burgfrieden, 5591 Beilstein, ✆ (02673) 1432, fax 1577 (DM100–110). Well-run hotel on the very edge of town, in the shadow of the castle. Spacious rooms and an in-house sauna and solarium.

Gute Quelle, Marktplatz 34, ✆ (02673) 1437 (DM60–80). Snug little guesthouse on the market square.

Bernkastel-Kues

Hotel Doktor-Weinstuben, Hebegasse 5, ✆ (06531) 6081, fax 6296 (DM140–160). Atmospheric converted 17th-century tithe-house. Richly decorated and efficiently run.

Hotel zur Post, Gestade 17, ✆ (06531) 2022, fax 2927 (DM130–180). Attractive 19th-century building with a tendency to knotty pine and wicker lampshades. The front rooms can be noisy as the hotel is on the busy riverside road.

Burkhard, Burgstraße 1, ✆ (06531) 2380 (DM76–90). Simple, lovingly run guesthouse that has been owned by the same family for over a century. It has been completely modernized and rather fussily decorated, but has lost none of its personal touch.

Eating and Drinking

Cochem

Scloßbergkeller, Schloßstr. 15, ✆ (02671) 3060 (DM20–40). Big, vaulted, candle-lit cellar on the road up to the castle. Inevitably touristy, but well worth a visit for the delicious homemade farm bread and smoked ham (made according to an old family recipe).

Alte Gutsschänke, Schloßstr. 6, ✆ (02671) 8950. Cosy wine tavern with stone walls, thick wooden beams—and a cast-iron fireplace from Norwich.

Café Flair, Moselpromenade, ✆ (02671) 7212. Large balcony and terrace, and the wickedest cream cakes on the Promenade.

Alte Thorschenke, Brückenstr. 3, ✆ (02671) 7059 (DM40–70). Hotel restaurant which serves good local dishes—especially game felled by their own hunters and eel from the Mosel.

Beilstein

Zenthaus-Keller, Marktplatz, ✆ (02673) 1850. Dim 16th-century cellar with furniture hewn from ancient wine vats. Mosel wines and superb local cuisine—such as *Weincräwes* (pork ribs cooked in wine, served on a mound of sauerkraut and potato purée).

Gute Quelle, Marktplatz 34, ✆ (02673) 1437 (DM20–40). Good home cooking in a friendly family restaurant. There is nearly always fresh trout, and also traditional dishes such as *Schoales*, a light meat and potato pie.

Café Klapperburg, 5591 Beilstein, ✆ (02673) 1417. On the ascent to the church. Scrumptious homemade cakes and a collection of coffee mills.

Bernkastel-Kues

Ratskeller, Am Markt 30 (DM30–60). Busy but comfy restaurant in the old 17th-century Rathaus. Tasty local fare such as *Wingertspoal*—pork marinated wine herbs and various peppers, then grilled on a skewer.

Rotisserie Royale, Burgstr. 19, ✆ (06531) 6572 (DM40–60). *Gutbürgerlich* cooking in stylish surrounds—try the pork marinated in Mosel wine and juniper berries, with solid helpings of vegetables.

The countryside immediately to the north of the Mosel is known as the **Mayen-Land**—soft, rolling grassland, dotted with little villages. Wildflowers and wheatfields add patches of yellow as they come into season. It is easy walking country (some jokingly call it *Rentnerferienland*—pensioner holiday territory). Further north the meadows gather themselves up into the stumpy **Eifel** range. This is a relatively deserted spot of the country, popular mainly with Germans on activity holidays. The hills, heathlands, nature parks and volcanic lakes offer all sorts of opportunities to indulge in cross-country skiing, vigorous hiking and healthy watersports. The only part of the Eifel subject to regular tourist invasion is the postcard-pretty **Ahr Valley**, famed for its hearty red wines. (The Ahr runs through the middle of the region and joins the Rhine near Remagen.) To the east, near Andernach, is the vast **Laacher See** and the beautiful Romanesque abbey of **Maria Laach**.

The Benedictine abbey of Maria Laach, 15km from Mayen (Bus 6032 from Mayen, or Bus 6031 from Andernach on the Rhine) is one of the finest examples of Romanesque architecture along the Rhine. A pale building of yellow stone, set in the middle of meadows beside a lake (the Laacher See), it maintains a stately serenity despite the hordes of tourists that invade it daily. The church was begun in the 11th century, though finished only in the 13th, and contains some superb stonecarving—look out especially for the lion fountain and frieze of demons in the **Paradise Portico**, enclosing the western choir. Other highlights include a splendid six-columned **baldachin** over the high altar and the brightly coloured, freestanding tomb of the founder, Count Palatine Henry II.

For more information on the Mayen-Land and Eifel see Directory entries for Mayen, Bad Münstereifel, Daun and Prüm. For towns in the Ahr Valley see Bad Neuenahr-Ahrweiler and Altenahr.

Trier

Sieh um Dich (Look Around You) is the name of a quiet alley beside Trier's cathedral—and nowhere in Germany is an invitation so compelling. Germany's oldest city was once one of the most important in the world—the *Roma Secunda* (Second Rome). A chronicler in AD1 called it *urbs opulentissima* (a most opulent city). Four centuries later the compiler of an almanac mentions it in the same breath as Constantinople, Alexandria and Rome. Six emperors ruled from here, including Constantine the Great. The ruins of their magnificent city are so impressive that they have quite justifiably earned Trier its present nickname—the Rome of the North.

The people of Trier live happily with this heritage. Bits of Roman wall crop up in back gardens. Every time someone digs a deep foundation they unearth something more. (Property developers have a hard time.) The sunny southern temperament seems to have stayed on, too. Trier is a friendly, open place, big enough to swallow up the tourists that flood the rest of the region. It sparkles with the bonhomie that so often goes with wine-producing towns. (The surrounding vines are among the best in the Mosel and a lot of the produce doesn't get beyond the city gates.) There is a new (alarmingly modern) university, so students add to the ragout of tourists, townsfolk and farmers. And to add spice to the pot there are the pilgrims to the birthplace of the city's most famous son, Karl Marx.

History

ANTE ROMAM TREVERIS STETIT ANNIS MILLE TRECENTIS (Trier existed 1300 years before Rome) boasts a 17th-century plaque in the town. This is not really true. Trier was founded by the Emperor Augustus in 16 BC, some 730 years after Romulus and Remus had pottered about the Seven Hills. The city was called Augustus Treverorum, after its founder and the local Celtic tribe he had vanquished. Later this was shortened to Treveris—the French still call the city Trèves.

Roman rule lasted for 500 years, during which Trier became capital of Gaul in AD 268, and later, when Constantine took up residence in 306, capital of the Empire. In 324 Constantine decided that Trier wasn't safe enough to be an imperial capital (it had already been sacked once by the Alemanni), and so he packed up and went to Byzantium, leaving the city to slow decline and further invasion by wandering barbarians. By the end of the 5th century Trier was in the hands of the Franks. In AD 800, under Charlemagne, the local bishops were promoted to archbishops and the city enjoyed a new lease of life as capital of the Electorate of Trier—a position of ecclesiastical and temporal power it enjoyed for the next 1000 years. In AD 882, however, the city was razed to the ground by Vikings who came sailing up the Mosel. In the 11th-century the Archbishop Poppo rebuilt the city almost from scratch.

As the Holy Roman Empire declined, so did Trier. It was one of the first cities to be occupied by the French Revolutionary forces, and never really regained its status in the 19th century. Today it is a provincial town with 100,000 inhabitants (roughly the same as in Constantine's day) who exist largely on the pickings of the tourist and wine industries.

Getting Around

By car: Trier is 118km from Koblenz on Autobahn 48. The more scenic route along the Mosel (B49 and B53) twists through 185km. Trier is 48km from the French border, 72km from the Belgian border, 10km from the Luxembourg border, and just 46km from Luxembourg itself. A small part of the centre of town is pedestrianized, and you can get to most of the main sights on foot. Most **parking** garages are in the streets south of the Hauptmarkt.

Mitfahrzentrale: Karl-Marx-Str. 15, ✆ (0651) 44322.

By train: The Hauptbahnhof is 10 minutes' walk to the north-east of the centre (along Theodor-Heuss-Allee). There are hourly connections to Koblenz (1hr 10min), Cologne (1½hr) and Luxembourg (50min).

By boat: For passenger services along the Mosel *see* **Getting Around** at the beginning of this chapter. Saar-Personenschiffahrt, Laurentiusberg 5, Saarburg, ✆ (06581) 5605, offer cruises on the Saar.

Public transport: A **Tageskarte** (day ticket, DM5) allows one adult accompanied by up to three children to travel anywhere on the city bus network for a 24-hour period. With a **Wochenend-Familienkarte** (Weekend Family Ticket, DM6) three adults and three children can travel on both Saturday and Sunday. The tickets are for visitors to Trier only and are available at the tourist information office.

Taxis: ℰ (0651) 72 525 or 33 030.

Bicycle hire: Bicycles can be hired from the parcel counter at the Hauptbahnhof. The tourist office has maps and suggestions for bicycle tours.

Tourist Information

The **tourist information office** is at the Porta Nigra, ℰ (0651) 978 080, fax 44759 *(May–Aug Mon–Sat 9–6.45, Sun 9–3.30; Sept–Oct Mon–Sat 9–6; Nov–Apr Mon–Fri 9–5, Sat 9–1)*. Staff can help with arranging accommodation and sightseeing tours, booking tickets and can supply maps and information.

Police: ℰ 110.

Medical and pharmaceutical emergencies: ℰ 4 55 55, night service ℰ 1150.

Banks: You'll find branches of the main German banks around the Kornmarkt, Porta Nigra and along Simeonstraße. There is an after-hours exchange at the Hauptbahnhof.

Post office: The main post office is on Bahnhofplatz next to the Hauptbahnhof.

Festivals

Trier has its fair share of **wine festivals**. The main one is at the end of July or beginning of August and involves much dressing up and Bacchanalian campery. At the **Moselfest** (June) there are all sorts of cultural events as well as the usual merry-making. **Carnival** is celebrated with nearly as much fuss as along the Rhine, and there is a big **flower festival** on the first weekend in July.

The Porta Nigra and the Simeonstift

The **Porta Nigra** (Black Gate), probably built at the end of the 2nd century, was the north gate of the old Roman city. Some 30m high and 36m wide, it is the biggest and best preserved Roman gate in the world—a triumphant and defiant pile that looks even more imposing now that age has blackened its yellow sandstone. The tons of masonry were held together by iron clamps, which made the gate nigh on impregnable to puny human assailants. Any that did manage to get through the first portcullis found themselves up against a second one—and open to a storm of missiles, hot oil and molten lead, rained down on them from a gallery inside the arch. After the Romans had left Trier, metal thieves stole the wall-clamps from all the other gates around the city, and then everyone else pillaged the masonry. The Porta Nigra alone was left standing because a holy hermit called

Simeon had lived in it. In 1035 the innovative Archbishop Poppo saw that if he lopped off one of the towers, roofed over the inner courtyard and filled in the arch up to the first floor, he would have a rather nice *Doppelkirche* (Double Church, *see* p. 86). He called the new church St Simeons—and so it remained until 1802 (a Romanesque choir was added in 1150). The gate has now been restored almost to its original state—but viewed from the city side you can clearly see the cut-off tower and rounded Romanesque protrusion. If you look up from inside the arch you can see decorative Rococo carvings around what was once the missile-hurling gallery.

Archbishop Poppo built a religious college, the **Simeonstift**, on the west side of the gate. Its cloister (oddly, on the first floor) is the oldest in Germany. Today the Simeonstift is home to the tourist office, a café and the **Städisches Museum** (City Museum) *(Tues–Fri 9–5, Sat and Sun 9–3; adm DM2)*—a far more interesting institution than the usual dreaded *Heimatsmuseum*. Here you can see the original Market Cross and Steipe statues (*see* below); paintings, furniture and folkloric knick-knacks from Gothic to present-day Trier; a glittering collection of Venetian glass; and Coptic textiles dating back to AD 4.

Simeonstraße and the Hauptmarkt

Simeonstraße, a busy shopping thoroughfare which runs from Porta Nigra to the Hauptmarkt, follows the route of the old Roman high street. The pink house (now an optician's) opposite the tourist office was Marx's home for most of his childhood, though he was born on the other side of town. Further along, at No. 19, is the **Dreikönigenhaus** (House of the Three Wise Men, 1230), a fortified patrician mansion. When it was built there would have been no entrance at ground level. You can see the original front door on the first floor—people had to climb in and out on a retractable wooden ladder.

The **Hauptmarkt** is a colourful pot-pourri of architectural styles from Gothic to Baroque, and human types from rosy-cheeked flower-sellers to drug-dazed (though amiable) punks. The latter seem drawn to the gaudy **Petrusbrunnen**, a replica of a 16th-century fountain (the original is in the Städtisches Museum). Next to it is a replica of the original **Market Cross** that was erected in AD 958. The main building on the Markt is the **Steipe** (1430–83), a festival hall named after the base of pillars and Gothic arches that seem to suspend it disdainfully above the daily bustle of the square, like a high-born lady lifting her skirts through the mud. Replicas of statues of the city's patron saints and of two armoured giants (guardians of civil liberty) adorn the façade. One knight looks out across the market, the other 'blind and deaf' with his visor down faces the cathedral—a direct snub to the archbishops, who tried to supress the rise of civic power. Next door is the curly-gabled, aptly named **Rotes Haus** (Red House, 1684). Here you can read the inscription proclaiming Trier to be older than Rome.

A little way further down Dietrichstraße is the **Frankenturm**, a Romanesque tower-house. On the south side of the Markt a chunky **Baroque portal**, wedged between two houses, leads through to **St Gangolf**, a Gothic church with a massive white tower put up by the burghers in 1507 to get one up on the archbishop. This tower was taller than any on the cathedral—but not for long. The archbishop retaliated by extending one of the steeples on his church in a determined display of his authority.

The Domfreihof

To the west of the market is the Domfreihof, a complex of buildings centring on the **Dom**. To celebrate the 20th year of his reign (AD 326) Emperor Constantine began to build four churches: St Peters in Rome, the Church of the Holy Sepulchre in Jerusalem, the Church of the Nativity in Bethlehem, and the cathedral at Trier (an indication of how important Trier was at the time). Constantine's cathedral was built on the site of a church founded by his mother, the Empress Helena, in a wing of her palace. Recently some magnificent ceiling paintings from the original Roman stateroom were discovered under the altar platform. After years of painstaking restoration, these are now on display in the **Diözesanmuseum** (*see* below). All that is left of Constantine's cathedral (which was, in fact, a complex of two different churches) are two of the four 12.5m-high columns that supported the ceiling. One is in the courtyard between the present cathedral and the Liebfrauenkirche, the other (known as the **Domstein**) is at the south portal. Legend has it that this pillar was thrown to the ground in anger by the Devil, who had been tricked into transporting the other three in the belief that he was helping to build an enormous drinking tavern. Various invaders have gutted the Trier cathedral. There were two major early attempts at rebuilding it—one in the 6th century, and one (by Archbishop Poppo) in the 11th. Most of what you see today is Poppo's church. Later additions pale beside this solid edifice, but one of the delights of the cathedral is its mixture of styles—the Gothic extension to one of its square Romanesque towers, bits of earlier Frankish masonry in the walls, a gorgeous 18th-century stuccoed ceiling and a beautifully crafted swallow's-nest organ, built in 1974.

Inside, the cathedral is light, airy and relatively plain. **Hans Rupprecht Hoffmann**, the local sculptor responsible for the Petrusbrunnen, contributed a **pulpit** (1570–72) and the **Ali Saints' Altar** (1614), both encrusted with figures and flourishes. The Romanesque **tympanum** (1180–1200) over the portal leading to the Liebfrauenkirche is a simpler, more poignant affair. Christ sits between St Peter and the Virgin, all three draped in delicately carved robes that bear traces of the original colouring. You'll also find the relic to top all relics—the **Seamless Robe of Christ**, allegedly brought from Jerusalem by the Empress Helena. This is kept locked tight inside a modern shrine in the Baroque **Heiltumskammer** at the east end of the church. The last time the robe was displayed for pilgrims was in 1959. Rumour has it that you could strike lucky again in 1996. Nearby is the entrance to the **Schatzkammer** *(Apr–Oct Mon–Sat 10–12 and 2–5, Sun 2–5; Nov–Mar Mon–Sat 10–12 and 2–4; adm DM1)*, where the main attraction is an odd 10th-century portable altar containing the **foot of St Andrew**, which looks like a jewel-encrusted bootblack's box.

From the **cloister** off the south side of the cathedral you get the best view of the mosaic of masonry and styles that make up the Domfreihof—from bits of Roman wall to extensions dating from the 18th century. Next door is the Gothic **Liebfrauenkirche**, almost as old as Marburg's Elizabethskirche (*see* p. 200), but already showing signs of French ornament. The ground plan resembles a rose (face down, with the steeple as its stem)—a symbol of the Virgin. The interior of the church is a murky forest of columns—one for each of the apostles—faintly lit through modern, deeply coloured stained-glass windows.

To the north of the cathedral is the **Bischöfliches Dom und Diözesanmuseum** (Diocesan Museum) *(Mon–Sat 9–1 and 2–5, Sun 1–5; adm DM1)*, where the highlight is the superb Roman ceiling painting transferred from the ruins of the Empress Helena's palace. It took experts years to piece together all the fragments; arguments raged for weeks about the positioning of a single chip. Most of the panels are intact, showing frolicking cherubs and larger portraits in astonishingly bright colours. You can also see a model of Constantine's original cathedral, and a collection of important statues from local churches.

South of the Domfreihof

Following Liebfrauenstraße south from the Liebfrauenkirche you pass the **Palais Kesselstatt**, a Baroque patrician palace tucked neatly into a curve in the street, yet still mustering a sumptuous portal. Today it houses wine-tasting rooms (if you ask the staff you can also visit the candle-lit cellars, lined with oak vats). Further along, across Konstantinplatz, you come to the **Konstantinbasilika** *(Easter–Oct Mon–Sat 9–1 and 2–6, Sun 11–1 and 2–6; Nov–Easter Tues–Sat 11–12 and 3–4, Sun 11–12; adm free)*, a gigantic brick throne room built by the Emperor Constantine (a man who never did things by halves). The Porta Nigra itself could fit inside the hall twice over. When German tribes invaded Trier they set up a whole village within the walls of the audience chamber.

Romans entering the hall would behold their Emperor, raised in a semi-circular apse, across a full 70m of heated marble floor, and lit by sunlight filtering through rows of thin alabaster window panes. The vast, wooden 30m-high free-hanging ceiling was such a triumph of design that builders reconstructing the basilica in the 1950s couldn't repeat it, and cheated by using reinforced concrete. In Roman times the building was richly decorated and covered in red plaster (you can still see remnants in the window apses). After the Romans withdrew, the building fell into decay. In the 19th century it was restored as a Protestant church, and given the austere interior you see today. Underneath the basilica is a network of **catacombs** and a 1st-century street *(guided tours, daily 3pm; adm free)*.

Adjoining the Konstantinbasilika is the **Roter Turm** (Red tower), the best preserved part of the 17th-century **Kurfürstliches Schloß** (Archbishop-Elector's Palace), which was destroyed during the Second World War. Next door is the **Rokoko-Palais der Kurfürsten**, a pink and white palace built with delicious flair by Johannes Seiz, one of Balthasar Neumann's brightest pupils, for an 18th-century archbishop who didn't like the old palace. The archbishop's successor didn't like the new palace either, and went to live in Koblenz where he built himself a more fashionable Neoclassical Residence. The Rococo palace was relegated to being a guest house, spent a couple of centuries as a barracks and was finally bombed to bits in the Second World War—all except the façade which survives in perfecly restored splendour overlooking a classical **garden** dotted with dozing students and Rococo statuary.

At the southern end of the garden is the **Rheinisches Landesmuseum** *(Mon 10–4, Tue–Fri 9.30–4, Sat 9.30–1, Sun 9–1; adm free)*, a treasure trove of Roman pottery, figurines and other relics. The burial monuments rank with the finest known, there are superbly preserved mosaics and masterpieces of early pottery fit for the tables of the opulent imperial capital. The museum's prize possessions are the **Diatretglas**, an elegant vessel surrounded by a filigree net cut from a single piece of glass, and the famous **Neumanger Weinschiff**, a carving of a Roman wine ship found at Neumagen-Dhron, just down the Mosel. The boat is complete with crew and barrels, which means it was transporting local produce—Roman wine came in amphorae.

A few minutes' walk west of the Landesmuseum, at Weberbach 25, you'll find the **Schatzkammer der Stadtbibliothek** (Municipal Library Treasure Room) *(Mon–Fri 1–5, Nov–Easter Wed 1–5; adm DM2)*. Here there are further rich surprises, including a Gutenberg Bible; the **Ada Evangel**, a 9th-century book with a 4th-century cameo of Constantine on the cover; the lavishly illustrated 10th-century **Codex Egberti**; letters from Goethe and Karl Marx and a 5m-long 19th-century railway map.

The Kaiserthermen and the Amphitheater

At the end of Weberbachstraße you'll find Trier's most evocative Roman remains, the **Kaiserthermen** (Imperial Baths) *(Jan–mid-Mar Tues–Sun 9–1 and 2–5; mid-Mar–Sept daily 9–6; Oct daily 9–1 and 2–5; Nov Tues–Sun 9–1 and 2–5; Dec daily 10–4; adm DM2)*. This massive bathhouse extended as far as the Konstantinbasilika and way beyond the busy modern streets that now hem in the ruins (a map at the east entrance gives you an idea of the layout). Emperor Constantine began work on the baths, but left for Byzantium before they were fully completed so the complex was never used in its entirety. Bathing in Roman times was a serious business. After a good steam you soaked in the *caldarium* (hot bath), splashed about a while in the luke-warm *tepidarium*, then plunged into the icy *frigidarium*, before romping about energetically on the *palaestra* (sports ground). Here the *caldarium* (at the east entrance) is the best preserved of the rooms—a towering structure of elegant brick arches that later served as a model for the western wing of Archbishop Poppo's cathedral, and as a city gate from medieval times up to the beginning of the 19th century. You can also see the outline of the small round *tepidarium*, and dip underground into the network of low passages through which slaves carried fuel to heat the floors. These tunnels—pieced together from the cellars of bombed out houses after the Second World War—give you a better impression of the baths' extent than anything on the surface.

Ten minutes' walk north-east of the Kaiserthermen, along Olewiger Straße, is the **Amphitheater** *(same times and prices as Kaiserthermen, closed Dec)*, Trier's oldest Roman ruin. Twenty thousand people would crowd into this hollowed-out hilltop to watch bloody gladiatorial clashes. You can still see the tiers for the stone seats, the cages where the wild animals were kept, and the square holes in the floor through which gladiators were brought to the surface by lift—and into which dead bodies were thrown at the end of the contest. On the western, imperial, side there is a tunnel leading into the arena so that (when he was quite sure it was safe) the emperor could nip down and show off a little.

West of the Hauptmarkt

A stroll from the Hauptmarkt, down Fleischstraße to Brückenstr. 10, brings you to Marx's birthplace, the **Karl-Marx-Haus** *(Nov–Mar Mon 3–6, Tues–Sun 10–1 and 3–6; Apr–Oct Mon 1–6, Tues–Sun 10–6; adm DM3)*. The founder of modern communism was born to well-to-do Jewish parents in 1818, though he spent much of his adult life in Paris and London. The museum devotes itself to dry expositions of his economic and political theory, rather than dwelling on gossipy aspects of his life (such as the affair with his maid and his troublesome spotty bottom), but you can see some hand-written love poems (almost as soppy as his prose is turgid), first editions of *Das Kapital* and rare early editions of the Communist Manifesto.

Further down towards the Mosel are the **Barbara-Thermen** *(same times and prices as Kaiserthermen, but closed Dec and Mon in Oct)*. These 2nd-century baths were once the second biggest in the Roman Empire, though these days little remains except an outline—fragments of the lower walls and the under-floor heating system. On the banks of the river itself you can see two old **cranes**, one from the 18th-century and one dating back to 1413. Nearby is the **Römerbrücke**, a modern bridge resting on massive Roman pillars. In Roman times there was an altar halfway across the bridge, and travellers would toss coins into the water as an offering to the gods—so today at low tide the muddy banks swarm with treasure hunters with metal detectors.

Further afield

Fifteen minutes' walk south of the centre (along Saarstraße and Matthiasstraße, Bus 3 or 4) is the **St Matthias Basilika** *(daily 7–6 except during services)*, a freshly restored Romanesque Benedictine abbey church with grand Baroque embellishments. The church contains the only Apostle's grave north of the Alps—that of St Matthias. He replaced the traitor Judas Iscariot after drawing lots with the rival candidate, Joseph Barsabas. The most beautiful parts of the abbey are the early Gothic cloisters and dormitory, but these can only be seen after smooth talking and an appointment (℗ (0651) 32634).

On the other side of town near the Hauptbahnhof (down Reichsabtei, Bus 3 or 4) is **St Paulin** *(daily 8–6, closed Fri mornings)*. Balthasar Neumann designed the church in 1757 for Archbishop-Elector Felix (a member of the von Schönborn family, whose members monopolized Neumann's talents). The austere exterior belies what the building has in store for you. Neumann's idea was that entering the church should be like passing through the gates of heaven. Sunlight floods in through tall windows, almost hidden behind the pillars, giving you the impression that the whole crisp white interior—dangling with Rococo cherubs and stucco foliage, encrusted with gold and adorned with pale, ethereal ceiling paintings—is glowing with a soft unearthly light of its own. Look out especially for the high altar and main choir stalls, designed by Neumann and made by the court sculptor Ferdinand Tiez.

The best **view** over Trier is from the **Weißhaus** across the Mosel. You can get there by **cable car** *(Mon–Fri 9–6, Sat and Sun 9–7; DM4 single, DM5 return)* from Zurlaubener Ufer, near the Kaiser-Wilhelm-Brücke (walking time 15min). The best time to go is in the early evening—as the sun sets and the monuments of Trier light up. Wine-buffs might like to take a trip out along Olewiger Straße (Bus 6 or 26), just past the amphitheatre. Once a **wine village**, though now a suburb of Trier, Olewig is home to many of the city's best wine producers (*see* **Mosel Wines**, p. 212). The **Trier Weinlehrpfad** (Educational Wine Trail) takes you through the vineyards to show how wine is made. Maps and explanatory leaflets are available from the tourist office, who can also help with details of **wine tastings** and **cellar visits**.

Trier ℗ (0651–)   ### Where to Stay

expensive

Hotel Dorint Trier, Porta-Nigra-Platz 1, tel. 27010, fax 2701170 (DM200–270). Swish, slickly run, central hotel with views across to the Porta Nigra. Famed for the groaning board at its breakfast buffet.

moderate

Altstadt Hotel, Porta-Nigra-Platz, ℗ 48041 (DM150–200). Smart, well-run, though otherwise unremarkable. Somewhere to fall back on when everywhere else is full. No restaurant.

Villa Hügel, Bernhardstr. 4, ✆ 33066, fax 37958 (DM140–175). White Jugendstil villa on a hill in the south of town. Upmarket in an understated way. Creature comforts include a sauna, an indoor pool and a roof terrace.

Petrisberg, Sickingerstr. 11–13, ✆ 41 181 (DM125–150). Modern hotel right in the middle of the vineyards, overlooking Trier. Run by a friendly family attentive to your every need.

Hotel Christophel, Simeonstr. 1, ✆ 74041, fax 74732 (DM110–120). Small hotel next to the Porta Nigra, well-run with a friendly, personal atmosphere.

inexpensive

Weingut Becker, Olewiger Str. 206, ✆ 938080, fax 938 0888 (DM80–110). Rustic wine-grower's house with its own cellar, good wines, good cheer and comfortable rooms.

Zur Glocke, Glockenstr. 12, ✆ 73109 (DM70). Hearty student drinking inn with a few rooms upstairs. Lively but comfortable.

Uranus, Mosel-Oberstau, ✆ (06502) 5880 (from DM22 per person). Youth hostel atmosphere on a boat moored on the Mosel. Single and double rooms too.

Youth Hostel: Maarstr. 156, ✆ 29292.

Eating and Drinking: Restaurants and Taverns

Tucked behind the Kaizer-Wilhelm-Brücke, trailing along the Mosel is a stretch of pretty little houses, painted in bright colours—once part of the fishing village of **Zurlauben**. Most of the cottages are now restaurants, with Mediterranean-style terraces under the vines. **Bagatelle** is the pick of the cheaper cafés, and also serves well-prepared salads and light meals. **Pfeffermühle**, ✆ 26133 (DM75–110), serves classic French cuisine, with an outstanding goose-liver paté and perfectly cooked salmon.

Zum Domstein, Hauptmarkt 5, ✆ 74490 (DM40–60). When the Grachers were digging out a new cellar under their restaurant near the cathedral, they unearthed hundreds of Roman cooking artefacts. The likelihood that her restaurant was on the site of the Empress Helena's kitchen inspired Rosemary Gracher to years of fervent research. The result is a Roman dining cellar, decorated with the bits and pieces that were dug up, where you can eat meals taken directly from the world's oldest cookbook, a 2000-year-old tome by Marcus Gavius Apicius. From the simplest *Mustea* (roll made with wine and cheese) to *Cervus assus* (venison with plums, honey, wine and vinegar) or *Copadiae* (veal in a pine-nut sauce with herbs and onions), the menu is a delight. You can round off the meal with a fruit soufflé and wash it down with Etruscan wine. Upstairs you can get tasty *gutbürgerliche* and vegetarian dishes (DM15–35).

Palais Kesselstatt, Liebfrauenstr. 9, ✆ 40204 (DM40–60). Converted 18th-century wine cellar with superb range of wines and a good, changing menu.

Historische Keller, Simeonstr. 46, © 469496 (DM20). Beneath the Karstadt department store. An odd place for a medieval cellar—but this was yet another surprise, discovered when the shop was building extra storage space. Good place for a cheap and tasty lunch.

Löwenbrauerei-Ausschank, Bergstr. 46, © 74846 (DM15–25). Leafy beergarden serving good local specialities. Try the Schwenkbraten (marinated pork grilled on beechwood) or baked fish.

Bars and Cafés

Zur Glocke, Glockenstr. 12, © 73109. Old pub with the atmosphere of a Heidelberg student tavern.

Café Brunnenhof, Im Simeonstift, © 48584. In the calm, pretty cloister of the Simeonstift, just behind the tourist office. Good for a coffee and elaborate ice-cream.

Mephisto, Am Irminen Freihof. Trendy pub with big, packed beer garden and cheap tasty food.

Asterix, Karl-Marx-Str. 11. Laid-back student bar with a quiet terrace and an abundance of good-value food.

In Flagrante, Viehmarkt 13. Ageing students in their umpteenth semester, and graduates who can't bring themselves to leave town.

South of the Mosel

Between the Mosel and the River Nahe, which runs almost parallel to it in the south, is the **Hunsrück**, a lonely, hilly region of forests and small villages known mainly for its semi-precious stones. The outside world (apart from jewellers and gem-cutters) would hardly know of the Hunsrück if it were not for Edgar Reitz's 15-hour film epic **Heimat**. Reitz was born here in 1932, and his saga of the fortunes of the Simon family between 1919 and 1982 is based on his memories. Local villages cash in on being part of the amalgam that made up his imaginary town of Schabbach.

See Directory entry for Idar-Oberstein.

Southwest of the Nahe is the **Saarland**, one of the poorest of Germany's *Länder*. There are some attractive wooded bits nearer the Hunsrück, but most of the *Land* is given over to coal-mining, steelworks and other heavy industry—all of them these days pretty much in the doldrums. Over the centuries the Saarland has ping-ponged between Germany and France, though nowadays French influence is detectable only in the odd *Salü* in place of *Guten Tag* and in a gallant Gallic attempt to brighten up local cuisine (which seems to consist mostly of potato dishes). East of the Saarland, just north of the French border is the **Pfälzer Wald** (Palatinate Forest), a thick, unspoiled forest, most of which has been declared a nature reserve, which shelters a few sleepy villages and lonely castles. Further east, back on the Rhine, you come to the rather elegant little town of Speyer.

See Directory entries for Saarbrücken, Annweiler and Worms.

Speyer

Speyer began as a Celtic, and then a Roman, settlement, but had its glory days at the beginning of the second millenium, when Conrad II, the first of the **Salian Emperors** built a great cathedral here as a suitable spot for his new dynasty to have their tombs. The town was dealt savage blows by both the Thirty Years' War and the 17th-century Palatine War of Succession, and limped through the following years with most of its population in exile, and its buildings in ruins. It was only in the 19th century, when Speyer became a seat of provincial administration, that the town began to recover. Today many of the old buildings have been impressively restored, and the town is certainly worth a few hours' visit.

Getting Around

By car: Speyer is just off Autobahn 9, 56km from Karlsruhe. You can also get there along Autobahn 5 from Frankfurt (90km).

By train: A local train runs to Ludwigshafen, where there are connections to Mainz (1¼hr), Frankfurt (2hr) and Saarbrücken (1¼hr). The Hauptbahnhof is 10 minutes' walk northwest of the centre, along Bahnhofstraße. Once in the town you'll find all the sights within a few minutes' walk of each other.

Tourist Information

The **tourist information office** is at Maximilianstr. 11, © (06232) 14395 *(Mon–Fri 9–5, Sat 10–12)*.

The Dom

Speyer's cathedral, begun in 1030, is arguably the peak of Rhineland Romanesque. It is a massive church—the biggest of the Romanesque period—with a delicately patterned façade and a plain, airy interior. This simplicity is less by design than the result of centuries of pillaging and looting. The cathedral burned down during the 17th-century Palatine Wars of Succession and barely survived the invasion of the French Revolutionary armies a hundred years later, when anything flammable was thrown on a huge bonfire in front of the west portal. In 1794 a devastated townsman wandered about the shell of the church and saw 'all the altars smashed dreadfully and the torsos of the shattered statues of the best craftsmen lying around... Organ, pulpit and all the chairs, be it in the choir, be it in the nave, have vanished.' Only Napoleon's desire to use the front façade as a triumphal arch saved the cathedral from demolition or conversion into a pig market. Rebuilding during the 19th century was slow and sporadic, and most of what you see today dates back to a concerted effort in the 1950s.

The order and simplicity of the interior can be seen to best effect in the **crypt** which, with its gentle arches and coloured pillars, has a peaceful mosque-like quality. Here you'll find the tombs of eight emperors and kings—including Rudolph von Hapsburg, the first of that line to be a German monarch.

To the left of the choir is a replica of the miraculous **Speyer Madonna**. The original 13th-century statue allegedly used to chat with St Bernard of Clairvaux, while he carried out his daily custom of making three large jumps towards the altar. One day the Virgin rebuked the saint for being late and he muttered '*Mulier tacet in ecclesia*' ('Women should be silent in church'). The statue remained suitably mute from then on.

Around the Dom

Just in front of the cathedral's main portal is the **Domnapf** (1490), a huge bowl that used to be filled with wine whenever a new bishop came to town. The crush to empty it again was so great that people fell in, and had to be carried home half-drowned and completely drunk. In the **Domgarten**, an informal English park laid out south and east of the cathedral, you can see the **Mount of Olives**, a 15th-century shrine with oddly effeminate statues, carved in 1856 to replace originals destroyed by the French. Further into the gardens you'll come across one of the two surviving bits of the medieval city wall, the **Heidentürmchen** (Heathens' Tower).

North of the cathedral (across Edith-Stein-Platz and down Sonnengasse) is the **Kloster St Magdelena**, a working Dominican nunnery. Parts of the complex date back to the 13th century, but the peaceful chapel is rather subdued Baroque.

Diagonally across from the cathedral, on Domplatz, is the **Historisches Museum der Pfalz** (Historical Museum of the Palatinate) *(daily 9–5; adm DM2)* where the prize exhibits are the conical **Golden Hat of Schifferstadt**, made in the 14th century from a single sheet of gold, and what is claimed to be the world's oldest bottle of wine, dating back to AD 300. In the old Jewish quarter, just north of the museum (up Große Pfaffengasse and along Judengasse) you can see a 12th-century **Mikwe** (ritual bath-house) *(Apr–Oct daily 10–12 and 2–5; adm DM1)*.

Around Maximilianstraße

Speyer's broad main street parades from the cathedral door past brightly painted Baroque buildings up to the solid, four-square **Altpörtel** *(Apr–Oct Mon–Fri 10–12 and 2–4, Sat and Sun 10–5; adm DM1)*, the only other surviving part of the city wall, dating back to 1230. From the gallery at the top (added in the 16th-century) you get a good view out over the town. Along Maximilianstraße you'll also find the red **Rathaus** (1712–26) and the **Alte Münze** (Old Mint, 1749), with a Dutch-style gable. On Große Himmelgasse, which runs alongside Maximilianstraße, you can see the **Retscherhof**, a ruined patrician palace, and the **Dreifaltigkeitskirche** a Baroque Protestant church with a lavish interior, put up after the town was razed in 1689.

Hotel Domhof, Bauhof 3, ✆ 13290 (DM180–260). Classy hotel in one of Speyer's historic courtyards. Tastefully decorated rooms and a beergarden that serves a delicious in-house brew.

Hotel Goldener Engel, Mühlturmstr. 27, ✆ 13260 (DM140–190). A comfortable old hotel near the Altpörtel that has been run by the same family for well over a century.

Hotel Luxhof, An der Speyerer Rheinbrücke, 6832 Hockenheim, ✆ (06205) 3030, fax 30325 (DM115–140). Family-run hotel set in trees overlooking the Rhine, near the Speyer Bridge. Commodious rooms, beer terrace and a sauna.

Gasthaus Grüne Au, Grüner Winkel 28, ✆ 72196 (DM60 without private facilities–DM80). Well-run little guesthouse in a quiet corner of town. Friendly service, and convenient for all the sights.

Youth Hostel: Geibstr. 5, ✆ 75380.

Eating and Drinking

Zum alten Engel, Hotel Goldener Engel, Mühlturmstr. 27, ✆ 132680 (DM25–50). Cosy cellar restaurant which serves good *Bretzel* (crispy, salted bread—a local speciality), tasty fish dishes and bakes.

Pfalzgraf, Gilgenstr. 26b, ✆ 74755 (DM25–60). Sedate restaurant with excellent game dishes.

Gasthaus zum Domnapf, Domplatz 1, ✆ 75454 (DM20–40). Hearty *Pfalz* cuisine, with especially good fish dishes and a filling Bretzel soup.

Zum Halbmond, Nikolausgasse 4, ✆ 24539 (DM20–50). Historical 17th-century half-timbered inn, near the somewhat pungent Speyerbach stream. Serves Hungarian food—spicy goulashes and soups you can stand your spoon up in.

Rabennest, Korngasse 5, ✆ 74446 (DM15–30). Simple *Weinstube* in a pretty side-street off Maximilianstraße. Haunt of locals with a reputation for good food (menu changes daily—look out for asparagus dishes in season).

Café Plusch, Korngasse. One of the many attractive watering holes along Korngasse, where Speyer's trendies foregather.

Baden-Württemberg

Baden-Württemberg is the source of sticky chocolate cake, cherry brandy and Mercedes-Benz. It boasts Germany's highest waterfall, sunniest town, twistiest railway and the tallest church steeple in the world. The names of the lofty local nobility—Hohenstaufen, Hohenzollern and Hohelohe—resound throughout German history, and over this region, from fortresses *hoh* atop the hills of the Swabian Jura. The landscape is dotted with chunky thatched cottages and encrusted with Baroque cloisters, and it has the densest concentration of castles in the country. You can wander through wildly romantic forests, ski on Alpine slopes, swim in vast, limpid lakes or banish your rheumatism in thermal spas.

This variety is the result of a rather curious match. The slender Duchy of Baden once trailed the Rhine from Heidelberg, through the Black Forest—dark haunt of hobgoblins and wood-spirits—and on to the temperate climes and crisp air of Lake Constance. Its folk were Roman Catholic and festive, as the bells and pom-poms of their national dress would suggest. In 1952 Baden was, rather reluctantly, yoked to the robust and hilly Württemberg, home to the Swabians—earthy Protestants with a reputation even among Germans for being ploddingly industrious.

A 19th-century British traveller wrote that the Swabians were 'hardy fatteners of snails and distillers of cherry water, a tribe, however, of whose intelligence their fellow countrymen entertain so low an opinion, that, all over Germany, a piece of gross stupidity is proverbially termed a *Schwabenstreich*.' Even today the *Schwob* is the butt of many a German joke—perhaps because of the faintly comic, bumpkin drawl with which they speak High German. Their pithy turn of phrase in the homeground of their own dialect, though, seems to inspire envy. *Leck mi am Ärschle* (kiss my arse) has acquired national currency, though it's still euphemized as 'the Swabian Greeting'.

Homespun sloggers they may be, but the Swabians can claim credit for the invention of the car, the bicycle, the airship, jet turbines and diesel engines, the astronomical telescope, calculators and cuckoo clocks, even the mouth organ and teddy bear. Local bright sparks include the philosophers Schelling and Hegel, writers Schiller and Hölderlin, and also Albert Einstein and Field-Marshal Rommel. Ingenuity and industry are a good mix, and despite the jokes, Baden-Württemberg has become the richest *Land* in the Federal Republic. The glossy high-tech factories that generate the wealth nestle unobtrusively in picture-book countryside. Tourists flock in and everyone seems very happy indeed—though beneath the blissful surface, tribal currents still pull strongly in different directions.

Unsuspecting travellers, fresh from the breezes of Rhineland or Black Forest bonhomie, sometimes find the Swabian atmosphere a little stifling.

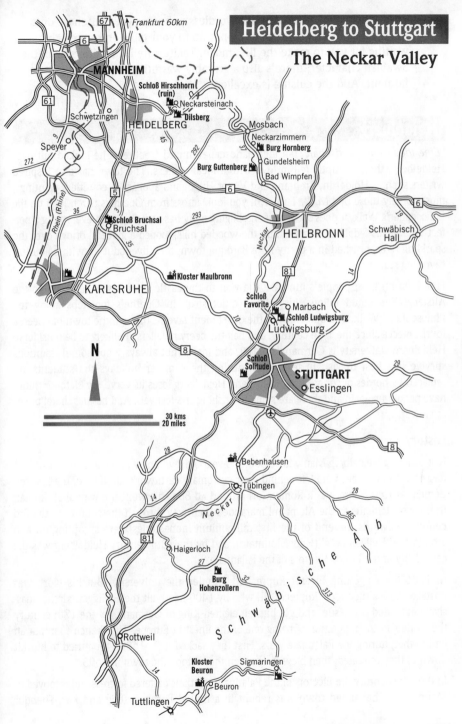

Frankfurt 60km

MANNHEIM

Schloß Hirschhorn (ruin)

Neckarsteinach

Dilsberg

HEIDELBERG

Schwetzingen

Mosbach

Neckarzimmern

Burg Hornberg

Gundelsheim

Speyer

Burg Guttenberg

Bad Wimpfen

Rhein (Rhine)

Schloß Bruchsal
Bruchsal

HEILBRONN

Schwäbisch Hall

Kloster Maulbronn

KARLSRUHE

Schloß Favorite

Marbach

Schloß Ludwigsburg

Ludwigsburg

N

Schloß Solitude

STUTTGART

Esslingen

30 kms
20 miles

Bebenhausen

Tübingen

Neckar

Haigerloch

Burg Hohenzollern

Schwäbische Alb

Rottweil

Kloster Beuron

Sigmaringen

Beuron

Tuttlingen

Don't worry when the assistant wordlessly thumps your purchase onto the shop counter, or the waiter lopes up to your table and stares glumly waiting for you to make the first move. Taciturnity is just one side of the Swabian character; there's also a grumbly warmth and a doughty sense of humour. And the cuisine is excellent.

Heidelberg

'*Eine idealische Landschaft*' (an ideal landscape) mused Goethe as he looked out over Heidelberg, then promptly fell in love with a local poetess. The town has also inspired writers such as Hölderlin, Brentano and Victor Hugo, and appears in countless paintings, most notably those by J.M.W. Turner. If you look across from Goethe's perch high on the Philosopher's Walk, it does seem as if an obliging deity has come up with everything a perfect vista needs—dabbed a castle onto the wooded hills, looped a graceful bridge over the sparkling river, brushed in a pretty little Baroque town, then livened it up with colourful, cavorting students.

First item on most people's itinerary is a visit to the castle, then a wander through the Altstadt. You could follow this with a quiet stroll in Goethe's footsteps along the Philosophers' Walk, or a pub crawl of the old student taverns (though the town has been a tourist mecca since the 19th century, and half the beery revellers are likely to be outsiders). Heidelberg University is Germany's oldest, and many (not always wholesome) traditions survive. It's best to visit in term-time: during the summer holidays the students are replaced by hordes of congress delegates, and Heidelberg loses its verve. By October things have perked up again and there are some flourishing arts festivals. And besides, hotel prices are lower.

History

Not counting Heidelberg Man whose 600,000-year-old jawbone was unearthed in 1907, or forgotten Celtic tribes who left behind their customary earthworks in 400 BC, the first settlement at Heidelberg was a Roman fort around AD 80. This went the way of all Roman frontier settlements as the Alemanni marauded their way through the country in the 3rd century. Towards the end of the first millennium monasteries were sprouting on and around the 'Heiligenberg' (Holy Mountain), and by the 13th century Heidelberg was the capital city of the Prince Electors of the Palatinate.

In 1386 the go-getting Elector Ruprecht I founded the university. But his work was upstaged by his successor, Ruprecht III, who by 1400 had built the Heiliggeistkirche, massively extended the castle, and got himself elected King of Germany. By the 17th century the castle had the reputation of being one of the finest in Europe. The French soon put an end to that, during the Palatinate wars. First they sacked it (in 1689), then tried to burn it down as they retreated, then blew it up when they retook the town in 1693.

In the 18th century the Electors of the Palatinate left their battered fortress and removed to Mannheim. The ruined town was rebuilt in a muted Baroque style and Karl-Theodor attempted to restore the castle, but was foiled in 1764—this time by an act of God, lightning. The abandoned and gloomy ruins inspired German Romantic writers and in the 19th century Heidelberg revelled in new-found popularity. The university flourished, and by the 1930s was producing record numbers of Nobel Prize winners. The town was spared by Allied bombers during the Second World War, and was subsequently chosen as the location for the US European Army Headquarters. The military presence, branches of two US universities in town and the relentless popularity of the American operetta *The Student Prince* (about a Heidelberg student who falls hopelessly in love with a barmaid) ensure that Heidelberg sits comfortably near the top of the itineraries of most visitors from the States. Some nights over 10 per cent of the people going to bed in Heidelberg are US citizens.

Getting Around

By air: Heidelberg is served by **Frankfurt Airport**. From here you can use a door-to-door minibus service (dep. 'Meeting Point' Hall B, duration one hour, DM40; reservation necessary, © (06221) 1 00 99 or fax 16 27 80).

By train: Heidelberg's **Hauptbahnhof** deposits you in a dismal quarter 1½ kilometres west of the centre. (Tram 1, or Bus 11 or 34 take you quickly to the Altstadt). There are rail connections to Munich (3hr), Frankfurt (55min), Stutttgart (¾hr) and Karlsruhe (½hr).

By car: Traffic is tunnelled under and channelled around the Altstadt, leaving the old streets blissfully silent and open only to pedestrians and flocks of bicycles. You can park in any one of 14 garages around the periphery for around DM15 a day, and hire yourself a **bicycle** from the parcel counter at the Hauptbahnhof.

Car hire: Avis, Karlsruher Str. 43, © (06221) 22 215; Hertz, Kurfürsten-Anlage 1, © (06221) 23 434.

Mitfahrzentrale: Kurfürsten-Anlage 57, © (06221) 24 646.

Public transport: Once in the old town you'll find that all you want to see is within easy walking distance. If you do want to use public transport it is a good idea to invest in a **Ticket-24-plus** (DM7), which offers a day's free travel not only on trams, but also on the **Bergbahn** (funicular railway) up to the castle. Single tickets on the Bergbahn (which leaves from Kornmarkt) are DM3.50 (return) to the Schloß and DM5.50 (return) right to the top of Königstuhl.

By boat: The **Rhein-Neckar-Fahrgastschiffahrt** (© (06221) 20181; offices at the Stadthalle (Congress Hall) operates cruise boats up and down the River Neckar and to resorts on the Rhine.

Tourist Information

The three main **tourist information offices** are at the Hauptbahnhof, © (06221) 21341 and 27735 *(Mon–Sat 9–7, Mar–Oct, also Sun 10–6, Nov and Dec Sun 10–5)*; at the Schloß, Neue Schloßstr. 54 *(daily 10–5)*; and at Neckarmünzplatz coach park *(Mon–Fri 9–6.30, summer only)*. They can supply you with maps, ideas for walks or pack you off on a city tour (DM16—a good way to find your feet in the city). The Hauptbahnhof office not only helps with accommodation, but offers good value package tours with museum passes, meals and glasses of Glühwein.

Post office: The main post offices are in Belfortstraße, Sofienstraße and Grabengasse.

Bureau de change: There is an after-hours exchange at the Hauptbahnhof, open normal banking hours and also on Sun and holidays 10–1.

Market days: Marktplatz Wed and Sat, Friedrich-Ebert-Platz Tues and Fri 7–1.

Festivals

Summer is the main season for festivals, and the Schloß is the favourite venue. On the first Saturdays in June and September, and the second in July, costume pageants and fireworks attract hordes of onlookers and there are open-air concerts and plays on most evenings in July and August (with *The Student Prince* making a predictable annual appearance). **Carnival** is celebrated here with gusto, and the best traditional **fairs** are the *Heidelberger Frühling* (early June) and the *Heidelberger Herbst* (late Sept), both held on the Karlplatz.

The Schloß

Note: There is free access to the courtyards and gardens of the Schloß at all times, though you can only see the interior by **guided tour** *(Apr–Oct daily 9–5, Nov–Mar 9–4; adm DM4, which includes entry to the Großes Faß; check the notice board for times of English tours)*. But it is the ruined courts and exterior of the Schloß that are most inspiring, and it's far more pleasant to wander about in your own time.

'A ruin,' wrote Mark Twain during his visit to Heidelberg in 1878, 'must be rightly situated, to be effective. This one could not be better placed. It stands upon a commanding elevation, it is buried in green woods, there is no level ground about it, but on the contrary there are wooded terraces upon terraces, and one looks down through shining leaves into profound chasms and abysses where twilight reigns and the sun cannot intrude.'

The massive Schloß that broods over Heidelberg grew up over four centuries, and is a haphazard mixture of Gothic and Renaissance styles. Today, the main route up to the castle, Neue Schloßstraße, is a gauntlet of ice-cream kiosks, souvenir stalls and parked coaches. For an experience closer to Mark Twain's, you should walk up the Burgweg (off the Kornmarkt). This winds its way up through the terraces, and brings you round the back of the Schloß through gloomy vaulted passages. On your way up, you pass the aptly named **Dicker Turm** (Fat Tower, 1533), half of its bulk blasted into oblivion. Between this and the octagonal **Glockenturm** (Bell Tower, 1525) stretches the **Altane**, a long balustraded terrace with a fine view back across the river. The Burgweg leads you through an arch in the **Friedrichsbau**, then drops you suddenly right in the central courtyard. Here the vast red sandstone mass of the Schloß dissolves into straggling ruins and grandiose façades.

Solid towers spawn graceful arches, which in turn burst into splendid Renaissance ornament before collapsing into a garden, or tumbling out onto a panoramic terrace. Flowers, even trees, grow out of cracks in the stone, vines garnish the statues and masses of creeper drape over the rough, rocky edges. In this fantasy landscape it is almost possible to ignore the swarms of tourists. (Since the castle never closes, to avoid the crowds you could creep up here at night, when it's eerily lit, or even arrive at the dewy first light of dawn.)

The Friedrichsbau was built in 1607 by the noisy, inebriate Friedrich IV and is decorated with enormous statues of his Wittlesbach ancestors, from Charlemagne onwards. It is one of the few parts of the castle to have been fully restored. The guided tour takes you inside to see the moulded ceilings and heavy, carved doorways. Another legacy of Friedrich IV is a diary consisting largely of entries such as 'Blotto again last night.' By the time he was 30 he was tottering about on crutches, and six years later he was dead. Students seem to detect a soul-mate, however, and he's still celebrated in drinking songs.

Working clockwise from the Friedrichsbau around the vast courtyard you can see the **Saalbau** (Hall of Mirrors Building, 1549) with graceful arched loggias. A festival hall on the first floor, lined with Venetian mirrors, gave the building its name, but the whole lot burnt down after the castle was struck by lightning in 1764. Then comes the **Ottheinrichsbau** (1556), a sheer Renaissance façade, silhouetted starkly against the empty sky and adorned with cherubs, copies of Roman coins from the 16th-century Elector Ott-Heinrich's collection, images of his favourite Old Testament heroes and statues of hunky Greek gods and lithe godesses. Next come the plainer **Ludwigsbau** (1524) a product of the simpler tastes of Ludwig V, and the **Ökonomiegebäude** (Service Quarters, 1508–44), now a restaurant. In the south-west corner of the courtyard is the oldest surviving part of the castle, the Gothic **Ruprechtsbau** (1400). The western flank of the courtyard is closed off by the **Bibliotheksbau** (Library, 1520–35) and **Frauenzimmerbau** (Women's Rooms, c. 1540). Also examples of Ludwig V's unostentatious taste, these buildings suffered most in the Thirty Years War. Through a gap in the southern part of the courtyard you can see the imposing red **Thorturm** (Gate Tower, 1541), the only tower to have survived all attacks intact. To the left is the gloriously collapsed, and again aptly named, **Gesprengter Turm** (Exploded Tower, c. 1460), a powder store blown clean in two by the French in 1693, revealing a neat cross-section of the rooms inside.

Down in the gardens along the western walls is a graceful arch, the **Elisabethentor**. This elaborate garden gate was built in one night by Friedrich V as a birthday surprise for his teenage wife, Elizabeth Stuart. The spirited daughter of the English King James I bewitched Heidelberg for five years with masques and balls, filled the gardens with talking statues and singing fountains and was whisked off by her husband to become Queen of Bohemia for a few short months before his defeat at the outbreak of the Thirty Years War. This last brief reign earned her the nickname of the 'Winter Queen', though her many gallants remembered her as the 'Queen of Hearts'.

Before leaving, have a look into the **Apothecary Museum**, located beneath the Ottheinrich building *(Apr–Oct daily 10–5; Nov–Mar Sat, Sun and holidays only 11–5; adm DM3)*. It contains reconstructed alchemist's workshops from all over Germany, with shelves of skulls, curious instruments and suspect jars. You could also join the long queue and pay your DM1 to see the **Großes Faß** (Great Vat) *(Apr–Oct 9–7, Nov–Mar 9–6)*, beneath the Friedrichsbau. Mark Twain holds it up for a dose of his characteristically irreverent ridicule: 'Everybody has heard of the great Heidelberg Tun, and most people have seen it, no doubt. It is a wine-cask as big as a cottage and some traditions say it holds eighteen hundred thousand bottles, and other traditions say it holds eighteen hundred million barrels. I think it likely that one of these statements is a mistake, and the other one is a lie. However, the mere capacity of the thing is of no sort of consequence, since the cask is empty, and indeed has always been empty, history says. An empty cask the size of a cathedral could excite but little emotion in me. I do not see any wisdom in building a monster cask to hoard up emptiness in, when you can get a better quality, outside, any day, free of expense.'

Current opinion is that the barrel holds 221,726 litres and was connected by pipes to the adjacent King's Hall where consumption averaged 2,000 litres a day. Guardian of the vat in the 18th century was the diminutive red-haired court jester Perkeo—himself no mean sozzler. He is reputed to have downed 18 bottles of wine daily, responding to all offers of a drink with an Italian *perchè no?* (why not?)—hence his nickname. He died of shock after sipping water by mistake, but survives as a sort of patron saint of Heidelberg's carnival.

The Altstadt

The Altstadt, below the castle at the foot of the hill, centres on two main squares, the Marktplatz and the Universitätsplatz. After the French had razed Heidelberg to the ground in 1693, the town was hastily rebuilt. To cut costs and save time, new structures were often lumped onto old foundations, so sober Baroque buildings are often seen jostling and twisting down narrow Gothic alleyways. The 18th-century centre remains plain, uniform and largely intact. Even the local McDonald's hides behind a Baroque façade, once the rather imposing court Apothek.

You're unlikely to be bowled over by sumptuous architecture in the Altstadt. Rather, it is a pleasant (mainly traffic-free) spot where you can stroll about and soak up the university-town atmosphere. Keep an eye open for the orange plaques, which give architectural pedigrees and chronicle past residents.

The university is properly called the Ruprecht-Karls-Universität (or Ruperto Carola) after its 14th-century founder, Elector Ruprecht I, and Margrave Carl Friedrich of Baden, who gave the institution a boost in the early 1800s. There were three teachers and just a handful of students at its inaugural mass, but by the end of the 19th century, Heidelberg University ranked with the best in the world. It never really seemed to recover from the massive exodus of academics during the Nazi regime and, some say, given the egalitarian national education policies of the past three decades, it never will. German universities are not allowed to select on merit. Legislation to this effect has existed since the 1960s, and has led to a great levelling of standards and a controversy similar to the one surrounding comprehensive schools in Britain. One of the results of the system is that universities tend to attract mainly local students, and to be all very much the same—though a famous professor might enhance a reputation in a certain field. Ruperto Carola certainly doesn't carry any extra status in the way that, in some circles, the Oxbridge or Ivy League universities still do. In the eyes of most Germans, Heidelberg is no different from any other national university. Gone are the days of haughty Prussian Junker heirs. Today's students are most likely to be hearty Badeners, or American—and now there are women students as well as men.

The so-called **Alte-Universität** (Old University), built in the 18th century, is on Universitätsplatz, right in the centre of the Altstadt. Across the square is the Neue-Universität, built in the early 1930s largely with American money including hefty donations from Henry Ford. Academic departments are scattered around town, and a brand new campus is growing up on the north-west banks of the Neckar.

Behind the rather stolid Old University building you'll find the entrance to the **Studentenkarzer** (Students' Prison) *(Apr–Oct Mon–Sat 9–5, Nov–Mar Sat 9–1; adm DM1)*, used until early this century. Before then students weren't subject to civil legislation. Miscreants were tried (in their absence) by university authorities, usually for drunkenness, unseemly behaviour or disturbing the peace. A university constable would then call on the errant young gentleman and invite him, at his own convenience, to occupy the students' jail. He lived for three days on bread and water, then imported sumptuous meals from outside. He was allowed out for lectures and could socialize with other prisoners. Sentences varied from a few days to four weeks. No self-respecting young man could possibly graduate without having spent some time in one of the cells, which were fondly given names such as the 'Grand Hotel' or 'Sanssouci'. Today the chairs and tables are rough with initials carved by past inmates, and the walls are still covered with the photographs and silhouettes left to commemorate their stay. Graffiti—painted, scratched or smoked on with candle soot over every inch of the remaining wallspace—boasts of crimes and protests innocence. 'For misinterpreted gallantry,' wails one unfortunate. A less penitent incarcerate smirks:

Polyp geneckt	Provoked a cop
Amtmann zitiert	cited an Alderman
Karzer gesteckt	chucked in jail
Fein amusiert	what fun!

Negotiate the cross-currents of bicycles on Universitätsplatz to head for Grabengasse, which leads to a busy thoroughfare named Plöck, and the **Universitätsbibliothek** (University Library) *(Mon–Sat 10–5; adm free)*. Here you'll find, among other beautifully illuminated, handwritten books from the University's collection, the **Codex Manesse**, a 14th-century collection of troubadours' lyrics, brilliantly adorned with 137 illustrations. The original rests in dim light under layers of glass, but dotted around the corridors are facsimiles that allow you a closer look.

Further down Plöck (as it crosses Friedrich-Ebert-Platz) is the former Institute of Natural Sciences where **Robert Wilhelm Bunsen** worked from 1853 to 1888. He discovered how to separate the colours of the spectrum, but is more familiar to budding chemists for the Bunsen Burner, standard equipment in any school laboratory.

If you cut down Akademiestraße onto Hauptstraße, you are immediately confronted with the 19th-century **Friedrichsbau** (now the Physiology and Pharmacology Department). Behind this, in a former Dominican Monastery, is the **Anatomy Department** (in the Anatomie-Gebäude). The rapidly expanding university took over the monastery in 1801 and within weeks students were dissecting cadavers in the chapel and using the sacristy as a morgue.

Hauptstraße and Marktplatz

Hauptstraße is the longest (and at times one could believe the busiest) pedestrian zone in Germany. A walk back east will take you past the **Kurpfälzisches Museum** (Palatinate Museum) at Hauptstr. 97 *(Tues–Sun 10–5, Thurs 10–9; adm DM3)*, housed in the Palais Morass, an 18th-century mansion built for a law professor. The garden courtyard, complete with dancing fountain, is a haven from the hurly-burly of shoppers and tourists. Inside the largish museum you'll find a plaster cast of Heidelberg Man's jawbone (the university guards the original under lock and key), reconstructed period rooms with outrageous chandeliers, local historical memorabilia and the **Windsheim Altar** (1509), a limewood carving by Tilman Riemenschneider which portays Christ and twelve beautifully characterized apostles.

Further down Hauptstraße (at No. 151) **Clemens Brentano** shared a house with his brother-in-law **Achim von Arnim**. Together they compiled an anthology of folk-poetry *Des Knaben Wunderhorn* (The Boy's Magic Horn) which excited the German Romantics, and inspired the Brothers Grimm to do the same with prose tales.

The Hauptstraße leads back past Universitätsplatz to the **Marktplatz**. Most of the square is hogged by the dull Gothic **Heiliggeistkirche** (1400). Traders have built stalls between its buttresses in retaliation. From 1706 to 1936 the church was divided in two by a screen. Catholics worshipped in the choir, and the Protestants had the rest. The latter have now bought out the former completely. The church once housed 55 tombs of Palatine princes, but in 1693 the invading French army turfed the bodies out into the street, and made off with the valuable pewter coffins. Today the only grave left is that of King Ruprecht I and his wife Elizabeth von Hohenzollern. Some 60 years earlier the invading General Tilly had despatched the church's other prized possession—the **Bibliotheca Palatina** (at the time said to be the greatest library in the world)—as booty to the Vatican. There it remains, though a few manuscripts, such as the Codex Manesse, have found their way back to the University Library. Opposite the church is a nondescript Baroque **Rathaus** and on the southern side of the square you can see one of the few Renaissance buildings to have survived the wars, a patrician townhouse, now the Hotel Zum Ritter St Georg. In earlier times Marktplatz was the scene of merry persecution of petty criminals, who were spun about in a cage where the Hercules fountain now stands, duels to the death, public executions and the burning of witches. 'Seven heedes were chopped off, and threye thir fingeres' remarked a traveller casually on his way through in 1525.

Further on down the Hauptstraße lie **Zum Sepp'l** and **Roter Ochsen**—two of the most famous student pubs (*see* below). A wander through the alleys to the south will bring you to the banks of the Neckar. In Pfaffengasse is the house where **Friedrich Ebert** (1871–1925), the first president of the Weimar Republic was born. Nowadays it is a small memorial museum *(Tues–Sun 10–6, Thurs 10–8; adm free)*. West along the river is the **Marstal** (arsenal, *c.* 1510), a stone pile with pixie-capped towers which now serves as a student Mensa (dining hall). If you nip in through an arch in the side you'll find the grassy courtyard where today's students fortress themselves against tourist invaders.

The graceful **Karl-Theodor-Brücke**, with its elegant twin-towered gate, crosses the Neckar to the east of the Marstall. On the north bank a precipitous flight of steps leads from the bridge to the **Philosophenweg**. The 'Philosophers' Walk' is a path through gardens and orchards, high above the Neckar, said to have inspired centuries of poets and formed the leafy backdrop for many a musing stroll and sauntering debate. Today it is peopled by jogging businessmen, students, stray tourists and lovers—also frail old biddies who simply *must* have a secret path up. The view across the rooftops to the castle and wooded hills beyond is unequalled. As the sun sets it picks out the red roofs of the Baroque town, then finally just the pink, glimmering castle. Birdsong mingles with the bells for evening mass, then there is a hush, and the city lights up 'like a fallen Milky Way', as Mark Twain put it.

Shopping

The seemingly endless Hauptstraße is packed with shoppers and is home to leading High Street chain stores and souvenir shops. For a more studenty atmosphere head for Untere Straße (off the Fischmarkt) where you'll find second-hand clothes shops, dinky grocery stores and alternative cafés.

Heidelberg ✆ (06221–) **Where to Stay**

Heidelberg is a popular tourist destination. To ensure accommodation in the centre it is worth booking well in advance. As always the tourist office (Hauptbahnhof branch) can help with reservations, though beware of being exiled to a dull and distant part of town.

expensive

Hotel Zum Ritter St Georg, Hauptstr. 178, ✆ 2 02 03/2 42 72, fax 1 26 83 (DM220–295). Occupies an historic 16th-century town house, though the interior borders on antique-hotel kitsch.

moderate

Park Hotel Atlantic, Schloß Wolfsbrunnenweg 23, ✆ 16 40 51, fax 16 40 54 (DM140–190). Stately hotel high up in a park behind the Schloß.

Goldene Hecht, Steingasse 2, ✆/fax 16 60 25 (DM165–225). Pleasant hotel right near the Altebrücke on the Neckar, and above a jolly traditional inn.

Hackteufel, Steingasse 7, ✆ 2 71 62, fax 16 53 79 (DM150–220). An elegant, quiet, family-run hotel with some romantic timber-beamed bedrooms.

Schönberger Hof, Untere Neckarstr. 54, ✆ 2 26 15/2 49 88, fax 16 48 11 (DM160–180). Quiet hotel overlooking a garden and the Neckar. Good value.

inexpensive

Elite, Bunsenstr. 15, 2 57 34, fax 16 39 49 (DM85–95). Fairly spartan, despite its name, but a good cheaper option that is still quite central.

Brandstätter, Friedrich-Ebert-Anlage 60, ✆ 23944 (DM89–99). Simple hotel, convenient for the Altstadt, but on a busy main road.

Youth Hostel: Tiergartenstr. 5, ✆ 41 20 66.

Eating and Drinking: Restaurants and Taverns

expensive

Simplicissimus, Ingrimstr. 16, ✆ 13336 (set menus from DM88). The town's best-kept secret. A tiny restaurant down a back street (near the Marktplatz), run by an Austrian couple. They fly in fresh ingredients from around the world, come up with delicious dishes such as steamed sea bass in orange-scented cream sauce and, to the envy and astonishment of the big boys in town, have just landed Heidelberg's first Michelin star.

Zur Herrenmühle, Hauptstr. 239, ✆ 1 29 09 (around DM90). Situated in a pretty 17th-century house. Upmarket and pricey, but with subtle Franco-German cuisine.

moderate

Zieglerbrau, Bergheimerstraße, off Bismarkplatz (DM30–40). A little out of the way, but popular locally. Good house brewery with German fare that includes such adventures as turkey fillets in port sauce.

Kurpfälzisches Museum, Hauptstr. 97, ✆ 24050 (DM45–60). Sedate and gloomy museum restaurant. Waitresses in black dresses silently dispense steaming dishes of tasty stews and casseroles.

Perkeo, Hauptstr. 75, ✆ 163 719 (DM35–55). Hearty German cooking and cheery tourist clientele. Great knuckles of pork and generous helpings.

Bars and Cafés

Tourists are thinner on the ground along **Untere Straße** (off the Fischmarkt) and the surrounding alleys—and this is where a lot of today's students socialize. Bars range from the hyper-trendy to bare rooms for serious drinking.

Punkt, Untere Straße. Posey but fun.

Zum Mohren, Untere Straße. Popular student hangout.

Starfish, Steingasse. Friendly and fairly tourist-free.

Cave 54, Kramergasse 2. Good live jazz, and sometimes dancing, too.

Eckstein, Untere Straße. Pulsating with the latests sounds. A place to be seen, but certainly not heard.

Zum Karpfen, Neckarstaden. In the shadow of the Theodor-Heuss-Brücke. A quiet spot for a drink on the river, if you want to get away from the boisterous student atmosphere for a while.

Schafheutle, Hauptstr. 94. Ever so refined. Champagne truffles, renowned marzipan, calorie-laden cakes and heavy bills.

Knösel, Haspelgasse 20. Traditional Konditorei. This is where the students come for their coffee and choccies.

Max, Marktplatz. Trendiest and most pleasant of the cafés on the market square.

Student Inns

A visit to one of the old student inns (*Kneipen*) is *de rigueur*. The taverns are cluttered with photographs, swords, drinking horns and other student paraphernalia, accumulated over centuries; and the heavy wooden tables are chunky with carved initials. Students are in the minority these days, but they're still there, and you can sometimes see the remnants of the old fraternities, in their odd caps, meeting to select a *Bierkönig* (Beer King). The title goes to whoever can down the most beer in one evening—alarming totals of around 50 litres are not uncommon. 'No stomach could hold that quantity at any one time, of course,' Mark Twain noted, 'but there are ways of frequently creating a vacuum, which those who have been much at sea will understand.'

An even less pleasant ritual, which has now all but died out (save for a fervent few) is the *Mensur*. Pairs of students from rival corps were protectively padded and goggled, and placed an arm's length apart. Then they slashed at each other with razor-sharp swords in what was less a duel than a ceremony of tribal scarring. The idea was to go for the bare skin on the face, and of course never to flinch or step back, and to try to last out fifteen minutes or until referees judged it was life-threatening to continue. Winning seems to have been less important than acquiring a visible scar (salt was rubbed into wounds to accentuate the effect), which was cherished as a symbol of manly, Germanic values. The tradition began in Heidelberg, and spread throughout Germany. Still today you will see the occasional senator or industrial magnate with an ugly slash across the forehead or cheek. It is said that the contests persist behind closed doors around town.

The old student inns also offer good food—usually pretty basic *gutbürgerliche Küche* at reasonable prices.

Zum Seppl', Hauptstr. 213. Biggest and most famous of the student taverns. It has been going continuously since 1634. Also famed for its cheap, meaty grub.

Roter Ochsen, Hauptstr. 217. A relative new-comer (it opened in the 18th century) and a little more upmarket (there are tables with cloths in one corner).

Schnookeloch, Haspelgasse 8. Oldest, but least touristy, of the three main taverns.

Entertainment and Nightlife

There is much in Heidelberg to entertain you apart from the traditional pub crawl (for which see **Student Inns** below). The tourist office publishes a short **listings magazine** called *Heidelberg diese Woche* (available at the tourist office and venues around town). There is a central ticket reservation agency at Konzertkasse, Theaterstr. 8, ✆ (06221) 583 520.

Classical music concerts take place in the Kongresshaus Stadthalle on the banks of the Neckar and in churches around town. More adventurous programmes find their way to the university's Alte Aula. **Student theatre** productions can similarly be seen at odd venues around town, though the standard isn't particularly high. **Mainstream theatre** is staged at the Städischen Bühnen, Theaterstraße, ✆ (06221) 58279. For **live music and dancing** head for the Schwimmbad-Musikclub, Tiergartenstraße 13, a public swimming pool which doubles as a disco featuring everything from Indie to Psycho and straight rock. Fischerstübchen, Obere Neckarstraße 2, is a student favourite for dancing, and Zigarillo, Mittermaierstr. 8, is a popular disco in an old factory.

South of Heidelberg

Schloß Bruchsal

Halfway between Heidelberg and Karlsruhe, set in bland countryside alongside the unremarkable village of Bruchsal is the building that travel writer Patrick Leigh-Fermor called 'one of the most beautiful baroque palaces in the whole of Germany'—Schloß Bruchsal *(Tues–Sun 9–1 and 2–6, DM3)*. He spent a night in the Schloß in 1933 on his walk to Constantinople, and in the morning was stopped dead in his tracks by the extravagance and sheer beauty of the state rooms and central staircase. A decade later, the palace was a burnt-out shell, but it has since been sumptuously restored, and is certainly worth an hour or two of your time.

Building began on the Schloß in 1720. It was to be the resplendent new seat of the Prince-bishop of Speyer, Cardinal Damion Hugo von Schönborn. The architectural big guns of the time—such as Maximilian von Welsch and Balthasar Neumann (*see* p. 59)—were wheeled in to obliterate any competition from the neighbours (in this case the Cardinal's own brother in Würzberg).

The yellow, red and white exterior of the Schloß is a cheeky exercise in *trompe l'oeil*. All the decoration, except the pilasters, is painted on. But the *ne plus ultra* is Neumann's staircase, which sweeps round a central cylinder and up to the state rooms. It is capped by a stunning painted dome, one of the greatest works of the master painter Januarius Zick (*see* p. 60). An extraordinary feat of *trompe l'oeil*, it appears to extend the dome infinitely upwards, past scenes of the history of the diocese, right up into the heavens. The state rooms, while awesomely grand, are pristine, empty of furniture and a little soulless.

But there are further delights in store. The Schloß also houses a **Museum Mechanischer Musikinstrumente** (Museum of Mechanical Musical Instruments) *(guided tours on the hour 10–5, except 1pm; adm DM6 includes entry to the Schloß)*. The tours are in German, but that doesn't really matter, as the real point is to show some of the 200 or so intruments in action. There are musical boxes, mechnical pianos, chairs that break into tune when you sit on them, and exquisitely made cabinets that play original compositions by great composers. A big 1925 cinema Wurlitzer has buttons for creating movie sound effects (including birds, doorbells and a police siren) and there is an entire brass band of mannequins whose eyes open and close. One extraordinary 1928 Parisian invention is the dummy of a dashingly good-looking accordionist and his cheeky young drum-playing partner. While they play, they grin, arch their eyebrows and look about flirtatiously—with uncanny naturalism.

Also part of the Schloß is the **Landesmuseum** *(same hours as Schloß; adm free)* where you can see the furniture and fittings that survived the Second World War bombs, including some very fine Beauvais tapestries.

East of Heidelberg: the Neckar Valley to Bad Wimpfen

Castles, Rude Knights and Devils in Disguise

The **Neckar**, which winds its way from the heart of the Swabian Jura through vineyards and wooded hills to meet the Rhine at Mannheim, is a slower moving, more placid river than the Rhine or Mosel. Castles, in various stages of ruin or restoration, pepper the hilltops. From time to time there is a gash of red, where the paths of road or rail have cut into sandstone; little blue granite cliffs line some stretches of the river. It all looks very pretty and seems rather low-key, but there's an underlying sense of dogged industry. On the sunny southern slopes, sturdy, wrinkled women in headscarves and cotton prints tend the vines by hand. Barges laden with sand and cement ply the river and chug impatiently in the locks. High-tech factories hum away discreetly in the greenery.

The B37, which closely follows the path of the river, is known as the **Burgenstraße** (Castle Road) for the fortresses along the way. **Burg Dilsberg** *(9–12, 1–6; adm)* and **Schloß Hirschhorn**, part of a parade of castles above **Neckarsteinach** (15km from Heidelberg), both command dramatic views over the valley. At **Neckarzimmern** (40km further on) up a road twisting through the vineyards, you come to the romantic, partially ruined **Burg Hornberg** *(Apr–Oct daily 9–5; adm DM3.50)*, seat of the 16th-century robber knight Götz von Berlichingen. He is famed for giving the German Kaiser the 'Swabian Greeting' (*see* p. 234) when he felt his traditional freedom was being threatened. At **Burg Guttenberg**, the owner, Claus Fentzloff, a local nobleman, shows off his falconery skills *(daily 11am and 3pm, Mar and Nov 3pm only; adm DM6)*. There's also a museum with a fascinating herbarium in which dried plants are stashed away in trick wooden boxes, carved to resemble books. This is also a good place to stop off for coffee or a bite to eat.

The best walks in the area are in the glades around **Zwingenberg** (halfway between Neckarsteinach and Neckarzimmern). Nearby is the **Wolfsschlucht** (Wolf's Glen). Follow the signposts from the main road to the lair of Samiel, the devil in the guise of a hunter. He would offer eager huntsmen his seven magic bullets. The first six invariably found their mark, but with the final one Samiel claimed his victim. After a visit to the glen in 1810, Weber used the story in his opera *Der Freischütz*.

Mosbach (near Neckarzimmern, *see* Directory) is a pretty, half-timbered town with a buzzing market, but the gem of the area is Bad Wimpfen. *See also Directory entries for Mannheim, Heilbronn, Schwetzingen, Schwäbische Hall.*

Bad Wimpfen

The village of Bad Wimpfen must have one of the prettiest skylines in Germany. Solid fortress towers, loops of Romanesque arches, a cascading step-gabled façade and a prickle of delicate pinnacles line up along a riverside ridge. Behind the town walls, narrow stairways wind steeply between bent and buckled half-timbered houses. (An old sign threatens punishment to anyone so unsociable as to squeeze a wheelbarrow through the alleys.) There's a comfy, country quiet about the place. Fresh breezes blow off the surrounding plains, and rosy-cheeked villagers greet each other in the street.

Yet once Bad Wimpfen was so important that there was a circle of 15 castles in the surrounding countryside to protect it. It was a favourite residence of the powerful 12th-century Staufian emperors. The Thirty Years' War wiped out 90 per cent of the population, but the town struggled back to life as a salt trading centre and remained a Free Imperial City up until it was captured by Napoleon. It was here, during the 13th century, that the young rebel King Henry VII was captured by his grandfather Emperor Frederick II. The boy king had been left to rule Germany by the greying emperor, who himself rarely set foot in the place, preferring to govern from Italy. Crowned at the age of 9, and married at 14 (to the 20-year-old Margaret of Austria), young Henry loved Bad Wimpfen. He gave the townsfolk a forest, 15km up the river. Thirty-five residents still have rights to firewood there. But at the age of 21 King Henry began to get a bit uppity. Frederick II swooped into Germany (for the second time in his life), threw his grandson into the deepest dungeon, and despatched the damsel queen to a nunnery.

As the **Pfalz** (imperial palace) fell into decay, its stones became garden walls. Tall houses grew up out of the old moat, with the main entrances leading off the street behind, right into the rafters. But significant parts of the old *Pfalz* remain, and are some of the best examples of lay Romanesque architecture you'll see in Germany.

Just behind the Rathaus, off the main village square, is the **Blauer Turm** (Blue Tower) *(Apr–Oct Tues–Sun 9–12 and 1.30–5; adm DM3)*, part of the original fortifications. It gets its name from the blue stone used in its construction (although this is not readily apparent). You can climb 169 stairs all the way to the rather eccentric pinnacled tower atop the sturdy base. This was added in 1848 after a fire had burned off the old one. The bay window, with a hole in the base, just above the front door was once a long-drop loo—but then the main entrance was elsewhere. Across from the Blauer Turm is the **Steinhaus** *(Apr–Oct Tues–Sun 9–12 and 2–5; adm DM3)*. Built by Barbarossa for the empress and her retinue, it was later the castle commandant's house, then a storeroom (hence the double doors up the side). Nowadays it's a museum—though the old murals, and the little nooks in the walls on the first floor (where the ladies used to sit and dream) are a better reason for visiting than the exhibits on the town's history.

A series of exquisite Romanesque **arcades** leads along the city wall from the Steinhaus. The patterned bases, tops and columns of the pillars reappear in different permutations all the way along, without a single repetition. A little further on you find the **Kaiserkapelle** (Palace Chapel) *(Apr–Oct, daily 10–12, 2–4.30; adm DM1)*, now a small ecclesiastical museum—though again the delicate frescoes are more exciting than the exhibits. In emergencies, after a hasty prayer, the emperor could make a quick getaway through a passage which led to the palace keep, the Roter Turm.

The **Roter Turm** (Red Tower, but about as red as the Blue Tower is blue), with its 3m-thick walls, was the ruler's last refuge, though if things really got hot, there was a secret passage to a boat hidden on the river. A little fast talking at the tourist information office will get you a key. Once inside you can see the arched nook for the emperor's bed; the rest of the family slept on the floor, and the servants had to drape themselves about the rafters. There's another alcove for the dining table and a crooked (apparently odour-reducing) passage leads to the loo.

Next door is the perky little half-timbered **Nürnberger Türmchen**, a reminder of the relief offered to the devastated town by the burghers of Nuremberg after the ravages of the Thirty Years' War.

As you explore the rest of the town, look out for **Mayor Elsässer's House** (in Untere Blauturmgasse) with its *Naitkopfer*—domestic gargoyles to ward off evil spirits. The prettiest streets are **Klostergasse** and **Apothekestraße**. At Apothekestraße 69, you can see one of the three five-storey gabled houses to survive the Thirty Years' War. Outside the **Stadtkirche** is a movingly sculpted *Crucifixion* by Hans Backoffen (*see* p. 55). At the eastern end of Hauptstraße is the **Hohenstaufen Tor**, once the main entrance to the imperial palace.

There are two more parts to Bad Wimpfen—the **Kur**, a modern spa complex on the northern outskirts, and **Wimpfen in Tal**, down in the valley. Here the Gothic church—at present shrouded in plastic as part of a four-year restoration project—has breathtaking medieval carvings by Erwin von Steinbach, who also built much of Strasbourg cathedral. It is worth risking official ire and poking your head through the scaffolding to see the south portal and the chancel. The restoration has revealed some of the original colouring.

The friendly and enthusiastic **tourist information office** is in the Rathaus, Marktplatz 1, ✆ 5 31 51, fax 5 31 29 *(Mon–Fri 9–12, 2–4, also Sat and Sun Apr–Sept 10–12 and 2–4)*.

Bad Wimpfen ✆ *(07063–)*   **Where to Stay and Eating Out**

Your best bet all round is to head for the recently restored **Hotel Sonne**, Hauptstr. 87, ✆ 245 (DM130), which dates back to 1563. It's efficiently run by a friendly family, has its own bakery and a good café/restaurant. The same family own **Weinstube Feyerabend** just up the road. Here you not only get good food, but a fine selection of local wines. If the Sonne is full try **Hotel Weinmann**, Marktplatz 3, ✆ 8582 (DM130) or **Hotel Blauer Turm**, Burgviertel 5, ✆ 225 (DM130), which also has a pleasant terrace café.

Stuttgart

Stuttgart is the capital of Baden-Württemberg and the centre of Swabian civilization. At each end of the high street are the totems of the city's success: the Mercedes-Benz symbol, neon-lit, rotates slowly on the Bahnhof roof; facing it, through an avenue of chic shops, an equally brilliant giant Bosch sparkplug pokes up into the sky. The Swabian philosophy of *Schaffe, spare, Haüsle baue* (work, save, build a house) has made Stuttgart into the richest city in the EC, but hardly a vortex of sizzling delight. A local poet paints the picture of Swabians living with a fence around the garden, a car in the garage, the shutters closed and the front door shut—a suburban nightmare summed up by the smug lines *Was ma hot/des hot ma* ('What you've got/You've got'). A sober Protestantism lurks behind the industriousness. At one time you could be reported to the police for doing housework on a Sunday. Even today, the town dies after midnight when, with characteristic Swabian thrift, the Mercedes badge is switched off.

Stuttgart lies in a hollow, hemmed in by green hills and besieged by thick forests. One vineyard makes it nearly all the way to the Bahnhof. Gracious villas poke up through this luscious greenbelt. Beyond it, industry sprawls out unchecked, gobbling up surrounding towns and villages. But down in the city centre, Stuttgart seems quite small, even rural; sometimes beautiful—but seldom congenial.

History

When Julius Caesar tried to take Gaul, some of the most dogged resistance he met came from Ariovistus and his fearless Suevians. The Suevians later succumbed to the Alemanni, but the name 'Swabian' has stuck. The Alemannic Duke Liovic of Swabia was a fine horse-breeder who, in about AD 950, set up a stud farm (*Stutengarten*) on the banks of the Neckar—and the settlement that grew up around the farm was so named.

In 1079 control of the land around Stuttgart passed to the Hohenstaufens. Then, from the late 13th to the 16th centuries, it ping-ponged between the Hapsburgs and the increasingly powerful Württemberg dynasty. Counts and Dukes came and went—then, in the 18th century, the Württembergs built a new palace and came to stay. The *Grafschaft* (county) of Württemberg, which had been upped to a Duchy in 1495, became a kingdom in 1806 and, for Stuttgart, a boom period followed. Schiller and Hegel nurtured the city's psyche, Gottfried Daimler and Robert Bosch took care of its pocket. Today Daimler-Benz and Bosch Electronics still form the backbone of Stuttgart's industry, and manufacturing and engineering companies (including Porsche) flesh out the rest. Stuttgart is also home to some 200 publishing companies. The Lord Mayor of Stuttgart (in the early 1990s it was Manfred Rommel, son of the Desert Fox) presides over a shining, comfortable and ordered city.

Getting Around

By Air

Stuttgart's spanking new **airport** is only 13km from the centre of town, with connections to London, Birmingham and other major cities in Europe and the USA. There's an express coach into the City Air Terminal in the town centre, and frequent S-bahn connections to the Hauptbahnhof.

By Train

The **Hauptbahnhof** is on the main Frankfurt–Munich line and offers direct connections to surrounding European countries and many other German cities (Karlsruhe, 1hr; Frankfurt 1hr 20min (ICE); Munich 2hr 10min). The Hauptbahnhof opens out directly onto the pedestrianized city centre. Below ground level you'll encounter the **Klett Passage**, a warren of snackbars, delicatessens and after-hours shops—and haven for Stuttgart's human rejects. The good burghers shop on, heedless of the sad-eyed Turks, ineffectual punks, junkies and alcoholics who line the walls and stare.

By Car

Stuttgart is on the A8, 90km east of Karlsruhe. In this city of the car, there are plenty of parking garages, filled with shiny, expensive motors. However, the extensive pedestrianized zone and a perfidious one-way system can reduce the uninitiated driver to a sobbing wreck.

Car Hire: Avis, Katharinenstraße, © (0711) 241 441, Airport, © (0711) 790 1415; Sixt Budget, Leonhardsplatz 17, © (0711) 243 925, Airport, © (0711) 790 1504.

Mitfahrzentrale: Lerchenstr. 68, © (0711) 221 453.

Public Transport

An efficient network of trams, buses, U-bahn and S-bahn whisks you about the city, and a **24-hour ticket** (DM8) gives you unlimited access to them all for a day.

The **tourist information office** (*i-Punkt*) is opposite the Hauptbahnhof at Königstraße 1A. For information telephone (0711) 222 8240/1/6. There's a free room reservation service on (0771) 222 8230/1/2/3. For DM19 you can go on a 2-hour city tour, and for a further DM3 the tour is extended by another hour and a couple of glasses of wine at the Weinbaumuseum (Wine Museum, *see* p. 258).

Post office: The main office is behind the Königsbau on Schillerplatz. A branch at the Hauptbahnhof stays open until 11pm and offers exchange facilities.

Medical emergencies: ✆ (0711) 280 211.

Emergency pharmacy: ✆ (0711) 224 310.

Police: ✆ 110.

Market days: Fruit and veg daily in the Markthalle; flower market Tues, Thurs and Sat morning on Schillerplatz; fleamarket Sat morning on Schloßplatz.

Festivals

Stuttgart has four main festivals. For two weeks in September and October visitors and locals knock back 1.5 million litres of beer and polish off 300,000 chickens during the **Cannstatter Volksfest**, a beano second in size only to Munich's Oktoberfest. The Volksfest was founded in 1818 as a harvest festival, and the focal point of the revelry is still a phallic tower laden with flowers, fruit and wreaths. Wanton merrymaking, however, does not seem a natural part of Swabian culture, and the other trappings of the feast—green felt hats with feathers, waitresses wearing dirndls, and lederhosen-clad oompah bands—are all imported from neighbouring Bavaria.

The **Weinachtsmarkt** (Christmas Market, commencing last weekend in November) is Germany's largest—sprawling out of Schillerplatz, up Kirchstraße and onto the market square. The **Spring Festival** (April/May) is a milder, more indigenous version of the Volksfest; and at the end of summer there's a 10-day wine festival, the **Stuttgarter Weindorf**, a popular feast of superb Swabian cooking and Württemberg wines.

The City Centre

From the Hauptbahnhof **Königstraße** sweeps you into the heart of Stuttgart. It is a wide, glitzy pedestrian walkway, lined largely by post-1945 glass and concrete. Well-heeled customers linger in the smart shops or set off up the avenue on irrevocable missions of consumer spending. At night the average age drops to around 25. Little clusters of onlookers politely applaud the buskers who place themselves at regular intervals up the length of the street. Everyone else just mills around, eventually coming to rest in one of the side-street cafés.

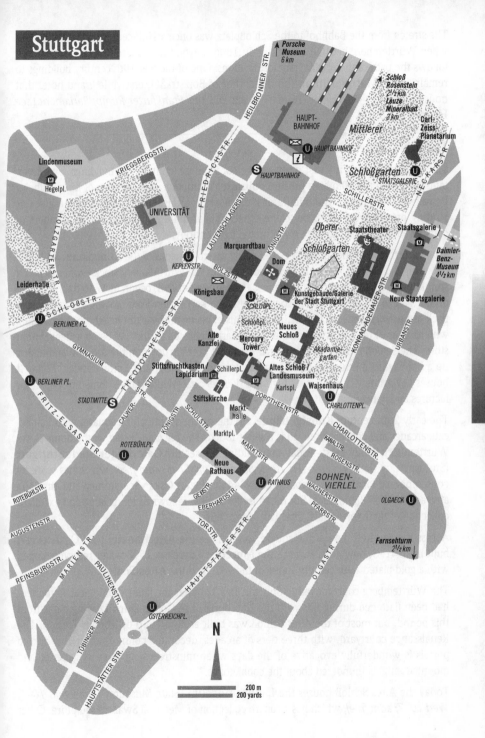

Stuttgart

Porsche
Museum
6 km

HEILBRONNER STR.

Schloß
Rosenstein
2¹/₂ km
Leuze
Mineralbad
2 km

HAUPT-
BAHNHOF

Mittlerer

Carl-
Zeiss-
Planetarium

Lindenmuseum

KRIEGSBERGSTR.

Hegelpl.

☒ ☑ HAUPTBAHNHOF
ⓘ

S HAUPTBAHNHOF

Schloßgarten
STAATSGALERIE ⓤ

UNIVERSITÄT

FRIEDRICHSTR.

SCHILLERSTR.

NECKARSTR.

LAUTENSCHLAGERSTR.

Marquardtbau

KÖNIGSTR.

Oberer

Staatstheater

Staatsgalerie

ⓤ
KEPLERSTR.

BOLZSTR.

Dom

Schloßgarten

Daimler-
Benz-
Museum
4¹/₂ km

Leiderhalle

U. SCHLOSSTR.

Königsbau

☒

Kunstgebäude/Galerie
der Stadt Stuttgart

Neue Staatsgalerie

ⓤ
BERLINER PL.

GYMNASIUM

ⓤ
SCHLOßPL.

Schloßpl.

Neues
Schloß

KONRAD-ADENAUER-STR.

URBANSTR.

HOLZGARTENSTR.

Alte
Kanzlei

Mercury
Tower

Akademie-
garten

ⓤ BERLINER PL.

THEODOR-HEUSS-STR.

Stiftsfruchtkasten /
Lapidarium

Schillerpl.

Altes Schloß /
Landesmuseum

FRITZ-ELSAS-STR.

STADTMITTE S

CALWER STR.

Stiftskirche

DOROTHEENSTR.

Karlspl.

Waisenhaus

ⓤ
CHARLOTTENPL.

KÖNIGSTR.

SCHULSTR.

Markt-
halle

CHARLOTTENSTR.

BOHNEN-
VIERTEL

ⓤ
ROTEBÜHLPL.

Marktpl.

KANALSTR.

ROSENSTR.

ROTEBÜHLSTR.

GERBSTR.

Neue
Rathaus

MARKTSTR.

ⓤ RATHAUS

WAGNERSTR.

EBERHARDSTR.

AUGUSTENSTR.

MARIENSTR.

PAULINENSTR.

TORSTR.

HAUPTSTÄTTER STR.

PFARRSTR.

OLGASTR.

OLGAECK ⓤ

REINSBURGSTR.

Fernsehturm
2¹/₂ km

TÜBINGER STR.

ⓤ
ÖSTERREICHPL.

N

200 m
200 yards

The stretch from the Bahnhof to the Schloßplatz was once a 19th-century showpiece, built when Württemberg became a kingdom in 1806. Beyond the square 'Upper' Königstraße follows the path of the original city fortifications. One of the few 19th-century buildings to remain is the **Marquardtbau** (on the corner of Bolzstraße), erstwhile grand hotel that housed the likes of Wagner, Bismark, Liszt and the *Frankfurter Rumpf-Parlament* (*see* **History** p. 43).

The Schloßplatz

The Schloßplatz itself is a vast, open square bordered by monumental buildings. Two fountains, and even the 60m-high **jubilee column** (commemorating 25 years of King Wilhelm I's reign), seem lost in the middle of it all. Mere mortals, sitting about on the grass or striding bravely from one side to the other, appear quite out of place, and numbers of comatose tramps seem to have given up the fight entirely.

The western end of the square is closed off by the colonnades of the **Konigsbau**. Built as a ballroom and concert hall in 1856, it today houses the Württemberg stock exchange and a sprinkling of upmarket shops. Opposite is the **Neues Schloß**, begun in 1746 by the people of Stuttgart to stop the petulant 16-year-old Duke Karl Eugen from moving the family seat back to Ludwigsberg (*see* below). Perhaps this explains their lack of loyalty to the building which, after extensive war damage, was nearly replaced in the 1950s by a department store. The Schloß took 60 years to build (part of it burning down in the process) and ended up a haphazard mixture of late Baroque, Rococo, Classicist and Empire styles. Today it houses government ministries, though the *Weisser Saal* (White Hall) is sometimes open for lectures and concerts.

The early 20th-century **Kunstgebäude**, on the northern side of the square, with its delicate arcades and copper dome, adds a softer touch. The big golden stag on the dome is the Württemberg family crest. Today the building houses the **Galerie der Stadt Stuttgart** (Stuttgart City Gallery) *(Tues–Fri 10–6, Sat and Sun 11–5; adm free)*, which has work by contemporary local artists, most notably Adolf Hözel, Oskar Schlemmer and the jolly abstracts of Willi Baumeister. But the museum is most renowned for its large and excellent collection of the Expressionist Otto Dix (*see* p. 65).

Across the southern end of the square you can see the **Alte Kanzlei** (Old Chancellery, built in 1541–3, now a restaurant), the **Mercury Tower** (a 1598 water reservoir tipped with a gold-plated 19th-century statue of the god), and the **Altes Schloß**.

The Württemberg court moved to Stuttgart in 1321 after the family home near Rotenberg had been flattened during tiffs with the Hapsburgs. The Gothic **Dürnitz** wing dates from this period, but most of the Altes Schloß was built around 1550 by Aberlin Tretsch. The Renaissance courtyard, with three tiers of arcades, decorated columns and richly carved portals is wonderfully evocative of the days when minstrels sang from its galleries and mounted knights thundered about the cobbletones.

Today the Altes Schloß houses the **Landesmuseum** (State Museum) *(Tues–Sun 10–5, Wed 10–7; adm free)*, which has a superb collection of Medieval Swabian sculpture. Other booty from surrounding monasteries includes stained glass from Bad Wimpfen and Alpirsbach and a lovingly detailed 16th-century portal from Ochsenhausen, on which fearsome little gargoyles and grumpy caryatids eye each other across the doorway. There are vast arrays of Roman and Frankish weapons and jewellery, and the entire contents of the grave of a Celtic prince. At the top of one of the towers you can see the Würtemberg crown jewels, and on the way up there's a case of exquisite 15th-century gold-leaf playing cards, divided into suits of dogs, ducks, falcons and deer. There's also a world famous collection of clocks and some old musical instruments, which get played at Sunday recitals.

If you ask at the porter's desk for a key, you can see the **Schloßkirche**, the first church in Germany specifically designed to meet Protestant requirements, with emphasis placed on the pulpit rather than the altar. In 1865 King Karl renovated the church, encrusting it with neo-Gothic grotesquery.

The Schillerplatz

The Altes Schloß and Alte Kanzlei form one corner of Schillerplatz, which has far more of a quiet old world charm than its neighbour, especially on flower market days (*Tues, Thurs, Sat*). An early 19th-century statue of the poet Friedrich Schiller (1759–1805), who was born nearby and spent several years in Stuttgart, is in the middle of the square. He was forced to flee the city after writing *Die Räuber* (The Robbers), a tirade against tyranny too hot for the absolutist Würtembergs.

On the southern side of the square is the **Stiftskirche**, a late-Gothic church built largely by Aberlin Jörg, who was responsible for many of the other churches in Stuttgart. The church turns its chancel on Schillerplatz, so you have to walk around to Stiftstraße for a good view of the mismatched towers and modern bronze doors designed in 1984 by Jurgen Weber. Most of the church fittings are modern, following severe war damage, but it's worth a look inside for the superbly carved **Grafenstandbilder** (ancestral gallery) of the Würtembergs, carved by the Swabian Sem Schlör in 1576. Next door to the church is the **Stiftsfruchtkasten**, once a wine and grain warehouse. A jolly Bacchus sports himself on top of the high Renaissance façade.

Markthalle and the Marktplatz

Nearby, in Dorotheenstraße, is the **Markthalle**, a big undercover market. Intriguing touches of the original Art Nouveau design survive, such as exotic gryphons above the arches, fish and fruit reliefs and a fading mural of jolly peasants. Inside the bright hall traders compete above the noise; glossy fruits, banks of flowers and peculiar sausages, scents of spices, cheeses and roasted coffee beans lure you this way and that. You can climb above the fray to a little café in the gallery, to take the whole scene in at once.

South of the Markthalle, on Marktplatz, is the hideous 1950s **Neue Rathaus**, but to the north you'll find Karlsplatz, and (on Saturdays) a small fleamarket with the usual piles of old leather suitcases, used telephone cards and suspect Dresden china. The yellow **Waisenhaus**, along the eastern end of the square, was built as a barracks in 1705, but spent most of its life as a jail and orphanage.

A busy highway thunders past, but you can cut back towards the Bahnhof through the **Akadamiegarten** and the southern end of the **Schloßgaarten**. Here you can have a look at the elegant curved façade of the **Staatstheater**, the opera house built in 1912 by the famous theatre architect, Max Lipmann.

The Staatsgalerie

On the other side of the hectic Konrad-Adenauer-Straße is Stuttgart's most controversial recent building: Scottish architect James Stirling's (d.1992) 1984 extension of the **Staatsgalerie** *(Tues–Sun 10–5, Tues and Thurs open until 8; adm free)*. Its cheeky postmodernism upset the sober Swabians, as had a statue by fellow Britisher Henry Moore some 10 years earlier. But the dark mutterings turned to murmurs of pride when the rest of the world erupted in enthusiastic praise of the building. Now it features in all the tourist brochures and even the Moore has been brought out of its old hiding place in the bushes and displayed prominently in front of the museum.

The Neue Staatsgalerie is a breathtaking building which thoroughly deserves all the praise and attention it is getting. Built largely from the same materials as the 19th-century Staatsgalerie, Stirling's building gracefully emanates from the old museum and curves round a vine covered inner courtyard, dotted with classical statues and evocative of a Roman arena. Other architectural quotes abound—Romanesque windows, hard Bauhaus lines, bright coloured handrails and trendy pink fluorescent tubes. The new extension has also done wonders for the museum's attendance figures—in the first year that it was open, annual admissions rose from 210,000 to 1.3 million. That is a good thing, for the collection is a fine one.

The works of art are divided along much the same lines as the buildings. The Alte Galerie houses work up to the early 20th century, and modern and contemporary pieces are displayed in the Neue Galerie. The early collection is especially strong on Old German Masters, featuring Swabians such as Bartolomäus Zeitblom and the Master of the Sterzing Altar. The most startling piece in the gallery is the enormous *Herrenberger Altar* (1519), a suitably extravagant work by the bolshy political activist Jerg Ratgeb, who has filled panels with a welter of quirky detail—lizards and scorpions scuttle around the base of the cross, the remains of the drunken guards' card came lie scattered outside Christ's grave. Look out also for paintings by another rather idiosyncratic artist, Hans Baldung *(see* p. 58), one time pupil of Dürer; some fine pieces by Cranach the Elder; and a sombre, almost monotone *Flight to Egypt* (1505) by the Master of Frankfurt.

There's a solid selection of Dutch Masters, including Rubens, Ruisdael, Hals and some early Rembrandt, and Tiepollo and Tintoretto make their appearance in the Italian section. The 19th century is largely given over to Swabian Romantic painters, but there's also a superb eight-piece cycle by Edward Burne-Jones depicting an androgynously beautiful Perseus as he rescues a limp Andromeda from the clutches of the Gorgon Medusa.

The highlight of the Neue Galerie is the excellent Picasso collection, the largest and most important in Germany. As well as instantly recognizable images, such as the *Woman in a*

Vest, there are some surprises, among them his sculpture *The Bathers*—a witty group of wooden figures standing on a pebble beach.

The rest of the gallery is a carefully selected Who's Who of a century of art, ranging from French Impressionists through Dali, Magritte and German Expressionism on to Andy Warhol, Jackson Pollock and the avant-garde. You can trace the development of Max Beckmann (1884–1950, *see* p.64) from an early (albeit frantic) classicism to his more familiar disturbed Expressionism. There are magnificent paintings by the contemporary painter Anselm Kiefer, and delightful and bizarre figures made by local artist Oskar Schlemmer (1888–1943) for the *Triadischen Ballet* in 1922. There's a whole room of the usual Joseph Beuys bits of felt, metal and broken machinery—but also the uncharacteristic and rather charming *Friedenhase* (1982), a golden rabbit nestling among cheap baubles behind thick plate glass. The museum also stages contemporary exhibitions, and the down-stairs café is a popular rendezvous for Stuttgart's arty set.

The Outskirts

The Schloßpark is nearly 4km long and leads eventually to the River Neckar on the northern edge of town. The park is narrow and fairly cultivated, but at the northern end it opens out into **Rosensteinpark**. Here there are wild flowers and open meadows that stretch out to the vineyards beyond, but there is an odd sense of desolation which seems to attract lonely, depressed men who sit motionless under the trees. At the top of the hill is **Schloß Rosenstein** (at the time of writing closed for renovations), built in 1824 as a royal country seat. Local legend has it that a fortune-teller told King Wilhelm I that he would die if he ever slept there. He assiduously avoided staying over at the Schloß. But one foul night in 1864 the court doctor persuaded the elderly king, after a long journey, to bed down at Rosenstein rather then struggle the last few kilometres back to Stuttgart. It was his first night in the Schloß, and his last anywhere.

Across the Neckar is **Bad Canstatt**, once a famous spa town but now more noted for its Volkfest (*see* **Festivals** above). At the **Lautenschlagerbrunnen** (lute-player fountain) in front of the old Kurhaus you can join the queue of old men laden with bottles, thirsty cyclists and harrassed mums waiting for a sip of the cool, fizzy, faintly metallic water. The Kurpark runs into Gottfried Daimler's back garden, where you can see the (much reno-vated) shed where he invented the first petrol engine. Now it's a small museum *(daily Apr–Oct 11–4; adm free)*, where you can see a motorcycle, boat, train and motorized car-riage, all built before 1888 and all sporting a Daimler engine.

For a view over the whole town—even as far as the Alps on a clear day—head for the 217m-high **Fernsehturm** (Television Tower) at Jahnstr. 7 *(8am–midnight; adm DM5)*, built in 1956, the first of its kind. The observation platform and restaurant are 150m high.

Mineral Baths

Stuttgart's mineral waters are certainly more enjoyable to swim in than to drink (*see* **Bad Cannstatt**). The best place for a rejuvenating dip is the modern **Leuze Mineralbad**,

Am Leuzebad 2–6 *(daily 6–9, last tickets 8; adm DM8 for 2 hours)*. Here you can be pummeled by massage jets, float about in cool, fizzy water, paddle through indoor and outdoor pools at a variety of temperatures, or frolic among the floor whisks, bubble pools and water spouts. If you don't mind having instructions shouted at you by a little man in white, you can even join in the communal underwater exercises. Afterwards you can sunbathe on the grass, have a sauna, jog about the keep fit trail, or just get drunk in the café. As well as a swimming costume, you will need a bathing cap (men too); a shower cap will do, and the ticket office sells disposable plastic ones.

Classic Cars

A little way out of town, but a must—even for those usually bored by the achievements and foibles of motoring—is the **Daimler-Benz Museum** at the Daimler-Benz Factory, Mercedesstraße *(Tues–Sun 9–5; adm free; Bus 56, S-Bahn line 1 to Neckarstadion)*. In the 1880s, with odd coincidence, Gottfried Daimler and Karl Benz simultaneously invented the motor car—Daimler in his garden shed in Stuttgart, and Benz just 150km away in Mannheim. The two firms only completely merged in 1960. It was Daimler's top salesman, Emil Jellinek, who called the new 1899 model after his own daughter, Mercedes. (Thankfully, modesty prevented him from using his own name.)

You are whisked by private bus from the entrance gates to a vast glass hall filled with gleaming cars. There are gracious early models with leather upholstery, brass switches and carved wooden knobs; 1920s sports cars and streamlined racers such as the Blitzen-Benz which clocked up 228kph (140mph) in 1909. You can also see some delightful oddities— including the inappropriately named Mercedes Simplex (1902) with a bewildering array of valves and pedals, and the 1935 Type 150 Sport Roadster, a jumped-up Noddy car. The elegant designs reach their height with the limousine designed for Emperor Hirohito and the first Popemobile, with a single armchair in the back. There's a recorded commentary (in English), films, interactive computer screens and a multi-media show.

The **Porsche Museum** at the Porsche Factory, Porschestraße *(Mon–Fri 9–12, 1.30–4; adm free; Bus 52, 90, 99 or S-Bahn line 6 to Neuwirtshaus)* is smaller and more low-key, but here you can tour the production line (prior reservation necessary; © (0711) 827 5685).

A World of Beer and Wine

In the suburb of Vaihingen the **Schwäbisches Brauereimuseum** (Swabian Brewery Museum) at Robert-Kochstr. 12 *(Tues–Sun 10.30–5.30; adm free; Bus 84, Tram 1 or 14, S-Bahn 1, 2 or 3)* is an interesting museum which takes you through five millenia of beer making around the world. In Uhlbach, set among the vineyards high above the city, the **Weinbaumuseum** at Uhlbacherplatz 4 *(Sat 2–6, Apr–Oct also Sun 10–12; adm free)* does much the same for wine, and also organizes tastings of local products.

The main shopping drag is the Königstraße, a pedestrian precinct which runs south from the Hauptbahnhof. Here you'll find major department stores and high-street shops. More upmarket establishments are on Stiftstraße and Eberhardstraße southeast of the Markt. Calwerstraat, parallel to Königstraat, has smaller, more interesting shops.

Entertainment and Nightlife

Stuttgart is the cultural centre of the region, and offers high-quality theatre and music. The **listings magazines** *Stuttgarter Monatsspiegel* or **Lift** will tell you all you need to know about what's happening in the theatres and concert halls. Their trendy counterpart, *Stuttgarter Strip* will let you in on the hippest night-life tips. The tourist office can help with **advance booking** for most events.

The home of the state opera and ballet is the **Staatstheater**, located in the southern part of the Schloßgarten, Oberer Schloßgarten 6, information © (0711) 20320, bookings © (0711) 22 17 95; the Großes Haus stages opera and ballet, the Kleines Haus puts on ballet and drama, and the Kammertheater houses more off-the-wall productions.

In the 1960s and early 1970s the **Stuttgart Ballet** under the direction of the legendary John Cranko, was by far the best in Germany. **Theatre** and **opera** under the control of Walter Erich Schäfer was equally visionary. Today the ballet company is led by Cranko's prima ballerina, Marcia Haydée, and still ranks highly, though it has lost its edge; theatre and opera now seem at their best under visiting directors, such as the innovative Peter Zadek. There's a blossoming experimental and **alternative theatre** scene (especially at Irrlicht-Theater, Augustenstr. 14 and Forum Theatre, Gymnasiumstr. 21) and two companies stage **plays in Swabian dialect** (Schwaben-Bühne, Frauenstr. 5 and Stäffelesrutscher, Rotebühlstr. 109b).

The chief **classical music** venue is the modern **Liederhalle** in Schloßstraße (bookings © (0711) 22 17 95), where the main auditorium is in the shape of a grand piano, surely a high-watermark of architectural kitsch. The **International Bach Academy**, formed in 1981, has already earned a strong international reputation under the leadership of Helmuth Rilling. Its ensembles are frequently to be heard around town, especially at the Stiftskirche. The **Stuttgart Kammerorchester** has a strong international reputation for Baroque music.

To sample the best of Stuttgart's nightlife, head for the bars and cafés in the Bohnenviertel (*see* below). Otherwise try Perkins Park, Stresemannstr. 39, a big, flash **disco** where everyone is on the lookout for visiting stars. The Altes Schützenhaus, Burgstallstr. 99, plays more **live music** and has more of a party atmosphere. Röhre, Neckarstr. 34–2, built in a disused railway tunnel and once *the* place to be, still hosts a variety of good bands. The trendies have headed off to Das Unbekannte Tier, Bolzstr. 10, or the DDR Bar in Theodore-Heuss-Straße.

The Dixieland Hall, Marienstr. 3b, swings with **trad jazz**, while Rogers Kiste, Hauptstätter Str. 35, and Oktave, Eberhardstr. 49, have a cosier atmosphere, host a range of jazz bands and sometimes erupt into spontaneous jam-sessions.

Stuttgart ✆ *(0711–)* **Where to Stay**

Property in the centre of Stuttgart ranks with the most expensive in the world. Hotel prices reflect this, though there are some bargains to be had.

expensive

Am Schloßgarten, Schillerstr. 23, ✆ 2 02 60, fax 20 26 888 (DM340–400). Stuttgart's top address. Here you live in pampered luxury and have splendid views over the Schloßgarten.

Queens Hotel Bristol, Wilhelm-Haspel-Str. 101, Sindelfingen, ✆ (07031) 6150, fax 87 49 81 (DM250–350). Calm and briskly efficient business hotel 20 minutes out of Stuttgart on the A81. Here you can banish the strains of the day in the sauna or jacuzzi before a meal in the gourmet restaurant.

moderate

Azenberg, Seestr. 114–116, ✆ 221 051, fax 297 426 (from DM180). Well-equipped hotel with pool and views over the city. (Bus 43 to Hölderlinstraße).

Hotel Ketterer, Marienstr. 3, ✆ 20 39 0, fax 2 03 96 00 (DM173–255). Close to the centre, yet a step back from the noisy mainstream. A modern hotel with a warm, friendly atmosphere.

Hotel Rotenberg, Stettenerstr. 87, ✆ 33 12 93 (DM120). Out of town in the eastern suburbs, with fine views over the vineyards.

Waldhotel Degerloch, Guts-Muths-Weg 18, ✆ 765 017, fax 765 3762 (from DM160). Quiet, hillside suburban hotel with garden. (U-Bahn 15 or 16 to Ruhbank).

inexpensive

Pension Märklin, Friedrichstr. 39, ✆ 29 13 15 (DM80–90 without breakfast). Cheap and convenient. Situated in a trendy but rather noisy part of town.

Eckel, Vorsteigstr. 10, ✆ 29 0995 (DM80). Small, family-run pension, not too far from the centre (bus 40 to Hölderlinplatz).

Youth Hostel: Haußmannstr. 27, ✆ 241 583.

Eating and Drinking

Liaber meh essa als zwenig trinka
(Rather eat more than drink too little).

Erst s'Om-de-Romm ond s Lass-mi-ao-mit machts Leba schee
(It's sociability and 'Let me join in' that make life so wonderful).

Two Swabian Proverbs

Stuttgart's convivial taverns, when you find them, are among the best things the city has to offer. Swabian cuisine is robust and delicious—with beefy stews, lots of onions and an abundance of noodles—and is usually washed down with quantities of local wine.

Specialities include *Zwiebelkuchen*, spicy breads made with onions, sour cream and bacon that are the perfect seasonal accompaniment to new autumn wine; and *Gaisburger Marsch*, a soporific stew of *Spätzle*, potatoes, beef and onions. The most ubiquitous local fodder is the *Maultasche* ('snout pocket'), a sort of giant ravioli with a variety of spicy fillings—often very tasty. Wily Catholics supposedly invented *Maultaschen* to hide the fact that they were eating meat on a Friday. When Queen Elizabeth visited Stuttgart, the name on the menu was changed to *Mundtasche* (mouth pocket), in deference to delicate royal sensibilities. **Spätzle** (delicate-tasting noodles) also crop up everywhere.

The **Calwerstraße**, which runs parallel to the top end of Königstraße, survived the Second World War and 1960s development unscathed. The pretty 15th–19th-century façades now front countless chic restaurants and cafés. Money is a great leveller, though, and the establishments are fairly indistinguishable. (If you're in Calverstraße during the day, pop into No. 39, a grocery store which still has its original 19th-century fittings.) Across the highway that hurtles down the east side of town, and up towards the red-light district, you come to small quarter of crumbly old houses known locally as the **Bohnenviertel**. Here, on the patch where market-gardeners once grew vines and beans (*Bohnen*), you'll find some good restaurants and cosy old wine taverns. If you would prefer somewhere more central, try the handful of good cafés and restaurants that cluster around the **Hans-im-Glück-Brunnen** (up Geißstraße, behind the Rathaus).

Württemberg Wines

Württemberg wines have a low international profile only because locals guzzle virtually the entire harvest: the average Stuttgarter gets through 60 litres a year. Wine comes in generous *Viertele*—quarter litre glasses with handles. Stuttgart's own vineyards produce rich reds from the Trollinger grape (grown only in Württemberg), but the Rieslings are also good. In November, some growers hang a broom or wreath above their front door to show that you can drop in for a taste of the new wine. These informal **Besenwirtschaften** ('Broom pubs') are allowed to stay open until March. Near to the centre of town they tend to be a bit commercialized, but if you're travelling around Stuttgart keep an eye open for an old *Besen*—you could very well end up *Viertele schlótza* (literally 'sucking on' wine) with local farmers in someone's front parlour.

Restaurants and Taverns

Alte Post, Friedrichstr. 43, ✆ 29 30 79 (DM70). Reputedly Stuttgart's best restaurant. Serves superb Swabian-inspired dishes.

Paulaner, Calwerstraße (DM25–45). Stuttgart's only surviving Baroque mansion (next to the Postbrunnen) is a *Brauerei* and restaurant with more charm than the others in Calwerstraße. Good beer and meaty cuisine.

Drei Mohren, Pfarrstraße (DM35–50). Quiet restaurant in the Bohnenviertel. Candle-lit nooks, local lovers and hefty Swabian cuisine.

Costas, Rosenstraße (DM25–35). Busy Bohnenviertel tavern where local Greeks go for a taste of home cooking.

Kachelofen, Hans-im-Glück-Brunnen (DM25–45). Snug restaurant that serves soul-warming Swabian dishes. Ideal for a cold winter's night.

Bars and Cafés

Schellenturm, Wagnerstraße. Tiny wine bar in a tower of the old city wall with a strong core of friendly regulars.

Kiste, Kanalstr. 2. A Bohnenviertel legend. Once the favoured haunt of an incognito King Wilhelm I (it was owned by his coachman), the Weinstube now attracts yuppies and would-be artists, and is preferred for its wine rather than the food.

Stetter, Rosenstraße. The most atmospheric Weinstube in the Bohnenviertel. It has a wine shop attached, but both are only open during the day.

Charlottenkeller, off Karlsplatz. Through an iron gate in the Waisenhaus on Karlsplatz, you'll find a secluded but popular Bierkeller which spills out into the courtyard during the summer.

Day Trips from Stuttgart: Palaces and Monasteries

Schloß Ludwigsburg

Make sure you have a good night's sleep, take an extra cup of coffee at breakfast and put on comfortable shoes before visiting Schloß Ludwigsburg, 15km north of Stuttgart (S-Bahn line 4 or 5, motorway A8 or A81) *(guided tours only; 4–5 daily Apr–Oct, 2–3 daily in winter; information © (07141) 91 02 52; duration 1¼ hours; adm DM4.50).* Not only is this Germany's biggest Baroque Schloß (modelled on Versailles), but it has acres of garden too.

The Schloß began as a modest hunting lodge commissioned by Duke Eberhard Ludwig of Württemberg in 1703. But the fashion-conscious young ruler got a glimpse of Versailles during wars with France and returned in 1714 fired with much grander ideas. The Renaissance hunting lodge grew into a 452-roomed, ochre-coloured Baroque pile, quite out of proportion with either the Württembergs' income or their status.

Lesser mortals were at first reluctant to come and live in the palace's shadow: not even the offer of free land, building materials and exemption from taxes could lure them. So the duke appealed to even baser instincts, and promised to move his official seat from Stuttgart to Schloß Ludwigsburg as soon as it was finished. The population of the town of Ludwigsburg subsequently shot up from 18 to 5000. The duke's successor moved back to Stuttgart four years later.

On the guided tour you barely skim the surface, visiting a mere 50 rooms of Baroque opulence. Italian stucco artists and fresco painters commissioned by the Duke became locked in a frantic competition to outdo each other, and it shows. If one designed a grand stairway, another would upstage it with elaborate statues, then a third would daub some nifty *trompe l'oeil* painting nearby to distract your attention even further. Mounds of gilding, cascades of silk drapery, lakes of parquet and forests of marble leave you limp and wondering how the residents ever managed to get through a day without lying down for a large proportion of it with their eyes shut. Amidst all this splendour is the dinky palace theatre, built in 1758, but redecorated in a more modest Neoclassical style half a century later. It boasts the world's first revolving stage.

A stroll through the garden offers no relief. There are 30 hectares of it. Arabesques of blossoms and coloured pebbles, vast fountains and geometric hedges adorn the formal section. The wilder English garden plunges into a valley and is dotted with fake ruins. There are lakes, flamingos, peacocks and, in the Japanese garden, a few scraggly Bonsai trees. In the *Märchengarten* (fairytale garden), giants rise booming out of castles, Rapunzel lets down her hair and real, live children leap, screaming with joy, as giant plastic frogs spit at them from a pond. Bridal couples pose wherever you look, and there are tourists *everywhere*. From April to October the gardens are the scene of *Blühendes Barock* (Baroque in Bloom), a huge floral festival.

Just 400m to the north of the palace is the summer residence, **Schloß Favorite** *(guided tours Tues–Sun 10–12 and 1.30–4; adm DM3)*, a petite building re-decorated at the end of the 18th century in a milder Classicist style. Fewer people make it up to Favorite, but its light and delicately designed rooms make it worth the walk. There's a mechanical organ which plays the same tune for you as it did for Duke Friedrich two centuries ago; and a stunning porcelain urn designed by the famous Karl Friedrich Schinkel (*see* **The Arts and Culture** p. 60).

Two Types of Solitude

A few kilometres west of Stuttgart, and closer to town, is **Schloß Solitude** *(Apr–Oct Tues–Sun 9–12 and 1.30–5, Nov–Mar 10–12 and 1.30–4; adm DM2.50; Bus 92)*. A pretty Rococo building with cake-icing stucco and elaborate parquet floors, the Schloß was built in 1764 by Duke Carl Eugen as a summer palace. A straight road ran the 13km to Ludwigsburg in the north. As the weather warmed up, furniture and provisions were carted down from the main palace, and up to 1500 guests would follow to dance and feast in the oval White Hall, or play blind man's buff in the garden. There's a pricey, but very elegant restaurant in the outbuildings.

Forty kilometres northwest of Stuttgart, on the B35, lies **Kloster Maulbron** *(Apr–Nov 8.30–6.30, Nov–Apr Tues–Sun 9.30–1 and 4–5; adm DM4)*, the beautifully preserved Cistercian monastery which Herman Hesse used as a setting for his novel *Narziss and Goldmund*. The entrance to the monastery is enclosed by a village-sized courtyard—a cosy jumble of stone and half-timbered buildings where the lay-brothers had their forge, apothecary, mill and storerooms. In the southeast corner you can see the **Faustturm**, residence of the real-life Doctor Faustus, one Johannes Faust, an early 16th-century scholar. He died in an inn in Staufen in the Black Forest as the result of a chemical explosion (*see* p. 285). The pong of his ultimate experiment—together with his rather dubious reputation as an alchemist—sparked off the rumour that he was a necromancer. This legend was later recorded (by an anonymous author) in the *Faustbuch*, the book that inspired Goethe and Christopher Marlowe. Today most of the old buildings in the courtyard are restaurants or cafés. There's also a **tourist information office**, © (07043) 1030 *(Apr–Nov Mon–Fri 8–12, Mon and Thurs also 1–5.30, Tues and Wed also 1–4.30, Sat and Sun 11–5; Nov–Apr Fri 8–12, Sat and Sun 11–5)*.

In the monastery itself, a fountain splashes in the cloister, there's a smell of old wood from the heavily carved 15th-century choir stalls and light shines through the empty Gothic window frames and plays softly over Romanesque arches. There's a quiet simplicity about the building, and an almost austere calm. You wouldn't be at all surprised to see a line of cowled monks file in from around the corner, but in fact there are no longer any monks living there. The graceful lay refectory dates from the beginning of the 13th century, and in the monks' refectory you can see the beginnings of some frescoes commissioned from the fiery Jerg Ratgreb (*see* p. 58). Instead of finishing them, he went off to join the Peasants' Revolt (*see* **History** p. 41) and ended up in four pieces in Pforzheim market square.

Tübingen

Tübingen, like Heidelberg, is a university town on the Neckar. Unlike Heidelberg, students and teaching staff are not outnumbered by tourists: they make up nearly half of Tübingen's population. It is a beautiful town with jumbles of brightly coloured half-timbered houses, prised apart by narrow, steeply winding stone stairways. Along the river are lines of grand old villas, and a solid Schloß keeps check from the hill above. But it is the university that breathes life into Tübingen. 'We have a town on our campus,' quip the locals. Everywhere people stride about with purpose, clutching little piles of books. They talk earnestly on street corners between lectures and brood over cups of strong coffee and roll-up cigarettes in the cafés. There is a serious, hardworking atmosphere in Tübingen, but also a university-town air of home-grown entertainment. Narrow streets echo with the sound of impromptu sitting-room concerts, couples punt lazily up the Neckar, students picnic in the parks—and even, on fine summer evenings, in the market square.

The university was founded in 1477 by Duke Eberhard the Bearded, and has a strong tradition of academic excellence and liberal thought. (This has rubbed off on the town— Tübingen is a centre of Green politics and has one of the few left-wing councils in Baden-Württemberg.) Johannes Kepler, the founder of modern astronomy, was a student here, and the most famous alumni—Hegel, Hölderlin and Schelling—all shared the same room in 1790–1. For years Catholic priests in the theological faculty have co-habited openly with their 'housekeepers', and in the 1970s the theologian Hans Küng was stripped of his offices by the Vatican for writing books questioning papal infallibility. Walter Jens, the left-wing critic and novelist, teaches in the classics department. More gentle flowers have grown in this hothouse of radicalism, including the 16th-century botanist Leonhard Fuchs, after whom the fuchsia is named.

By train: The **Hauptbahnhof** is five minutes' walk from the town centre. A branch line connects Tübingen with Stuttgart (1hr). All the main sights are within easy walking distance of the Bahnhof.

By car: Tübingen is about 40km south of Stuttgart on the A27a.

By boat: Boats and punts can be hired at the base of the Neckarbrücke.

The **tourist information office** is on the Neckarbrücke, © (07071) 3 50 11 *(Mon–Fri 9–6.30, Sat 9–5, Apr–Nov also Sun 2–5pm)*.

The Altstadt

Tübingen's **market** is a bright and bubbling brew of townsfolk, students and local farmers with heaps of fresh fruit and giant vegetables. At one end is a delightfully gaudy (mainly 15th-century) **Rathaus**, covered with 19th-century frescoes and with a pompous little pulpit jutting out of the first floor. An ornate gable surrounds the **astronomical clock**, made by Johannes Stiffler in 1511, which wheezes on the hour to a very slow chime. The Rathaus is not strictly a tourist attraction, but if you stride in with enough confidence, you can see (in the *Große Sitzungsaal* on the first floor) some of the original huge oak supporting beams and pillars. In the *Empfangsaal* on the second floor are some 16th-century grisaille frescoes.

Beside the Rathaus, the **Burgsteige** ascends past some of the oldest houses in Tübingen and brings you to the ornate Renaissance portal of **Schloß Hohentübingen** *(guided tours of prison and great vat Apr–Sept Sat 5pm, Sun 11am and 3pm; adm DM3)*. The gate, built between 1604 and 1606 in the form of a Roman triumphal arch is the best part of the Schloß, which is otherwise worth the climb only for the views. Experts will spot the riband of the Order of the Garter curled around the Württemberg coat of arms. Queen Elizabeth I had bestowed the honour on Duke Friedrich just before the gate was built.

Back down the Burgsteige, and to the right, you'll come to Münzgasse, which leads you to the heart of the old university district. Today the university is centered mainly north of the town, along Wilhelmstraße, but Münzgasse and the adjoining Holzmarkt is still a hub of student life, with bookshops and smoky cafés in the alleys, and buskers and fledging public orators on the square.

Everything is very much in the shadow of the enormous Gothic **Stiftskirche**. Highlights inside the church include a finely-carved late-Gothic canopied pulpit, an altar painting by Hans Schaufelein (a pupil of Dürer's) and thirteen richly carved tombs of members of the ruling House of Württemberg. On the square around the church you can see the bright pink **Buchhandlung Heckenhauer**, where Hermann Hesse worked for four years (learning bookbinding after dropping out of university) and the **Cottahaus**, Munzgasse 15, once headquarters of the famous publishing company. Under Johann Friedrich Cotta, the

Cotta-Verlag published Schiller and most of the stars of the German Enlightenment, and set up the liberal *Allgemeine Zeitung*. Nearby is the Baroque **Alte Aula**, the old University Hall and at Münzgasse 20 you can see the old **Studentenkarzer** (student jail) *(Sat only, guided tour at 2pm; adm DM1)*. Up Pfleghofstraße, behind the square, is the daunting **Pleghof**. Once a nursing home and then a tithe barn for the Bebenhausen Monastery (*see* **Outside Tübingen** below), its seemingly impregnable walls now enclose the police station and student residences.

Below the Alte Aula, right on the water's edge, is the **Hölderlinturm** *(Tues–Fri 10–12 and 3–5, Sat and Sun 2–5; adm DM1)*. The poet Friedrich Hölderlin lodged here with a carpenter's family from 1807 until his death in 1843. He paced the length of the long hall 'every day, with tremendous strides', coming up with highly charged, complex poetry—some of the best in the language—and slowly sinking further and further into insanity. Today the tower houses a small memorial museum. Across the river is the **Plantenallee**, a long island park which is a favourite student gathering place (reached from the Neckarbrücke).

Further up the street is the pink **Bursa**, built between 1478 and 1482 as a student dormitory. It is still used for lectures. At the top of the street is the **Evangelisches Stift**, the Protestant theological college where Hegel, Hölderlin and Schelling shared their room.

The Altstadt spreads out to the north of the Marktplatz. Here you can see parts of the old city wall, and some impressive half-timbered buildings. The **Fruchtschranne** (an enormous 15th-century fruit warehouse) in Schmiedtorstraße and the 14th-century **Nonnenhaus** (Nun's House) off Langestraße are both worth the walk. The **Kornhaus** (1453) has been deftly converted into the city museum.

Tübingen ℂ (07071–)   ***Where to Stay***

Hotels are pricey, and few and far between, especially in the Altstadt.

Hotel Krone, Uhlandstr. 1, ℂ 3 10 36, fax 3 87 18 (DM220–250). The town's most upmarket hotel. Attentive care and comfort, but little flair and situated on a busy traffic junction.

Hotel an Schloß, Burgsteige 18, ℂ 2 10 77, fax 5 20 90 (DM95–135). Pick of the bunch. Ancient inn right up against the castle gate. Friendly staff.

Hotel Hospiz, Neckarhalde 2, ℂ 26002, fax 26385 (DM130–170). Unpretentious hotel near the Schloß. Pleasant rooms, some with a good view over the town.

Pension Binder, Nonnengasse 4, ℂ 52643 (DM103–140). Quiet; in the Altstadt.

Youth Hostel: Gartenstr. 22, ℂ 23002.

Eating and Drinking: Restaurants and Taverns

Mauganeschtle, Burgsteige 18, ℂ 210 7779 (DM20–40). The place to come if you've developed a taste for *Maultaschen* (*see* p. 261). You can choose from 26 different types.

Forelle, Kronenstr 8, ✆ 22938 (DM30–45). Good old-fashioned *Weinstube* with excellent game and trout dishes.

Ristorante Est! Est!, Neckargasse 22, ✆ 24216 (DM15–40). Cosy, circular pizzeria in the tower at the beginning of the Neckarbrücke.

Bars and Cafés

Tübingen is very much a student town. During vacations it can be very quiet. In term time activity centres on the Marktplatz and surrounding alleys.

Marktschänke, Am Markt 11. On the market square. Traditional venue for a lively night's drinking with students.

Tangente, Pflegerstr 10. Also popular with students, but has a more trendy edge.

Hades, Halengasse. Quite sedate—despite its name and the red light outside. Patronized by an older crowd.

Alte Tübingen, Haaggasse 8. A cosy place for a slow drink and long chat.

Around Tübingen

Bebenhausen

Just north of Tübingen, on the edge of a nature reserve, is the beautiful hamlet of Bebenhausen, with its Cistercian **Kloster**. The abbey dates from the 12th century, but has 16th and 17th-century embellishments. From 1806 to 1918 it served time as hunting lodge to the Württembergs, and King Wilhelm II lived there in exile after his abdication in 1918. He died three years later, but Queen Charlotte lived on until 1946. After her death, Bebenhausen was used by the *Land* parliament of Württemberg until the unification with Baden in 1952. You can still see some of the dark, panelled, decorated rooms of the Hunting Lodge *(Tues–Sun, tours on the hour 10–4 inclusive except 1pm; adm DM2.50)*, but the main attraction is what remains of the old abbey *(Tues–Sun 10–12 and 2–5; adm DM2, combined ticket DM4)*. Especially impressive are the 16th-century Winter Refectory (where the carved ceiling is supported by three slender wooden columns) and the Lay Refectory. Here the painted vaulted roof has survived, completely unrestored, since 1530.

Monks at Bebenhausen led a hard life. The Cistercians were a silent order, and the brothers were allowed to speak for only 10 minutes a day (in the *Parlatorium*). They were called to prayer seven times every 24 hours and, in winter, were allowed only one hour a day near the fire in the 'warming room'. Even the times that they went to the toilet were prescribed—but they could wash daily (the whole body on Saturdays) and were allowed a bath at Christmas and Easter (a lot for those days).

Where to Stay and Eating Out

Landhotel Hirsch, Schönbuchstr. 28, Tübingen-Bebenhausen, ✆ (07071) 68027, fax 600803 (DM200). A haven for anyone who wants to escape the cares of the world, with a good restaurant, too.

Burg Hohenzollern

In the gently rolling green countryside 30km south of Tübingen on the B27, perched on top of a conical hill, is Burg Hohenzollern *(Apr–Oct 9–5.30, Nov–Mar 9–4.30, guided tours only; adm DM 5)*, the towering ancestral home of the powerful Hohenzollern dynasty, who schemed and battled through centuries to emerge in 1871 as rulers of the newly unified German Empire *(see* p. 43). You can see it from miles around, a little like the giant's castle in a fairytale. You spiral higher and higher up through the woods to reach the Schloß (a 15-minute walk from the car park, though you can take a mini-bus for DM3.50 return). Guided tours begin from the outer courtyard.

Although the Hohenzollerns first built a castle on the hill in the 10th century, the present Schloß is largely a 19th-century Neo-Gothic reconstruction with hefty Prussian fortifications. The **St Michael Kappelle**, with Gothic stained glass and some Romanesque reliefs, is all that survives from earlier buildings. Inside, the Schloß seems surprisingly modest for the seat of so grand a family, though there is some beautifully-worked parquet flooring. Look out for the charming portrait of Prince Waldemar, painted in 1876 by his mother the Empress Victoria (daughter of the British Queen) and one of Fredrick the Great, looking just a little tired and ruffled 'On his return from the Seven Years War'. In the **Schatzkammer** (treasure chamber) you can see the crown of Prussia, and some bejewelled snuff boxes (including one that saved the life of Frederick the Great by absorbing a bullet).

Rottweil

Thirty kilometres further south along the B27 is **Rottweil**, ancestral home of fierce, ugly dogs. The town itself, however, is friendly and bustling with brightly painted old houses which have survived unmolested by warfare since the 17th century. Winding streets of ancient pot-bellied dwellings suddenly open out to reveal astonishing views, for Rottweil is squeezed onto the top of a precipitous spur.

The Gothic church, the **Heilig-Kreuz-Münster** (Münsterplatz), has a severe interior that puts you firmly in your place on the Divine hierarchical scale, but the cheerful Baroque ornamentation of the **Kapellenkirche** (in Hochbrucktorstraße) will provide an antidote. The most compelling reason for visiting Rottweil, however, is the **Dominikanermuseum** at Am Kriegsdamm *(Tues–Sun 10–1 and 2–5; adm DM3)*. Here you can see the 2nd-century **Orpheus Mosaic** from Arae Flaviae, the Roman settlement that preceded Rottweil. Orpheus plays his lyre to an array of birds and beasts. Upstairs is the **Sammlung Dursch**, a stunning collection of 14th–16th century Swabian wood carving.

Rottweil is off the tourist routes, and is a good place to come for a really authentic taste of **Fastnet** (Carnival). The highpoint of the celebrations is *Narrensprung*

('Parade of Fools') on Shrove Tuesday. You can see some of the beautifully carved wooden masks used in the *Narrensprung* parade (as well as other interesting displays on the town's history) in the **Stadtmuseum** at Hauptstr. 20 *(Mon–Thurs and Sat 9–12 and 2–5, Fri 9–12, Sun 10–12; adm free)*.

See also Directory entry for Haigerloch.

Tourist Information

The **tourist information office** is at the Altes Rathaus, ✆ (0741) 49 42 80.

Where to Stay and Eating Out

Hotel Lamm, Hauptstr. 45, ✆ (0741) 45015, fax (0741) 44273 (DM95–140). An informal, family-run hotel in the middle of town.

Hotel zum Sternen, Hauptstr. 60; ✆ (0741) 7006, fax (0741) 23950 (DM185–220). Romantic old hotel with heavy wooden beams in some rooms.

Gasthaus Liederhalle, Präsenzgasse (DM25–45). Specializes in schnitzels and soups and has a fine view over the surrounding countryside.

Brüderschaftstube, Brüderschaftstraße. *Weinstube* celebrated for its home cooking.

Karlsruhe

If your taste is for Neoclassical architecture, or Jugendstil, or if you like looking at paintings and pottering around museums, you should do as the Margrave of Baden did in 1715, and break your journey at Karlsruhe. Margrave Karl Wilhelm so liked the spot he chose for a rest during a hunting trip, that he named it in honour of the occasion (*Ruhe* means 'rest') and announced that he had 'graciously decided to have a princely palace built, as a place of rest for the future'. While he was napping under a tree, so the story goes, he dreamt of a fan that his wife had lost earlier in the day, and hit upon the idea of surrounding his palace with a fan-shaped city. This he did, and the centre of Karlsruhe still follows this plan.

The Margrave was a child of his time, with aspirations to the absolutist grandeur of Versailles, but without the cash to realize them. His palace had to be fairly modest—but to compensate he made sure that none of the houses in his new city was more than a single story high. He also thoroughly indulged his passion for flowers, surrounding himself with acres of garden.

His successor, Karl Friedrich, commissioned the important German Neoclassical architect, Friedrich Weinbrenner, to redesign the Schloß. Karl Friedrich was one of the few German rulers to become chummy with Napoleon, with the result that during his long reign (1746–1811) he was elevated first to the status of Elector, then to Grand Duke (in 1806). The Grand Duchy of Baden flourished, and Karlsruhe became one of the most fashionable courts in Europe. Brahms opined that any decent man should visit Karlsruhe at least once a year. As favoured court architect, Weinbrenner got commissions all over town. Invading Prussians, and the city's position in the demilitarized zone after the First World War, put an

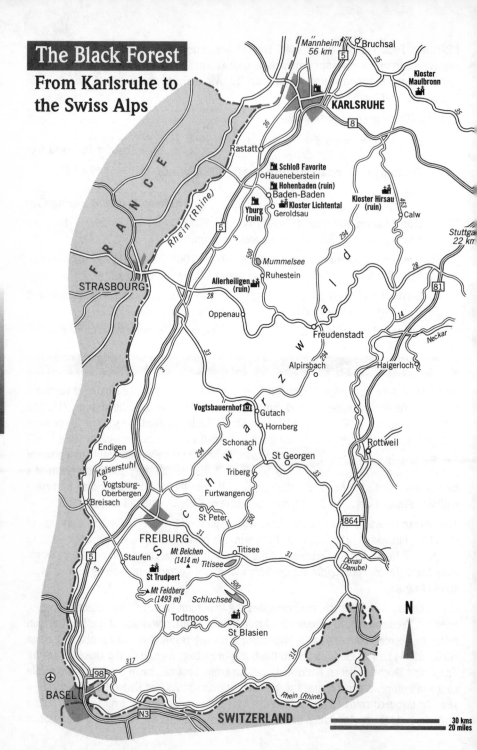

The Black Forest

From Karlsruhe to the Swiss Alps

Mannheim 56 km · Bruchsal

Kloster Maulbronn

KARLSRUHE

Rastatt

Schloß Favorite
Haueneberstein
Hohenbaden (ruin)
Baden-Baden
Yburg (ruin) · Kloster Lichtental
Geroldsau

Kloster Hirsau (ruin) · Calw

Stuttga 22 km

Rhein (Rhine)

STRASBOURG

Mummelsee
Ruhestein

Allerheiligen (ruin)

Oppenau

Freudenstadt

Alpirsbach · Haigerloch

Neckar

Vogtsbauernhof · Gutach
Hornberg

Schonach

Endigen

Kaiserstuhl
Vogtsburg-Oberbergen
Breisach

St Georgen · Rottweil

Triberg

Furtwangen

St Peter

FREIBURG
Staufen · Mt Belchen (1414 m) · Titisee
St Trudpert
Mt Feldberg (1493 m) · Schluchsee

Todtmoos
St Blasien

Donau (Danube)

N

BASEL

Rhein (Rhine)

SWITZERLAND

30 kms
20 miles

end to Karlsruhe's heyday. Today Karlsruhe is a large industrial town, but still enjoys the Margrave's heritage. Nearly half of its area is parkland, and some fine Neoclassical architecture survives. Years of intelligent acquisition have also provided Karlsruhe with some really good museums.

Getting Around

By train: The **Hauptbahnhof**, ☎ (0721) 19419, is a good 20 minutes' walk south of the centre (Tram 3, 4 or 6). There are connections to Heidelberg (½hr), Frankfurt (1hr 10min) and Stuttgart (¾hr).

By car: Karlsruhe is 60km from Heidelberg on the B3 (or the parallel Autobahn 5). The A5 also takes you to Frankfurt (140km). Stuttgart is about 80km away on the A8.

Car hire: Hertz, Kriegstr. 5, ☎ (0721) 374 040; Sixt Budget, Schauenburgstr. 15, ☎ (0721) 86 447.

Mitfahrzentrale: Rankestr. 14, ☎ (0721) 33 666.

Public transport: Once you're in the centre all the sights are within walking distance, though if you do need to make use of the bus and tram network a *Tageskarte* (day card; DM6) is good value as it gets two adults and two children around town for 24 hours.

Taxis: ☎ (0721) 3 00 33.

Tourist Information

The friendly **tourist information office** is opposite the grand Jugendstil Bahnhof, Bahnhofplatz 6, ☎ (0721) 35 530 *(Mon–Fri 8–7, Sat 8–1)*. It is worth checking here before you book a room as they often have special offers for local hotels and packages including cut-price accommodation deals, entry to museums and even trips into the Black Forest.

Post office: Kaiserstr. 217.

Bureau de change: There is a branch of the Deutsche-Verkehrs-Kredit-Bank at the Hauptbahnhof *(Mon–Sat 7–8 and Sun 9–1)*.

Police: ☎ 110.

Medical emergencies: ☎ (0721) 558 055.

Festivals

Karlsruhe's jolliest bash is the **Brigande-Feschd** held on the market square in early May. The original 'Brigands' were the Calabrian builders who came to construct the Schloß in the 18th century—and the name has stuck as a nickname for all Karlsruhers. Bands oompah well into the night, local beer and wines flow and there are prodigious amounts of food (including the famous local *Maultasche*—a sort of giant ravioli).

The Schloß and the City Centre

The pale yellow sickle-shaped **Schloß** still dominates the town, but nowadays the populace have overrun it. Architecture students swarm over the walls, taking measurements and making perspective drawings; crocodiles of schoolchildren emerge from an art class inside, clutching dripping paintings and peculiar lumps of clay; dogs bounce around the fountains and impromptu football teams churn up the garden turf. A wild forest stretches out behind the palace; indoors is the **Landesmuseum** *(Tues–Sun 10–5.30, Thurs to 9; adm free)*.

The museum's selection of antiquities is superb (particularly the Cycladic and Phoenician displays). Rather than being overwhelmed by cabinet after cabinet of dull repetition, you're offered only the choicest, quirkiest and most interesting finds. There is a good folk art section, with examples of the gaudy bridal hats that are part of the local traditional dress—3kg heaps of baubles, mirrors and bells. Lovers of Jugendstil will have a field day, finding everything from an exquisitely embroidered evening bag with a gold nymphette as a clasp, to a dining room suite inlaid with rare woods and mother-of-pearl. Glass acquisitions include the best from Bohemia, Vienna and Bavaria, as well as some delightful kitsch such as the model of Golgotha in a bottle. Margrave Ludwig Wilhelm ('Türkenlouis') campaigned boisterously against the Turks. His rich Ottoman booty has almost a floor to itself.

On the southwest corner of the Schloßplatz, you'll find the **Staatliche Kunsthalle** (State Art Gallery) *(Tues–Fri 10–1 and 2–5, Sat and Sun 10–6; adm free)*. The collection of Old Masters is superb. The highlight is Grünewald's tortured *Crucifixion* (*c.* 1500), and two earlier works—characterful monochromes of *St Elizabeth of Thüringia* and *St Lucia*. Look out also for works by the idiosyncratic artist Hans Baldung (*see* p. 58). In his *Nativity* (1539) a grumpy baby Jesus looks almost blasphemously like his terrestrial dad. A rather touching *Melancholy* by the 16th-century painter Matthias Gerung shows the artist lonely and oppressed in a grotesque Hieronymous Bosch-like world.

Lack of space means that you'll only see part of the Dutch collection—but that is certain to include some fine Rembrandt and Rubens and Ruisdael. There's a particularily strong 19th-century German section, with works by Anselm Feuerbach (1829–80), whose portaits of strong, pensive women are among the best products of the period. The one-time director of the museum, Hans Thoma (1839–1924), is best represented by his delicate character studies, though he sometimes shows a taste for large dollops of 19th-century sentiment.

Modern art is housed next door in the **Orangerie** *(Tues–Fri 10–5, Sat and Sun 10–6; adm free)*. This is a modest flit through 20th-century art, but it alights on most of the famous names. The best paintings are those by members of the German Expressionist group, the *Blaue Reiter* (*see* p. 64).

Directly across from the main entrance to the Schloßgarten is the narrow **Marktplatz** with two of Weinbrenner's best Karlsruhe buildings, the simple, understated **Rathaus** (1805) and the rather imposing temple-like **Evangelische Stadtkirche** (1807). Margrave Karl Wilhelm's remains lie under a pyramid in the middle of the square. Weinbrenner knocked down the church that stood over them when he needed more room for his own buildings. Other Weinbrenner buildings include St Stephan's church (Erbprinzenstr. 14) and the

Staatliche Münzstätte (Stephaniestr. 28a). If you are really taken by his work, the tourist office can give you the map of a walk which takes in everything he did in the town. If you prefer something a little more frivolous, head for Baischstraße, where you'll find some well-preserved Jugendstil houses.

Karlsruhe © (0721–)   **Where to Stay**

Hotels cater largely for the business market, and are on the pricey side—though the tourist office often offer special package deals at lower prices (*see* **Tourist Information** above).

expensive

Queens Hotel, Ettlinger Str. 23, © 37 27 0, fax 37 27 170 (DM275). Smart and modern with fine views over the city from the upper storeys. A well-equipped business hotel, with a friendly, efficient management who create a genuinely welcoming atmosphere.

moderate

Hotel Bahnpost, Am Stadtgarten 5, © 3 49 77, fax 3 49 79 (DM160–220). Charming hotel that nestles up against the side of the Stadtgarten, and is quiet and comfortable.

Hotel Kaiserhof, Karl-Friedrich-Str. 12, © 26615, fax 27672 (DM190). Stolid *bürgerliche* hotel on the busy market place.

Hotel Eden, Bahnhofstr. 15–19, © 18 180, fax 181 8222 (DM170–190). On the edge of the Stadtgarten. Reliable and efficiently run—somewhere to fall back on when the others are full.

inexpensive

Hotel Erbprinzenhof, Erbprinzenstr. 26, © 2 38 90, fax 2 69 50 (DM120–150). The pick of the cheaper central hotels. Peaceful and convenient for the sights. No restaurant.

Pension am Zoo, Ettlinger Str. 33, © 33678 (DM100 without private facilities). Cheery, family-run pension, just a peacock's squawk from the zoo.

Youth Hostel: Moltkestr. 2b, © 2 82 48.

Eating and Drinking

The best area of town for cafés and restaurants is around the triangular, leafy **Ludwigsplatz**, and along neighbouring Waldstraße. Here people crowd into atmospheric pubs and spill out onto shady terraces in good weather. Most cafés also serve food.

Restaurants and Taverns

Scala at the Queens Hotel (see above) (DM70–100). *The* place for a gourmet meal.

Dudelsack, Waldstr. 79, ✆ 2 21 66 (DM35–65). Famed for its excellent game and fish dishes—a good place to sample French-influenced Baden cuisine. Try the delicious guinea fowl, or salmon and basil lasagne. There is a pleasant garden out the back, where you can eat in fine weather.

Salmem, Ludwigsplatz (DM20–35). Both a café on the square, and a bistro around the corner in Waldstraße where you can get large helpings of delicious Baden food and healthy salads.

Bars and Cafés

Vogelbräu, Kappellenstr. 50. A local brewery which dishes up a murky, unfiltered beer—a must for aficionados. The pub is popular with students and unless you're there early in the evening you won't get a seat.

Krokodil, Waldstr. 63. Friendly café with a warren of different rooms and a clientele that ranges from punks to university professors.

Baden-Baden

The famous mineral springs, muttered a 19th-century traveller, 'collect to Baden all the fashion and disease of this part of Europe.' Mark Twain was even less impressed: 'It is an inane town, full of sham, and petty fraud, and snobbery, but the baths are good... I had had twinges of rheumatism unceasingly during three years, but the last one departed after a fortnight's bathing there, and I have never had one since. I fully believe I left my rheumatism in Baden-Baden. Baden-Baden is welcome to it. It was little, but it was all I had to give. I would have preferred to leave something that was catching, but it was not in my power.'

The baths are still good, and though Baden-Baden is not nearly so fashionable as it once was, it still attracts its share of the *beau monde*. The combination of the aged, the well-off and those racked with rheumatism might not promise exciting chemistry, but there is a style and romance about Baden-Baden that makes it irresistible.

It was the Roman Emperor Caracalla who first eased his aching joints in the healing springs, around AD 215 (*baden* means to bathe in German). Then in the 13th century the Margraves of Baden built a castle on the hill, and made it their seat. During the Reformation the family split into a Protestant and a Catholic branch—the Baden-Durlachs and the Baden-Badens—hence the town's double-barrelled name (though this has only been used officially since the 1930s). Visiting diplomats and notables stewed happily in the baths, and the spa's reputation began to spread. By the 18th century even the best royal households began to take note, and when Napoleon made Baden a buffer state in 1806, the newly created Grand Duke seized the chance of filling state coffers. Baden-Baden reached its zenith in the mid-1800s as the 'summer capital of Europe'. Powerful monarchs (including Queen Victoria, Czar Alexander and Emperor Franz Josef), and hosts of the rich and famous (Dostoyevsky, Wagner, Brahms and Disraeli, during one season) would come to take the waters, listen to the orchestra and have a flutter at the casino. Then they'd head south to do much the same thing in Monte Carlo for the winter. During this period the leading Neoclassical architect, Friedrich Weinbrenner, virtually rebuilt the town, creating most of the public buildings still used today.

Getting Around

By train: You can arrive in Baden-Baden on the Orient Express. Even if you're travelling less luxuriously, you'll find the town easily accessible on the main Frankfurt–Basel line (Karlsruhe, 20min; Frankfurt, 2hr). The new **Bahnhof** is 4km northwest of the city (in the suburb of Oos), but Bus 1 or 3 will get you speedily to the centre. Then everything is within walking (or tottering) distance.

By car: Baden-Baden is just off the A5, about 30km from Karlsruhe.

Tourist Information

The **tourist information office** is in the Haus des Kurgastes (Spa Visitors' Centre) Augustaplatz 8, © (07221) 27 52 00 or 27 52 01 *(daily 9am–10pm)*. The staff can help with accommodation, book you into concerts or on city tours, and offer information on spa cures.

The Baths and Sights

The first place to head for, as visitors have done for over a century, is the cool, beautifully manicured **Lichtentaler Allee**, a promenade park that follows the trickling River Oos, just behind the Haus des Kurgastes. There's a whiff of facepowder and bracing after-shave in the air. Thin-legged ladies hobble about, mirroring the gait of their nervous chihuahuas. Dapper octogenerians whizz past, using their walking sticks more as a means of propulsion than support. Creaking couples limp from bench to bench. You get the sneaking suspicion that white-coated attendants are lurking in the bushes waiting to pick up anyone who falls.

At the northern end of the park, past an elegant **theatre**, built in 1862 in the style of the Paris Opera House, you come to the **Kurhaus**. Here is the hub of Baden-Baden social life with spa rooms, banqueting halls, restaurants and the famous **casino**. A tree-lined walkway of exclusive shops leads up to the Kurhaus garden. Each has a small table outside in the shade, where the best customers can rest, toy with the roses and sip a drink. In the formal garden people wander around aimlessly, or sit in front of the pavilion and listen to the orchestra. On one side the sparkling white Kurhaus itself stands poised and serene. Between its eight slender Corinthian columns is a neat row of white chairs. On fine days well-coiffured women in owl-lensed sunglasses sit here, eyes gently closed against the sun. The occasional tubby pink husband dozes off nearby, his panama hat balancing on his knee.

There are guided tours of the casino *(daily Apr–Sept, 9.30–12, in English by appointment, © 2 10 60; adm DM3)*, but it's a much better idea to come back at night and experience the real thing (*see* **Entertainment** below). To visit the rest of the Kurhaus (apart from the restaurants) you either have to take a cure (*see* **Activities** below) or be invited to a ball.

Next door to the Kurhaus is the orangey-pink arcade of the **Trinkhalle** (pump room) *(open Good Friday to All Saints' Day (1 Nov), 10–5.30; adm free)*, built between 1839 and 1842 by Heinrich Hübsch, a disciple of Weinbrenner. You can stroll its 90m length looking at vivid frescoes which depict scenes from local legends, by the Romantic painter Jakob Götzenberger. Then pop in to sample the waters. There are two types, dispensed by attendents who will charge you DM2 a glass if you're not staying in Baden-Baden and so haven't paid your 'Kurtax'. Their sour expressions may be because they've drunk too much water from the Friedrichsquelle, which is warm, salty and quite vile. The Heinrichsquelle is worse.

Behind the Trinkhalle, on top of the Michaelsberg, is the heavily ornate Orthodox **Stourdza-Kapelle** *(daily 10–6; adm DM1)* built in 1863 by Leo von Klenze (famed for his buildings in Munich). It is the mausoleum for the teenage Prince Michael Stourdza of Romania, whose father was living in exile in Baden-Baden when the young prince was murdered in Paris.

Very little remains of medieval Baden-Baden, which was razed to the ground by the French in 1689. But on the hill opposite the Kurhaus (in the Marktplatz) you'll find the **Stiftskirche**, a Romanesque-Gothic church with bravura Baroque flourishes. The jewel of the church is a superb sandstone *Crucifixion* (1467) carved by Nicolaus Gerhaert von Leyden. You can also see the burial monument of the bloody campaigner against the Ottomans, Margrave Ludwig Wilhelm ('Türkenlouis'). It is an outrageous Rococo creation with allegories of Courage, Wisdom and Justice, and also drums, canon balls, skeletons and bits of human limb, all meticulously carved in marble.

In a car park behind the Stiftskirche you can peer through glass at the remains of the old **Roman Baths** or, if you are really interested, pay DM2 to get in *(open 10–12 and 1.30–4)*. Next door is the magnificent **Friedrichsbad** (*see* **Entertainment and Nightlife** below), which still functions as a bathing palace.

Just after construction began on the Friedrichsbad in 1869, Baden became part of the North German confederation and subject to a Prussian ban on gambling. With the casino so peremptorily closed, the town desperately needed another focus for its social life. So the authorities put their all into making the Friedrichsbad the sort of place where the princes of Europe would not balk at taking off their clothes and whiling away a few hours.

On the hill behind the Friedrichsbad is the **Neues Schloß** *(tours of interior Mon–Fri 3pm; adm DM3)*, originally built in 1437 for the Margraves of Baden. The present building, however, dates largely from the 18th and 19th centuries and is worth visiting mainly for the views across the town. There's a mediocre café (with a good view) and a small **museum** *(Apr–Oct 10–12.30 and 2–5; adm DM2)* full of kitchen utensils and displays on the town's history. An even better view can be had from the ruined **Altes Scloß**, 3km out of town (along Leopoldstraße, Bus 5). You can climb the tower and look out right across the Black Forest, before descending for a well-earned drink in the café.

Banks and main high-street stores are to be found along the pedestrianized stretches of Lange Straße, Gernsbacher Straße and Sophienstraße—though you will find quirkier and more romantic shops in the smaller streets leading off these busy thoroughfares up towards the Schloß.

Entertainment and Nightlife

Fynes Moryson, an English gentleman travelling through Germany in 1616, noted that the waters of Baden-Baden helped bathers 'shun all sadness' and were good for 'a colde braine, and a stomack charged with rhume'. Today's brochures promise relief from rheumatism, respiratory ailments and 'sexual disturbances'. If you really would like to take a cure, contact the tourist office, which offers a variety of packages, ranging from two days, with a quick visit to the baths, to three weeks of the full treatment with medical check-ups. Alternatively, you can visit the **Caracalla Therme** *(daily 8am–10pm; adm DM15 for 2 hours)*, a vast modern complex with indoor and outdoor pools, waters of various temperatures and drinking fountains.

Far more fun, and worth every pfennig of the extra cost, is the **Friedrichsbad** *(baths open Mon–Sat 10–10; mixed bathing all day Wed and Sat and 4–10 on Wed and Fri, otherwise segregated—bathing takes place naked, latest adm 2 hours before closing; other facilities generally available Mon–Sat 8–5; prices vary according to treatment)*. The Friedrichsbad is a sumptuous neo-Renaissance building with marble baths and halls, arches and domed ceilings, elaborate stucco and exotically painted tiles. Daylight diffuses through steam and frosted glass, imparting a soft glow to the gilding and the creams, blues and pinks of the décor. Notices request silence, but conversation seems naturally hushed.

Here you can undergo everything from electrotherapy to underwater massage, but you should not leave Baden-Baden without succumbing to the delights of the famous **Röisch-Irische Bad** (Roman Irish Bath), so called because the process of alternating hot and cold treatments was supposedly invented by the Irish *(adm DM38)*. For around two hours you progress through 15 different rooms experiencing showers that squirt at you from every conceivable direction, warm air baths, hot air baths, steam of different temperatures and fragrances, thermal soakings, scrubdowns and an invigorating massage. Finally you're cocooned in warm towels and blankets and laid out to rest. It leaves you dreamy and refreshed for days.

Even if you have no intention of gambling, a visit to the overwhelmingly splendid **casino** *(daily 2pm–2am; adm DM5; minimum age 21)* is a must. Marlene Dietrich thought that it was the most beautiful gaming house in the world. Few would disagree. The same team who were responsible for the Paris Opera came up with the design—a cross between *La Belle Epoque* and Versailles. The glass doors slide back, and you step into another world, a realm of plush and gold, of glimmering crystal chandeliers, rich carving and dark, warmly coloured paintings. This is where

Dostoyevsky gambled obsessively while writing *The Idiot*, and where once you could have met the royalty of Europe. Today as you walk to the bank to collect your chips you might still brush shoulders with a dowager countess, a German millionaire or a magnetically arrogant young Arabian prince. There's a low hum of conversation from the roulette rooms, but the card tables attract more edgy, serious gamblers who scribble earnestly on their notepads, working and reworking complicated systems, and waiting for the right moment to pounce. Here there is silence, save for the croupier's *danke schön, bitte schön*, the click of chips and the patter of the fountain outside.

The minimum stake is DM5, though you can come in just for a look around. Take your passport and go appropriately dressed (a suit, or jacket and tie is acceptable for men—if you wear evening dress you'll look like a croupier). If you have never gambled before, you can have the rules explained at special sessions during the evening (ask the commissionaire), or on Friday mornings (10.30–11.30). There are bars and a buffet inside the casino, and you should get a good evening's entertainment out of DM100, even if you don't come away with any change.

The **Theatre**, which opened in 1862 with the premiere of Berlioz's *Beatrice and Benedict*, still maintains an exceptionally high standard, and hosts festivals which feature the likes of Placido Domingo and Julia Migenes.

At Iffezheim, the local **horse-racing track**, the Spring Meeting (end of May) and Grand Week (end of August) attract the international jetset, and are accompanied by rounds of banquets and balls. On the Fremersberg, to the west of town, is an 18-hole **golf course** which the late Duke of Windsor called 'a real pearl' *(℗ (07221) 2 35 79 for details of times and green fees)*.

Baden-Baden ℗ (07221–)   ***Where to Stay***

expensive

Brenner's Park-Hotel, Lichtentaler Allee, ℗ 9 00 0, fax 3 87 72 (DM458–998). The grandest survivor from Baden-Baden's golden years, a plush palace overlooking the park where you're treated with the same quiet deference as Queen Victoria must have been a hundred years ago.

Steinberger Europäischer Hof, Kaiserallee 2, ℗ 2 35 61, fax 2 88 31 (DM230–430). Similar location and atmosphere to the Brenner's Park, but doesn't presume that you can draw on state funds to pay your bill.

Der Kleine Prinz, Lichtentaler Str. 36, ℗ 3464 (DM225–325 DM). Run by an ex-director of the New York Hilton and Waldorf-Astoria. One of the most charming hotels in town, with individually furnished rooms (some with open fireplaces).

Queens Sport Hotel, Falkenstr. 2, ℗ 2 19 0, fax 21 95 19 (DM200–300). For those of energetic bent. It has its own gym, sauna and swimming pool, and well-equipped comfortable rooms.

moderate

Hotel am Friedrichsbad, Gernsbacher Str. 31, ✆ 27 10 46, fax 3 83 10 (DM130). Old inn with well-modernized interior. Overlooks a quiet pedestrian area with an Altstadt atmosphere.

inexpensive

Hotel am Markt, Marktplatz 18, ✆ 22 747 (DM98). Pleasant no-nonsense hotel in the cheaper price range.

Pension Cäcilienberg, Geroldsauer Str. 2, ✆ 7 22 97 (DM77). Small, good value guesthouse on the edge of town (about 20min from the centre; take buses going to Geroldsau).

Youth Hostel: Hardbergstr. 34, ✆ 5 22 23.

Eating and Drinking: Restaurants and Taverns

Der Kleine Prinz, Lichtentalerstr. 36, ✆ 3464 (DM70). Excellent gourmet food in a muted, classical setting.

Molenkur, Quettigstr. 19, ✆ 33257 (DM25–35). Solid *gut bürgerliche* cooking, an arty clientele and a pretty garden for summer meals.

Münchener Löwenbräu, Gernsbacher Straße (DM20–30). Occasionally raucous Bavarian-style beer garden where you can get large hunks of pork to accompany your beer.

Most restaurants in Baden-Baden are aimed at the tourist market and are fairly run-of-the-mill. Locals head out to the surrounding wine villages for a good meal out. Try:

Varnhalt **Popisil's Merkurius**, Klosterbergstr. 2, Varnhalt, ✆ (07223) 54 74. Enjoys a reputation for good Bohemian cuisine.

Neuweier **Schloß Neuweier**, Mauerbergstr. 21, Neuweier, ✆ (07223) 5 79 44 (set menus DM48–120). Intimate, romantic garden restaurant in the courtyard of a 12th-century castle. The Schloß makes its own wine and serves superb Baden and gourmet food. The menus change seasonally and come up with delicacies such as oxtail stuffed with nuts and herbs in a burgundy sauce.

Bars and Cafés

Café Palais Gargarin, Lichtentaler Allee. The place to be seen sipping your morning bubbly. It has a terrace overlooking the goings-on along the promenade.

Café Italia, Langestraße. Where locals stop off from shopping for ices and coffee.

Weinstube im Baldreit, Küfer Str. 3. Secluded wine bar in the Altstadt, with a quiet courtyard terrace.

On the southern outskirts of the town, just off the main road, is **Kloster Lichtental** *(Mon–Sat 2.30–5, Wed and Sun 10.15–12, closed first Sun in month; adm DM1.50)*. Behind its serene façade the nuns beaver away making soul-warming liqueurs, which they sell in their shop. Just up the road, at Maximilianstr. 18, is the **Brahms Haus** *(Mon, Wed and Fri 3–5, Sun 10–1; adm DM1)*, where you can see the attic room in which the composer lived from 1865 to 74.

Baden-Badeners escape the tourists by heading out to the **Geroldsauer Waterfall** (leave town by Geroldsauerstraße, and take the last turning left in the village of Geroldsau). This is a peaceful forest paradise with footpaths following a series of waterfalls and rapids. Just beyond the point where cars are no longer allowed, a **Gaststätte** nestles in banks of rhododendrons and dishes up delicious meals.

The **Rebland** (winelands), to the west of Baden-Baden offer wonderful opportunities for walks and rootling out cheery local inns. At one point a road spirals upwards through vineyards and thick forests to the **Yburg**, a ruined 13th-century castle with views across the borders to France. Nowadays the castle is an inexpensive café that serves *Maultaschen* (*see* p. 261) and hearty home-made soups.

North of Baden-Baden, near the village of Haueneberstein, is **Schloß Favorite** *(guided tours Mar–Oct on the hour 9–5 except 1pm; adm DM3)*, built between 1710 and 1712 as a summer residence for Margravine Sybilla Augusta, who ruled as regent after the death of her husband, 'Türkenlouis'. The Margravine indulged her taste for the heavy ornament of her native Bohemia and built what Mark Twain said was 'in every way a wildly and picturesquely decorated house', its interiors lavishly covered in mirrors, rare wood, coloured marbles and semi-precious stones. Her famous collection of porcelain is also on display.

The Margravine was a notorious fast-liver, but from time to time would collapse in remorse, and hole herself up in the **Penitents' Chapel** in the Schloß grounds, with no company but wax models of the Holy Family, for months on end. Twain relates how after one 'final, triumphant and satisfying spree' she shut herself up in the chapel for the last two years of her life, castigating herself with whips, wearing hairshirts and sitting down to meals with the Holy Family: on one side of the table the rigid wax figures with their fishy glass eyes and corpsy complexions, and on the other the 'wrinkled, smouldering old fireeater... mumbling her prayers and munching her sausages in the ghostly stillness and shadowy indistinctness of a winter twilight'.

The Black Forest and Freiburg

Germans have an almost mystical relationship with their *Wälder* (forests). '*Deutscher Wald, deutsche Romantik, deutsches Gemüt*' (literally, German forest, German Romanticism, German feeling) the saying goes—the woods exercise a grip over the national spirit similar to the American Dream. Polls showed—even at the height of the Cold War—that Germans were more worried about *Waldsterben* (the dying of the forests caused by pollution) than the arms race or the threat of nuclear attack. On any day of the week, whatever the weather, there will be people in stout shoes (and sometimes bright socks and knee-britches too) striding over the hills or through the acres of German woodland.

The mother of all German forests, for locals and tourists alike, is the *Schwarzwald* (Black Forest)—stretching from Baden-Baden to the Swiss Alps, and occupying most of southwest Baden-Württemberg. Blankets of dark conifers shroud the hills. You climb up and up in a church-like gloom, then pop out somewhere high to glimpse the sun sparkling on damp pine needles, and wisps of mist floating from the tree-tops. Then you plunge back down again, past waterfalls and lakes out onto rolling meadowland, past spa towns, *Luftorte* ('fresh air resorts') and busy timber farms, fragrant with newly cut wood. In summer the shady woods and manageable hills entice you into long, vigorous walks. In winter, if you're lucky, you'll wake up one morning to find the pines jet-black against a backdrop of crisp new snow. Sudden dark storms can make high drama in the forest. Black clouds roll in, lightning flashes across the hilltops and everything is drenched in a hammering rain. Then, just as suddenly, the rain stops. There's a sharp silence, and brilliant shafts of sunlight beam down onto the soaked foliage, drawing out warm and musty scents.

This is the land of hobgoblins and will-o'-the-wisps, of wood-spirits, water-demons and witches. Here you'll still see people in *Tracht* (traditional dress), not only for tourists' benefit, but also for weddings, church services and festivals. The virgins of Gutach adorn their hats with 2kg of bright red pompoms; elsewhere brides wear hats weighty with mirrors and beads. Wooden, barn-like thatched houses (a design little changed since the Alemanni first built them) dot the hillsides. On your walks you could meet badgers, silver foxes and hosts of birds.

Tourists descend on the Black Forest in coachloads—to snatch up cuckoo clocks, gobble down the famous cherry and chocolate cake and snap away at the scenery. Luckily, most tourist activity is centered on a few resorts. But from the smaller villages it is still possible to go on long, relatively lonely walks. This section offers a few tips on where to find these; the very touristy places are consigned to the Directory. However, if you really want a quiet holiday in unspoiled German forest, you should head for eastern Bavaria—*see* p. 380.

On the other hand, if the idea of the quiet life seizes you with panic, if you're naturally gregarious, or just prefer cities, then go to Freiburg, in the heart of the *Wald*—one of the most beautifully situated towns in Germany, and offering an attractive contrast to country life with its splendid architecture and jolly university-town atmosphere.

Getting Around
By Train

The **Schwarzwaldbahn** (Black Forest Railway, information from any local station) trundles along miles of scenic track between Offenburg and Donaueschingen, ducks in and out of tunnels and at one point climbs 500m between two villages only 11km apart (winding back and forth over 26km to do so). The really stunning (and at times hair-raising) stretch is between Hornberg and St Georgen in the north.

The best way to visit more remote villages is using your own transport. Of the marked tourist routes the **Mountain Road** (B500) is the best, beetling along the hilltops between Baden-Baden and Freudenstadt. The **Panorama Road** wanders about in the area around Freiburg, and the **Spa Road** leads you to various healing waters. (Information on all the routes is available from the Freiburg tourist office.)

Public Transport

The **Freizeit Bus** (information ℭ (07441) 4085), a bus service centred on Freudenstadt, can take you to many of the smaller resorts. It is a good idea to enquire about the *Freizeit Pass* and other special ticket offers. Local tour buses ply the more popular routes (especially in summer).

Hiking

By far the best way to see the Black Forest is **on foot**. There are marked trails all over the forest which give you the option of anything from an afternoon stroll to a fortnight's serious walking. Tourist offices can give you advice on walks and sell maps of the trails. Some travel companies organize group hikes, and will cart your luggage on ahead of you, so that you can stroll unimpeded to the next cosy inn. Again, tourist information offices can help here. Ask for information on 'Wandern ohne Gepäck'.

Tourist Information

The tourist information offices at **Baden-Baden** (*see* p. 274) and **Freiburg** (*see* p. 287) both carry extensive information on the Black Forest. There are also well-signposted **local offices** in most of the smaller resorts—usually in the Rathaus or Kurhaus administration building—where you can find out about accommodation and hiking routes.

The Black Forest North of Freiburg

The northern part of the forest offers dense woodland, stubby hills, drifts of wildflowers, banks of bracken, and energetic bands of hikers. As you get closer to Freiburg, down the Gutach and Kinzig valleys, the countryside opens up a little, the quaint wooden farmhouses become more profuse, and cuckoo clocks are rife.

If you turn off the B500 at Ruhestein, you come—down a narrow winding road—to **Allerheiligen**, the gaunt ruins of a 12th-century monastery reposing in quiet, leafy surrounds. A bright stream flows along nearby, then tumbles over a succession of falls in one of the prettiest nooks of the Black Forest. Nowadays there's a private school at Allerheiligen, and although it is a popular spot, it provides a welcome sanctuary from the tourist traps. The nearby village of **Oppenau**, while in itself not particularly special, makes a good base for ventures into the forest.

Freudenstadt is where tourist traffic comes to a halt for the night, but if you venture a few miles further on along the A294, you come to **Alpirsbach**, a sleepy town with a clutch of rustic hotels, a graceful Romanesque monastery and a glass-blowing workshop (open to the public during office hours).

South of Alpirsbach the first cuckoo clocks make their ominous appearance. In **Schonach** you can see the largest one in the world (a grim experience). By the time you reach **Triberg** you can hardly move for cuckoo clock shops, factories and museums—and tourists happily carrying off wrapped boxes of various sizes. Triberg is a frantic, but pretty town, trailing steeply down a hill deep into the valley below. Perched on a rock above the town is **Maria in der Tanne**, a pilgrimage church built on the spot where a leprosy-curing stream miraculously spouted from stone in 1644. Today the stone is no longer to be seen, and it is hardly worth the climb to see the church's outrageously tinselly Baroque altar. At the **Schwarzwaldmuseum** *(May–Oct daily 9–6, Oct–May daily 10–12 and 2–5, closed 15 Nov–15 Dec; adm DM3)* you can see a bright array of *Tracht* (traditional costumes), and chunky, powerful carvings by Karl Josef Förtwangler (known locally as 'Woodcarver Joe'). At the upper end of the town is the highest waterfall in Germany—the **Gutacher Wasserfall**—which makes its 162m descent gradually, through seven stages.

Further south, at **Furtwangen** where, supposedly, the first cuckoo clock was modelled on the local Rathaus, you will find the **Deutsches Uhrenmuseum** (German Clock Museum) at Gerwigstraße 11 *(Apr–Nov daily 9–5; adm DM3)*, which looks beyond the cuckoo clock to timepieces from around the world.

If you want relief from the tourist throngs, head west from Schonach into the **Prechtal**, a cosy valley of little farmsteads, or south from Triberg to **St Peter**, a traditional Schwarz-wald village with a rather oversized Baroque church.

See also directory entries for Freudenstadt, Mummelsee, Vogtsbauernhof.

Tourist Information

Alpirsbach: Kurverwaltung, Hauptstr. 20, ✆ (07444) 614 281.

Triberg: Kurverwaltung, Luisenstraße, ✆ (07722) 81230.

Where to Stay and Eating Out

This part of the Black Forest is well-geared to the tourist market and abounds with places to eat or spend the night. What follows is a brief personal selection.

Allerheiligen

Allerheiligen Gaststätte (DM30–60). Comfy Gaststätte next to the ruins. Specializes in smoked trout, game dishes and death-by-chocolate Black Forest cake.

Gasthaus Hirsch, Straßburgerstr. 5, ✆ (07804) 732 (rooms from DM60; meals DM25–45). Rustic guesthouse in Oppenau. Good restaurant which specializes in trout dishes.

Alpirsbach

Hotel Rössle, Aisbachstr. 5, ✆ (07444) 2281, fax (07444) 2368 (DM100). Stay in high Schwarzwald style in a friendly family hotel.

Gasthof Schwanen-Post, Marktstr 5, ✆ (07444) 2205 (from DM80). Comfortable hotel in traditional Black Forest building.

Pension Waldhorn, Kreuzgasse 4, ✆ (07444) 2411, fax (07444) 4469 (DM90). Small, friendly pension which offers just the sort of slap-up breakfast you need before an energetic day's walking.

Triberg

Parkhotel Wehrle, Gartenstr. 24, ✆ (07722) 86020, fax (07444) 860 290 (DM135–200). Elegant hotel which has been run by the same family since 1702. (They seem to have saved their best furniture along the way—the place is crammed with antiques.) A circular restaurant opens out onto a lush garden and serves fine food and good teas.

Gasthaus Krone, Schulstr. 37, ✆ (07722) 4524 (DM75). Comfortable rooms and hearty local cuisine.

Zur Sonne, Zähringstr. 2, St Peter, ✆ (07660) 203 (rooms from DM90; meals DM25–45). The perfect down-to-earth village inn, filled with delicious aromas from the kitchen.

The Southern Black Forest

The southern Black Forest is one of the sunniest areas in Germany. In the eastern part you can cool off in limpid lakes during hot summer days. Further south you can ski until March, then descend to the Rhine where the cherry trees will be in blossom, and the vines just beginning to sprout.

Down the B500 from Furtwangen, past the hectic lakeside resort of **Titisee**, you come to the rather more deserted waters of the **Schluchsee**. Trees reach right down to the shore, broken by little stretches of sandy beach. A few people splash about at the water's edge, while the odd windsurfer or yacht streaks by. A few miles further on you come to **St Blasien**, an almost comically incongruous, giant Neoclassical church—modelled on St Peter's in Rome and plonked down in the middle of the forest by Benedictine monks. Locals have nicknamed it the 'Dom' (cathedral). Inside the huge, symmetrical rotunda, the pews, walls and dome are all dazzling white; the floor is cold grey marble. The effect is breathtaking, though at times you get the impression you are in an incredibly grand public lavatory.

Working your way back up towards Freiburg on the forest roads that weave between the B3 and the B500, you come to the two highest points in the Black Forest—**Mt Belchen** (1414m) and **Mt Feldberg** (1493m). Both offer spectacular views, and lots of company. Well-signposted paths take you from the road to the summit. To the northwest of Mt

Belchen lies the **Munstertal**, a serene valley full of munching cows and wooden Schwarzwald houses. On the road that passes through the village of Münstertal, you'll find another monastery: **St Trudpert**. It is an attractive, rather subdued Baroque building with elegant stucco-marble side altars and a rather odd pulpit canopy, in which Christ appears in an apocalyptic chariot drawn by mythical beasts. Outside, a modern statue of the Saviour that sheds real tears stops just a hair's breadth short of kitsch.

As the river Münster trips along to join the Rhine, the valley widens and the thick forests bow out to vineyards and grassland. Here you'll find **Staufen**, a town of richly coloured old houses, idling beneath the ruins of an old castle. At the Gasthaus zum Löwen the real **Doktor Faustus** came to a smelly end while trying to make gold for the bankrupt local count (*see* p. 263).

The road winds on past Staufen through orchards and terraced vineyards, around knobbly hills and on to **Breisach** on the Rhine, high on a promontory overlooking France. 'Whoever the war was between, and whatever it was about, Alt Breisach was sure to be in it,' Jerome K. Jerome wrote in *Three Men on the Bummel*. This presented a problem for the troubled citizen of Breisach: 'One day he would be a Frenchman, and then before he could learn enough French to pay his taxes he would be an Austrian. While he was trying to discover what you did in order to be a good Austrian, he would find that he was no longer an Austrian, but a German...' Poor battered Breisach still retains much of its heavily fortified city ramparts, and the burghers are now firmly German. The town isn't particularly attractive, but is worth a stop for the art treasures in the **Münster**. There's a graceful late Gothic **rood screen** and a vast **fresco cycle** (1490) by Martin Schongauer (*see* p. 57). The superb composition, delicate, rather wistful characterization and subtle colouring make it one of the masterpieces of German church art. The curious, exquisitely carved **altar** (by the unknown 15th-century Master HL), has bizarrely anachronistic Baroque-like cherubs and drapery, and sections that could be mistaken for Art Nouveau.

Beyond Breisach, in an area of rugged little hills, you come to the **Kaiserstuhl** ('Emperor's seat'), an odd, stepped volcanic slope that looks like the beginning of a giant's stairway. Legend has it that Frederick Barbarossa lies asleep deep in the mountain, waiting for the right time to reappear and save the world. It is a lush area, a butterfly hunter's paradise, and in between the vineyards you'll find banks of wild flowers—poppies, roses and even orchids. On the northern slope of the mountain is **Endingen**, a pretty village with a fancy, gabled 16th-century Rathaus and a 17th-century Kornhaus.

See Directory entry for Titisee.

Tourist Information

Breisach: Werd, off Rheinstraße, © (07667) 83227.

St Blasien: Kurverwaltung, Am Kurgarten 1–3, © (07672) 41430.

Staufen: Rathaus, © (07633) 80536.

As always in country areas the best bargains (and often the tastiest breakfasts) are to be had in private accommodation. Look out for the ubiquitous *Zimmer Frei* signs, or enquire at local tourist offices. Rooms go for around DM30 per person including breakfast.

Staufen

Gasthaus zum Löwen, Hauptstr. 47, ✆ (07633) 7078 (DM145). Scene of Dr Faust's sudden demise—you can even sleep in the room where he died (Room 5).

Hotel Hirschen, Hauptstr. 19, ✆ (07633) 5297 (DM90). A pleasant, less diabolical option than the Gasthaus zum Löwen.

Breisach

Gasthaus Bayrischer Hof, Neutorstr. 25, ✆ (07667) 289 (rooms DM70, meals DM25–45). Small but comfortable rooms. The restaurant is popular with locals at lunchtime (good food but brusque service).

Vogtsburg-Oberbergen

Gasthof Schwarzer Adler, Badbergstr., ✆ (07662) 715 (rooms from DM100, meals DM70). Gourmet restaurant in a small village near the Kaiserstuhl. There are a few guest rooms upstairs.

Baden Wines

The thin strip of vineyards that trails through the Black Forest from Baden-Baden almost to Basle produces nearly 25 per cent of Germany's wine—some 400 different ones annually. Most of these are put out by the ZBW (Zentralkellerai Badischer Winzergenosenschaft) co-operative. The wines are of good quality, but no match to those of the Mosel, Rhineland and Franconia. Rather they are perfectly respectable quaffing wines, which may occasionally offer pleasant suprises. The hefty red Spätburgunders (made from the Pinot Noir grape) are popular, though recently crisp dry Rieslings have been taking over as local favourite. The rich, honey-toned Ruländer whites (made from Pinot Gris) and spicy Gewürztraminer varieties are also well worth a taste, and can hold their own against the smokiest of sausages. The steep slopes and volcanic soils of the Kaiserstuhl produce the best wines in the region (especially Rülander and Spätburgunder).

Freiburg

Locals ('Bobbeles') say that there are two types of people in Germany: those who live in Freiburg, and those who want to live there. It is the sunniest town in the country, is completely surrounded by the Black Forest, has no heavy industry and its cathedral boasts 'the most beautiful spire in Christendom'. So many people retire there that it has been nick-named 'Pensionopolis', but larky students and wine-quaffing locals give the city life and flair. Its other epithet is 'the northernmost town of Italy'.

Freiburg enjoys scorching summers (when the Bobbeles abandon their town to tourist invaders), and long, golden autumn evenings. In the spring you can shed your jersey here earlier than anyone else in Germany, and winter mornings are crisp, icy and brilliant. Whatever the season, you can hike through the Black Forest before lunch, spend the afternoon in a good museum, then—after an evening walk through the alleys and along the canals of the Altstadt—let your hair down in a student pub, or chat the night away in a welcoming Weinstube. It is the sort of life that can ensnare you for days.

Freiburg received its charter from the Duke of Zähringen in 1120, a good century before the foundation of most other German cities. Tucked into a corner between France, Austria and Switzerland, Freiburg has been beseiged, fought over, plundered and occupied by the French, Austrians and various German tribes throughout its history. Local innkeepers have profited greatly by the healthy trade from passing nobility. Austrian emperors from Maximillian onwards all checked in at local hostelries; Napoleon and Czar Alexander I both stayed the night, and Marie Antoinette swept through with 36 carriages and 450 horses on her way to Strasbourg to marry the Dauphin of France. In the Second World War the hapless town suffered not only under Allied onslaught (an air attack in November 1944 destroyed most of the Altstadt), but was also bombed in error by the Germans. The Bobbeles, however, have become adept at rebuilding their town, and have not only returned old buildings to their former glory, but have added some tasteful new ones too.

Getting Around

By air: The nearest **international airport** is the Airport Basel-Mulhouse-Freiburg in France, just a few minutes away on a regular bus shuttle service.

By train: Freiburg is on the main Mannheim/Karlsruhe/Basel line, and so is served frequently by very fast **trains** (Basel ¾hr; Karlsruhe 1hr; Frankfurt 2hr 10min ICE). Travel on an east/west axis, though, involves hip-hopping on small branch lines. The **Hauptbahnhof** is just west of the Altstadt.

By car: Freiburg is just off the A5, 130km from Karlsruhe and 60km north of Basel.

Car hire: Europcar, Wilhelmstr. 1a, © (0761) 31066.

Mitfahrzentrale: Belfortstr. 55, © (0761) 36749.

Public transport: An environment-conscious city council has ensured a comprehensive public transport system. *Regiokarten* (from DM9) offer cheap unlimited travel in the city and out into the Black Forest, but you'll find all the city sights easily accessible on foot.

Tourist Information

Tourist Office: Rotteckring Str. 14, © (0761) 368 900.

Carnival (or *Fastnet* as it is called here) is celebrated with parades, partying and traditional jesters. There is a **Spring Festival** in May and an **Autumn Festival** in October, both of which involve funfairs and generous quantities of food and wine. You can also sample local wines at **Wine Festivals** in June and mid-August.

The Altstadt

Freiburg's Altstadt isn't the pristine museum-piece you'll find in so many German towns. It is a jumble of old houses and modern shops; narrow alleys that flash you sudden glimpses of the mountains or Münster spire, and broad highways that shoot out to the edge of town. Over 5000 people still live in this 700m-wide pocket in the centre, so day and night there is a genial neighbourhood buzz.

On the streets, you can still see craftsmen painstakingly chipping away at Rhine pebbles (as they've done for centuries) to make the brightly coloured mosaics that cover the pavements. Little channels of icy water gush alongside the road—the bane of foreign cyclists and pedestrians, but a boon to carefree toddlers and the footsore in the summer. These **Bächle** have existed since the Middle Ages. They were intended not as sewers, but to course sparkling drinking water from mountain streams throughout the city, to cool the streets in summer and to provide handy sluices for dousing fires.

The Münsterplatz

The market on Münsterplatz is one of the most tantalizing in Germany. A bouquet of bright umbrellas fans around the Münster. Near the main portal the flowersellers peek out from behind banks of blooms. Around the northern side, local farmers pile baskets and barrels with prodigous quantities of bright fruit and earthy vegetables, and spread out long tables of mouthwatering homemade goodies. Along the southern buttresses you'll find imported foods and cheerful stalls of local crafts. Street-actors and musicians battle bravely against the general hubbub, and with polite regularity the cathedral bells join in the fray.

Opposite the south face of the Münster is the startlingly red, arcaded **Kaufhaus**, with a decorative oriel on each corner. This was built as a finance and customs centre in 1520. The city merchants were keen to display their power to the bishop across the way, and to drive their point home decorated the Kaufhaus façade with statues and coats of arms indicating the city's links with the Hapsburgs. The Kaufhaus is flanked by two grand Baroque palaces. On the right is the **Erzbischöfliches Palais** (residence of the archbishop since 1832, not open to the public). The house on the left was built by the artist Christian Wenzinger as his own residence. It is soon to open as a History Museum, which will allow you to see the fine ceiling paintings and the sumptuous staircase he created for himself. At the eastern end of the square stands the 18th-century **Hauptwache** (guardhouse). These days it is a public urinal, the only one in Germany to be listed as a national monument.

The Münster

The **Münster** was begun in 1200 and completed by 1513, making it a rarity in that it was entirely finished in the Middle Ages (most German Gothic cathedrals got their finishing touches during the 19th-century Romantic revival). In contrast to the hectic architectural hotch-potch of other churches built over the same period, the Romanesque transept and Gothic choir and chancel of the Freiburg Münster (all in the same red sandstone) blend with quiet harmony. The best place to appreciate this is from the arcade of the Kaufhaus.

The Münster began life as a parish church (it was granted cathedral status only in 1827), and so was allowed just one tower. Smarting under the indignity of this restriction, the church's patrons—the wealthy citizens of Freiburg—put their all into this single steeple. It starts off on a square base, resolves into an octagon of bristling lancets and bayonet windows, then finishes off with a flourish in a pyramid of Gothic tracery. At night it lights up from the inside, hanging over the town like an enormous fairy lantern. The label of 'the most beautiful tower in Christendom' was given to it, not by the tourist brochures, but by Jacob Burckhardt, the famous 19th-century Swiss art historian—and for once such praise doesn't seem an exaggeration.

The main portal is equally impressive. The whole of Christ's life story is meticulously carved into the tympanum, angels and prophets ascend the arches, and the wise virgins gaze at their rather forlorn-looking foolish counterparts across the porch. The devil—in his guise as a handsome 'Prince of the World' eyes a voluptuous maid. But if you take a peek behind him, you see that he is being devoured by hideous worms, serpents and lizards.

The densely-coloured windows in the aisles are the church's greatest treasures. They were commissioned by various trade guilds in the 13th and 14th centuries; pretzels, scissors and other clues incorporated into the designs show who the patrons were. The painting at the High Altar, representing the life of the Madonna (1512–16), is one of the best works of the idiosyncratic Hans Baldung Grien (*see* p. 58), and shows his usual, very individual flair with colour and his dramatic sense of light. To get a view of the reverse side, you need to join a guided tour *(DM1, times posted up at the entrance)*; this will also give you access to more art treasures in the ambulatory chapels.

Around the Münsterplatz

West of Münsterplatz, you can see the **Altes Rathaus** and the **Neues Rathaus** side by side on Rathausplatz. The two are in fact contemporary Renaissance buildings, but the Neues Rathaus was used by the university until 1896. In the middle of the square is a statue of the mild 14th-century monk and alchemist Bertold Schwarz, who stumbled across the formula for gunpowder while trying to make gold. Today the square is a resting place for sandwich-munching students, weary tourists and pensioners, and a Lear-like tramp who sometimes wanders in from the Black Forest with flowers in his hair.

Around the corner, in a lane behind the simple Franciscan monastery of **St Martin** (*c.* 1300) is the decorative **Haus zum Walfisch** (built 1514). The Dutch humanist Erasmus lived here for two years after fleeing from Basel in 1529. Nearby, on Kaiser-Josef-

Straße, the impressive 15th-century palace known as the **Baseler Hof** also housed religious refugees from the Swiss city: it was the residence in exile of the Chapter of Basle Cathedral.

The little alleys off the eastern end of Münsterplatz (dark and mysterious at night, when they're lit only by gas lamp) lead through an area of old clerical and seminary buildings to the **Konviktstraße**, a part of the Altstadt renovated in the 1960s to much acclaim from the architectural world. Original roof levels and house widths were kept, although often very modern materials and ideas were used. The result is a charming area that preserves a medieval atmosphere without descending into twee nostalgia. Even the massive parking garage has been successfully integrated. From the top terrace you'll get one of the best views of the Münster.

Konviktstraße ('Konvict' = seminary) leads to the 13th-century **Scwabentor** (Swabian Gate), one of the oldest buildings in the city. From here you can wander past **Zum Roten Bären** (Germany's oldest inn, with records dating back to 1311) and down into the **Inseln** and **Fischerau**—charming, higgedly-piggedly medieval artisans' quarters crowding the banks of an old canal (*see* **Eating Out** below).

On Augustinerplatz (between Inseln and Fischerau), is the **Augustiner Museum** *(Tues–Fri 9.30–5, Sat and Sun 10.30–5; adm free)*. This converted monastery is an ideal setting for a strong collection of medieval art. Of all the fine altar-pieces, the *Passion Altar* (1480) by the Master of the Housebook is the most stunning—richly coloured and with a characterization that seems to prefigure later Dutch masters. There are some first-rate paintings by Matthias Grünewald and Lucas Cranach and some typically quirky work from Hans Baldung Grien, including his evil-eyed 'Cupid with a Burning Arrow' (1530). You can also see statuary, stained glass and other treasures from the Münster, and some exquisite smaller woodcarvings by the mysterious Master HL, carver of the altar at Breisach (*see* p. 285). Upstairs you'll find the usual, run-of-the-mill collection of furniture, porcelain and restored period rooms. The 19th and 20th-century glassware, though, is a must—even if you're not a connoisseur. Right at the top of the building you can see some early models of Freiburg with the castle still intact.

Nearby, but not quite as impressive, is the **Museum für Neue Kunst** (same times and prices). The old school building has a cheery, friendly atmosphere. There is a good stock of German Expressionists, a modest range of international modern art, as well as temporary exhibitions.

A stroll back westwards will take you past the 13th-century **Martinstor** (nicknamed McDonald's Tor for its present tenant) to the present **university**, housed mainly in 19th-century red sandstone buildings, though there is an interesting Jugendstil lecture theatre. You can slip in for a look at it between sessions.

For a good view over the whole town climb up **Schlossberg** (a steep mound just east of the Schwabentor), or the 1284m-high **Schauinsland** (a hill 15km from the centre; take tram 2 to Günterstal, then bus 21, then the cable car).

expensive

Colombi, Rotteckring 16, ✆ 21 060 (DM320–370). The grandest hotel in town. Sleek realm of Hollywood staircases, panelled dining rooms and fresh flowers daily.

moderate

Hotel zum Bären, Oberlinden 12, ✆ 36913 (DM210–230). Germany's oldest inn, built in the 12th century, retains many original features and offers good service.

Park Hotel Post, Eisenbahnstr. 35, ✆ 31 683 (DM190–210). Comfy old hotel which overlooks vineyards in the middle of town, and is convenient for the Hauptbahnhof.

Schwarzwälder Hof, Herrenstr. 43, ✆ 32 386, fax 30 853 (DM100–160). Simple but good value hotel in the heart of the Altstadt.

Zur Sichelschmiede, Insel 1, ✆ 35 037 (from DM130). Small rooms, but friendly service. Above a *Weinstube* in a delightful corner of the Inseln quarter.

inexpensive

Hotel Schemmer, Eschholzstr. 63, ✆ 272 424 (DM70 without private facilities). Behind the Hauptbahnhof. Clean and well-run. No restaurant.

Am Stadtgarten, Bernhardstr. 5, ✆ 28290 (DM80–104 without breakfast). Centrally situated and good value. TV in rooms.

Youth Hostel: Karthäuserstr. 151, ✆ 67 656.

Eating and Drinking

Across the tracks from the Hauptbahnhof you'll find the Stühlinger district, full of beautiful but unloved 19th-century buildings. Here are the trendier bars and student dens. The Altstadt is the most fertile ground for good restaurants and cafés. The Inseln and Fischerau quarters are at their best at night. The crumbly old buildings wedged up against the canal have escaped prissy restoration. You'll find noisy beergardens and intimate candle-lit restaurants, tiny squares and courtyards, soulful buskers and genial merrymakers. Half the enjoyment of going out in Freiburg is in exploring the backstreets yourself to find that arty *Weinstube*, or unknown restaurant deserving a Michelin star; but here are a few starters.

Restaurants and Taverns

Zur Traube, Schusterstr. 17, ✆ 32 190 (DM80). The chef comes up with mouth-watering game and fish creations (such as pike wrapped in bacon and served with red lentils).

Zur Sichelschmiede, Insel 1, ✆ 35 037 (DM20–30). *Gemütliche* nook where you can get pizzas and simple Schwarzwald food.

Schinderhannes, Schwabentorplatz 7, ✆ 39 390 (DM20–40). Popular wine bar with good Baden food. Try the *Schäufele*—spicy smoked shoulder of pork.

Engler's Weinkrügle, Konviktstr. 12, ✆ 383 115 (DM20–40). Specializes in Black Forest trout. Set menus under DM20.

Zum Stahl, Kartäuserstr. 99, ✆ 33 402 (DM20–35). Just east of the Altstadt, on the edge of the Black Forest. Long tables under the trees in the summer, and serves delicious Baden food (you pay by weight for meat dishes). Studenty clientele.

Markthalle, through the double doors at the end of Martinsgasse. An old factory that has been converted into an eating hall lined with small stalls selling local, Chinese, Indian, Greek, Italian and French dishes—and much more besides. Only open during the day, so a good spot for lunch.

Bars and Cafés

Hausbrauerei Feierling, Gerberau 46. A cluster of bars, at many levels, centred on the enormous copper vats of the in-house brewery; opposite is a large, usually packed, beergarden.

Babeauf, Klarastraße. Student favourite in the Stühlinger district.

Ex, Klarastraße. Punky, loud music and murky, coloured lighting.

Brazil, corner of Escholz and Wannerstr. Big and bright with a token palm tree and cheap food.

Osteria, Grünewaldstr. 2. Trendy Italian wine bar in the Altstadt. Good selection of local and Italian wines, and a friendly crowd.

Ulm

Ulm is perhaps best known to trivia quiz fanatics as the birthplace of Albert Einstein, the site of the world's tallest steeple and the home of Albrecht Berblinger, the 'Tailor of Ulm', who fell into the Danube in 1811 while making one of the first serious attempts to fly. Hermann Hesse called Ulm an 'extraordinarily beautiful and unusual city'. On his tramp south in the 1930s, Patrick Leigh-Fermor marvelled at the medieval atmosphere of the town, the warrens of artisans' workshops, 'storeys that beetled and almost touched' and 'roofs that retreated in confusion' up the banks of the Danube. A few years later, however, Allied bombers laid waste to 80 per cent of Ulm, and when the city rose again it was (as Leigh-Fermour noted on a later visit) 'in a geometry of skyscraping concrete blocks'. But the cathedral and pockets of the old town survived, and restorers have patched up many of the scars. As you hurtle between Stuttgart and Munich, or pass by on the Romantische Straße (*see* p. 311), a stop-over in Ulm will be time well spent.

Ulm is on the banks of the Danube (a natural frontier), right on the border of Bavaria and Württemberg and within a few days' march of France and the Alps. Hannibal, Charlemagne, Fredrick Barbarossa and Napoleon have all swanned past on their conquests;

great armies have plundered it, then recoiled as they got their come-uppance. Ulm has been tossed back and forth between the Alemanni, the Franks, the Swabian Hohenstaufens, the Bavarians, the Austrians and the French. Yet in 1397 its citizens won unique rights to self-government with the *Grosser Schwörbrief* (Big Oath Letter—a German Magna Carta), and for centuries Ulm was a *Kaiserstadt*, managing to hang onto this 'Free Imperial City' status until 1802. Today Ulm is part of Baden-Württemberg, although its satellite town, Neu-Ulm, is in Bavaria.

Getting Around

By train: Ulm is on the main northbound rail route from Munich, and so is served by about 40 express trains a day (Munich 1hr 10min ICE; Frankfurt 2¼hr ICE; Stuttgart ¾hr ICE). The **Hauptbahnhof** (information ℰ (0731) 102 1440) deposits you right in front of a monument to Einstein, from where all the sights are within easy walking distance.

By car: Ulm is on the A8 100km southeast of Stuttgart and 130km west of Munich.

By taxi: ℰ (0731) 64000.

By boat: Rheinhold Kräß, Kramgasse 3, ℰ (0731) 62751, offers round-trips on the Danube ranging from DM9 for an hour's tour.

Tourist Information

The **tourist information office** on the Münsterplatz, ℰ (0731) 64161 *(Mon–Fri 9–6, Sat 9–12.30)*, is the usual cornucopia of advice, maps, information and assistance with bookings and guided tours.

Post office: The main post office on Bahnhofsplatz offers exchange facilities.

Police and emergencies: ℰ 1881.

Festivals

June and July are good times to catch Ulm in a celebratory mood. The **Stadtfest** fills the Münsterplatz with carousels, side-shows and food stalls for most of June, and on the penultimate Monday of July—**Schwörmontag**—the mayor takes an oath (11am in the Weinhof) to commemorate the *Grosser Schörbrief*, then there is a barge procession along the Danube. Every four years you can see **Fischerstechen** (fisherman's jousting), in which boats are used in place of horses. The next tournament is in July 1994.

The Münster

Ulm Münster's famous steeple launches itself heavenwards, like a giant stalagmite, tapering swiftly to a point 161.6m above the ground. Blue-grey stone and delicate tracery make it almost transparent against the sky. In churches with open spires like this, remarks Leigh Fermor, 'one could understand how congregations thought their orisons had a better start than prayers under a dome where the syllables might flutter around for hours. With steeples they follow the uprush of the lancets and make an immediate break for it.'

The citizens of Ulm wanted a church to outstrip all others (especially nearby Strasbourg's) as a triumphant display of the city's wealth and independence. The architects (succeeding members of the Parler and Ensingen dynasties, top masons of the day) came up with a building that would hold 20,000 people—double Ulm's population at the time. In 1377 construction began. Two centuries later the builders were still at it when they were over-taken by the Reformation, and work ground to a halt. Building resumed only in 1844 and the tower was completed (following a 15th-century plan) in 1899.

The medieval townsmen emptied their coffers to commission some of the best artists of the time to decorate the church. Despite the ravages of the iconoclasts, some fine works remain. Particularly worth seeking out are the superb **choir stalls** (1469–74), carved with life-size human busts by Jörg Syrlin the Elder and Michel Erhart, local craftsmen. Syrlin's son, Jörg the Younger, is responsible for the **pulpit canopy** (1510), a delicate needle of turrets and finials that echoes the main spire. Further symbolic bridges to Heaven are the soaring **Tabernacle** (*c.* 1470), which bristles with little figurines of prophets and saints, and the gilded canopy to the **font** (1474).

Most of the church is cast in the usual cathedral gloom, but rows of windows, high up in the central section, flood the top half of the nave with light, lending a preternatural glow to the enormous **fresco** of the Last Judgement that arches over the choir. Just to the right of the choir arch is the anguished *Man of Sorrows* (1429). The sculptor, Hans Multscher, went on to become one of the greatest artists of the period. Already, the energy and fluidity of this early work set it quite apart from the stiff, static carving of Multscher's contempo-raries. The statue really belongs in the main portal, but was brought inside to protect it from the ravages of pollution—a replica deputizes outside.

Of the side-chapels, the most impressive is the **Besserer-Kapelle**, to the right of the chancel. There's a crucifix by Michel Erhart, and some rich **stained glass** (1431) by Hans Acker. Like Multscher, Acker pioneered the late Gothic realism. His windows display a wealth of sensitive characterization and fine detail—one of the saints at Abraham's feast is munching a sausage.

A climb of 708 steps up the steeple *(daily 9–5; adm DM2)* could be rewarded (on a clear day) with a view of the Alps.

The Altstadt

South of the Münster, huddled between two rushing streams and the Danube, is the **Fischerviertel** (Fisherman's Quarter), a cluster of old *fachwerk* houses inhabited in medieval times mainly by artisans. On Fischergasse you can see a boatman's house (No. 18), a baker's (No. 22) and a fisherman's cottage (No. 23). The island between the streams attracted tanners and millers. Today the Fischerviertel bristles with cafés and smart galleries, but it is also still a residential district. Strings of washing flap across some alleys, and the feet that cross the little wooden bridges and the squares belong as much to locals as to visitors. As you potter about, keep an eye open for the alarmingly wonky **Schiefe Haus** (Crooked House, *c.* 1500) on the river off Fischergasse.

From the Fischerviertel you can follow the old town wall along the Danube, an eerie experience at night, when the yellow floodlights cast strange shadows on the stonework. A little way along you'll find the **Metzgeturm** (Butcher's Tower, 1345), a brick tower with brightly coloured glazed roof tiles that leans precariously (about 2m from the vertical). Local legend blames the tilt on corpulent butchers who were imprisoned in the tower for making their sausages too short.

North of the Metzgeturm is the Marktplatz where the **Fischkasten**—a fountain created by Syrlin the Elder in 1482—and the 14th-century **Rathaus** vie with each other in gaudy brilliance. The Rathaus wins by a long chalk, thanks largely to the frescoes (recently restored to much the same vividness they had when they were painted by Martin Schaffner in 1540) and a large 16th-century astronomical clock. Inside the Rathaus you can see a replica of the unfortunate Albrecht Berblinger's flying machine.

Albrecht Ludwig Berblinger: 'The Tailor of Ulm'

 Berblinger was a master tailor in the city of Ulm at the beginning of the 19th century. While stitching and unstitching, however, his mind was on greater things. He wanted to fly, and was determined that he could do so. He set about making a flying machine out of wood, bone and silk. Its large, leaf-shaped wings were rigidly fixed to a central harness—more like a modern hang-glider than a flapping imitation of bird wings. Berblinger was the butt of particularly nasty derision from his fellow townsmen, and so practised early in the morning or at dusk. In 1808 he succeeded in making a short flight from the top of his garden shed. However in 1811, in front of an audience that included the king and most of the local aristocracy, he attempted to fly across the Danube from the top of the Adlerbastei. A few minutes later he was being fished out of the water by passing fishermen.

Berblinger gave up the idea of flying and spent most of the rest of his life working on a (rather ingenious) design for an artificial leg. He died defeated and bankrupt— though a recent reconstruction of his glider has shown that it *can* work. The Tailor of Ulm was just too inexperienced in using his invention, and didn't have enough knowledge of how to manage wind currents to control his flight.

At the far end of the square is the **Ulm Museum** *(Tues–Sun 10–5, Thurs 10–8; adm free)* where you'll find displays on the city's history (including a slide show of the Second World War devastation), a good collection of Swabian religious carving (with more work by Multscher and Erhart) and a diverting collection of modern art.

Very little remains in Ulm by way of atmospheric hotels. Most were built after the war and are functional and standardized.

Stern, Sterngasse 17, ✆ 63091, fax 63077 (DM140–175). Plain but efficient hotel just north of the Altstadt.

Ulmer Spatz, Münsterplatz 27, ✆ 68081, fax 602 1925 (DM135–160). Modern hotel with small garden opposite the cathedral.

Goldener Bock, Bockgasse 25, ✆ 28079 (DM130). Erstwhile brewery near the Kornhaus, now a comfortable hotel.

Baümle, Kohlgasse 6, ✆ 62287 (DM75–90). The best place to stay in Ulm, and also one of the cheapest. A cosy, friendly small hotel, and the only one which still occupies a pre-war building. No restaurant.

Anker, Rabengasse 2, ✆ 63297 (DM78). Simple hotel slap next to the cathedral.

Youth Hostel: Grimmelfinger Weg 45, ✆ 384455.

Eating and Drinking

The best areas for atmospheric restaurants and interesting cafés are the **Fischerviertel** and the poky lanes around **Rabengasse**, just north of the Münster. Fish is a local speciality—even in medieval times live trout were stored in large perforated tanks in the Fischerviertel.

Restaurants and Taverns

Forelle, Fischergasse 25, ✆ 63924 (DM50). Heavy wooden beams, head-bumpingly low ceilings and an excellent kitchen—trout and other fish dishes are a speciality.

Fischhaus Heilbronner, in Rebengasse (not to be confused with Rabengasse, just a few yards away). Here, behind a well-stocked fish shop, there is space for about 30 non-smokers to enjoy superb, inexpensive, plainly cooked fish. Lunchtime only.

Barfüßer, Lautenberg 1. Brews its own beer and sells good wholesome food.

Bars and Cafés

Zunfthaus der Schiffleute, Fischergasse 31. The 15th-century fisherman's guildhall right at the heart of the Fischerviertel. A good place to start off the evening with a drink; it serves food, but it isn't that special.

Historisches Brauhaus Drei Kannen, Hafenbad 31–1. Lively Brauhaus with a beergarden beside an Italianate loggia that looks like a film set.

Ulmer Weizenbierhaus, Kronengasse 12. A must for *Weizenbier* fans—you can choose from more than 20 different varieties.

Note: The churches mentioned below all function as such. This means that there is no admission charge, and that the buildings are open from early morning to around 6pm. Most discourage casual visitors during Sunday services. The monasteries themselves are not usually open to the public, though you are usually free to wander around the out-buildings.

South of Ulm you leave sober Protestant Swabia behind. Here, in the mid-17th century, the Counter-Reformation triumphed. Abbots set about rebuilding their monasteries, stimulated by the sinuous movement, colour, light and sheer fantasy of the new Baroque (and later Rococo) styles. Here were architectural forms that could exalt the Virgin, glorify the saints, and provide splendid backdrops for the pomp and ceremony of popular worship. The result of the abbots' fervour is that the rather dull countryside in this south-east corner of Baden-Württemberg is today enlivened by vivacious outbursts of Baroque architecture.

Kloster Wiblingen (5km south of Ulm off the B28; Bus 3) was begun as late as 1772, and shows some degree of Neoclassical restraint. The sparkling white interior, with its domed ceilings and Corinthian pillars, is rather cautiously gilded, but there are energetic ceiling frescoes by Januarius Zick (*see* p. 60). In his depiction of the Second Coming, above the nave, clouds through which little figures float up into the sky swirl ever higher. There's also a finely painted Last Supper in the choir apse. The dramatically realistic altar crucifix is probably by the Gothic sculptor Michel Erhart (*see* **Ulm Münster** above).

In an adjoining building, upstairs, past rows of medical text books (the monastery is now used by Ulm University), you come to the **library**, built in 1744 *(Tues–Sun Nov–Mar 2–4, Apr–Oct 10–12 and 2–5; adm DM2)*. Here the stuccatori have let loose with Rococo swirls and flourishes all over the window jambs and ceilings. The body of the library is gently Baroque, with a gallery that seems to hover above the bookshelves on top of slender marbled pillars.

Münster Zwiefalten (about 60km southwest of Ulm, on the B312) was built between 1744 and 1765 by Johann Michael Fischer (who was also responsible for much of the design of the church at Wiblingen). The interior was fashioned by Johann Joseph Christian, one of the leading sculptors of the day. Here Rococo fantasy reaches hallucinogenic proportions. Tumbling cherubs carry drapes of gilded cloth (part real, part painted). The pulpit drips with stucco stalactites and is laden with leaves, putti and cartoon clouds. There is even more finicky foliage around the confessional, which with exotic fronds and lichen looks rather like a fairy grotto.

Another 60km further, on the banks of the Danube, lies the Benedictine **Kloster Beuron** (the monastery is not open to the public, though you may visit the church during the day). Beuron is the most beautifully situated of the monasteries around Ulm. Here the Danube really is blue, and winds between steep hills. Grey rocky cliffs jut out of the forest, and in Autumn the valley blazes with colour. Founded in 1080 as an Augustinian monastery, it was entirely rebuilt during the Baroque period. The Benedectines took over at the beginning of the 19th century, and are today in equal parts famous for their excellent sausages and sublime Gregorian chant. The former can be bought from the Kloster's own butcher's shop, while the latter can be heard at High Mass *(Mon–Sat 11.15am, Sun 10am)* or Vespers *(Mon–Sat 6pm, Sun 3pm)*. The Baroque church is fairly tame by the standards of its neighbours, but the richly decorated Byzantine chapel—built in 1898 to house a 15th-century Pietà—makes up for any shortcomings.

Back on the B312, near the Bavarian border, you'll find **Ochsenhausen**, a 14th-century Benedictine monastery that also received a complete Baroque facelift. However, the gaunt Gothic bones show beneath the rejuvenated pink and white surface. The long, narrow nave seems quite at odds with the Baroque decor. Nearby (on the B30) is **Steinhausen** where, according to the tourist brochures, you'll find 'the most beautiful village church in the world'. It is certainly an impressive confection of pink and blue paint, white cake-icing stucco and bright ceiling frescoes. Whether or not it deserves its epithet remains a matter of

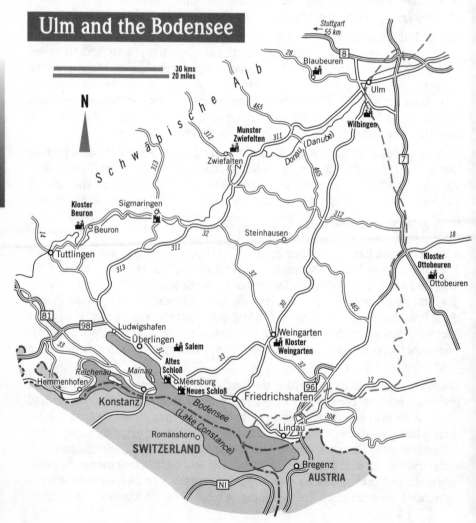

personal taste. Further down the B30, towards Lake Constance (about 85km from Ulm), is the enormous **Kloster Weingarten**, which vies with Ottobeuren (*see* below) for the title of the German Escorial. The imposing **Basilika** is modelled on St Peter's in Rome, and the monastery complex is the largest in the country. Inside the Basilika you can see a particularly grand organ made by the famous 18th-century organ builder, Joseph Gabler.

Even if your preference is for the plain and simple, you should not miss the Benedictine abbey at **Ottobeuren**, just across the Bavarian border, about 50km south of Ulm. Once again Johann Michael Fischer played the largest part in its construction. Johann Joseph Christian and the Augsburg artist Johann Michael Feichtmeyer were the driving force behind the interiors. You enter through a deliberately dimmed porch into a vast, exhilaratingly bright hall. There are pulpits way above your head, abundant flocks of putti, and licks and curls of stucco and gold. Behind all this joyous abandon, however, you sense a strong controlling hand. Especially worth seeking out are the richly carved choir stalls and the reliquaries in the side altars. Entire human skeletons recline on two of the tombs, decked out in gauze, velvet and gold. The three organs, built by the master Karl Joseph Riepp, rank with the most beautiful church organs in the world.

In the adjoining **Museum** *(Mon–Sat 10–12 and 2–5, Sun 10–12 and 1–5; adm DM2)* you can see more religious carving and painting, some exquisite 18th-century inlaid furniture and visit the small **Baroque theatre** and elegant **library**.

See also Directory entries for Blaubeuren, Sigmaringen.

Where to Stay

These monasteries are isolated, or attached to small villages. Often the most comfortable and convenient accommodation is to be found in **private rooms** (about DM25–30 per person including breakfast, look out for signs reading *Fremdenzimmer* or *Zimmer Frei*). The most attractive place to stay in the region is Beuron.

Zur Linde, opposite the church at Steinhausen, ✆ (07583) 2381 (DM60–85). Friendly, pleasant guesthouse with a good restaurant.

Waldhorn, Karlstr. 47, Weingarten, ✆ (0751) 405 125 (DM75–90). Clean and comfortable, also with restaurant.

Hotel Pelikan, 7792 Beuron, ✆ (07466) 406 (DM80–140). Family-run establishment with a restaurant attached.

The Bodensee (Lake Constance)

Most foreign tourists see the Bodensee (known in the English-speaking world as Lake Constance) with noses pressed to the train window as they whizz between the Black

Forest and Bavaria. Yet if you stop for a moment and allow the Bodensee to exercise its charms, you might find it very difficult to draw yourself away. The clear lake, 80km long and 13km wide, is set against the resplendent backdrop of the Alps. A trip around the shores takes you through three different countries (Germany, Austria and Switzerland), into thick forests and medieval towns, past vineyards and abundant orchards and along the edges of quiet, isolated nature reserves. Windsurfers glide about on the water and children mess about in boats. You can sample the various national cuisines, go on long country walks, visit old churches and castles, or dance till the early hours.

German tourists know this, and come here in their droves, though there are plenty of quiet spots to be found, and the Bodensee is a far better place to spend your time than the over-rated Bavarian lakes.

Getting Around

One of the delights of the area is border hopping to sample the different cuisines, and to enjoy the changing landscapes. Border formalities are fairly relaxed, but do remember to carry your passport with you.

By train: There are regular rail connections along the lake between Konstanz and Lindau; between Munich and Lindau, and between Frankfurt, Stuttgart, Basel and Konstanz.

By car: The B31 hugs the entire northern shoreline and is connected by a short Autobahn (A98) to the B33, which follows the lake from Radolfzell to Konstanz. There are two **car ferries**, one between Konstanz and Meersburg (20 minute journey; about DM15 for a medium-sized car) and one from Friedrichshafen to Romanshorn (40 minutes; DM23).

By boat: The **Weiße Flotte** (White Fleet; information ✆ (07531) 281 389) operates cruise ships that follow the northern shore between Schaffhausen in Switzerland and Bregenz in Austria. The average ticket price is DM15, though you can buy special 7 and 15-day passes.

Bicycle hire: By far the most pleasurable way of seeing the countryside is by bicycle. Most of the land around the lake is fairly flat, and there is a comprehensive network of cycle routes (maps and details from tourist offices). You can hire bicycles very cheaply from the parcel counters at most German Rail stations (*see* **Travel** p. 13).

Tourist Information

The tourist information office at **Konstanz**, Konzilstr. 5, near the Bahnhof, ✆ (07531) 284 376 *(Mon–Fri 8.45–6, Sat 9–1 and 4–6, Sun 4–6)* can help with general information about the Bodensee and Swiss areas as well as about the town itself. The **Lindau** tourist office, opposite the Bahnhof, ✆ (08382) 26 000 *(Mon–Fri 8–12 and 2–6, Sat 9–12.30)* can also help with information on Bregenz.

Konstanz is an old town (dating from before AD 600), straddling the Rhine at the point where it drains out of the Bodensee. The backstreets are cobbled and lined by little white houses with blue shutters. Grander buildings are adorned with brighter colours and startling frescoes. There's a gay, Mediterranean air to the town, and students from the big new university give it a youthful edge.

Its **Münster**, set on a mound slightly higher than the rest of the Altstadt, has grown up in fits and starts since the 8th century. The crypt dates back to these Carolingian times, and evokes the mystery and pagan ritual of early Christianity. Stumpy, wierdly decorated pillars prop up the low arches; on the walls hang four giant gilt-copper medallions (c. 1000), embossed with ancient designs. The basilica preserves much of its original, magnificent Romanesque stature, while the west front rises up in a sheer block of three fused towers (c. 1100–1400). A rather ridiculous neo-Gothic spire (1866) balances on top. Don't miss the superbly carved 15th-century Hauptportal (main entrance, in the west porch between the towers) and choir stalls (both by the local craftsman Simon Haider), and an exceptional winged altar (1524) in the St Konrad's Chapel (down a staircase off the northern transept).

The other sights in Konstanz comprise mainly historical façades of buildings not normally open to the public. The most fruitful area for exploration is just south of the Münster, where you will find rows of gaudy Renaissance mansion fronts. Walk down Hohenhausgasse and branch off into Zollernstraße, or into Kanzleistraße and then Obermarkt and Hussenstraße. The 16th-century **Rathaus** (in Kanzleistraße) sports bright 19th-century frescoes, but go through the main arch to find a quiet Florentine-styled courtyard decorated with milder Renaissance wall-painting.

To the east of the Münster is the Stadtgarten through which you can stroll, past bobbing yachts moored alongside the promenade, to the imposing **Konzilgebäude**, an old storehouse that in 1417 is said to have accommodated the conclave that elected Pope Martin V (nowadays it is used as a festival hall). West from here, across the broad Marktstatte, you come to Rosgartenstraße (which gets its name not from a rose garden, but as a euphemism for the horse abattoir that once stood here—in German *Roß* = horse). Here you will find the **Rosgartenmuseum** *(Tues–Sun, 10–5; adm free)*, an atmospheric museum still fitted out with its original 19th-century display cases, crammed full of archaeological finds and exhibits from the Middle Ages.

Konstanz © (07531–)   ***Where to Stay***

Steigenberger Insel Hotel, Auf der Insel 1, © 1250, fax 264 02 (DM265–450). One of Germany's top-ranking hotel chains has carpeted the cloisters and dolled up the cells of an old monastery to create the most luxurious hotel in town, right on the lake and surrounded by its own gardens.

Hotel Barbarossa, Obermarkt 8–12, ✆ 22 021, fax 27 630 (DM98–185). Smartly modernized, historic hotel in one of the most atmospheric parts of town. Old Redbeard himself signed a peace treaty with the Lombards here in 1183, and there has been an inn and dancing hall on the site since 1419.

Hotel Germania, Konradigasse 2, ✆ 23 735, fax 23 797 (DM120). Small hotel in the Altadt, run with a personal touch.

Youth Hostel: Zur Allmanshöhe 18, ✆ 32 260.

You can also stay in **Gottlieben** (*see* below):

Hotel Drachenfels, CH-8274 Gottlieben TG, ✆ (072) 691 414 (DM150–320). On the shore of the lake. Splendid period-furnished rooms and impeccable service.

Hotel Krone, CH-8274 Gottlieben TG, ✆ (072) 692 323, fax (072) 692 456 (DM170–190). Slightly cheaper option than the Drachenfels, but also comfortable and on the water's edge.

Eating and Drinking: Restaurants and Taverns

Seehotel Silber, Seestr 25, ✆ 63 044 (DM60 DM). Serves delicious food beside the lake. Good fish dishes.

Zum Kelch, Halfhade 7 (DM40). Intimate little place with an imaginative menu that changes seasonally.

For a really superb meal and splendid setting cross the border to the tiny Swiss village of **Gottlieben**, close enough to be almost a suburb of Konstanz (don't forget your passport, though). Gottlieben is a cluster of old buildings (most of them owned by the same family), idyllically situated on the lake, overlooking a nature reserve. Here, on Sunday mornings, yachts more alongside the restaurant terrace and people disembark for long, late breakfasts. The best time of all to come is in the evening, when swans glide past on the glimmering pink water, and you can have a languid meal as the sun sets.

Waaghaus, ✆ (072) 691 4 14 (DM60–90). Terrace restaurant on the water, where you can eat delicately smoked meats, fish poached in subtle juices and irresistible deserts.

Fischerstube, next door to the Waaghaus (DM30–50). Here you can wear your muddy boots, swill beer and enjoy simpler fare from the Waaghaus kitchen.

Drachenberg, ✆ (072) 691 414 (DM70–100). Superb French cuisine in warm, wood-panelled environs. Ideal for winter.

Bars and Cafés

Theatre Café, Konzilstr 3. Konstanz's arty set wake up slowly over a late breakfast and big cups of coffee. You can also get good pastas and salads.

Tantris, St Johanngasse, near the Münster. The place to be seen sipping cocktails.

Schlößli, Hornstaader Str. 43. Popular bar and beergarden in nearby Horn, much fraternized by students.

Kulturladen, Bücklestr. 33. Packed and pulsating with the latest live music.

Reichenau, Mainau and the Untersee

West of Konstanz is the **Untersee** (Lower Lake), a secluded pocket of water tucked away from the normal tourist beat. Much of the surrounding countryside is nature reserve on which you cannot set foot, and there are also thick forests on the peninsula north-east of Konstanz, fragrant orchards, and stretches along the shore with scrubby grass and stumpy trees, rather like Greek island farmland. Flocks of 20 or 30 swans swim about quietly, then fly off with a laborious, thundering rhythm. This is superb country for walking, cycling and seeking out good restaurants (*see* below)—though from time to time one of the yacht-flattening storms that suddenly sweep across the lake might send you dashing into a *Weinstube* a little earlier than you had planned. The best part of the shore is between Radolfzell and Stein am Rhein.

The island of **Reichenau**, in the Untersee, can be reached by causeway from the B33. The monastery founded there in the 8th century became an international centre of learning, and built up immense wealth, owning land all over southern Germany. The 430-hectare island basks in its own temperate micro-climate, and is now largely given over to fruit, flower and lettuce growing. On summer days uncoordinated irrigation sprinklers turn the quiet country paths into obstacle-courses.

Most visitors, however, come for the three superb Romanesque churches on the island. **St Georg** is a peaceful little 9th-century church in the middle of the fields. Inside you will find some superb 10th-century frescoes depicting Christ's miracles, and St George's skull (the Reichenau monks had quite some purchasing power when it came to relics). The **Münster**, the main abbey church built in 816, is the least attractive of the three, but has an interesting *Schatzkammer* (treasure chamber) which contains an exquisite 5th-century ivory pyx and shelves of sparkling reliquaries. Around the back of the church is an aromatic herb garden. **St Peter und Paul**, at the water's edge, is decorated in an odd jumble of styles, with 11th-century murals above the altar and Rococo stucco on the ceiling.

The islet of **Mainau** is in the main body of the lake, and can also be reached by causeway. It is the seat of the octogenarian Count Lennart Bernadotte, a member of the Swedish royal family, who some years ago excited local gossip by marrying his young secretary. The old count still fuels *Weinstube* conversation with such exploits as his televized drinking of neat lakewater to prove that it is not polluted. Mainau is famed for its gardens. There are banks of tulips and rhodendendrons in May and June, formal gardens with witty bursts of topiary, orchids, banana trees and peacocks. In high season, between 10,000 and 30,000 people *a day* pay their DM8 and stream onto the little island—though if you go for an evening meal in the restaurant (*see* below) you are excused entrance fees and have the gardens a little more to yourself.

Reichenau

Salatstube, Untere Rheinstraße (DM15–25). Sample Reichenau salads farm-fresh in the middle of the lettuce fields.

Hotel Mohren, Pirminstr. 141, © (07534) 485 (DM140–210). Traditional hotel in the middle of the island. Attentive staff and a relaxed atmosphere.

Hotel Seeschau, An der Schiffslände 8, © (07534) 257 (DM160–190). Charming, privately owned hotel by the lake. Good fish restaurant (meals DM60–70).

Hemmenhofen (near Stein-am-Rhein)

Sporthotel Höri, Uferstr. 20–40, © (07735) 8110 (rooms DM180–290). On the water's edge. Not a particularly attractive place to stay at, but does an afternoon cream-cake buffet that will totally wreck any good your long walk has done you.

Haus Stern Am See, 7766 Gaienhofen-3, (07735) 2015 (DM60–130). Charming small guesthouse with gruff owner. The water laps almost to the front door and wooden balconies hang over the lake.

Moos (near Radolfzell)

Hotel Gottfried, Böhringer Str. 1, © (07732) 4161, fax (07732) 52502 (rooms DM140, apartments from DM240, meals from DM80). Fine place for a longer stay. Large, well-appointed rooms and swimming pool, tennis courts and a sauna; yet still maintains a small family-run hotel atmosphere. The fairly unprepossessing exterior hides one of the best restaurants on the Bodensee. Owner-chef Klaus Neidhart's mouthwatering fish dishes are flavoured with subtle and imaginative sauces, and accompanied by a variety of homemade breads and tasty salads. The wine list is extensive and offers a careful selection of top quality regional and foreign wines. There's a garden terrace for sunny days, but the hotel isn't on the water.

The Northern Shoreline

The shore between Ludwigshafen and Lindau is the most tourist-intensive part of the lake, though there are still villages where you can escape the throngs, and some sights that make it worthwhile joining the queues.

Just east of Überlingen is the pilgrimage church of **Birnau**, standing all on its own above steep terraces of vineyards that run down to the lake. Inside, the *Honigschlecker*—a cheeky cherub stealing honey from a hive and licking his finger—has usurped the saints as an object of popular veneration. The Rococo church is a dazzling *tour de force* by some of the best artists of the day. Peter Thumb was the architect, and the fresco painter Gottfried Bernard produced the superb ceiling paintings. In the cupola Divine Light travels via the

Virgin to a real mirror (borne by putti), whence it is deflected onto the onlooker. If you position yourself correctly, you become part of the fresco. The mirror has a dual function. It also covers a hole in the ceiling which ensures a constant draught around the dome, thus preventing flies from settling and soiling the picture.

A few miles inland is **Salem** *(Apr–Oct Mon–Sat 9–5, Sun 11–5; adm DM8)*, erstwhile Cistercian monastery, now the seat of the Margrave of Baden and also Germany's most prestigious boarding school. It was founded in the 1920s by Dr Kurt Hahn, who went on to found Gordonstoun in Scotland. (In term time your tour is accompanied by distant sounds of banging desks and breaking voices.) The detour is worth it if only for the spectacular stucco ceilings in the Margrave's rooms. The Gothic church has some fine Baroque embell-ishments—especially the organ, resplendent with palm-tree-climbing cherubs. A Gasthaus just outside the school gates makes a handy lunchtime stopover.

Back on the shores of the Bodensee, you reach **Meersburg**, a pretty (though very touristy) old town, with two castles perched high above the lake. The **Altes Schloß** *(Mar–Oct daily 9–6, Nov–Feb 10–5; adm DM6)* is the oldest inhabited castle in Germany. Inside you'll find the usual kitchens, dungeons and suits of armour, but also the quarters once occupied by Germany's greatest female poet, Annette von Droste-Hülshoff. Little has changed in the two modest rooms since she died here in 1848, pining with unrequited love for the nov-elist Levin Schücking, 18 years her junior. The **Neues Schloß** *(Apr–Oct daily 10–1 and 2–6; adm DM3)* is really only worth visiting for the grand staircase built to plans by Balthasar Neumann. From time to time the Meersburg Boys' Brass Band (in red coats and fur-trimmed hats) or other ensembles give concerts in the halls. The **Zeppelin Museum** *(Apr–Oct daily 9–6; adm DM3.50)* has a large collection of airship memorabilia—including burnt-out bits of the Hindenburg—of interest mainly to aviation buffs.

Tourists flock (by car and on foot) across the causeway to the island resort of **Lindau**, but here they are swallowed up by the bustling, colourful, rather Mediterranean town. Lindau is an architectural bouillabaisse, with little bits of everything from 13th-century fortification towers to the spanking new Inselhalle recreation centre. The entrance to the tiny **harbour** is guarded by a weatherbeaten lighthouse and a haughty Bavarian lion (Lindau is just inside Bavaria). In town (on Reichsplatz, near the harbour) look out for the delightfully eccentric 15th-century **Altes Rathaus** with its curly gables, witty *trompe l'oeil* and gaudy assort-ment of frescoes. On Marktplatz, to the north, is the **Haus zum Cavazzen**, a Baroque patrician palace with rather more muted murals. This houses the **Stadtmuseum** *(Apr–Oct Tues–Sun 10–12 and 2–5; adm DM5)*, an ideal museum for a rainy day. There's nothing very spectacular here, but lots to keep you entertained. Downstairs there are *Totentafeln*, wooden fold-out tablets from the 17th century, used to depict a dead notable's life and achievements. On the first floor are some fine period rooms, and further up into the rafters you'll find old clocks, dolls houses and traditional painted furniture—and get occasional glimpses out across the red rooves of Lindau. The collection of mechanical musical instru-ments *(guided tours only, 30min, 2pm–5pm)* is a good place to round off your visit.

Across on the other side of town, beneath the multi-turreted **Diebsturm** (Thief's Tower, built in 1350) is the earthy little 11th-century church of **St Peter**, which houses a superb

Passion Cycle by Holbein the Elder—his only surviving frescoes. The church is now a very simple war memorial.

See also Directory entries for Überlingen, Friedrichshafen.

Tourist Information

Meersburg: Kurverwaltung, Kirchstr. 4, ✆ (07532) 82 382 *(Mon–Fri 9–12 and 2–5.30, Apr–Sept also Sat 10–2)*.

Lindau: The tourist office is opposite the Bahnhof, ✆ (08382) 26 000 *(Mon–Fri 8–12 and 2–6, Sat 9–12.30)*.

Where to Stay and Eating Out

This part of the Bodensee is a popular holiday spot with the Germans themselves, and in the summer, or over long weekends, you'd be advised to make advance bookings for accommodation.

Meersburg and Hagnau

In Meersburg it is best to avoid the hectic lake shore and head up to hotels and restaurants in the Altstadt. In the village of Hagnau (2½km further east) life is quieter and prices are lower.

Hotel/Weinstube Löwen, Marktplatz 2, Meersburg, ✆ (07532) 6013, fax (07541) 71 357 (rooms DM140–175, meals DM30–40). Romantic old hotel in the upper city. Tasty *gutbürgerlich* cooking in the *Weinstube*.

Pension Winzerstube, Seestr. 1, Hagnau, ✆ (07532) 6350, fax (07532) 2999 (DM100–150). Clean, modern waterside *Pension*.

Erbguth's Landhaus, Neugartenstr. 39, Hagnau, ✆ (07532) 6202 (DM100). Secluded guesthouse with friendly owners.

Rebgut Haltnau, ✆ (07532) 9732 (DM25–45). Wine-farm restaurant on the road between Meersburg and Hagnau. Locals come here looking for a good meal and a little peace. Good wines, fish dishes and solid beef and pork casseroles.

Lindau

Hotel Reutemann, Seepromenade, ✆ (08382) 5055, fax (08382) 505 5202 (from DM210). Large, efficiently run hotel set slightly back from the throngs on the promenade.

Hotel Stift, Stiftsplatz 1, ✆ (08382) 4038, fax (08382) 5586 (DM140–162). Relaxed, friendly hotel in the Altstadt.

Gästehaus Lädine, In der Grub 25, ✆ (08382) 5326 (DM80). Cheap and cheerful pension in convenient location. No restaurant.

Zum Sünfzen, Maximilianstr. 1, ✆ (08382) 5865 (DM30–45). Converted 14th-century house in the Altstadt that serves good, plain meals.

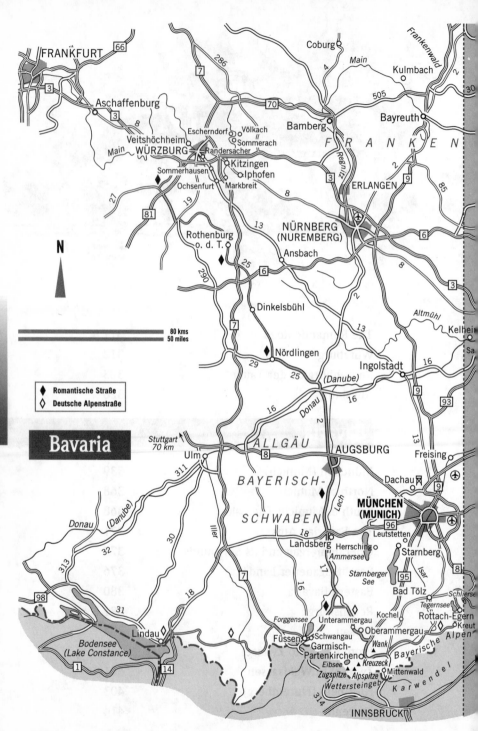

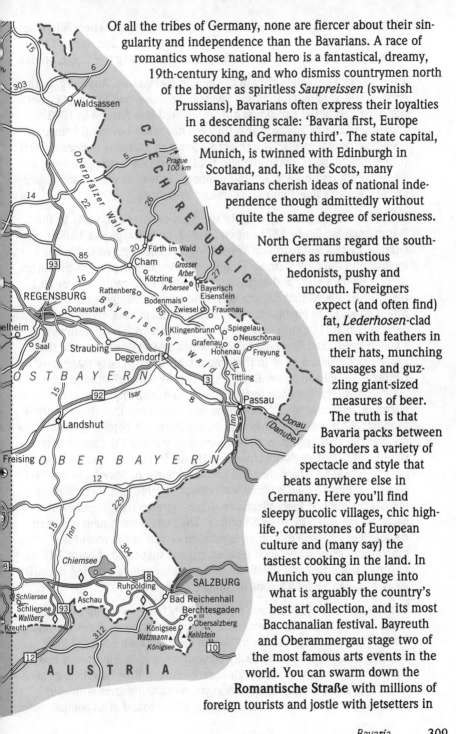

Of all the tribes of Germany, none are fiercer about their singularity and independence than the Bavarians. A race of romantics whose national hero is a fantastical, dreamy, 19th-century king, and who dismiss countrymen north of the border as spiritless *Saupreissen* (swinish Prussians), Bavarians often express their loyalties in a descending scale: 'Bavaria first, Europe second and Germany third'. The state capital, Munich, is twinned with Edinburgh in Scotland, and, like the Scots, many Bavarians cherish ideas of national independence though admittedly without quite the same degree of seriousness.

North Germans regard the southerners as rumbustious hedonists, pushy and uncouth. Foreigners expect (and often find) fat, *Lederhosen*-clad men with feathers in their hats, munching sausages and guzzling giant-sized measures of beer. The truth is that Bavaria packs between its borders a variety of spectacle and style that beats anywhere else in Germany. Here you'll find sleepy bucolic villages, chic highlife, cornerstones of European culture and (many say) the tastiest cooking in the land. In Munich you can plunge into what is arguably the country's best art collection, and its most Bacchanalian festival. Bayreuth and Oberammergau stage two of the most famous arts events in the world. You can swarm down the **Romantische Straße** with millions of foreign tourists and jostle with jetsetters in

Alpine ski resorts, or you can wander into a tiny village where life potters on in much the same way as it has done for centuries and head off into the unspoiled backwoods of the Bavarian Forest, along the Czech border.

There is just as much variety in the people themselves. Augsburg, in the west, is still very much in placid Swabian territory; and Franconia (the northern part of the *Land*) was only integrated into Bavaria in 1803. Locals here can be adamant that they are *not* really Bavarian. Franconia even has its own capital, Nuremberg—home to a famous *Weinachtsmarkt* (Christmas Market). Franconia also boasts Germany's strongest beer, a 12-per-cent-proof brew made in Kulmbach, as well as what many regard as the country's finest vineyards around Würzburg.

Bavaria was a kingdom up until 1918, ruled over for 700 years by the Wittelsbach family. In 1871, when 'mad' King Ludwig—the builder of fairytale castles and patron of Wagner—reluctantly agreed to Bavaria's inclusion in the new German Empire, the kingdom kept many privileges, such as its own army and embassies abroad. A 19th-century Prussian historian exploded that Bavaria was 'eine lebensunfähige, politische Mißbildung, recht eigentlich ein Zwerg mit einem Wasserkopf' (a political deformity that is unfit to survive, in fact a dwarf with an abnormally swollen head), and deserved to be smashed by the Prussians, and the Wittelsbachs locked away in their mountain castles. Today many north-Germans would still agree. Bavaria is fervently Roman Catholic. This means lots of holidays and festivals, but also a staunch, sometimes alarming, conservatism. It is perhaps no coincidence that Hitler centred so much of his activity on Munich, Nuremberg and Berchtesgarten. Since the war the state government has been firmly under the control of the right-wing Christian Social Union (CSU), for most of this period ruled over by would-be Chancellor and unofficial 'king' of Bavaria, Franz-Josef Strauss. When he died without a successor in 1988, numbers of party members switched their allegiance to the extreme-right Republikaner party, which is led by an ex-SS officer. The State government has been responsible for some draconian legislation—such as the recent law sanctioning mandatory blood tests on anyone suspected of being HIV positive, and arrest and indefinite detention for people carrying the AIDS virus who don't follow a code of 'proper behaviour'.

But as a visitor to Bavaria, you're more likely to be swept up by good cheer than fiery politics. Take the advice of the favourite Bavarian saying: *Mir san mir* (literally, 'we are us'—take us as we are). Soon the local greeting *Gruß Gott* will trip easily off your tongue. You may even end up peppering your conversation with unselfconscious little blasphemies such as *Gott sei Dank* (thank God), or find yourself linking arms with your neighbours in a beer garden and swaying to the sound of an oompah band.

The Romantic Road (Die Romantische Straße)

The prominence of the Romantic movement in German art, literature and music might lead you to expect that Germany's oldest tourist route is in some way associated with Wagner's powerful operas or Caspar David Friedrich's dramatic paintings, but the Romantische Straße is, in fact, 'romantic' with a small 'r'—more in the style of *Love Story* than *Wuthering Heights*; of cosy firesides and soft focus grassy meadows, rather than surging passions and dramatic scenery.

The route sets off from the university town of Würzburg and meanders through vineyards and rolling countryside, past the showy medieval gems of Rothenburg and Dinkelsbühl. Then it marches on south through the Fugger family stronghold of Augsburg. From here you follow the path of the Via Claudia Augusta—the ancient road that connected Augsburg and Rome—and end with a flourish in Füssen, in the Alpine foothills, a total of 343km altogether. Your progress is punctuated by stops in Baroque palaces, grand churches and cute *fachwerk* villages, and as you near the mountains you find Neuschwanstein and Hohenschwangau—two of Ludwig II's whimsical castles.

Not only did the Romans tread this road. So also have rampaging emperors, crusaders and pilgrims to various churches along the route. Nowadays your fellow travellers are most likely to be busloads of tourists, devoutly following the route signs and alighting at the marked sights. But even the smallest deviation from the very well-beaten track can take you to forgotten corners, ignored by the throngs pounding by.

Getting Around

This really is motoring country. The route is well signposted (in both directions) and for visiting some of the sights and doing your own exploring, a car is essential. A determined driver could cover the full 343km in a day, but there would be little point. Most of the delights of the Romantic Road are architectural, and it takes time to savour them. Simply trundling through the pretty, but uneventful countryside would be monotonous. Allow five days to a week for a reasonably unhurried tour.

It is possible, though time-consuming and tedious, to attempt the journey by a combination of rail and local buses. A far better idea, if you are relying on public transport, is to take the **Romantic Road Bus** (Eurobus Line 190 A; information and advance booking: Deutsche Touring GmbH, Am Römerhof 17, 6000 Frankfurt/Main 90; © (069) 790 3256; fax (069) 70 4714). It is a festive coach, popular with backpackers and trippers from around the world. The bus runs daily from May to October, stopping at all the main sights. Often stops are only long enough for a quick look around, but you can also stay overnight and catch the next bus through. A ticket for the full 10-hour journey costs DM85, but the company also accepts German Rail Passes.

You can of course also travel the Romantic Road from south to north (the bus runs both ways), but the route builds up in a more logical crescendo if you start in the vineyards of the north and end up in Ludwig's castles in the Alps.

Würzburg is wine, water and light. To the west the brawny Marienberg fortress swaggers above the town; to the east the Baroque Residenz rests gracefully in its gardens; through the middle flows the Main—'like a child between father and mother', remarked the writer Heinrich von Kleist in 1800. Vineyards slope right into the centre of the town. On sunny days the sharp light reflects off the Main and throws everything into vivid relief.

Around AD 500 the Franks systematically began to wipe out local tribes, and by AD 650 had established a Duchy at 'Virteburch'. A few decades later the wandering Irish bishop, Kilian, came to preach Christianity, and was killed for his troubles (thus ensuring canonization). But Kilian had done his work well: by AD 742 Würzburg was a bishopric, and in the 12th century it got its own cathedral. In 1397 King Wenzel the Lazy promised to make Würzburg a free imperial city—but he never got round to doing so. It wasn't until the late 17th century, with the arrival of the powerful Schönborn family as Prince-Bishops, that Würzburg really came into its own.

This early Würzburg—a dreamy town of Baroque palaces, *fachwerk* houses, narrow alleys and shady corners—was flattened in 20 minutes by Allied bombers on 16 March 1945. Of the 108,000 inhabitants, barely 5000 crawled out of the ruins, and Würzburg became known as the *Grab am Main* (grave on the Main). Much of the new city is modern, but the monuments have been carefully restored, and you can still find quiet old courtyards, madonnas in niches on the streets, elaborate Baroque fountains and poky, gas-lit alleys.

The best time to visit Würzburg is in the autumn, when the grapes are being harvested, and you can huddle in Weinstuben, at the end of long 'golden days', sipping freshly fermented wine. The city is popular with Germans for short break holidays. In season it becomes crowded over weekends, but is much quieter during the week and outside August and October.

Getting Around

By car: Würzburg is on the A3, 110km from Frankfurt and 130km from Nuremberg.

Car hire: Europcar, Am Hauptbahnhof, ✆ (0931) 12060; Hertz Höchberger Str. 10, ✆ (0931) 41 5221.

Mitfahrzentrale: Bahnhofsvorplatz-Ost, ✆ (0931) 12904.

By train: Würzburg is on the main ICE **rail** route from Hamburg to Munich. Connections to other cities in Germany are fast and frequent, and there's an hourly train to **Frankfurt Airport** (1hr 20 minutes away). For ticket and timetable information, ✆ 1 94 19. Once in town, all the tourist sights are within walking distance.

Public Transport: If you do find you need to use public transport, you could invest in a 24-hour pass (DM5, DM4 over weekends). The main bus station is just outside the Hauptbahnhof.

Taxi: ✆ (0931) 19 410.

Tourist information offices: Hauptbahnhof, ✆ (0931) 3 74 36 *(Mon–Sat 8am–8pm)*; Haus zum Falken, Market Square, ✆ (0931) 3 73 98 *(Mon–Fri 9–6, Sat 9–2)*.

Post office: Bahnhofsplatz 2 (open until 8pm, even on Sundays and also runs a **bureau de change**).

Emergency numbers: Police ✆ 110; doctors and dentists ✆ (0931) 1 92 22.

Würzburg holds a world-renowned **Mozart Festival** annually in June. Concerts are held in the Residenz—with the highlight being the *Kleine Nachtmusik* concert (first and last Saturdays) performed by lamplight in the gardens. There is also a **Bach Festival** towards the end of November. On the first Saturday in July Würzburg erupts with the **Kiliani**, a procession followed by a fortnight of partying to celebrate St Kilian's Day. In the last weeks of September there is a huge **wine festival** beside the Friedensbrücke, where all the local producers present their wares, but a more intimate alternative is the **Burgerspital Wine Festival**, held towards the end of June in the Burgerspital courtyard.

The Residenz

Situated to the east of the city (follow Kaiserstraße and Theaterstraße from the Hauptbahnhof) the Prince-Bishops' **Residenz** *(Apr–Sept Tues–Sun 9–5, Oct–Mar 10–4; adm DM4.50)* is its pearl , and a good place to start your visit. In 1720 the new Prince-Bishop Johann Philipp von Schönborn decided he wanted to build a palace that was altogether grander and more modern than the draughty old Marienberg fortress that had housed his predecessors. The problem of how to finance his vision was handily solved when he was obliged to confiscate the 600,000 florin fortune of a disloyal chamberlain. Johann Philipp's uncle—Elector of Mainz and Prince-Bishop of Bamberg—wrily suggested that a monument dedicated to the hapless official should be erected in front of the palace.

The Schönborns were an influential family (spawning at least a dozen bishops), infected with the *Bauwurm* (literally 'building worm'—the lust to build) and graced with good taste. Johann Philipp showed remarkable foresight in choosing as his chief architect a young bell-founder and cannon-maker who had showed some flair as an amateur draughtsman (having designed his own house and come up with a city plan for Würzburg). Balthasar Neumann went on to become one of the greatest German architects of the age, and through him the Prince-Bishop realized his dream of building a *Schloß über die Schlösse* (castle to beat all castles)—a massive, U-shaped Baroque sandstone pile that stands resplendent in its own square. After its completion, the Residenz became the talk of the civilized world. Half a century later it still impressed Napoleon, who quipped that it was 'the loveliest parsonage in Europe'.

The **Vestibule** (entrance hall—big enough for a coach-and-six to do a comfortable U-turn in) has a low ceiling with a rather half-hearted *trompe l'oeil* dome and a few licks of restrained classical decoration. Neumann's original design was even plainer—perhaps to intensify by contrast the surprises he had up his sleeve.

Guests stepped out of their carriages right onto Neumann's magnificent **staircase**. Here the low vaulting of the vestibule seems to break open to reveal the blue sky and wispy clouds of a ceiling **fresco** high above. The painting (by the celebrated Venetian artist Giovanni Battista Tiepolo) depicts allegories of the four known continents paying tribute to the Prince-Bishop. Neumann himself sits astride a cannon on the cornice below his patron, proudly surveying his work. (Neumann, and the staircase, can also be seen on a DM50 note).

At 18m by 32m, the fresco is the biggest in the world, yet it arches over the staircase without the support of a single pillar. Neumann carried off this spectacular feat of engineering by having the ceiling built out of feather-light pumice stone. Nobody believed it would work. A rival architect threatened to hang himself by the neck from the roof, confident that it would collapse under his weight before he could be strangled. An irritated Neumann suggested that the Prince-Bishop have a battery of artillery fired off in the stairwell to prove the strength of his design. Neither test was carried out, but Neumann's confidence was vindicated in 1945, when Allied bombs destroyed most of the rest of the Residenz, but not the stairway or its vaulting.

Each step is only a few centimetres high (designed to prevent shocking flashes of ladies' ankles), and they are perfectly spaced, inducing an exhilarating Hollywood glide as you sail up and down. At the top of the stairs, you come to the **Weißer Saal** (White Hall). Here the renowned stucco artist Antonio Bossi, who was already on the brink of madness, was given free reign and he let loose a feverish blaze of stucco work, before completely succumbing to his psychosis. The room is painted entirely white (now a little grey), to give full prominence to the stucco, but also to rest the eyes before the onslaught of the State Rooms.

The first of these, the oval **Kaisersaal** (Imperial Hall—the German Emperor used the Residenz whenever he was in the area) was also decorated by Tiepolo and Bossi. The frescoes, showing scenes from Franconian history, rank with Tiepolo's finest work. They bristle with life and play delightful tricks, at times even popping out into 3-D relief. The vast supporting cast of classical dieties get just the same meticulous treatment as the leading players. (One amorous couple has even been featured in *Playboy* magazine.)

To 70m right and left of the Kaisersaal stretch the Imperial Apartments. This is the part of the Residenz that suffered most from Allied bombing, but it has been lovingly rebuilt. As you walk from room to room, you get a sense of the restorers' growing confidence as they refine their skills at the old crafts. Two rooms shouldn't be missed: the sumptuous **Spiegelkabinett** (Mirror Cabinet), with its hand-painted mirrors and glittering gilded stucco, and the **Grünes Zimmer** (Green Cabinet) with exquisite Rococo lacquer work.

Back downstairs, off the eastern end of the Vestibule is the **Gartensaal** (Garden Hall). Gardens offered an escape from the strictures of formal 18th-century courtly behaviour. Beyond the palace walls you could let your hair down a little. (Courtiers often got into the spirit of things by dressing up as carefree peasants.) The Garden Hall, which opens out directly into the grounds, was a sort of buffer zone used for serving up food and as a setting for musicians. In his stucco work Bossi has hidden mirrors that flicker with a magical, mysterious light when the chandeliers are lit. The fresco (by Johann Zick) explores the contrast between stiff courtly formality and happy abandon. Smaller pictures of putti wickedly send-up the more serious treatment of a 'Banquet of the Gods' in the main painting.

There are more cheeky putti on the bastions in the garden behind the Residenz, carved by the court sculptor Peter Wagner. Things take a more disturbing turn south of the building, where rape is the theme, with two heavy statues, the 'Rape of Prosperine' and the 'Rape of Europe'. Before leaving, have a look at the Court Chapel (in the southern wing of the building), another Neumann triumph, with spiralling columns, curving balconies and graceful arches.

Around Town

The town centre, bound by gardens which follow the line of the old city wall, is nicknamed the *Bischofs Hoed* (Bishop's Mitre) by the locals, because of its shape. Würzburg is not a museumpiece, but in amongst the everyday bustle you will suddenly come across quiet pockets that belong to another age, or will turn a corner to a surprise view, past the glass and concrete to the river or mountains and vineyards beyond.

The Dom

A walk from the Residenz down Hofstraße will bring you to the **Dom**. The 12th-century church seemed to have survived the 1945 air raid relatively intact (though the heat from surrounding fires melted the bells), but one year later the roof of the nave collapsed, and the cathedral had to be substantially rebuilt. It is worth a visit mainly for the vast array of Franconian sculpture—seven centuries worth of bishops' effigies. By far the most impressive is the portrait of the 92-year-old Rudolf von Scherenberg (1499), carved with an almost discomforting realism by Germany's most eminent late-Gothic sculptor, **Tilman Riemenschneider** (1460–1531). Riemenschneider arrived in Würzburg in 1483, and as well as being a prolific sculptor twice managed to become *Bürgermeister*. He was imprisoned in 1525 for persuading the city council to join the Peasants' Revolt. Some say he was tortured, and his hands were left crippled, others say it was his spirit that was broken—but after his release he never carved anything of note again.

Look out also for the intricately carved lectern (possibly also by Riemenschneider) and a 13th-century Epiphany group where the Kings' robes are patterned with the heraldic eagle, rose and *fleur-de-lis* to represent Germany, Britain and France, then the world's leading nations.

The Neumünster

After the timeless hush of the Dom the city centre seems hectic. To the right, on Küschnerhof, you'll find the **Neumünster**, built in the 11th century to house the remains of St Kilian and his fellow missionaries, but now largely dramatic, sweeping Baroque. Beyond the northern exit of the church is the peaceful **Lusam Garden**, where you can see one remaining wing of the original 12th-century cloisters—a dainty row of carved Romanesque pillars and arches. In one corner, the minstrel Walther von der Vogelweide (d.1230), Germany's equivalent of Chaucer, lies buried. There are little shallow water-bowls on each corner of the memorial, in answer to the poet's last wish that birds should always have a reason to visit his grave. He was wildly popular in his time, and 750 years on locals still make sure that the grave is never without flowers.

The Marktplatz

West of the Neumünster you can cut through intriguing alleys of shops to the **Marktplatz**. On the northern side of the square is the pretty **Haus zum Falken**, built as a priest's house in the 14th century, but given a dextrous Rococo stucco façade when it became an inn in 1751. Next door is the Gothic **Marienkapelle**, most interesting for its exterior carvings. On the tympanum above the north portal is a rather odd Annunciation. God communicates with the Virgin through a speaking tube, down which the baby Jesus can be seen surfing earthwards. Riemenschneider's lithe, erotic Adam and Eve on the south portal caused a scandal when they were first seen, mainly because a beardless Adam was thought disrespectful. The statues you see are 19th-century copies; the originals are in the Mainfränkisches Museum (*see* below), safe from corroding fumes. Balthasar Neumann (*see* pp. 59 and 313) is buried in the church (which was only called a 'chapel' because it was built by burghers, and the stuffy bishop refused to grant it the status of a parish church).

There was a constant and hard-fought battle between townsfolk and clergy of Würzburg, where one in five of the population was a priest. The **Rathaus** on the western side of the square was bought by the burghers in 1316, and continually enlarged to cock a snoot at the bishops—but it remains very much in the shadow of Würzburg's ecclesiastical buildings. Inside is the fine Romanesque **Wenzel Hall**, where in 1397 the burghers set out to to wine, dine and woo King Wenzel into granting the city free imperial status—a brave but fruitless attempt to snatch power from the bishop. (The hall is visitable during office hours, when not in use.)

Along Juliuspromenade

Halfway along Theaterstraße, east of the Marktplatz, you come to the **Bürgerspital**—almshouses, founded in the 14th century, that derive their income from large, excellent vineyards. A narrow arch leads you to the quiet courtyard, where sturdily shod grannies sit happily on benches along the walls. A possible explanation for their contented smiles is that the Bürgerspital administration traditionally grants residents a glass of wine a day, and a bottle over weekends.

Around the corner on the Juliuspromenade is another worthy institution, the **Juliusspital**, founded by the prince-bishop in 1576 and now used as a hospital. Pop in for a look at the Baroque **Fürstenbau** (erstwhile residence of the prince-bishop) and wander through to the peaceful gardens at the back. At harvest time this little park buzzes with activity as grapes are carted in to the Juliusspital's winery.

Further down the Juliuspromenade you come to the River Main, and a twin-armed 18th-century **crane** built by one of Balthasar Neumann's sons. From here it is a pleasant walk south along the river to the **Alte Mainbrücke**, a beautiful old bridge dating largely from the 17th century, and decorated with 12 enormous statues of saints.

Festung Marienberg

Across the bridge, on the hill, is **Festung Marienberg**, a hotch-potch of fortifications, some dating back to the 13th century, that formed the Prince-Bishops' palace prior to the building of the Residenz. The buildings are all carefully restored, but devastation by the Swedes during the Thirty Years' War, the Prussians in the 19th century, and Allied bombs during the Second World War have left little of the original interiors intact. You can, however, visit the dinky 8th-century **Marienkirche** (one of Germany's oldest) and an impressive 105m-deep **well**, chipped out through solid rock in 1200 to ensure a water supply when the fortress was under siege. The **Zeughaus** (arsenal) now houses the **Mainfränkisches Museum** *(Apr–Oct Tues–Sun 10–5, Nov–Mar closes 4; adm DM3)* which has a superb collection of Riemenschneider sculpture and a wine museum.

On top of the next hill is the **Käppele**, a compact pilgrimage church (the devout climb the hill on their knees) built by Neumann in the 1740s. However you've managed your passage to the top, you'll find the view back across town exhilarating.

Würzburg ✆ (0931–)   ***Where to Stay***

Hotels in Würzburg are not particularly cheap. In the summer and early autumn booking at least a fortnight ahead is advisable.

moderate

Hotel Würzburger Hof, Barbarossaplatz 2, ✆ 5 38 14, fax 5 83 24 (DM160–230). Has been run by the same family for nearly a century and is getting gradually grander all the time. It is centrally situated, and double-glazed against traffic noise.

Hotel Zur Stadt Mainz, Semmelstr. 39, ✆ 5 31 55, fax 5 85 10 (DM180–200). An old inn, recently renovated and fitted out with comfortable old furniture. All rooms have TV and double glazing.

Hotel Alter Kranen, Kärrnergasse 11, ✆ 5 00 39, fax 5 00 10 (DM130). The best bargain in town. It is a central, cosy hotel, with friendly management. Front rooms overlook the Main with views up to the Marienberg and the vineyards.

Hotel Am Klein-Nizza Park, Friedrich-Ebert-Ring 20, ✆ 7 28 93 (from DM90 without private bath). A simple hotel which overlooks a park behind the Residenz. About the cheapest conveniently situated hotel.

Youth Hostel: Burkarder Str. 44, ✆ 4 25 90.

Eating and Drinking

Local wines are renowned as among the best in Germany (*see* below). If you come to Würzburg at harvest time, try a glass of *Federweißer* (known locally also as *Bremser*)—a cloudy, fermenting grape-must that tastes like fruit juice, looks like scrumpy cider, and has you under the table within minutes. A slow glass with a slice of home-made *Zwiebelkuchen* (a sort of onion quiche), is a fine way to end an autumn day.

Moszuppe, a rich wine and cream soup, makes a tasty starter. Committed gourmands can follow this up with one of the heartier Franconian dishes, such as *Schmeckerli* (stomach of veal). Alternatively, you could nibble on a *Blooz* (a plate-sized salty cracker) or a couple of *Blaue Zipfel* (sausages poached in spicy vinegar). These go an odd blue colour when cooked, but taste delicious. Würzburgers love fish and cook it well. Carp comes baked or served up 'Sud' (poached in heavily-spiced wine and vinegar). *Meefischli* is whitebait from the Main. Locals say the fish should never be longer than the little finger of St Kilian's statue on the bridge, and that they should swim three times—in water, fat and wine.

Restaurants and Taverns

expensive

Haus des Frankenweins, Mainpromenade, next to the old crane, ✆ 1 20 93 (DM100). As well as being a vortex for oenophiles, the restaurant lures gourmets to its fresh carp, exotic roulades and upmarket versions of an old Franconian *Brotzeit*.

moderate

Bürgerspital, Theaterstr. 19, ✆ 13861 (DM20–45). Cellar restaurant of famous local wine producer which offers the complete range of in-house wines (the dry Kerner is particularly good) and tasty Franconian dishes.

Juliusspital-Weinstuben, Juliuspromenade 19, ✆ 54 080 (DM20–40). Atmospheric, though cavernous. Their wines are world-renowned and they serve a good harvest-time *Federweißer*. The Franconian cooking is good too.

Fischbäuerin, Katzengasse 7, ✆ 42487 (DM25–55). The best place to try *Meefischli* and other seasonal fish dishes.

Hotel zur Stadt Mainz Restaurant, Semmelstr. 39, ✆ 5 31 55 (DM25–55). Run by the sort of cook who can turn the simplest ingredients—like oxtail and brown sauce—into a heavenly experience, but on some nights it seems that every visitor to Würzburg has heard about her.

Weinhaus Schnabel, through a plain door at Haugerpfarrgasse 10, ℂ 53 314 (DM15–25). A good no-nonsense establishment with stolid waitresses, bright lights and inexpensive servings of many Franconian specialities.

Bars and Cafés

Locals call their cafés *Bäcken*. In the summer there is a jovial temporary beergarden on the east bank of the Main, in front of the Haus des Frankenweins. Sitting on the wall with your legs dangling over the water, looking up across the old bridge to the Marienberg, you can sip your drink in one of the best spots Würzburg has to offer.

Zum Stachel, Gressengasse 1. Was the headquarters for local farmers during the Peasants' Revolt, and gets its name ('the Spike') from a mace hanging outside the door. The tiny courtyard is a jigsaw of balconies, loggias and stairways, draped with creepers—rather like a tightly designed set for a Shakespeare play.

Sternbäck, Domstraße. A welcoming bar squeezed into an old house, though in the summer people sit outside under the trees.

Brückebäck, Alte Marienbrücke. Across the Alte Mainbrücke from the centre. A trendy bar where students and the youthful smart set line up against the plate glass windows, and look out across the river.

See also Directory entry for Aschaffenburg.

Franconian Wine

'Dagegen sende mir noch einige Würzburger; denn kein anderer Wein will mir schmecken und ich bin verdrüßlich wenn mir mein gewohnter Lieblingstrank abgeht.' (Send me some more Würzburger, for no other wine is so much to my taste, and I get grumpy without my favourite drink).

Goethe in a letter to Christiane Vulpius; 1806

Goethe put his money where his mouth was: he ordered 900 litres of Franconian wine (Frankenwein) in 1821 alone. The superb wines from the vineyards around Würzburg are one of Germany's best kept secrets. Most of the vines are tucked away between stretches of forest and pasture (wherever they can best escape the crippling frosts), so you hardly notice that they are there. Yields are small, which means that when the wines do make it past the voracious locals to the outside world, they are expensive, and hence often ignored. Yet it was a Franconian wine that was chosen to represent Germany's viticulture at Queen Elizabeth II's coronation banquet, and for the Pope to tipple when he visited Germany in the 1980s.

The wines come in dumpy, flat, round-shouldered flasks known as *Bocksbeutel*. These were supposedly invented by grape-growing monks who wanted to smuggle wine out into the fields—and so were around long before Mateus Rosé was even a gleam in a publicist's eye. Almost exclusively white, the wines are mostly dry, pithy, flavoursome—often similar to Burgundies—and heartily alcoholic. At one time most Franconian wines were made from the Silvaner grape—a bit of a non-starter in other regions, but here producing rich, honeyed wines. Sadly, Silvaner has been supplanted by the ubiquitous Müller-Thurgau, the wine-drinkers' equivalent of easy listening. Yet even this usually wimpish grape manages to pack a few beefier punches in Franconian wines.

Heavy frosts and short summers mean that growers have something of a struggle getting Riesling grapes to ripen, but when they do (in hot years like 1976) the results are extraordinary.

In Würzburg, Riesling and Silvaner grapes bake away on the heat-retaining limestone slopes below the Marienberg fortress and in the famous Stein vineyard south of the city. These supply three of Germany's greatest wine producers: the **Bürgerspital**, Theaterstraße/Semmelstraße *(cellars open Mon–Thurs 7.30–12 and 1–4.45, Fri 7.30–12; shop open Mon–Fri 9–6 and Sat 9–12)*; the **Juliusspital** *(bulk purchases from Klinilkstr. 5, open Mon–Thurs 8–12 and 12.30–4.15, Fri 8–12; smaller quantities from Koellikerstr. 1–2, Mon–Fri 9–6, Sat 9–1)*; and the **Hofkeller**, Residenzplatz *(Mon–Fri 8.30–5.30, Sat 8.30–12)*. Each offers wine-tastings, but if you'd prefer a more general introduction to local wines visit the **Haus des Frankenweins** on the Main next to the old crane *(open Mon–Fri 10–6 and Sat 10–1)*, which offers a wide selection from all over the region and can give helpful guidance and advice. You should certainly sample some Rieslings and Silvaners from the Stein vineyards, but some of the newer wine varieties can be just as exciting. Kerner, in particular (a blend of red Trollinger and Riesling) can produce a strong, fruity, dry white wine.

A Wine Tour around Würzburg

A drive out of town south along the B13 will take you to **Randersacker**, where the Pfülben vineyards produce good Rieslings. There's a growers' co-operative at Maingasse 33 *(open Mon–Fri 8–12 and 2–6, Sat 8–12)*, and a good private estate is Weingut Gebrüder König, Herrngasse 29, *(open daily 8–6)*. The village of **Sommerhausen**, a few kilometres on, is an enchanting cluster of grey stone houses, with vines and geraniums bursting out of cracks in the walls. There's a 16th-century Rathaus with pinnacled gables, and a Renaissance castle in the high street. In autumn the whole village bustles with the urgencies of harvest, and you catch fragrant whiffs of ripe pears, and the musty odour of crushed grapes. A colony of artists works here, and sometimes contributes to the small **Christmas Market** during Advent—the best (and most kitsch-free) in the area. There is also a minuscule theatre above the old tower gate, that attracts audiences from as far away as Würzburg. **Weingut Konrad Schwarz**, Schleifweg 13 (✆ (09333) 221 for appointment) uses grapes from the excellent Ölspiel vineyards to make velvety Spätburgunder reds.

If you turn eastwards, past the villages of Ochsenfurt and Marktbreit (both with typically Franconian red-and-grey half-timbered houses), you come to **Kitzingen**. Here, walk past the Rathaus and into a yard behind the Landratsamt and you'll come to the cellars of the **Alte Kitzinger Klosterkeller**, part of an 8th-century Benedictine nunnery. Hadeloga—the stalwart sister of the Frankish King Pippin the Short—got over the shock of seeing her paramour dancing in the local market with another woman by founding (rather than running off to) a nunnery. As Mother Superior she set her noble nuns to work in the fields, and soon they were producing excellent wines. Today you can visit their cellars (the oldest in Germany) and sit among the huge old vats sampling wines. Here you could try one of the more recent grape varieties—such as the fruity, rather flowery Bacchus. Tastings are conducted under the deft guidance of erstwhile German Wine Queen, Karin Rickel, © (09321) 700589 *(shop open Wed, Thurs and Fri 9–12 and 1–6, Sat 10–1)*. Kitzingen also has the official German Carnival museum, the **Deutsches Fastnachtsmuseum**, at Im Falterturm *(Apr–Nov Sat and Sun 2–5; adm DM2)*, with costumes, masks and other bits and bobs from the pre-Lenten revels.

From Kitzingen, you can follow the B8 south to **Iphofen**, where the fertile red marly soils produce delicious, mouth-filling wines. Here even Müller-Thurgau grapes manage a heady aromatic bouquet, and it is a good place to try some of the newer hybrids (such as Scheurebe or Perle).

The town itself seems dreamily lost in time. Much of the old town wall is intact. The quaint 13th-century *fachwerk* **Rödelseer Tor**, with its jumble of different roofs, seems to prop itself up by leaning in all directions at once. A sumptuous Baroque Rathaus comes as a surprise after narrow streets of half-timbered houses, and in the late-Gothic St Veit's church, you can see some fine Riemenschneider carving. Rieslings from the Julius-Echterberg and Kronsberg vineyards are superb. (These were the wines chosen for Queen Elizabeth and the Pope.) **Weinbau Hans Dorsch**, Rödelseer 8, © (09323) 13 75 *(Mon–Sat 8–6, Sun 9–12)* makes good wines from these vines, and also from the superior Kalb slopes.

North of Iphofen, off the B286, you come to **Volkach** a busy little wine town propelled by its ebullient Ratsherr (Councillor) and 'Wine Ambassador', Waldemar Sperling. When he isn't dolled up in medieval garb for a wine tasting or festival, he runs the tourist office, or whizzes around town making sure that everyone is organized and contented. There's a 16th-century Rathaus and some romantically crumbly bits of old city wall. Down a side-street off the Marktplatz is the **Schelfenhaus**, a Baroque residence (now converted for public functions) where you can see some fine stucco work by a Bamberg artist named Vogel (= bird), who used to sculpt a bird somewhere into his work as a trademark. On a hill above the town, in the little church of Maria im Weingarten, is one of Riemenschneider's most exquisite works, the *Madonna im Rosenkranz* (Madonna in a wreath of Roses; 1524). It shot to international fame when it was 'art-napped' and held for a ransom in 1962. The poor parish couldn't come up with the money, so the editor of *Stern* offered DM100,000 for its return. The original was easily picked out from the numbers of fakes that sprouted up in response to the reward, because (unbeknown to most) it had a hollow back.

At **Weinbau Max Müller I**, Hauptstr. 46, © (09381) 12 18 *(open Sat and Sun)*, you can taste some Rieslaner wines—a new hybrid fast becoming a local speciality. Near Volkach, at the top of the **Vogelsburg**, you can admire the fine view while sipping spicy Traminer wines made by local Augustinian nuns. The village of **Escherndorf**, back down the hill, is famed for a vineyard called Lump, which produces some of the region's best wines.

Tourist Information

Randersacker: Markt Randersacker, Maingasse 9, ✆ (0931) 70 82 82.

Sommerhausen: Rathaus, ✆ (09333) 216.

Kitzingen: Schrannenstr. 1, ✆ (09321) 2 02 05.

Iphofen: Marktplatz 27, ✆ (09323) 30 95.

Volkach: Rathaus, ✆ (09381) 4 01 12.

Festivals

Winegrowing towns have the best festivals of all—less raucous than beer festivals, but with more style and an infectious conviviality. The townsfolk will often elect a Wine Queen (as much for her knowledge of wine as good looks and personality) and there is much eating, dancing and drinking of local wines. As well as the Würzburg wine events (*see* above), there are well over 100 smaller village festivals held between May and November. Rather like traditional British fêtes, many of these are organized by local associations such as Voluntary Fire Brigades or sports clubs. Look out for wayside signs advertising a **Weinfest** in the early summer and autumn, especially in the villages around Volkach.

Where to Stay

It is possible to base yourself in Würzburg and visit the wine villages on a day trip. The most idyllic of the villages for a longer stay is **Sommerhausen**. The **Pension am Schloß**, Hauptstraße, ✆ (09333) 13 04 (DM110) is right at the heart of things. All rooms have television, and guests can hire bicycles for jaunts into the vineyards. Private rooms in Sommerhausen cost around DM30 per person. (Try Frau Brand, Zwischenweg 7, ✆ (09333) 14 58—or enquire through the tourist office.)

In **Iphofen** you'll find the charming **Gästehaus Fröhlich**, Geräthengasse 13, ✆ (09323) 3030 (DM70–90), run by German-Canadian Ruth Perry. All the rooms are warmly and individually decorated with old furniture, and there is a café downstairs that serves delicious homemade cakes.

For something grander, head for **Volkach** and the **Hotel Vier Jahrezeiten**, Hauptstr. 31, ✆ (09381) 37 77, fax (09381) 47 73 (from DM120), built in 1605 as a residence for the Prince-Bishop. The rooms are sumptuously decked out with antiques and cabinets of Bohemian glass. **Zur Schwane**, across the road at Hauptstr. 12, ✆ (09381) 515 (DM110–170), is a family-run hotel with its own vineyard and schnapps distillery, and a breakfast buffet that even locals try to get in on.

expensive

Restaurant von Dungern, Hauptstr. 12, **Sommerach**, ✆ (09333) 1406 (around DM70). People travel out from Würzburg to sample Franconian cuisine, here elevated to gourmet heights with local mushrooms, wines, guinea fowl and rabbits all helping in the ascent.

Hotel Zur Schwane Restaurant, Volkach (*see* above) (around DM100). Deserves its place in the list of the top 444 restaurants in Germany, with adventurous concoctions such as venison in a red cabbage and walnut sauce.

moderate

Gasthof Goldener Stern, Maxstr. 22, Iphofen, ✆ (09323) 3315 (DM25–45). Looks fairly ordinary from outside, but serves scrumptious food. The owner, Rainer Steinruck, forages around local markets and comes up with simple, but inspired dishes-of-the-day (such as turkey fillets with wild mushrooms in a wine and cream sauce) to supplement his usual menu. Iphofen is renowned for its asparagus, and in season this gets onto the menu in a variety of guises.

Weinstube Torbäct, Hauptstraße, Volkach (DM20–45). A good place for a hearty board of sausages, breads and cheeses (or homemade *Zwiebelkuchen*) to knock back with your harvest-time *Federweißer.*

Scloß Hallburg, between Volkach and Sommerach, ✆ (09381) 2340. Converted Schloß, most popular on Sunday mornings when you can have a delicious brunch (with some Franconian wine or *Sekt*) to the accompaniment of a live jazz band, and then wander around the romantic gardens. Lunch menus include such treats as local trout with brown sauce.

Rothenburg ob der Tauber

Sixty kilometres south of Würzburg, along the route of the Romantic Road, lies Rothenburg ob der Tauber. A prosperous town until the 17th century, Rothenburg never really recovered from an exhausting sequence of occupations during the Thirty Years' War. No new building took place for centuries. Although it was badly bombed in the Second World War, Rothenburg was painstakingly rebuilt, and today survives almost perfectly intact as a medieval museum piece. It takes half an hour to skirt the town on the **sentry walk** atop the old city wall. Steep roofs crush right up against the ramparts, and you get a splendid view of the *fachwerk* alleys, pointy gables, turrets, spires and decorated façades that draw coachloads of tourists all year. It is all very pretty: 'gingerbread architecture', sniff some people contemptuously—and, like gingerbread, a little of Rothenburg goes a long way.

See also Directory entries for Dinkesbühl and Nördlingen.

The **tourist office** on the Marktplatz, ✆ (09861) 4 04 92 *(Mon–Fri 9–12 and 2–6, Sat 9–12)* can give you a small map marked with suggested walks, as well as plentiful information on the town.

On Whit Monday locals in the appropriate garb act out *Burgermeister* Nusch's drinking feat, though no one really attempts to match it (*see* below); and one Sunday each month in the spring and summer you can see the jolly *Schäfertanz* (Shepherd's Dance) in front of the Rathaus (the dance supposedly began as a celebration of Rothenburg's deliverance from the Plague). Vast crowds turn out to watch both events. The Advent *Christmas Market* has a long-established reputation as one of the best in Germany.

The best time to see the town is very early in the morning, before the hordes hit the streets. As the mist drains out of the alleys down to the River Tauber in the valley far below, you might quite expect to see someone in tights and a floppy hat trundle past in a heavy wooden cart. Even when the streets (and side-streets) fill up with tourists, Rothenburg doesn't entirely lose its medieval atmosphere. In the **market square** farmers rub shoulders with trinket-sellers. In the autumn there are stalls selling *Federweißer* wine direct from the barrel, and during Advent a *Christmas Market* clusters around the side of the Rathaus, up against St Jakobskirche.

In the gable of the **Ratsherrntrinkstube** overlooking the square, little figures in the windows near the clocks act out Rothenburg's most historic moment *(on the hour from 11am to 3pm and also at 9pm and 10pm)*. In 1631, during the Thirty Years' War, the formidable General Tilly captured the town, but agreed to spare it if one of the councillors could down the contents of a *Meistertrunk* (a 3-litre tankard of wine) in one go. Georg Nusch, a former *Bürgermeister*, took up the challenge. He saved Rothenburg in ten minutes, but needed three days to sleep off the effects.

On the western side of the square is the **Rathaus**. The front part of the building is Renaissance, but behind that an earlier Gothic hall pokes up a slender, 61m-high tower. Inside you can see the bare Imperial Hall *(daily 8–6; adm free)*, and descend to the gloomy dungeons. Just behind the Rathaus is Rothenburg's famous **Christkindlmarkt**, a shop which sells all the traditional trappings of a German Christmas the whole year round.

Impressive old mansions line the **Herrngasse**, (which extends westwards past the Rathaus), though the city's grandest home is the **Baumeisterhaus** in Schmied-gasse. Statues of the Seven Virtues grace the first floor, while the Seven Deadly Sins frolic on the floor above. (Nowadays the Baumeisterhaus is a restaurant—*see* below). North of the market looms the Gothic **St Jakobskirche**, where you can see the superb *Heiligblut-Altar* (1504), carved in limewood by Tilman Riemenschneider.

If miserable weather makes wandering the streets uncomfortable, then you could head for one of the small museums. The best are an originally furnished **Handwerkhaus** (Craftsman's House) at Alter Stadtgraben 26 *(Easter–Oct daily 9–6 and 8pm–9pm; adm DM3)* and the **Kriminalmuseum** at Burggasse 3 *(Apr–Oct 9.30–6, Nov–Feb 2–4; adm DM3.50)* with its collection of medieval punishment and torture instruments. The **Puppen und Spielzeugmuseum** (Doll and Toy Museum), Hofbronngasse 13 *(daily 9.30–6, Jan and Feb 11–5; adm DM3.50)* has a vast selection of dolls from all over the world, and some exquisite doll's houses; and the **Reichstadtmuseum**, Klosterhof *(Apr–Oct daily 10–5, Nov–Mar 1–4; adm DM2.50)*, housed in a former Dominican convent, preserves many of the old fittings and equipment, as well as relics, of Rothenburg's 13th-century Jewish community.

Rothenburg ob der Tauber ✆ (09861–)   **Where to Stay**

Most of the visitors that pour into Rothenburg are day-trippers. An overnight stay is not as expensive as you might expect in such a tourist trap, and it does mean that you can see the town at its quietest.

moderate

Hotel Reichs-Küchenmeister, Kirchplatz 8, ✆ 20 46, fax 8 69 65 (DM120–180). Attractive modern conversion of a 16th-century patrician house, with its own sauna, steamroom and jacuzzi.

Hotel Roter Hahn, Obere Schmiedgasse 21, ✆ 50 88, fax 51 40 (DM125–180 DM). A cosy, family-run hotel in a 14th-century building that was once an inn run by relatives of the *Meistertrunk*-downing *Bürgermeister*.

inexpensive

Hotel Hornburg, Hornburgweg 28, ✆ 84 80 (DM90). A capacious old Franconian villa—some of the rooms are enormous. Just outside the town wall. The staff are friendly, and happy to lend books and bicycles to guests. No restaurant.

Private rooms in the Altstadt work out at around DM50 for a double. Try Herr Hess (Spitalgasse 18, ✆ 61 30), or Herr Schneider (Alte Stadtgraben 11, ✆ 32 11)—or enquire at the tourist office. In the elegant little town of Dinkesbühl, a few kilometres further south, you will find accommodation a bit cheaper and just as romantic.

Eating and Drinking

Baumeisterhaus, Obere Schmidgasse 3, ✆ 34 04 (DM30–65). One of the most atmospheric places to eat in Rothenburg—albeit popular with tourists. You can sit in heavy-beamed dining rooms, or the medieval courtyard draped with creepers. There is a café where you can munch on *Apfelgebäck*, and a restaurant serving fine Franconian food (try carp dipped in egg and breadcrumbs, then fried until it shines).

Rothenburger Bierstube, Klingengasse 38 (DM25–35). More off the beaten track, nestling up against the city wall in a quieter part of town. Good beer and *gut-bürgerliche* cooking.

Glöcke, Am Plönlein 1 (DM25–35). Popular with locals for tasty, simple cuisine.

Augsburg

Augsburg has been hoarding treasure for over 2000 years. Its Romanesque cathedral is out-shone by the Gothic St Ulrich's, and both are eclipsed by the Renaissance Rathaus. Garlands of Baroque gables hang between Rococo palaces. The streets are so wide, that some look more like squares. A 17th-century Italian visitor enthused that the roads were wide enough to fit 10 waggons abreast.

The host of luminaries connected with the city includes the Roman Emperor Augustus (after whom it was named), Hans Holbein the Elder and Younger, Martin Luther, Mozart (whose father was born here, and who often returned to give recitals) and the 20th-century engineers Rudolf Diesel and Willi Messerschmidt. Augsburg doesn't commemorate Messerschmidt because of his Nazi sympathies; and for a long time they also ignored another famous son, the left-wing playwright Berthold Brecht, who dismissed his home-town as a bourgeois *Scheiss-stadt*.

Augsburg was founded by Tiberius (step-son of the Emperor Augustus) in 15 BC, and soon became a prosperous trading city on the Via Claudia Augusta, the road to Rome. By the 13th century it was a Free Imperial City, and reached its zenith in the 15th century with the rise to power of two local merchant families, the Fuggers and the Welsers. Despite being constantly locked in battles of one-upmanship with each other, they amassed fabu-lous amounts of money, and wielded the most extraordinary international influence. Between them they came to own entire countries in South America, propped up the finan-cially ailing royal houses of Europe and made Augsburg the financial centre of the world. Their wealth put the Medicis' fortunes in the shade.

Yet as well as this grand heritage, Augsburg also has the world's first social housing com-plex (built by the Fuggers in 1514), charming alleys and crumbly stone houses. It is a university town with a warm café life that takes the hard gloss off its stately façade.

Getting Around

By car: Augsburg is on the A8, 60km northwest of Munich and 160km southeast of Stuttgart.

Car hire: Avis, Klinkerberg 31, © (0821) 3 82 41.

By train: Augsburg is a busy rail junction. Over 90 trains a day can take you to and from all parts of Germany (Munich, ½hr ICE; Würzburg, 2hr ICE; Frankfurt, 3 hr). The **Hauptbahnhof** lands you west of the centre amidst unpromising modern buildings, but it is only a 15-minute walk to the Altstadt, past the tourist office and local bus station.

Public transport: A day ticket for the trams and buses costs DM5, though you are unlikely to need it unless you are staying in the suburbs.

Taxis: ✆ (0821) 35 025.

Tourist Information

The main **tourist information office** is near the Railway Station, Bahnhofstr. 7, ✆ (0821) 50 20 70 *(Mon–Fri 9–6, Sat 9–1)*. Its staff can supply you with maps and information, offer city tours and guided city walks in English and can book your accommodation. There is a smaller information office on Rathausplatz *(open Mon–Wed 7.30–4, Thurs 7.30–5.30 and Fri 7.30–12)*.

Post office: Viktoriastr. 3 (near the main station).

Medical emergencies: ✆ 1 92 22.

Police: ✆ 110.

Festivals

There are two big **folk festivals**—one at Easter, and the other at the beginning of September. Both have accompanying street markets in the Jakobviertel. The **Christkindlmarkt** during Advent is one of the best Christmas markets in Germany (after Nuremberg and Munich), and is especially renowned for the quality of its live music, and for its 'alternative' Christmas stalls selling environmentally sound and politically correct products.

The Rathausplatz

The city's elegant **Rathaus** is a good place to start your tour. Augsburg's 17th-century Master Builder, Elias Holl (1573–1646), was one of the most important architects of the German Renaissance. In 1614 Holl returned from a trip to Italy brimming with new ideas. His rhetoric was as skilful as his draughtsmanship. Within weeks he had persuaded the city council to rip down the old Gothic Rathaus, and commission him to build a more majestic expression of their might. Holl's monumental building, with its simple, clean proportions and twin onion-domed towers is a gem of civic architecture. Inside you'll find the magnificent **Goldener Saal** *(free access during office hours)*. Burnt out during an air raid in 1944, it was finally restored (to a somewhat over-pristine state) only in the 1980s. Every crinkle, twirl or protruding finial of the carved wooden ceiling has been lavishly gilded. Set among all this nutwood, limewood and gold, 14 metres above your head, are panels of richly coloured paintings depicting personal and civic virtues. Thankfully, grisaille wall frescoes and a gentle pastel-coloured marble floor help subdue the riot.

Next door to the Rathaus is the 70m-high **Perlachturm**. The foundations date from the 11th century, but most of the rest was built 200 years later to serve as a watchtower. Then in 1615 Elias Holl rounded it off with a dome to complement those on his Rathaus, and to house the bells from the old city hall. The word 'Perlach' comes from the Old German for 'bear dancing', and was probably the name of a Roman amphitheatre on the site. Today the bruins could jig to merry Mozart tunes played *(at 11am, 12 noon, 5pm and 6pm)* on a carillon installed in 1985 to celebrate Augsburg's 2000th anniversary.

In the middle of Rathausplatz stands the ornate **Augustusbrunnen**, a fountain built in 1594 to honour Augustus Caesar, the city's founder. In the summer, this vast square is packed with tables, benches and umbrellas, and becomes one enormous *Bierstube*, while on the far side of the square, in hushed, carpeted cafés, spruce pensioners keep each other company over *Kaffee und Kuchen*.

The Dom

A short walk northwards up Hoheweg, brings you to the **Dom** (begun 1060)—a hotchpotch of different architectural styles. Shadows of the original Romanesque arches can be seen above later Gothic windows; the twin spires date back to the 11th century; the high altar was installed in 1962; and there is a bright and sugary Rococo chapel (a favourite for weddings) off the north aisle. The cathedral's art treasures should not be missed. The series of **Prophet Windows** (1140) is the oldest cycle of stained glass in the world. Five prophets are depicted in bold colours and simple designs. All (except David, who is crowned) wear the peculiar pointed hats that medieval Jews were required to wear. There is an outstanding **bronze portal**—most of it dating back to the 12th century—and an eloquent cycle of paintings by **Holbein the Elder**, showing scenes from the life of the Virgin. In the crypt you can pay your respects to past Bishops of Augsburg, who were being buried on this spot a century before work on the Dom was even begun. In the courtyard outside the Dom, are the ruins of the foundations of the ancient church of St John the Baptist (*c.* 960), which include a full-immersion font that was probably part of a secret Christian baptistry in the cellars of a 6th-century Roman house.

Just beyond the Dom, you'll find the **Mozart-Gedenkstätte** (Mozart House) at Frauentorstr 30 *(Mon, Wed and Thurs 10–12 and 2–5, Fri and Sun 10–12; adm free)* which mainly documents the life of Mozart Senior, who was born in Augsburg but soon upped sticks for Salzburg and Vienna. Young Wolfgang frequently gave concerts in his father's home town, his recitals on one occasion coinciding with a heady 15-day romance with his cousin Bäsle.

Luther and the Fuggers

A wander back down Annastraße brings you to **St Anna's**, built as a Carmelite monastery in 1321. You would be forgiven for thinking that this church was the wrong way around, for a memorial chapel built in 1509 by Jakob Fugger and his brothers fills the *whole* of the west chancel and completely upstages the rest of the simple basilica. This **Fuggerkapelle**, with superb marble carving by Hans Daucher, became the touchstone for Renaissance design in Germany.

In the east cloister, a flight of simple wooden stairs (the **Lutherstiege**) leads up to a set of rooms housing an exhibition on the life of Luther. Unfortunately, most of the exhibits are textual, and commentary is in German only.

In 1518 Luther was summoned to a court of the inqustion in Rome. His patron, Johann Friedrich of Saxony, fearing for the priest's life, persuaded the Pope to hold the hearing in Augsburg. The pretext was that an ailing Luther couldn't make the journey to Rome (though he did manage to walk the full 500km from Wittenberg to Augsburg, where he stayed at St Anna's). He was interrogated by Cardinal Cajetan at the home of Jakob Fugger between 12 and 14 October, but they couldn't reach an agreement. On 20 October, under threat of arrest, Luther slipped out of town.

At the next Diet, in 1530, the Augsburg Confession laid out the basic tenets of the Lutheran faith, but it wasn't until 1555, with the signing of the Peace of Augsburg that the struggle between the two churches in the Holy Roman Empire was resolved (see p. 42). Later, St Anna's became a Lutheran church. Jakob Fugger, a fervent Roman Catholic who imported bands of Jesuits to try and tip the balance in Augsburg, must be turning in his monumental grave.

From here make your way across to Maximilianstraße, which leads south from Rathausplatz. Until 1957 Maximilianstraße was named after King Maximilian I Joseph of Bavaria. Then it was decided to rename the street after Emperor Maximilian I (1459–1519), a great lover of Augsburg. This odd gesture in effect changed nothing at all. Two very stylish 16th-century fountains grace the street—the first topped with a statue of Mercury, the second with a robust Hercules. They were designed by Dutch sculptor Adrian de Vries to symbolize Augsburg's merchants and master craftsmen respectively.

Just before the Hercules fountain, at Maximilianstr. 36–38, is the conglomeration of three houses that formed the 16th-century **Fuggerpalast**. The building is still home to Fugger descendants, but you can nip around the back for a look at the **Damenhof**, a pretty little Italianate courtyard with arcades of Etruscan pillars, a musicians' balcony and traces of the original frescoes.

The Fugger family fortune was largely established by Jakob Fugger the Rich (1459–1525). The youngest son of a *nouveau-riche* merchant family, he wanted to become a priest but at the age of 19, following the deaths of his father and older brothers, he was hauled back out of the monastery to run the family firm. He went off to Venice for business training, and was so fired by the Italian way of life that on his return he almost single-handedly introduced the Renaissance to Germany. (The buildings he commissioned became models for the movement throughout the country.) He also brought with him double-entry bookkeeping, took risks in buying up some flooded mines and ended up with monopolies over Hungarian copper, Austrian silver and Spanish quicksilver. Soon he had amassed a fortune that historians estimate was the equivalent of the combined assets of today's top ten multinational companies. The rulers of Europe came to him to borrow money to pay their armies, and for the bribes needed to put a new emperor on the throne. (The election of Emperor Charles V in 1519 was financially secured through 543,585 florins from the Fuggers and 143,333 florins from their arch-rivals the Welsers.) In return Jakob Fugger extracted concessions and favours that increased his wealth and power even more.

In his late forties he married a woman half his age. For 20 years he showered her with gifts and they entertained lavishly—but had no children. Jakob died in 1525, leaving his fortune to his nephew Anton. His wife re-married three weeks later—to some scandal, but very little surprise.

Anton ran the firm well, but lost his nerve a little over the dangerous trade with the Americas and the West Indies. (Charles V had given the Welsers control over Venezuela, the Fuggers were offered Chile and Peru, but declined as Anton felt that pirates and conquistadors made the venture too risky.) The family fortune gradually crumbled. Today's Fuggers own a bank and some property, but are not nearly as well off as their predecessors.

Further down Maximilianstraße (just opposite the Hercules Fountain) is the **Schaezler Palais** *(Tues–Sun 10 am–5 pm, Oct–Apr to 4 pm; adm free)*, built in 1770 for a wealthy silversmith. Inside is a compact Rococo ballroom, almost in its original resplendent shape with deep mirrors, glittering crystal chandeliers and a ceiling painting showing Europe as the centre of the world. Marie Antoinette (who was on her bridal procession from Austria to France) popped in for three minuets during the grand opening ball, and the room at once became the social hub of Augsburg. Today the candles on the rows of chandeliers are lit only for an occasional Mozart concert.

Much of the Schaezler Palais is given over to a mediocre collection of Baroque art, but at the back it connects up with a 16th-century convent, now the **Staatsgalerie** *(times as above)*. Here you can see a striking portrait of Jakob Fugger in his favourite Venetian brocade cap by Albrecht Dürer (1518), and a series of paintings of Roman basilicas (1499–1504) by Holbein the Elder and local artist Hans Burgkmair (1473–1531).

Maximilianstraße runs up to the church of **St Ulrich and St Afra**—a lofty Gothic structure with a Bavarian onion spire added in the 16th century. Shrines to Ulrich and Afra are inside, and three golden altars (1607), packed with saints and cherubim tower up above the choir. The adjacent **Ulrich Lutheran Church** used to be a sort of clerical souvenir shop, selling trinkets and indulgences, but after the 1555 Peace of Augsburg was given to the Lutherans as a gesture that they could live in happy harmony with the Catholics right next door.

The Jakobviertel and Fuggerei

If you duck east off Maximilianstraße, you come to the **Jakobviertel**, once the poorer part of town. Now, among the clutter of restored medieval houses and narrow streets, you find galleries, craftshops and museums. The **Römisches Museum** (Roman Museum) at Dominikanergasse 15 *(Tues–Sun 10–5, Oct–Apr to 4 pm; adm free)* is housed in an old Gothic hall church. The highlight of the collection is an AD 2 bronze horse's head, probably part of an equestrian statue. The **Holbein Haus** at Vordere Lech 20 *(Tues–Sun 10–5)* commemorates its famous resident with a few documents, but is mainly used for contemporary art exhibitions.

Still smarting from the insults Brecht heaped upon them, the citizens of Augsburg only recently swallowed their pride and opened the **Brecht Haus**, Auf dem Rain 7 *(Tues–Sun 10–5, Oct–Apr to 4pm; adm free)*. The playwright was born here in 1898, the son of a paper factory owner, and went off to study medicine in Munich in 1919, where he first tried his hand at theatre. The exhibition centres mainly on Brecht's life in Augsburg—which isn't the most enthralling part of his career.

Jakob Fugger wanted to be sure that he would go to heaven. Reliable sources had it that this was a difficult feat for a rich man—but that a good stock of prayers on the right side of the Doomsday Book could ease the passage. So in 1523 Fugger built a housing estate for Catholics who had been made poor 'through no fault of their own', setting the rent at one Rhenish guilder per annum—and one 'Our Father', one 'Hail Mary' and one 'Creed' daily, in his favour. Today the **Fuggerei** in Jakoberstraße is still financed and run by the Fugger family; residents pay DM1.72 rent a year (the equivalent of a Rhenish guilder) and still offer up the prescribed prayers for their benefactors.

The estate, designed by Thomas Krebs, is a model of social housing, way ahead of its time. Houses are separated by wide lanes; there are trees, fountains and individual gardens. The houses are divided into two parts, each with separate entrances: one tenant has the attic, the other the garden. Every bell pull is different to give front doors a little individuality.

Mozart's great-grandfather lived at No.14. He had been ostracized and reduced to poverty after burying the corpse of an executioner. Next door, at No.13, you can visit a house in its original state *(Mar–Oct 9–6; adm DM1)* to marvel at the ingenuity of the design. The bright front room (used as a workroom) has windows onto the street, and back into the kitchen. A special handle allows you to open the front door to customers without leaving the work bench. The stove that heats the workroom is loaded from behind the wall in the kitchen (to reduce fire risk). Upstairs in the bedrooms there are niches for candles (also to prevent fires). The cottages are cosy and compact, and modern residents look blissfully content—even though they have to put up with streams of staring tourists and pay a 50-pfennig fine to the nightwatchman if they come home after 10pm.

Augsburg ☏ (0821–)   **Where to Stay**

expensive

Drei Mohren Hotel, Maximillianstr. 40, ☏ 51 00 31, fax 15 78 64 (DM274–340). Mozart, Goethe and any number of archdukes and princes have stayed here before you. This is the poshest address in town, though bland modernization has all but destroyed the old atmosphere.

moderate

Hotel Ost, Fuggerstr. 4–6, ☏ 3 30 88, fax 3 55 19 (DM160–185). A quiet hotel near the centre, with friendly management. The Bahnhof is a five-minute walk away, and there's a parking garage nearby. No restaurant.

Hotel Post, Fuggerstr. 5–7, ☏ 3 60 44 (DM130–150). Just across the road from the Hotel Ost, with decor that veers from the spartan to the impressively kitsch. The owner, Frau Weiss, is popular with the local American military for her motherly care and hearty cuisine.

Pension Georgrast, Georgenstr. 31, ✆ 5 02 61 (DM72–96). Very good value. It is central, quietly situated and even offers special deals on Chinese massage and health cures. No restaurant.

Bayerischer Löwe, Linke Brandstr. 2, ✆ 70 28 70 (from DM62). Among the cheapest and most cheerful of the group of pensions in the north-eastern suburb of Lechhausen. No restaurant.

Youth Hostel: Beim Pfaffenkeller 3, ✆ 3 39 09.

Eating and Drinking

Though it is technically in Bavaria, Augsburg is really the easternmost outpost of Swabia, and the cooking is appropriately refined. You'll find Spätzle (shredded noodles) with nearly everything. They are delicious straight from the pot, covered with brown butter and breadcrumbs or cheese and fried onions. *Zwetschgendatschi* is a local speciality so popular that it has earned Augsburgers their nickname ('Datschiburgers'). It is a yeasty lump of pastry smothered with plums and cinnamon sugar, and you'll find it in cafés all over town.

Restaurants and Taverns

expensive

Bistro 34, Hunoldsgraben 34, ✆ 3 92 94 (DM50). Crammed with junkshop furniture and draped with pearls and feather boas. It serves whatever inspires the Italian, Greek and Swabian chefs (the fillets of pork in Armagnac are delicious).

Welser Küche, Maximilianstr. 83, ✆ 3 39 30 (DM70). Hosts a nightly banquet where meals from Philippine Welser's original 16th-century cookbook are served.

moderate

7-Schwaben-Stuben, Burgermeister-Fischer-Str. 12, ✆ 31 45 63 (DM25–45). Popular tavern serving Swabian cuisine. While you are looking through the menu nibble on some of the delicious dark bread with *Griebenschmalz* (lard with chopped onion and apple).

Fuggerei-Stube, Jakobstr. 26 (DM25–45). At the Fuggerei, and one of the best places in town for Swabian food. Try *Krautspatzen* (noodles with bacon and sauerkraut—surprisingly delicate, and far tastier than it sounds).

inexpensive

Bücher Pastet, Korneliusstraße. Restaurant in the cellar of a bookshop. For around DM7 you'll get the dish of the day (usually something delectably Swabian)—and can refill as many times as you like. They also serve a spicy home-brewed beer.

Kreßlesmühle, Barfüßerstr. 4, © 3 71 70. An arts centre in an old mill. *The* place to be if you're a student, school truant or jazz fan. There's a café (with a popular beer garden), live music (anything from blues singers to wandering sephardic balladeers), and also good theatre and film.

Kahnfort, Riedlerstr. 11. A wooden chicken-run of a bar right on the river's edge. On summer's afternoons (for a small fee) you can make off in one of the boats bobbing underneath the windows.

Perlach Bar, tucked into the wall of the church at the Perlachturm, and overlooked by nearly everyone. A cupboard-sized-bar where you can sip a schnapps on a freezing winter's afternoon.

Zeughaus, Zeugplatz. The beergarden is popular with thirty-somethings who are reluctant to shake off their student years. A restaurant inside serves good, inexpensive meals.

Café Eber, Rathausplatz. The best place to join the Datschiburgers at their favourite culinary pastime.

Ludwig's Castles and the Wieskirche

Soon after Augsburg, the faint smudge on the horizon begins to resolve itself into the peaks and shadows of the Alps. As you travel nearer, the atmosphere seems to sharpen, there's a growing chill in the air and the countryside begins to erupt in rocky outcrops.

In the middle of the rolling fields that lead up to the foothills, you'll find the **Wieskirche** (which tourist brochures rather alarmingly refer to as 'The Church of our Flagellated Lord in the Meadow'). This is a pilgrimage church. The object of veneration is a wooden statue of Christ, that was rejected (for being too ugly) from the local Good Friday procession. Later it was found that, if you prayed hard enough, the figure shed real tears. Pilgrims flocked from afar, and in 1746 Abbot Marianus II decided to build a grand church to accommodate them. The result was one of the finest examples of Rococo architecture in Germany. The architect, Dominikus Zimmerman (*see* p. 60) was so pleased with it that he came to live nearby for the rest of his life. Light streams in through the windows, reflects off the brilliant white walls and pillars and picks out the curls and licks of gilded stucco. Cherubs and angels peek out from behind garlands of foliage, and in the middle of an effervescent ceiling fresco (by J.B. Zimmerman), the resurrected Christ sits resplendent on a rainbow.

Sadly, despite its isolated setting, the Wieskirche swarms with tourists. There are clusters of coaches and souvenir kiosks all the way up to the door. You even have to endure piped music. When the church was finished in 1754, Abbot Marianus used his diamond ring to scratch into the window of the prelates' chamber the words: 'At this place abides happiness, here the heart finds peace'. He must be turning in his grave.

Just as you get to the Alpine foothills you come to Neuschwanstein and Hohenschwangau, two castles which once belonged to the dreamy, eccentric King Ludwig II of Bavaria (1845–86).

King Ludwig II of Bavaria

 In the 19th century Bavaria was ruled by a fairytale King. He had piercing blue eyes and carefully curled dark locks. He built fantastical castles in the mountains and was so excited by German legends that he used to dress up and act them out with his friends. The official story has it that he was quite mad, and drowned himself in the Starnberger See—but exactly what happened in the last days of his life is obscured by half-truth and deceit on the part of his scheming ministers.

In Germany King Ludwig II has cult status. Perhaps his hopeless, self-destructive romanticism appeals to the national psyche. To foreigners he is known mainly as the builder of Neuschwanstein, the white castle made famous by the film *Chitty Chitty Bang Bang* and featured in countless German tourist leaflets. But Ludwig's real contribution to the world is a far more significant one. He appreciated and championed the operas of the composer Richard Wagner at a time when that alone would have been enough to have him certified. Without the king's sustained, enthusiastic and generous support it is doubtful that Wagner would ever have had the opportunity to produce the work he did.

Ludwig was born on 25 August 1845. Three years later his grandfather, King Ludwig I, was forced to abdicate following a scandalous affair with the 'Spanish' dancer Lola Montez (alias Mrs Eliza Gilbert, a British housewife who later ran off with, and bigamously married, an Old Etonian guardsman). The infant Ludwig's father became Maximilian II of Bavaria, but reigned for just 16 years, so it was at the tender age of 19 that the pretty young prince assumed the throne. He was fastidious about his appearance ('If I didn't have my hair curled every day, I couldn't enjoy my food', he said) and enjoyed the costumes that came with his new role (though he sometimes paraded under a parasol with his helmet under his arm, so as not to spoil his coiffure). Mundane affairs of state, however, held little appeal, and the young king soon antagonized his cabinet.

Even as a toddler Ludwig had begun to reveal the proclivities that were later to seal his fate. His mother, Queen Marie, noted in her diary that the infant Ludwig loved art, would build churches and monasteries with his toy bricks, enjoyed dressing up (usually as a nun) and was always giving away his toys and money. As he grew older Ludwig came to revere the Bourbons of France, especially Louis XIV, the 17th-century 'Sun King'. The splendours of Versailles (which Ludwig visited in 1867) and the rich romance of German legends such as that of Lohengrin, the Swan Prince, inspired him to build three dream castles: Neuschwanstein (1869, *see* p. 338), a shrine to Lohengrin, Tannhäuser and other medieval German heroes; Herrenchiemsee (begun 1878, *see* p. 370), a mock Versailles; and Linderhof (1879, *see* p. 374) with its magical grotto. All in all, these three castles cost around 31 million marks. This was approximately the amount of the indemnity paid, without a peep of protest, to Prussia after the Seven Weeks' War—but Ludwig's frittering such money away on beautiful buildings put his ministers in a flap.

Another cause for ministerial complaint was the king's infatuation with Richard Wagner. Ludwig heard his first Wagner opera (*Lohengrin*) in 1861. In the words of an attendent courtier the music had 'an almost demoniacal' effect on the young prince, who became so convulsed with excitement that he seemed in danger of having an epileptic fit. At that time Wagner's music was considered by many to be cranky, ugly and even dangerous. Ten years later Mark Twain was to write (also of *Lohengrin*): 'The banging and slamming and booming and crashing were something beyond belief. The racking and pitiless pain of it remains stored up in my memory alongside the memory of the time I had my teeth fixed... the recollection of that long, dragging, relentless season of suffering is indestructible.' (He did admit that the now famous Wedding Chorus was 'one brief little season of heaven and heaven's sweet ecstacy and peace during all this long and diligent and acrimonious reproduction of the other place'.) Today Twain's opinion might still find some sympathizers. Certainly in the 1860s Ludwig's conviction that no-one could 'possibly remain unmoved by this magical fairytale, by this heavenly music' was not a common one—though it also hints that the monarch (whose lack of musical ability had driven at least one teacher to despair) was captivated less by Wagner's music than by the world of fantasy the operas evoked.

As soon as he became king, Ludwig set about tracking down his hero. Wagner had gone into hiding. The *Ring des Nibelungen* and *Die Meistersinger* were unfinished, all the leading opera houses had declared *Tristan* impossible to stage, and the extravagant composer had run up enormous debts. Cabinet Secretary Pfistermeister spent three weeks in pursuit of the elusive Wagner, who was certain that powerful creditors were on his tail. The hapless secretary travelled from Vienna through Switzerland and finally unearthed his quarry in Stuttgart. Wagner was whisked back to Munich for an emotional meeting with the king. An intense and passionate friendship developed between the two—amounting to far more than straightforward royal patronage: Ludwig worshipped the composer. Wagner wrote of Ludwig that 'he knows and understands everything about me—understands me like my own soul,' and later: 'He is like a god! If I am Wotan, then he is my Siegfried.' He wrote (to others) of the tremendous inspiration he derived from Ludwig, and the two kept up a relentless and gushing correspondence, even when they were seeing each other almost daily.

The king paid off Wagner's debts, set him up in a villa in Munich, granted him a stipend that exceeded that of a senior minister and promised him an enormous sum on completion of the *Ring*. Although the money that Ludwig lavished on Wagner was from his personal fortune, not state coffers, the cabinet became increasingly alarmed at the influence the composer wielded. Cabinet Secretary Pfistermeister and

Minister-President von Pfordten (nicknamed Pfi and Pfo) connived to get rid of Wagner, and in the end they succeeded. In December 1865 Ludwig, convinced by Pfi and Pfo that his behaviour was alienating his subjects, asked Wagner to leave Munich, but the friendship continued at a distance, and the king continued to pour money into Wagner's projects, including the establishment of the Bayreuth Festival.

Ludwig's relationship with Wagner was almost certainly platonic. The king *was* a homosexual but, when he wasn't agonizing over what he considered to be a mortal sin and swearing himself to months of celibacy, he was in love with a succession of grooms, handsome cousins, and attentive aides-de-camp. In 1867 Ludwig had proposed to his cousin Sophie, the daughter of Duke Max in Bayern, but after postponing the wedding date a number of times, he finally admitted that he couldn't go through with it and broke off the engagement. The only woman he had any real time for was Sophie's sister, the Empress Elizabeth of Austria (*see* p. 348). He loathed his mother, saying that her 'prose' destroyed his 'poetry'. He avoided her as much as possible and referred to her alternately as 'that old goose', 'the widow of my predecessor', or by an honorary title—'the Colonel of the Third Artillery Regiment'. Ludwig and Elizabeth, however, adored each other. They had been friends from childhood—she 'the dove', and he 'the eagle'—and they remained deeply attached until his death. Apart from Elizabeth, Wagner and a few long-lasting loves (notably his equerry Richard Hornig), Ludwig had few close friends. He was a shy and solitary figure who slept most of the day, and went for long lonely rides in the dead of night. At Linderhof there was even a device which lowered his entire dining table into the kitchens, where it could be replenished with food so that the king could be quite alone when he ate.

More and more Ludwig began to inhabit his dream-world, increasingly neglecting affairs of state. He ran up huge debts building and decorating his castles, and had to borrow millions of marks from the Bavarian State Bank. By 1884 there seemed a real possibility that Linderhof and Herrenchiemsee would be repossessed by creditors—but nothing could dissuade Ludwig from his mission. Finally, the cabinet decided that the king had to go. As Ludwig's brother, Otto, was insane, his mild-mannered uncle Prince Luitpold had to be persuaded to act as regent. The easiest way to ensure Luitpold's backing was to have Ludwig declared insane too.

There was a history of madness in the family. Apart from brother Otto (who had suffered from convulsions since childhood) there was a string of odd, bewildered souls on his mother's side, and also the Princess Alexandra—a highly strung aunt who was convinced that she had swallowed a grand piano made of glass. Ludwig's own bizarre behaviour was a rich source of evidence for a case to be made against him. Early in 1886 the Minister-President Freiherr von Lutz and some cabinet colleagues, set about having Ludwig certified. A thick wad of 'evidence' was put together—much of it gossip from servants, many of whom had been dismissed and had a grudge against the king. The prominent alienist Dr Bernhard von Gudden certified Ludwig on the basis of this report, without having once examined his patient.

Certainly Ludwig was subject to violent outbursts of frenzied temper and was obsessively shy of the public; at banquets he would hide behind banks of flowers and have the band play so loudly that conversation was impossible. His admiration for the Bourbons gave him a taste for absolute monarchy: he once spoke of selling Bavaria and using the money to buy a kingdom which he could rule with supreme power. He occasionally demanded that he be dressed in full regalia (which had to be fetched from a strongroom in Munich) for his midnight rides; after reading a book on the Chinese court he went through a phase of demanding that servants prostrate themselves before him; he would mete out extraordinary medieval punishments ('Pluck out his eyes') to those who had offended him, though courtiers took these with a pinch of salt, and only pretended to carry them out. His nocturnal lifestyle, solitary habits and theatricality make him seem very odd indeed, but there is little hard evidence of true madness. Rather, Ludwig was a dreamy eccentric with the power, money and position to pamper his whims and make his fantasy-world real. Naturally, he cast himself as king of this world, and demanded the deference that this implied. He could, and did, commission private performances of operas he loved, and have scenes he particularly enjoyed repeated again and again; build grottos, gardens and entire castles which made fairytales come to life; dress up and live for a while the life of one of his legendary heroes. But (much though he loathed his administrative role) he had an astute understanding of international affairs and was capable of rational, intelligent political argument, even at the height of his so-called 'madness'. He could also be disarmingly down-to-earth, and was adored by local peasants as the tall and handsome king who would suddenly appear from nowhere, plonk himself down next to some woodcutters and share their lunch, or chat knowledgeably about cattle with a cowherd.

The night that Dr Gudden and a deputation from the cabinet came to apprehend Ludwig was cold and rainy. The party arrived at Hohenschwangau around midnight, planning to cross the valley to neighbouring Neuschwanstein, where the King was staying, the next morning—but a loyal coachman cottoned on to what was happening and warned the king. When the officials (who had been feasting sumptuously) noticed that the coachman was missing, they suspected that the secret of their mission was out, and set off at 3am, in formal dress and somewhat the worse for wear, for Neuschwanstein. Here they found their paths blocked by the police, the fire-brigade and crowds of loyal locals who had come to protect their king.

The members of the commission were arrested, but the machinery of Ludwig's downfall was already in motion. Ludwig failed to heed advice either to flee to the Tyrol, or to appear in public in Munich in order to show that he was not mad, and on 12 June 1886 a second commission arrived to take him to the castle at Berg, on the Starnberger See. Ludwig was devastated, drinking heavily and threatening suicide. The next evening, though, he seemed calm enough to go for a walk in the grounds with Dr Gudden, unaccompanied by warders. The two never returned. Later that night both of their bodies were fished out of shallow water at the edge of the lake. Exactly what happened remains a mystery. Perhaps Ludwig attempted suicide, and Gudden drowned while trying to save him—or maybe Ludwig vengefully murdered Gudden, but suffered a heart attack while doing so. (He *was* overweight, but also a good swimmer—so it is hard to believe that he could drown in just a few feet of water.) Whatever the explanation, Ludwig's death was tragic and pointless. The Empress Elizabeth, who perhaps understood him better than anyone, burst out when she heard the news: 'The king was not mad; he was just an eccentric living in a dream-world. They might have treated him more gently...'

Towards the end of his life, Ludwig became preoccupied with building grand, theatrical castles (*see* also pp. 370 and 374). The king himself drew up plans for **Neuschwanstein** *(Apr–Sept 8.30–5.30, Oct–Mar 10–4; adm DM8)*, with the help of a stage designer rather than an architect. Work was begun in 1869 and went on right up to Ludwig's deposition in 1886. The sparkling white Schloß, with its prickles of spires and turrets became a prototype for Walt Disney fairytale castles. (It stars in the film *Chitty Chitty Bang Bang*.) Neuschwanstein opened as a museum three weeks after Ludwig's apparent suicide, and has been a tourist trap ever since. Notices command you to obey all members of staff, not to stray from your tour group and warn that you are not guaranteed a tour in the language of your choice. You are churned through the castle in groups of 60, as guides mechanically reel off their spiel in 35 minutes flat (probably about half as long as you waited in the queue for a ticket). Then it's off down the hill and up the other side to Hohenschwangau to start all over again.

For all that, Neuschwanstein is well worth the battle. The castle is ingeniously situated. From one side you look out across flat grassland to the shimmering Alpsee; other windows open straight onto an Alpine gorge with bounding cascades. You slip giddily from stagy Byzantine halls into heavily carved wooden dens. (Fourteen woodcarvers toiled for nearly five years just to finish the king's bedroom.) Corners, windows and doorways are draped in rich brocades (usually in Ludwig's favourite blue) and the walls are painted with scenes from the legends that inspired Wagner's operas.

Hohenschwangau *(same times and prices)* is not as impressive. King Maximilian II (Ludwig's father) rebuilt it from the ruins of a 12th-century castle in the 1830s. It was here that Ludwig grew up and spent much of his reign. (He only ever stayed in the fantasy castle across the valley for six months.) Lohengrin, the Swan-King, is supposed to have lived in the original Schloß. Ludwig was obsessed with swans, and with the legend *(see* p. 335). He loved to dress up as Lohengrin, and often got Prince Paul von Thurn und Taxis (a young favourite) to act out the story in a swan-shaped boat on the Alpsee, while a band played appropriate snippets from Wagner's opera.

For the most part, the rooms in Hohenschwangau are tame, rather homely Neo-Gothic. When Ludwig became king he changed the ceiling fresco in the Royal Bedroom from a day to a night sky—with an artificial moon and twinkling stars lit by lanterns from behind. This bedroom was the scene of a fracas between a young Ludwig and the seasoned actress Lila von Bulyowsky. Afterwards, *she* claimed that she had been shocked by the nude women in the murals and, besides, would never dream of seducing a mere boy. *He* claimed that she had chased him around the room. They both said that they spent most of the evening sitting on the bed reciting *Egmont*—up to the scene of the kiss.

See also directory entry for Füssen.

Where to Stay and Eating Out

Of the three Gaststätte that have been built next to the Wieskirche, the **Moser** is the best value. Like the others, it serves up Bavarian tourist favourites, with lots of cheese and beef from the ubiquitous Allgäu cows.

The comfortable **Schloßhotel Lisl**, Hohenschwangau, © (08362) 8 10 06, fax (08362) 8 11 07 (DM100–240) is in the valley between Ludwig's castles, and has good views of both. It sets itself high standards, despite being in such a popular location, and staff are attentive and courteous. The hotel has a beer garden, and two restaurants serving good Bavarian food. In the nearby village of Schwangau, the cosy **Pension Neuschwanstein**, Schwangau, © (08362) 82 09 (DM90) has a perfect view across to Neuschwanstein and the Alps. It is in the style of a traditional Bavarian Alpine chalet, so all rooms have a small wooden balcony (though not every one has a view). The café downstairs serves tasty homemade cakes.

München (Munich)

> *'Der Deutsche Himmel.'*
>
> ('It's the German Heaven', Thomas Wolfe)
>
> *'Voilà, une capitale'*
>
> (Charles de Gaulle, on his first visit)

Bavarians see Munich as the 'secret capital' of Germany. Berliners sniffily call it the *Millionendorf,* a big provincial village. King Ludwig I of Bavaria proclaimed it the 'Athens on the Isar', and the tourist brochures settle for '*Weltstadt mit Herz*' (the metropolis with a heart). Munich herself can't make up her mind whether she is the sophisticated courtier, or boisterous village wench. Her architectural wardrobe is a resplendent, somewhat too grand, array of royal cast-offs, and her jewelbox dazzles—yet one whiff of hops and she's dancing on the table. Here is the stratosphere of German high society, one of the world's great opera houses, a transcendent collection of art—and also the Oktoberfest, the world's beeriest beano. Munich is fast-moving, high-powered and modern, yet everyone seems fresh-faced, exuberant and relaxed. Businessmen dart out of flashy new office blocks, shed their pinstripes and sunbathe by the River Isar. In smart cafés, wealthy *Schickies* show off designer versions of Bavarian *Tracht*, while in cellars and beer gardens jolly families in real *Lederhosen* and feathered hats swill beer and try to drown out the oompah band. The Berliners are right. Munich *is* parochial. That is what makes it so enticing.

Most Germans dream of living in Munich. The popular press (especially in Bavaria) often prints polls showing that (if they had to leave their *Heimat*) this is the city most Germans would choose. This despite the patriotic smugness of the locals—Munich is simply the best in everything and *Zugereiste* ('newcomers') remain so for decades—and the Föhn. The Föhn is a warm wind that blows off the Alps, clearing the sky to a crystal blue and causing headaches and bolshy bad-temper in otherwise cheery Müncheners. Even the Föhn is wary of *Zugereiste*. You have to live in Munich for five or so years before you begin to feel its effect. So if you're bouncing around with other happy visitors on an apparently perfect day, don't be surprised by growling barmen and snappy shop assistants.

Apart from the style, conviviality and super-elegant architecture, what attracts people most to Munich is its setting and size. In the time that it takes other city-dwellers to get to work, Müncheners can be in the Alps. The city itself is compact and manageable. In the centre, on the left bank of the Isar, is the Altstadt, a racing heart of swish streets and rollicking *Brauhaüser*. To the north is the erstwhile bohemian quarter of Schwabing (now tamed and gentrified), the main museum complex and the vast, green Englischer Garten. To the west is the grand Schloß Nymphenburg. Across the river and to the south you'll find the quirkier corners, pockets of immigrants and artists and the biggest technical museum in the world.

History

In 1158 the Emperor Frederick Barbarossa was called on to settle a dispute between his uncle, Bishop Otto von Freising, and his cousin, Henry the Lion. Otto had controlled a very profitable toll bridge across the Isar—directly on the lucrative salt route. With his customary leonine ferocity, Henry had simply burnt the bridge down, and built his own further along the river. He called the settlement that subsequently sprang up 'Munichen', after the monks who had built a new church nearby. A cautious Barbarossa decided in favour of his cousin, though in 1180 Henry fell from grace (for refusing military help to the emperor) and power was handed over to the Wittelsbach family. They ruled Bavaria continuously right up until 1918.

At first the capital of the region was Regensburg. The first Wittelsbach to set up home in Munich was Duke Ludwig the Severe, who built a suitably plain Residenz in 1255. By the beginning of the 16th century Munich was capital and the official family seat.

The salt trade boomed, and Munich got fat. Even the Thirty Years' War, which devasted the rest of Germany, left the town relatively undiminished. (King Gustavus Adolphus of Sweden called it 'the golden saddle on a scraggy nag'.) In the 18th century, Baroque style blossomed here as hardly anywhere else north of Italy. Then in 1806 Napoleon made Bavaria a kingdom. The first King, Ludwig I, with his penchant for Neoclassical architecture, set about creating his Athens of the north, but a love affair with the Spanish dancer Lola Montez caused a scandal which eventually led to his abdication. Ludwig's son, Maximilian II, also had the building bug, and Munich grew even grander. The next king, Ludwig II, brought Wagner to Munich (see p. 334), but hated the capital and spent most of his time in the mountains, dressing up and building fantastical castles.

In the 1900s, under Prince Regent Luitpold, Munich became one of the centres of European intellectual life. Jugendstil germinated here, and during the first part of the century, in smoky cafés in the Schwabing district, you could have met the likes of Trotsky and Thomas Mann, the painters Marc, Kandinsky and Klee or the playwright Bertolt Brecht.

Hitler put an end to this Golden Age. In 1919 he established his Nazi party headquarters in Munich, and though his 1923 putsch failed (see p. 45), he made Munich the 'Capital of the Movement'. It was here that Chamberlain signed the agreement he was sure meant 'peace in our time' in 1938. Within months war was declared. Munich was the centre of a gallant anti-Nazi resistance movement, the White Rose, but the organization was crushed and the leaders executed. In the last years of the war, heavy Allied bombing destroyed 40 per cent of the city centre. However, most of the Baroque buildings (and, alas, some of Hitler's monstrosities) survived. Restoration work has been careful and sensitive, and there are few high-rise blocks or ugly concrete sprawls.

Today Munich still has a flourishing artistic life. There are more theatres here than in any other city in Germany, and it is the centre of the German film industry (Fassbinder lived and worked here for years). Nearly one fifth of the city's population are scholars or students, and there is a busy publishing industry. Above a bohemian undercurrent lies a glossy layer of prosperous bankers, insurance brokers and hi-tech industrialists. The twinkle in Munich's social sheen is still the Wittelsbach family. They are an unofficial local royalty. Bavarians still address the Duke of Bavaria as 'Your Royal Highness', and the Wittelsbach parties at Schloß Nymphenburg are the *ne plus ultra* of the Munich social calendar.

Getting Around

By Air

Munich's spanking new **Franz Josef Strauß Airport** (© (089) 97 52 13 13) has non-stop flights to New York (8hr), London (2hr) and most other European capitals. Line S8 on the S-Bahn gets you to the Hauptbahnhof in 39 minutes, for only DM10. The Airport Bus also goes to the Hauptbahnhof (Arnulfstraße entrance). It takes 45 minutes and costs DM12. Both services leave every 20 minutes.

By Train

Munich's cavernous **Hauptbahnhof** deposits you just west of the city centre, and immediately locks into the extensive metro system. Munich is a hub of rail travel, and Europe's fastest trains will speed you all over Germany and across its borders. For train information ℂ (089) 1 94 19, for reservations ℂ (089) 12 23/23 33.

By Car

Munich is also a major node on Germany's autobahn system, though the Munich–Berlin route barely copes with post-unification traffic. Pedestrians rule in the middle of town, and though some parking is available, it's better to use one of the parking lots south of the centre, or around the Bahnhof, and rely on public transport.

Car hire: Europcar, Schwanthalerstr. 10a, ℂ (089) 594 723.

Mitfahrzentrale: Lämmerstr. 4; ℂ (089) 59 45 61.

Public Transport

A fast and efficient system of trams, buses and S-bahn and U-bahn trains will whisk you all over the city between 5am and 1am. A single ticket costs DM2.50, but you may find it more cost effective to buy a *Tageskarte* (Day Ticket; DM8 for central zone, DM16 for entire metropolitan area). This entitles two adults, three children and a dog to unlimited travel from 9am on one day to 4am on the next. There is no expiry date on a *Streifenkarte* (Strip Ticket; DM10 for 20 strips). Two strips are valid for travel (with appropriate hops and changes) for two hours in any one direction. *Streifenkarten* and single tickets must be validated at the beginning of each journey, and *Tageskarten* should be stamped before setting out on your first journey. (Validating punches are found on buses and trams and at the entrance to stations.) You can buy tickets from dispensing machines at the stops, tobacconists and newsagents with a white K in the window, or on buses and trams. For bus and tram information ℂ (089) 23 80 30 (for S-Bahn information ℂ (089) 55 75 75).

Taxi: ℂ (089) 21610 or (089) 19410.

By Bicycle

If you take the S-Bahn out into the countryside around Munich, you'll find that many railway stations also operate an inexpensive bicycle rental service (ask at the parcels counter). Radius Touristik, Arnulfstr. 3; ℂ (089) 59 61 13, near the Hauptbahnhof, rents out bikes at DM15 per day (DM45 per week) and also offers guided cycle tours.

Tourist Information

Tourist information offices: Hauptbahnhof, Bayerstraße entrance, ℂ (089) 23 91 256/7 *(daily 8am–10pm)*; Airport, ℂ (089) 97 59 28 15 *(Mon–Sat 8.30am–10pm, Sun 1pm–9pm)*; Rindermarkt, Pettenbeckstraße *(Mon–Fri 9.30–6)*. They supply brochures and maps, and for DM5 will book you a room (no phone bookings).

Post office: Opposite the Hauptbahnhof *(open 24 hours)*. It has ranks of telephones and fax machines, and a good **Bureau de Change**.

American Express: Promenadeplatz 6, ℭ (089) 2 19 90, and you'll find main branches of most German **banks** in the immediate vicinity.

Ambulance: ℭ 1 92 22.

Emergency medical service: ℭ (089) 55 86 61.

Emergency pharmacy service: ℭ (089) 59 44 75.

Police: ℭ 110.

Consulates

American: Königinstr. 5, ℭ (089) 2 88 81.

British: Bürkleinstr. 10, ℭ (089) 21 10 90.

Canadian: Tal 29, ℭ (089) 22 26 61.

Festivals

The first thing to note about the famous **Oktoberfest** is that it takes place in September. In just over two weeks (from mid-September to the first Sunday in October), crowds of revellers get through over five million litres of beer, half a million sausages, 650,000 chickens, 70,000 knuckles of pork and usually around 70 oxen. Most of the drinking is done in enormous beer tents on the Theresienwiese (the 'Wies'n'—a vast fairground just behind the Hauptbahnhof), under the watchful eye of the towering statue of Bavaria. Those who have had their fill of beer and oompah bands spill out of the beerhalls to whoop it up on the dodgems, big dippers and various other stomach-churning spins and rides in the surrounding funfair. The autumn air is pungent with the smell of roasting meat, spilt beer and toasted almonds.

During the Oktoberfest there are balls and parties all over town, and two spectacular parades. The **Opening Parade** of landlords and brewers starts at 11am on the first day of the *Fest*. Landlords and their families ride to the fairground in ornate carriages or prettily decorated horse-drawn drays. You can jostle with the crowds in Schwanthalerstraße, or get a better view from the grandstand in Sonnenstraße (tickets DM36 from the tourist office). On the first Sunday of the festival there is a two-hour-long **procession** of bands, coaches, decorated floats, people in traditional dress, thoroughbred horses, prize oxen and even the odd goat. The route goes from the Max II Denkmal, through the city centre to the fairground. Grandstand seats will set you back DM55, but there's an enclosed standing area at Odeonsplatz where you can avoid the worst of the crush for DM16 (tickets from the tourist office).

Rather wisely, there is **no parking** around the Oktoberfest grounds, so people are encouraged to use public transport. The **U-Bahn** to Theresienwiese (Lines 4 and 5)

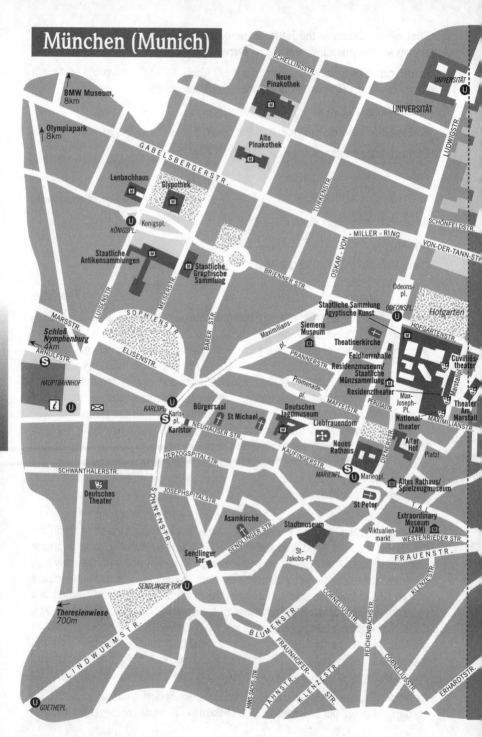

München (Munich)

BMW Museum,
8km

Olympiapark
8km

SCHELLINGSTR.

Neue
Pinakothek

UNIVERSITÄT

UNIVERSITÄT

GABELSBERGERSTR.

Alte
Pinakothek

Lenbachhaus

Glypothek

TÜRKENSTR.

LUDWIGSTR.

SCHÖNFELDSTR.

Königspl.

KÖNIGSPL.

MILLER - RING

VON - DER - TANN-STR.

OSKAR - VON

Staatliche
Antikensammlungen

Staatliche
Graphische
Sammlung

BRIENNER STR.

Odeons-
pl.

ODEONSPL.

Hofgarten

MARSSTR.

SOPHIENSTR.

BARER STR.

MESERSTR.

LUISENSTR.

Staatliche Sammlung
Ägyptische Kunst

HOFGARTENSTR.

Schloß
Nymphenburg
4km

ELISENSTR.

Maximilians-
pl.

Siemens
Museum

Theatinerkirche

Cuvilliés-
theater

ARNULFSTR.

PRANNERSTR.

Feldherrnhalle

Residenzmuseum/
Staatliche
Münzsammlung

Marstall-pl.

HAUPTBAHNHOF

Promenade-
pl.

PERUSASTR.

Residenztheater

Max-
Joseph-
Pl.

Theater
Am
Marstall

KARLSPL.

Karls-
pl.

Bürgersaal

St Michael

MAFFEISTR.

Deutsches
Jagdmuseum

National-
theater

MAXIMILIANSTR.

Karlstor

NEUHAUSER STR.

Liebfrauendom

DIENERSTR.

Alter
Hof

HERZOGSPITALSTR.

KAUFINGERSTR.

Neues
Rathaus

Platzl

SCHWANTHALERSTR.

JOSEPHSPITALSTR.

SONNENSTR.

MARIENPL.

Marienpl.

Altes Rathaus/
Spielzeugmuseum

Deutsches
Theater

St Peter

TAL

Asamkirche

Stadtmuseum

Viktualien-
markt

Extraordinary
Museum
(ZAM)

WESTENRIEDER STR.

Sendlinger
Tor

SENDLINGER STR.

St-
Jakobs-Pl.

FRAUENSTR.

SENDLINGER TOR

KLENZESTR.

Theresienwiese
700m

BLUMENSTR.

CORNELIUSSTR.

REICHENBACHSTR.

CORNELIUSSTR.

LINDWURMSTR.

FRAUNHOFER

HANS-SACHS-STR.

JAHNSTR.

KLENZE STR.

ERHARDTSTR.

GOETHEPL.

Siegestor

SCHWABING

Chioesischer Turm

Mónopterus

Englischer Garten

Japanisches Teehaus

Haus der Kunst Ⓜ

Museum für Vor- und Frühgeschichte Ⓜ Bayerisches Nationalmuseum

PRINZREGENTENSTR.

Schackgalerie Ⓜ

LERCHENFELDSTR.

WIDENMAYERSTR.

Isar

Maximilian- anlagen

PRINZREGENTENSTR.

Villa Stuck Ⓜ

Ⓤ LEHEL

Theater am Marstall

BÜRLEINSTR.

KARL-SCHARNAGL-RING

MAXIMILIANSTR.

Werkraumtheater

HILDEGARDSTR.

Staatliches Ⓜ Museum für Völkerkunde

ISMANINGER STR.

Maximilianeum

MAXIMILIANSBRÜCKE

THOMAS-WIMMER-RING

Isartor/ Karl Valentin Museum

Ⓢ ISARTOR

THIERSCHSTR.

STEINSDORFSTR.

MAX- WEBER- PL.

Max- Weber- Pl. Ⓤ

ZWEIBRÜCKEN- STR.

Wiener Pl.

INNERE WIENER STR.

HAIDHAUSEN

PREYSINGSTR.

N

ERHARDT STR.

LUDWIGSBRÜCKE

KELLERSTR.

LILIENSTR.

ROSENHEIMER STR.

Gasteig Kulturzentrum

300 m
300 yds

Ⓜ
Deutsches Museum

is very crowded; Lines 3 and 6 to Goetheplatz or Poccistraße are easier going and deposit you a short walk from the southern end of the grounds.

Munich's **Stadtgründungsfest** (City Anniversary, mid-June) is a much smaller affair, but in many ways more fun. This is the festival the locals keep for themselves. From Marienplatz to Odeonsplatz and in the courtyards of the Rathaus you'll food stalls, long beer tables and *ad hoc* cafés. Lots of people dress up in traditional *Tracht*, and even those who don't are prone to bouts of folk-dancing. Aromas of pretzels, fresh chocolate, crispy pork and countless other local and foreign foods fill the air. Oompah bands, local choirs and visiting musicians keep up a steady beat. There is an intimate, birthday-party atmosphere, no uncomfortable crush and only a scattering of tourists.

Those with a liking for fleamarkets should keep an eye open for the **Auer Dult**, an outdoor fleamarket on Mariahilfplatz that takes place three times a year (for eight days at the ends of April, July and October). The **Christkindlmarkt**, Munich's Christmas market, is on Marienplatz from the end of November. Stalls sell gifts, kitsch and trivia, but also charming German handmade decorations and lots of *Gluhwein* and food. Every evening at 5.30pm you can hear live Christmas music.

Munich has its own lively carnival tradition—here the celebration is called **Fasching** (*see* p. 127). Hi-jinks last from mid-January to Shrove Tuesday, with rounds of Costume Balls and jolly doings at the Victualenmarkt on the final day.

On the cultural side there is the **Münchener Opernfest**, an opera festival of world renown which takes place from mid-July until the beginning of August. Tickets are hard to come by, so it is a good idea to contact the tourist office or the Nationaltheater, ✆ (089) 221 316, long before the event if you wish to attend. During the festival there are also special concerts held all over town.

Marienplatz and the Southern Altstadt

Marienplatz has been the centre of Munich since the town began. It started life as a corn market, then became a public execution site and jousting arena. In 1315 Emperor Ludwig the Bavarian affably decreed that the square should never be built on, so that it would remain 'all the more jolly, attractive and leisurely for gentlemen, citizens and friends'. And so it has—though today it is a touch more frenetic than leisurely.

There is no motor traffic in 'Munich's parlour' (as locals call it), just two types of people: those criss-crossing the square with purpose, and those sitting about in randomly scattered white metal chairs, chatting sociably or cricking their necks to look up at the points and pinnacles of the Neo-Gothic **Neues Rathaus**.

The Neues Rathaus, which fills the entire northern edge of Marienplatz, was built between 1867 and 1909 to supersede the far more graceful, real Gothic **Altes Rathaus** (built 1475, on the east side of the square). The modest tower of the Altes Rathaus contains a small **Toy Museum** (*see* **Museums** below). The tower of the 19th-century upstart is a full 80m high, and sports an elaborate *Glockenspiel*. Every day, at 11am *(May–Oct also noon and*

5pm), carved figures re-enact the wedding festivities of the 16th-century lovers, Duke Wilhelm V and Renata von Lothringen. At a few minutes past the hour (marked with reckless lack of synchronization by all the bells of the city), the *Glockenspiel* creaks and jangles into life. The carillon hammers out a haphazard and tinny tune as trumpeters, banner-waving citizens and jousting knights jerk past the impassive couple. Below them, figures revolve in the *Schäfflertanz* (coopers' dance)—a joyful jig from 1517 that celebrated the end of the plague. Finally a cock pops out and crows thinly, and its all over. A trickle of applause runs through the crowd, and they divert their gaze to the buskers on the square.

Just beyond the Altes Rathaus, on Platzl, the famous **München Hofbräuhaus** (literally 'Court Brewery') roars and trumpets its way well into the night (*see* **Bars and Cafés** below). Nearby is **Alter Hof** (Old Court), built up from the sparse ruins of Ludwig the Severe's 13th-century Residenz, but requiring quite a feat of imagination to endow it with any medieval atmosphere.

Just off the south-east corner of Marienplatz, looking loftily out over the town, is **St Peter's**, Munich's oldest church. First records appear in 1169, though most of the present structure was built between the 15th and 17th centuries. The church is no architectural stunner, but locals love it. They call it *Alter Peter* (Old Peter) and come in their hundreds for weddings and Sunday services (after which, in good Munich fashion, they file out for a quick drink in one of the surrounding bars). Visitors can clamber up the tower for a fine view over the city.

South of St Peter's, the **Victualenmarkt** (produce market) sprawls between ancient chestnut trees. The wooden stalls are daily piled high with bright fruit and flowers. There are choice cuts of game, exotica such as banana leaves and dried worms, and more types of sausage than you could dream of. As you thread between the barrels of wine, piles of eggs and Winnie-the-Pooh honeypots, you get whiffs of freshly baked bread, tangy spices, cheeses and ground coffee. Everything is very much under the control of rosy-cheeked women vendors, renowned for their earthy wit, but notoriously grumpy if you handle their wares. The little alleys (such as Heiligestraße) around the market are lined with long-established family food shops, and are great fun to explore. The Victualenmarkt is a favourite lunchtime feasting spot for Münchners. In good weather people sit in the midst of it all, drinking beer under the dense shade of the chestnut trees—or duck off into one of the many surrounding Gastätte (*see* **Eating and Drinking** below).

East of the market, in Westenrieder Straße, are Munich's quirkiest museums. Seven of them are collected under one roof at **ZAM**, *Das Zentrum für Aussergewöhnliche Museen* (The Centre for Unusual Museums) *(daily 10–6; adm DM8 for the lot)*. The **Corkscrew Museum** and the **Padlock Museum** are cabinet-sized and merit but a quick glance; the others are more intriguing. Two millenia's worth of potties fill the **Chamber Pot Museum**—Roman ones with dumpy handles, Chinese porcelain ones with lids, pompous Royal Doulton and nifty Art Deco ones, humble workers' potties and some that met very grand royal bottoms. The **Bourdalou Museum** features the delicate porcelain containers, shaped rather like gravy boats, that discreetly served the needs of 18th and 19th-century society ladies trapped for long hours in toiletless courts. Children can skip off to the **Easter**

Bunny Museum (thousands of the creatures), but you'll probably want to join them in the **Pedal Car Museum**. Pedal cars hit the streets soon after the first horseless carriages. There are bone-shaking contraptions from the 1880s; flash mini-Bugattis, Buicks and Morgans; Noddy cars, pert little French numbers and solid British bangers. The **Sisi Museum** is not what English speakers might expect, but a shrine to one of Bavaria's heroines, Elizabeth ('Sisi'), the favourite cousin of Ludwig II, who married the Emperor of Austria.

Elizabeth, Empress of Austria ('Sisi')

 Sisi is the nation's most revered tragic royal, a sort of 19th-century Princess Di. She was born in 1837 to Duke Max in Bayern and his wife Ludovika, sister of the Grand Duchess of Austria. She was a plain child (with the looks of a peasant maid, her aunt complained), but made up for it in sweetness, charm and good humour. By the time she was 16, the ugly duckling had grown into a graceful, rather fetching young woman—so much so that when she bumped into her cousin, Emperor Franz Joseph of Austria, one summer evening in the spa resort of Bad Ischl, he fell head over heels in love with her. The emperor was just seven years Sisi's senior. The match seemed ideal, and it wasn't long before an engagement was announced—despite Sisi's private misgivings. (She kept these doubts to herself, though spelled them out in sorrowful poems in the *Versbuchlein* she kept.)

Sisi's caution was justified. Her aunt and mother-in-law, the domineering Grand Duchess Sophie (perhaps the most politically powerful woman in Europe since Maria Theresa) developed an antagonism to the young bride and made her life at court unbearable. Her relationship with her new husband was also not a success. Sisi began to put herself through punishing fasts. Soon the 1.72m-high empress weighed just 50kg and had a waist measurement of 50cm. She developed fevers and coughs, which immediately disappeared once she was away from Vienna, her husband and her mother-in-law. Publicly, though, Sisi was wildly popular. She had blossomed into an exceptionally beautiful woman, was spirited and sympathetic, and spent her time visiting hospitals and old people's homes. When family pressure got too much for her, she would take herself off to Italy or Greece for 'rest cures' lasting months on end, until the emperor arrived to take her back home. But even these long absences didn't alienate her subjects, who continued to adore their nobly suffering empress.

In 1872 Grand Duchess Sophie died (Sisi nursed her through her final illness and was continually at her bedside), but this did not really ease the lot of the hapless empress. In 1886 her cousin, and one of her closest friends, King Ludwig II of Bavaria drowned in mysterious circumstances (*see* p. 337). Then in 1889 her son the Crown Prince Rudolph and his mistress were found dead in an apparent joint suicide. From now on Sisi wore only black, and sank into a deep melancholy. When she was cautiously asked if she didn't feel a sense of rebellion against her fate, she replied coolly '*Nein, ich bin von Stein*' ('No, I'm made of stone'). On 10 September 1898 while, heavily veiled, she was taking an evening walk, she was fatally stabbed by an Italian anarchist who had, in fact, mistaken her for someone else.

Today, like her cousin Ludwig, Sisi has a cult following (especially among Germany's gay community). The museum of her memorabilia in Munich has a shrine-like atmosphere, cafés have been named in her honour and a recent TV series on her life broke viewing records.

Westenrieder Straße leads up to the **Isartor**, one of the three remaining medieval town gates. Here, in one of the towers, is an even odder collection, the **Karl Valentin Museum** *(Mon, Tues, Fri and Sat 11.01–17.29, Sun 10.01–17.29; adm 299 pfennigs, children and fools [sic] 149 pfennigs)*. Karl Valentin (1882–1948) was the German Charles Chaplin and still has a cult following. His spindly statue in the Victualenmarkt always has fresh flowers in its hand and little offerings about its feet. Brecht and Hermann Hesse were fans, but Valentin's humour can leave foreigners a little perplexed. His most famous joke is: 'Why does St Peter's have eight clocks?' 'So that eight people can tell the time at once.' The tower is chock-a-block with memorabilia, cartoons and jokey exhibits such as a melted snowman and a nest of unlaid eggs, but the labels are all in German. Right at the top is the cosiest café in town *(see* below).

If you wander back through the Victualenmarkt and out off its western side you'll come to the more conventional **Stadtmuseum** in St Jakobs-Platz *(Tues–Sun 10–5, Wed until 8.30pm; adm DM5)*, housed in a late-Gothic arsenal. The heart of the museum is an excellent local history collection, where you can see Erasmus Grasser's vibrant *Moriskentänzers* (Morris Dancers, 1485) carved for the ballroom of the Altes Rathaus. The turn of an ankle, a fold of cloth and the angle of the hands gives the wooden figures uncanny life and grace. These statues alone make a visit worthwhile, but the Stadtmuseum has a brood of other collections under its wing. The **Museum of Musical Instruments** is of world renown, though unimaginatively presented. (Look out, though, for periodic concerts, when you can hear the instruments in use.) The **Puppet Museum** has around 25,000 exhibits from all over the world, ranging from life-sized marionettes to quaint creatures cobbled together out off junk (though, again, rather statically presented). As well as the expected shelves of historical equipment, the **Photography Museum** has some interesting old pictures of Munich. Ludwigomanes can delight in some rarely seen photographs of the eccentric king. Film buffs should keep an eye open for the daily-changing programme of rare movies. The temporary exhibitions are usually superb and, appropriately for Munich, there is also a **Brewery Museum**.

Beyond the Stadtmuseum is Sendlingerstraße, which leads up to **Sendlinger Tor**, another of the medieval town gates. Halfway along the street is the florid Rococo **Asamkirche** (1746), designed by the brothers Cosmas and Egid Quirin Asam *(see* p. 60), and considered a highpoint of their long partnership.

The third medieval gate, **Karlstor**, is to the north on Karlsplatz, a vast but seedy square where shifty adolescents hang out around a modern fountain. Locals call Karlsplatz 'Stachus' (supposedly for one Eustachius Föderl who had a beer garden here long ago)— and nowadays even underground train-drivers say *Stachus* when they announce the stop.

Munich's busiest shopping precinct connects Karlsplatz and Marienplatz. In the midst of the pedestrian hubbub the **Liebfrauendom** (or 'Frauenkirche') points two knobby towers skywards. The two steeples date from 1525. Their tops look rather like beer mug lids, and have become something of a city symbol. The church itself is a huge, but disappointingly plain, Gothic hall, built between 1468 and 1494. It contains the oldest Wittelsbach vault, and a mysterious black footprint (reputedly that of the Devil) burned into the marble floor. The more interesting Wittelsbachs (including 'mad' King Ludwig II) are buried in **St Michael's** church, a little further along on Neuhauser Straße. The church was built between 1583 and 1597 for Duke Wilhelm V (he of the *Glockenspiel*). In a niche on the strong Renaissance façade, the Archangel Michael delivers the finishing blow to the forces of Evil (a satyr). The capacious interior is primly dressed with white stucco and covered by a barrel vault second in size only to St Peter's in Rome. Nearby is the **Bürgersaal**, an 18th-century oratory. The church itself is upstairs; at ground level there is a dimly lit hall where you'll invariably find a handful of people lighting candles at the grave of Father Rupert Mayer. This popular priest was packed off to a concentration camp for his brave resistance to the Nazis, but his congregation created such an uproar that he was later released and kept under house arrest at Kloster Ettal (*see* p. 374). He survived to preach a few more times at the Bürgersaal, but died in 1945.

The Northern Altstadt and the Residenz

In the 19th century, three successive Wittelsbach rulers turned the patch north of Marienplatz into one of the most sustainedly elegant suites of squares and boulevards of any city in the world. It all began at the turn of the century, when King Max I Joseph laid out Max-Josef-Platz and built the Opera House, raising the enormous sums required by imposing a local beer tax. His son, King Ludwig I, returned from a seven-month tour of Italy and Greece so struck with classical architecture that he declared he would not rest 'until Munich looked like Athens' (a more comprehensible ambition in the 19th century than it would be today). By the time he died, he had done so much to achieve his aim that his son, King Max II, cautiously wondered: 'Do you think I am allowed to build something different?' Max was not plagued by self-doubt for long, but hatched the graceful 'Maximilian style', and in 1851 built **Maximilianstraße**, now Munich's grandest shopping boulevard.

Maximilianstraße sweeps away to the east of Max-Josef-Platz, over the Isar and up the opposite bank to the **Maximilianeum**—a striking pile of pale, glimmering stone and home to the Bavarian State Parliament. From a perch on the roof, an archangel loftily surveys the *crème de la crème* of Munich society gliding in and out of the classic boutiques and exclusive cafés. The *Vier Jahrzeiten*, one of the world's most prestigious hotels, stands in their midst with quiet composure.

Max-Josef-Platz itself is boxed in by the Doric colonnade of the Hauptpost (originally a 19th-century family palace), the imposing classical façade of the Opera House and the mighty **Residenz**—once the Wittelsbach family home, but now a splendid museum *(Tues–Sun 10–4.30; adm DM4)*. The palace is so large that guided tours manage only half of it at a time (you come back later in the day for the other part). Even if you wander about in your own time, you would be advised to set aside at least half a day for the visit, and to invest in the *Residenz Guidebook*, an exhaustive room-by-room guide available from the ticket office. (Note that you'll need to buy further tickets for admission to other museums in the complex.)

When the Swedes conquered Munich during the Thirty Years' War, King Gustav Adolf looked over the Residenz and sighed, 'If only it had wheels!.' Luckily for Münchners, he could not take it back to Sweden with him, and left it pretty much intact. Today, the Residenz is considered one of the finest Renaissance palaces in Europe, though the buildings that cluster around the seven inner courts in fact date from the 16th to the 19th centuries, and are a jumble of Renaissance, Rococo and Neoclassical styles. After Second World War bomb damage, the complex had to be almost entirely rebuilt—but most of the sumptuous furniture was saved and is on display.

The oldest part of the palace is the **Antiquarium**, a cavernous barrel-vaulted hall, wildly decorated with views of Bavaria, grotesques and grumpy putti. It was built in 1571 (though the décor came a decade or so later) to house the Wittelsbachs' collection of antiquities. The Antiquarium leads off the **Grotto Court**, one side of which is a playful cavern of volcanic rock inset with mussel shells and colourful chunks of crystal. Duke Wilhelm V had the grotto built in 1586 as a 'secret pleasure garden'. Other highlights on the ground floor include the **Nibelungen Halls** (just to the left of the main entrance) decorated for Ludwig I between 1827 and 1867 with glossy paintings of the Nibelung legends; the **Ancestral Gallery** (along the northern side of Königsbauhof), a rich Rococo corridor lined with (often imaginary) portraits of past Wittelsbachs; and a 17th-century **Court Chapel**. The rooms around the Grotto Court house a dazzling collection of **porcelain**.

Most spectacular of all are the aptly named **Rich Rooms** on the upper floor—Rococo extravaganzas designed by François Cuvilliés (*see* below). They lead through to Duke Maximilian I's tiny **Secret Chapel** (*c.* 1615), an outrageous nook of marble and lapus lazuli, flecked with gold tendrils and coloured stone. In an adjoining room you can see the duke's impressive collection of reliquaries, including those containing the heads of John the Baptist and his mother.

You need another ticket for the **Schatzkammer** *(same times; adm DM4)*. Here you can see the Bavarian crown jewels, other crowns dating back to the year 1000 and a striking collection of jewellery and precious objects—golden stags with coral antlers, carved rhino-horn drinking vessels and beautifully inlaid boxes. Look out especially for Duke Wilhelm V's private altar (1580), carved from ebony, and laden with gold, enamel, precious stones and pearls; and the breathtaking Statuette of St George (1590). St George sits astride an agate stallion (draped with rubies and diamonds) and slays an emerald dragon with a crystal sword. If you could lift up his jewel-encrusted visor, you would see a tiny painted face.

Yet another ticket is needed for the **Altes Residenztheater** (or Cuvilliés-Theater), entrance off the Brunnenhof *(Mon–Sat 2–5, Sun 10–5; adm DM2.50)*, a Rococo triumph by the erstwhile court jester, François Cuvilliés. Elector Max Emanuel spotted the Belgian dwarf's talent as a designer soon after he arrived at court, and sent him off to Paris to study. Cuvilliés returned to give Rococo flair and flourish to buildings all over Germany. In 1943 all the boxwood panels of the plush, gilded interior were dismantled and safely stored.

Later, after Allied bombs had burnt out the old building, a modern **Neues Residenztheater** was built within the walls; the old interior was reconstructed on the present site.

François Cuvilliés

 When Elector Max III Joseph of Bavaria (1745–77) decided to build a new palace theatre in 1750, he chose as an architect the deputy head of his Office of Works, François Cuvilliés. Cuvilliés was born in Hainault in Belgium in 1695, and had joined the Elector's grandfather's court as a dwarf jester at the age of 11. Later, *le nain Cuvilliér*, became a cadet and made such a mark that, despite his small stature, he was promoted to the Elector's own regiment in 1717. Here he proved especially clever at mathematics and the theory of fortification—so much so that the emperor personally paid for him to be sent to study court architecture at the Académie Royale in Paris (though Cuvilliés himself would have preferred to be drafted to the Hungarian front).

When he arrived back in Germany in 1726, design commissions flowed in thick and fast, including one to decorate the interior of the palace at Brühl (1728, for Prince Bishop Clemens August, brother of the Elector of Bavaria, *see* p. 142), and for the Amelienburg in Munich's Nymphenburg Park (1734, *see* p. 357). Cuvilliés, now approaching middle age, was at the forefront of a golden age of Rococo which was just begining in Bavaria. When Max III Joseph approached him to build the new Residenztheater he was at the zenith of his career, and produced what is still one of the most splendid interiors to be seen in Munich.

The Residenz also accommodates the **Staatliche Münzsammlung** (State Coin Collection) *(Tues–Sun 10–4.30; adm DM2.50)*, the largest and oldest of its kind in Germany. To the north of the palace is a stiffly formal **Hofgarten**, once the royal park.

The Hofgarten opens out onto **Ludwigstraße**. At the beginning of the 19th century this was a vegetable garden. King Ludwig I flattened it with a broad, grand avenue that runs in a dead straight line from Odeonplatz to the solid eminence of the **Siegestor**, a triumphal arch built in 1850 to honour all Bavarian armies. Odeonplatz is dominated by the **Feldherrnhalle** (1841) an insufferably pompous monument to Generals Tilly and von Wrede (of the Thirty Years' and Napoleonic Wars respectively). It was here that 14 Nazis were shot dead during Hitler's unsuccessful 1923 putsch. The gay yellow Rococo façade and twirly-topped towers of the **Theatinerkirche** (designed by Cuvilliés in 1768) brightens the mood of the square, but the rest of Ludwigstraße is very much four-square and solid. Suitably, the stately buildings that line the street house such august institutions as the state Archives and library, the government offices and the university.

Beyond the Siegestor the mood changes completely. Tall trees line the street, cafés spill out onto the pavement, and knots of students and *Schickies* chatter under the bright umbrellas, or wander in and out of the trendy shops and galleries. This is **Schwabing**, no longer the shocking hotbed of Bolsheviks and bohemians it was at the turn of the century, but still vibrant and fun to explore. It is one of the most fruitful areas in town for cafés, restaurants, fringe theatres and night life (*see* listings below). The central axis is Leopoldstraße. Here you'll find the glitzier cafés. The student bars, quirky shops and cheaper restaurants are mainly to the west of Leopoldstraße. Hopeful young artists ply their wares, and snack bars double as galleries. The east of Leopoldstraße, towards Wedekindplatz and Münchener Freiheit, is more the province of black clothes, sharp haircuts and pounding discotheques.

In its heyday Schwabing was a honeypot to artists, writers and thinkers from all over Germany. From collaboration around a *Stammtisch* in the Alte Simpl café came *Simplicissimus*, the leading satirical magazine of the time. Another local publication, *Jugend* (Youth), gave its name to Jugendstil, the German equivalent of Art Nouveau. The novelist Thomas Mann, the poet Rainer Maria Rilke and the painter Lovis Corinth, as well as countless other lesser-known artists, all lived and worked here. Even Lenin put in a brief appearance (calling himself Meyer) between 1900 and 1902. (There was later a Bolshevik revolution in Munich, in 1918, and for a few months Bavaria was declared a republic.)

Many of the artists became famous and moved to grander parts of town. Hopefuls, would-bes and property speculators moved in. Nowadays Schwabing is fashionable but expensive, and has lost its edge. The truly trendy are to be found in Haidhausen (*see* **Cafés** below).

The Museum Quarter

Munich has more museums than any other city in Germany, and the quality of the collections puts even Berlin in the shade. The credit (or blame) for this lies with the pillaging Wittelsbachs. All around Bavaria and the Palatinate (which was ruled by a branch of the family), museum directors will sulkily reel off lists of treasures that went south to Munich.

Most of the important museums are clustered north of the Altstadt. The Alte Pinakothek (14th–18th-century masterpieces), the Neue Pinakothek (18th and 19th-century), the Glypothek (Classical sculpture), the Staatliche Antikensammlungen (Greek, Roman and Etruscan art) and the Lenbachhaus (Munich painters from Gothic to contemporary) are distinguished neighbours in the area west of Ludwigstraße. East of the boulevard, along Prinzregentstraße, are the Haus der Kunst (20th century art), the Bayerisches National Museum (Wittelsbach booty from the Middle Ages onwards), the Schack Galerie (19th-century painting) and the Villa Stuck (Jugendstil). There is enough to keep you here for days. All state museums are free on Sundays and public holidays; otherwise a *Verbunden-eintrittskarte* (joint entrance ticket) makes a good investment at DM20.

The **Alte Pinakothek** *(Tues–Sun 9.15–4.30; adm DM7)* ranks easily among the world's top art collections. An incomparable array of early German Masters will give you the clearest art history lesson on the period you're ever likely to get; the few Italian paintings are pearls; and there is more Rubens than you can find in one spot anywhere else. Yet, despite its eminence, this is a quirky collection, reflecting the tastes and foibles of the Wittelsbachs who put it together over a period of nearly 400 years. Elector Maximilian I (1597–1651) had a penchant for Dürer, and tracked down pieces all over the country. His court artists could imitate the master impeccably, and 'corrected' smaller paintings to a size deemed more appropriate for the vast Residenz walls. Elector Max Emanuel, who was

Governor of the Spanish Netherlands from 1692 to 1701, is responsible for acquiring many of the Flemish works. It took Brussels dealers, and the Bavarian treasury, some time to recover from one spending spree, in which Max Emanuel allegedly got through 200,000 francs in half an hour. A century later, King Ludwig I brought crates of paintings back from his Italian journey. He also spent a fortune on contemporary art.

The Early German collection is in the left wing on the lower floor, and overflows into a few rooms upstairs. The lower right wing is taken up by paintings (from all countries) between the Renaissance and Baroque. Upstairs, working from left to right (after the Early German and Early Netherlandish rooms) you will find Italian, Flemish and Dutch works, and finally painting from France and Spain. Confusingly, room numbering begins afresh upstairs, and is done in a mixture of Roman and Arabic numerals.

Highlights on the ground floor left wing include *The Golden Age* (1530, Room IIa) by Lucas Cranach the Elder. Cranach, one of the first German artists to dare to paint naked figures, fills an Eden-like garden with frolicking nudes. Look out also for Bernhard Strigel's warmly realistic *Guard with a Crossbow* (1521, Room IIb) and Wolf Huber's dramatically charged *Christ Taken Prisoner* (1530) hanging nearby. Jesus is set upon by a relentlessly ugly mob (one of whom seems intent on reporting on what he can see up the Saviour's robe). This dramatic realism was the result of the influence of Netherlandish painters, and is used with powerful effect in the vividly coloured *Kaisheim Altar* (1502) by Holbein the Elder and *Crucifixion* (1450) by the Master of the Benediktbeueren Crucifixion, both in Room III.

The line between Flemish and German painting is sometimes hard to draw. One of the leading artists of the Late-Gothic Cologne School, Bartholomew Bruyn, was, in fact, Flemish. You can see Bruyn's work, and more fine Cologne School painting (such as *St Veronica* (1420) by the Master of St Veronica) in Cabinets 1–3. But to see the best work from the Cologne School (by Stefan Lochner, and the Masters of the Bartholomew Altarpiece and of the Life of the Virgin) you should go to Room III upstairs. South German painters were more under the influence of the Italians—as you can see from the harsh light and clear shadows of Michael Pacher's altarpiece hanging in the same room.

Albrecht Dürer was the first European artist to paint self-portraits. In Room II upstairs you can see his Christ-like *Self-Portrait with Fur-Trimmed Robe* (1500), which he inscribes with delightful self-assurance: 'Thus I, Albrecht Dürer of Nuremberg, painted myself in imperishable colours at the age of 28.' Room II is a treasure trove, with many of Dürer's finest works such as *The Four Apostles* (1526) and also superb paintings by his contemporaries. Look out for Hans Burgkmair's exotic *Altarpiece of St John the Evangelist* (1518), populated by monkeys and colourful birds; Albrecht Altdorfer's seething *Battle of Issus* (1529); and Matthias Grünewald's intricately worked *Saints Erasmus and Maurice* (1520).

A wander through the Italian rooms takes you past choice paintings by Botticelli, Fra Filippo Lippi and Raphael, including his tender *Tempi Madonna* (1507), which King Ludwig I battled for 20 years to own. You can see Leonardo's earliest known painting—the *Madonna with a Carnation* (1473)—and superlative works by Titian and Tintoretto.

The vast Rubens collection fills the rooms at the heart of the upper floor. The 65 pieces on display range from hasty *modellos*, run off for his workshop, to enormous canvases of the Last Judgement (Room VII). Look out especially for *Drunken Silenus* (1616, Room VII), where a flabby old Silenus (Bacchus's tutor) stumbles about in bleary intoxication, and is mocked by his retinue and goosed by a Moor. The Flemish and Dutch collections continue with paintings by Van Dyck, Rembrandt and the much-neglected Jan Steen.

After a glimpse of some frothy French painting by François Boucher and Nicolas Lancret (Room XII), and the darker moods of El Greco and Murillo (Room XIII), you can pop back downstairs to see Pieter Breughel's witty *Land of Cockaigne* (1566). Three fat men lie sprawled on the ground in this Promised Land of Gluttons (they would have had to chomp their way through a mountain of buckwheat porridge to get there), while around them are fences made of sausages, pigs that come equipped with a carving knife, and ready-capped eggs that run about on little legs waiting to be eaten. Nearby is Jan Breughel the Elder's densely populated *Harbour Scene* (1598).

Across the way from the museum is the shiny modern **Neue Pinakothek** *(same times and price, or DM7 for both)*, lean fare after the banquet of the Alte Pinakothek, but still worth a visit. The collection begins with artists (such as David, Gainsborough, Goya and Turner) who broke with Baroque traditions and set the style for 19th-century painting, but it is the Germans who get the strongest look-in. Keep an eye open for Arnold Böcklin's dreamy *Pan in the Reeds* (1859), Anselm Feuerbach's statuesque *Medea* (1870), the murky, mysterious paintings of Hans von Marées and the huge translucent Greek and Italian landscapes produced by Ludwig I's court artists. There is a respectable range of French work, including Manet's *Breakfast in the Studio* (1868) and Degas' *Woman Ironing* (1869)—a change from the usual ballet dancers. You can also see a version of Van Gogh's *Sunflowers* and familiar works by Gaugin, Egon Schiele and Gustav Klimt.

Nearby, the **Glypothek** *(Tues, Wed, Fri–Sun 10–4.30, Thur noon–8.30pm; adm DM3.50)* and **Staatliche Antikensammlungen** *(Tues and Thur–Sun 10–4.30, Wed noon–8.30; adm DM3.50; joint ticket for both museums DM6)* occupy two daunting Neoclassical piles on either side of an otherwise barren Königsplatz. King Ludwig I commissioned the buildings to house his collection of antiquities. The Glypothek is the more interesting of the two, with an entire pediment plundered from the Aphaia Temple in Aegina, the outrageously erotic *Barberini Faun* and fine statues from the Hellenistic period. The chief attraction of the Antikensammlungen is the glittering array of Greek and Etruscan gold jewellery.

Directly across Luisenstraße is the **Lenbachhaus** *(Tues–Sun 10–6, Thurs to 8pm; adm DM5)*, the elegant, Italianate villa of the highly paid 'painter prince', Franz von Lenbach (1836–1904). Many of the rooms keep their original fittings and furnishing, but most of the villa is now the Municipal Museum. The main reason for a visit is the extensive collection of paintings by Kandinsky and fellow members of the *Blaue Reiter*, such as Klee, Marc and Macke (*see* p. 64). Ironically, the conventional, established von Lenbach was the group's greatest foe. Most of the works on show here were part of a secret hoard stashed away for years by Gabriele Münter, Kandinsky's jilted mistress. The Russian-born Kandinsky had to leave Munich at the outbreak of the First World War, and left everything he owned in her charge. While he was away he met and married someone else. Years later Gabriele gave him back his furniture, but held onto all the artworks he had left behind. Well into her eighties, she handed the lost collection over to an astonished city council, who, in the search for somewhere large enough to display all the works, came up with the Lenbach villa. The museum often also holds good exhibitions of contemporary German work.

Over on Prinzregentstraße you'll find the **Haus der Kunst**, a nasty 1930s building that still has swastikas carved into the stone above the doorways. The State Gallery of Modern Art, usually housed in the west wing, is indefinitely closed for renovation. In the meantime, parts of the superb collection of 20th-century art pop up as temporary exhibitions in other museums around town.

The **Bayerisches Nationalmuseum** *(Tues–Sun 9.30–5; adm DM3)* is almost next door. The core of the sprawling museum is once again a Wittelsbach collection—this time of art and artefacts from all around Europe. Highlights are sculptures by Tilman Riemenschneider *(see* p. 55) and a collection of nativity scenes dating from the 17th to 19th centuries. Another division of the museum contains folk art. Another has applied art, with especially good displays of porcelain and clocks.

A little further down the street is the **Schack-Galerie** *(daily except Tues 9.15–4.40; adm DM2.50)*, a cosy little museum very much worth a visit for its excellent collection of works by 19th-century artists Anselm Feuerbach, Arnold Böcklin, Franz von Lenbach and Moritz von Schwind—painters often unfairly ignored outside of Germany.

Just over the river, past the glittering **Angel of Peace** high on her stone column, and across Europaplatz is one of Munich's gems, the **Villa Stuck**, Prinzregentstr. 60 *(Tues–Sun 10–5, Thurs to 9pm; adm DM2)*, home and studio of the painter Franz von Stuck (1863–1928). Perhaps his greatest gift was for interior design, and the villa is a monument to Jugendstil, with patterned parquet floors, richly painted walls and stylish furniture.

The Englischer Garten and the Isar

The **Englischer Garten** is an enormous park stretching for over 5km along the Isar, north of Prinzregentstraße. Icy brooks criss-cross its broad meadows, and skip along through thick forests and past cultivated lawns. At times all you can hear is birdsong and splashing water—and you can't see the city at all. It is easy, indeed pleasant, to get lost. People stroll about, play ball games and sunbathe (completely naked in the grass around the Eisbach), but the Garten is most famous for its large, shady **beer gardens** *(see* below).

The idea for the park came in the late 18th century from an American, Benjamin Thompson, inventor of the cast-iron stove and later made Count Rumford by a grateful Elector Karl-Theodor, who was entranced with the garden. Near the south entrance there is a **Japanese Teahouse** built in 1972 *(traditional tea ceremonies second and fourth weekends of the month, Sat and Sun 3pm, 4pm and 5pm)*. Further into the park you'll find the **Monopterus** (a 19th-century temple with a fine view back over the city) and the **Chinesischer Turm**, a fragile pagoda in the middle of the most popular beer garden.

South of the Englischer Garten, you can follow the Isar past rows of grand 19th-century buildings and some very elegant old bridges. In summer the sandy banks are spread with more sunbathers, and between Wolfrathausen and Thalkirchen enormous log rafts float gently downstream, laden with revellers, beer barrels and sometimes even small bands and portaloos. On Museumsinsel, just past the Ludwigsbrücke is the **Deutsches Museum** *(daily 9–5; adm DM8)*, a gigantic museum of science and technology (you would have to walk over 16km to take in everything).

You can see a model of a bow drill from the fourth millenium BC and a space capsule; the first German submarine, the original Puffing Billy and a Wright Brothers aeroplane. You can go down a coal mine or sit under the stars in the Zeiss Planetarium. There are sections on metallurgy, hydraulic engineering, carriages and bicycles, telecommunications, new energy techniques, physics and photography—and that's just for starters. The Aeronautics and Space Travel exhibitions are the most interesting, but even Power Machinery can come up with intriguing surprises. You can clamber in and out of many of the exhibits, and even operate a few. Children love it. The museum shop is a treasure trove of models, toys for boffins and splendidly illustrated books—and they also sell a very necessary floor guide.

Nymphenburg

When, after ten years of hoping, the Electress Henriette Adelaide finally gave birth to a son in 1662, her husband celebrated by building her a small palace 5km to the west of the city. She called the Italianate villa *Castello delle Ninfe*. Later generations of Wittelsbachs added a succession of symmetrical wings, and as **Schloß Nymphenburg** *(Tues–Sun 9–12.30 and 1.30–5; adm DM2.50 for Schloß, DM6 including pavilions and Amelienburg; Tram 12, Bus 41)* it became their favourite summer residence.

This stately palace is set in acres of Versailles-style park. Inside, the rooms are suitably lavish—mainly Rococo and High Baroque. In the notorious *Schönheitengalerie* (Gallery of Beauties) there are 36 portraits of women who took King Ludwig I's fancy between 1827 and 1850, including one of his scandalous mistress, Lola Montez. (The king cherished his favourites, chatted to them during the sittings, and even selected husbands for a few.) The palace also contains a collection of Nymphenburg porcelain (the famous factory moved here in 1761) and a coach museum. The outrageously ornamented sleighs and carriages created for King Ludwig II are not to be missed.

The interiors of the **Amelienburg** (a hunting lodge behind the south wing of the palace, designed by Cuvilliés) surpass anything in the main building. Cuvilliés gives the dinky lodge the sumptuousness and splendour of a grand palace, but with a refined lightness of touch. He even manages a diminutive Hall of Mirrors without violating the boundaries of good taste.

As you wander about the park, keep an eye open for the **pavilions**: the **Magdalenen-klause** (1728), a 'ruined' hermitage retreat with a grotto; the **Pagodenburg** (1719), a chinoiserie party house; and the **Badenburg** (1721), a Baroque bathing house where the pool has handy underwater benches.

Munich's Other Museums

This is one city where you will never be at a loss for something to do on a rainy day. Here is but a selection of some of the other museums you can find around town.

Staatliche Sammlung Ägyptische Kunst, Hofgartenstr. 1 *(Tues–Sun 9–4; adm DM2.50)*. Mummies, Coptic robes and artworks from the Wittelsbachs' Egyptian phase.

Staatliche Graphische Sammlung, Meiserstr. 10, © (089) 55 91 490 *(Mon–Wed 10–1 and 2–6.30, Thurs to 6pm, Fri 10–12.30; adm free)*. An enormous selection of drawings, woodcuts and etchings—not all are on display, but may be viewed in the Study Hall by prior arrangement. Particular strengths are the collections of 15th-century German woodcuts and graphics by German Expressionists.

Deutsches Jagdmuseum, Neuhauserstr. 53 *(daily 9.30–5; adm DM4)*. Equipment, clothes and end-products of huntin', shootin' and fishin'. This is the place to come to see the world's largest collection of fish-hooks.

Museum für Vor- und Frühgeschichte, Lerchenfeldstr. 2 *(Tues–Sun 9–4; adm DM2.50)*. Bits and bobs from Bavarian households from prehistoric times to the early Middle Ages.

Staatliches Museum für Völkerkunde, Maximilianstr. 42 *(Tues–Sun 9.30–4.30; adm DM5)*. Well-stocked ethnological museum with good Asian and Oriental collections.

Siemens Museum, Prannerstr. 10 *(Mon–Fri 9–4, Sat and Sun 10–2; adm free)*. Hi-tech, hands-on electronics museum.

BMW Museum, Peteulring 130 *(daily 9–5; DM4.50)*. Massive public relations job for the car company. Flash modern exhibits rather than vintage oddities.

Spielzeugmuseum, Alte Rathaus *(daily 10–5.30; adm DM4, children DM1, family card DM8)*. A towerful of cases crammed with toys from carved Futurist figures to Barbie dolls.

Shopping

Along Maximilianstraße even the shops have crystal chandeliers. Here you'll find the Chanels, Cartiers and Cardins. Further into Schwabing, the rents are lower and the fashion shops trendier. Happy consumer-culture department-store shopping goes on in the pedestrian walkways of Neuhauserstraße and Kaufingerstraße, and along Sendlingerstraße. Just behind the Rathaus, in Dienerstraße, is a 300-year-old delicatessen, Dallmayr's, which still supplies the Wittelsbachs with teas and coffees from its wooden chests, sticky sausages from its racks and lobster and caviar from beneath its gushing fountain. For even headier tastes and aromas try the Victualenmarkt (*see* p. 347.). At Loden-Fry in Maffeistraße, you can buy Bavarian hats and *Lodentracht*, the hardy green Alpine wear lately favoured by British Foreign Secretary Douglas Hurd. Nearby, in the Wallach-Haus, it can cost up to DM700 for a hand-made dirndl, though you could run up your own from hand-printed textiles at around DM80 a metre. The humbler Hans-Sachs-Straße (south of the centre, near Sendlinger Tor) is a quaint street of ethnic stores, secondhand shops, galleries and quirky clothes shops, and in Schellingstraße there are *two* English bookshops (Anglia's at No. 3 and Words Worth's at No. 21a).

Activities

Jogging, walking and cycling in the Englischer Garten is a favourite Munich activity. You could also join the locals for a swim in one of the lakes or rivers in the park (they are quite clean enough). In colder weather try the **Volksbad** *(variable opening times)*, a graceful turn-of-the-century indoor swimming pool just across the Ludwigsbrücke.

To the northwest of Schwabing, just off the Georg-Brauchle-Ring (U-Bahn Line 3 or 8, S-Bahn Line 8) is the **Olympiapark**, a vast complex of sports facilities created for the 1972 Olympic Games including an enormous swimming pool, an ice rink and a cycle track. The buildings are set in landscaped parkland beside an artificial lake and are also used for concerts and festivals in the summer.

Where to Stay

expensive

Hotel Vier Jahreszeiten Kempinski, Maximilianstr. 17, © 23 03 90, fax 23 03 96 93 (DM548–628). From its classic wood-panelled lobby to the glass-walled, roof-top swimming-pool, this is the Grand Duchess of the world's top hotels. An exalted guest list (the Windsors and Gorbachevs have been here before you), palatial period suites, smart modern rooms and award-winning restaurants come together with a genuine warmth of atmosphere and discreet, impeccable attention to your every need. This is the one hotel in Germany to splash out on, even if your budget doesn't usually stretch so far.

Hotel Insel-Mühle, Von-Kahr-Str. 87, © 8 10 10, fax 8 12 05 71 (DM250–380). A converted 16th-century mill on a gushing stream in a leafy spot just beyond Schloß Nymphenburg. Run with love and flair. The rooms are cosy, and most look out over a small park.

Queens Hotel, Effnerstr. 99, © 92 79 80, fax 98 38 13 (DM310–345). Glitzy modern hotel, peacefully detached from the throb of the city, but only 10 minutes away by car. Business visitors will find swift service and hi-tech back-up. The 'Bavarian Suites' are decked out in country-cottage nouveau, with pine four-posters and repro tiled stoves.

moderate

Hotel Olympic, Hans-Sachs-Str. 4, © 23 18 90, fax 231 89199 (DM165–240). Centrally located in a trendy street just to the south of the Altstadt. It hugs a pretty little garden courtyard—and most rooms get a peek. The proud new owners give it a friendly, personal touch.

Hotel Am Markt, Heiliggeiststr. 6, ✆ 22 50 14 (DM120–140). Tucked away in an alley beside the Victualenmarkt. The owner has plastered the walls with photographs of his favourite opera singers, and runs his establishment with appropriate verve. The rooms are comfortable, but not diva-sized.

Hotel Dollmann, Thierschstr. 49, ✆ 23 80 80, fax 23 80 83 65 (DM165–225). A sober 19th-century patrician mansion with pastel colours, soft lighting and hushed guests. Situated near the Isar, in a peaceful street just off Maximilianstraße.

Hotel Lettl, Amalienstr. 53, ✆ 28 30 26, fax 2 80 53 18 (DM165–210). A touch 1970s, this hotel occupies a quiet court in the heart of Schwabing. Rather grumpily managed.

Hotel Nymphenburg, Nymphenburgerstr. 141, ✆ 18 10 86, fax 18 25 40 (DM180). Well-appointed rooms and a pocket-sized garden. Away from the Alstadt bustle, on the road to Schloß Nymphenburg.

Gästehaus Englischer Garten, Liebergesellstr. 8, ✆ 39 20 34 (DM152–172). Idyllic, creeper-covered *Pension* on the edge of the Englischer Garten. Avoid the Annexe, though, where the rooms are quite spartan.

Hotel Galleria, Plinganserstr. 142, ✆ 723 3001, fax 724 1564 (DM170–240). An elegant Jugendstil villa, with spacious rooms, 10 minutes south of the centre (S-Bahn, Line 7 to Mittersendling).

inexpensive

Pension Am Kaiserplatz, Kaiserplatz 12, ✆ 34 91 90 (DM67–75). Good value pension run by a sweet old lady with a very individual flair in interior design.

Pension Frank, Schellingstr. 24, ✆ 28 14 51 (DM80–90 without private bath). A haven for cheery backpackers in the heart of Schwabing. Big rooms and a helpful management.

Pension Carolin, Kaulbachstr. 42, ✆ 34 57 57 (DM110–118). Friendly, well-run *pension* just behind the university.

Pension Steinberg, Ohmstr. 9, ✆ 33 10 11 (DM98–125). Bright Schwabing *pension* with a well-founded reputation for its slap-up breakfast.

Youth Hostels: DJH München, Wendl-Dietrich-Str. 80, ✆ 13 11 56 (DM19) (age limit 27); Jugendgästehaus München, Miesingstr 4, ✆ 723 6550 (DM24) (age limit 27); Haus International, Elisabethstr. 87, ✆ 12 00 60 (DM40) (no age limit).

Eating and Drinking: Restaurants and Taverns

expensive

Aubergine, Maximilianplatz 5, ✆ 59 81 71 (DM 150–200). Perennially Munich's top restaurant. Lavender, rather than aubergine, décor, an intimate atmosphere and top-class cooking by gourmet chef Eckhart Witzigmann.

Grüne Gans, Am Einlaß 5, ✆ 26 62 68 (DM100). Private dinner party atmosphere in tiny restaurant, personally supervised by cooks Julius and Inge Stollberg. Delicious classic cuisine, without fuss or pretension.

Kay's Bistro, Utzschneiderstr. 1, ✆ 2 60 35 84 (over DM100). Above your head minute fairylights glitter between drapes of muslin. Around you are bits of Neoclassical paraphernalia, nobs, snobs and wealthy tourists. Rich sauces abound, and you get the impression that this restaurant rides a little on its reputation of being one of the city's chicest.

moderate

Deutsche Eiche, Reichenbachstr. 13 (central). A cosy old-fashioned Gastätte that was Fassbinder's local. It attracts an arty crowd, and the matronly owner cooks splendid, simple meals—occasionally surprising customers with duck or curry.

Halali, Schönfeldstr. 22, ✆ 28 59 09 (central). A rarity: rustic Bavarian décor that isn't kitsch, and a chef that experiments with local cuisine and comes up with wonders. Wild boar, venison and strange local mushrooms abound.

Weichandhof, Betzenweg 81, ✆ 811 1621 (Obermenzing, S-Bahn Line 2). Folksy ambiance, riverside setting and standard Bavarian fare. Get tucked into a hearty *Hirschragout* (venison stew) or *Böfflamott* (from *Boeuf à la Mode*, a Napoleonic boil-up of beef, herbs and wine).

Augustiner-Großgaststätten, Neuhauserstr. 16, ✆ 551 99 257 (central). In the big, domed middle-room, quaintly decorated with seashells and hunting trophies, you can devour mounds of *Weißwurst* (boiled veal sausages) and pretzels. *Weißwurst* is *the* south-Bavarian speciality. They must be fresh (one of the ingredients is brain) and you shouldn't eat the skin.

Gaststätte Leopold, Leopoldstr. 50, ✆ 39 94 33 (Schwabing). Good, old-fashioned Gaststätte with walls browned by decades of tobacco and cooking smoke. Try the *Leberkäs mit Ei*—meatloaf with egg (ordered by the 100g), eaten with pretzels.

Weinhaus Neuner, Herzogspitalstr. 8, ✆ 260 3954 (central). Through the door on the left is a well-stocked wine bar, on the right there is a busy restaurant serving good, tasty food.

Haxnbauer, Münzstr. 8, ✆ 22 19 22 (central). Strictly for carnivores. Enormous grilled knuckles of pork disappear with astonishing rapidity down the throats of even the frailest-looking customers.

Amaranth, Steinstr. 42, ✆ 448 7356 (Haidhausen). Upmarket vegetarian restaurant with adventurous, herby risottos and crêpes.

Osteria Italiana, Schellingstr 62, ✆ 272 0717 (Schwabing). The best of Munich's many Italian restaurants, popular with academics, film people and para-mafiosi.

Shida, Klenzlestr. 32, Haidhausen. Popular Thai restaurant with a mouth-watering menu of spicy soups, delicate curries and fish dishes.

Nürnberger Bratwurst Glöckl am Dom, Frauenplatz 9, ℭ 29 52 64 (central). Home of the grilled *Bratwurst*. You order them in pairs with sweet mustard and bread rolls, and eat them out under the trees beside the Frauenkirche in summer, or in the snug wood-panelled *Stüberl* in winter.

Bratwurstherzl, Heiliggeiststr. 3, ℭ 22 62 119 (central). Quick-stop beer-and-*Brotzeit* pub with mounds of delicious sausages, *Leberkäse* and *Obatze* (a classic snack made with mature camembert, peppers and spices).

Crêperie Normande, Pariserstr. 34, ℭ 48 69 39 (Haidhausen). Crêpes and galettes with flair (try the Roquefort-and-apple compote flambéed with Calvados). Also more conventional fillings.

Anti, Jahnstr. 36 (central). Gaudy décor, bouzouki music, Greek ex-pats and food that takes you right back to that idyllic island holiday.

Primo, Maximilianstr. 30 (central). Stand-up *Imbiß par excellence*, with superb wines, deli-delights and a posh clientele. The **Victualenmarkt**, Blumenstraße 7–11, is the best place of all for a cheap snack. Try a *Wurstsemel* (roll with sliced sausage) or a *Schinkensemml* (with ham) direct from one of the butchers, or steaming soup from the Müchener Suppenküche. Lots of booths sell Bratwurst and Weißwurst, which you can then take along to the beergarden. The *Ausgezogene* (heavy doughnuts, a.k.a. *Schmalznudel*) at Café Frischut, on the market, are reputedly the best in town.

Bars and Cafés

Central

Hofbräuhaus, Platzl 9. Munich's most famous beerhall bursts at the seams with raucously singing Australians, Americans and Germans from the provinces. Everyone sways to the resonant oompah band, and many feel moved to dance. The Hofbräuhaus is the subject of a drinking-song that is almost the Bavarian national anthem, but few locals go anywhere near the place.

Schumann's, Maximilianstr. 36. Perennial favourite of the rich and famous, with suitably arrogant waiters and inflated prices. Keep an eye open for Boris Becker and assorted megastars. *Stammtische* here are holy territory, and will remain empty even when the rest of the bar resembles the U-Bahn at rush hour.

Nachtcafé, Maximiliansplatz 5. Bright, buzzing and open until 6am. Full of bleary disco flotsam, fashion victims and high-fliers who never sleep. There is also good live music, and snacks to appease late-night hunger pangs.

Heiliggeiststuberl, Heiliggeiststraße. A minute, cosy wooden box of a bar, tucked away in a little alley beside the Victualenmarkt.

Jahreszeiten Bar, Maximilianstr. 17. Rich mahogany, enveloping leather chairs and live piano music surround incurable romantics and journalists on expense accounts.

Iwans, Josephspitalstr. 15. Once the vortex of Soviet chic—now just black polo-necks and designer denim minus the hammers and sickles. Rather incongruously, they sell hot Ovalmaltine.

Café Luitpold, Brienner Str. 11. Traditional cakes-and-coffee café. Aunties' favourite.

Café Kreuzkamm, Maffeistr. 4. A defeating array of delicious cream cakes and *haute couture*. There's a flicker of excitement in the atmosphere—as if coffee drinking were still a vice.

Schwabing

Pavement cafés line Leopoldstraße, Wedekindplatz and Müenchner Freiheit, but at weekends Schwabing loses any vestige of its past bohemian atmosphere. BMWs with spoilers and jazzed-up Opels line the streets; their sunbed-bronzed owners fill the bars. Girls in Benetton outfits eye designer labels, dream of becoming filmstars and gossip about school. Old Schwabing does make a gallant attempt to fight back, but most of the real trendies are in Haidhausen on the other side of town.

Alter Simpl, Türkenstr. 57. The pub where the satirical magazine *Simplicissimus* was germinated, where Thomas Mann stood on a chair to read from his novels and Frank Wedekind sang to a lute accompaniment. Children and grandchildren of the original clientele come back to enjoy a living-room atmosphere that has somehow survived the commercialization of the rest of Schwabing.

Café Extrablatt, Leopoldstr. 7. Owned by gossip columnist Michael Graeter, and once *the* café in Schwabing. Nowadays it is populated by glamour goblins and aspiring media stars who haven't done their research properly. (Their hoped-for Svengali, no doubt, being already half-sozzled in the Augustiner-Keller.)

Munich, Leopoldstr. 9. Another wannabe showroom. Lots of cheek-pecking and darting glances.

Café an der Uni, Ludwigstr. 24. Cosier café with agreeable student crowd.

Drugstore, Feilitzschstr. 12. It has never quite forgotten its 1960s heyday, but now this gives it a nostalgic charm for a new wave of young trendies.

Haidhausen and Further Afield

Glimpse through the windows in Haidhausen and you'll see Bavarian kitsch, Turkish textiles and bright new canvases. Immigrants, artists and ageing Munich originals live side by side in one of the liveliest quarters in town. Between the Isar and the Ostbahnhof, in the streets around Wiener Platz and Max-Weber-Platz, and in the 'French Quarter' around Orleansplatz and Rosenheimer Platz, you'll find galleries, good restaurants, bars and cafés galore. A walk of just a few yards down

Wörthstraße is a good example of what the area has to offer. You can have a slap-up breakfast for around DM10 in a trendy café (**Café Voilà** at No. 5), down a beer in a workers' bar (**No. 7**), bop to live music in the **Snoopy Music Club** (No. 9), or visit a **Café Theatre** and winebar (No. 11).

Café Giesing, Bergstr. 5. Owned by a local pop star, who programmes good live music for a young, arty, friendly crowd of drinkers.

Casino, Kellerstr. 21. Solid blue walls throw faultless haircuts and bright Caribbean cocktails into stark relief. Perfect for posing.

Café Größenwahn, Lothringerstr. 11. A party atmosphere prevails. Drunken musicians break into impromtu performances, and crowds of thirty-somethings have a jolly good time.

Café Wiener Platz, Innere Wiener Straße. Nothing special to look at, but it has one of the warmest atmospheres of any café in the district. The crowd is a mixed bag of actors, students and local shopkeepers.

Hofbräukeller, Innere Wiener Str. 19. Thundering beerhall full of big round tables and big round men.

Ballhaus, Klenzestr. 71. Odd chandeliers flicker with electric candles and wistful couples nibble at plates of sushi in a downbeat but carefully trendy café.

Café Stöpsel, Preysingstr. 16. Comfy hideaway for afternoon tea and a good read.

Those who are too up-to-the-minute even for Haidhausen head west to the battered concrete suburb of **Neuhausen**.

Café Freiheit, Leonrodstr. 20. Currently Munich's 'in' café. Crowded, unpretentious and friendly, but subject to poisonous exhaust fumes from the hectic Mittleren Ring.

Ruffini, Orffstr. 22–24. A quieter alternative, famed for its soups and Sunday breakfasts (when you have to arrive early to get a seat).

Beer Gardens

The entire population of Koblenz (all 110,000 of them) could descend on Munich in one swoop, and each find a seat in a beer garden. Müncheners—with a little help from their visitors—get through prodigious quantities of beer annually (five million litres during the Oktoberfest alone). In great beer tents during festivals, out under the trees in the summer, and in noisy halls and cellars the whole year round good burghers, grannies, *Schickies* and punks rub shoulders and down hefty *Maße* (litre mugs) of beer. Clusters of tourists join in, curious as to whether the fat men in feathered hats are for real (they are), and all too often destined to become one of the *Bierleichen* ('beer corpses') that litter the ground at the end of the evening. You can get hearty helpings of Bavarian nosh in most beer gardens (sausages, roast pork and grilled fish are the standard fare), and it is perfectly acceptable to take your own picnic. Kick-off time is around 10am, and the hardy keep going to midnight and beyond. In bad weather you can usually retreat into an adjacent beerhall. What follows is a selection of watering holes to start you off. A little knowledge of local terminology is also useful:

Maß (a.k.a. *Helles*): A litre of conventional beer.

Dunkles: Strong malt beer, popular at festivals.

Weißbier: Beer made from wheat instead of barley, and served with a slice of lemon.

Radler-Maß: A 50/50 lager and lemonade shandy.

Russn-Maß: *Weißbier* shandy.

Isar-Maß: Mixture of *Weißbier*, apple juice and Blue Curaçao. Not for delicate constitutions.

Stammtisch: Table for regular customers.

Central

Franziskaner-Garten, Perusastr. 5. A good place for a beer-and-sausage breakfast, right in the heart of town. There's been an inn on the site for 500 years, and Emperor Franz Joseph had a *Stammtisch* here.

Augustiner-Keller, Arnulfstr. 52. A leafy surprise off a tatty street behind the station, much favoured by staff from *Bayerischen Rundfunk* (the Bavarian TV station). If you sit at one of their *Stammtische* just near the entrance, the waiters will give you short shrift. The house-brewed beer is excellent, and the aroma of *Steckerlfisch* (char-grilled skewered fish) fills the neighbourhood.

Englischer Garten

Chinesischer Turm, southern end of Englischer Garten. Known to locals as the 'China-Turm'. On sunny days you'll find more students here than at the university, and cheery bands of young tourists too. **Aumeister**, Sondermeierstr. 1; north end of Englischer Garten. The best place for a picnic under the chestnut trees. Anything you bring to eat will be better than the food on sale, but the beer is a tasty Hofbräuhaus brew.

Seehaus, on the Kleinhesseloher See. Respectably quiet lakeside garden, full of dewy-eyed couples barely noticing the sunset.

Osterwald-Garten, Keferstr. 12. Hairy academics and paunchy Schwabing diehards drink slowly and have grumbly conversations. For once the food is good—try the *Schweinsbraten* (roast pork) which comes with giant dumplings.

Further Afield

Kloster Andechs, just east of the Ammersee (*see* **Around Munich** p.370). The local monks brew potent beers, which you can drink on a terrace overlooking the valley below the monastery. In deference to the surroundings, there are signs commanding *Singen und Lärmen nicht gestattet* (No noise or singing allowed). The *Bock-Bier* is so powerful that it is now only served during the week—over weekends it caused too many motor accidents. The Kloster kitchens come up with delicious fare (try the creamy Beer Soup).

Schloßgaststätte Leutstetten, Altostr. 10, Leustetten (off the A95, or train in Starnberg direction). In a small village south of Munich. The real thing, with waitresses in traditional dress, FC Bayern football team at their *Stammtisch* and the best *Schweinsbraten* (roast pork) for miles.

Waldwirtschaft Großhesselohe (A bit of a mouthful which locals shorten to *Wawi*, Georg-Kalb-Str. 3, Großhesselohe (S-Bahn Line 7, 27). A large beer garden on the Isar with a jazz band usually in full swing by mid-afternoon. This is the best place to sample *Ausgezogene*—alcohol-absorbent doughnuts, fried in lard and dipped in sugar. The *Stecklerlfisch* (char-grilled skewered fish) ranks with the best.

Entertainment and Nightlife

Munich has possibly the best opera company in Germany, two top-class orchestras, over 40 theatres, a vibrant film industry, the country's leading theatre school, two excellent music academies and a lively jazz and modern music scene. The local listings magazines *Münchner Stadtmagazin* (available from newsagents) and *In Munich* (free from cafés and theatres) will guide you through the maze.

Opera and Classical Music

The **Opera House** on Max-Joseph-Platz has an advance ticket sales office on Maximilianstr. 11, ☎ 22 13 16 *(Mon–Fri 10–1 and 3.30–5.30, Sat 10–12.30pm)*. Operas often sell out well in advance, but you can get standing room and student tickets from DM5 at the box office in the Opera House one hour before the performance. The **Opera Festival** in July and August ranks with those in Salzburg and Bayreuth. The **Staatstheater am Gärtnerplatz**, ☎ 201 67 67 *(Mon–Fri 10–1 and 3.30–5.30, Sat 10–12.30pm)* presents a frothier programme of operetta, ballet and musicals, with similar last-minute ticket offers. Classical concerts take place in churches all over town, in the **Herkulessaal** (Residenz, ☎ 29 06 71) and in the Gasteig (*see* below). Keep an eye open also for concerts in the beautiful Cuvilliés Theatre. The best place to buy advance tickets is at the central **Theater- und Konzertkasse** (Neuhauserstr. 9, ☎ 12 04 0). The *Münchner Philharmonie* (under the baton of Sergui Celibidache, a front-rank conductor who refuses to record) and the *Bayrisches Rundfunk Sinfonie Orchester* (under Sir Colin Davis) are Munich's leading orchestras, but the *Münchner Kammerorchester* and ensembles from local academies also keep a high standard. Munich's largest concert hall is the Philharmonie Hall, part of the new **Gasteig Kulturzentrum**, Rosenheimerstr. 5, ☎ 4 80 98 614 *(general box-office open Mon–Fri 10.30–2 and 3–6, Sat 10.30–2)*. Amidst much controversy, the city recently built this huge, incongruous, glass and brick arts centre just across the Isar at a cost of 350 million Deutschmarks. It is now the focal point of much of the city's best music and theatre, and also hosts the annual film festival.

Theatre and Cinema

Munich has eleven major theatres, as well as a plethora of fringe and cabaret venues (amply supplied by out-of-work actors from the national drama academy). Performances are almost always in German and, even if your German is good, the cabaret (which relies heavily on in-jokes and dialect) can be glumly incomprehensible. The outer reaches of the avant-garde, on the other hand, are equally confusing to all, no matter what your mother-tongue is. Hardy perennial Alexeij Sagerer continues to bewilder the establishment with performances involving live pigs, mud and lots of noise. The **Deutsches Theater** (Schwanthalerstr. 13, ✆ 51 44 360) sometimes imports foreign musical and dance companies. Mainstream local theatre is to be seen at the **Residenztheater** (Max-Joseph-Platz, ✆ 22 57 54). **Werkraumtheater** (Hildegardstr. 1, ✆ 23 72 1328) and **Theatre im Marstall** (Marstallplatz, tickets from Residenztheater box-office) stage more experimental work, and the most established cabaret venue is the **Münchner Lach-und Schiesgesellschaft** (Ursulastr. 9, ✆ 39 19 97). **Hai** (Rosenheimerstr. 123–5), in Haidhausen, is the liveliest venue to head for at present, with a bar, exhibitions, occasional discos, cabaret—and often Alexeij Sagerer. The annual Munich Film Festival in June and July gives you the opportunity to see new cinema from around the world. Failing that, head for **Museum-Lichtspiele** (Lilienstr. 2, ✆ 48 24 03), a complex of three cinemas that shows films in the original language (usually English)—a rarity in Germany.

Nightlife and Live Music

The *Münchner Jazz-Zeitung* (available in music shops and jazz clubs) will tell you what's on in town. Avant-garde jazz and improvised music are particularly strong in Munich—**Unterfahrt** (Kirchenstr. 96) in Haidhausen being the venue for the adventurous. More mainstream fare can be had at **Alltoria** (Türkenstr. 33). Madonna and Prince-sized rock concerts are held in the **Olympiahalle** (Olympia-Park) and the **Circus-Krone-Bau** (Marsstr. 43), with tickets on sale at agencies around town (such as the one in the Marienplatz U-Bahn concourse). For up-and-coming German bands and the best visitors from abroad, check the programme at **Backstage** (Graubünderstr. 100, ✆ 18 33 30—good on rap, reggae and Afro), **Theaterfabrik** (Föhringer Allee 23, ✆ 950 56 56) and **Café Giesing** (*see* **Cafés**). The **babalu club** (Leopoldstr. 19) is currently the most popular dance spot, with US rap teams, Techno sounds and the best local DJs. During the summer you can bop about in the open air at **Sound Garden** (Schleißheimer 393) to everything from punk to sixties oldies. **Station West** (Berduxstr. 30) presents a mixed-bag of discos, live concerts and curious theatre, but the chicest place to dance is the **Park-Café** (Sophienstr. 7)—though here you can pay up to DM20 just to get in. Early in the week many clubs offer free or reduced admission, otherwise you can expect to pay around DM10 to get in, and often the same again for a drink.

About 20km north-west of Munich is the **Dachau Concentration Camp Memorial** *(Tues–Sun 9–5; adm free; S-Bahn Line 2 to Dachau, then Bus 722 to the* Gedenkstätte (Memorial); *Autobahn 8 Exit Dachau/Fürstenfeldbruck, then follow signs to KZ, Konzentrationslager).* Dachau was the Nazi's first concentration camp, set up in March 1933 on the site of an old munitions factory. It was used mainly for political prisoners, so, unlike Auschwitz and Belsen, was not primarily a 'death camp'. Nevertheless, a visit is a sombre, disturbing and eye-opening experience.

The camp is a bleak, windswept expanse of gravel and concrete (Allied soldiers razed the wooden barrack huts to the ground in 1945). Next to the entrance gate, which bears the cynical motto *Arbeit macht Frei* (Work brings Freedom), is the old kitchen and laundry, now a **museum**. Here there is a display of photographs and documents relating to the camp that is at once chilling and depressing, and a short but harrowing **documentary** film is shown *(11.30 and 3.30 in English).* Across from the museum are two reconstructed **barrack huts**. Each hut was built to accommodate 208 prisoners, with only two washrooms between them. By 1938 up to 1600 people were crowded into each barrack. Inside you can see how the original prisoners' bunks were redesigned to become wooden three-tiered shelves on which the inmates slept, crammed against each other and stacked to the ceiling. The sites of the other 28 barracks are marked by neat gravel oblongs. At the end of the row is a Jewish Temple, an International Memorial, and Catholic and Protestant Churches. A path from the far corner of the camp takes you to the ovens and crematorium, and the gas chamber—camouflaged as a shower room. Lethal gas was to be surreptitiously channelled in through holes in the ceiling. You can still see the holes, though the gas chamber was never used. Dachau prisoners selected for gassing were transported to Hartheim Castle near Linz in Austria, where 3166 were executed between 1942 and 1944 alone.

On fine days thousands of Münchners flock out to the southern **lakes** to swim, waterski, windsurf, sunbathe and enjoy all the commercial trappings of German *Freizeit* ('leisure time'). In just one hour you can be out of the city, breathing bracing Alpine air at the seethingly popular Ammersee or Starnbergersee, or at the smaller Tegernsee or Schliersee. The more distant Chiemsee has the added attraction of King Ludwig II's grandest palace.

Getting Around

Ammersee: 40km south-west of Munich, off Autobahn 96, S-Bahn Line 5 to Herrsching (1hr). **Ferries,** run by Schiffahrt auf dem Ammersee (© (08143) 229) cross the lake to quieter spots.

Starnberger See: 30km southwest of Munich, off Autobahn 95, S-Bahn Line 6 to Starnberg (40min). Bicycles to rent at S-Bahnhof (DM6 per day with S-Bahn ticket, otherwise DM10). **Ferries** ply the shores (DM17.50 round-trip or DM5.50 per stop).

Tegernsee and **Schliersee**: Two lakes 8km apart and 50km south of Munich off Autobahn 8. Rail connections from Munich Hauptbahnhof (just over 1hr).

Chiemsee: 80km southeast of Munich on Autobahn 8. There are frequent rail connections from Munich Hauptbahnhof to Prien am Chiemsee (1hr) and ferries will take you across to the islands (Chiemsee Schiffahrt, Seestr. 108, ✆ (08051) 6090; DM8.50 round-trip).

Tourist Information

Ammersee: Rathausplatz 1, Schondorf, ✆ (08192) 226.

Starnbergersee: Kirchplatz 3, Starnberg, ✆ (08151) 13008.

Tegernsee: Kuramt, Rathaus, Tegernsee, ✆ (08022) 180 122.

Schliersee: Kurverwaltung, Schliersee, ✆ (08026) 4069, ✆ (08026) 2325.

Chiemsee: Rathausstr. 11, Prien am Chiemsee, ✆ (08051) 3031.

The Lakes

The **Ammersee** and the **Starnberger See**, just a few kilometres apart, are both large, pretty lakes lined with rich Münchners' holiday villas. In places it is hard to find a stretch of public beach, and when you do it is likely (in good weather) to be packed with fellow pleasure-seekers. Both lakes allow waterskiing (banned on most other Bavarian lakes), and the water is skimmed with power-boats, yachts and windsurfers. The main resort on the Ammersee is **Herrsching**, which can get very crowded (you can find quieter public beaches by following the path around the lake). From Herrsching you can walk up through the woods (5km, not all easy going) or catch a bus (951 or 956) to **Andechs**, a beautiful 14th-century hill-top monastery. The Gothic church has a fussy Rococo interior and the tomb of the composer Carl Orff, but the Benedictine brothers are more famous for their potent beer (*see* **Eating Out** below). Most of the eastern shore of the Starnberger See is private property (though there are public beaches at Berg, Leoni and Ammerland).

Starnberg, right at the top of the lake, is the main resort. From here the cafés, icecream stands and windsurfer hire shops spread out down the western shore—a peculiar mixture of Alpine charm and seaside tack. The main beach is at Possenhofen, where King Ludwig II drowned (*see* pp. 337–8). Today a small wooden cross (occasionally stolen by devotees) marks the spot where he was found, and there is a chapel to his memory nearby.

Tegernsee, surrounded by forests and lush countryside, against a backdrop of the Alps, is a parade ground for Munich's nouveau riche and wealthy industrialists from the north. The frantic displays of wealth give the resorts around this beautiful lake an unpleasant edge, and the flood of 'Ruhr roubles' bumps up the prices. The best thing to do is to join the hang-gliders on the peak of the 1722m-high **Wallberg** *(cable car from the southern village of*

Rottach-Egern; DM18 return), from where you get a detached and spectacular view. The Benedictine Kloster dates from the early 16th century. Maximilian I turned it into a summer home, and nowadays it is a beer tavern. The tiny **Schliersee**, on the other hand, is far less crowded and uptight, and has a charming country atmosphere. People still wear traditional dress on feast days for their own sakes, and not for tourist photographs. You can mess about in little boats with no fear of being flattened by something fast, and the hang-glider air traffic is not quite so thick. It is also a pleasant place to swim, as the water in summer can reach 25°C, a good 5°C warmer than the larger lakes.

Chiemsee, 40km further west, is a vast lake popular with watersports enthusiasts, but best known as the location of **Schloß Herrenchiemsee** *(daily 9–5; adm DM4)*, Ludwig II's final and most ambitious building project. Ludwig idolized the Sun King, Louis XIV of France, and was determined to build a replica of Versailles in Bavaria. With this in mind he bought **Herreninsel**, an island on the Chiemsee, in 1873. The cornerstone of the new palace was laid five years later. Ludwig's generous patronage of the composer Wagner, and earlier fantasy castles at Linderhof and Neuschwanstein, had all but bankrupted state coffers. This time the king's ministers tried to temper his ambitious plans, but in the end Ludwig got his own way. He sent back plan after plan drawn up by the architect George Dollmann, until finally his proposed palace reached the dimensions of the French original. The garden façade at Herrenchiemsee is an exact replica of the Versailles garden façade, but money ran out in 1885 after only the central part of the palace had been built.

The ferry *(see **Getting Around** above)* drops you off at a wooden jetty on the northern end of the island. After running the gauntlet of souvenir kiosks, you follow leafy avenues across the meadows, to come somewhat abruptly upon the formal gardens and splendid façade of the Schloß. You can only see the interior on a guided tour, but this is well worth it for the sumptuous Parade Chamber (an Audience Hall even more ornate than the one in Versailles); the king's bedroom with its rich, blue, heavily gilded boat-like bed; the Dining Room with a 'magic table' like the one at Linderhof *(see p. 374)* and an exquisitely worked 18-arm Meißen porcelain chandelier; and the stunning Gallery of Mirrors (an exact replica of its Versailles counterpart, with nearly 2000 candles in the chandeliers and candelabras).

Before Ludwig bought Herreninsel, there was a monastery on the island. **Fraueninsel**, a few hundred yards across the water, was (and still is) the site of a Benedictine nunnery. Most visitors head back to the mainland after seeing Herrenchiemsee, so Fraueninsel is left to the relative calm of the nuns, birds, fishermen and a scattering of holiday residents and tourists. The whitewashed church is a quaint mixture of Romanesque, Gothic and Baroque. Next to it is a distinctive 9th-century octagonal bell-tower, topped with a 16th-century onion dome. The **Torhalle** (gatehouse) *(May–Oct daily 11–6; adm free)* has a chapel in the upper storey containing splendid Carolingian frescoes.

Where to Stay/Eating Out

Kloster Andechs, Ammersee. Has a terrace where you can drink strong beer and eat scrumptious food *(see **Munich Beer Gardens** p. 364)*.

Bräustüberl, north wing of the Kloster, Tegernsee. A beer hall popular with thirsty local farmers. Spirited (at times rowdy) alternative to the chic cafés elsewhere on the lake.

Herrenchiemsee Beer Terrace, Herreninsel, near jetty. Shady spot with a fine view over the lake. Despite being in such a tourist trap, the food (schnitzels, sausages and other tourist standards) is well-cooked and reasonable (DM15–30).

Kloster Café, Fraueninsel, adjoining the Kloster. Charming café overlooking the lake on the pretty and reposeful nuns' island. You can sip the fiery *Klostergeist* (a liquer distilled by the nuns themselves) with your coffee or after a meal (DM15–25).

Seehotel Überfahrt, Überfahrtstr. 7, Rottach-Egern, Tegernsee, ✆ (08022) 6690 (DM200). Large, chichi lakeside hotel with its own pool and health centre.

Fischerstüberl am See, Seestr. 51, Tegernsee, ✆ (08022) 4672 (DM90–110). Cosy inn with a leafy terrace overlooking the lake. The restaurant serves superb fresh fish.

Haus Huber am See, Seestr. 10, Schliersee (from DM80). Simple, cheery boarding house within a few minutes' walk of the lake.

The Bavarian Alps

The craggy Bavarian Alps stand shoulder to shoulder, just an hour's drive from Munich. At times they plummet abruptly to the edges of icy, sparkling lakes, or stretch out into luscious meadows and rolling forest-land. The air is invigorating, fragrant with wildflowers in the spring, and clear—the hesitant, mournful tune of cowbells carrying for miles across the valleys. The hillsides are dotted with traditional chalets—some with white-washed lower storeys and wooden upper halves, their long balconies cascading with flowers; others entirely of wood with low-pitched roofs and decorative little belfries; yet others with gaudily painted façades.

In winter people in startlingly bright ski-clothes shoot about the snow-covered slopes and crowd into warm *Gaststätte* to drink *Glühwein* or hot chocolate. In summer the Alps become delightfully rural. You can see women in headscarves working in the fields, cowherds leading a handful of prized animals up to mountainside grazing lands, and village-folk resplendent in traditional *Tracht* (costume) for a wedding or feastday. This is a part of the country that will appeal mainly to nature-lovers and winter-sports enthusiasts, though you will also find King Ludwig II's most charming and eccentric castle, and high culture in the form of the famous Oberammergau Passion Play.

See also Directory entries for Bad Reichenhall and Inn-Salzachgau.

Getting Around

By car: The **Deutsche Alpenstraße** (German Mountain Road) is a signposted tourist route that winds from Lindau on the Bodensee to Berchtesgarten in the east.

It is one of the most spectacularly beautiful of all the German Tourist Roads, though it is not quite finished and at times you have to duck into Austria or dip down onto the plains. Even the minor roads are well-made, though some passes are steep and twist tortuously. In winter it is a good idea to fit snow tyres or carry chains if you are intending to leave the main roads.

By train: The only track that runs the length of the Alps is across the border in Austria (connecting Feldkirch in the west with Innsbruck and Salzburg). However, there are numerous rail routes radiating out of Munich (Garmisch-Partenkirchen (1hr 20min; a *Sonderrückfahrkarte* (special round-trip ticket) almost halves the price: DM28, return or DM70 return including cog-railway and cable car to Zugspitze), Mittenwald (1hr 40min), Oberammergau (1hr 40min), Berchtesgarten (2½–3hr).

By bus: Private bus companies offer tours from Munich to Alpine resorts. Try **Panorama Tours** (Arnulfstr. 8, ✆ (089) 591 504), who offer a variety of trips including Berchtesgarten (DM65) and Linderhof/Neuschwanstein (DM65).

Walking: Walking is one of the most rewarding and refreshing ways of exploring the region. Local tourist offices can often suggest routes and provide maps. The Bavarian state government has declared six areas of pasture to be common land. Here you can walk about as you please, and will come across mountain cabins offering snacks and fresh milk from the herds. The designated zones are around Garmisch-Partenkirchen, Berchtesgarten, Kreuth (south of the Tegernsee), Schliersee, Aschau (south of the Chiemsee) and Ruhpolding. (Apply to local tourist offices for details.)

Tourist Information

Oberammergau: Eugen-Papst-Str. 9a, ✆ (08822) 1021.

Mittenwald: Dammkarstr. 3. (08823) 33981.

Garmisch-Partenkirchen: Kurverwaltung, Bahnhofstr. 34, ✆ (08821) 1800.

Berchtesgarten: Königseestr. 2 (near Bahnhof), ✆ (08652) 5011.

Festivals

The **Oberammergau Passion Play** began in 1634 after residents of Oberammergau, worried by the first signs of plague in the village the previous year, had vowed that if the pestilence developed no further their descendents would perform the Passion of Jesus every ten years, into eternity. No-one in Oberammergau died of the disease, and for generations townsfolk have honoured the pledge—though in 1680 the performance date was altered to coincide with the beginning of each new decade (the next one is in AD 2000). The text has had a chequered history. A rather bawdy original was cleaned up in 1750 and put into high Baroque verse. The 19th century saw the first prose version, and recent modernizations have expunged some rampant anti-Semitism. Nowadays the Passion takes place in a vast open-air theatre which was built in the 1930s. The spectacle lasts the whole day (with a two-hour break for lunch) and nearly half a million people get to see the 100 or so performances between May and September. *Passion Oberammergau* is Village Hall Nativity Play writ enormous. Only locals (1500 of them) may take part, many men cultivating biblical beards for months before the event. Even the props are made by Oberammergau craftspeople alone, and tradition dictates that a local virgin plays Mary. There was outrage in 1990 when not only was the Mother of God portrayed by a mother-of-two, but (even worse in Bavaria) another of the lead actors was a *Protestant.*

As a Roman Catholic stronghold, Bavaria has a number of **religious festivals**—often involving street processions, dressing up in *Tracht* and feasting. At **Corpus Christi** you'll see the richest collection of local dress, especially around Oberammergau where the men wear knee-britches, bright waistcoats and heavy leather belts and the women are resplendent in brocaded dresses and otter-fur bonnets. On **Palm Sunday** the rites have intriguing pagan undertones. Churches, streets and homes are decorated with *Palmbosch'n* (silvery willows) festooned with ribbon-like *Geschabertbandl* (dyed woodshavings). Two little cuts are made in the bark to let out witches and druids (not viewed as favourably in Bavaria as they are in Wales). Children carry the branches to church to be blessed, and then out into the fields where they are left to ensure protection for the year ahead.

The autumn **cattledrive** is the most colourful of all village events. Hardy cowherds (men and women) decorate their animals with elaborate *Faikl*—head-dresses made of ribbons, leaves, feathers and flowers, sometimes up to a metre high—and bring them down from the high Alpine pastures where they have spent the summer. This takes place around *Michaeli* (29 September), though much depends on the weather and it is better to make enquiries locally. In May or June the cowherds and their charges head back for the mountains—but this is done without quite so much display. The cattle drives take place in towns throughout the mountains and foothills. The earliest autumn drive is usually in Garmisch-Partenkirchen (early September), and the last is in Königsee (sometimes as late as October), where the cows have to make the last part of their journey by boat.

Oberammergau and its Surrounds

Oberammergau, about 90km south-east of Munich on the B23 (off Autobahn 95), is a small town crushed right up against a sheer granite mountainface and—Passion Play or no—teeming with tourists nearly the whole year through (*see* **Festivals** for details of the Passion Play.) Most come simply because the town is famous, and are surprised by how pretty it is. You can visit the empty **Passionstheater** *(May–Oct daily 9.30–12.30 and 1.30–5; Nov–Apr Tues–Sun 10–12.30 and 1.30–4.30; closed Jan)*, but despite the exhibition on past Passion Plays in the foyer, this is a dull and rather pointless exercise. A far more rewarding experience is a wander through the streets to look at *Luftmalerei*—the bright frescoes that adorn many Alpine homes. These paintings (usually of biblical scenes) became the rage during the Counter-Reformation, when such displays of religious zeal were encouraged. Fresco painting was an expensive business, but Oberammergau was a prosperous town, fat with the takings from Passion Play tourism and woodcarving even in the 18th century. Old *Luftmalerei* abounds, and the tradition continues. Some of the best examples are by a local artist, Franz Seraph Zwinck (1749–92). His **Pilatushaus** (in Verlegergasse) is an exquisite work of controlled design and skilful *trompe l'oeil* that far surpasses other façades in town—some of which seem wilfully kitsch.

When they aren't donning biblical robes and learning lines, a large proportion of Oberammergauers are chipping away at blocks of wood. The town is renowned for its **woodcarving**, and the streets are lined with shops selling crucifixes, cherubs, nativity scenes and chunky toys. Some shops (such as Holzschnitzerei Josef Albl in Devrientweg, and the Pilatushaus, which is now a crafts centre) have workshops attached where you can watch the craftsfolk chiselling out piece after piece.

Four kilometres down the B23 you come to **Kloster Ettal**, a 14th-century Benedictine monastery that got a massive Baroque facelift during the Counter-Reformation. Ettal pales by comparison with the other Baroque churches in the region (*see* pp. 298 and 299), but it does have a rather splendid cupola fresco by the Tyrolean artist Johann-Jakob Zeiller.

Ten kilometres to the west is **Schloß Linderhof** *(daily Apr–Sept 9–12.15 and 12.45–5.30, Oct–Mar 10–12.15 and 12.45–4; adm DM6 including Grotto and Kiosk)*, the oddest and most bewitching of King Ludwig II's castles. Ludwig was an absolutist, deeply opposed to his father's namby-pamby ideas of constitutional monarchy. He hero-worshipped the French Bourbons, especially Louis XIV. When he became king in 1864 he wanted to replace Max II's modest hunting lodge at Linderhof with a massive copy of the palace of Versailles, which he planned to call Meicost Ettal (an anagram of Louis XIV's motto *L'état c'est moi*). He later changed his mind and set his ersatz Versailles on Herreninsel (*see* p. 370). Linderhof became a retreat for the dreamy king. Here, in the 1870s, he built a modest 'Royal Villa' (in which the bedroom is by far the biggest room) and set about filling the surrounding parkland with quirky pavilions and life-size stage sets where he could re-enact scenes from Wagner's operas. Like an enchanted prince, Ludwig would descend on Schloß Linderhof in a golden Rococo sleigh, with a retinue of attendants in period livery.

The **Schloß** itself is a modest, rather dumpy, Baroque imitation—crispy white and heavily ornamented, like a small over-iced wedding cake. It is periodically upstaged by a 30m spurt of water from the gilded **fountain** *(every hour on the hour 9–5)* which is set at the entrance in the middle of a formal parterre garden. In one corner of the garden, at odds with the strict symmetry, is the old Linden tree that gave the castle its name. Inside, the palace is encrusted with gilded stucco and smothered in tapestries, rich fabrics and exotic carpets (one of them made out of ostrich plumes). The highpoint is the enormous **bedroom** with its 2.7 bv 2.1m blue velvet bed, fenced off by a carved and gilded balustrade. In the garden outside, an artificial cascade (built to cool the room in summer) tumbles almost up to the window. In the dining room you can see Ludwig's famous **magic table** which sank through the floor to be loaded up by lackeys in the kitchens below, so that the reclusive king could eat alone, often dressed up as Louis XIV or the Swan Prince.

Beyond the formal parterres, a wilder 'English Garden' extends for another 50 hectares, gradually blending into the Alpine countryside. This was the park that Ludwig intended to fill with romantic and fantastic buildings. He didn't realize all his plans, and not everything he built has survived, but his favourite, the **Venus Grotto** (1876), has. This is a 10m-high artificial cavern with a small lake, designed to reproduce the scene in the first act of Wagner's *Tannhäuser*. Garlands of roses hang between sparkling stalagmites and stalactites, all made from canvas, cement and lustrous stones. Hidden lights, some of them underwater, throw streaks of bright, changing colour across the shadows—a spectacular feat of electrical engineering for the time. The gilded shell-shaped boat in which Ludwig loved to be rowed about waits empty on the water.

The **Moorish Kiosk** nearby was built for the 1867 Paris Exhibition and bought by the king in the 1870s. Its stylish minarets look quaintly out of place against a backdrop of the Alps. Inside, the enamelled tail-feathers of the birds on the **Peacock Throne** stand out even against the kaleidoscopic colours of the walls and windows. At the eastern edge of the park is the simple wooden **Hunding's Hut**, based on Wagner's stage directions for the first act of the *Walküre*. It is a recent replica of the original hut (which burnt down in 1945), and isn't really worth the walk unless you're an avid Ludwig- or Wagnerphile.

Garmisch-Partenkirchen and Mittenwald

Garmisch-Partenkirchen, Germany's leading ski resort, lies a few kilometres south of Oberammergau along the main road (B2) at the foot of the lofty Wetterstein range. Two villages, one on each side of the railway line, have merged to form the present town, but retain quite different atmospheres. Garmisch is glitzy, modern and expensive, while Partenkirchen across the track has been more tenacious in holding onto its Alpine village charm and is a little cheaper. Ludwigstraße in Partenkirchen even has some traditional *Luftmalerei*—though not as impressive as in Oberammergau. Most people scuttle out of Garmisch-Partenkirchen as quickly as possible, either to ski, or for the magnificent views from the surrounding mountaintops. The **Zugspitze** (2963m) has the highest peak in Germany. There are two ways of getting to the top by public transport: *Zugspitzbahn* (electric railway) from central Garmisch to Eibsee followed by a dizzy ride on the *Eibseebahn* cable car to the summit; or *Zugspitzbahn* to Eibsee, then rack railway (through a tunnel) to Hotel Schneeferhaus (2645m, good skiing during the winter season) then the *Gipfelbahn* cable car the rest of the way. *(Both methods cost DM50 return (DM30 single) in summer and DM43 (DM29 single) in winter. A 7-day pass costs DM65 (June–Oct) and special ski-*

passes cost DM112 (3 days) and DM225 (7 days).) A cheaper option, with nearly as panoramic a view, is **Wank** (1780m), where the cable car from the outskirts of Garmisch costs only DM19 return (DM13 single) and where souvenir kiosk proprietors are bemused by the high turnover of postcards sold to British visitors. **Hikers** might like to tackle the challenging **Alpspitze** (2628m), or to strike out along a path hewn from the rock in the dramatic **Partnachklamm** gorge, southeast of Garmisch.

Mittenwald (20km further south-east, just off the B2) is prettier, less touristy and has a far more authentic atmosphere than Garmisch-Partenkirchen. Chalets with bright frescoes and low overhanging eaves snuggle together in the shadow of jagged peaks, neighbours greet each other brightly in the street, occasionally an ancient tractor chugs through town. The pews in the local church still have family name-plates fixed on the end. In Obermarkt and around Im Gries you'll see some of the richest *Luftmalerei* in the district.

In 1683 Mathias Klotz, a local farmer's son who had spent some time working in Cremona with the great violin maker Niccoló Amati, returned to teach his craft to local woodcarvers. Today Mittenwald violins, violas and cellos are coveted by musicians around the world. The tiny **Geigenbaumuseum** at Ballenhausgasse 3 *(May–Oct Mon–Fri 10–11.45 and 2–4.45; adm DM3)* displays some of the finest instruments and documents the history of the craft. There is also an open studio where you can watch a violin maker at work.

Mittenwald's pet mountain is **Karwendl** (2385m). The views from the top—over the valley and the Wetterstein range—are even more breathtaking than those from the peaks around Garmisch *(cable car DM23 return, DM14 single).*

Berchtesgadener Land

In the south-east corner of Germany, on the Austrian border, is the **Berchtesgadener Land,** where (local legend goes) dawdling angels who had been commanded to distribute wonders and beauty around the globe were so startled by a divine command to hurry along that they dropped the lot here. Some of the mightiest mountains of the Alps crowd around a slender lake and a lush valley that is now a National Park.

At the beginning of the 12th century some Augustinian monks struggled through the snow from Salzburg, built a priory at Berchtesgaden, and established what was to become one of the smallest states in the Holy Roman Empire. Later, in 1515, the discovery of hugely rich deposits of salt ('white gold') made the Prince-Archbishops of Berchtesgaden just as wealthy and powerful as their neighbours in Salzburg ('Salt City'). In the 19th century the state was incorporated into Bavaria, and the ruling Wittelsbachs secularized the priory and converted it into a royal residence. But for many, the name Berchtesgaden has a more sour historical connotation: it was here, in a village just above the town, that statesmen (including Britain's Neville Chamberlain) came to visit Hitler in his rented country retreat, in the vain hope of preventing an invasion of the Sudetenland (*see* p. 46). Hitler enjoyed meeting foreign dignitaries in this awe-inspiring mansion and film footage of the Führer on the grand stairway is indeed impressive (*see* **Obersalzberg** below).

The hillside town of **Berchtesgaden** teems with tourists. The frantically busy main road that winds through the centre almost puts the kibosh on any Alpine charm, but Berchtesgaden has more to offer than pretty houses and winter sports. In the elegant Renaissance rooms of the Wittelsbach **Schloß** *(May–Sept Sun–Fri 10–1 and 2–5, Oct–Apr Mon–Fri 10–1 and 2–5; adm DM4.50)*, you can see part of the extensive collection of sacred art put together by Crown Prince Ruprecht, son of the last King of Bavaria, who lived here from 1923 to 1955. The German woodcarving (with some fine pieces by the celebrated Tilman Riemenschneider) is especially good, and there is also a good collection of porcelain and Italian furniture. A charming Romanesque cloister and Gothic dormitory survive from the earlier medieval priory.

In the simple **Franziskanerkirche** at the southern end of town you can see a graceful Baroque carving of Christ, and (in the adjoining graveyard) convincing testimony to the healthy mountain air—the tomb of one Anton Adner who lived from 1705 to 1822.

A tour of the disused shafts of a working salt mine, the **Salzbergwerk** *(May 1–Oct 15 daily 8.30–5; Oct 16–Apr 30 Mon–Fri 12.30–5.30; adm DM12.50; tour 1½hr)* may not sound enticing, but is an experience not to be missed. Men don the traditional thick protective miners' clothing: a felt hat and leather bum-pad. Women get a blue hat and baggy white trousers (it's not a good idea to wear a skirt). Then you huddle together astride a wooden waggon that carries you down a long tunnel deep into the mine. Next you slide down a 30m-long chute (this is the reason for the leather pad) into an enormous vault, glittering with salt crystals. Here you're shown a film and a real miner explains how the equipment works. Then it's off down another long chute to an enormous underground lake where, a little like Ludwig II in his magic grotto, you are borne across the black water on a wooden boat. Finally you're whisked back up to the surface by lift and train.

The **Königsee** (5km south of Berchtesgaden, buses from Hauptbahnhof) is a thin, fjord-like lake that hooks itself around the foot of the **Watzmann** (2713m), Germany's second highest mountain. Crowds flock here whatever the weather; escape them by taking the electric ferry which makes a round trip (DM15) past dramatic mountain and forest scenery.

High in the mountains east of Berchtesgaden is the little village of **Obersalzberg** (cable car DM10 return), the site of Hitler's **Berghof**, his mountain retreat. The house was badly bombed during the war, and reduced to rubble by US troops in 1952—and so it remains, overgrown and unsignposted. A better reason for visiting Obersalzberg is the 'Eagle's Nest', a restaurant at the summit of the **Kehlstein** (1834m) (special buses take you from the village up a magnificent winding road, and then you travel the last 124m in a lift inside the mountain). The Eagle's Nest was built as a teahouse and given by Martin Bormann (Hitler's adviser and private secretary) to his boss as a 50th birthday present, but the Führer seldom used it. Today it is very commercialized, but nothing can detract from the splendour of the view across the Alps—as far as Salzburg in clear weather.

Shopping

For centuries **Oberammergau** dealers have been creaming off the best **woodcarvings** from local family workshops and selling them in town. Most of this carving has a religious theme, and much is churned out for the souvenir market, but there are some fine artists at work. If you pay a bit extra, you can commission a piece from someone whose work takes your fancy. Where you shop will be very much a matter of personal taste, but try Toni Baur (Dorfstr. 27) for really vibrant secular pieces and Josef Albl (Devrientweg 1) for more traditional religious work. There is a craft centre and co-op at the Pilatushaus (in Verleger-Gasse), where prices are a little lower. In **Berchtesgaden** the carvers concentrate more on dolls and toy horse-carriages. The local speciality is *Spanschachteln*, brightly painted wooden boxes. You can get all of these at Schloß Adelsheim (Schroffenbergallee 6).

If you have DM10,000 to spend on a **violin**, head for **Mittenwald**, where Anton Maller (Stainergasse 14) sells instruments of world renown. If your budget isn't up to that you can settle for a chocolate or marzipan version, on sale all over town.

Activities

The best **skiing** is in the western part of this region. Garmisch-Partenkirchen hosted the 1936 Winter Olympics and is still a World Cup downhill, super giant slalom and ski jump centre—and it's easier on the pocket than most Swiss resorts. Good and intermediate skiers should head for the Zugspitze and Kreuzeck Hausberg (where there are two classic black pistes); beginners will be happier on the gentler slopes of Wank. Mittenwald and Oberammergau specialize in cross-country skiing. The season is generally from December to April—though in this region it can last a little longer. Further east, around Berchtesgaden, the runs are not as exciting (though they are pretty). However, the town is a vibrant centre for **other winter sports** such as tobogganing, skating, curling and ice-skittles.

Hikers are very well catered for. Alpine refuges are dotted all over the mountains and offer shelter, refreshment and often overnight facilities as well at minimal cost. There are some excellent marked routes, especially around Königsee and in the Berchtesgaden National Park. Maps and details of these are sold at local tourist offices. Local mountaineering schools (such as the Bergersteigerschule Karwendl-Wetterstein, Dekan-Karl-Platz 29, Mittenwald, ✆ (08823) 2341; or the Deutsche Alpen- und Kletterschule, Ettalerstr. 36, Oberammergau, ✆ (08822) 1772) offer climbing courses and individual guides.

Hang-gliding, **ballooning**, **cycling** and **white-water rafting** are popular; you can hire equipment and get tuition in most of the main resorts (try Outdoor Club Berchtesgaden, Bahnhofstr. 11, Berchtesgaden, ✆ (08652) 66066; or Heinzelmann-Reisen, In der Artenreit 13, Schönau am Königsee, ✆ (08652) 2530).

Where to Stay

expensive

Hotel Böld, König-Ludwig-Str. 10, Oberammergau, ✆ (08822) 3021, fax 7102 (DM168–246). Smart hotel with a lick of Alpine charm and a herbal sauna, steam bath, solarium and jacuzzi—in fact most of what you need for a hedonistic holiday.

Hotel Geiger, Berchtesgadener Str. 103–105, Stanggaß, Berchtesgaden, ✆ (08652) 5055, fax 5058 (DM150–300). Large converted farmhouse in the valley just outside town. Heavy furniture and a solidly respectable atmosphere.

Posthotel Partenkirchen, Ludwigstr. 49, Garmisch-Partenkirchen, ✆ (08821) 51067 (DM150–220). Atmospheric old coaching inn in grand Bavarian style.

moderate

Hotel Wolf, Dorfstr. 1, Oberammergau, ✆ (08822) 3071, fax 1096 (DM98–180). Modern Bavarian-style hotel a few minutes' walk from the Passionstheater. Rooms in the top two storeys have wooden balconies, banks of flowers in the window boxes and mountain views.

Hotel Alte Post, Dorfstr. 19, Oberammergau, ✆ (08822) 1091, fax 1094 (DM80–138). Rustic Bavarian hotel braving a busy junction in the middle of town.

Die Alpenrose, Obermarkt 1, Mittenwald, ✆ (08823) 5055 (DM120–150). A 13th-century merchant's house with painted ceilings, panelled nooks and individual flourishes of carving in the bedrooms—right in the centre of one of the prettiest towns in the region.

Post Hotel, Obermarkt, Mittenwald, ✆ (08823) 1094 (DM140–190). Considers itself a dash above the Alpenrose up the road. It is more upmarket, but not as cosy.

Hotel Vier Jahreszeiten, Maximilianstr. 20, Berchtesgaden, ✆ (08652) 5026, fax 5029 (DM140–180). Sleepy old hotel that has sprouted an angular modern extension. Ask for one of the rooms with a balcony and mountain view.

Hotel Krone, Am Rad 5, Berchtesgaden, ✆ (08652) 62051 (DM90–150). Quiet, family-run hotel with fine views, away from the bustle of town. Done up with local painted furniture, and with a sunny terrace for summer breakfasts.

inexpensive

Haus Alpenruh, Schillerweg 2, Mittenwald, ✆ (08823) 1375 (DM60–80). Charming little *Pension* at the edge of the village.

Pension Almrose, Purschlingweg 3a, Oberammergau, ✆ (08822) 4369 (DM42–56 without private bath). Clean and friendly, with an Alp at the bottom of its garden.

Pension Haus am Berg, Am Brandholz 9, Berchtesgaden, ✆ (08652) 5059 (DM68–96). Good value *Pension* perched on the hillside overlooking the town. Most rooms have their own balcony.

Ohlsenhof, Von-Brug-Str. 18, Garmisch-Partenkirchen, ✆ (08821) 2168 (DM60–80). Friendly, well-run guesthouse popular with younger travellers.

Youth Hostels: Mahlensteinweg 10, Oberammergau, ✆ (08822) 4114; Jochstr. 10, Garmisch-Partenkirchen, ✆ (08821) 2980; Buckelwiesen 7, Mittenwald, ✆ (08823) 1701.

Private rooms in local houses go for DM20–30 per person (including breakfast). Look out for *Fremdenzimmer* signs or ask at the tourist office. You will have most luck in Oberammergau, or nearby Unterammergau, an authentic little farming village with a whiff of dung in the air.

Eating and Drinking

Oberammergau

Zauberstuberl, Eugene-Papst-Str. 3a (DM10–30). Cosy spot for lunch, especially in winter when the chef comes up with five or six different thick, warming soups.

Berggasthof Kolben-Alm, take Kolben-Alm cable car, ✆ (08822) 6364 (DM20–35). Small hillside guesthouse that serves great cold-meat platters and steamy noodle-rich Bavarian food. You might catch a *Hüttenabend*, when locals and hikers get together for a festive sing-song.

Café Hochenleitner, Faistemantelgasse 7, ✆ (08822) 1312. The best place to head for if you want to sample Bavarian country baking—here is good coffee and a tempting array of *Torte*.

Gasthof Gries, Im Gries 41, (DM25–35). Sausages, noodles and hunks of meat swimming in thick gravies—all hearty local fare.

Zur Brücke, Innsbrucker Str. 38, ✆ (08823) 1388 (DM25–50). The place to go if you like good beer, zither music and yodelling with your meal.

Arnspitze, Innsbrucker Str. 68, ✆ (08823) 2425 (DM30–50). Mountain views and mother's own cooking.

Berchtesgaden

Vierjahrszeiten, Hotel Vierjahrszeiten, Maximilianstr. 20, ✆ (08652) 5026 (DM30–50). Popular restaurant that serves excellent fish dishes (such as perch cooked in foil with shrimps and mushrooms).

Garmisch-Partenkirchen

Alpenhof, Bahnhofstr. 74, ✆ (08821) 59055 (DM20–70). Wide variety of local cuisine—from sausage snacks to finely-cooked fish—served up in defeatingly generous portions.

Eastern Bavaria

From a natural fountain in a palace garden near the Black Forest, the River Danube flows swiftly eastwards across Germany on its route to the Black Sea. One of the most captivating stretches is in eastern Bavaria, just before the river crosses the border into Austria. It wends its way through fertile meadows, glides under medieval bridges, past castles and monasteries and through the wealthy merchants' city of Regensburg. Then it flows past the

Bavarian Forest—the largest natural wilderness in Europe—before slipping by the Italianate town of Passau and out of Germany.

During the Cold War this eastern corner of Bavaria, wedged between the Alps and Czechoslovakia, was all but ignored by the Germans themselves, let alone foreign visitors. Today it is still removed from mainstream tourism and offers intriguingly different architecture, unrivalled natural beauty and glimpses of a way of life that has barely changed this century. Folk traditions and festivals thrive here as nowhere else in Germany, and people participate for their own enjoyment rather than as a performance for tourists.

Getting Around

By car: Autobahn 3 (from western Germany) joins the Danube at Regensburg and travels along the river to Passau. Autobahn 92 (from Munich) leads past Landshut and, within 100km, to the heart of the area. Travelling by car is the best way to see the Bavarian Forest; there are local buses, but services are sporadic.

By train: There are main-line connections to Regensburg and Passau from Munich and from the west and north of Germany. Local trains will take you to the main towns in the Bavarian Forest.

By boat: Cruise boats operate between Regensburg and Passau—a delightful way to see the region. Local companies also offer cruises, round trips and excursions into Austria (*see* **Getting Around** sections below).

Regensburg

Regensburg is a mosaic of romantically crumbly plasterwork in yellow ochre, pale green, faded pink and terracotta, with the odd sooty bump of Roman wall and flounce of medieval stonework. Despite an august history as an important trading and administrative centre, it is an intimate, lived-in old slipper of a town—its fabric patched, darned and lovingly restored, but never charmlessly pristine. Modern Regensburgers prefer to inhabit old buildings, rather than simply revere them. As you trundle your trolley through the supermarket, you may have to manoeuvre around Romanesque pillars; a dress shop changing-room might be wedged under a Gothic arch; the deli across the road was probably once a chapel. In the early evenings, as the lights come on in first floor apartments, you can glimpse vaulted ceilings, rich Gothic carving and dark panelled walls.

A university town with first-rate breweries, Regensburg brims with good cheer. Visitors from Charlemagne to Mozart and Goethe have been struck by its felicitous position on the Danube. Some choice museums and the angelic Domspatzen (literally 'Cathedral Sparrows', a world-famous boys' choir) add to the attraction.

History

The French call Regensburg *Ratisbonne*, from the old name of Radasbona, which suggests early Celtic origins. But the first known settlement at this point on the Danube was **Castra**

Regina, a Roman fortress established by Emperor Marcus Aurelius in AD 179. Despite hostility between the Romans and surrounding Celtic and Teutonic peoples, there must also have been some fraternizing, for soon a mixed-race tribe, the Baiuvarii, outnumbered everyone else. By the 6th century the last Romans had disappeared, and the new **Duchy of Bavaria** was ruled by the Agilofing dynasty—Burgundians installed by the Merovingian kings. The Agilofingers made Regensburg their seat, and under the Carolingian king **Charlemagne** (who resided here from 791 to 793) it remained a city of administrative and ecclesiastical importance, playing host to the occasional **Imperial Diets**. When the Diets became permanent in 1663—in effect the first German parliament—the Regensburg Rathaus was chosen as their venue, and remained so until 1803.

Meanwhile, because of its position on the Danube (an important east–west European thoroughfare) and near the Brenner Pass over the Alps to Italy, Regensburg flourished. Medieval Regensburger coins have been found from Venice to the Scandinavian coast, and as far away as Kiev. Arbeo of Freising, an 8th-century monk, marvelled at the 'gold and silver, purple cloths, iron, wine, honey and salt' that filled the city's warehouses and weighed down the boats on the Danube. Later a brisk trade in slaves and weapons further swelled local coffers to make 13th-century Regensburg the largest and richest city in south Germany. By the time it became a **Free Imperial City** in 1245 Regensburg was also a centre of culture and learning. Two of the first epic poems in German, the **Kaiserchronik** and the **Rolandslied** originated here. Generations of wealthy merchants built show-piece townhouses—first cosy Romanesque, then more swanky Gothic. Fortified mansions with high towers, inspired by Italian city villas, rose up all over town. At the peak of Regensburg's prosperity there were over 60 of them, and around 20 still survive. (Apart from a battering at the hands of Napoleon, the city has been relatively unscathed by war.)

The Wittelsbachs succeeded to the duchy in 1180, and moved the capital first to Landshut, and then to Munich. New trade routes by-passed Regensburg and by the end of the 14th century the town had been overtaken as a trading centre by Nuremburg and Augsburg. Regensburg has never forgiven the Wittelsbachs. The bitterness became even more intense in the 19th century when the rulers plundered Regensburg's monasteries and churches for art treasures to add to their private collections and to top up state funds. Locals speak of 'the largest art-robbery of the 19th century': 'They would have taken the cathedral if they could have moved it.' In 1853 the relatively poor town scraped together what money it could to build a Royal Villa, in an attempt to lure the Wittelsbach monarchs for at least an occasional visit. King Ludwig III treated this gesture of apparent reconciliation with contempt, dismissing the little palace as 'an aviary' and finally carting off its furniture too. Even today Regensburgers bristle at the fact that the Royal Villa is neglected and used as goverment offices and has not been restored as a museum (like other Wittelsbach residences in Bavaria). One the other hand, they counter brightly, the centuries of neglect meant that Regensburg became a 'Sleeping Beauty', unable to replace its historic buildings with new ones and ignored by rampaging armies. So today the town remains pretty much in its original medieval shape, although the establishment of the University in 1967, new BMW, Toshiba and Siemens factories, and a blossoming tourist industry have provided an awakening kiss.

By car: Regensburg is about 120km from Munich (on Autobahn 9 and 93) and 100km from Nuremberg (on Autobahn 3).

Car hire: Sixt Budget, Im Gewerbepark 6, Gebäude A1, ✆ (0941) 401 035.

Mitfahrzentrale: Jakobstr. 12, ✆ (0941) 57400.

By train: Trains run frequently to Munich (1½hr) and Nuremberg (1hr), and seven times daily to Cologne (5¾hr) and to Vienna (4¼hr). The **Hauptbahnhof** (information ✆ (0941) 19419) is about 15 minutes' walk from the centre of town (straight down Maximilianstraße).

Boat trips: Gebrüder Klinger (Steinerne Brücke, ✆ (0941) 55359) offer excursions and round trips on the Danube (a trip to Walhalla and back takes about two hours, a one-way cruise to Passau takes most of the day). You can also go on short city cruises to see Regensburg's skyline, and brave the whirlpools under the Steinerne Brücke (DM7.50). City trips leave from near the Historische Wurstküche and most Danube cruises leave from Werfstraße on the island of Untere Wöhrd. Short trips through the Donaudurchbruch gorge leave from Kelheim (20km southwest of Regensburg off the B16, or rail to Saal then DB bus). Boats run daily from mid-May to early September (9.15am, 10am then every 30 minutes until 5pm; DM7 return).

Public transport: Regensburg is compact, so everything you're likely to want to see is within easy walking distance. If you do find that you need buses you can pick up a route plan from the information office at Ernst-Reuter-Platz 2 (near the station).

Taxis: ✆ 57000.

Tourist office: Altes Rathaus, ✆ (0941) 507 2141 *(Mon–Fri 8.30–6, Sat 9–4, Sun 9–12)*.

Post Office: Main post offices are on Domplatz and next to the Hauptbahnhof.

Police: ✆ 110.

Medical emergencies: ✆ 19222 or 73073.

Market days: Fruit and vegetable Market, Alter Kornmarkt and Neupfarrplatz *(Mon–Fri 6–12)*. Flower Market, Altdorferplatz *(Mon–Sat 6–12)*.

The biggest bash of the lot is the **Altstadt Festival** (held in the summer) with jugglers and street theatre, a morality play about Emperor Charles V and Barbara Blomberg (see below), folk music and loads of food and drink. There are also two big **beer festivals**, the *Frühjahrsdult* (two weeks in May) and *Herbstdult* (two weeks in Aug/Sept). Of the many annual music festivals the **Bach-Woche**

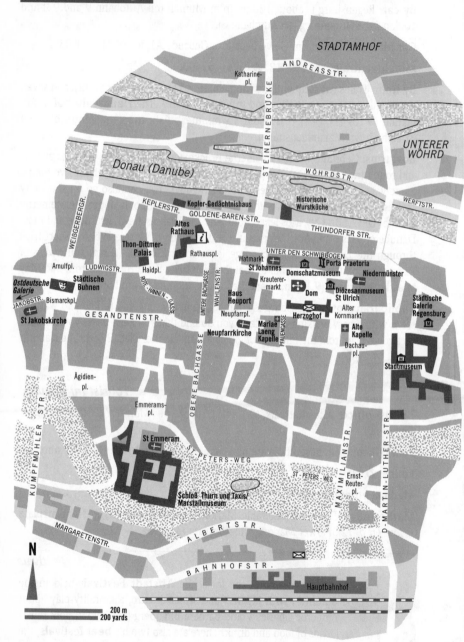

Regensburg

STADTAMHOF

ANDREASSTR.

Katharine-pl.

UNTERER WÖHRD

STEINERNEBRÜCKE

Donau (Danube)

WÖHRDSTR.

WERFTSTR.

KEPLERSTR.
Kepler-Gedächtnishaus

Historische Wurstküche

WEIßGERBERGR.

GOLDENE-BAREN-STR.

THUNDORFER STR.

Altes Rathaus

Thon-Dittmer-Palais

Rathauspl.

UNTER DEN SCHWIBBOGEN

Arnulfpl.

LUDWIGSTR.

Haidpl.

Watmarkt

Porta Praetoria

Ostdeutsche Galerie

Städtische Buhnen

St Johannes

Domschatzmuseum

Niedermünster

JAKOBSTR.

Bismarckpl.

RÖTE-HANNEN-GASSE

UNTERE BACHGASSE

WAHLENSTR.

Krauterer-markt

Dom

Diözesanmuseum

St Ulrich

Städtische Galerie Regensburg

St Jakobskirche

GESANDTENSTR.

Haus Heuport

Neupfarrpl.

Herzoghof

Alter Kornmarkt

Mariae Laeng Kapelle

Alte Kapelle

Neupfarrkirche

PFAUENGASSE

Dachau-pl.

Ägidien-pl.

OBERE BACHGASSE

Stadtmuseum

Emmerams-pl.

St Emmeram

ST-PETERS-WEG

MAXIMILIANSTR.

D-MARTIN-LUTHER-STR.

KUMPFMÜHLER STR.

Schloß Thurn und Taxis/ Marstallmuseum

ST-PETERS-WEG

Ernst-Reuter-pl.

MARGARETENSTR.

ALBERTSTR.

N

BAHNHOFSTR.

Hauptbahnhof

200 m
200 yards

(Bach week, June or July) is the most renowned, and the **Bayerisches Jazz-Weekend** (July) is the jolliest, with up to 50 amateur jazz bands blasting away in bars, squares and normally secluded courtyards. As well as the usual **Christmas Market** (on Neupfarrplatz), there is a special **Crafts Christmas Market** on Haidplatz, where you can buy local carving, weaving and all types of hand-made gifts. The **Domspatzen** (cathedral choir) perform right through the year, but give special concerts at the Christian festivals.

Around the Cathedral

Regensburg's giant **cathedral**—the finest Gothic church in south Germany—looms over the town's low red rooftops, looking rather as if it had been dropped there by accident. Construction began soon after 1260 on the site of an earlier Romanesque building but, as with so many German Gothic churches, it was only completely finished when the twin towers went up in the 19th century. In the cathedral's back courtyard is the **Eselsturm** (Donkey Tower), a remnant of the original Romanesque church, called after the donkeys who used to wind their way up the ramps inside carrying building material. The architect of this church made a bet with the builder of the Steinerne Brücke that he would finish first (*see* **Along the River** below). He lost rather dismally: the bridge was finished in 11 years, long before the cathedral. If you look up onto the roof of the Eselsturm, you can see a little statue of the hapless architect. He threw himself off the tower when he lost the bet.

Work on the present cathedral came to a complete halt for 100 years during the Reformation, when the Protestant city fathers wouldn't grant the bishops any money. When work resumed in the 17th century, the interior was decorated according to the new Baroque fashion—which meant that all the medieval stained-glass windows were replaced with clear glass. Recent restoration work has tried to recapture the old Gothic mood, and all that remains from the Baroque period is a splendid gold and silver altar. One set of 14th-century windows was left (in the south transept), containing parts of windows (exquisitely made with fingernail-sized pieces of glass) from the original Romanesque church. Across in the north transept is a modern window in a bold, rather ethnic design. This caused a local rumpus when it went up in 1986—people said it looked like a totem pole. Other highlights of the church include 13th-century statues of the Annunciation, with a beaming Gabriel and suitably stunned Mary, both wrapped in swathes of perfectly carved cloth; and two niches at the western nave entrance containing grotesque little figures of the Devil and his grandmother.

To see the **cloisters** you must go on a guided tour *(May–Oct Mon–Sat 10am, 11am and 2pm, Sun 12 and 2; Nov–Apr Mon–Sat 11, Sun 12; adm DM2.50)*. This is worth it for a look at the **Allerheiligenkapelle**, a graceful Romanesque chapel with traces of original 12th-century frescoes, and the 11th-century **Stephanskapelle** which still has its original altar (with openings at the base where the faithful would pop in notes with requests to their saint, whose relics lay inside). On the north side of the cathedral, the **Domschatzmuseum** (Cathedral Treasures Museum) *(Apr–Oct Tues–Sat 10–5, Sun 11.45–5; Dec–Mar Fri and Sat 10–4, Sun 11.45–4; adm DM2)*, housed in a former bishop's palace, has richly embroidered vestments dating back to the 11th century and rooms of sacramental treasures—including some fine Jugendstil pieces. The **Diözesan-museum St Ulrich** *(Apr–Oct Tues–Sun 10–5; adm DM2, DM3 for joint ticket)*, around the back of the cathedral, is worth a visit for the building itself, a 12th-century court chapel. The supremely elegant arches inside are covered in ornamental frescoes from the 16th to 17th centuries. Most notable of the collection of paintings and sculptures to be seen here is the aptly named *Beautiful Madonna* by the great Regensburg painter Albrecht Altdorfer (1480–1538).

Altdorfer's Madonna once hung in the tiny Gothic church of **St Johannes**, just at the entrance to the cathedral and formerly its baptistry. Early in 1992 the priest in charge of St Johannes decided that its tower needed a clock and, much to the consternation of the purists, he raised the money and put one up—a rather elegant timepiece complete with musical bells.

Across the square, directly opposite the cathedral, is a former patrician palace, the **Haus Heuport**. In the porch you can see the 14th-century carvings of a wicked seducer (with a snake crawling out of his back) luring a virgin with an apple. The maid has just spilt her cup of oil. The exact history of the statues isn't known, but love letters (written in Latin), found buried under the stairs just a few months before this guide went to print, might throw some light on the affair.

A few strides south brings you to Neupfarrplatz. Stranded on a concrete island in the middle of this expanse of tarmac and paving is the **Neupfarrkirche**, a rather plain church built on the site of a synagogue which had been destroyed in 1519. Just before the church was finished the city council adopted the Reformation, so this became Regensburg's first Protestant church. Nearby, on Pfauengasse (just off the south side of Domplatz) through an unassuming little door, is Regensburg's smallest chapel, the **Mariae Laeng Kapelle**. In the 17th century the notion arose that if you wrote out your prayer on a piece of paper as long as Mary, your request would be granted. The Church didn't approve, but the belief proved tenacious and the chapel is still cluttered with flapping notes and framed messages of thanks.

A walk back eastwards across the Domplatz brings you to the Alter Kornmarkt, where you'll find the **Herzoghof** (Ducal Court), a 13th-century mansion with a stone tower, probably the site of the first Agilofinger residence (nowadays it belongs to the Post Office). On the south side of the Alter Kornmarkt is the **Alte Kapelle**, a sober church from the out-side, but a Rococo riot within; while off the northern end of the square is the **Niedermünster**, a Romanesque basilica, now the cathedral parish church. Recent excava-tions have uncovered Merovingian, Carolingian and even Roman predecessors (these can be viewed by appointment only, © 560 200). Down towards the river, on Unter den Schibbögen, you can see the heavy stone blocks of **Porta Praetoria**, once the northern gate of the Roman fort. Part of the tower and one of the arches are still preserved.

Along the River

After the cathedral, Regensburg's most prominent landmark is the **Steinerne Brücke**, a stone bridge of 16 graceful arches that spans the Danube. It was built between 1135 and 1146 in preparation for a crusade (the wooden bridge it replaced would have collapsed under the massed ranks of a departing army). The builder supposedly made a pact with the Devil. If the Devil helped him to win his bet with the cathedral's architect by finishing the bridge first, then the first soul that crossed it would be despatched immediately to Hell. The wily builder won his bet, and foxed Satan too: first to cross the bridge was a donkey. As the only strong and defendable river-crossing along the entire length of the Danube at the time, the Steinerne Brücke contributed greatly to Regensburg's success as a trading town. Two of the three **gates** on the bridge were blown up by Napoleon, but you can see the third—which he left intact as a fitting frame for his triumphal entry into the city. The bridge still rests on its original foundations—sturdy piles of stone that have never had to be repaired and that confuse the powerful Danube into a series of whirlpools. Legend had it that only a virgin could sail across these rapids and survive. Undaunted by this, local companies offer boat trips across them. Alongside the gate is the **Salzstadel** (City Salt Store, now a restaurant), built between 1616 and 1620. Boats carried the precious 'white gold' along a canal that went right into the building. Inside you can see the lift shaft up which the salt was hauled to safe storage. If you look carefully at the old wooden beams in the ceiling, you'll see that they are still encrusted with white crystals. Next door is the **Historische Wurstküche** (*see* **Eating and Drinking** below), a sausage kitchen probably built as the bridge workers' canteen. Mozart munched the delicious Regensburger *Wurst* here, and lodged across the way in the **Zum Weissen Lamm** (as did Goethe some years later).

A short walk west along the River brings you to Keplerstraße named after Johannes Kepler (1571–1630) whose work on planetary motion ranks him with Copernicus as a founder of modern astronomy. He lived on and off in Regensburg throughout his life, and died in the house at No. 5, now the **Kepler-Gedächtnishaus** *(guided tours Tues–Sat 10am, 11am, 2pm and 3pm, Sun 10 and 11; adm DM2.50)*, which contains a less than riveting collection of period furniture and instruments, and displays on Kepler's life and works. Also on Keplerstraße, however, is the **Runtinger Haus**, one of the best preserved Regensburg patrician palaces. It was built for the Runtinger family around 1400. Matteus Runtinger joined together two older houses by building a grand banqueting hall, seating nearly 120 (it is still hired out for grand parties) and had his architect copy features of Italian villas he had seen on his travels. Unfortunately, you can't visit the house, which is now the offices of the Bavarian Monuments Bureau. Rich merchants such as Runtinger, bringing back these new architectural ideas from Italy, sparked off a fashion for **fortified mansions** with solid castle-like towers. The towers were (like the number of horses you had) merely a status symbol: most were completely empty, save for a chapel at ground level. The houses were built around courtyards, which were entered through an arch large enough to drive a coach through, and closed off by a heavy wooden door. All around town you can glimpse these courtyards—often with Italianate first-floor loggias.

The Merchant Quarter

The **Altes Rathaus**, on Rathausplatz just west of the cathedral, was the centre of medieval Regensburg. The oldest section was built in the mid-13th century. A banqueting hall was incorporated in about 1360, and a Baroque eastern wing was added in the early 18th century. From the outside the Rathaus is an unassuming building with just one flourish—a decorative Gothic balcony from which the Holy Roman Emperor would wave to a respectful populace. The square itself was the scene of much imperial pomp. When Ferdinand III was crowned in the 16th century, the streets as far as the cathedral were covered in red, white and yellow cloth, coins were thrown to the crowd and a fountain gushed red and white wine.

To see the magnificent **interior** of the Rathaus you need to go on a guided tour *(May–Sept Mon–Sat 3.15pm in English; Mon–Sat 9.30, 10.30, 11.30, 2, 3, 4 and Sun 10, 11, 12 in German; adm DM3, tickets from the tourist office—ask for* Reichstagmuseum Führung). The highlight of the tour is a visit to the **Imperial Hall** (once the banqueting chamber) where the Perpetual Imperial Diet of the Holy Roman Empire sat from 1663 to 1806. It is a small, but sumptuously decorated room with an impressive free suspended wooden ceiling, and is laid out just as it was when nobles from around the empire came to wrangle about imperial policy. There is a simple canopied chair for the emperor, and punishingly hard, colour-coded benches (green for princes, red for Electors) for the rest. The tour also includes a well-equipped **Torture Chamber** (torture was only abolished in 1806).

The streets around the Rathaus still follow Roman and medieval lines. **Wahlenstraße**, south of Rathausplatz, and the surrounding alleys, such as Untere-Bachgasse, Obere-Bachgasse and Kramgasse are the most rewarding spots for looking at historic city architecture. Wahlenstraße is the city's oldest street. Here you will find the **Goldener Turm**, the highest remaining patrician tower (now with a wine bar at the top). Obere-Bachgasse 7 was the painter **Albrecht Altdorfer's house**, and at No. 15 are the remains of one of the **private chapels** that used to grace the merchants' towers.

Obere-Bachgasse, at its northern end, becomes Untere-Bachgasse. From here, if you duck down the quaint little medieval alley of Hinter der Grieb, then along Rote-Hahnen-Gasse, you come to **Haidpaltz**. This vast square was once a jousting arena and the scene of a bloody battle in the 10th century between one Krako the Hun and a local hero called Dollinger. Dollinger won, and earned himself (as well as the usual purse of gold) immortality in the form of the Dollinger Ballad, still recited today. These days Haidplatz is the stomping ground of scruffs with ghettoblasters.

On the northern end of the square is the former inn **Zum Golden Kreuz**, which from the 16th to the 19th century was the grand lodging place of princes visiting the town to attend the Diet. The 46-year-old **Emperor Charles V** caused tongues to wag when he used the hotel as a trysting place during his affair with the local teenage beauty **Barbara Blomberg**. One of the results of the liaison was a son, Juan de Austria, who was born here in 1547. He banished his mother to a nunnery (she had continued her errant ways long after Charles V died) and went on to become an heroic soldier and Governor of the Netherlands. Further along the square is the big Neoclassical **Thon-Dittmer Palace**, which unites several earlier Gothic houses and is now an arts centre with an elegant wood-panelled concert hall. The large courtyard is surrounded by graceful Renaissance galleries and is used in the summer for outdoor performances.

A few minutes' walk west of Haidplatz (along Ludwigstraße, then down Drei-Mohren-Straße and across Bismarckplatz) is the mysterious old **St Jakobskirche**. It is also known as the *Schottenkirche* (Scots' Church) after the Irish monks who founded it in 1090. (The Irish were at that time referred to as *Schotte*—ironically the monastery became a Scottish one in the 16th century, and remained so until its dissolution 300 years later.) The Romanesque portal is covered in puzzling pagan-like designs. The whores and hangmen that crowd together with mermaids, monsters and more conventional Christian iconography, defy modern attempts at interpretation. The two most feasible theories are that the carvings depict a scene from the Last Judgement, or tell the story of the original Irish monks' voyage across the seas in answer to Charlemagne's call. The dim interior, with its low arches and oddly carved pillars, evokes an early Christianity, rich with ancient rites and rituals. In the Byzantine apse is a carved 12th-century crucifixion group with a dramatically miserable Virgin and Mary Magdalene.

Further west at Dr.-Johann-Maier-Str. 5, but worth the extra 10 minutes' walk, is the **Ostdeutsche Galerie** (East German Gallery) *(Apr–Sept Tues–Sat 10–1 and 2–5, Sun 10–1; Oct–Mar Tues–Sat 10–1 and 2–4, Sun 10–1; adm DM2.50; Bus 11 or 6)*, an interesting collection of 19th- and 20th-century paintings, graphics and sculpture by artists who lived or worked in the former East Germany. As well as pieces by such notables as Otto Dix, Lovis Corinth and the expressionist Karl Schmidt-Rottluff, there is some odd, rather kitschy surrealist work from the 1960s and 1970s. There is also a good collection of early 20th-century sculpture, which includes Käthe Kollwitz's poignant *Soldatenfrauen* (1937).

South of the Centre

Obere-Bachgasse leads south to Emmeramsplatz, which is dominated by the church of the **St Emmeram** monastery, founded in the 8th century on the site of an old Roman church, and for centuries one of the most important centres of learning in Europe. In the 19th century the monastery was secularized. Its new owners, the Princes von Thurn und Taxis (*see* below) kitted it out with such new-fangled inventions as flushing toilets, hot and cold running water and electric lights. The church itself, however, remains in use. Part of the interior was splendidly reworked in 1730 by those famous Baroque designers, the Asam brothers—though the older parts of the church (most notably the 12th-century vestibule) have more charm and mystique. Around the right-hand side of the main altar you can see fragments of a wall that dates back to Carolingian times, and in the crypt there are remnants of 8th-century wall-paintings.

The **Schloß Thurn und Taxis** is immediately behind the church. The fortune made in pioneering a European mail service in the 16th century (and cornering the monopoly well into the 19th) has made the 'T und T's' probably the richest family in Germany. They own 17 per cent of Regensburg, vast tracts of forestland in Germany and Canada, and the largest private Bavarian brewery (locals nickname the beer *Tod und Teufel*—Death and the Devil). The present Fürst (prince) is not yet in his teens, but his mother, Gloria, (who was some 30 years her late husband's junior) cuts a dash on the Munich social scene. In Regensburg she is known as 'the punk princess', and at the Café Princess in town you can buy succulent chocolates called *Kese Gloria* ('saucy Gloria'). Her Regensburg home boasts more rooms than Buckingham Palace, and some of the finest furniture in the land. The family sold up castles in the west of Germany just before the Second World War, and removed the contents to Regensburg, which escaped bombing.

If the family is not at home, you are allowed in for a glimpse at the breathtaking **interiors** *(guided tours only, Mon–Fri 2pm and 3.15pm, Sun 10 and 11.15; adm DM3, information © (0941) 504 8181)*. The tour includes the beautiful former **cloisters** which exhibit the range of Gothic style from the 12th to the 14th centuries. There is also a **Marstallmuseum** (Museum of the Palace Mews) *(guided tours, Mon and Wed–Sat 2 and 3.15, Sun 10 and 11.15; adm DM3)*, a glittering collection of carriages, sleds and sedan chairs.

East of the Centre

Two more museums are a short walk east of the Alter Kornmarkt. The **Stadtmuseum** at Dachauplatz 2–4 *(Tue–Sat 10–4, Sun 10–1; adm DM2.50)*, housed in an old Minorite monastery, ploughs through 2000 years of Regensburg history. Its 100 rooms of exhibits make viewing quite a task, but displays are well laid out. There is an interesting cutaway model of a Roman house, and another of the Steinerne Brücke with all three gates intact. Regensburg's most famous artist, Albrecht Altdorfer (1480–1538), has a room to himself. He was a painter of the **Danube School**, who were known for the elaborate landscapes they used as backgrounds to their work—lush Austrian and Bavarian scenery that often completely overwhelmed the main subject of the painting. Altdorfer's art made him rich, and he became a town councillor and official city architect.

The **Städische Galerie Regensburg** (Municipal Gallery) *(Tues–Sat 10–4, Sun 10–1; adm DM2.50)* is in a converted 15th-century house known, aptly, as the *Leerer Beutel* (empty purse). Here you'll find a rather thin collection of 19th- and 20th-century German art.

Entertainment and Nightlife

There is a thriving **classical music** scene in Regensburg, with concerts taking place in a variety of atmospheric old halls and churches. The tourist office publishes a **Monatsprogramm** (Monthly Programme) of what's on, and also offers a **ticket reservation service**. The city's main theatre, the **Städtische Bühnen**, Bismarckplatz 7, © (0941) 59156, stages mainly opera and dance. The most vibrant venue in town is the **Thon-Dittmer-Palais**, Haidplatz 8, © (0941) 507 2432, offering a varied fare of jazz, classical music and theatre. In summer it holds performances outdoors in its graceful Renaissance courtyard. The **Turmtheater im Goliathhaus**, Watmarkt 5, © (0941) 562 233, sparkles with cabaret and small-scale musicals. Children enjoy the **marionettes** at the **Figurentheater**, Dr.-Johann-Maier-Str. 3, © (0941) 28328 (performances Sept–May, Sat and Sun 3pm).

Nightlife in Regensburg centres mainly on cafés and beer gardens (*see* below), but if you feel like dancing, head for the Sudhaus in Unterebachgasse. The town's noisy and frustrated youth frequent cafés and discos (such as Scala) in the Pustet Passage, off Gesandtenweg near Haidplatz.

Regensburg ℂ (0941–)   *Where to Stay*

expensive

Altstadthotel Arch, Haidplatz 4, ℂ 502 060, fax 502 0668 (DM164–280). The connoisseur's address. A grand old patrician palace which has been stylishly converted. The nickname ('Ark') comes from its odd, bulging boat shape. Most rooms are spacious and all are tastefully decorated.

Bischofshof, Krauterermarkt 3, ℂ 59086, fax 53508 (DM175–200). A richly fitted-out inn that was once the bishop's palace. The rooms are elegant and comfortable and the service impeccable. These days the hotel is the meeting place for everyone who is anyone in Regensburg local politics.

moderate

Münchner Hof, Tändlergasse 9, ℂ 582 6265, fax 561 709 (DM120–140). Smart, newly renovated hotel. The rooms are small, but often have quaint features such as a Gothic wall-niche or old wooden beams. Service is brisk and friendly.

Kaiserhof am Dom, Kramgasse 10–12, ℂ 54027, fax 54025 (DM120–125). Old, family-run hotel in the shadow of the cathedral. Convenient but a bit spartan.

Hotel Rote Hahn, Rote Hahnengasse 10, ℂ 560 907 (DM110). Simple but atmospheric hotel in a 16th-century building in the Merchant Quarter. Some of the rooms are a little small, but still good value and the staff are friendly and attentive.

inexpensive

Spitalgarten, St Katharineplatz 1, ℂ 84774 (DM60 without private bath). Romantic old building with the Danube and a beer garden right outside.

Stadlerbräu, Stadtamthof 15, ℂ 85682 (DM54). Fairly basic, but clean and comfortable guesthouse situated across the Danube in a lively student quarter.

Eating and Drinking

On a fine evening in Regensburg you can have great fun wandering about the medieval alleys and nosing out a restaurant, an old courtyard café or beer garden hidden behind high stone walls. First just the clinking of glasses gives them away, then a shaft of light leads you through an arch or up a passage to a drink and good cheer. Here are a few tips to start you off.

Historiches Eck, Watmarkt 6, ✆ (0941) 58920 (DM50–80). Coolly decorated establishment with suave service and a well-prepared, imaginative menu. You can have simple, succulent venison steaks, or delicate fare such as perch with an asparagus sauce, served with onion confit and wild mushrooms.

Zum Krebs, Krebsgasse 6, ✆ (0941) 55803 (DM50–70). Upmarket restaurant in a medieval house. Tasty Franco-German cuisine.

Hotel Bischofshof am Dom, Krautermarkt 3, ✆ (0941) 59086 (DM40–70). The chef worked for the T und T's for over a decade. Now he runs this smart hotel and makes sure the restaurant is one of the best in town. Delicious variations on traditional German dishes.

David im Goliathaus, Watmarkt 5, ✆ (0941) 561 858 (DM40–60). Attractive restaurant with a roof-garden where you can eat such well-tried perennials as prawn cocktail and duckling with orange.

Bräuerei Kneitinger, Arnulfpaltz 3, ✆ (0941) 52455 (DM15–25). Good, inexpensive Bavarian food in an old tavern atmosphere. Try pancake soup or baked carp.

Historische Wurstküche, An der Steinerne Brücke, ✆ (0941) 59098 (DM10). The medieval McDonalds. For 850 years the little hut on the Danube has dished out Regensburger pork sausages—grilled over beechwood fires and served with sweet mustard and sauerkraut. The same family has owned the *Wurstküche* for the past 200 years. In the summer you sit at long tables beside the river. In winter you crowd into the minuscule, smoke-filled restaurant-cum-kitchen.

Dampfnudel-Uli, Watmarkt 4, ✆ (0941) 53297 (DM5–15). Cluttered and eccentric little restaurant that occupies what was once a private chapel in the base of the medieval Bamburger tower. Uli and Vroni Deutzer serve sweet Bavarian dumplings smothered in a variety of sauces—ranging from simple vanilla to concoctions of fruit, beer and wine.

Bars and Cafés

Hemingway's American Bar, Obere Bachgasse 3–5, ✆ (0941) 561 506 (DM20–40). Fashion victims, dynamic young things with designer spectacles, and the occasional Bogart *manqué* eye each other up as they drink cocktails or eat salads out of huge glass bowls. Homesick Americans will find comfort in the menu.

Café Kominski, Hinter der Grieb 6. Another place to see and be seen as you sip your *Feierabend* drink.

Café Orphée, Untere Bachgasse 8, ✆ (0941) 52977. Wood-panelled French-style café and crêperie. Around the back there is a pretty little garden with a fountain.

Altstadt Café, Hinter der Grieb 8, ✆ (0941) 52646. Traditional café with attractive courtyard garden—popular with locals for long breakfasts.

Türmchen, Wahlenstr. 14. Cosy wine bar at the top of a high fortified tower.

Café Prinzeß, Rathausplatz 2, ☎ (0941) 57671. The oldest Konditorei in Germany. It opened in 1686 to serve pralines to the French delegates at the Imperial Diet, and still produces mouthwatering chocolates and cakes.

Beer Gardens

Bischofshof, Am Dom, ☎ (0941) 59080. Beautifully situated right at the foot of the cathedral in what used to be the bishop's palace garden. The beer garden is still owned by the Bishop of Regensburg, and everyone drinks here—from tourists to the mayor. You can get delicious *Brotzeit* (meat and cheese snacks, DM6–10) to go with your beer.

Spitalgarten, Katharineplatz 1, ☎ (0941) 84774. Right on the Danube, tucked in between the Steinerne Brücke and an old hospital. Popular with laid-back locals.

Kneitinger Keller, Galgenburgerstr. 18. Rip-roaring 1200-seater beer garden within staggering distance of the University.

Zum Gravenreuther, Hinter der Grieb 10, ☎ (0941) 53348. Old inn with a charming little courtyard garden. Work up an appetite first for the hearty Bavarian fare, such as liver dumplings or roast pork with caraway seeds.

Around Regensburg

Shining white on a hill above the Danube, 11km east of Regensburg, stands **Walhalla** *(Apr–Sept daily 9–6; Oct 9–5; Nov–Mar 10–12 and 1–4; adm DM1.50)*, a pompous monument modelled on the Parthenon. It was put up by King Ludwig I in 1842 to honour Germany's heroes, though some have slipped in with dubious qualifications. Featured among the 200 or so plaques and busts of soldiers, artists, philosophers and other notables, you'll find the Dutch humanist Erasmus, Copernicus (a Pole) and scatterings of Austrians and Swiss. It is not a very enthralling site to visit, but the views over the Danube are pretty, and the surrounding park is good picnic territory. You can get to Walhalla by car (take the road along the north bank of the Danube, through Donaustauf), though it is more interesting to go by boat (*see* **Getting Around** above).

An even more attractive boat trip follows the section of the Danube just west of Regensburg. You board at **Kelheim**, 20km southwest of Regensburg (*see* **Getting Around** above). (Just outside Kelheim, on top of the Michelsberg, is another of Ludwig I's monstrous carbuncles, the **Befreiungshalle** (Liberation Hall) *(Apr–Sept daily 8–6; Oct–Mar 9–12 and 1–4; adm DM1.50)*, a rotunda erected to commemorate Bavarians killed in the Napoleonic wars.) The boats pass through the dramatic **Donaudurchbruch** gorge, where the river squeezes through chalk cliffs just 80m apart. The gorge ends suddenly, and the river bends round a wide sandy beach on which stands the solid, faded yellow **Kloster Weltenburg** *(8–7 daily, also accessible by road from Kelheim)*. The Kloster is Bavaria's oldest monastery, but these days is best known for the captivating

Baroque church (decorated by the Asam brothers) and its strong dark beer—buy it from the **Klosterschenke Weltenburg** *(© (09441) 3682; from DM10)* which serves up the monks' brew in the Kloster courtyard and in atmospheric old rooms in the abbey. There's a wide range of food too, from fat pretzels to hunks of roast meat and subtle fish dishes.

See also Directory entry for Straubing.

Passau

All over Europe towns with a few canals or more than one river flowing through them are flattered with Venetian epithets. Passau, the 'Bavarian Venice' is one of the few that comes anywhere near deserving the hype. Napoleon felt it was quite the most beautiful town he had overrun in all Germany. The 18th/19th-century traveller and naturalist, Alexander von Humboldt, ranked Passau among the seven most beautifully situated cities in the world. If you stand on the high battlements of the Vesta Oberhaus fortress and look out over the Altstadt, you might be inclined to agree. Most of Passau is packed onto a peninsula at the confluence of the rivers Danube, Ilz and Inn. Light reflecting off the water blanches the pastel shades of square, Italianate buildings, giving Passau the air of a sunny Mediterranean town. Only when you look closer, and notice how the outdoor tables with their bright umbrellas have been ranged in strict orderly rows, are you reminded that the *piazza* is a *Platz.*

Few foreigners know about this little town at the eastern edge of Germany. Yet in the 14th century Passau was a flourishing trading centre, with turnover on the three rivers more than double that on the Rhine. For centuries the burghers battled with the powerful Prince-Bishops who owned the town. The wealthy merchants hoped for independence, like their neighbours in Regensburg. But the Bishops, ensconced in one of the most impenetrable fortresses in the land, always won. Passau craftsmen did, however, succeed in developing the finest sword blades in Europe, and a 13th-century Bishop of Passau spent his quieter moments writing down the *Nibelungenlied*, Germany's most popular epic poem.

In 1662 a fire reduced the medieval town to rubble, and the present Baroque town was built by fashionable Italian architects. But, as with Regensburg, Passau's fortunes were already on the wane and the city's only recent claims to fame are that Wagner almost chose it over Bayreuth as the site for his music temple, and that a local photographer invented the picture postcard. Today Passau is a university town with a small student population and a reputation for unpleasant right-wing politics.

Getting Around

By car: Passau is just off Autobahn 3, 90km from Linz in Austria, 170km from Munich, 100km from Regensburg and 225km from Nuremberg. If you are travelling from Nuremberg or Regensburg, then the regional road B8, which follows the Danube, is a more **scenic route**. Most **parking garages** are to be found along the southern bank of the Danube.

Car hire: Europcar, Hauptbahnhof, © (0851) 54235.

By train: The **Hauptbahnhof** (information © (0851) 55001) is 10 minutes' walk west of the Altstadt. There are frequent connections to Linz (1hr 10min), to Vienna (3hr), Munich (2hr), and to Regensburg (1hr 10min).

Boat trips: Passau is one town really worth viewing from the water. The leading shipping company on this stretch of the Danube is **Wurm & Köck** (Höllgasse 26, © (0851) 929 292). They offer a 45-minute **Dreiflüsse Rundfahrt** (Three Rivers Cruise, DM7) as well as longer trips as far as Linz (DM30 return). The **Donau-Dampfschiffahrts-Gesellschaft** (DDSG, Im Ort 14a, Dreiflußeck, © (0851) 33035) can take you to Vienna. Most boats leave from the Luitpold-Hängebrücke.

Taxis: © 57373.

Tourist Information

The **tourist information office** at the Neues Rathaus, Rathausplatz *(Mon–Fri 8.30–6, Sat and Sun 10–2; Nov–Mar Mon–Fri 8.30–5)* can help out with maps and leaflets about Passau. The **Infostelle** *(Mon–Fri 9–5, Sat and Sun 9–1)*, alongside the Hauptbahnhof can also give you information on the region—including Austria and the Bavarian Forest.

Police: © 110.

Medical emergencies: © 1 92 22.

Post office: Next to the Hauptbahnhof *(Mon–Fri 8.30–12.30, 2–5.30, Sat 8–12)*.

Market days: Fruit and vegetable market, Tues and Fri mornings on Domplatz.

Festivals

During the **Maidult** in May, the whole town seems to become one large, bright market, and its citizens give themselves over to almost continuous beer-drinking. For the **Burgerfest** at the end of June the formula is enriched by dance, music and sports such as bunji-jumping. At the other end of the scale, the long-established **European Weeks** (EW) from June to August attract to Passau some astonishing European names from the worlds of opera, ballet and classical music.

The Altstadt

Even at close quarters, Passau's Altstadt—with its arcaded streets, narrow alleys, archways, covered stairways and wrought-iron gates—seems more Italian than German. That said, once you've wandered about and soaked in the general atmosphere, there is not very much to see. **St Stephan's Cathedral** is the best place to begin a walkabout. The church is at the highest point in the Altstadt, largely because it rests on the heaped-up ruins of numerous predecessors and of the original Roman Fort Batavis. Today's Baroque church was built in the 17th century to replace a Gothic one all but destroyed by the town fire.

The interior is heavily laden with white stucco, but has an impressive gilded canopied pulpit, crawling with cherubs and angels. The **organ** is the largest in the world. With 231 stops and 17,388 pipes it is roughly twice the size of the one in London's Royal Albert Hall. If you come at 12.30pm on weekdays (during summer) or on Thursdays at 7pm, you can hear a recital *(adm DM3 lunchtimes, DM6 evenings)*.

Residenzplatz, behind the cathedral, is a small cobbled square lined with patrician mansions. From here you get the best view of the controlled and rather elegant late-Gothic east end of St Stephan's. Alongside is the grand 18th-century **episcopal palace**. A walk down Schrottgasse brings you to the Gothic **Rathaus**, which defiantly faces the bishops' fortress across the river. The building was the home of the wealthy Haller family, who for generations led citizens' rebellions, and as early as 1298 had given up some rooms for use as a town hall. Lovers of rich décor can pop inside for a look at the **Großer Saal** *(Easter–Oct Mon–Fri 10–12 and 1.30–4, Sat and Sun 10–4; adm DM1)*, a weighty conglomeration of Baroque marble, 15th-century stained glass and enormous 19th-century wall paintings.

On the other side of the Rathausplatz in the Hotel Wilde Mann is the **Passauer Glasmuseum** *(daily 10–4; adm DM3)*, a vast and excellent collection of glassware, well worth a visit even if you're not a connoisseur. Exhibits range from the exquisite to the wacky— room after room resplendent with painted glass, clear glass, garish colours and curious shapes. The Jugendstil and Art Deco pieces are particularly good, and there is some finely painted 19th-century work. East of the Rathaus, on Bräugasse, you'll find the **Stiftung Wörlen** (Wörlen Foundation museum of modern art) *(Tues–Sun 10–6; adm DM5)*. There is no permanent collection, but visiting exhibitions are of a high standard and the building, with its pretty arcaded courtyard, makes an attractive setting whatever is on show.

Vesta Oberhaus

The medieval bishops' fortress of Vesta Oberhaus looms over the town from the top of a rocky outcrop across the Danube. It is easy to see how the building became the focus of the citizens' anger, and also why it proved hopelessly unassailable over the centuries. Today the fortress has been converted into a warren of **museums** *(Tues–Sun 9–5, closed Feb; general adm DM3)*. You can reach Vesta Oberhaus by crossing the Luitpoldbrücke, then walking up a precipitous flight of stairs cut into the rock. If that seems a little daunting, you can catch a bus from the Rathausplatz *(Apr–Oct, half hourly from 11.30–5)*. Once there you can wander through the old rooms and courtyards and see early Passau picture-postcards and maps of Bavaria in the **Lithograph Museum**; some nondescript contemporary art in the **20th-Century Gallery**; Gothic painting and sculpture in the **Diocesan Museum**; an interesting collection of craftsmen's tools, and sculpture by the city's most famous artist, Hans Wimmer, in the **City Museum**; and some rickety old waggons in the **Fire Brigade Museum**. But by far the best reason for visiting the fortress is for the magnificent views over Passau and the three rivers. The pale Danube, the muddy Inn and the Ilz, turned a deep green-black by the marshy soils of the Bavarian Forest, swirl together in marble colours, before continuing eastwards. Interestingly, although the Inn is deeper, broader and has travelled further to get here than the Danube, it is still regarded as a tributary.

expensive

Hotel Wilder Mann, Am Rathausplatz, © 35071, fax 31712 (DM130–230). A converted 11th-century palace on the Danube, and one of the best hotels in the region. The rooms are sumptuously decorated—mostly with antiques (the best ones are at the back, with balconies overlooking a quiet garden). The service is relaxed and friendly, there's a Michelin-starred restaurant, a swimming pool in the Gothic vault, and even an in-house museum (*see* above).

moderate

Hotel König, Untere Donaulände 1, © 35028, fax 31784 (DM 140–150). Recently modernized hotel with comfortable rooms looking out across the river to the Vesta Oberhaus. The new architects managed to slip a sauna and solarium into the design.

Altstadt Hotel, Braügasse 23–29, © 3370, fax 337 100 (DM120–160). Smart, modernized hotel with a terrace-restaurant overlooking the point where the three rivers meet. The hotel has its own underground garage.

inexpensive

Pension Rößner, Braügasse 19, © 2035, fax 36247 (DM80–90). Family-run *pension* right on the Danube. The rooms are small, but cosy.

Pension Weißes Lamm, Theresienstr. 10, © 2219 (DM47–50). Clean pension in the modern, pedestrianized shopping precinct, but within easy walking distance of all the Altstadt sights.

Eating and Drinking: Restaurants and Taverns

Heilig-Geist-Stiftschenke, Heilig-Geist-Gasse 4, © 2607 (DM25–35). A *Weinstube* that dates back to 1358. Heavy wooden tables under low arches, bread in baskets and good wine thumped down in ceramic jugs. The food is mouthwatering—with fish from their private waters and a lengthy pancake menu (the wild mushroom fillings are delicious).

Zum Jodlerwirt, Schrottgasse 12, © 2422 (DM25–45). The venue for *Weißbier* aficionados, with yodelling and jolly folk music on Saturdays and hearty Bavarian cuisine, such as venison ragout and potato dumplings.

Ristorante Zi'Teresa, Theresienstr. 26, © 2138 (DM15–40). Homemade pizzas and pasta in a popular restaurant with a small garden. **Drei Linden**, Steinweg 6 (DM20–30). Cosy Gasthof near the cathedral. Good local and Austrian dishes—especially fish and game.

Theresiencafé, Theresienstr. 14. Tranquil daytime café with a small courtyard garden. Ideal for late breakfasts and lunches.

Café Kowalski, Obersand 1. Away from the tourist crush, but crammed with local trendies and students. The tiny balcony overlooking the Inn is popular at sundown.

Café Duft, Theresienstr. 22. Central café with a neighbourhood atmosphere—the honeypot of local gossip. You can also get a bite to eat.

Café Aquarium, Unteresandstr. 2. Aptly named chrome-and-glass box where people go to be seen.

Goldenes Schiff, Unteresandstr. 8. Popular student drinking tavern with a tiny garden round the back. Serves good cheap grub too.

The Bavarian Forest and the Upper Palatinate

The **Bavarian Forest** (German: *Bayerische Wald*), which gives its name to the eastern-most strip of Bavaria, is one of the last wild areas in Europe. It spreads way into Bohemia across the Czech border, and merges in the north with the **Upper Palatinate** (German: *Oberpfalz*). This confusing echo with the Rhineland region arises because the area was ruled by the powerful Electors Palatine of the Rhine, a senior branch of the Bavarian Wittelsbachs. This is an idyllic land of meadows and wild-flowers, forests in unimagined shades of green, hidden lakes and fast, chuckling streams. When the mists come down the woods seem secret and isolated—but more often than not the sun is shining, the air seems honey-scented and is filled with the warbles and chirrups of birdsong. This is one of the few places where the roadsign showing a leaping deer can be taken literally.

City Germans scoffingly refer to this out-of-the-way part of their country as the 'Bavarian Congo', yet this gives you the clue to its charm. Here life goes on in much the same way as it has done for centuries. There are story-book farmyards, colourful local festivals and hardly any foreign tourists at all. The food is excellent, and accommodation encouragingly cheap.

Despite the lush appearance of the countryside, the soil is rocky and hard to farm—but it does contain large silica deposits. This, and the abundance of firewood for furnaces, led the medieval woodsmen to take the cue from their Bohemian neighbours and begin blowing glass. (Town names that end in '-hütt' or '-reuth' derive from the old German word for a glassworks.) Today **glass-blowing** is still more an individual craft than a large industrial affair. Most larger factories use traditional methods, and dotted around the forest towns are workshops where you can watch craftspeople puffing and sweating beside glowing furnaces.

Getting Around

By car: A car is essential if you really want to get about the area easily and explore remoter corners. Roads are all well-made. The most scenic routes are along and around the B85 and the B22.

By train: If you are coming by train, head for Grafenau or Furth im Wald, both of which are handy bases for exploring the countryside. Trains leave from Regensburg and Passau, but you will have to change two or three times, and the journey will take up to three hours.

Hiking: As always in Germany this is well-organized, with marked routes around the forests, and mountain huts where you can sleep the night. Tourist offices and bookshops can supply you with detailed maps. The most determined hikers could try the 180km *Nördliche Hauptwanderlinie* (Furth im Wald to Dreisesselberg, 7–10 days). The *Südliche Hauptwanderlinie* (105km, Rattenberg–Kalteneck, 5–7 days) in the rolling hills near the Danube valley is easier on the legs. An even softer option is the route through the middle of the forest from Kötzing (near Cham) to Bayerisch Eisenstein (on the Czech border; 50km, 2 days).

By bicycle: Perhaps the ideal way to see the area—you can get about at a civilized speed, stop where you like, and really appreciate the countryside. You'll need a bike with gears though, as some parts of the Forest can be quite hilly. Again, there are all sorts of marked routes ranging from those you can knock off in a few hours to some that take days. The Bavarian Regional Tourist Office (Landesfremden-verkehrsverband Bayern e.V., Prinzregentstr. 18, 8000 München 22, ✆ (089) 212 3970) brings out a detailed brochure (available from tourist offices throughout the area) which grades routes according to difficulty and also suggests those which are suitable for children.

Tourist Information

Bavarian Forest National Park: The Visitor Centre, Hans-Eisenmann Haus, Böhmstr. 35, Neuschönau (near Grafenau), ✆ (08558) 1300 *(Mon–Sat 9–5)* runs slide-shows about the Park and the dreaded *Waldsterben* ('forest death', *see* below). They also offer tours of the park, sell maps, and can give hiking suggestions.

Cham: Cordonhaus, Propsteistr. 46, ✆ (09971) 4933.

Furth im Wald: Schloßplatz 1, ✆ (09973) 3813.

Grafenau: Rathausgasse 1, ✆ (08552) 42743.

Kötzing: Herrenstr. 10, ✆ (09941) 602 150.

Waldsassen: Town Administration, Johannisplatz 11, ✆ (09632) 8828.

Festivals

Roman Catholic farmers find lots of excuses to celebrate, and the towns around the Bavarian Forest are alive with colourful religious parades, seasonal festivals with ancient pagan roots, and busy fairs. Festivities take many forms—from costume parades requiring months of preparation, to a village bash in a beer tent, accompanied by a man on an electric accordian. Early spring and summer, Easter and

Corpus Christi are the most rewarding times of the year to catch the local revels.

The most famous festival in the region, and one of Germany's largest, is the **Drachenstich** in Furth im Wald on the second and third Sundays in August. There is a fair, lots of food and beer and an opening procession with 200 horses and many hundreds more people in *Tracht*. The highlight is a re-enactment of St George's battle with the dragon (a spectacle which goes back over 900 years, making it the oldest piece of folk theatre in Germany). A local lad dons armour and slays an 18m luminous green (and these days mechanized) monster, which dies dramatically, spurting blood all over the delighted onlookers. The performance lasts 75 minutes and is repeated at intervals throughout the festival. Tickets cost from DM5 (standing) to DM30 and can be booked through the *Drachenstichfestausschuß* (Stadtplatz 4, © (09973) 9254).

The **Pfingstritt** is an impressive procession of decorated horses and men in *Tracht* that makes its way, on Whit Monday, from Kötzing (near Cham) to the pilgrimage church at Steinbühl, 7km away (starts 8am). There a couple are symbolically married, and the whole show returns to Kötzing for a knees-up in the town square.

From Passau to Zwiesel

The first stop out of Passau, 20km up the B85, is **Tittling**, where you'll find the **Museumsdorf Bayerischer Wald** *(daily 9–5.30; adm DM5)*, an impressive outdoor museum of some 50 reconstructed farmhouses dating from the 15th to the 19th centuries. A little further along the B85, a side-road ducks off to Grafenau, Spielgau and Frauenau, three towns that border the vast National Park. The towns, while not in themselves particularly attractive, are thick with *pensions* and rooms to let and make convenient bases for ventures into the forest. **Grafenau** is the most touristy, with a railway station and intermittent invasions of coach parties. At **Frauenau** you can visit the **Freiherr von Poschinger Kristallfabrik**, Moosauhütte, © (09926) 703 *(guided tours Mon–Sat 9.45–11.30 and 12.45–1.30; adm DM1.50)*, a glassworks that has been in the same family for 14 generations and which achieved worldwide fame for its Jugendstil pieces. Although the company now employs over 200 workers, they still use traditional glass-blowing methods. **Glashütte Valentin Eisch**, Am Steg 7, © (09926) 279, also admits visitors and has a reputation for zanier, more avant-garde work. The **Glasmuseum**, Am Museumpark *(daily 9–5; adm DM3)* has a collection of glass from ancient Egyptian to modern times (though not as impressive as the one in Passau) and gives you a thorough technical introduction to glassmaking in the area. The nearby village of **Zwiesel** is a centre for many of the individual glassblowers and smaller firms—most of whom don't mind if you pop your head in for a look.

The **National Park** itself is 13,000 hectares of rolling moorland, lush forest and mountains. It is dotted with inns and private guesthouses, and in some places there are preserves for animals (such as bears, lynx and buffalo) that used to roam freely. The air here is as unpolluted as in the centre of an ocean, but sadly the forests are succumbing to

Waldsterben, the killing disease that has affected nearly 80 per cent of Germany's trees. Many blame acid rain caused by pollution from British factories, but recent research points the finger at exhaust fumes from the millions of cars that shoot about the German Autobahns. Despite the alarming statistics, the forests appear healthy enough.

From Zwiesel to Waldsassen

Country roads winding north of Zwiesel bring you to **Bodenmais**, a bustling resort that seems made up entirely of glassware shops and *pensions*. It is, however, a good base for visiting the **Arbersee**, a dark lake squeezed between forested slopes at the foot of the region's highest mountain—**Grosser Arber** (1456m). The summit of the mountain, and a panoramic view, can be reached by chair lift. You can also hike along the river Arber, which drops in a series of falls and cascades through the **Risslochschlucht** gorge.

A few kilometres further on you come to the towns of **Kötzing** and **Furth im Wald** (*see* **Festivals** above). The fearsome *Drachenstich* dragon can be seen all year round in a lair near the Furth im Wald tourist office. There is also a display on the history of the pageant. Nearby is the small walled town of Cham, a hub of local transport and famous for its beers. The local Hofmark brewery produces the malty *Würzig-Mild* and tasty, somewhat bitter *Würzig-Herb*. Here the countryside opens out, and the B22 takes you north through a lonely landscape dotted with copses, isolated farms and the odd ruined castle. The town of **Waldsassen**, 130km up the road from Cham, is, however, very much worth the journey for its impressive Baroque **Stift** (collegiate church) and **Stiftsbibliothek** (library) *(summer Tues–Sun 10–11.30 and 2–5, winter 10–11 and 2–4)*. The library is a rich mixture of old volumes and elaborate woodcarving. Its upper gallery is supported by a series of figures carved to represent everyone connected with books. At times the connections become a little strained (such as the figure of the shepherd: the skins of his flock were used as book-binding). From Waldsassen it is only a short journey west to Bayreuth or Nuremberg.

Where to Stay

Accommodation in the Bavarian Forest is plentiful and cheap. You can get private rooms from as little as DM16 per person. Many of these are in farmhouses or in cottages in the woods, and are often a much better bet than hotels. Look out for the *Fremdenzimmer* or *Zimmer zu vermieten* signs. Small villages such as the romantic **Klingenbrunn** (5km from Spiegelau, right on the edge of the National Park) are better alternatives to the towns, and will almost always have empty rooms.

Grafenau

Steigenberger Hotel Sonnenhof, Sonnenstr. 12, © (08552) 4480, fax 4680 (from DM200). A smart modern hotel designed to pamper your every whim. All the rooms have balconies, and in-house facilities include tennis courts, a steam bath, sauna, swimming pool, jacuzzi and hunky ski instructors.

Säumerhof, Steinberg 32, ✆ (08552) 2401 (DM120–180). Comfortable, tastefully decorated rooms, and personal attention from the owner—who also cooks superb meals.

Hohenau

Die Bierhütte, Bierhütte 10, Hohenau, ✆ (08558) 315, fax 2387 (DM150–170). Cosy hotel between Grafenau and Freyung, set beside a small lake. The romantic old building was once a glassworks and brewery, and is these days run with tender loving care by the Störzer family.

Bodenmais

Bayerwaldhotel Hofbräuhaus, 8373 Bodenmais, ✆ (09924) 7021, fax (09924) 7210 (from DM90). Traditional Bavarian hotel, owned by the same family for over 100 years. It is friendly, *gemütlich* and also offers a Fitness Centre and indoor pool.

Furth im Wald

Hotel zur Post, Stadtplatz 12, ✆ (09973) 1506 (DM60–90). Comfortable hotel in the middle of town.

Hotel Gasthof Himmelreich, Himmelreich 7, ✆ (09973) 1840 (DM70–80). Quiet pension, set a little back from the busy High Street.

Hohenbogen, Bahnhofstr. 25, ✆ (09973) 1509 (DM60–80). Cheery, down-to-earth pension with spotless rooms. Also serves good meals (DM20–40).

Eating and Drinking

Dotted all over the forest are inns and small villages with guesthouses where you can have a good meal for under DM20 a head. The following suggestions might start you on your way.

Brauerei-Gasthof Eck, Eck 1, Böbrach, ✆ (09923) 685. Picture-book hillside inn with an in-house brewery. Excellent cuisine and good beer.

Brauereigasthof Kamm, Bräugasse 1, Zenting, ✆ (09907) 315. House brewery serving hearty Bavarian dishes such as venison ragout and wild mushroom pancakes.

Säumerhof, Steinberg 32, ✆ (08552) 2401, Grafenau (DM35–50). Superb, imaginative cuisine using local produce and game, and a relaxed friendly atmosphere.

If you would like to spend some time on a **farm**, or learn how to make traditional Bavarian Sunday roast pork and dumplings, some local farmers take in guests between May and October, and are happy to show you around their farms and farm kitchens. Prices vary according to the length of your stay, but work out at around DM160 per person per week, including breakfast. The following are renowned for their scrumptious Sunday roasts: Marile Geier, Emminger Str. 23, Schöllnach, ✆ (09903) 347; Hannelore Koller, Alberting 35, Grafling, ✆ (0991) 25326; Anni Weiherer, Eidsberg 36, Grafling, ✆ (0991) 25756.

Nürnberg (Nuremberg)

Nuremberg is Bavaria's second largest city and the capital of Franconia. It is a 'city with a past', most recently remembered as the scene of vast Nazi rallies and the 1945–9 war crimes trials. Before Allied bombers flattened 90 per cent of the Altstadt in a single air-raid on 2 January 1945, Nuremberg had been considered one of the most beautiful towns in Germany.

It was a centre of art, science, trade and craft; home to Albrecht Dürer, Germany's most famous painter, to Hans Sachs (the original *Meistersinger* of Nuremberg), and to the inventors of the first world globe, the pocket watch and the lead pencil. Luther wrote that 'Nuremberg shines throughout Germany, like a sun among the moon and stars'. Pope Pius II praised the town's dazzling splendour and wrily remarked that 'the Kings of Scotland would be glad to be housed so luxuriously as the ordinary citizens of Nuremberg'. Adalbert Stifter, a 19th-century poet, enthused that the entire city was a work of art whose 'gracefulness, serenity and purity' of line filled him with irrepressibly gratifying feelings.

These days you would be forgiven for not getting quite so excited about Nuremberg. It is an odd mixture of dull modern architecture and painstakingly restored old buildings. No longer a vortex for art and industry, it is, however, an attractive and lively town, justifiably famous for its Christmas Market, scrumptious sausages and chewy gingerbread. There is some first-rate art to be seen, and the German National Museum, based here since 1852, has one of the most varied and impressive collections in the country.

See also Directory entries for Coburg and Kulmbach.

History

Nuremberg's zenith was in the Middle Ages. It had been declared a Free Imperial city by Frederick II in 1219 and was at a nexus of the western world's main trade routes: from the Balkans to Antwerp, from Hamburg to Venice and from Paris to Prague. The city was also famed for its bell-founders, candlestick-makers, woodcarvers, glass-painters and, above all, for producing precision scientific instruments. By the 16th-century Nuremberg had become equally celebrated for its painting and sculpture, and was beginning to achieve an almost mythical status in the eyes of many Germans. That is why, even after new trade routes to the Americas had robbed the city of its wealth (by diverting trade with the east from land to sea), Nuremberg became the focus for the Pan-German movement in the 19th century. Later the Nazis were to warp this symbolism even further. Hitler commissioned huge monuments to his 1000-year Reich to be built at the edge of the city, and Nuremberg became the scene of rousing Nazi rallies. The Allies, too, seemed to recognize this symbolic importance when they chose Nuremberg as the venue for bringing the surviving Nazi leaders to trial after the war.

Today Nuremberg still produces pencils and scientific instruments, and is noted in the industrial world as a leading manufacturer of children's toys. But, though it is a mecca for street entertainers in the summer, Nuremberg has lost any claim to being the cultural centre of Germany.

By air: Nuremberg **airport** (information ✆ (0911) 350 6200) is just 7km north of the centre. There are frequent flights to local German airports, and also connections to London, Amsterdam, Paris, Milan and Brussels. A bus shuttle service will run you to the Hauptbahnhof in 20 minutes (every 30min, 5am–11.30pm).

By train: The **Hauptbahnhof** is south of the Altstadt, just outside the old city wall. Intercity trains run hourly, with connections to Hamburg (4hr), Frankfurt (2¾hr) and Munich (1½hr).

By car: Nuremberg cowers in the middle of one of Europe's biggest motorway junctions: Autobahns connect you to every major city in Germany. One word of warning—since reunification the A9 to Berlin has become treacherously busy, and in some places isn't quite up to the load—traffic is heavy, and sometimes jams fast.

Car hire: Avis, airport, ✆ (0911) 528 966; Europa, Fürther Str. 31, ✆ (0911) 260 308.

Mitfahrzentrale: Allersberger Str. 31a, ✆ (0911) 446 9666.

Public transport: The Altstadt is quite small enough to get about on foot. However, should you need it there is a comprehensive network of buses, trams and U-Bahn lines. The same tickets are valid on all three. Prices depend on how many zones you cross, and can be bought at most stops.

Taxis: ✆ 20555.

The main **tourist information office** is opposite the Hauptbahnhof, ✆ (0911) 233 632 *(Mon–Sat 9–8)*. There's a branch in the Altstadt at Hauptmarkt 18, ✆ (0911) 233 634 *(Mon–Sat 9–1 and 2–6, Sun 9–1 and 2–4)*.

Post office: Next to the Hauptbahnhof at Bahnhofplatz 1. It also offers **exchange facilities**.

Police: ✆ 110.

Medical emergencies: ✆ 533 771.

Market days: There is a good week-day fruit and vegetable market on the Marktplatz. At the beginning of the asparagus season in May, this becomes a market devoted to asparagus.

Nuremberg has the largest and most famous **Christkindelsmarkt** (Christmas market, literally: Christ-child's market) in Germany. At the beginning of the 17th century it became the fashion to give children presents at Christmas rather than at New Year, which had previously been the custom. The market that grew up in Nuremberg to meet the demand for carved toys and tasty goodies became the prototype for similar fairs now held in nearly every town in the country.

From the Friday before Advent until Christmas Eve the Market Square is transformed into an enchanted land of wooden stalls and bright bunting, smothered in pine leaves and lit by lanterns. Despite the market's enormous popularity, you'll find little kitsch or tatty commercialism. Vendors pile their stalls with hand-carved wooden toys, traditional decorations and all kinds of craftwork. Aromas of *Glühwein*, grilling sausages and freshly-baked ginger *Lebkuchen* soften the sharp winter air. You can buy the *Rauschgoldengel* (gold foil angels), *Zwetschgenmännle* (odd figures made from crepe paper and prunes) and the kind of straw wreaths that have decorated Nuremberg homes at yuletide for centuries. At dusk on the first day a 'Christ-child' ringingly recites a prologue from the balcony above the entrance to the Frauenkirche, and little terrestrial angels peel off carols down below. A few days later, together with strings of school-chums all bearing home-made lanterns, they wind in procession up the hill from the Market Square to the castle.

The **Altstadtfest** in late September is ostensibly a celebration of Franconian folk culture, but it is really a rollicking knees-up, with mounds of food from all over the world and beer flowing freely. The **Toy Fair** (the largest of its kind in the world) held every February is peopled mainly by mums, dads and business folk walking between the stacks of teddies and playing the latest computer games. Big boys' toys whizz about during the **Norisring car races** in late June. Roads to the southeast of the city are closed off to make a long racetrack, traffic piles up, and you are deafened by car and helicopter engines for days on end.

Cultural events tend to cluster around the summer months. At the end of May you can catch **Musica Franconia**, a week of concerts of ancient music played on period instruments. Then the **Kulturzirkus**, an international theatre festival of increasing renown, is held in June—as is Europe's oldest sacred music festival, the **Orgelwoche** (literally 'organ week'). Buskers and street entertainers descend on the city's streets for a fortnight in July/August for the **Bardentreffen** ('Bards' Meet'). They're joined by more established names who also give open-air concerts. In October the Ost-West Jazzfestival hosts bands playing anything from Dixie to free jazz.

The Kaiserburg

The Kaiserburg *(daily Apr–Sept 9–12 and 12.45–5, Oct–Mar 9.30–12 and 12.45–4; adm DM3, guided tours only)*, lording it on a rock over the northern edge of the Altstadt, gives Nuremberg its unmistakable skyline of odd stone blocks and quirky towers. The view back down over the jumble of red-peaked roofs transports you back to medieval times, and gives you a good idea of the layout of the town.

The eccentric cluster of buildings that makes up the Kaiserburg grew up over centuries, and is, in fact, two castles merged into one. On the **eastern spur** of the rock is the **Burgrave's (Count's) Castle**. From the 11th until the end of the 12th century this was a fortress belonging first to the Salian kings (an ancient Frankish line) and then to the local Burgraves of Nuremberg. When the last of the line of the original Burgraves died in 1190, he was succeeded by his son-in-law, Frederic I of Zollern, founder of the Hohenzollern dynasty. During the 13th and 14th centuries the castle was the Hohenzollern's chief seat in Western Franconia, but the burghers of Nuremberg didn't take too kindly to their rule. After a number of hostile clashes the Hohenzollerns were finally defeated, and they sold the castle to the city in 1414.

The **Imperial Castle** on the **western spur** was a seat of the powerful Hohenstaufen line in the 12th century. The Hohenstaufens provided Holy Roman Emperors from 1138 to 1254. Even after the family's decline the castle continued to play an important role in empire politics. In 1356, in a decree known as the **Golden Bull**, Emperor Charles IV had commanded that the first Diet summoned by any newly elected German king had to be held at the castle. This held true for two centuries (until the Diet moved permanently to Regensburg), making Nuremberg one of the political centres of the empire. In 1427 the western spur too was taken over by the town and incorporated into the city defences, but it remained the property of the Holy Roman Empire.

The oldest part of the Kaiserburg is the gloomy **Fünfeckturm** (Pentagonal Tower, c. 1040), the only part of the original Salian building to survive. It now shares the eastern spur with the solid **Luginslandturm**, a tower put up in one go during the 14th century by burghers keen to keep a watchful eye on what was happening in the Burgrave's castle. Once they had ousted the Hohenzollerns, the citizens joined the two towers with a Gothic **Kaiserstallung** (Imperial Stables, built 1494, now a Youth Hostel).

The main body of the castle is on the western spur. The late-Gothic **Palas** was the Hohenstaufen family living-quarters. Only the east wall of the original Romanesque building remains, the rest was built by Emperor Frederick III in the 15th century. The guided tour takes you through rather bare state rooms and suites. Most of the Kaiserburg had to be rebuilt after the Second World War. The outside of the castle is impressive, but interiors tend to be empty and devoid of any atmosphere. One building that did survive the Allied bombs is the **Kaiserkapelle**, a *Doppelkapelle* (*see* p. 86) with an airy upper tier for the emperor and his family, and a squat, dim lower storey for humbler beings. There is a crucifix in the Upper Chapel said to be by the renowned local carver, Veit Stoss. The Nuremberg *Doppelkapelle* is the only one known to have an additional west gallery and choir tower—the solid **Heidenturm** (Heathens' Tower). Out in the forecourt you can see the **Tiefer Brunnen**, a well probably as old as the castle itself and so deep that it takes 6 seconds for a stone dropped from the top to hit the water.

The Northern Altstadt

Just below the Kaiserburg is the **Tiergärtner Tor**, one of four gates in the wall which still surrounds the medieval Altstadt. The area around the Tiergärtner Tor is one of the most attractive parts of the Altstadt. Lanes of half-timbered houses open out onto a cobbled Platz that, especially in the summer, is a hive of buskers, back-packers and other merry youth. Just outside the city wall (west along Johannisstraße) is the **Johannisfriedhof** *(Apr–Sept*

7–7, Oct–Mar 8–5), one of Germany's oldest and best-known cemeteries. Elaborate 16th- and 17th-century tombstones depict the scenes from the lives of the deceased. Among locals buried here are the *Meistersinger* Hans Sachs (*see* p. 71), the sculptor Veit Stoss and the artist, scientist, writer and politician, Albrecht Dürer.

The **Albrecht-Dürer-Haus** *(Mar–Oct and during Christkindelsmarket Tues–Sun 10–5, Wed 10–9; Nov–Feb Tues–Fri 1–5, Wed 1–9, Sat and Sun 10–5; adm DM3)*, where Germany's most complete Renaissance Man lived from 1509–28, is just across the square from the Tiergärtener Tor. The house is worth a visit for its cosy atmosphere and authentic medieval interiors, though you won't find any original Dürer paintings. There are, however, a few engravings and first editions of his treatises. Modern artists have also contributed some rather odd homages to the great man.

Down Bergstraße (also just across from the Tor), in the **Altstadthof** (a 16th-century court-yard) you'll find the **Hausbrauerei** *(hourly guided tours Mon–Fri 2–7, Sat and Sun 11–7; adm DM4.50)*, a working antique brewery, with cellars deep under the Kaiserburg. After your visit you can taste the murky beer in an adjoining pub. Further south, down Albrecht-Dürer-Straße and across Weinmarkt, you come to **Weißgerbergasse**—the most attractive lane of half-timbered houses in the city, now mainly given over to restaurants and cafés. Down Karlstrasse, which also leads off Weinmarkt, is the **Spielzeugmuseum** (Toy Museum) *(Tues–Sun 10–5, Wed 10–9; adm adults DM5, children DM2.50)*. At the time of writing the museum was closed for renovations, but if it has been re-opened it should be worth a visit for its vast collection of mainly 18th–20th-century toys. Germany was Europe's main manufacturer of toys—notably mechanical and tin toys—in the 19th century. Back eastwards along Schustergasse you come to the twin-towered **St Sebalduskirche** (1225–1379), Nuremberg's oldest parish church. Inside, resting on 12 bronze snails, is the richly decorated brass **Shrine of St Sebald**. Cast by Peter Vischer in 1391–7, it is generally considered to be the highpoint of German Renaissance metal work. There is a moving **crucifixion scene** by Veit Stoss on the pillar behind the Shrine. On a pillar in the nave is a charming, delicately coloured early 15th-century carving of **Mary with a halo**.

Around the corner on Burgstraße is the **Stadtmuseum Fembohaus** *(Mar–Oct and during Christkindelsmarket Tues–Sun 10–5, Wed 10– 9; Nov–Feb Tues–Fri 1–5, Wed 1–9, Sat and Sun 10–5; adm DM3)*, really only worth a visit for a look at the heavy stucco ceilings and wood-panelled rooms transferred here from other patrician mansions around town. A far more rewarding museum is the intimate **Tucherschlößchen** at Hirschelgasse 9 *(guided tours Mon–Thurs 2, 3, 4pm, Fri 9, 10, 11am, Sun 10 and 11am; adm DM1.50)* a few minutes' walk up towards the university in the northeastern corner of the Altstadt. This was the Renaissance mansion of the Tucher family, who made their fortune manufacturing astronomical instruments, and later importing textiles and brewing beer. The house was destroyed during the war, but completely restored by the family themselves. There is a loving, personal touch to the displays of fine furniture and painting. The highlight of the tour is the **Tucherbuch** (1590–6), a family chronical with stunningly beautiful illustrations. Tours are in German only, but you can ask for a printed English translation.

Around the Hauptmarkt

The **Hauptmarkt** is the centre of town, and scene of a bustling, countrified daily **market** of stalls laden with fruit, fresh herbs and homemade cakes and breads. Across the northern end of the square is an exuberant Renaissance **Altes Rathaus**, built in the style of a Venetian *palazzo*. Here you can visit the **Lochgefängnisse** *(Apr–Sept Mon–Fri 10–4, Sat and Sun 10–1; adm DM3)*, medieval prison cells complete with a fully-equipped torture chamber. Outside, on the western side of the square, is a replica of the completely over-the-top **Schöner Brunnen** (Beautiful Fountain), a filigreed Gothic spire, gaudily painted and crowded with figures of electors, prophets and other church heroes. The trickles of water that spout from the base seem quite gratuitous.

The pretty step-gabled **Frauenkirche**, erected by Emperor Charles IV in 1355, is just across the square. Although the church was badly bombed, the intricately carved **tympanum** above the entrance porch survived intact. In the 16th century a pretty oriel and clock were added to the façade. Above is a gold and blue ball that shows the current phase of the moon. Below is a Glockenspiel (nicknamed the **Männleinlaufen**) that commemorates Charles IV's 'Golden Bull' (*see* above). At noon the carillon rings out merrily and figures of the seven electors circle three times around a statue of the emperor. Above the main altar in the church is the painting called the **Tucher Altar** (1445), a lively composition by the best artist working in Nuremberg prior to Dürer, an unknown painter now named the 'Master of the Tucher Altar'.

West of the Hauptmarkt (along Augustinerstraße, then down towards the River Pegnitz) is the big, half-timbered **Weinstadel**, a medieval wine store. Willows on the river banks and the covered wooden **Henkersteg** ('Hangman's Bridge') make a picture-postcard scene. South of the Hauptmarkt you can cross the river over the Museumbrücke. From here you can see the sprawling stone buildings of the **Heilig-Geist-Spital** (a medieval hospital) on the left, and the neat **Fleischbrücke** (modelled on Venice's Rialto Bridge) on the right.

The Southern Altstadt

By crossing the Museumsbrücke, and following Königstraße (a brash, modern shopping precinct), you come to the **St Lorenz-Kirche** (1250–1477). From the outside St Lorenz looks almost identical to St Sebalds, begun some 25 years earlier: the communities on either side of the river were in fierce competition with each other at the time. The parishioners of St Lorenz did eventually show a little more imagination. Instead of merely imitating their rivals' building, they turned to models in France. The interior of the church is spectacular High Gothic, with a glittering **rose window**, and a prickly 20m-high **tabernacle**, by the local mason Adam Kraft. Above the high altar you can also see more fine carving by Veit Stoss—his polychrome **Annunciation**.

Outside the church is an eye-catching fountain, the **Tugendbrunnen**. The Seven Virtues look a little nonplussed as water squirts from their breasts, and from the up-raised trumpets of supporting cherubs. Across the square is the oldest house in the city, the 13th-century Nassauer Haus, with a turreted upper storey and prettily carved oriel window.

Huddling around the **Königstor** (at the end of Königstraße, in the south-eastern corner of the Altstadt) is the **Handwerkerhof** (Artisans' Courtyard) *(Mon–Sat 10–6.30)*. Here candlemakers, tinworkers, dollmakers and others ply their crafts in a twee medieval atmosphere while tourists look on and buy, and also consume vast quantities of *Bratwurst* and *Lebkuchen*.

The Germanisches Nationalmuseum

The imposing Germanisches Nationalmuseum *(Tues–Sun 10–5, Thurs 10–1; adm DM5)* is on the Kornmarkt (just off Königstraße, across Hallplatz). Its enormous collection of German art and artefacts—gathered from earliest times to the 20th century—is housed in the **Karthaus**, a 14th-century Carthusian monastery. Modern buildings have been integrated into the old Gothic fabric: plate glass and sharp angles contrast quite startlingly with gentler lines and worn stone. Floor plans are available at the entrance, but this museum is fun to explore at random. You can wander through cloisters resplendent with fine carvings, duck through low doors into dim little rooms stuffed with old furniture, climb up narrow stairs to see cabinets of seemingly forgotten cultural ephemera. You can be diverted for hours, and can get quite enjoyably lost.

The **Ground Floor** is devoted to medieval art, prehistoric artefacts and collections of musical instruments and hunting equipment. The pick of the painting and sculpture is in rooms 8–14. There is work by famous Würzburg woodcarver **Tilman Riemenschneider** (*see* p. 55), as well as notable pieces by the local artist and villain **Veit Stoss**. In his exquisite *Raphael and Tobias* (1516) the swirls and billows of the angel's cloak seem to float in the wind. He finished the carving soon after he had been convicted of forging promissory notes, branded on both cheeks, imprisoned and stripped of his status as a Master Craftsman. Two paintings are especially worth seeking out. The gentle, touchingly intimate *Madonna of the Sweet Pea* (1410) by the **Master of St Veronica** is one of the finest examples of the 'soft style' of the Cologne School (*see* p. 56). This stands in contrast to the powerful, naturalistic 'hard style' of later painters such as **Konrad Witz**. His *Annunciation* (1444) shows an attempt to portray perspective and a treatment of light that was revolutionary for the time.

In the south-west wing of the ground floor you'll find the magically named **Golden Cone of Ezelsdorf-Buch** (1100 BC). The cone, stamped with intricate patterns, is over 88cm high and made from a single piece of paper thin gold (crushed up, it would fit easily into a matchbox). The south-east wing contains a superbly displayed collection of musical instruments. There is a 12 minute slide show introducing the collection, and headphones dotted around the hall give you a chance to hear recordings of the instruments you're looking at.

The upper floor is haven to a variety of traditional costumes, toys and domestic objects, sculpture and painting from the Renaissance onwards, arts and crafts of the 20th century and the first ever world globe (designed by Martin Behaim in 1491). The **Behaim Globe** has pride of place in Room 35. Nicknamed the *Erdapfel* (Earth Apple) it is, apart from the absence of Australia and the Americas (both then unknown to the Western world) and the odd bit of distorted coastline, remarkably accurate. Behaim based his globe on the latest charts supplied by Portuguese navigators, as well as Ptolemy's map of the 2nd century AD—information which led Columbus to believe that he had reached the Far East when he came across the Americas (and so called its people Indians).

Renaissance and Baroque paintings are hung in Rooms 33–64. Here you can see an extensive collection of works by **Dürer**, such as the eloquent portrait of his bright-eyed, octagenarian teacher, *The Painter Michael Wolgemut* (1516). There is also fine work by **Lucas Cranach the Elder**. Look out for the wrily detailed *Venus with Cupid stealing honey* (1530). **Hans Baldung** (nicknamed 'Grien' because of his preference for green clothes) is also well-represented. In his **Sebastian Altar** (1507), the artist himself (in a dashing red hat and the inevitable green cloak) stands next to the martyred saint, and confidently eyes the viewer.

Most impressive of all are the objects and instruments from Nuremberg's Renaissance heyday as a centre of crafts (Rooms 65–74). The artistry of the **Schlüsselfelder Ship**, a gilded silver tablepiece made around 1503, is breathtaking. A mermaid supports a three-masted ship which is finished in meticulous detail. The rudder can move and the deck and rigging swarm with 74 minute, individually cast sailors.

The 20th-century art in the museum is less exciting. However, in Room G (in the northernmost wing) you can see **Ernst Kirchner's** rather wretched *Self-portait as a Drunkard* (1915) one of this Expressionist's best works.

South of the City Wall

Just outside the Altstadt boundaries (in Lessingstraße, off Frauentorgraben) is the **Verkehrsmuseum** (Transport Museum) *(daily 9.30–5; adm DM4)*. Here, among the old post coaches and model trains you'll find 'Adler', the **first German railway locomotive**. It ran on a track which opened in 1835 between Nuremberg and nearby Fürth.

The grey, looming, half-finished piles built by Hitler as monuments to his Third Reich are to be found in **Luitpoldhain** *(Tram 12)*, a park in the south-eastern suburbs. This is the setting for the images we are familiar with through old newsreels: from the podium draped with swastikas Hitler made his ranting speeches to the vast stadium filled with a roaring sea of spectators all raising their hands in the *Sieg Heil* salute. Today the buildings are supposedly a memorial to the Nazis' victims, but there seems something distasteful in the fact that they are still used as sports halls and decked out in bunting for fairs and pop concerts.

At the northern entrance to the park is the **Luitpoldarena**, scene of SS parades. Behind that is the **Kongresshalle** (modelled on the Colosseum in Rome, but never completed). Across an artificial lake is the **Zeppelin Tribune**, designed by star Nazi architect Albert Speer for the massive September rallies. The torches and colonnades have been stripped off the podium, but the massive stadium (holding 70,000) remains. It is windswept and overgrown, but still used by the US Army as a sports ground and during the Norisring motor races (*see* **Festivals** above).

Shopping

For pewter, stained-glass, pottery, jewellery and handmade knick-knacks, head for the Craftsmen's Courtyard (*see* **Southern Altstadt** above). Much of the centre of Nuremberg is taken up by the usual pedestrianized shopping zone. In Königstraße, Karolinenstraße and Kaiserstraße you'll find all the major department stores and a few swish boutiques. Schmidt's bakery on the Hauptmarkt sells *Lebkuchen* cooked to a recipe that has been a family secret for centuries.

Entertainment and Nightlife

The local **listings magazine** is *Plärrer* (DM3.50 from news stands). The tourist office brings out a monthly *Monats Magazin* (DM2) and **Sommer in Nürnberg**, a free guide to summer events.

The best music, theatre and opera in Nuremberg happens during the summer arts festivals (*see* **Festivals** above). At other times the city tends to be outshone by Munich. The local **Opernhaus** and **Schauspielhaus** on Richard Wagnerplatz (south of the Altstadt just outside the city wall; box office ☎ 231 3808) keep up a reasonably high standard. The local **orchestra**, the Nürnberger Symphoniker, plays at the Meistersingerhalle in Luitpoldhain (Tram 12, box office ☎ 492 011). You can also pre-book tickets at a booth on the second floor of the Karstadt department store, opposite the Lorenzkirche.

The Roxy (J. Lossmannstr. 116, ☎ 48840, Tram 8) has a wide-ranging, frequently changing, programme of **films** in the original language. The trendiest **disco** in town (often with live music) is Mach 1 (Kaiserstr. 1–9), hotly followed by Tanztempel One (Rothenburger Str. 29). The **Green Goose** (Vordere Sterngasse 25) has a friendly crowd, and plays New Wave and rock. Das Boot (Hafenstr. 500, Bus 67) offers standard chart music in a converted ship. Over weekends it will cost you around DM10 to get into a disco or nightclub, though this sometimes entitles you to a free drink.

Big time **pop stars** perform at the Serenadenhof (Bayernstr. 100, ☎ 55554). Dixieland is the sole fare at Schmelztiegel (Bergstr. 21), a small **jazz** cellar near the Tiergartenertor. There's a less hearty atmosphere, but better music, at Steps (Johannisstr. 83, Bus 34).

Nürnberg ☎ (0911–)   **Where to Stay**

expensive

Atrium Hotel, Münchener Str. 25, ☎ 47480, fax 474 8420 (DM234–398). Classy, glassy modern hotel in the Luitpoldhain Park, with its own pool, sauna, gym and sun terrace.

Merian-Hotel, Unschlittplatz 7, ✆ 204 194, fax 221 274 (DM165). Stylish, well-run hotel in a pretty area of the Altstadt. Comfortable, tastefully decorated rooms—some look out over a shady square with a fountain—and impeccable service.

Burghotel, Lammgasse 3, ✆ 204 414, fax 223 458 (DM160). Folksy hotel at the foot of the Burg. Facilities are smart and modern, and it has a swimming pool.

Hotel Elch, Irrerstr. 9, ✆ 209 544, fax 241 9304 (DM150–185). Lovely medieval half-timbered inn in the Altstadt. Rooms can be a bit on the small side, but the atmosphere and friendly, personal service make up for it.

Hotel Marienbad, Eilgutstr. 5, ✆ 203 147, fax 204 260 (DM138–170). One of the best of a bunch of nondescript hotels around the Hauptbahnhof. It is clean, efficiently run and there to fall back on if everywhere else is full.

Alt-Nürnberg, Breite Gasse 40, ✆ 224 129 (DM50–60 without private bathroom). Comfortable, centrally situated guesthouse.

Fischer, Brunnengasse 11, ✆ 226 189 (DM67 without private bathroom). Cheap, clean and cheerful.

Vater Jahn, Jahnstr. 13, ✆ 444 507 (DM65–85). Good value, relaxed *pension* near the Hauptbahnhof.

Eating and Drinking

Nuremberg has two culinary claims to fame: **Nürnberger Bratwurst** (sausages the size of your little finger) and **Lebkuchen,** a spicy gingerbread made with honey and nuts. Traditionally *Lebkuchen* are sold only at Christmas, but nowadays you can eat them all year round. *Nürnberger Bratwurst* should be made entirely of pork. The sausages are served on pewter plates, with sauerkraut, potato salad or hot white radish. Six is the minimum order, 'real men' knock back a dozen at a time and if you order more than ten you get them on a heart-shaped plate. Snack stalls sell them '*Zwaa in an Weckla*' (two in a roll). Usually *Bratwurst* are grilled over wood fires, but you can also get them *Nackerte* ('Naked'—raw, peeled, mixed with onions, pepper and paprika and spread on black bread), or as *Blaue Zipfel* (marinated in spiced vinegar—reputedly a good hangover cure). *Bauernseufzer* are long, smoked *Bratwurst* which can be eaten raw or boiled.

Restaurants and Taverns

expensive

Entenstub'n, Günthersbühler Str. 145, ✆ 598 0413 (DM80–100). Elegant Michelin-starred restaurant with a shady garden terrace. Famed for its asparagus mousse and fine fish dishes.

Heilig Geist Spital, Spitalgasse 16, ✆ 221 761 (DM45–60). The 15th-century eating hall of the old hospital, extending right out over the River Pegnitz. Excellent, wide-ranging menu with good game and veal dishes.

Goldenes Posthorn, An der Sebalduskirche, ✆ 225 153 (DM45–60). Romantic old inn. Dürer's local, founded in 1498 and still serving up good Franconian meals. There's a delicious potato soup, and tasty asparagus dishes in season.

moderate

Der Nassauer Keller, Karolinenstr. 2–4, ✆ 225 967 (DM35–50). Low ceilings, low lights and strategically placed suits of armour in the cellar of Nuremberg's oldest house. Renowned for their saddle of lamb and old Franconian cookery.

Böhms Herrenkeller, Theatergasse 19, ✆ 224 465 (DM35–50). Traditional tavern with a good wine list and hearty Franconian dishes. Try the *Schweinebraten* (roast pork with potato dumplings) or *Krautwickala* (stuffed cabbage leaves).

Irrer Elch, Irrerstr. 9, ✆ 209 544 (DM25–50). Cosy medieval tavern with good home-cooking. Game and carp dishes are a speciality.

inexpensive

Prison St Michel, Irrerstr. 2 (DM20–35). Popular French restaurant that serves everything from scrumptious galettes (wholemeal pancakes) to standards such as duckling with orange.

Bratwurst-Häusle, Rathausplatz 1, ✆ 227 695 (DM15–25). The huge chimney puffs out grilled-sausage aroma right across the square. Locals and tourists pack inside for the best *Bratwurst* in town.

Bratwurst-Glöcklein, Im Handwerkerhof, ✆ 227 625 (DM15–25). In the Craftsmen's Courtyard and very touristy, but serves up good *Bratwurst.*

Bars and Cafés

Café Sebald, Weinmarkt 14, ✆ 225 225. Lively, trendy café in the midst of a cluster of half-timbered houses. Also serves good salads and light meals.

Ruhestorung, Tetzelgasse 31, ✆ 221 921. Busy bar in the northern Altstadt, popular with students.

Weinkruger, Wespennest 6–8, ✆ 232 895. Popular wine tavern in the cellar of an old monastery. In the summer it spills out onto a riverside terrace. There's a large wine list, and also good meals.

Tücherbrau am Opernhaus, Frauentorgraben. Busy and attractive beer garden along the city wall, opposite the Opera House.

Café Kröll, Hauptstr. 6–8, ✆ 227 511. Traditional café on the Hauptmarkt. Good coffee and mouth-watering cakes.

Before the border with the old DDR came down, Bayreuth was a sleepy little town, forgotten in an isolated pocket of West Germany and brought out into the light just once a year for the famous Wagner Festival. The inhabitants were prosperous and conservative, and seemed to begrudge the appearance of the new Bayreuth University in the late 1970s, belittling it with the diminutive *Universitäla*. The hordes that poured in a decade later—stuffed five to a Trabant, rubbing holes in the steamed up windscreens and peering out at the wealthy West—were almost too much to bear. Bayreuth is still reeling from the shock. It is now a bustling town on the main Berlin/Munich axis of Germany. The burgeoning numbers of students are asserting their presence and give the town a little life and flair. This, and some fine 18th-century architecture, make Bayreuth worth a visit in its own right.

The Baroque and Rococo buildings are mostly the legacy of the Margravine Wilhelmina, sister of Frederick the Great. In 1731 the cultured, intelligent and passionate Wilhelmina was married to the Margrave of Bayreuth. Had it not been for her father's inept, bungled matchmaking, she could probably have been Queen of England. Instead she was lumped with a provincial Margrave with a reputation as a crushing bore. Not to be defeated by this, Wilhelmina set about transforming Bayreuth into a glittering centre of the arts, and employed some of Europe's top architects to give the town a face-lift. A century later the composer Richard Wagner chose Bayreuth as the centre for staging his operas. He came to live here with his wife Cosima and her father Franz Liszt, built a theatre and laid the foundations for the annual festival. However, Wagner's nationalism and anti-Semitism appealed to the Nazis and the Bayreuth Festival, as Germany's cultural mecca, became tainted with a fanaticism that it is only just beginning to shake off. Many blame Wagner's English daughter-in-law, Winifred, for cultivating Hitler's patronage, and having him to stay as a house guest when he came to Bayreuth for festivals during the 1930s.

Getting Around

By car: Bayreuth is 85km north of Nuremberg on Autobahn 9, the main route between Berlin and Munich (230km away). Much of the centre of town is pedestrianized. The main parking lots are north-east of the centre off the Wittelsbachring.

Car hire: Avis, Marktgrafenallee 6, © (0921) 26151; Hertz, Erlanger Str. 43, © (0921) 51155.

By train: The **Hauptbahnhof** is 10 minutes' walk north of the city centre. There are hourly trains to Nuremberg (1hr).

Tourist Information

The **tourist information office**, Luitpoldplatz 9, © (0921) 88588, can help with booking accommodation and offers good walking tours around the town.

Police: © 69182.

Medical Emergencies: © 22222.

Every year, for the five weeks from July to the end of August, around 60,000 people cram into Bayreuth for the **Wagner Festival**, the biggest and most important celebration of the composer's work in the world. The festival was founded by Wagner himself. After much bitter wrangling with the Bavarian finance ministry, but with the ardent patronage of King Ludwig II, the Maestro set about designing a theatre and creating a temple to his own art. The first festival (which opened with the *Nibelungen* in 1876) was a complete flop. Wagner even had to sell the costumes to try and recoup costs. It was his second wife, Cosima, who really established the event. She reigned over the festival until 1908, when she handed over to her son Siegfried. Administration remains very much a family affair. Today the show is run by the composer's grandson Wolfgang. Performances take place in the original red-brick **Festspielhaus** *(guided tours Tues–Sun 10–11am, 1.30–3, closed Oct; adm DM3)* on a hill north of the centre (past the Bahnhof, along Bürrgerreuther Straße). An imposing, but not particularly beautiful building, it has punishingly hard seats and brilliant acoustics. Official ticket prices range from DM30 to DM230, and tickets go on sale from mid-November. How they are meted out remains a mystery to outsiders (even to the Bayreuth tourist office, who will not be able to help you at all). Agencies around the world get batches—but with no regularity or apparent reason behind the allocation. Individuals have to apply in writing the year before they hope to attend (to Kartenbüro, Festspielleitung, Postfach 10062, 8580 Bayreuth). The pattern here seems to be that you will strike lucky every fifth or seventh year.

The townspeople's answer to these shenanigans is the **Frankische Festwoche** (Franconian Festival), which usually occurs concurrently with the **Bayreuther Volkfest** (Folk Festival) for a week in May/June. Here, as well as top-rate cultural fare from the likes of the Bavarian State Opera, you'll find beer tents, a funfair and much jolly merrymaking.

The City Centre

Margravine Wilhelmina's most impressive contribution to Bayreuth architecture is the **Markgräfliches Opernhaus** *(guided tours Tues–Sun 9–11.30 and 1.30–4.30; adm DM2.50)* on Opernstraße, just east of the tourist office. The Margravine commissioned the great Bolognese theatre builder Giuseppe Galli Bibiena and his son Carlo to design the Opera House. From the street it is a plain, rather insignificant building. Even the simple grey foyer with wooden cut-out balustrades doesn't lead you to expect much, but beyond the auditorium doors lies one of the most beautiful and atmospheric theatres in the land. The entire Rococo interior is made of wood—carved, gilded, marbled and painted in deep, subdued greens. There's a tasteful scattering of garlands and putti, and some rich ceiling paintings. The wood gives the theatre intimacy and warmth (as well as excellent acoustics), and also an odd sense of artifice. The theatre itself seems to have all the magic of a stage set. The bell-shaped stage is 27m deep—the largest in Germany until 1871. Its size and good acoustics helped lure Wagner to Bayreuth, but he later decided that even the Opernhaus couldn't cope with the grand productions he had in mind, and built the even bigger Festspielhaus on the hill. Margravine Wilhelmina was an accomplished painter, writer, actress and composer: on the tour of the theatre you get a chance to sit down, soak in the atmosphere, and listen to a recording of one of her works.

Running west from Opernstraße is the town's main shopping street, **Maximilianstraße**. At No. 57 you can see the high triangular gable of the 400-year-old sandstone pharmacy, the **Mohren Apotheke**. The northern side of the street is dominated by one of Bayreuth's landmarks, the Baroque **Altes Schloß**, now a tax office. The Schloß has twice had to be completely rebuilt: once in recent history, after Allied bombing in 1945, and once in 1753 after it had burnt down. (Some say the Margrave started the fire deliberately, as he wanted a new palace and his wife's extravagance had already drained and alienated the Treasury.) An elegant 16th-century octagonal stone tower juts up behind the Schloß. A ramp inside allowed the Margraves to ride their horses right to the top, but today you can climb up for a splendid view of Bayreuth only if you go on the official City Tour.

In Kanzleistraße, which runs south off Maximilianstraße, is the **Stadtmuseum** *(July and Aug Mon–Fri 10–5, Sept–June Tues–Fri 10–5; adm DM2)*, a run-of-the-mill museum enlivened by the model ships and miniature cannons used at the beginning of the 18th century by Margrave Georg Wilhelm for the spectacular naval battles he used to stage on the artificial lake behind his palace. Further on is the **Stadtkirche**, with a quaint stone bridge connecting the tops of its delicate towers. The church is the only building in town which predates the Renaissance. At the back of the church is the diminutive **Schwindsuchts-häschen**, the town's smallest house, barely as wide as a car. Kanzleistraße leads into **Friedrichstraße**. Here Margrave Friedrich gave away land cheaply and donated building materials to anyone who would build acccording to plans approved by his architects (who were firmly under the control of Wilhelmina). The result is a sustained and grandiose stretch of Baroque architecture.

Off the northern end of Maximilianstraße (across the Wittelsbachring, at Kulmbachstr. 40) is the **Brauerei- & Büttnerei-Museum** (Brewery and Cooper's Museum) *(guided tours Mon–Thurs 10am)*. The half-hour-long tour takes you through the fully functional 19th-century steam brewery, and ends up with free samples in a 1920s-style beer bar.

The Neues Schloß and Villa Wahnfried

If you follow Ludwigstaße, south of Opernstraße, you soon come to the sumptuous **Neues Schloß** *(guided tours Tues–Sun 10–11.30 and 1.30–4.30; adm DM3)*, built when the Altes Schloß burned down. Wilhelmina herself had a hand in much of the interior design. The showpiece of the castle is the **Zedernsaal** (Cedar Chamber), a warm, wood-panelled dining hall. In the curious **Spiegelzimmer** (Mirror Room), Wilhelmina intended the irregular fragments of mirror that line the walls to be a comment on the vanity of an age that was overly concerned with appearances.

A shady **Hofgarten** extends behind the Schloß. At the eastern end of the garden you come to **Villa Wahnfried**, once Wagner's home and now the **Richard-Wagner-Museum** *(daily 9–5; adm DM2.50, DM3.50 in July and August)*. Wagner designed the house himself, and lived here from 1874 to 1883 with his second wife Cosima (whom he had stolen from his leading conductor Hans von Bülow. The house is built around a large central reception hall, where the best musicians of the day gave recitals, and the Wagners held soirées with royals, intellectuals, musicians and artists dancing in attendance. The museum houses an interesting collection of Wagner memorabilia, and costumes and photographs of past productions. In the cellar is an intriguing collection of set-designers' models. Wagner and Cosima lie buried in a simple grave behind the house.

The Eremitage

Set amidst wheatfields and woodland on the eastern borders of town (along Königsallee—Bus 2 from Marktplatz) is the romantic **Eremitage** *(guided tours Tues–Sun 9–11.30 and 1–4.30; adm DM2)*. Originally built by Margrave Georg Wilhelm (Friedrich's predecessor) as an ascetic retreat (hermitage) from his reputedly voluptuous court, the Eremitage and its park were later given to Margravine Wilhelmina as a present. The frustrated Margravine gave vent to the passionless tedium of her marriage by turning the spartan retreat into a glamorous country seat. She escaped here with her talented friends, and poured her heart out in emotional memoirs which caused a scandal when they were published decades after her death. The palace itself is a mildly interesting Rococo building: the real attraction of the Eremitage lies in the gardens. They include extravagant **fountains** and a **water grotto**, an **artificial ruin** used as an open air theatre where Wilhelmina herself played Racine's *Bajazet* with Voltaire, and the **Sonnentempel** (Sun Temple). This dumpy dome, to one side of the main palace, is covered with a sort of 18th-century pebbledash of blue and green stones that sparkle in the sunlight. On top is a gilded statue of Apollo driving a chariot pulled by three rearing horses.

Bayreuth ✆ (0921–) **Where to Stay**

Standard prices are given below. Expect an increase of *at least* 20 per cent during the Wagner Festival. Rooms over this period are booked out months in advance.

expensive

Bayerischer Hof, Bahnhofstr. 14, ✆ 22081, fax 22085 (DM150–250). Plush modern hotel close to the station and convenient for the Festspielhaus. The rooms are well-appointed, the staff unobtrusively attentive and the hotel has its own swimming pool and loads of parking space.

moderate

Hotel Goldener Anker, Opernstr. 6, ✆ 65051, fax 65500 (DM140–200). Old-style hotel with smallish but comfortable rooms. Right near the old Opernhaus, and convenient for all the city sights.

Gasthof zum Edeln Hirschen, Richard-Wagner-Str. 77, © 64141, fax 52115 (DM90–110). Well-run family guesthouse with simple, comfortable rooms.

Fränkischer Hof, Rathenaustr. 28, © 64214 (DM95–120). Small, central hotel with friendly management.

Gasthof Goldener Löwe, Kulmbacher Str. 30, © 41046, fax 47777 (DM96–110). Charming, countrified brewery-cum-guesthouse in a quiet spot still quite close to the centre of town.

inexpensive

Gasthof Zum Herzog, Herzog 2, Kulmbacher Str., © 41334 (DM78–86, some rooms without private bathroom). Clean, comfortable and good value.

Youth Hostel: Universitätsstr. 28, © 25262 (Bus 4).

Eating and Drinking: Restaurants and Taverns

Annecy, Gabelsbergerstr. 11, © 26279 (DM40–60). Relaxed atmosphere and good, unpretentious French cuisine—scrumptious casseroles and poultry dishes.

Wölfel, Kirchgasse 12, © 68499 (DM25–50). Cosy tavern, ideal for a meal after a drink at the Eule. Serves excellent Franconian cuisine. You can get delicious baked carp, or ham cooked in a doughy pastry.

Brauereischänke am Markt, Maximilianstr. 56, © 64919 (DM20–40). A little touristy, but with a jolly atmosphere and hearty Franconian fare: good sausages and pork with raw dumplings.

Bars and Cafés

Rosenau, Badstr. 29, © 65136. Good beerhall with beer garden and a friendly atmosphere.

Herzogkeller, Hindenburgstraße, © 43419. Vast beer garden which is popular with students.

Eule, Kirchgasse 8, © 57554. Known as Bayreuth's *Künstlerkneipe* (artists' pub). Musicians and singers used to gather here after festival performances. The walls are covered with photographs that span decades of Wagnerian stars. It's the nearest the town comes to a Festival Museum, and worth a visit (even though today's celebrities tend to stay outside Bayreuth and socialize in their private apartments).

Café Florian, Dammallee 12a, © 56757. Festival or no, the watering-hole for Bayreuth's 'in' crowd.

Operncafé, Opernstr. 16, © 65720. Elegant café next to the old Opernhaus. A good place for coffee and gooey cakes.

*Das ist eine Stadt, die steckt voller Raritäten, wie die Kommode einer
alten Großmama, die viel zusammenscharrte. ('This is a city stuffed
with more rarities than an old, hoarding granny's chest of drawers.')*

Karl Immerman (19th-century traveller).

Bamberg is a vibrant university town, just west of Bayreuth, built on seven hills along the
River Regnitz. It is a hot contender for the title of the most beautiful town in Germany, yet
is inexplicably ignored by most foreign tourists. The Thirty Years' War and the Second
World War—which together caused the ruin of so many German cities—left Bamberg relatively unscathed. It has managed to salvage at least one good example of every European
architectural style from Romanesque onwards. Without losing its medieval structure or
charm, the town enjoyed a Baroque building boom when some of the era's greatest architects slipped decorous mansions in between the wonky half-timbered houses that prop
each other up along Bamberg's steep, winding alleys.

Bamberg also has a splendid cathedral, boisterous student life, a symphony orchestra of
world repute, and ten excellent local breweries—just the sort of mixed bag that can make
a small German town a delight.

Getting Around

By car: Bamberg is just off Autobahn 70, which links it to Würzburg (100km) and
Bayreuth (70km), and Autobahn 73, which runs south to Nuremberg (60km). The
biggest and most convenient undercover parking garage in the city is beneath
Maximilianplatz, near the Rathaus.

By train: The Bahnhof (information ℂ (0951) 19419) is 15 minutes' walk from
the centre. (To get to the Rathaus walk down Luitpoldstraße, turn right into Obere
Königstraße and then cross the Kettenbrücke.) There are hourly connections to
Würzberg (1hr) and frequent trains to Nuremberg (¾hr) and Munich (2½hr).

Taxis: ℂ 15015.

River cruises: You get superb views of Bamberg from the river, especially in the
early morning. Tickets for boat trips can be bought from Bamberger
Veranstaltungstdienst (Langestr. 24).

Tourist Information

The **tourist information office**, Geyerswörthstr. 3, ℂ (0951) 871 161, is on an
island in the Regnitz *(Apr–Sept Mon–Fri 9–7, Sat 9–5; Oct–Mar Mon–Fri 9–6,
Sat 9–2).*

Post office: Ludwigstr. 25, near Bahnhof *(Mon–Fri 7–7, Sat 7–2, Sun 11–1).*

Banks: Branches of most German banks are situated along Hauptwachstraße/
Grüner Markt.

Police: ✆ 110.

Medical emergencies: ✆ 19222.

Roman Catholic Bamberg's main festival is **Corpus Christi** (May/June) when there is a church procession with many people dressed in *Tracht*. There is more traditional dress and dancing, as well as water-jousting during the **Sandfest** in August.

The Lower City

The lower part of the city is the scene of Bamberg's day-to-day commercial life. The hub of all the activity is **Maxplatz**, where there is a busy weekday fruit and vegetable market. On the northern side of the square stands the ponderous, imposing **Rathaus** (originally a seminary) designed by the great Baroque architect, Balthasar Neumann. Grünermarkt, a wide boulevard of Baroque buildings, leads south off Maxplatz. The most impressive façade belongs to **St Martin**, a stately Jesuit church built in 1686–83 by the Dietzenhofer brothers (who designed many of Bamberg's best Baroque buildings). Inside there is a rather clever *trompe l'oeil* dome.

Grüner Markt leads on to the Obere Brücke, a bridge over the River Regnitz. Linking the Obere Brücke and the Untere Brücke, a few yards downstream, is the **Altes Rathaus**, certainly the oddest town hall in Germany. The Rathaus completely covers an island in the middle of the river, so it seems to float like a rather gaudy boat tethered to the two bridges. The basic structure is Gothic, though this was given a Rococo boost in the late 18th century. A soaring stone gateway arches over Obere Brücke. On one side of the arch stretches a wing emblazoned with bright murals, on the other side a little half-timbered addendum hangs out over the water.

From the Untere Brücke you can see **Klein-Venedig**, a cluster of half-timbered fishermen's houses that come right up to the water's edge. On the other side of the river the hills bristle with a variety of church spires. To the east of the bridges, in streets lined with faded ochre buildings reminiscent of Italy, you'll find two of the most ostentatious Baroque mansions in the city. The **Böttingerhaus** (Judengasse 14) has an opulent portal and courtyard, bulging with stucco work by the local artist Vogel. The house was built by the Franconian chargé d'affaires in 1707–13. Later he built himself a summer river-palace almost next door. The **Concordia** (at the end of Concordiastraße) is, however, best viewed from across the water. This you can do by ducking down an alleyway at the bottom of Concordiastraße and over the bridge onto the Geyerswörth island.

The Nonnenbrücke takes you from the island across to Schillerplatz back on the northern river bank. Here you will find the **E.T.A. Hoffmann-Haus** *(May–Oct Tues–Fri 4–6, Sat and Sun 10–12; adm DM1)*. E.T.A. Hoffmann (1776–1822) was a Romantic painter, composer and writer who is today most remembered for his bizarre short stories. Two of his tales inspired Romantic ballets—Delibes' *Coppelia* and Tchaikovsky's *The Nutcracker.* Hoffmann himself (who had an eccentric, even schizophrenic personality) is the subject of Offenbach's opera *The Tales of Hoffmann.* For most of his life Hoffmann was a civil servant, but while he lived in Bamberg (1808–13) he tried to make a career of his various artistic talents. The museum contains a large collection of memorabilia, but is really only worth a visit if you are a Hoffmann fan.

The Domstadt

In the 11th century Emperor Henry II first established the Bishopric of Bamberg in the hope that the city would become the capital of the Holy Roman Empire and rival Rome in importance. His dreams weren't realized, but Bamberg did become a famous centre of learning in the Middle Ages, and the prince-bishopric he created was to last until Napoleon's secularization. The cathedral and ecclesiastical palaces that crown Bamberg's main hill are known as the Domstadt (Cathedral City), in contrast to the commercial town down below. From the Altes Rathaus you wind through narrow alleys and up precipitous stairways to the large, sloping **Domplatz**. This square presents a magnificent spectrum of European architecture from Romanesque beginnings in the cathedral to Gothic, Renaissance and Baroque in the surrounding buildings.

The Cathedral

The first **cathedral**, commissioned by Emperor Henry II, burnt down twice. Construction on the present one began around 1215 and lasted until 1237—two decades that saw the flowering of Gothic architecture. The east chancel of the cathedral is earthy, rounded Romanesque; the west chancel flighty, pointed Gothic. Between them the nave is a perfect illustration of the Transitional style. The four towers mirror each other with just a slight distortion that reflects the changes that those two important decades produced: the spires on the western end are a touch lighter, sharper and more delicate than their solid Romanesque counterparts.

The **Fürstenportal** (Prince's Portal, 1228) on the north side of the nave is a supreme feat of Romanesque carving. Apostles and Old Testament prophets line arches that recede towards a heavy wooden door. On the tympanum, Christ presides authoritatively over the Last Judgement. Inside, gathered around the east choir, are more fine early **13th-century sculptures**. A youthful, pregnant Virgin, swathed in superbly worked folds of cloth, is flanked by an aged Elizabeth (also known as 'The Bamberg Sibyl'). Two much simpler female figures, *Synagogue* and *Ecclesia*, represent the Old and New Testaments. Synagogue is blindfolded, skinny and wears a thin, seemingly transparent shift. Ecclesia has a crown, fuller garments and a smug smile. Most famous of all is the statue of the **Bamberger Reiter** (Bamberger Rider *c.*1235). No-one knows who the horseman is—possibly Constantine the Great, maybe one of the Magi. He sits proud on his steed, reins in check, staring far into the distance. The whole statue quivers with energy, but holds unfortunate memories for many. Hitler saw it as a pinnacle of German artistic perfection, and during the Third Reich reproductions adorned public buildings everywhere. The **Imperial**

Tomb in the centre of the nave contains the remains of the saintly 11th-century ruler Emperor Henry II and his consort Kunigunde. The top and sides are covered in carvings depicting events from their lives by the famous medieval sculptor Tilman Riemenschneider (*see* p. 55). To the left of the west chancel you can see the deeply burnished, though sadly unfinished, **Weinachtsaltar** (Nativity Altar, 1520–3), one of the last works of the Nuremberg sculptor Veit Stoss.

The **Diözesanmuseum** (Diocesan Museum) *(Easter–Oct Tues–Sun 10–5.30; adm DM2)* is across the cloisters in the chapterhouse (another Balthasar Neumann building). Here you'll find some richly woven ecclesiastical vestments, including robes belonging to Henry II and Kunigunde and the papal vestments of Pope Clement II—the only pope to be buried in Germany. He died in 1047, and his tomb is in the western choir, but not accessible to the public.

The Alte Hofhaltung

Alongside the cathedral is the Alte Hofhaltung, a motley complex which comprises the former imperial and episcopal palace and old imperial Diet Hall. The **Ratstube**, a graceful Renaissance building on the corner nearest the cathedral, now houses the **Historisches Museum** *(May–Oct Tues–Sun 9–5; adm DM2)*, a missable collection of bits and bobs relating to the city's history. Next to this is a grand Renaissance stone gateway, the **Reiche Tor** (Imperial Gate). It is flanked by allegorical figures of the Regnitz and Main rivers and shows Henry and Kunigunde carrying a remarkably accurate model of the cathedral. Through the arch you come to the big, uneven cobbled **inner court**. All around the edges are striking, four-storey, 15th-century half-timbered buildings with wooden galleries and heavy, drooping eaves.

The Neue Residenz

The rest of the Domplatz is taken up by a later palace, the huge L-shaped Neue Residenz *(Apr–Sept daily 9–12 and 1.30–5, Oct–Mar 9–12 and 1.30–4; adm DM3)*. The palace is yet another product of the powerful Schönborn family (*see* p. 312), whose mutual one-upmanship resulted in a scattering of grand buildings across Germany. The Baroque Residenz was commissioned by Prince Bishop Lothar Franz von Schönborn (who was also Archbishop and Elector of Mainz), and built by Leonhard Dientzenhofer in 1697–1703. The **interior** is worth a visit for a look at the bright frescoes in **Kaisersaal**, and a finely painted **Chinesische Kabinett**. The building also houses the small **Staatsgalerie**, a not particularly notable collection which includes works by Cranach the Elder and Hans Baldung Grien. Around the back of the palace is a **rose garden**, a fragrant retreat with serene statues, a Rococo summerhouse (now a café) and a magnificent view over Bamberg.

Michaelsberg and Altenburg

A footpath leads up from Aufseß-Straße (behind the Residenz), through orchards to the top of Michaelsberg, another of Bamberg's seven hills. The Benedictine **abbey** of St Michael on top of the hill is now an old people's home, but you can visit its Baroque church which has delicate paintings of over 600 medicinal herbs on the ceiling. The abbey cellars house the **Fränkisches Brauereimuseum** *(Tues–Fri 1–4.30, Sat and Sun 1.30–4; adm DM3)*, a small museum of beer and brewing history. Outside a spacious terrace looks out over Bamberg and the surrounding countryside, and there is a small café under the trees.

Retracing steps down Michaelsberg and continuing along Maternstraße, you reach the **Karmelitenkloster**. The church is another Dientzenhofer Baroque showpiece, but the **cloisters** *(daily 8–11 and 2–5.30)* are serenely Romanesque. Nearby, on Unterkaul, is Bamberg's finest Gothic church, the **Obere Pfarrkirche**, while uphill (along Altenburger Straße) is the **Altenburg** (1109), a ruined castle complete with moat and bear pit.

Bamberg ℗ (0951–)   ### Where to Stay

expensive

St Nepomunk, Obere Mühlbrücke 9, ℗ 25183, fax 26651 (DM190–240). Stylish hotel that teeters over the Regnitz on stilts. The rooms are sumptuously decorated and the service is impeccable.

moderate

Hotel Alt Ringlein, Domanikanerstr. 9, ℗ 54098, fax 52230 (DM130–180). Spruce, newly modernized hotel, part of which has been an inn since 1545. It nestles in the shadow of the cathedral, and is run by a capable and attentive family.

Barock-Hotel am Dom, Vorderer Bach 4, ℗ 54031, fax 54021 (DM125–145). A beautiful old Baroque building in a quiet, shady street behind the cathedral. The rooms aren't very imaginatively furnished, but they're comfortable enough and the management is helpful and friendly.

Weierich, Lugbank 5, ℗ 54004, fax 55800 (DM95–120). Rustic, cosy inn, centrally situated.

inexpensive

Spezial, Obere Königstr. 10, ℗ 24304 (DM80). Comfortable tavern run by a local brewery, a few minutes walk from the lower city.

Fässla, Obere Königstr. 21 (DM90). Also owned by a local brewery, but a little more upmarket with TV in the rooms and a hearty breakfast buffet.

Youth Hostel: Wolfsschlucht, Obere Leinritt 70, ℗ 56002.

Eating and Drinking

Bamberg is most famous for its beer. There are ten local breweries, which together produce around 30 different kinds. Locals rate highly the *Rauchbier* (smokey beer) made from smoked malt following a 16th-century recipe. The taverns owned by the breweries are also often recommendable places for tasty good-value meals.

Zum Schenkerla, Domanikanerstr. 6, © 56060 (DM25–35). Lively 17th-century tavern. Good beer and light meals.

Spezial, Sternartstraße (DM25–35). Beer cellar with garden, popular with locals and serving well-prepared food.

Dom-Terrassen, Unterer Kaulberg 36 (DM25–45). Unassuming *Gaststätte* near the Karmelitenkloster. Splendid terrace with views over the Domplatz.

Michaelsburg. There's a small café for *Kaffee und Küche*, as well as a larger *Gaststätte* (meals DM25–55) on the Michaelsburg. Both have terraces overlooking the town.

Café Domherrenshof, Karolinerstr. 24. Big basket chairs, high Baroque ceilings and a terrace with a view up to the Neue Residenz. Good place for breakfast or a lunchtime snack.

Entertainment and Nightlife

The **Bamberger Symphoniker**, once the *Deutsches Orchester* of Prague, skipped the border as the Iron Curtain was falling. They give concerts all over town, but one of the most enchanting ways to hear them is at the regular candlelit performances in the Kaisersaal of the Neue Residenz. Members of the *Symphoniker* also form the **Bamberg Baroque Ensemble**, which plays chamber music, and there are various other groups of high quality performing around town. **Tickets** for all concerts can be obtained from Bamberger Veranstaltungsdienst, Lange Str. 24, © 25255. Nearby is **Downstairs** (Lange Str. 16), the **nightclub** most popular with Bamberg's trendies.

See Directory entry for Pommersfelden.

Thuringia and Saxony

All the towns in this chapter lie in what used to be the DDR. Nowhere else in Germany did the Iron Curtain conceal quite so many wonders. Here, in Dresden, Leipzig, Weimar, Gotha and Eisenach were palaces, legendary art collections and venerable universities. You hop along the line of towns in the footsteps of Goethe, Schiller, Luther, Cranach and Bach—all of whom lived and worked here for important periods in their lives. South of this constellation, in the Thuringian Forest and among the Erz Mountains, craftspeople turn out brightly painted woodcarvings and musical instruments, in much the same way as they have done for centuries. Then, in the furthest corner of Germany, squeezed between the Czech and Polish borders, you will find one of the country's most dramatic sights—the haunting jagged rocks of 'Saxon Switzerland'.

MAGDEBURG

Elbe

184

81

9

Wittenberg

71

DESSAU

6

Saale

184

Mulde

HALLE

80

LEIPZIG

2

95

Naumburg

Buchenwald

ERFURT 7

Weimar

87

9

7

Eisenach

Gotha

Jena

GERA

92

Marienglashöhle

88

Friedrichroda

4

4

T H Ü R I N G E N

(T H U R I N G I A)

ZWICKAU

Thüringer Wald

Saalfeld

281

Schneeberg

169

Feengrotten

282

72

Blankenstein

R

Klingenthal

92

283

Markneukirchen

Thuringia

• — △ •   the Rennsteig
    R

In the days before the *Wende* the few foreigners who managed to penetrate this region would come back saying how *nice* the East Germans were. Somehow living under an oppressive regime made them gentler

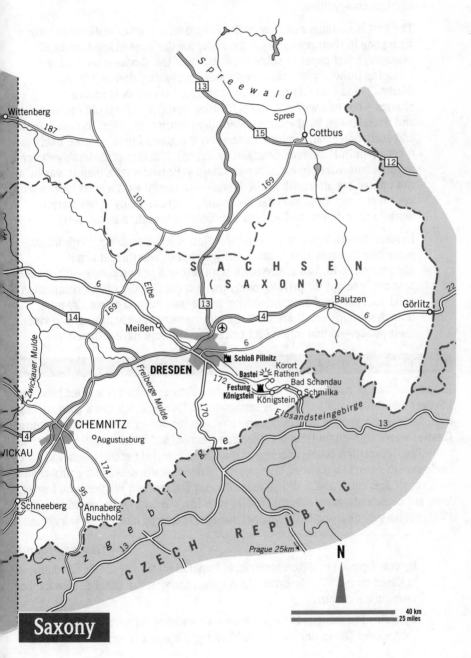

Saxony

and warmer than their wealthy, go-getting Western cousins. The best way to survive if you didn't join the Party was in a small, self-supporting group of trusted family and friends, and this trust made human relations closer and less competitive.

The east is no longer so unworldly. People who used to walk about with a string bag in their pockets—at the ready for the sudden appearance of sausages, toilet paper or some other rarity in the shops—now fill their shopping trolleys with consumer goods. In chasing after an affluent lifestyle some East Germans have abandoned their sweet-natured charms—but you will still find refreshing vestiges of their old openness and friendliness. By the same token, the notoriously sullen shop assistants and surly hotel staff are now thinner on the ground (you're more likely to meet them in Hannover, Stuttgart or Berlin). It is also considerably easier to find somewhere to eat, sleep or fill up your petrol tank than it was in the immediate aftermath of the *Wende*—though it isn't a good idea to let your fuel gauge drop too near the 'empty' mark as many petrol stations work to shop hours, and are more difficult to find than in the west.

In some towns, however, accommodation is still a problem. With hotels, especially, the question is often not which, but whether. It is not uncommon to find an entire town with just one or two hotels—often the best bet is to opt for private rooms (most tourist offices offer a reservation service). Paucity of accommodation in the past pushed prices sky-high, though as more hotels are built the old ones are quickly having to revise their policy—so you might find prices quoted here have dropped.

Eisenach

Eisenach, a town of gracious old villas which stand quietly at the foot of wooded hills, was J.S. Bach's birthplace and a seat of the Landgraves of Thuringia. It is also a good starting point for an exploration of the Thuringian Forest. On the outskirts of town is **Wartburg Castle**, where Luther translated the Bible into German, and which inspired Wagner to write *Tannhäuser* (thus doubly affirming its place as an object of national pilgrimage). The castle gave its name to a puttering little car, the DDR's only alternative to the smaller and even noisier Trabant. After the *Wende* people forsook Trabants and Wartburgs for flashier, faster and considerably more efficient Western cars. The Wartburg factory closed forever in 1991, though new Opel and BMW factories managed to soak up much of the workforce.

Getting Around

By car: Eisenach is 180km northeast of Frankfurt on the A5, and 85km southeast of Kassel on the B7. It is just off the A4, the Autobahn that connects most of the towns in this chapter.

By train: The Bahnhof is a few minutes' walk east of the town centre. There are connections (about one every two hours) to Frankfurt (1½hr), Erfurt (50min),

Leipzig (2¼hr) and Dresden (4hr).

Walks: Eisenach is the start of one of Germany's most famous marked walks, the 168km long **Rennsteig**. The trail was laid out in the 19th century (when the passion for organized hikes through the countryside began), and you can still follow the original stone markers all the way through the Thuringian Forest almost to the Czech border. There are shelters and places to stay at regular intervals all along the way. The Eisenach tourist office can furnish you with maps and detailed information.

Tourist Information

The **tourist information office**, Bahnhofstr. 3–5, © (03691) 76162 *(Mon 10–6, Tues–Fri 9–6, Sat 10–2)* has information about Eisenach and the Thuringian Forest. There is also a special **Wartburg Information Centre**, Am Schloßberg 2, © (03691) 77072 (same hours).

Festivals and Events

In the final weeks of March you can catch the region's most important music festival, the **Thuringian Bach Festival** in and around Eisenach. Around Easter, during the **Eisenacher Sommergewinn** a sungoddess vanquishes icy Winter, houses are decorated with bright flower mosaics, there is a parade of floats through town and painted eggs, pretzels and beer abound.

The Wartburg

The Wartburg *(Apr–Oct 8.30–4.30, Nov–Mar 9–3.30; adm DM5, or DM10 including Palas tour)* is undoubtedly Eisenach's main attraction, especially for Germans who have been pouring in by the coachload since the borders came down. It is a good idea to arrive early and avoid the crush. The castle is on the southern edge of town. You can get there by bus (10 or 10a from the Bahnhof, DM2.50 return) or by car—though this involves driving up a twisting road with a 13 per cent gradient, and parking (at a cost of DM4) still quite some distance from the entrance. Mini-buses ('Prendelbus') run from the parking lots and main road to the castle (DM4 return). A pleasant alternative is to walk up through the forests. (Take Wartburgallee out of town, then follow the signs; 20–30min). The last part of the walk is steep, but there is always the Prendelbus to help you on your way. Children can go up by donkey (DM3).

The Wartburg is a rambling castle, founded in 1067 and sprouting towers, halls and gateways for centuries afterwards. Yet it is small-scale and homely rather than awe-inspiring. The reason the castle holds such attraction for Germans is that **Martin Luther**, after ducking his Roman Catholic interrogators at the Diet of Worms, stayed here for 10 months as a guest of the Landgrave of Thuringia, hiding behind a forked beard and the persona of *Junker Jörg* ('Farmer George'). To pass the time he translated the New Testament from Greek into the vernacular, thus helping to cast German into the mould of a literary language (in much the same way as the King James Bible did for English). Wartburg had always had a reputation for being a cultured court. It was here, in the 12th and 13th centuries, that competitions of **Minnesänger** (minnesingers: minstrels) attracted the best poets in the land, such as Walther von der Vogelweide (*see* p. 68) and Wolfram von Eschenbach, author of *Parzifal*. Centuries later, after a stay in the castle, Richard Wagner used the contest as the setting for his opera *Tannhäuser*.

The Romanesque **Palas** *(guided tour only, 1 hour)* contains over 200 finely carved **pilasters**. In the diminutive **Sängersaal** (scene of the troubadour contests) is an impressive fresco cycle by the Romantic painter **Moritz von Schwind** (part of a 19th-century restoration effort). In the 'Elizabeth Bower' glittering Jugendstil mosaics tell the story of another famous resident, the self-sacrificing young **St Elizabeth of Thuringia**, who preferred to tend the poor and elderly rather than join in jolly court life, and ended up being cast out to fend for herself in Marburg (*see* p. 200). At the top of the building is the splendid **Festsaal**, built in the 19th century when the Sängersaal proved too small, and still occasionally used for concerts. From here you can cross into the **museum** (another 19th-century addition) which houses Cranach's portraits of Luther's parents and a superb collection of local medieval woodcarving (displayed here while the Thüringer Museum in town is closed for restoration). From here you follow the Wehrgang (sentry's walk) to the **Lutherstube**, the bare wood-panelled room where the Reformer worked. Luther was evidently much harrassed at his work by the Devil, who appeared in a number of seductive and irritating guises, finally assuming the form of a large blue fly. At this Luther lost his temper and hurled an ink bottle at the Prince of Darkness, leaving a stain on the wall. Over the centuries souvenir hunters have chipped away at the blot, so that all that now remains is a hole. You can, however, see the whale vertebra on which Luther rested his feet.

Around Town

At the foot of the Wartburg, just off the main road, is the elegant **Reuter Villa** *(Tues–Sun 10–5; adm DM3)*, home of the Low German writer and artist Fritz Reuter, but more appealing to foreign visitors for its original 19th-century furniture and exhibition on Wagner (including an excellent Wagner library). Carrying on along Wartburgallee towards the town centre you pass the **Automobilbaumuseum** *(Tues–Sun 9–5; adm DM3)*, a small glass-walled museum that looks more like a car sales showroom than a museum. Inside is a collection of Wartburgs, from the first to the last. (The Wartburg was a speedy and stylish car before becoming the box-shaped saloon of the past few decades.)

A little further on, and left along Grimmelgasse, you come to Frauen-Plan, a spacious square (now mainly car park) on which you'll find the **Bachhaus** *(Apr–Sept Mon 12–5.45, Tues–Sun 9–5.45; Oct–Mar Mon 1–4.45, Tues–Sun 9–4.45; DM3)*, thought to be J.S. Bach's birthplace. Today it contains a small collection of old musical instruments, and displays on the achievements of the talented musical family. Johann Sebastian Bach was born in 1685 into a family of musicians and spent all his life in Thuringia, mainly in Weimar and Leipzig. Oddly, during his lifetime he was known more as a virtuoso organist than as a composer. He produced hundreds of compositions—mainly to order for churches, as practice pieces for students or for court entertainment—but managed to keep up a consistently high standard. His precise (though often intensely spiritual) Baroque work was swamped by the new Classical style that followed, and after his death in 1750 Bach the composer was quickly forgotten. A century passed before Felix Mendelssohn fished out his forgotten works and almost singlehandedly restored him to a state of grace.

Lutherstraße leads off the Frauen-Plan to the **Lutherhaus** *(Oct–Apr Mon–Sat 9–1 and 2–5, Sun 2–5; May–Sept Mon–Fri 9–1 and 2–5, Sat and Sun 9–1 and 1.30–5; adm DM3)*, the 15th-century half-timbered house where Luther boarded from 1498 to 1501 while he was a pupil at the local school. Inside is a not particularly riveting exhibition from the local Protestant church archives. From the Lutherhaus it is just a few minutes' walk north to the Marktplatz, where you can see a deep red **Rathaus** and a modest Rococo **Stadtschloß** (closed indefinitely for renovations) that was the palace of a local branch of the Saxon Wettin dynasty (*see* p. 42). In the middle of the square is the **Georgenkirche**, where Luther sang as a choirboy and where Bach was baptized; there is a powerful statue of the composer in the porch. More recently the church was an important meeting point for demonstrators against the DDR regime, in the events that eventually led to its collapse.

Off the western end of the Markt is the **Predigerkirche**, which will one day house a remarkable collection of 11th- and 12th-century Thuringian carving, though for the moment it, too, is closed for repair. (Part of the collection can be seen at Wartburg.) East of the Markt is a Romanesque city gate, the **Nikolaitor**, with the simple, rather beautiful late-Romanesque **Nikolaikirche** alongside.

Eisenach ✆ (03691–)　　　　　　　　　　　　　　　　　　　　　　　　***Where to Stay***

Hotel Auf der Wartburg, Auf der Wartburg, ✆/fax 5111 (DM160–280). Friendly staff, luxurious rooms and a dreamy setting alongside the castle.

Hotel Fürstenhof, Luisenstr. 11–13, ✆ 5371, fax 3682 (DM160–260). Charming, eccentrically designed turn-of-the-century hotel rescued in the nick of time from ungracious decay. It is on a prime site above the town and the rooms (many with wooden balconies) look across to the Wartburg. The service is impeccable.

Christliches Hospiz Glockenhof, Grimmelgasse 4, ✆ 5216, fax 5217 (DM180). Comfortable converted Jugendstil villa. Part of a group of hotels that offers 'Christian hospitality'—evident more in the warmth of greeting and genuine friendliness than in any overt evangelizing.

Hotel Burghof, Karlsplatz 24–6, ✆ 3387. Well-run hotel in the shadow of the Nikolaitor. Due for renovation. The new prices haven't been decided but it will be in the inexpensive to moderate range.

Pension Klostergarten, Am Klosterholz 23, ✆ 625 166, fax 625 148 (DM80). Bright victim to the owner's penchant for pink and white. On the western edge of town. No restaurant.

Café Swing, Karlsplatz 10, ✆ 71545. Trendy café near the Nikolaitor. Drinks, ice-cream and light meals.

Alt Eisenach, Karlstr. 51, ✆ 76088 (DM40–50). Steaks and other meaty dishes brought on sizzling platters to your table.

Ritterstube, Schmelzerstr. (DM25–30). Fish specialities, including shark steak.

Burghof, Karlsplatz 24–6, ✆ 3387 (DM15–20). Hotel restaurant serving simple, well-cooked and inexpensive meals.

The Thuringian Forest

The Thuringian Forest (German: *Türinger Wald*) stretches to the south-east of Eisenach. Forests cover the hills, then suddenly clear to offer views over meadowy uplands. Forgotten villages of half-timbered houses alternate with ugly hostels and hotels put up by trade unions under the DDR. Mild summers make this ideal hiking country (*see* the Rennsteig under **Getting Around**, above), and it is possible to ski in the winter. Two of the best-known sights are underground. At Friedrichroda, in the northern part of the forest, is the **Marienglashöhle** *(Mid-Apr–Sept daily 9–5, Oct–mid-Apr daily 9–4; adm DM3)*, an enormous cave, complete with subterranean lake and sparkling crystal walls. (The crystals were used to decorate statues of the Madonna—hence the cave's name.) Outside Saalfeld, further south, you'll find the considerably more commercialized **Feengrotten** (Fairy Grottos) *(Feb–Oct 9–5; adm DM5)*, an abandoned vitriol mine in which bizarre formations of stalagmites and stalactites are lit up and given evocative names, such as the **Märchendom** (Fairytale Cathedral).

Gotha

Gotha, 30km east of Eisenach, has a special resonance to British ears. Saxe-Coburg-Gotha was the name of the British royal family before they patriotically opted for 'Windsor' at the outbreak of the First World War. ('Saxe' is the English prefix for any branch of the Wettin dynasty (*see* p. 42).) The duchy split after the war, when Coburg became part of Bavaria.) The town has two other, rather contradictory, claims to fame. A local publishing firm used to bring out the famous *Almanach de Gotha* (a German equivalent of *Debrett's Peerage*); and it was here, in 1875, that the Socialist Worker's Party of Germany (the ancestor of today's **Social Democratic Party**), was formed. Today Gotha is a pretty town, with some beautifully restored old buildings. It makes a good base for ventures south into the Thuringian Forest.

By car: Gotha is 30km east of Eisenach on the A4 (or B7). At the time of writing the latter is still a maze of detours. There is a **petrol station** on Huttenstraße (carry on northwards up Bahnhofstraße).

By train: The Bahnhof is a few minutes' walk south of the centre (along Bahnhofstraße). There are connections to Leipzig (2hr) and Erfurt (25min).

Public transport: The **Thüringerwaldbahn** (information ✆ (03621) 52402) is one of the two surviving rural tramways in Germany (the other is in Saxon Switzerland). Line 4 of the city tramway picks you up at the Bahnhof, then tootles off beyond the city boundaries into the heart of the Thuringian Forest, taking you all the way to the Marienglashöhle caves (*see* above) for a mere DM3.50.

Tourist Information

The **tourist information office** is at Blumenbachstr. 1–3, ✆ (03621) 54036 *(Mon–Fri 9–5, Sat 9–12)*.

The Altstadt and Schloß Friedenstein

Gotha's little red Renaissance **Rathaus** shows off its fancy gables from a position bang in the middle of the elongated Hauptmarkt. To the north and east are **Am Brühl** and the **Buttermarkt** which, with their half-timbered and Renaissance houses, are the most atmospheric spots in town. Down Jüdenstraße to the west is the **Augustinerkloster**, a 13th-century monastery with a quiet, rose-covered cloister.

At its southern end, the thin Hauptmarkt sweeps up, past a series of artificial cascades, to **Schloß Friedenstein** *(daily 9–5; adm DM5 including admission to all museums; museums only adm DM3 each)*. This graceless white pile was built in 1643–54 for Duke Ernst I when he came to rule over the newly created duchy. In the **Schloßmuseum** there is an interesting collection of Egyptian and Greek antiquities, and an entire gallery of handsome, glinting white Neoclassical statues by the French sculptor Jean-Antoine Houdin (1741–1828). The picture gallery contains a substantial array of Cranach; the 16th-century *Gothaer Tafelaltar* (fold-out tablets bearing 157 different scenes from the life of Christ, each lovingly filled out with scenes of contemporary Germany); and a touchingly tender painting known as *The Lovers of Gotha*, done in 1484 by one of Germany's most skilful early artists, the **Master of the Housebook**. The Schloßmuseum also shows off some of the palace's **interiors** ranging from grotesquely heavy Baroque stucco to the restrained Pompeii room, decorated in the 18th century in imitation of rooms uncovered during the Pompeii excavations.

The **Regionalmuseum** consists of the usual array of furniture and craftsman's tools—but attached to the museum is Gotha's gem, a completely intact **Baroque theatre**, installed by Ernst I in the 1640s when the palace was built. The state-of-the-art technical equipment included a revolving stage (the mechanism still works—you can't visit it, but there's a model in the room next door). The theatre is named after **Konrad Ekhof** (1720–78) who founded Germany's first permanent resident acting company here in 1775. The set and backdrop (showing a formal French garden) are original, dating from 1774. There is no orchestra pit—the band used to sit at a table in front of the stage. The theatre is still sometimes used for concerts.

Upstairs is a small museum of **photographic portraiture**, which includes a signed photograph of Bismarck. Higher still is a compact, but impressive **Cartography Museum**. In the extensive **Schloß Gardens** there is a boating lake, a fake Doric Temple and an elegant Orangery (now a music library). Behind the Schloß looms a gargantuan neo-Renaissance building now housing the **Museum für Natur** *(daily 9–5, DM3)* where you can see well-presented displays of the flora and fauna of the Thuringian forest.

Gotha ✆ *(03621–)*   **Where to Stay**

Hotel Slovan, Hauptmarkt 20–21, ✆ 52047 (DM150–200). Newly converted, but not overly friendly.

Hotel Waldbahn, Bahnhofstr. 16, ✆ 53252 (from DM70). Adequate hotel on frantically busy street.

Pension Regina, Schwabhäser Str. 4, ✆ 53922 (from DM60). An ordinary little *Pension* near the centre.

Eating and Drinking

Bierstube am Brühl, Brühl 18, ✆ 53539 (DM15–25). Thuringian sausages and basic *gutbürgerlich* cuisine.

Ratskeller, Hauptmarkt 3, ✆ 54057 (DM25–60). Enthusiastic new team offer an internationally influenced menu, with fish specialities.

Kuhn und Kuhn, Hühnersdorferstr. Attractive bar and beergarden just off the Buttermarkt. Small snack menu.

Erfurt

Next stop along the A4 is Erfurt, the capital of Thuringia. Erfurt passed through the Second World War relatively unscathed—and though the town became drab and dilapidated under the communist regime, there is enough between the splendid cathedral and the curious Krämerbrücke to take up a good day of your time.

Erfurt weathered the *Wende* a little better than many of its neighbours—the local economy was based on horticulture and microelectronics rather than dinosaur heavy industries. A boost came in 1992 when, to celebrate the town's 1250th birthday, Erfurt re-established its university. Originally founded in 1392, the university had been one of the most important in Europe (numbering Luther among its students), but was closed by the Prussians in 1816.

Getting Around

By car: Erfurt is another 25km along the A4 from Gotha. Although the parallel B7 is slightly shorter, the motorway journey takes less time.

By train: The Hauptbahnhof is 20 minutes' walk south of the centre, along Bahnhofstraße. Erfurt is one of the region's main rail junctions, and there are frequent connections to Weimar (¼hr), Gotha (½hr), Leipzig (1hr 10min), Dresden (2½hr) and Kassel (2½hr).

Public transport: It is quite possible to walk between Erfurt's sights, but they are scattered and the tram connections are good and worth using. A day ticket for unlimited travel costs DM4.

Tourist Information

There are **tourist information offices** at Bahnhofstr. 37, © 26267, and Krämerbrücke, © 23436.

Festivals and Events

A permanent festival of flowers and plants, with seasonal exhibitions, is held at the **Internationale Gartenbauaustellung** (known as *iga*, daily 10 to dusk; adm DM4), an enormous garden show which takes place in a park on the outskirts of town. It is best seen in the spring, or during the special theme exhibitions. There are also orchid, cactus and tropical houses.

The Domhügel

Erfurt's **cathedral** stands grandly on top of the **Domhügel**, a small hill to the west of the city centre. At the foot of the hill is an enormous market place, stamped out by the Prussians as a parade ground. These days fruit and veg stalls and the occasional fair try bravely to fill the void, but it is better to visit the **Domplatz** at weekends when you have an unrestricted view across to the awe-inspiring stairway that—as if promising a path to Heaven—sweeps up to the cathedral door from the end of the square.

There has been a cathedral on this sight since AD 742. Today's light, playful Gothic building (begun in 1420) rests on a very solid base. Part of this dates back to an earlier Romanesque church and part is the bulwark-like **Kavaten** (which had to be built under the towers in the 13th century because the ambitiously designed cathedral extended over the edge of the hill). Light filters into the dim choir through towering spears of **stained-glass windows**, each densely populated with biblical figures. The richly coloured windows were made between 1370 and 1410; more than 70 per cent of the glass is original. The **choir stalls** are the work of two sets of carvers—13th-century craftsmen, and generations of choirboys who made their mark (often in elaborate Gothic script) over subsequent centuries. The cathedral's most renowned treasures are a **candelabrum** (1160) in the shape of a man (nicknamed *Wolfram*) and a quiet, simple **Madonna**, carved in the same year. (Both are in the south transept, just to the right of the choir.) Look out also for a **Cranach** Madonna and a fancy Renaissance **font** set in its own pavilion with an 18m-high spire. In the nave is the tomb of the **Count of Gleichen** and his two wives. The count was captured during the crusades by a Turkish sultan, and set to work as a slave—but the sultan's daughter fell in love with him. She helped him to escape and they ran away together. Ever the gallant, count Ernst felt that he had to marry her—even though he had a wife at home. The countess was only too happy to have her husband back, so the Turkish princess converted to Christianity, the Pope granted a special dispensation, the second marriage took place, and all three lived together happily ever after.

Standing next door to the cathedral, also on the Domhügel, the **Severikirche** makes a modest neighbour. Inside is the pink sandstone **tomb of St Severus**, carved by the 14th-century sculptor now known as the Master of St Severus; a Baroque organ bedecked with flames and angels; and a 15th-century relief of the Archangel Michael nonchalantly slaughtering a gruesome devil.

From the Domhügel to the Krämerbrücke

Behind the Domhügel is a second, larger, hill, the **Petersberg** which is covered by the **Zitadelle** (citadel), a windswept, depressing fortress begun in the 17th century but bearing the heavy stamp of both Prussian and DDR militarism. The fortress surrounds an earlier Benedictine abbey, but you can barely recognize the Romanesque **Peterskirche**, which was converted into an arsenal by the Prussians. (Moves are underway to restore the church, but this will be a long process.)

Marktstraße leads eastwards off the Domplatz. To the north of Marktstraße (around Allerheiligenstraße and Michaelisstraße) is one of the most atmospheric parts of town—quiet streets of wonky half-timbered houses running down to the sluggish River Gera. South of Marktstraße you will find the **Predigerkirche**, one of the many interesting old parish churchs around town. Inside, the original 15th-century structure is intact—including an opaque roodscreen that completely cuts off the monks' part of the church from the hoi polloi. On the choir screen is an exceptional stone carving of the Madonna (1350), and a painting of the crucifixion done in the same year.

Marktstraße leads up onto the **Fischmarkt**, once the centre for Erfurt's thriving medieval trade. Here decorative **Renaissance mansions** stand in the shadow of a heavy 19th-century **Rathaus**. A few minutes' walk beyond the Rathaus brings you to the city's most unusual sight, the **Krämerbrücke**. Like Florence's Ponte Vecchio, this 14th-century bridge is lined with little shops and houses—it is the only one of its kind north of the Alps. As you cross the bridge you have the impression that you are walking down a medieval lane. Duck down the stairs at Kreuzgasse, and you find yourself on the river bank, with a fine view back to the half-timbered houses that line the parapets, seemingly clinging to each other for support.

Around Anger

From the other end of the Krämerbrücke, Meienbergstraße takes you up to **Anger**, Erfurt's main shopping street and the hub of the public transport system. At the top end is the **Kaufmannskirche** (Merchants' Church), where Luther preached in 1522, and which still has a copy of the sermon taken down in shorthand by an enterprising member of the congregation.

Anger is lined with Erfurt's most opulent and ostentatious mansions (look out especially for the Jugendstil extravaganza at No. 23). At the far end the street forks. On the northern fork (Regierungstraße) is the **Statthalterei**, a Baroque palace that was the scene of the famous meeting between Goethe and Napoleon in 1808. (Napoleon showed a remarkably good knowledge of the poet's work.) The **Angermuseum** *(Wed–Sun 10–6; adm DM3)*, in a splendid Baroque mansion on the corner of Bahnhofstraße and Anger, is essential viewing. Downstairs you can see some excellent carving by the Master of St Severus, a ceiling rescued from the 14th-century Rathaus, and an exquisitely illustrated, handwritten astrological almanac dating from 1458. Upstairs there is a good collection of German painting, including works by Cranach and the eccentric Hans Baldung.

Erfurt © (0361–)   ### Where to Stay

Erfurt is pitifully short of hotels and most of those that do exist are due for closure and renovation. Prices fluctuate and you would be strongly advised to contact hotels in advance, or to enquire at the tourist information office (which also offers a reservation service for private rooms around town—probably your best bet).

Hotel Erfurter Hof, Bahnhofsvorplatz 1–2, © 51 151 (from DM150). Modern, central and the only really viable alternative to private rooms.

Hotel Thuringen, Juri-Gagarin-Ring 154, © 65 512 (from DM90). Functional hotel on hectically busy ring road.

Eating and Drinking

Zum Wenigemarkt, Wenigemarkt 13 (DM20–25). Quiet restaurant on the peaceful square at the eastern end of the Krämerbrücke. Simple but tasty food (such as chilli con carne and goulash).

Gildehaus, Fischmarkt 13, © 23273 (DM30–40). Old building on the Fischmarkt, panelled walls and heavy furniture with embroidered upholstery. This sets the scene for the cuisine which comprises dishes such as pot roast with fruit sauce and dumplings.

Penne-Keller, Große Arche 5, © 643 7470 (DM20–60). Frankfurt *Apfelwein*, a wide selection of beers, light meals and game dishes in season.

Café zur Krämerbrücke, Krämerbrücke. Ideal *Kaffee und Kuchen* café on the Krämerbrücke, with a terrace on the river bank offering a fine view of the bridge.

Café Arche, Große Arche 8. Friendly café in quiet alley off Marktstraße. Delicious icecream, good cakes and a long menu of different coffees and teas.

Weimar

Just 20km east of Erfurt is Weimar, the town whose name falls on the German ear as Stratford-upon-Avon does on the English. In the middle of the 16th-century Weimar became a seat of the Saxon Wettin dynasty. The dukes were patrons of the painter Lucas Cranach, who produced most of his work here. Later J.S. Bach spent nine years in Weimar as court organist. The writer Christoph-Martin Wieland came as a tutor in 1772 and, most important of all, Goethe arrived in 1775—and stayed for most of the rest of his life. Weimar became the cultural capital of Germany, attracting other writers such as Friedrich Schiller and Johann Gottfried Herder, and later composers such as Franz Liszt and Richard Strauss. Friedrich Nietzsche came here to die, and, at the beginning of this century, the local art school grew into the influential Bauhaus movement (*see* p. 64).

In 1919 the National Theatre in Weimar became a refuge for the German National Assembly, escaping a left-wing unrest in Berlin, *see* p. 45. Here it drew up the constitution for Germany's first democracy, the ill-fated Weimar Republic (*see* p. 45). Germany was never ruled from Weimar—the deputies scuttled back to Berlin as soon as the coast was clear.

Weimar escaped the Second World War relatively lightly, and was one of the towns pin-pointed for big investment and rapid redevelopment after the *Wende*. Today it is a bright and attractive town of fine period architecture, with a youthful, peculiarly Oxbridge air. The centre is small and quite manageable on foot. Here, more than anywhere else in Germany, it is possible to imagine what life was like in the compact capitals of the tiny German principalities, many with a cultural resonance way beyond their size.

Getting Around

By car: Weimar is 20km from Erfurt on the A4/B7. The same roads will take you to Dresden (225km); and Leipzig is 100km to the north, along the A9. There are **petrol stations** just off Theatre-Platz, and north of the centre along Karl-Liebknecht-Platz.

By train: The Hauptbahnhof is quite some way to the north of the town, along Carl-August-Allee.

Public transport: All buses run to Goetheplatz in the centre. After that the sights are all within easy walking distance of each other.

Tourist Information

The **tourist information office** is at Marktstraße 4, © (03643) 65384 *(Mon 10–6, Tues–Fri 9–6, Sat 9-1, in summer 9–4)*. The staff can supply maps and explanatory leaflets, and will also book you a hotel or private room.

Around the Markt

Weimar's small, busy Markt is a good point to begin your visit. Opposite a solid, rather dull 19th-century **Rathaus** is the wildly elaborate Renaissance **Cranachhaus**, where the painter lived for the last part of his life. On the south side of the square is the **Hotel Elephant** (familiar to readers of Thomas Mann's novel about Weimar's glory years, *Lotte in Weimar*). Next door is the **Bachstube** (now a restaurant), home to the composer during his spell as court organist. Bach's sojourn in Weimar came to an ignominious end. He was imprisoned for a month in 1717 after giving public vent to his rage at being passed over for the post of court musical director. Afterwards he left in a huff to take up another position at nearby Köthen.

The south-eastern part of the Markt leads onto an even larger square, the Platz der Demokratie, bound at its southern end by the tasteful Baroque **Fürstenhaus**. This is where Goethe had his audience with the young duke on arriving in Weimar. (Today the building is occupied by a music academy.) Another palace on the east side of the square houses the **Herzogin Anna Amilia Bibliothek**, a library named after the enlightened regent whose rule in the 18th century marked the beginning of Weimar's golden age. Inside is the **Rokokosaal** *(Mon–Sat 11–12.30, closed Nov–Mar; adm free)*, a galleried Rococo library still lined with shelves of old books.

Walking north from the Platz der Demokratie you come to the enormous **Schloß** *(Tues–Sun 9–1 and 2–6; adm DM4)*, a grand parade of different buildings (mainly Neoclassical) lined up around a vast courtyard. Inside is a **museum** with a number of excellent Cranachs, including a well-known portrait of Luther and the lewd *Battle of Naked Men and Lamenting Women*. There is also the famous pair of portraits by Dürer of the Nuremberg merchant Hans Tucher and his wife, and some immensely skilful Dutch *Pronkstileven* (still lives of ostentatious objects), as well as a small selection of Italian Renaissance paintings and Russian ikons. Upstairs is a collection of Romantic, 19th- and 20th-century art which is less impressive, but does include interesting work by Tischbein, Caspar David Friedrich and Arnold Böcklin. You also have the opportunity to see some of the Schloß **interiors**, the most impressive of which are the **Dichterzimmer**—rooms decorated to commemorate the famous poets who lived in Weimar.

West of the Schloß, along Mostgasse, is the **Herderkirche** (officially SS Peter and Paul, but known after the 18th-century poet who was its pastor for 30 years). Inside is a superb Cranach *Crucifixion*, which features the painter himself standing between John the Baptist and Luther at the foot of the cross. Up Jakobsstraße, off the northeast corner of Herderplatz, is the **Kirms-Krackow-Haus**, reputedly Weimar's finest example of 18th-century domestic architecture, but at the time of writing closed indefinitely for renovations. A little further north is the **Jakobskirche**, where Cranach lies buried. This was the church where, in 1806, Goethe finally placated Weimar society by marrying Christiane Vulpius, the woman he had lived with for 18 years. (He told her he was doing it to reward her for her bravery in the face of the French troops who had occupied the town earlier that year.) Kaufstraße, off the southern end of Herderplatz, will take you back to the Markt.

The Museum Houses

If you walk down the side of the Rathaus, along Windischenstraße then left up Am Palais, you come to the **Wittumspalais** *(Tues–Sun 9–12 and 1–5; adm DM3)*. This was the Regent Anna Amilia's retirement palace. Here, every Friday, the brilliant duchess and Goethe would preside over intellectual discussions at a round table. The palace has been superbly restored and is filled with fine period furniture; it includes the famous *Tafelrundenzimmer* (Round Table Room), as well as a *Festsaal* designed by Goethe himself. There is also a small display devoted to **Christoph-Martin Wieland** (a contemporary of Goethe's regarded as one of the major poets and philosophers of the time, but now rather neglected).

Diagonally across Theaterplatz from the Wittumspalais is the **Nationaltheater**, scene of the 1919 National Assembly and the premieres of many of the great plays in the German language. Even in Goethe's time, though, the quality of the productions had begun to deteriorate. The great dramatist objected to the cheap French melodramas that seemed to be taking over the German house of culture. One evening, during a performance of *The Forest of Burgundy* (in which the hero—a bull mastiff—had been taught to ring a bell by means of a sausage tied to the rope), the poet stormed out of the theatre in a rage, demanding that the play be withdrawn. Unfortunately the voluptuous leading lady had 'a peculiar sort of influence' over the Grand Duke. The play ran on, and Goethe never returned to the Nationaltheater.

South of the Wittumspalais, along Schillerstraße (a shady pedestrianized shopping street), you come to the **Schillerhaus** *(Wed–Mon 9–5; adm DM5 to house and museum)*. Behind the house where Germany's second great dramatist lived for the last three years of his life, is a spacious modern museum devoted to his life and works. This is a step up on the usual collection of manuscript facsimiles and memorabilia, with models of theatre sets and documentation of early performances.

At the end of Schillerstraße a right turn into Frauentorstraße brings you to the Frauenplan and the **Goethe Wohnhaus and Goethemuseum** *(Tues–Sun 9–5; adm DM5 to house and museum)*, a point of pilgrimage for many Germans. Even in his own lifetime Goethe was an object of veneration, and people would travel to Weimar just for a glimpse of him. John Russell, an Englishman passing through in 1823, wrote: 'Though [Goethe] is now 74 years old, his tall imposing form is but a little bent; the lofty open brow retains all its dignity, and even the eye has not lost much of its fire'; but he goes on to remark the poet's frustration at being followed around town by gawping tourists, and notes, 'sometimes he shuts his door and often his mouth for the dread of being improperly put into books.'

The poet's Baroque mansion is the more interesting of the two sections. Here you can see the study where he worked, his library (behind bars) and the narrow bed where he died. There is also a cabinet containing his favourite cloak and a moulting top hat. However, the stream of visitors destroys any remnant of atmosphere. Oddly, Goethe's ghost seems to linger more in a neglected shed off the main courtyard. Here the 20th century is completely cut out, and his small coach looks as if it could be harnessed up and ready for him in five minutes.

In the museum section you can see memorabilia ranging from playing cards used by Goethe's mother to portraits of his many mistresses. There are also some first editions and manuscripts, though little in the poet's own hand: he used to dictate everything but his shorter poems to a secretary.

South of Frauenplan (across Wielandplatz and down Marienstraße) is the **Liszthaus** *(Tues–Sun 9–12 and 2–5; adm DM2.50)*, the most atmospheric of the museum houses. The dashing Hungarian composer and virtuoso pianist, Franz Liszt, came to live here in 1848 and worked for 11 years as director of the local orchestra and opera company. Later he complained of Weimar's conservatism, and went to live with his son-in-law, Richard Wagner, in Bayreuth—but returned to Weimar every summer for the last 17 years of his life. Here you do not have to peer through bars and chained-off doorways, but can walk about the rooms and touch the furniture. Look out for the collection of carved walking sticks, a favourite Liszt accessory (he was a stylish dresser and notorious womanizer).

Weimar ℗ (03643–)   ***Where to Stay***

Telephone numbers are still subject to change. If you have problems getting through, check with German directory enquiries (℗ 1188) or the tourist information office.

Hotel Elephant, Markt 19, ℗ 61471, fax 65310 (DM270–400). Weimar's most famous hotel, once again raised to the heights of luxury and exclusivity.

Christliches Hotel Amalienhof, Amalienstr. 2, ℗ 5490, fax 549 110 (DM186–196). Newly converted from typical Neoclassical Weimar mansion. Friendly staff. One of the few hotels near the centre.

Hotel Liszt, Lisztstr. 1–3, ℗ 61911, fax 419 836 (DM140–180). Simple hotel, not too far from centre.

Pension Savina, Rembrandtweg 13, ℗ 600 797 (DM90). Cheapest in town. Clean and functional. Near the Hauptbahnhof.

Youth Hostels: Humboldtstr. 17, ℗ 64021; Zum Wilden Graben 12, ℗/fax 3471.

Private Rooms: (DM30–60). Apply through the tourist information office.

Eating and Drinking

Residenz Café, Grüner Markt 4, ℗ 501 883. Classical music, lots of polished wood and piles of newspapers and magazines.

Café Goethe trift Nina, underneath Residenz Café. Café/gallery with friendly alternative crowd.

Elephant Keller, Hotel Elephant, ℗ 61471 (DM25–25). Successful Weimar businessmen meet over Thuringian pot roast and game stews.

Kürschners, Schillerstraße, opposite the Schillerhaus (DM20–30). Trendy café with good changing menu (usually with fish, chicken and turkey dishes).

Zum weißen Schwan, Am Frauenplan, ✆ 61715 (DM60–80). A 16th-century wood-panelled inn where Goethe had a *Stammtisch*. Thuringian and international cuisine, including dishes such as boar stuffed with mushrooms with herb and mustard paste.

Buchenwald

A few miles north of Weimar is the site of one of the Nazi's most horrific concentration camps, **Buchenwald** *(May–Sept 9.30–5.45, Oct–Apr 8.45–4.45)*. This was not a designated extermination camp, but of the 240,000 people incarcerated here from 1937 to 1945, 56,000 died of starvation, disease or as the result of torture. The liberating Red Army in their turn rounded up hundreds of Nazi suspects, then tortured and killed them in the forests near Buchenwald (mass graves were uncovered in 1990). Today the camp is a barren, sobering memorial to the Jews, communists, gypsies, homosexuals and other victims of Nazism. There is a small museum with displays on Nazi atrocities. The camp itself has largely been demolished, but the site seems disturbingly haunted by the atrocities that took place there.

East of Weimar

Travelling east along the A4 you come to **Jena**, a lively university town dominated by the 120m-high cylindrical *Universitätshochhaus* (nicknamed the *Phallus Jenensis*), and then cross the border into **Saxony**, where the first major town is **Chemnitz** (known under the DDR as Karl-Marx-Stadt). Chemnitz has surprising pockets of beauty in between its Stalinist architecture, and is more worth a visit than its reputation as 'the Saxon Manchester' suggests. Below Chemnitz, trailing along the Czech border, are the **Erzgebirge** (literally 'Ore Mountains').

See Directory entries for Jena, Zwickau and Chemnitz.

The Erzgebirge

Rich deposits of metals—such as silver, tin and lead—all along the Erzgebirge range gave medieval Saxony its economic clout. In later centuries, as the ore began to run out, the locals turned to wood-carving and lace-making to earn their money. It was probably a brightly painted Erzgebirge nutcracker that provided the inspiration for Tchaikovsky's ballet. Erzgebirge wooden toys and pyramidical Christmas decorations were sold throughout Germany even before the *Wende* abolished trade restrictions.

Although the mountains are really no more than chunky hills, and despite the fact that fumes wafting over from Czech factories made this one of the most polluted parts of the country and all but killed the trees, the Erzgebirge was one of the most popular holiday resorts in the DDR. It is still worth a visit. Air quality has now much improved, this is reasonably good skiing country from quite early in winter and there are some charming villages that still exist mainly on carving and other crafts.

Roads B169/283 and B174, leading south from Chemnitz, take you through the most attractive part of the range—though **Augustusburg** (14km east of Chemnitz), a pretty town gathered around a huge Renaissance Schloß, is worth the short detour. **Annaberg** (just off the B174) and **Schneeberg** (just off the B283) are the most rewarding places to watch woodcarvers at work and buy their wares. The skiing is best at **Klingenthal** (a few kilometres further down the B283). A little further on, at **Markneukirchen**, is a long-established colony of musical instrument makers, whose products are used by orchestras all round the world.

See Directory entries for Annaberg and Schneeberg.

The countryside to the north and east of Chemnitz, once also poisoned by pollution, is much cleaner since local factories have stopped burning lignite, and now that fewer of the cute (but environmentally filthy) Trabants are on the road. However, this is not a region to visit for the landscape so much as for the cultural treasure troves of its main cities—Leipzig and Dresden.

Leipzig

Leipzig, like so many other east German cities, runs the full spectrum of colours between grey and brown. Unlike the others, Leipzig doesn't appear drab. Here the mood is one of an old Central European city—a hundred times closer to Vienna, Budapest or Prague than to its German neighbours.

The merchants who crowded into Leipzig from the 16th to the 19th centuries built their homes and warehouses around scores of small open-air markets. Then they began trading in the inter-connecting alleys. Today you will still find narrow passages lined with book-shops; damp, hidden courtyards with just one café, and elegant arcades with classy shops and eye-catching window displays (a rarity in eastern Germany).

For centuries Leipzig rivalled Salzburg and Vienna as a centre of European music. Telemann and Bach worked here (in bitter rivalry). Mendelssohn and Schumann presided over the Conservatory. The Gewandhaus orchestra played new work by Beethoven, Brahms, Liszt and Tchaikovsky, and the opera house was the second (after Bayreuth) to perform the complete cycle of Wagner's *Ring des Nibelungen*. Leipzig University was one of the most prestigious in Germany, attracting such stars as Goethe, Wagner, Leibnitz and Nietzsche. Progressive local publishers brought the cream of Germany's writers and thinkers to town—Lessing, Klopstock, Schlegel and Jean Paul held forth in the coffee shops. Schiller had such a good time here that he wrote the 'Ode to Joy' during his stay.

Something of this stimulating atmosphere has stuck. Coffee shop dissenters and sharp satirical cabaret survived in the austerity of the DDR regime (even more so than in Berlin). The demonstrations which eventually toppled the regime began in Leipzig. The university is bang in the middle of town, and students swarm everywhere. Whereas in nearby Dresden you'll find rampant consumerism and cafés fitted out with catalogue furniture, Leipzig has preserved a warmer, woodier, old European atmosphere, without a bit of stuffiness.

History

Leipzig gets its name from the Old Sorbian word for lime tree—*Lipa*. The Sorbs (a Slavic tribe, *see* p. 465) arrived here around AD 6, and soon found their sleepy agricultural settlement 'at the lime trees' becoming a centre of hectic trading activity—the town lay at a junction of trade routes between the Rhine and Russia, and Rome and the Baltic. In 1165 Leipzig was granted market rights, then in the 16th century Emperor Maximilian I boosted the ordinary markets to the status of Imperial Trade Fairs (a move that effectively quoshed competition anywhere less than a day's journey away). Local traders began to specialize in silks, calico and woollen cloth, doing a roaring trade with England. This suffered when Napoleon blockaded English ports at the beginning of the 19th century, but the French emperor got his come-uppance in 1813 at the Battle of Leipzig which led directly to his first downfall and exile on Elba.

Trade recovered and in the second part of the 19th century Leipzig became one of Germany's major industrial cities. This made it a prime target for Allied bombers during the Second World War. On 4 December 1943 nearly two thirds of the centre was destroyed in a single raid. Trade fairs continued after the war under the DDR government, and Leipzigers were less isolated from contact with the West than their compatriots. Perhaps this was the reason that Leipzig led the way in the peaceful revolution that toppled the communist dictatorship in 1989.

Getting Around

By Air

Leipzig's airport (© (0341) 2240) is 18km northwest of the city, at the junction of motorways A9 and A14. There is a regular shuttle service to the Hauptbahnhof. Flights are mainly to other German airports, but there is increasing traffic to other European destinations.

By Train

Leipzig's stunning Hauptbahnhof (*see* below; © (0341) 7240) is on the northern edge of the city centre. There are fast Intercity connections in all directions around Germany: Berlin (2hr), Dresden (1¼hr), Chemnitz (1hr 20min).

By Car

Leipzig is 116km west of Dresden on the A14 and 190km south of Berlin on the A9. Parking in town is very restricted, but there are numerous car parks outside the ring. There are 24-hour petrol stations on Marschnerstraße and Torgauer Straße.

Car hire: Avis, Hotel Stadt Leipzig, © (0341) 214 5844; Hertz, Maritim Hotel Astoria, © (0341) 722 4701.

Mitfahrzentrale: University courtyard, Kiosk 7–8, © (0341) 719 2097; Ritterstr. 15, © (0341) 286 221.

Leipzig has an excellent, inexpensive system of buses and trams. Tickets are sold from automatic dispensers (at major stops only) and cost 50 pfennigs for a 10-minute short hop, DM1 for 30min, DM1.50 for an hour. A City-Karte (DM3) allows you unlimited travel from 9am to midnight, and a *24-Stunde-Karte* (DM4) lets you go through to the same time the next day. All tickets should be validated by the stamping machine on boarding.

Taxi: ✆ (0341) 7411 or 594 171.

Leipzig's **tourist information office**, ✆ (0341) 795 9326, is near the Haupt-bahnhof, at Sachsenplatz 1 *(Mon–Fri 9–7, Sat and Sun 9.30–2)*. Here you can book tickets for concerts, reserve accommodation and pick up maps and brochures on the city.

Banks: The Deutsche Verkehrsbank at the Hauptbahnhof operates to extended hours and has a 24-hour exchange machine.

Post office: The main post office is on Augustusplatz.

Police: ✆ 110.

Medical emergencies: ✆ (0341) 211 5115.

Emergency pharmacy: ✆ (0341) 292 014.

Leipzig's two main festivals focus on classical music and are both of world repute. The **Gewandhaus Festage** at the beginning of October promotes new artists and hosts established orchestras on alternate years. There is a major international **Bach Festival** every four years (the next one is in 1997), featuring prizewinners from the prestigious **Bach Competition**.

The Hauptbahnhof and around Sachsenplatz

Leipzig's **Hauptbahnhof**—the biggest terminal station in the world—is a breathtaking introduction to the city. Immense arches hoop over the platforms. Passengers appear as tiny spots of colour against a Brobdingnagian sandstone backdrop. Until the Nazis centralized local administration, the Prussians ran the west side of the station and the Saxons looked after the east side. The Hauptbahnhof still has two entrances, and doubles up on nearly everything else.

The Hauptbahnhof opens out onto the Platz der Republik, a segment of the city **Ring**, scene of the famous **Monday demonstrations** in 1989. The demonstrations grew out of discreet protest prayer meetings held in the Nikolaikirche (*see* below). These grew in size

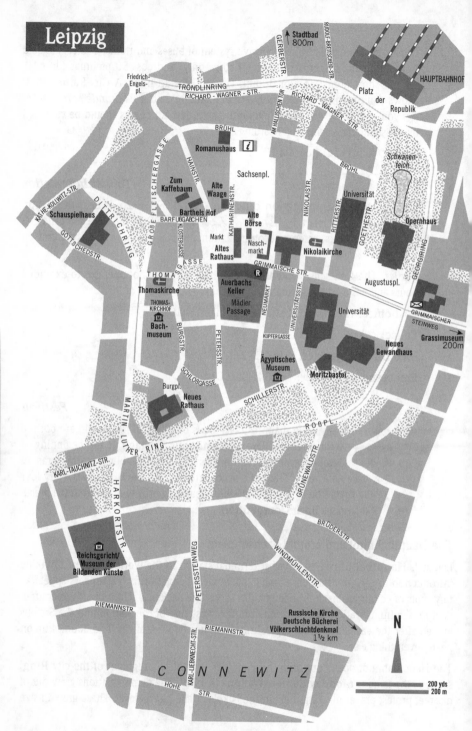

Leipzig

Stadtbad 800m

Friedrich-Engels-pl.

TRÖNDLINRING

RICHARD - WAGNER - STR.

RICHARD - WAGNER - STR.

GERBERSTR.

RUDOLF-BREITSCHEID-STR.

AM HALLISCHEN TOR

HAUPTBAHNHOF

Platz der Republik

BRÜHL

Romanushaus

ℹ️

Sachsenpl.

Schwanenteich

BRÜHL

NIKOLAISTR.

Universität

GROßE FLEISCHERGASSE

HAINSTR.

Zum Kaffebaum

Alte Waage

KATHARINENSTR.

RITTERSTR.

GOETHESTR.

Opernhaus

KÄTHE-KOLLWITZ-STR.

Schauspielhaus

DITTRICHRING

Barthels Hof

BARFUßGÄßCHEN

KLOSTERGASSE

Alte Börse

GEORGIRING

GOTTSCHEDSTR.

Markt

Naschmarkt

Altes Rathaus

Nikolaikirche

GRIMMAISCHE STR.

Augustuspl.

GRIMMAISCHER

GRIMMAISCHER STEINWEG

Grassimuseum 200m

THOMAS- GASSE

Thomaskirche

R

Auerbachs Keller

Mädler Passage

NEUMARKT

UNIVERSITÄTSTR.

Universität

THOMAS-KIRCHHOF

M

Bachmuseum

BURGSTR.

PETERSSTR.

KUPFERGASSE

Neues Gewandhaus

Ägyptisches Museum

M

Moritzbastei

Burgpl.

SCHLOßGASSE

Neues Rathaus

SCHILLERSTR.

ROßPL.

MARTIN - LUTHER - RING

GRÜNEWALDSTR.

KARL-TAUCHNITZ-STR.

HARKORTSTR.

BRÜDERSTR.

PETERSSTEINWEG

M

Reichsgericht/ Museum der Bildenden Künste

WINDMÜHLENSTR.

RIEMANNSTR.

RIEMANNSTR.

Russische Kirche Deutsche Bücherei Völkerschlachtdenkmal 1½ km

N

KARL-LIEBKNECHT-STR.

C O N N E W I T Z

HOHE STR.

200 yds
200 m

and bravado until, eventually, by 5pm on a Monday the city centre would be deserted, as around 200,000 candle-bearing Leipzigers marched around the Ring to protest peacefully against their repression. The movement started off similar demonstrations around East Germany, and led directly to the end of communist rule.

Diagonally across the Platz der Republik (and down Am Hallischen Tor) is the ugly expanse of Sachsenplatz. After the Second World War much of Leipzig was rebuilt in a harsh utilitarian style. **Sachsenplatz** is one of the greater misfortunes. Since the *Wende*, though, more of the old courtyards and arcades clustered around these big modern squares are being restored. Initially, traders who came to Leipzig for the fairs could not become *Lagerherren* ('store gentlemen') like the city residents, but had to conduct their business out in the open as *Sonnenkramer* ('sun traders'). As they grew wealthier these merchants settled here—but continued to trade outside in courtyards and passages between the buildings. Families lived at ground level, and the goods were hauled up to the top storeys for safe-keeping at night. Some of these courts and alleys are now chic arcades, but others retain their poky romantic air. There are some charming ones off the Hainstraße, on the western side of Sachsenplatz.

Off the northwest corner of Sachsenplatz (on Brühl) is the **Romanushaus**, an exuberant Baroque mansion named after the merchant who built it but ended up in prison for forging banknotes to pay for it all.

The Markt

Leipzig's Markt is just off the south-west corner of Sachsenplatz. Running the entire length of the square is the city's pride and joy, the Renaissance **Altes Rathaus** *(Tues–Fri 10–6, Sat and Sun 10–4; adm DM2)*, built in nine months in 1556 by the quirky local architect Hieronymous Lotter. Lotter insisted on making his building asymmetrical—positioning the clock tower well to the left, adding a skew-whiff window and even bending the walls a little. (This didn't go down at all well with the order-loving Germans. To this day the prefix *Lotter-* is used to mean slovenly or sloppy.) Inside you can see the 53m-long *Festsaal*, and a number of municipal relics—including the executioner's sword used to decapitate Woyzeck (later immortalized in Büchner's play) in the Markt in 1824. Upstairs is a room of furniture that once belonged to the composer **Mendelssohn** (Felix Mendelssohn-Bartholdy, 1809–47). He lived in Leipzig for 12 years, directed the Gewandhaus orchestra, founded the Conservatory and rescued the works of J.S. Bach from obscurity.

Behind the Rathaus is the perfectly proportioned **Alte Börse** (Old Stock Exchange), a Baroque beauty symmetrical to the last gilded acanthus leaf, while on the northern end of the square is the **Alte Waage** (Old Weighing House, 1555), another Lotter building (this one with an even, delicate gable). An alley off Hainstraße (to the west of the Alte Waage) brings you to **Zum Coffe Baum**, built in 1694 and the oldest and most famous of the Leipzig coffee houses. When coffee first came to Europe from Turkey in the 17th century, it was considered terribly wicked. Coffee houses only became socially acceptable when respectable musicians like Bach began to meet and play in them (he satirized polite society's attitude to the beverage in his *Coffee Cantata*). Above the doorway of Zum Coffe

Baum is a carving of a luxurious Turk, reclining under a coffee tree and offering a bowl of the drink to an innocent cherub. At the time of writing the coffee house is closed for renovations, but soon you will once again be able to join its distinguished roll-call of clients, which has included Goethe, Wagner, Liszt and Schumann. Just beyond Zum Coffe Baum (off Kleine Fischergasse) is **Barthels Hof**, the oldest trade fair courtyard in Leipzig. This one has a 'through-yard' so that waggons could unload and drive straight on to the next street, without having to turn.

At the southern end of the Markt is the **Mädler-Passage**, Leipzig's grandest arcade, built at the turn of the century and reminiscent of the *Galleria Vittorio Emanuele* in Milan. The much older **Auerbach's Keller** (a beer cellar under one of the malls) was made famous by a scene in Goethe's *Faust*, in which Mephistopheles bewitches the drinkers (*see* **Eating and Drinking** below).

Around the Thomaskirche

West of the Mädler Passage, in a quiet close off Thomasgasse, is the **Thomaskirche**. This is where Bach was organist and choirmaster from 1723 until his death in 1750. The **Thomanerchor** was (and still is) one of Germany's most renowned boys' choirs. (You can hear the *Thomanerchor* sing in the church on Friday evenings and Saturday afternoons.) The boys sang not only in church, but also at civic functions and private parties, and the vast quantity of work which Bach wrote for them ranks with his best. Bach was only the third choice for the job (the City Council wanted someone who could also teach the boys mathematics) and was constantly at loggerheads with the authorities.

Inside the church you'll find **Bach's tomb**. Bach enthusiasts found the neglected original grave in a nearby churchyard in 1895. When it was exhumed three skeletons were found. One showed signs of a spine disease peculiar to organists, and this is the one presumed to be Bach's, and interred here. Across the close from the church is the **Bachmuseum** *(daily 9–5; adm DM4)*, where (to the accompaniment of piped music) you can look at the composer's account book, the timetable showing when he taught the boys, and displays on the lives of Bach and his vast family. Bach married twice—first his cousin Maria Barbara Bach, who died in 1720, then Anna Magdalena Wilcken (in 1721). He had twenty children between them, several of whom became notable musicians and composers in their own right, including W.F. Bach (who worked mainly in Dresden and Halle), C.P.E. Bach (Berlin and Hamburg), J.C.F. Bach (Bückeburg) and J.C. Bach (London).

The Nikolaikirche and Augustusplatz

To the east of the Mädler Passage (along Grimmaische Straße and up Nikolaistraße) is the **Nikolaikirche**, scene of the fateful Monday prayer meetings. The sober medieval walls enclose a riotous **interior** of Neoclassical pillars that suddenly burst into palm fronds, and stucco work done by an artist obviously hankering after the freedom of Rococo.

Further east along Grimmaische Straße you come to the **University**. All that remains of the old university (which was founded in 1409) is a Neoclassical gateway by the Berlin architect, Schinkel. Anything that survived Allied bombs was demolished in the 1960s by DDR leader Walter Ulbricht—a native of Leipzig who wanted to make a mark with his new Karl-Marx-University. The ancient university chapel (which had survived the war intact) was reduced to rubble, and 1960s shoeboxes went up in its place. However, the centre-piece of the complex, a 34-storey **Universiteitshochhaus**, designed to resemble an open book, is so audacious that it deserves preservation as a period piece.

Flanking the university is the wide **Augustusplatz** (formerly Karl-Marx-Platz). At the northern end is a severe Opera House, and opposite that the **Neues Gewandhaus**, an unattractive modern building that is the new home to the renowned Gewandhaus Orchestra. Founded in 1743, this is the world's oldest symphony orchestra. Past directors have included Mendelssohn, Furtwängler and Bruno Walter. In the foyer is a superb Jugendstil statue of Beethoven by the sculptor Max Klinger. The figure caused a sensation when it was first unveiled because the great composer is naked, and sits with what appears to be a towel draped over his knees, looking as if he has just got out of his bath.

Behind the Gewandhaus is the **Moritzbastei**, the only surviving part of the city fortifications, and now a student café and arts centre (*see* **Eating and Drinking** below). On Schillerstraße, just beyond the Bastei is a small **Ägyptisches Museum** *(Tues–Fri 2–6, Sat 10–1; adm DM3)* with a regulation mummy, some interesting funerary models, and bits of pottery and statues ranging from 4000 BC to 1000 BC. Schillerstraße leads on to the **Neues Rathaus**, a grotesque turn-of-the-century building which looks like a cross between a giant's palace and a municipal prison.

Beyond the Ring

A ten-minute walk east of Augustusplatz (along Grimmaischersteinweg) is the **Grassimuseum** (Trams 6, 4 or 20), a sprawling Art Deco complex that is home to three museums. The **Museum des Kunsthandwerks** (Arts and Crafts Museum) *(Tues and Thurs 10–6, Wed 2–8, Fri 10–1, Sat and Sun 10–5; adm DM3)* has a superb collection of Meißen porcelain, glass, textiles and decorative art—though it displays only a small part of its hoard at any one time. The **Museum für Völkerkunde** *(Tues–Fri 9.30–5.30, Sat 10–4, Sun 9–1; adm DM3)*, a well-stocked and colourful ethnological museum, is just across the courtyard. Best of all is the **Musikinstrumenten-Museum** *(Tues–Fri 9–5, Sat 10–5, Sun 10–1; adm DM3)*, with a separate entrance at the side of the building. This is by far the most interesting musical instrument museum in the country. The collection is arranged chronologically and there are taped recordings available of some of the instruments. You can see superbly carved viols and exquisitely inlaid virginals. There is the world's first dated clavichord (1543) and the oldest original fortepiano (1726, built by Cristofori, the inventor of the modern piano). Despite the rare and priceless objects everywhere, the museum has a comfortable, slightly tatty ambience. The instruments seem loved and used, and the air has a warm, woody smell. The staff are relaxed, helpful and informed, and will even demonstrate instruments for you. Look out for some of the curiosities—an ancient Saxon horn, a *Tafelklavier* (piano cum make-up and sewing box) and the *Glasharmonika* (a more sophisticated adaptation of the squeaky finger-round-the-rim-of-a-wine-glass effect, in which glass bowls are spun by a pedal mechanism and played with both hands at once).

Lying to the southeast of the centre (along Windmühlenstraße or Prager Straße, Trams 15 or 20) is the splendid **Russische Kirche**, a narrow, towering Orthodox chapel built in 1913 to commemorate the 100th anniversary of the Battle of the Nations (*see* below). The dim, mysterious interior is choc-full of gilded ornament and 18th-century **ikons**. Just across the road is the **Deutsche Bücherei** *(Mon–Sat 9–4)*, the German copyright library. Inside is a missable **museum** of books and writing, from 3000 BC to the present day. A few stops further south is the **Völkerslachtdenkmal**, a grotesque lump of a monument, built on the site of the **Battle of the Nations** (a.k.a. the Battle of Leipzig) in which the Prussians, Russians, Austrians and Swedes combined forces to defeat Napoleon in 1813—at the cost of 61,000 lives.

Diagonally across the Ring from the Neues Rathaus is the **Reichsgericht**, a sumptuous neo-Renaissance palace that was Weimar Germany's supreme court. It is best known as the venue for the Nazi's show trial of those accused of starting the Reichstag fire (*see* **Berlin** p. 485). You can visit the grand courtroom upstairs, but the real attraction is the **Museum der bildenden Künste** (Museum of Plastic Arts) *(Tues–Sun 9–5, except Wed 1–9.30; adm DM3)*, which houses a first-rate collection of Dutch and Old German Masters and German Romantics, with outstanding work by Cranach, the Hamburg Master Francke and the 19th-century painter Arnold Böcklin.

Lepzig's up-and-coming trendy quarter is **Connewitz**, just south of the Reichsgericht. Check out the streets around Hohestraße, Riemanstraße and Karl-Liebknecht-Straße. Squatters have taken over some of the old villas, new bars and cafés are popping up and there is a bubbling social and night life.

A short journey north of the ring—but certainly worth the effort at the end of a tiring day—is the **Stadtbad**, Eutritzscher Str. 21, ☎ (0341) 7637 *(Mon 1.30–9, Tues–Fri 8am–9pm, Sat 8–7, Sun 8–1)*. Here, for DM7, you can steam, have a sauna and swim in an icy mineral pool in the original turn-of-the-century city baths. Then you can sip a drink in the relaxation area, which is decorated with vivid oriental designs and lined with mahogany changing booths. Take towels, but no swimming costume. There are separate baths for men and women, though on some days bathing is mixed.

Around Leipzig

Around Leipzig lies some of the most desolate and polluted land in Germany, though it is dotted with towns that various enthusiasts make the object of pilgrimage. **Halle** (40km west on the A14) was the birthplace of the composer George Frederic Handel, and has an appropriate museum. **Dessau** (70km north on the B184) was the real home of the influential Bauhaus school (*see* **The Arts and Culture** p. 64), and you can still see the college building whose design so astonished the world in 1919. In **Wittenberg** (67km north on the B2) the hitherto unknown monk, Martin Luther, nailed his 95 Theses to the church door and sparked off the Reformation (*see* **History** p. 41).

The one absolute must in the vicinity is the cathedral at **Naumburg**, 60km south off the A9 *(Nov–Feb Mon–Sat 9–4, Sun 12–4; Mar–Oct Mon–Sat 9–5, Sun 12–5; Apr–Sept Mon–Sat 9–6, Sun 12–6; adm DM3.50)*. This 13th-century cathedral contains statues by the medieval **Master of Naumburg** (working *c.* 1240) that hold their own easily in the catalogue of the world's most beautiful and significant works of art. We know little of the Master, other than that he trained in France, and did some work on the cathedral in Mainz (*see* p. 170). The stone-carvings you can see here form the most comprehensive collection and are the best-preserved examples of his work, and are centuries ahead of their time. They are matched by little else bar works by Michelangelo and the finest Classical sculpture. The rood screen in the west choir includes a life-sized Passion, in which a breathtakingly naturalistic Christ, Virgin and the Baptist are each racked with suffering. (Many of the other figures, though, are inept Baroque replacements.) The star pieces are the **Statues of the Founders** of the cathedral, beyond the screen in the dim choir. A care-worn Margrave Ekkehard II stands next to his wife Uta who, every inch the smouldering, seductive beauty, lifts the collar of her cloak alluringly to her cheek. Opposite stand another couple, the pensive Margrave Hermann and his spouse Reglindis, who is grinning with cheeky good humour. As well as the cathedral the Altstadt has some fine Renaissance and 18th-century burgherhouses and a parish church with two paintings by Cranach.

See also Directory entries for Halle, Wittenberg and Dessau.

Shopping

Leipzig has many more interesting and stylish shops than any other of the ex-DDR cities. The elegant Mädler Passage has interconnecting malls lined with excellent boutiques and luxury stores. More mundane High Street shops line Grimmaische Straße alongside the Passage. You can find romantic arcades off Hainstraße, Gr. Fleischergasse and Ritterstraße, though many of the famous old antiquarian book-shops that used to be here are, sadly, finding rents too high and moving out of the centre. Some book dealers are in Talstraße and Brüderstraße south-east of the Ring.

Leipzig © (0341–)   ## Where to Stay

Accommodation in Leipzig is expensive. You will have to battle to find anywhere for under DM200 a night. Prices may drop as competition increases, but in the meantime the best options are private rooms. These range from DM60 to DM80 and can be booked through the tourist office.

expensive

Maritim Hotel Astoria, Platz der Republik 2, © 2220, fax 722 4747 (DM336–456). Currently Leipzig's classiest address. Luxurious hotel near the Hauptbahnhof.

moderate

Corum Leipzig, Rudolf-Breitscheid-Straße 3, © 12510, fax 125 1100 (DM260–275). Smart new hotel near the Hauptbahnhof.

Deutscher Hof, Waldstr. 31–33, © 211 6005, fax 286 076 (DM240). Pleasant, well-restored hotel to the west of town.

Am Lisztplatz, Rosa-Luxemburg-Str. 36, ✆/fax 688 0592 (DM130). Spartan, but clean and close to town.

Nestor Hotel Leipzig, Gräfestr. 15a, ✆ 59630, fax 722 4747 (DM214–244). New, bland but well-run. Five minutes from the Hauptbahnhof on Tram 16.

inexpensive

Pension Am Zoo, Pfaffendorfer Str. 23, ✆/fax 291 838 (DM90–125). Acceptable *Pension* just west of the Hauptbahnhof. The best deal in town at this end of the market. No restaurant.

Pension Hilleman, Rosa-Luxemburg-Str. 2, ✆ 282 482 (DM70). Also near the station. Basic price is cheaper than Am Zoo, but you don't get breakfast and have to share the bathroom. No restaurant.

Youth Hostel: Käthe-Kollwitz-Str. 62, ✆ 470 530.

Eating and Drinking: Restaurants and Taverns

moderate

Auerbachs Keller, Mädler-Passage, ✆ 216 1040 (DM35–50). Go in through the right-hand door. If this is closed sneak through the main eating hall, down the passage past the toilets, then on through two more rooms, and eventually you'll find the 'Goethe room', complete with heavy carving, 16th-century paintings and pictures of Mephistopheles and Faust. Wherever you sit, the food is excellent—try the tomato and basil soup or one of the succulent steaks.

inexpensive

Bachstübl, Thomaskirchhof 12, ✆ 291062 (DM15–25). Comfortable Weinstube overlooking the quiet St Thomas church close. Inexpensive daily changing menu.

Bahnhof Restaurant, Hauptbahnhof main hall, level 2 (DM15–20). Through the station café (itself a turn-of-the-century classic with a high glass ceiling), behind a door marked Historisches Restaurant, you enter a time warp. The food (schnitzels and pastas) isn't much to rave about, but the restaurant, with moulded ceilings and carved wood, has hardly changed since it was built.

Vis à Vis, Rudolph-Breitsheid-Str. 33, ✆ 292 718 (DM15–30). Near the Hauptbahnhof, open 24 hours. Ideal for late-night munchies or nightcaps.

Pfeiffer's Weinstuben, Dittrichring 6, ✆ 281 323 (DM30–45), Tasty Swabian cuisine—pork or beef swimming in gravies and thick stock, and served with delicate noodles.

Paulaner-Palais, Klostergasse 3–5, ✆ 211 3115 (DM25–35). Capacious complex of rooms, courtyards and terraces belonging to one of Bavaria's best breweries. Pastas, sausages and nourishing meals as well as beer.

Mövenpick, Naschmarkt 1–3, ✆ 211 7722 (DM15–45). The national chain, which always serves good food, here has a branch on a prime site and with an amiable atmosphere too.

Café Concerto, Thomaskirchhof 13, ✆ 204 343. Immensely civilized. Arty, with a touch of old Vienna. Ideal for *Kaffee und Kuchen* and intelligent conversation.

Café Corso, Neumarkt 2, ✆ 282 233. Genteel, faded old Leipzig café, with the best cream cakes in town.

Moritzbastei, Universitätsstr. 9, ✆ 292 332. Lively student café and beer cellar under the city fortifications. Inexpensive snacks too. Sometimes there is live music (and an entrance fee) at night.

СПb , Hansa Haus, Grimmaische Str. 12. Cyrillic initials for St Petersburg. Very trendy bar in glassed-over trade fair courtyard. Soviet décor and loud music until the very last customer leaves.

el dry, Prinz-Eugen-Str. 5, ✆ 391 1161. Trendy bar with beer garden in Connewitz.

Entertainment and Nightlife

Leipzig does not suffer as badly from night death as other east German towns, and keeps up the traditional high standards of classical music. A comprehensive **listings magazine**, *Kreuzer* is on sale at most news agents. You can reserve **tickets** for most events at the Ticket-Galerie, Katharinenstr. 23, ✆ 559 929.

The Thomaskirche holds recitals by the **Thomanerchor** (Friday evenings and Saturday afternoons; you can sometimes even catch them for free at a Sunday morning service) and regular organ recitals. The **Neues Gewandhaus**, Augustusplatz 8, ✆ 71320, is the main venue for concerts by the renowned *Gewandhausorchester*, the excellent *Rundfunkchor* and major visiting orchestras. Opera and ballet are staged at the **Opernhaus**, Augustusplatz 12, ✆ 71680, and, if your German is up to it, Leipzig's famous **satirical cabarets** are still on the boil: Academixer, Kupfergasse, ✆ 200 849, and Pfeffermühle, Thomaskirchhof 16, ✆ 295 877. The **Moritzbastei**, Universitätsstr. 9, ✆ 292 932, and the lively **Beyerhaus**, Ernst-Schneller-Str. 6, ✆ 310 489, are the best venues for **jazz** and **live music**. The Moritzbastei also holds good late-night **discos**.

Dresden

Before Allied saturation bombing reduced Dresden to a pile of rubble on the night of 13–14 of February 1945, the city had been known as the 'Baroque Florence', and generally regarded as one of the most beautiful cities in Europe. This acclaim was due largely to the efforts of Augustus II (1670–1733), head of the powerful Wettin dynasty that had ruled over Saxony since 1423, and his son Augustus III.

Augustus II is popularly known as **Augustus the Strong**, as much for his sexual prowess (he is supposed to have sired a child for every day of the year and kept a small harem of mistresses) as for his physical strength—which he displayed willingly by snapping horse-shoes with one hand, twisting iron banisters into rope, and holding fully-armoured soldiers aloft in his palm. In 1697, three years after becoming Elector of Saxony, Augustus was made King of Poland. To celebrate the fact, and to advertise his glory, the new king set about commissioning palaces to make Dresden worthy of its new status as a royal capital. The altogether milder Augustus III initiated one of the greatest art collections in Europe, founded the state opera and orchestra, and filled his father's grand buildings with cultured and erudite courtiers.

The bombing raid that destroyed Dresden was the most horrific of the war. At the time official figures stated that 35,000 people were killed, though there is clear evidence that the actual death toll was at least three times that amount. The attack may have been designed to send an unequivocal propaganda message that the tide had turned, but it is hard not to read into it a desire for humiliation and revenge. After the war the Soviets denied complicity, officially branding the attack 'the terror-raid of the barbaric imperialists'. Winston Churchill pretended that he had known nothing about it, and blame fell on Sir Arthur 'Bomber' Harris, head of Bomber Command. (Harris was the only service chief not to get a peerage after the war, and the recent unveiling by the Queen Mother of a memorial to him caused outrage throughout Germany.)

The DDR's rebuilding of Dresden was hurried and ugly. Some of the old buildings were restored, but many were just left in ruins. Today Dresden is abuzz with construction and restoration, the opera holds its head up high among the best, and the art museums remain among the most spectacular in the world. If you intend visiting more than one museum in Dresden it is worthwhile investing in a DM10 **Tagekarte**, which allows you into all of the main collections on any one day.

Getting Around

By Air

Dresden's airport, 9km north of the city centre, serves primarily German destinations. A regular shuttle bus runs to and from the Hauptbahnhof.

By Train

The **Hauptbahnhof** (information ✆ (0351) 470 600) opens right into the centre of town. There are frequent connections to Meißen (¾hr), Leipzig (2hr) and Berlin (2½hr). A number of **narrow-gauge steam railways** operate in the Dresden area. The most scenic run from Freital (enquiries ✆ (0351) 461 2374), Radeburg (✆ (035208) 2251) and from the Hauptbahnhof itself (diesel service only).

By Car

Dresden is at the junction of two motorways: the A13 (which connects it to Berlin (180km)) and the A4 (which runs west through Saxony and Thuringia). Parking in the centre can be difficult, and theft from cars is commonplace. There is a **24-hour petrol station** on the corner of Wienerstraße and Gerhart-Hauptmann-Straße.

Car hire: Hertz, Hotel Bellevue, ✆ (0351) 56628; Sixt, Dresden Hilton, ✆ (0351) 484 1696.

Mitfahrzentrale: Bodenbacher Str. 99, ☏ (0351) 234 0121; Nürnberger Str. 57, ☏ (0351) 463 6060.

Public Transport

Dresden is well served by a network of tram, bus and S-Bahn lines. Tickets are sold from automatic dispensers (*not* at all stops) and cost DM2. A 24-hour card costs DM5 and you can get a special weekend family card (2 adults and up to 4 children under 16) for DM6.

Taxis: ☏ (0351) 459 8112.

By Boat

Dresden's **White Fleet** of riverboats was founded in 1836. You can still take a paddle steamer along the River Elbe all the way to Saxon Switzerland (round trip 8.30am–6.15pm, DM22.50), and it is possible to get off along the way. There are also short sightseeing trips through Dresden and as far as Meißen and special jazz and gourmet cruises. Prices range upwards from DM6. Boats leave from the Terassenufer (enquiries ☏ (0351) 502 3877).

Tourist Information

The main **tourist information office**, ☏ (0351) 495 5205, is a few minutes' walk from the Hauptbahnhof at Prager Straße 10–11 *(Apr–Sept Mon–Sat 9–8, Sun 9–1; Oct–Mar Mon–Fri 9–8, Sat 9–2, Sun 9–1)*. There is also a branch at Neustad in the pedestrian tunnel, ☏ (0351) 53539 *(Mon–Wed 9–6, Thurs 9–6.30, Fri 9–7, Sat and Sun 9–3)*. Both dispense brochures and maps, and offer the usual services of room reservation and guided city tours.

Banks: Branches of the main high-street banks can be found along Prager Straße. There is a 24-hour exchange machine in the Hauptbahnhof.

Post office: Next to the tourist information office on Prager Straße.

Police: ☏ 110.

Medical emergencies: ☏ 52251.

Prager Straße and the Altmarkt

The Hauptbahnhof opens out directly onto the the ugliest part of the centre. The broad walkway of **Prager Straße** is lined with concrete-box architecture on a grand scale. This is where thousands of people congregated in October 1989, hoping for a train to Prague and freedom (*see* **History** p. 50). After the *Wende* Prager Straße became the scene of frantic consumerism. Rows of banks opened in wooden prefabs, western goods spilled out of the shops and onto pavement stalls and the streets were filled with Ossis in cheap clothes, staggering off to their Trabbis weighed down with televisions and video equipment. Today the sight is even more colourful and just as hectic. Prager Straße is filled with ad hoc street traders' stalls and mobile fast-food booths, and everyone seems hell-bent on shopping. This is a world away from Leipzig's sophisticated arcades.

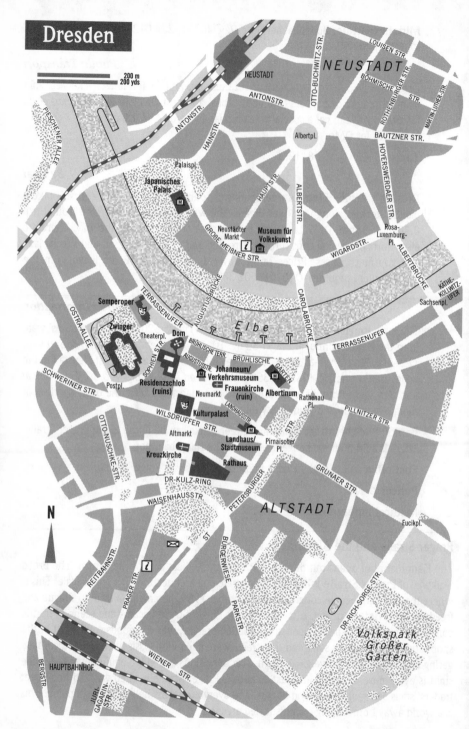

Dresden

200 m
200 yds

PIESCHENER ALLEE

NEUSTADT

NEUSTADT

ANTONSTR.

OTTO-BUCHWITZ-STR.

LOUISEN STR.

BÖHMISCHER STR.

ROTHENBURGER STR.

MARTIN-LUTHER-STR.

ANTONSTR.

HAINSTR.

Albertpl.

BAUTZNER STR.

HOYERSWERDAER STR.

Palaispl.

Japanisches
Palais

Neustädter
Markt

Museum für
Volkskunst

Rosa-
Luxemburg-
Pl.

ALBERTBRÜCKE

ALBERTSTR.

HAUPTSTR.

GROßE MEIßNER STR.

WIGARDSTR.

CAROLABRÜCKE

KÄTHE-
KOLLWITZ-
UFER

Sachsenpl.

TERRASSENUFER

AUGUSTUSBRÜCKE

Semperoper

OSTRA-ALLEE

Zwinger

Theaterpl.

Dom

E l b e

BRÜHLSCHE TERR.

BRÜHLSCHE

SOPHIENSTR.

AUGUSTUSSTR.

Johanneum/
Verkehrsmuseum

TERRASSENUFER

BRÜHLSCHER
GARTEN

Postpl.

Residenzschloß
(ruins)

Neumarkt

Frauenkirche
(ruin)

Albertinum

Rathenau
Pl.

SCHWERINER STR.

Kulturpalast

LANDHAUSSTR.

STR.

PILLNITZER STR.

WILSDRUFFER STR.

Altmarkt

Landhaus/
Stadtmuseum

Pirnaischer
Pl.

OTTO-NUSCHKE-STR.

Kreuzkirche

Rathaus

GRUNAER STR.

DR-KULZ-RING

WAISENHAUSSTR.

PETERSBURGER

ALTSTADT

Eucikpl.

N

ST

BÜRGERWIESE

REITBAHNSTR.

PRAGER STR.

PARKSTR.

DR-RICH-SORGE-STR.

Volkspark
Großer
Garten

BERGSTR.

HAUPTBAHNHOF

JURI-
GAGARIN-
STR.

WIENER STR.

At its northern end Prager Straße opens out onto the **Altmarkt**, now mainly a car park. The stark **Kreuzkirche** on the eastern side of the Altmarkt is home to a famous choir, the *Kreuzchor*. Inside you can see a cross made of nails from the rafters of the bombed-out Coventry Cathedral in England, a symbol of reconciliation between the two nations. Just off the Altmarkt (east down Wilsdruffer Straße) is the 18th-century **Landhaus**, now containing the **Stadtmuseum** *(Mon, Tues, Thurs, Sat and Sun 10–6, Wed 10–8; adm DM4)*. You can look in at the grand central stairway for free, but the displays on Dresden's history (from early times to the present day) though extensive, are not particularly riveting.

The Neumarkt and the Cathedral

Behind the ugly modern Kulturpalast that blocks off the end of the Altmarkt is the Neumarkt. The jagged ruins of the **Frauenkirche** rise up dramatically at one end. For years the church was left in this war-damaged condition as a memorial. Now, amid furious controversy, it is being restored to its former state.

Alongside the Frauenkirche is the **Johanneum**, built in 1586 as the royal stables, but now bristling with the statuary and stucco of an 18th-century face-lift. Part of the building now houses the **Verkehrsmuseum** (Transport Museum) *(Tues–Sun 10–5; adm DM4)*, a playground of old trams, model trains and strange flying machines. The best section is the one devoted to motor transport—ranging from a genuine horseless carriage (built in 1886) to a deluxe Trabant (i.e. with chrome trimming) and a cutaway new Audi turbo-diesel. Look out also for the wooden motorbike made in 1885. Down one side of the Johanneum, running the entire length of Augustusstraße (101 metres), is a glimmering frieze of painted Meißen tiles depicting the **Fürstenzug**—a parade of all the Wettin rulers up to the beginning of the 20th century. On the other side of this wall is a 16th-century Florentine-styled courtyard, complete with a long row of arcades decorated with antelope horns, and once the scene of jousting tournaments.

At the end of Augustusstraße stands the **cathedral**. In order to be eligible for the Polish throne, Augustus the Strong had to renounce the Protestantism that his family had so long championed and become a Roman Catholic. His son Augustus III, on the other hand, commissioned this church (the largest in Saxony) to assure the Pope of his allegiance. The interior is whitewashed and fairly plain, though there are some attractively painted side-chapels and an icecream cake pulpit. In the crypt the Wettins rest in their solid sarcophagi.

The Residenzschloß and Semperoper

Next door to the cathedral stood the enormous main palace, the **Residenzschloß**. This was devastated by Allied bombs, and is only now being repaired. Work is scheduled to finish in 2006—an optimistic forecast to coincide with Dresden's 800th anniversary. The domes were the first bits to be restored, and once again form a glittering part of Dresden's skyline. All you can see of the interior, however, is the **Spiegelzimmern** (Mirror rooms) *(Mon, Tues, Fri–Sun 9–5, Thurs 9–6; adm DM5)*, which alone survived the war. The entrance is behind the cathedral in Sophienstraße. Inside is an exhibition of Baroque glass, porcelain and carving. Only one or two of the old mirrors survive, but you can peer into a dim *Eck-kabinett* (corner cabinet) lined with gilded mirrors and containing a life-size dummy of Augustus the Strong in robes and armour.

Behind the cathedral, on Theatreplatz, is the noble, curved **Semperoper**, the State opera house, named after its designer Gottfried Semper. Semper's original theatre (built 1838–41) was badly damaged by fire in 1869, and was rebuilt once by his son Manfred, and then again after the Second World War. Wagner's *Tannhaüser* and *The Flying Dutchman* were premiered here, as were most of the operas of Richard Strauss. Even through the DDR years the resident opera company kept up its position as one of the best in the world. The interior is a palace of marble, ceiling painting and stucco. If you can't get into a performance, then it is worthwhile joining a **guided tour** *(approximately hourly, times chalked up on board outside, closed mid-July to mid-August; adm DM5)*. Beside the Semperoper is a neat Neoclassical building, the **Italienisches Dörfchen** (Italian village), so named because it stands on the site of the huts of the Italian (Roman Catholic) masons who were imported to build the cathedral in this Protestant heartland. (At the time of writing the building is being renovated, and will open—before 2006 it is hoped—as a classy café.) On the opposite side of the Theatreplatz stands the magnificent Zwinger.

The Zwinger

Dresden's gem, and Germany's prize piece of late Baroque architecture, is the Zwinger. It was built between 1710 and 1728 as a spacious pleasure palace for Augustus the Strong. The architect, Mattheus Daniel Pöppelmann, came up with a supremely elegant design comprising two-storey pavilions connected by single-storey galleries, enclosing a wide, open courtyard. The rows of tall, arched windows take up more space than the sandstone walls (which were richly decorated by the sculptor Balthasar

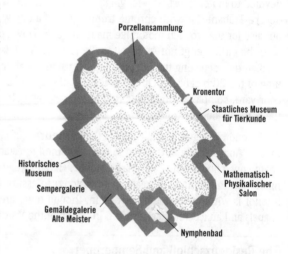

Permoser). Funds ran out before the north wing could be built, but this was made good by Gottfried Semper, who added a neo-Renaissance gallery in 1847–55. The most impressive entrance crosses a moat on the western side and passes through the **Kronentor**, named after the enormous Polish crown carved over the arch. Have a look also for the **Glockenspielpavilion**, which has a carillon of 40 Meißen porcelain bells, and the **Nymphenbad**, an elaborate fountain created by Permoser.

The Zwinger now contains a number of museums. The most important of these is the **Gemäldegalerie Alte Meister** (Gallery of Old Masters) *(Tues–Sun 9–5, Wed 9–6; adm DM7)*, housed in Semper's new wing. Augustus III and his successors demonstrated consistent good taste as they accumulated their hoard of European art, and as a result they built up one of the finest collections in the world.

You'll see hosts of familiar paintings from the **Italian Renaissance**—such as Raphael's wistful *Sistine Madonna* (most reproduced for the pensive pair of cherubs at the bottom) and important work by Correggio, Tintoretto and Botticelli. Look out also for the sensual *Sleeping Venus* painted by Giorgione and finished off by Titian, and the splendid series of the parables by Domenico Feti. There are also numerous scenes of Dresden by the court painter Bernado Bellotto, done very much in the style of his famous uncle Canaletto.

The Dutch and Flemish collection is awesome, with roomfuls of Rubens and Rembrandts, prime landscapes by van Ruisdael and two serene Vermeers (one of them is the famous *Girl Reading a Letter*). Look out for Rubens' disturbingly realistic *Rape of Leda by the Swan*, and Rembrandt's similarly uncomfortable *Rape of Ganymede* (in which an infant Ganymede is dragged off by the shirt-tails, wetting himself with fear). There is also an amusing portrait by Van Dyck of the three very grown-up-looking *Children of King Charles I of England*.

German painting doesn't feature quite so spectacularly, but there are good works by Cranach, Dürer and Holbein the Younger. There is also a small French collection and some superb painting by the Spanish Masters Velazquez and Murillo.

In the southeastern pavilion is the **Porzellansammlung** (Porcelain Collection) *(Mon–Thurs, Sat and Sun 9–5; adm DM3)*. The collection here isn't exclusively devoted to Meißen ware (also called Dresden china), and is, in fact, a touch disappointing. There are interesting cabinets showing early copies of Chinese originals, some elaborate gilded table-ware decorated with flowers and a few enormous religious creations. Ironically the entire collection is upstaged by a French piece—an exquisite bouquet of flowers made in 1749.

The Porcelain Story

 In the 17th and 18th centuries Europeans coveted the porcelain that began to arrive across the seas from China, and desperately wanted to manufacture it for themselves. Augustus the Strong decided that he was going to crack the problem, and with characteristic finesse locked up an alchemist with instructions to find out how to make the precious substance, or forfeit his freedom forever. Johann Böttger was this help-less alchemist's name, and in 1708, after seven unsuccessful years, he finally triumphed by producing a recipe for red porcelain—but he wasn't released. The King wanted white porcelain, so kept him incarcerated for a further five years, until Böttger found that by adding quartz and substituting kaolin for local clay he could make white porcelain. It was only in 1714 that Böttger (by then blinded by metal poisoning) was set free. He died five years later at the age of 37, but the porcelain factory at Meißen (just outside Dresden) went on to become one of the most famous in the world.

It dominated European porcelain manufacture until 1750 and devastated the Chinese porcelain trade. Other centres developed, notably Vincennes in France (1740)—moving to Sèvres in 1756, where it was under the control of Louis XV. The Chelsea pottery in London produced porcelain after 1745. European porcelain manu-facture quickly became the most sophisticated ceramic art-form the world has ever known, and the quality of 18th-century ware has never really been exceeded.

The Zwinger also includes the **Rüstkammer** *(Tues–Sun 10–6; adm DM3, or included in Gemäldegalerie ticket)*, a glittering collection of Wettin armour and weapons. The stylish, ornately decorated armour for generals and their horses, the beautifully wrought swords by Nuremberg silversmiths, and some of the early firearms are works of art rather than mere weapons. In the southern gallery there is a small natural history museum, the **Staatliches Museum für Tierkunde** *(Tues–Sun 9–4; adm DM1)*. Next door is an intriguing collec-tion of old globes, astronomical instruments and watches in the **Mathematisch-Physikalischer Salon** *(Fri–Wed 9.30–5; adm DM3)*.

The Brühlsche Terrasse and the Albertinum

Running east from the Theaterplatz along the Banks of the Elbe is the **Brühlsche Terrasse**, a terrace and pleasure-garden created out of the old city fortifications in 1726–43. The magnificent view up and down the river soon earned this promenade the nickname 'the Balcony of Europe'. The vaults below (now mostly wine bars and restaurants) were for a long time home to the unfortunate alchemist Böttger.

At the end of the Brühlsche Terrasse is the **Albertinum**, converted into a museum out of the former arsenal as early as 1884. Today it houses three museums. The **Gemäldegalerie Neue Meister** (Gallery of New Masters) was, at the time of writing, still undergoing renovations. It is renowned for its late 19th-century French painting, including works by the Impressionists, Manet, Degas and Van Gogh, as well as for its German Romantics. Downstairs in the **Skulpturensammlung** *(adm included in Grünes Gewölbe ticket, see below)* is a wide selection of Greek and Roman sculpture and vases.

The main draw in the Albertinum, however, is the royal treasury, the **Grünes Gewölbe** (literally, the Green Vault) *(Mon, Tues, Fri, Sat, Sun 9–5, Wed 9–6; adm DM5)*—the richest collection of treasures this side of the Topkapi Palace in Istanbul. The objects on display (only about a third of what is in the vaults) are the last word in extravagance, flamboyance and unashamed splendour, created for sheer visual delight as well as to show off a vast wealth in gold and precious stones. A 19th-century visitor summed the mood up perfectly when he called the Grünes Gewölbe a 'gorgeous toyshop'. The cases filled with ivory, amber, gold, silver and jewels display stunning virtuosity in craftsmanship. Here is wit, daring and outrageous ornament—but never bad taste. An early attempt at imitating china consists of a solid gold coffee-service delicately enamelled to resemble the real thing. Many of the best pieces are by Augustus the Strong's court jeweller, **Johann Melchior Dinglinger**. You can't miss his *Court of Delhi on the Birthday of the Great Moghul*, made up of 137 tiny gilded and enamelled figures of humans and animals, encrusted with over 5000 diamonds, emeralds, rubies and pearls. At the other end of the scale is an earring made out of a cherry pip—on which 185 different faces have been carved. There are bowls carved in agate, drinking cups made out of coral, jade and carved rhinocerous horn, and jewellery that looks ponderous enough to tear off your earlobes or break your neck.

The Neustadt

From Theaterplatz the Albertbrücke takes you over the Elbe to **Neustadt**, laid out as a Baroque extension to the city. At the end of the bridge is a showy gilded equestrian statue of Augustus the Strong. Beyond this is Hauptstraße, a more stylish version of Prager Straße, with trees down the middle, classier shops and a few original Baroque buildings. Hauptstraße leads on to a big traffic circus, Albertplatz. North and east of here (around Rothenburger Straße, Lutherstraße and Louisenstraße) is Dresden's trendy quarter. Fringe theatres, new galleries and arty cafés have opened here and are beginning to flourish.

East of Hauptstraße, along Große Meisener Straße, is the **Museum für Volkskunst** *(Tues–Sun 10–5; adm DM2)*, a museum of refreshingly earthy folk art. Painted wood and carving is a local speciality. There are air-born cherubs holding candles, beautiful cribs and beds, and odd chandeliers made out of wooden bobbles. Tucked away in a room at the back is a 19th-century mechanized Crucifixion with a Christ that drops his head at the appropriate moment, but sadly out of order.

expensive

Maritim-Hotel Bellevue, Große Meißener Str. 15, ✆ 56620, fax 55997 (DM448–538). The best in town. A lavishly furnished hotel with a splendid view across to the Semperoper, Zwinger and Brühlsche Terrasse.

Dresden Hilton, An der Frauenkirche 5, ✆ 48410, fax 484 1700 (DM395–495 without breakfast). Splendid new hotel overlooking the Frauenkirche. Usual Hilton efficiency.

moderate

Hotel Rothenburger Hof, Rothenburger Straße 15–17, ✆/fax 502 2808 (DM195). Friendly, imaginatively decorated hotel in the northern Neustadt.

Hotel Stadt Rensburg, Kamenzer Str. 1 (Tram 6, 11, 13 or 26), ✆ 51551, fax 502 2586 (DM145). Simple, clean hotel—but in northern Neustadt, a little way from the sights.

Hotel Glasewald, Berggasse 27, ✆ 75322, fax 75906 (DM110). Comfortable hotel in the forest at the northern edge of town. Spacious garden terrace. Bus 80 stops about 15 minutes' walk away.

Hotelschiff Elbresidenz, Terrassenufer PF 328, ✆ 459 5003, fax 459 5137 (DM180–210). Best value of the row of hotel ships moored along the Elbe. Close to the centre.

inexpensive

Pension Steiner, Plattleite 49 (Tram 11), ✆ 37376 (DM80–110). Among the grand villas of Loschwitz, east along the Elbe. The closest you'll get to the centre at this price.

Pension Haus Höhenblick, Wachwitzer Höhenweg 28, ✆ 36363 (DM80 without breakfast). Pleasant pension, also in hills over looking the Elbe.

Youth Hostel: Hübnerstr. 11, ✆ 471 0667.

Private rooms in Dresden cost between DM60 and DM90 and can be booked through the tourist office.

Eating and Drinking: Restaurants and Taverns

moderate

Altmarktkeller, Wilsdruffer Str. 19–21, ✆ 495 1212 (DM30–50). Good-value cellar restaurant on the Altmarkt. Steaks, local specialities such as stuffed cabbage, and tasty daily specials.

Laterne, Bautzner Str. 1, ℂ 53094 (DM30–50). Intimate 5th and 6th-floor restaurant with view over Neustadt to the famous Dresden skyline. Simple, tasty food (try the venison fillet with various forest mushrooms).

Rothenburger Hof, Rothenburger Str. 15–17, ℂ 502 2808 (DM30–50). Well worth the schlepp across Neustadt and the extra Deutschmarks for the friendly atmosphere and superb food. Try the pheasant breast in walnut sauce.

Kügelgenhaus, Hauptstr. 12, ℂ 52791 (DM30–45). Atmospheric restaurant in old Baroque house. Slow service but good local specialities—the potato soup is a must on wintry days.

Blockhaus, Neustädter Markt 19 (DM35–55). Belorussian restaurant in Baroque guardhouse looking across the Elbe to Dresden's grandest monuments. Intriguing dishes such as *Matschanka*—roast pork with salami, shallots, sour cream and butter beans.

inexpensive

Hebedas, corner of Rothenburger Str. and Böhmische Str. (DM15–20). Bright lights, formica tables and formidably solid German cooking.

Bars and Cafés

Café Sphinx/Café Prag, Altmarkt 16–17, ℂ 495 1135. Local favourite for people-watching on the Altmarkt.

Bierhaus Dampfschiff, An der Frauenkirche 5, ℂ 48410. Best of the touristy bars and cafés behind the Brülsche Terrasse.

Raskolnikoff, Böhmische Str. 34, ℂ 401 0457. Hole-in-the-wall bar with off-the-wall crowd. One of the best spots for a drink in the arty quarter north of the Neustadt.

Planwirtschaft, Louisenstr. 20, ℂ 57 0518. Popular café and beer cellar, also in the trendy quarter.

Kutscherstubchen, Hauptstr. 11. Quiet, candle-lit bar in the Neustadt.

Entertainment and Nightlife

Dresden's **listings magazine** is *Sax*, available at newsagents and in some museums. You can get **tickets** for State orchestras and theatres in the Schinkelwache on Theaterplatz (ℂ 48420, fax 484 2692).

Dresden's **opera** company and its orchestra, the *Sächsische Staatskapelle*, rank with the best in the world. They perform at the Semperoper, ℂ 48420, but tickets can be hard to come by and it is advisable to book months in advance. You can try for returns at the theatre just before the performance. The **Dresdner Philharmonie** also enjoys a good reputation as an orchestra. They can usually be heard in the Kulturpalast on the Altmarkt, ✆ 486 6286. There is good **main stream theatre** at the Schauspielhaus, Ostraallee 47, ✆ 48420. Projekttheater 7, Louisenstr. 47, ✆ 53041, has an exciting programme of **alternative theatre** and **dance**.

For **live music** try Music Circus, Pieschener Alle 1, ✆ 434 480, where you can dance as well, or Klub Neue Mensa, Bergstr. 47, ✆ 463 6495. Trendiest places to **dance** are currently Club für Dich, Martin-Luther-Str. 21, ✆ 51984, Café im Bärenzwinger (Brühlscher Garten) and Hauz II (Zellescher Weg 41c, entrance Teplitzer Straße).

South of Dresden

From Dresden you can follow the River Elbe in a paddle steamer, a train or by road. (If you are going by car the more attractive route is along Käthe-Kollwitz-Ufer out of town, then follow the banks of the river—rather than the offical B172 route). The terminus of Tram 9 and 14 is just a ferry hop from the Pillnitz (*see* below).

First stop is the suburb of **Loschwitz** on the steep hills lining the right bank. The elegant villas here escaped bomb damage (though crumbled gradually under the DDR). You could wander the steep streets for hours; admiring the architecture and glimpsing the view between the houses. It is a vista that appealed to Romantic painter Caspar David Friedrich, and to the architect Schinkel, both of whom had homes here.

Just beyond Loschwitz lies Pillnitz, where Augustus the Strong had his summer palace. **Schloß Pillnitz** is in fact two palaces, both heavily influenced by Oriental architectural styles. The **Wasserpalais** *(Wed–Mon 9.30–5; adm DM3)* contains a missable applied arts museum (mainly glass and porcelain). In the almost identical **Bergpalais** *(Tues–Sun, 9.30–5; adm DM3)* you can see some of the rather stark interiors. This Schloß, as well as **Schloß Albrechtsburg** (soon to be a new venue for the Dresdner Philharmonie) and a string of other grand homes further upstream, are perhaps seen at their best from a boat on the river.

As you near the Czech border (just 30km away) you come to the most spectacular sight in the region, a range of bizarre rocks, eerie ravines and fissured cliffs to rival the balancing boulders in Zimbabwe or the towering Meteora in Greece. Nineteenth-century Romantics nicknamed this outcrop of the Elbe Sandstone Mountains **Saxon Switzerland**, a name that has stuck, but does no justice to their drama and oddity. The most spectacular stretch along the river is between **Kurort Rathen** and the border town of **Schmilka**. From **Kurort Rathen** it is a 30-minute hike to the most remarkable formation of all, the sheer **Bastei**. From its 194m-high viewing platform from which you can see the whole of Saxon Switzerland. An 80m-long stone bridge spans the gorge to the 12th-century castle of **Felsenburg Neurathen**. Nearby is an open-air theatre, carved into the rock. At Königstein, a few kilometres further on, an enormous fortress **Festung Königstein** *(May–Sept 8–8, Oct–Apr 9–5; adm DM5)* seems to grow organically from the rock.

Johann Böttger, the inventor of European porcelain (*see* p. 460) was incarcerated here for a time, and it was used as recently as the 1950s as a prison for DDR dissenters.

Saxon Switzerland is great hiking country—in between the rocks are meadows, steep hills, and forests criss-crossed by icy streams. It is also fearsomely challenging ground for rock-climbers. The ideal base for exploring the area is **Bad Schandau**, a quiet village squeezed between the rocks and the river. From here you can catch the **Kirnitzschtalbahn**, an electric tram that runs out into the heart of the surrounding nature reserve, or shoot up vertically in a turn-of-the-century lift to the mountain-top suburb of wooden chalets.

North of Dresden

The famous porcelain manufacturing town of **Meißen** is 25km northwest of Dresden along the B6 (you can also get there by train or paddle steamer, *see* **Getting Around** above). Meißen is near the top of the list for special restoration funding. The town, which tumbles down a steep hill and along the river valley, escaped Second World War bombing virtually intact, and could become one of the prettiest towns in Saxony. But progress with renovation is slow. The streets can barely cope with the influx of new traffic, and there is an unfriendly, money-grubbing edge to what could well develop into Saxony's nastiest tourist trap.

The **Staatliche Porzellan-Manufaktur Meißen** (Talstr. 9, © (03521) 468 208) still produces sought-after wares in the classic Meißen tradition. The factory is just off the main road 1½km south of the centre (from the Markt follow Fleischer Gasse, then turn right into Neu Gasse). Here you can, usually after a long wait, join the throngs on a **guided tour** *(Tues–Sun 8.30–12 and 12.30–4.15; adm DM4)* through the different stages of porcelain manufacture. The tour lasts 40 minutes, and the only really interesting bit is watching the designs being painted on by hand. A far better prospect is the **Schauhalle** *(same times; adm DM5)*, a spectacular array of porcelain clocks, fancy figurines and tables groaning under glittering dinner services.

Meißen's other main attractions are the **Albrechtsburg** *(Feb–Dec daily 10–6; adm DM5)*, a 15th century castle high above the city, and the **Dom** *(daily May–Sept 9–4.30, Oct–Apr 9–3.30; adm DM2.50)*, resting safely in the fortress courtyard. The castle is known mainly for the odd vaulting and curious, twisting staircase—both the work of masterbuilder Anton von Westfalen. The Gothic Dom contains some fine carving, including works from the school of the Master of Naumburg (*see* p. 55), though not by the great sculptor himself.

Northeast of Dresden (54km along the A4) is **Bautzen**, cultural capital to the **Sorbs**. The Sorbs are Slavs (they still speak their own language, similar to both Czech and Slovak) who have for centuries lived in this corner of Germany (at one time called the province of Lusatia). Persecuted by the Nazis, they were championed as heroes by the Soviets and allowed to have their own schools and cultural institutions. Bautzen is the centre for the **Domowina**, the Sorb cultural organization, but you are more likely to hear the language, and see the colourful traditional costumes in the Spreewald to the north (*see* p. 512). The main Sorb **festivals**—horseback processions at Easter, and revelry on *Hexenbrennen* (literally, 'Witch-burning'), the night of the witches' sabbath, 30 April—are also less touristy outside of Bautzen.

Bautzen itself is an attractive Baroque town, and at the moment of writing is in far better shape than neighbouring Görlitz. It is very much worth a short stop-off for a look at the **cathedral**, a *Simultankirche*, divided into a Protestant and a Roman Catholic section and built at a slight curve to fit it into a small site. Also worth exploring is the Reichstraße, the main street lined with carefully restored Baroque houses, and the medieval fortifications, stretching high above the River Spree. You can see displays on the history and culture of the Sorbs at the **Sorbisches Museum** *(daily 9.30–12.30 and 1.30–4; adm DM3)*.

See also Directory entries for Görlitz and Cottbus.

Tourist Information

Meißen: An der Frauenkirche 3, ✆ (03521) 454 470.

Bautzen: Fleischmarkt 2, ✆ (03591) 42 016.

Where to Stay and Eating Out

Meißen

Pannonia Hotel, Hafenstr. 27–31, ✆ (0511) 540 7810 for reservations (DM250). Newly converted villa in a small riverside park opposite the Schloß.
Pension Plossenschänke, Wilsdruffer Str. 35, ✆ (03521) 2254 (DM100). Adequate and virtually the only other hotel in town.
Gaststätte Monasterium, Freiheit 13, ✆ (03521) 453 437. Serves microwaved food in a medieval seminary building.
Vincenz Richter, An der Frauenkirche 12, ✆ (03521) 453 285 (DM15–50). The best restaurant in town, serving everything from simple snacks to roast duck.

Bautzen

Bautzener Stüb'l, Steinstr. 5, ✆ (03591) 42 075 (DM125). A comfortable little *Pension* in the Altstadt.
Wjelbik, Kornstr. 7, ✆ (03591) 42 060. Offers good local cooking.

Berlin and the Spree

Dig deep into the land around Berlin and you will start turning up fine golden sand. Brandenburg was known as the 'sand-box of the Holy Roman Empire'—geologically an ocean-bed, botanically just one step up from a desert. Today the landscape, especially to the north of the capital, can be bleak. But follow the river Spree southwards and you come to the romantic forests and marshland of the Spreewald. Here you can punt about between the trees as if you were in the thick of a mangrove swamp, and meet the local Sorbs—not Germans at all, but Slavs, with their own language and conscientiously preserved traditions.

Desolate sandpit it might have been, but Brandenburg—on the border between eastern and western Europe and on the main trade route between Dresden and the Baltic—was of crucial strategic importance. Here the Prussians built up a powerful army, and set about subjugating the continent. Militaristic Prussia, with its heel-clicking formality, pig-headedness and discipline, is responsible for one of today's most negative stereotypes of the Germans, but Berlin, the capital of the Prussian Empire, has long been one of the country's most stimulating cities.

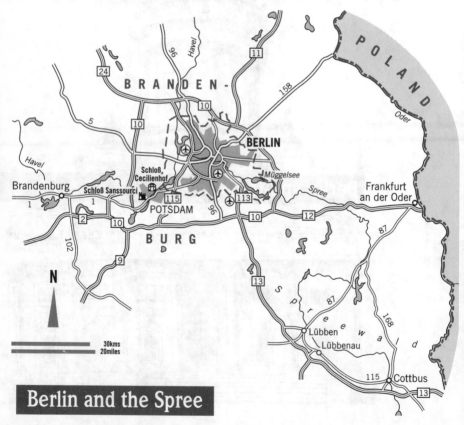

Berlin and the Spree

We called her proud, snobbish, nouveau riche, uncultured, crude, but secretly everyone looked upon her as the goal of his desires. Some saw her as hefty, full-breasted, in lace underwear, others as a mere wisp of a thing, with boyish legs in black silk stockings. The daring saw both aspects, and her very reputation for cruelty made them more aggressive.

Carl Zuckmayer, writing of Berlin.

Berlin is a city with two centres—the cluster of expensive hotels, bars, cinemas and shops round the Memorial Church ... and the self-conscious civic centre of buildings round Unter den Linden, carefully arranged.

Christopher Isherwood, *Goodbye to Berlin.*

Berlin was two cities long before the Wall cut through it, and, to some extent, is still so. The pompous Prussian capital seethed with bohemian intellectuals and artists. The 'divinely decadent', sexually free city of the 1920s and 1930s was all the time being squeezed more tightly in the Nazi's grip. The Cold War polarized the city completely, and even after the *Wende* Berlin's Ossis and Wessis seemed worlds apart and wary of each other. All the difficulties, contradictions and resentment of reunification were here distilled into one town.

Things are changing fast, though. Berliners are less likely than they were just after the *Wende* to add the tag East or West when they introduce themselves. People are beginning to venture beyond their familiar patches of town, and bright lights, new coats of paint and a scramble of construction make it ever harder to follow the line of the old divide. But in many ways *die Mauer in den Köpfen* ('the Wall in the mind') is still there. Many Berliners still bristle with *Neid* (envy)—the Ossis of the Wessis' material affluence and higher salaries, the Wessis of the Ossis' low rents. Shopkeepers do a brisk trade in T-shirts reading 'We want our Wall back'.

In the U-Bahn around midnight Berlin is, in another way, clearly two cities. Half the passengers are going home, half are just going out. Solid, respectable Berlin—soon to have its ranks swelled by senators, civil servants and more diplomats—is on the way home from the opera or dinner. Alongside, in leopardskin leotard, scruffy jeans or swathes of black, is the Berlin that still attracts artists, adventurers, shady characters, dreamy youth and simple hedonists from all over the world. Theirs is the Berlin where cafés only *begin* serving breakfast at 11am; of smoke-stained *Kneipe* with not a peep of background music, where the problems of the world are argued out; of night clubs that are open till dawn—a rough, improvised, cocky, abrasive city, perhaps nostalgic for 1920s insouciance, but with roots that go far deeper. Berlin once caused Goethe to remark, 'I see in everything that this is a city filled with such an impertinent species of mankind that one doesn't get far using delicacy with them; to keep above water in Berlin one has to be somewhat coarse oneself.'

Even if you have Zuckmayer's daring, and manage to yoke the two worlds together, you still will not be able to escape Berlin's cruelty. The city wears the scars of its difficult history, not with any pride or self-pity, but simply as a matter of fact. You will pass huge, cold monuments to Prussian imperialism, even more chilling Nazi showpieces, façades pock-marked by Second World War shrapnel, jagged concrete remnants of the Wall, and plaques commemorating those murdered while trying to cross it. Among it you'll find excellent museums, Europe's rudest shop assistants, pride, confusion and flair. Above all you will breathe *Berlin Luft* ('Berlin air'), the bracing atmosphere of a big, complicated, vibrant city.

Apart from the cluster of grand buildings and museums around Unter den Linden, Berlin's sights are scattered. Getting from one to another often involves a complicated journey on public transport. Frequently you'll be tempted to walk, as each destination seems a manageable distance from the last, but by the end of the day you will have trekked for miles. Unless you have wonder-thighs and very comfortable shoes you'll be hobbling for the U-Bahn by sundown and will be too exhausted to go out at night. A bicycle makes an excellent alternative (*see* **Getting Around** below).

A word, too, about museums. Many collections were split up after the Second World War, and led separate lives on either side of the Wall. After re-unification Berlin found itself with some duplicate museums, with many of those in the east badly in need of repair. Directors are haggling about what should go where, and entire buildings are closed for long periods of renovation. In the meantime the collections play a sort of museum musical chairs. This applies particularly to paintings and archaeological artefacts. Works are mentioned here where they appeared at the time of writing, but please don't be surprised if you find them somewhere quite different.

This chapter divides the city up into areas. You could visit each one individually, but if time is short and you need to be selective it is a good idea to target exactly what you want to see and to plan your journey so that you keep travelling in a circle. Otherwise you could end up spending most of your time on the U-Bahn.

History

Berlin even began life as two cities. **Coelln** (meaning 'sand bank'), a fishing settlement on the south side of the Spree and **Berlin** (meaning 'bog'), a trading town on the north bank, set up a common town council in 1307 (though they had been growing up separately for a good century before that). The towns joined the **Hanseatic League** and prospered—until robber barons pillaged them later in the century. In 1411 the councillors appealed to the Holy Roman Emperor, who sent **Friedrich von Hohenzollern**, Burgraf of Nuremburg to help, later making him Elector of Brandenburg. The Hohenzollerns stayed for 507 years.

The second Hohenzollern ruler, **Friedrich Irontooth** (so-called because once he had got his teeth into something he never let go) forced Berlin to leave the Hanseatic League, cruelly quashed a city rebellion and, to prove his point, changed Berlin's emblem from a bear rampant to a bear on all fours with an iron collar around its neck and a Hohenzollern eagle perched on its back. He was the first of many rulers, though, to complain of *Berliner Umwille* (unwillingness to follow orders).

Towards the end of the 17th century another of the line, **Elector Friedrich Wilhelm**, in an attempt to swell the population, gave refuge to **Huguenots**—Protestants fleeing religious persecution in France. The Huguenots brought sophisticated crafts (such as enamelling and watchmaking), Berlin's first public transport (sedan chairs) and *Weiße Bier*. The Elector was also tolerant towards **Jews**, and the influx of refugees formed the basis of what was to be one of Berlin's most influential communities.

Two generations later another Friedrich Wilhelm (known as 'the Drill Sergeant') set about building up the army with such application (billeting troops all over town and press-ganging virtually any man able to move) that the citizens tried to escape. The king (Prussia had become a kingdom in 1701) built a **city wall**—not to keep invaders out as was usually the case, but, ironically, to keep the burghers in.

The army continued to grow under King Friedrich Wilhelm's son, **Frederick the Great** (1740–86). The new king was also obsessed with culture and style (though himself an appalling musician and embarrassing poet). For years Voltaire lived at court and Berlin became a centre of high fashion and (Frederick liked to think) liberal thought, attracting the likes of the philosphers Hegel and Schlegel, the composer Mendelssohn and the writers E.T.A. Hoffmann and Gotthold Ephraim Lessing.

In the latter part of the 18th century Prussia began to emerge as a European power to be reckoned with. Although Napoleon briefly occupied Berlin, Prussian involvement in his defeat—notably at Waterloo—led to even more territory coming under the eagle's wing (*see* **History** p. 43). In 1848 King Friedrich Wilhelm IV came in for a taste of *Berlin Umwille* when a 10,000-strong people's revolt demanded more democratic rights. The king donned revolutionary colours and appeared in the streets promising free elections—though he reneged on all his promises once order was restored and embarked upon an even fiercer programme of repression.

In 1862 Friedrich Wilhelm's successor, **Wilhelm I**, appointed **Otto von Bismarck** Prime Minister of Prussia. Bismarck set about uniting Germany by 'blood and iron' (*see* **History** p. 43). He was another man who had trouble with *Berliner Umwille*—people kept voting for liberal candidates rather than the Iron Chancellor's favoured deputies. In 1871, during the Franco–Prussian War, King Wilhelm was crowned emperor (Kaiser) of a united Germany in the Hall of Mirrors at the Palace of Versailles. Berlin was now the capital of this new Germany. Its population rocketed and the city seemed well on the way to becoming the cultural and industrial centre of Europe. This period of prosperity, known as 'Wilhelmine' period (in German *Grunderzeit*—Founders' Time) spawned a distinctive style of furniture and Neoclassical architecture that became a Berlin trademark.

The First World War and Spartacus Revolt (*see* **History** p. 45) put the brakes on a little, but Berlin blossomed under the Weimar Republic. 'Weimar culture' was very much the *Berlin* culture of Brecht and Kurt Weill, Arnold Schönberg and the conductor Bruno Walter; of Dada, Josephine Baker, Marlene Dietrich, experimental cinema, transvestites and naked 'Beauty-dancers'. But this 'Golden Age' of the 1920s began to sour with the appearance of the Nazis.

Hitler also got a taste of *Berliner Umwille*—in the 1930 elections the city voted overwhelmingly for the Left. As Chancellor, though, the *Führer* put the clamps on. Communists were arrested and shot, 'decadent' cabarets and nightclubs were closed down, many artists were branded as traitors and the 'enemy within', the Jews, were subject to discrimination and persecution. On 9 November 1938, in response to a German diplomat being killed by a Jewish activist in Paris, the Nazis ran riot, smashing the windows of Jewish businesses and synagogues and houses. Later this destructive orgy became known as *Kristallnacht* (night of the broken glass). By the end of the war only 8000 of Berlin's 160,000-strong Jewish community remained. Many had fled abroad, but one third had died in the Nazi concentration camps.

As capital of the Reich and Hitler's headquarters, Berlin came in for some of the fiercest bombing of the war. (A cartoon of the time shows one Berliner looking up at the bombers flying over the shell of his city and remarking, with typical Berlin dry wit, 'Now they have to bring the houses with them'.) By the end of the war the capital's population had been reduced by nearly half to 2.5 million, 70 per cent of whom were women. Times were hard. Berliners were rationed to two potatoes and half a loaf of bread a day and had to cut down the trees in the Tiergarten for fuel. The Soviet blockade (*see* **History** p. 48) made the situation worse. Soon after the blockade was lifted, Berlin formally became two cities, with the eastern part under the DDR.

The building of the Wall in 1961 (*see* **History** p. 49) seemed to symbolize the irreversibility of the division. Even a few months before the hugs, tears and partying at the Brandenburg gate on 9 November 1989, few people believed that Berlin would ever be one city again (for more on the events leading up to unification. Cosy, if claustrophobic, West Berlin suddenly found itself part of a much larger metropolis. The lights that had glittered alluringly on the other side of the Wall from the East Berliners, were—at one swoop—part of their own city.

But for the first year or so after unification little seemed to change. Once the euphoria had worn off, East and West Berliners found that they had little in common with each other. Wessis were resentful of the extra tax imposed on them to pay for the *Wende*, and complained that their new neighbours expected too much for nothing. Ossis found that the streets of the West were not paved with gold and that some Communist institutions (such as free child care) were not so bad after all. Refugees from the eastern bloc countries flooded the city. Finding housing became nigh on impossible and the streets clogged up with traffic. Lack of money kept the Ossis at home in the East. Lack of inclination kept the Wessis in their familiar, well-stocked cafés in the West. Chancellor Kohl's promises of a rosy future after an initial period of belt-tightening disappeared into the gloom of a German recession.

But something is stirring. In the time that it took to write this book, a subtle (but sure) change came over Berlin. The city began to fuse. In the centre, at least, it became hard to tell the two Berlins apart. Trendy bars and clubs are sprouting in the eastern part of town—even one or two fashionable restaurants. Frustration, resentment and caution are still there, but Berliners seem to be finding common cause and building a new, unified city for themselves.

By Air

Berlin has three major airports, **Tegel** (℃ (030) 41011, about 15 minutes' drive north of the centre), which deals with most international and charter flights, **Schönfeld** (℃ (030) 67 870) in the southern suburbs, which still is mainly for eastern European traffic, and **Tempelhof** (℃ (030) 69 091) in the city centre, which is supposed to be for internal flights and smaller aircraft only, but seems to sneak in a few international connections too. Tegel, the main airport, offers connections to major cities all over the world. It is connected by bus to the U-Bahn network (Bus 109 or 700 to Jakob-Kaiser-Platz on Line 7, or Bus 128 to Kurt-Schumacher-Platz on Line 6). A taxi supposedly gets you into town in half the time and costs DM25, but heavy traffic can scupper all attempts at speed and push up your bill considerably. Schönfeld is directly connected to the S-Bahn (Lines 9 and 10), and Bus 119 takes you from Tempelhof to Kurfürstendamm in about 20 minutes.

Airline Offices:

American Airlines, Bundesallee 213, ℃ (030) 211 0032.

British Airways, Europa Centre, Budapester Str., ℃ (030) 261 1335.

Lufthansa, Kurfürstendamm 220, ℃ (030) 410 13844.

TWA, Kurfürstendamm 28, ℃ (030) 882 7096.

By Train

This is still a time-consuming business, often involving awkward transfers. Most trains from the west arrive at **Bahnhof Zoo**, in the centre of west Berlin. Trains arriving from other directions tend to end up in the eastern part of the city at **Bahnhof Lichtenberg** or the **Hauptbahnhof** (which is no longer a Hauptbahnhof at all—though it is gradually being used more). Both of the latter are on the S-Bahn system, about 20 minutes from Alexanderplatz. Some journey times are: Munich (7½hr), Hamburg (3½hr), Hannover (4½hr). **Information** on trains is available at stations or at the offices of the Deutsche Bundesbahn (Hardenbergstr. 20, ℃ (030) 19419).

By Car

Berlin has three main Autobahn approaches, the A24 from the north, via Hamburg (260km), the A2 from the west, via Hannover (290km), and the A9 from Munich (590km) in the south. Road surface conditions have improved vastly since DDR days, but the A9 can get frantically busy. The A2 is notorious for traffic jams and accidents, so if you're coming from north-west Germany it is a better idea to travel via Hamburg.

Parking in Berlin, even in some of the suburbs, is becoming a problem and unless your hotel has its own garage (which always costs extra) it is probably a good idea to park on the outskirts of town and use public transport. Large new petrol stations have sprung up all over eastern Berlin, so out-of-hours refuelling is no longer the problem it once was.

Car Hire: Avis, Budapester Str. 43, ✆ (030) 261 1881; Hertz, Budapester Str. 39, ✆ (030) 261 1053; InterRent Europacar, Kurfürstendamm 178–9, ✆ (030) 881 8093.

Mitfahrzentrale: Mitfahrzentrale im U-Bahn Zoo (just where it says, on Line 1 platform), ✆ (030) 310 331); Citynetz, Kurfürstendamm 227, ✆ (030) 19 444.

Public Transport

Berlin's **U-Bahn** and **S-Bahn** form an efficient and comprehensive network, and are fully integrated once again. However, there are some problems. Travelling from west to east can still be tricky and may involve time-consuming line changes—generally it is a better idea to use the S-Bahn for this (Lines 3, 5, 6 and 9 all run from Bahnhof Zoo to Friedrichstraße and Alexanderplatz). Also, no train at all makes the crucial journey across the Tiergarten, from the centre of western Berlin through the Brandenburg gate to Unter den Linden. Best bet for this is Bus 100, which is on the go 24 hours a day.

Trains run from about 5am to 1am. Lines U1 and U9 run all night on Friday and Saturday. Otherwise check out the **nightbuses** (numbers prefixed by an N:— routes are posted at bus-stops).

Tickets are valid on all three systems. Single tickets (DM3.20) allow you to travel anywhere for up to two hours. A **Sammelkarte** gives you four two-hour journeys for DM11, but the best value is the **24-hour travel card** for DM12. Weekly travelcards (Mon–Sat only) cost DM30. You can buy tickets from blue machines at stations, special ticket offices, or bus drivers. All tickets, even travel cards, must be validated by stamping machines (on platforms or in buses) when you commence your first journey. Without a valid ticket you are liable to a DM60 spot fine.

Taxi: It is more usual to go to one of the taxi ranks around the city than to try and flag down a cab in the street. Alternatively, you can phone for one on 6902 or 261 026. After 8pm, U-Bahn staff will call a taxi for women travelling alone.

Maps

The map printed with this chapter will help you to orientate yourself and get about between the sights. If you intend staying in Berlin for any length of time, or are going out exploring the night-life it would be a good idea to buy a more detailed map with a street index. The best ones are published by Falk. They are available in bookshops and newsagents all over Germany, and sometimes from good bookshops in other countries. Falk maps usually contain a plan of the public transport network too, though you can pick up handier versions from ticket offices at U-Bahn stations.

By Bicycle

A bike is a practical and relatively safe way of getting about in Berlin. Cycle paths are well laid out, and cover most of the city. Bicycle thieves are rampant, though, so be careful to lock your bike securely, preferably with a metal, U-shaped lock to something immovable. You can **hire a bicycle** for around DM10 a day, leaving your passport as a deposit, from:

Berlin by Bike, Möckernstr. 92, ✆ (030) 216 9177.

Fahrradverleih Rad Lust, Waldemarstr. 42 (Kreuzberg), ✆ (030) 651 925.

Boats and Cruises

Seven per cent of Berlin is covered by water. The **River Spree** and the **Landwehr Canal** flow through the middle of town. A tributary of the Spree, the **Havel**, flows along the western edge of the city, and breaks up into a patchwork of lakes. Numerous smaller canals and rivers criss-cross the suburbs. A short boat trip is a novel way to orientate yourself, and some parts of town, especially around the Mitte, seem quite romantic viewed from the water.

Stern & Kreisschiffart, Sachtelebebstr. 60, ✆ (030) 810 0040. Sightseeing cruises of the city, from DM8.50. The company also operates a **ferry service** on the Havel Lakes between Spandau, Wannsee and Potsdam.

Berliner Wassertaxi, Schloßbrücke, opp. Zeughaus, ✆ (030) 972 6124. City tours, DM9. More comfortable boat and English commentary, but the tour is not as extensive.

Tourist Information

Tourist information offices:

Europa Center: Budapester Str., ✆ (030) 262 6031 *(Mon–Sat 8am–10.30pm, Sun 9–9)*.

Tegel Airport: Main Hall, ✆ (030) 41 01 3145 *(daily 8am–11pm)*.

Bahnhof Zoo: ✆ (030) 313 9063 *(Mon–Sat 8–11)*.

Hauptbahnhof: ✆ (030) 279 5209 *(Mon–Sat 8–10)*.

Potsdam: Friedrich-Ebert-Str. 5, ✆ (0331) 21100 *(daily 8–6)*.

Consulates:

UK: Unter den Linden 32–4, ✆ (030) 10117.

USA: Clayallee 170, ✆ (030) 819 7465.

Australia: Berlin Hilton, Mohrenstr. 30, ✆ (030) 23 82 2041.

Police: ✆ 110.

Ambulance: ✆ 112.

Medical & pharmaceutical emergencies: ✆ (030) 31 00 31.

Emergency dentist: ✆ (030) 1141.

Banks: Branches of main banks can be found along the Kurfürstendamm. The Berliner Bank in the main hall of Tegel Airport is open daily 8am–10pm.

American Express: Friedrichstr. 172, © (030) 238 4102 or Uhlandstr. 173–4, © (030) 882 7575.

Post office: At Bahnhof Zoo (Mon–Fri 8–6, Sat 8–12; one 24-hr counter).

Lost and found: BVG Fundbüro, Lorenzweg 5, © (030) 751 8021 (for items lost on public transport).

Baby sitting: Babysitter-Service, Claudiastr. 6, © (030) 393 5981.

Markets: Fleamarket/Antiques: Straße des 17 Juni, Sat and Sun 8–3.30; Bahnhof Friedrichstraße (under the arches), Mon and Wed–Sun 11–6.

Street Markets: Maybachufer, Tues and Fri 12–6.30 (fruit, veg and exotica); Winterfeldplatz, Wed and Sat 8–1 (food, clothes and general market).

Festivals

East Berlin has lost all its Communist Party parades, and West Berlin never had much to offer in the way of organized beanfeasts. The one obvious date for celebration—9 November, the day the Wall came down—is also the anniversary of *Kristallnacht*, the massive 1938 anti-Jewish riot. That, and the fact that unification is not all a bed of roses anyway, puts a dampener on any festivities. **New Year** celebrations at the Brandenburg Gate seem to be taking the place of a 9 November party. May Day is also usually celebrated with gusto, with most of the fun (and usually a riot) happening in Kreuzberg. On a Saturday early in July around 20,000 of the city's nightclub ravers get up uncharacteristically early (around 3pm) don their gladrags and, together with 50 floats and a cacophony of their favourite DJs march through the centre of town on the annual **Love Parade**. Needless to say, this is followed by parties the whole night through.

The arts festival most worth catching is the **Berlin Film Festival**, held over two weeks in February. This is one of the cinema world's major showcases, and is always worth a look-in.

Around Bahnhof Zoo

Before the *Wende* Bahnhof Zoo (Zoologischer Garten) was West Berlin's main station, and the area around it became the centre of town. The station itself, however, was administered by the East German authorities, and was a dump. Bahnhof Zoo still acts as a magnet to hobos, junkies, alcoholics and all manner of shady characters, but the surrounding streets remain among Berlin's liveliest.

Long before the Wall went up, this patch of shops and cafés around the western end of the Tiergarten stood as a polar opposite to the sober, administrative 'Mitte' (literally 'middle') across the park.

The Kurfürstendamm

The **Kurfürstendamm** (or Ku'damm as you'll quickly come to call it) was built by Bismarck as an answer to the Champs Elysées in Paris. It was the heart of 1920s and 1930s Berlin, when High Society shopped in its stores, writers and artists lounged in its cafés, and everyone packed the theatres and cabarets nightly. American poet Thomas Wolfe called the boulevard the 'largest coffee house in Europe'. During the Second World War Allied bombs destroyed almost all of the fine houses on the Kurfürstendamm. When it was rebuilt, the Ku'damm re-emerged as a glittering concrete and glass showpiece for the capitalist West. Today the 53m-wide, shady avenue has slipped a notch downmarket but can still boast enough classy stores, genteel cafés and pulsating night-spots to satiate the hungry hordes of consumers that overrun it day and night.

Roughly parallel to the Ku'damm, a block or two north is Berlin's main bargain shopping street, **Kantstraße**, which has earned the disparaging nickname 'Warsaw Boulevard' because of the Poles who come by the coachload to stock up on things they can't buy at home. Kantstraße crosses **Sauvignyplatz**, an oddly restful square for this part of town, and the best spot for good, inexpensive cafés and restaurants (*see* **Eating and Drinking** below).

There is little to do on the Ku'damm but gawp, drink coffee and shop, but on Fasanen-straße (one of the roads leading south) you will find the **Käthe-Kollwitz-Museum** *(Wed–Mon 11–6; adm DM5)*—four floors of sculpture, lithographs and etchings by one of Germany's foremost 20th-century artists (*see* **The Arts and Culture** p. 64).

Breidscheidplatz

The Kurfürstendamm, at its eastern end, splays out into **Breidscheidplatz**, a vast expanse of concrete much beloved of skateboarders, winos and punks. Few share their affection for the square, but as Breidscheidplatz is the traffic hub of western Berlin, there is no escape. Passers-by march determinedly, eyes down, on criss-crossing paths to their destinations. In the middle stand the bombed out remains of the **Kaiser-Wilhelm-Gedächtniskirche** (Kaiser Wilhelm Memorial Church, known locally as the Hollow Tooth), once a stupendously vulgar Neo-Gothic church, built in the 19th century to glorify Prussia's military might. It was left in this ruined state after the Second World War as a *Mahnmal*, a 'warning to posterity' (moral, one local wag points out: 'Don't get bombed'). The American historian, Gerhard Masur, described the church as 'one of the few buildings to be improved by the fall of bombs and the ravage of fire'. You can judge for yourself by taking a look at what remains of the **interior** *(Tues–Sat 10–6, Sun 11–6; adm free)*. Cracked gold mosaics depict Christ and His earthly sidekicks, the Hohenzollerns. Next door is a startling hexagonal **tower** of blue glass. This is a modern part of the Memorial Church, built in the 1960s and known variously as the 'Lipstick' and 'Soul Silo'. Light filters through the blue glass to give the **interior** a calm, otherworldy atmosphere.

Opposite the *Gedächtniskirche* is the **Europa-Center**, an ugly 1960s skyscraper complete with a revolving neon Mercedes symbol. At the top is an **observation platform** *(daily 9–11; adm DM2)*. Apart from the view (in all directions except east) or a visit to the tourist

Berlin (East)

Spree

Reichstag

Soviet War Memorial

Unter den Linden

Brandenburger Tor (Brandenburg Gate)

S

TOLLERANZSTR.

LUISENSTR.

STRABE DES 17 JUNI

I Segessäule

Tiergarten

Hitler's Bunker

SITE OF BERLIN WALL

Kemper pl.

Musikinstrumenten-Museum

Philharmonie

KEMPER PL.

M **M**

Potsdamer Pl.

S
U *POTSDAMER PL.*

TIERGARTENSTR.

Kunstgewerbemuseum

Kammermusiksaal

M

M

Kulturforum

KLINGELHÖFERSTR.

VON-DER-HEYDT-STR.

Neue Nationalgalerie **M**

POTSDAMER STR.

Martin-Gropius-Bau

Bauhaus-Archiv

REICHPIETSCHUFER

Staatsbibliothek

Landwehrkanal

SCHÖNEBERGER

UFER

M *BERNBGR. STR.*

Topographie des Terrors **M**

LÜTZOWSTR.

KLUCK-STR.

KÖRNERSTR.

HALLESCHES

MÖCKERNSTR.

Nollendorf-pl. **U** *NOLLENDORF-PL.*

U *KURFÜRSTEN STR.*

GLEISDREIECK **M**
U

TEMPELHOFER

UFER

MÖCKERNBR.

U

BÜLOWSTR.

POTSDAMER STR.

TREBBINER STR.

MAABENSTR.

NOLLENDORFSTR.

M

Museum für Verkehr und Technik

N

MÖCKERNSTR.

GOEBENSTR.

YORCKSTR.

U

YORCKSTR.

HAGELBERGER STR.

500 metres
500 yards

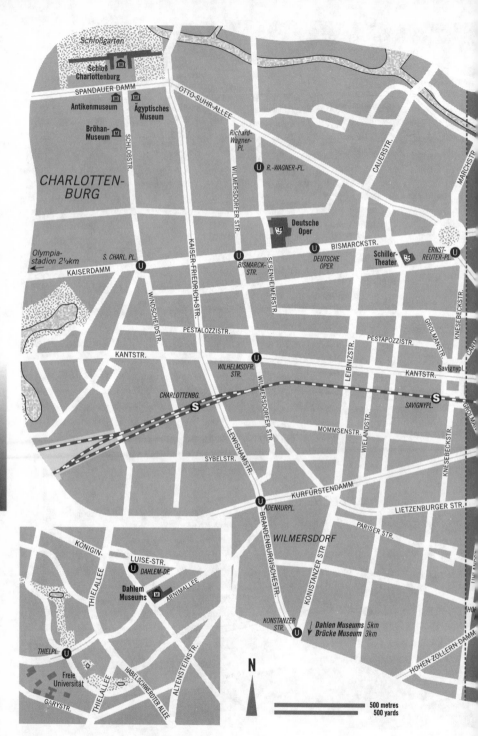

Berlin (West)

Bellevue

Spree

Tiergarten

⑤ HANSAPL.

ALTONAERSTR.

BACHSTR.

FLOTOWSTR.

Spree

MARCHSTR.

T i e r g a r t e n

Siegessäule 1

Tiergarten ⑤

STRAßE DES 17 JUNI

Neuer
See

HOFJÄGERALLEE

ERNST-
REUTER-PL.

Landwehrkanal

TIERGARTENSTR.

KNESEBECKSTR.

HARDENBERGSTR.

FASANENSTR.

CARMERSTR.

KLINGELHÖFERSTR.

VON-DER-HEYDT-STR.

☒ Bauhaus-Archiv

ghypl.

Zoologischer
Garten

Zoologischer
Garten

LÜTZOWUFER

LÜTZOWSTR.

UHLANDSTR.

ⓘ

BUDAPESTER STR.

GROLMANSTR.

⑤ Zoologischer
Garten

ⓤ ZOOLOG. GTN

Breitscheidpl.

⬜ Europa-
Center

KURFÜRSTENDAMM

SCHILLSTR.

KURFÜRSTENSTR.

Kaiser-Wilhelm-
Gedächtniskirche
(ruin)

TAUENTZIENSTR.

ⓤ KURFÜRSTENDAMM

JOACHIMSTALER STR.

Wittenbergpl.

ⓤ UHLANDSTR.

KaDeWe

WITTENBERG-
PL.

KLEISTSTR.

☒ Kathe-Kollwitz-
Museum

AUGSBURGER
STR. ⓤ

LIETZENBURGER STR.

Nollendorfpl.

NOLLENDORF-
PL. ⓤ

MAAßENSTR.

SCHAPERSTR.

FASANENSTR.

MEIEROTTOSTR.

NOLLENDORFSTR.

UHLANDSTR.

MOTZSTR.

WINTERFELDTSTR.

Winterfeldtpl.

ⓤ SPICHERN-STR.

PARISER STR.

REGENSBURGER STR.

ⓤ

V.-LUISE-PL.

LUTHER STR

GOLTZSTR.

HOHENZ.
PL.
ⓤ

NACHODSTR.

HOHENSTAUFEN-

STR.

BUNDESALLEE

MOTZSTR.

HOLSTEINISCHE STR.

NASSAUISCHE STR.

GÜNTZELSTR.

ⓤ GÜNTZELSTR.

ROSENHEIMER STR

↓ SCHÖNEBERG

office, the Europa-Center is eminently avoidable—especially the facile **Multivision Berlin**, a glossy 40-minute film on the city shown on the 2nd floor. Rather, hurry across Tauentzienstraße to **KaDeWe** (pronounced *kah-deh-veh*), short for Kaufhaus des Westens (the Department Store of the West). This is Berlin's answer to Harrods or Bloomingdale's, with a sumptuous upstairs food hall that rivals anything its competitors can offer.

Around the Tiergarten

The eastern reaches of Berlin's big inner-city park once came to a dead end up against the Wall. Today the Straße des 17 Juni, which runs through the middle of the Tiergarten, is once more a major thoroughfare connecting the eastern and western parts of the city. The park is not just a good place for a quiet stroll—along the southern edge of the gardens is a cluster of some of Berlin's best **museums**.

The Tiergarten (literally 'animal gardens') began life as a hunting estate for the Electors of Prussia. Friedrich Wilhelm the 'Drill Sergeant' turned most of the land into parade grounds (something he could barely resist doing to anything bigger than a courtyard), but in 1742 his successor, Frederick the Great, was the first to open the gardens as a public park. Today's lakes, meadows and thickets of trees are very close to the informal 19th-century design of local landscaper Peter Joseph Lenné, though the vegetation itself had to be renewed after the Second World War when the Tiergarten was bombed, denuded for firewood and planted with vegetables. You can picnic under the trees, wander about the pathways or disappear off to be alone in some forgotten corner of the park. Sunbathers show two great German enthusiasms. They all obediently lie crammed on the *Liegenwiesen* (officially designated sunbathing spots), no matter how temptingly empty adjoining stretches of grass appear, and they take off *all* their clothes.

The **Zoo** itself *(daily 9–sunset; adm DM7.50, Aquarium DM7, combined ticket DM11, children half-price)* is a pongy, dismal and expensive place at the far west end of the Tiergarten. There is little to distinguish it from other big zoos around the world, and you can get a reasonable impression of it by skirting the edges on your way to the park. On Budapester Straße, just south of the Zoo, members of the right-wing *Freikorps* attacked and murdered the leaders of the Spartacus revolt, **Karl Liebknecht** and **Rosa Luxemburg** (*see* **History** p. 45). Liebknecht was shot and thrown into a lake in the Tiergarten. Rosa Luxemburg was clubbed to death and her body dumped in the **Landwehr Canal**, which flows through the Tiergarten just behind the zoo.

The broad boulevard that runs across the Tiergarten is called the **Straße des 17 Juni**, after the date in 1953 when East German workers revolted against the occupying Soviets. (The Russians sent in tanks to crush the insurrection—*see* **History** p. 48). In the middle of the avenue is the **Siegessäule**, a 67m-high column topped with a gilded Winged Victory, yet another boast of Prussian military success. The monument makes an eye-catching orientation point, and you can climb to the top for one of the best **views** to be had over Berlin *(Apr–Nov Mon 1–6, Tues–Sun 9–6; adm DM2)*. The Straße des 17 Juni stretches on to the **Brandenburg Gate** (*see* below).

The Tiergarten Museums

Soon after the Landwehr Canal leaves the Tiergarten, it passes the **Bauhaus-Archiv** at Klingelhöferstr. 14 *(Tues–Sun 11–7; adm DM4)*. The Bauhaus movement (*see* **The Arts and Culture** p. 64) is much maligned as the progenitor of ugly 1960s concrete and glass boxes. In fact the school (founded by Walter Gropius in 1919) fostered a diversity of crafts from weaving to set design, and attracted artists of the calibre of Kandinsky, Moholy-Nagy and Paul Klee. The museum contains a superb collection of Bauhaus work, from the iron-framed furniture (much imitated by Habitat and IKEA), to tea services, bright textiles and Oskar Schlemmer's bizarre costume designs. There are also paintings and graphics by the group's major artists and illustrations of work by the architects Gropius and Mies van der Rohe (the museum is housed in a Gropius building).

A little further east, along Von-der-Heydt-Straße, is Berlin's biggest wasted architectural opportunity, the **Kulturforum**. Two concert halls, the State Library and a cluster of important museums occupy a prime site between the Tiergarten and the Landwehr Canal, but the buildings bear no architectural relation to each other (they are even oriented in different directions) and the land between them—which could be filled with greenery and outdoor cafés—lies barren and unused, except as a makeshift car park.

The first museum that you come across if you have followed the canal from the Bauhaus-Archiv, is the **Neue Nationalgalerie** *(Tues–Fri 9–5, Sat and Sun 10–5; adm free; Bus 29 or 83)*. The building is the work of the most inspired of the Bauhaus architects, Mies van der Rohe (creator of the Seagram building in New York). It is an exercise in classic simplicity, with sheer glass walls edged by clean, straight black lines. Inside, the bright, airplane-hangar-like ground floor is normally used for temporary exhibitions. Downstairs is an untaxing collection of 19th- and 20th-century art. There is a smattering of French Impressionists, some Picasso and Léger. The highlights are generally the German works— good paintings by the 19th-century artists Anselm Feuerbach and Arnold Böcklin, and some exceptional canvases from the 1920s and 1930s by Max Beckmann, Otto Dix, Ernst Ludwig Kirchner and George Grosz, including the latter's famous *Stützen der Gesellschaft* ('Pillars of Society', 1926), a grotesque parody of the Weimar Establishment. Just outside is the **Matthaïkirche**, a 19th-century red-brick church—a dwarfed oddity in this very 20th-century landscape. In the spruce white interior there are often exhibitions by local artists.

Opposite the Neue Nationalgalerie is the **Staatsbibliothek** (State Library) *(Mon–Fri 9–9, Sat 9–5)*, an enormous, gold-clad building that featured in local director Wim Wenders' film *Wings of Desire*. A little further north, up Potsdamer Straße, is another gold-clad monstrosity, this time with wings. It is easy to see how the **Philharmonie**, home to the Berlin Philharmonic under its famous conductor Herbert von Karajan (until his retirement in 1989), got the nickname 'Karajani's Circus'. The smaller **Kammermusiksaal** (Chamber Music Hall) next door is very much in the same idiom. Part of the complex houses the **Musikinstrumenten-Museum** *(Tues–Sat 9–5, Sun 10–5; adm DM4)*, a museum of musical instruments that focuses mainly on keyboards from ancient dulcimers to flashy Wurlitzers and early synthesizers. There is a Stradivari violin and a 2m-high contrabass saxophone. Everything is very clinically presented, though period recordings played through the headphone sets dotted around the exhibition space do help to give you some sense of atmosphere. Otherwise all is under a deathly hush—until some wag puts a coin in the mechanical jazz orchestra in the café downstairs.

To the west of the Philharmonie is the **Kunstgewerbemuseum** (Museum of Applied Arts) *(Tues–Fri 9–5, Sat and Sun 10–5; adm DM4)*, a charmless new building that houses a truly outstanding collection of precious objects such as jewellery, watches, reliquaries and priceless knick-knacks, mostly amassed as Prussian war booty. On the top floor you will find exhibits from the Renaissance to Rococo, the ground floor is mainly medieval, and the 20th-century collection is in the basement. The medieval section is the most impressive. You can see almost the entire contents of the **Welf dynasty treasury** from St Blasius in Brunswick—superb 11th to 15th-century goldsmithry including the **Welf Cross**, encrusted with jewels and poised on a delicate silver base. Also here is the **Lüneberg Municipal Silver**, the richest surviving treasure of its kind in Germany. Elsewhere you will find craft of mind-boggling intricacy by famous Nuremburg gold- and silversmiths, Venetian goblets and Dresden porcelain. The collection is rounded off by a display of Jugendstil and Art Deco jewellery, ceramics and objets d'art.

Next door to the Kunstgewerbemuseum, a new 'Museum of European Art' is under construction. The finishing date is uncertain, but if it has opened by the time you visit Berlin, it is likely that you will find the contents of the Dahlem Picture Gallery (*see* below) and also some eastern Berlin galleries relocated here. This will complete the plans for the Kulturforum, and this soulless clump of unfortunate buildings will have undeservingly become one of Europe's foremost museum complexes.

The Mitte

The Mitte—the 'city centre'—at the eastern end of the Tiergarten, beat the drum and blew the trumpet for the Prussian Empire. Here are the palaces, the pompous state buildings, an entire island of museums and the famous promenade of Unter den Linden. Here, too, is the grim Reichstag, so redolent of the Nazi regime, and chunks of the Wall that remind you of more recent oppression.

The DDR rulers built gargantuan concrete edifices on the old bombsites to make East Berlin a showpiece capital, while many of the older buildings slipped into disrepair. Today a massive reconstruction effort is wiping out most of the traces of the death strip that lined the

Wall, and is knocking the Mitte back into a shape considered more appropriate to an epi-centre of government.

The Brandenburg Gate and the Reichstag

The Straße des 17 Juni passes the rather stiff **Soviet War Memorial** (a monument to the members of the Red Army who fell at the taking of Berlin), and leads on to the **Brandenburg Gate**.

The Brandenburg Gate (built in 1791) has been the focus of so many important events in Berlin's turbulent history that it carries some very mismatched symbolic baggage. Architect Carl Gotthard Langhans modelled the arch on the entrance to the Parthenon in Athens, intending the temple-like appearance as a symbol of peace after the rather eventful reign of Frederick the Great. Two years later the gate was topped with the **Quadriga**—a statue of Nike in her chariot—and became a victory totem instead. Prussian hubris was deflated when this new role of triumphal arch was exploited by a conquering Napoleon, who marched between the columns in 1806 and took the Quadriga back with him to Paris. The gate (with the Quadriga back in place) was the rallying point for left-wing revolutionaries in 1848 and 1918, but also the scene of Nazi torch-light processions in the 1930s. Cut off just behind the Wall during the Cold War, the Brandenburg Gate came to stand for the division of Berlin, and then—on that night of tearful partying and hugging in 1989—heralded the re-unification of Germany as it was flashed up on TV screens all over the world.

Today traffic rushes under the arch again, as the Straße des 17 Juni becomes Unter den Linden. But one curious divide still exists. On the eastern side of the gate traders have set up makeshift stalls where they sell old Soviet badges and military caps, Russian dolls and cameras and chips off the Wall. An invisible barrier stops them spreading over to the western side.

In the wasteland that now stretches southwards along the path of Wall, you can see the lump of concrete that marks the site of **Hitler's Bunker**. This is where the Führer shot himself and his bride of one day, Eva Braun, on 30 April 1945, when Soviet tanks were just a few blocks away. Loyal lieutenants burned and buried the bodies, but rumours persist that Hitler did not commit suicide at all. One of the oddest stories is that Soviet authorities identified the charred corpse by comparing dental records, and that Hitler's teeth are still stashed away in a museum somewhere in east Berlin. The bunker was sealed up after the war to prevent its becoming a neo-Nazi shrine.

The **Reichstag**, just north of the Brandenburg Gate, also has a chequered history, a parlia-ment building which has seldom lived up to the dedication on its façade—*Dem Deutschen Volke*: To the German People. For the first 20 years after it was built in 1894, the Neo-Renaissance building was home to a puppet parliament of the Prussian aristocracy. Wilhelm II dismissed the Reichstag as a 'gossip shop', but it was from here that the SDP deputy announced the Kaiser's abdication, and the formation of the German Republic, in 1918. What followed, however, was a domino-line of collapsing governments, based not here but in Weimar (*see* **History** p. 45). Hitler relocated to the Reichstag in 1933, but destroyed any semblance of democracy when he blamed the fire which swept through the building on the night of 27 February 1933 on a simple-minded Dutch communist. The blaze was probably started by the Nazis themselves, but Hitler used it as an excuse to ban the communist party and later to take on dictatorial powers.

The Reichstag is soon to close for renovations in preparation for the grand transfer of government to Berlin from Bonn (though rumour has it that many of the senators would prefer to stay put in the quieter provincial town). Until then you will be able to see a bland multimedia (mainly photographic) exhibition on **Questions in German History** *(Tues–Sun 10–5; adm free)*. The questions are none too probing and, like the answers, are all in German (though you can get an English taped accompaniment for DM2).

Unter den Linden

Elector Friedrich Wilhelm planted the first trees along Unter den Linden ('Under the Lime Trees') when it was laid out as a bridle path leading to the Tiergarten just after the Thirty Years' War. By the 19th century the trees had grown to a majestic size. Friedrich Karl Schinkel, the architect of Neoclassical Berlin, added some splendid buildings, and Unter den Linden became the hub of Imperial Prussia. In the 1930s Hitler mowed down the trees to make a parade ground. The communists replanted half of them, but it was only after the opening of the Wall that the mile-long avenue once again got its full complement of limes. Today Unter den Linden can look a bit bedraggled, especially in winter, and it roars with traffic, but the grand old boulevard is swiftly being smartened up and elevated to its former state of grace.

A few hundred metres eastwards along the avenue, on the left, is the heavy Neoclassical **Staatsbibliothek** (State Library), which opened in 1910. Once famed for its collection (some 6 million books), it stagnated when its acquisitions from the West were minimal after the war, and its future direction is uncertain. In the middle of the avenue outside is a 19th-century **equestrian statue of Frederick the Great**, with some of the artists and philosophers he patronized depicted on the pedestal (but not Voltaire, who had had a rather bumpy fall from favour—*see* p. 499).

Next door to the library is the **Humboldt-Universität**, an august institution founded in 1806 by the philologist and education reformer Wilhelm von Humboldt. Marx and Engels studied here, and the Brothers Grimm and Einstein were once on the staff. The university had a strong liberal tradition, which is why Nazi propaganda minister Joseph Goebbels chose **Bebelplatz** (the square opposite) for the notorious **Buchverbrennung** (burning of books) on 11 May 1933. Thousands of 'immoral and destructive documents and books'—including works by Freud, Einstein, Marx, Heinrich Heine and Thomas Mann—went up in smoke as a prelude to Nazi persecution of intellectuals and Jewish authors.

The restrained design of the Humboldt Universität stands in contrast to the other buildings on Bebelplatz. On the western side is the **Alte Bibliothek**, the former royal library, known locally as the *Kommode* (chest of drawers) because of a pot-bellied façade strongly reminiscent of Baroque bombé furniture. Opposite is the **Staatsoper**, Prussia's first public opera house, built in 1743 by Frederick the Great's chief architect, Georg von Knobelsdorff. Knobelsdorff based his design on a simple Corinthian temple, but couldn't resist adding a few Rococo flourishes. Behind the theatre you can see the enormous dome of the **St Hedwigs-Kathedrale**, Berlin's first (and for some time only) Roman Catholic church. This is another Knobelsdorff project, begun in 1747 in imitation of the Pantheon in Rome. The architect's grand scheme ran into trouble, and the dome was finally completed only in the 19th century. The church was bombed during the Second World War, and has been restored with a modern, clinical (but nonetheless impressive) interior. Next door to the Staatsoper is the **Palais Unter den Linden**, a 17th-century building with a Baroque façade. At the beginning of the 20th century this was a famous exhibition space for modern art—particularly for the Expressionists. The Nazis closed it down in 1933, declaring its contents 'degenerate'. Nowadays the palace houses the grand **Operncafé** (*see* **Eating and Drinking** below). On the other side of Unter den Linden (next to the Humboldt-Universität) is Schinkel's first major commission, the **Neue Wache**, a guard house built in the form of a Roman temple in 1818. Since 1918 it has contained Germany's tomb of the unknown soldier. An unknown resistance fighter was added after the last war, and the communists later declared it a monument to the victims of fascism. Today it also commemorates those who fell prey to Stalinism. Next door is a fine Baroque building, the **Zeughaus** (arsenal), dating from 1695, nowadays home to temporary exhibitions on German history.

South of Unter den Linden: the Gendarmenmarkt and the Wall

If you take Charlottenstraße to the south of Unter den Linden, just before the Statue of Frederick the Great, a short walk will bring you to the **Gendarmenmarkt** (formerly the Platz der Akademie) which, after a recent facelift, is the leading contender for the title of Berlin's most elegant square. In the centre stands the **Schauspielhaus**, a copy of a Schinkel theatre (the original was bombed in 1945). It is now used for classical concerts. On fine summer evenings the tall double doors are thrown open at the end of a performance, and the audience spills down the wide stairway to stand chatting in the square. On some nights the Gendarmenmarkt itself is the auditorium, and swells with punters who gather for an open-air concert.

The Schauspielhaus is flanked by two matching churches, known as the **Deutscher Dom** and the **Französischer Dom** (the German and French cathedrals), both built in the 1780s. The churches' twin cupolas are modelled on two similar churches on the Piazza del Popolo in Rome. One church served the German Lutheran community, the other was for the French Huguenots. The Protestant Huguenots came to Berlin after 1685, when Elector Friedrich Wilhelm had declared religious tolerance by the Edict of Potsdam. Soon they made up nearly one third of Berlin's population, and gave Prussia a tremendous economic and cultural boost. Inside the Französischer Dom is a small **Huguenot Museum** *(Tues, Wed and Sat 10–5, Thurs 10–6, Sun 11.30–5; adm DM2)*. You can also climb the **tower** *(daily 10–6; adm free, no lift)* for a good view across the square and Unter den Linden.

Off the northern end of the Gendarmenmarkt, along Französiche Straße, is the **Friedrichwerdersche Kirche**, a church by Schinkel in an uncharacteristic Neo-Gothic (rather than Neoclassical) style. Inside the church is the **Schinkelmuseum** *(daily 10–6; adm DM4)*, a collection of period sculpture and a display on the life of Berlin's most revered architect—but not really worth the admission fee.

Further down Charlottenstraße, and back west along the frantically busy Leipziger Straße, you come to one of the last bits of the **Wall** left standing. The western side of the wall was covered in witty graffiti and vivid murals. (There are several books of photographs of what amounted at times to an art form—now crunched up by bulldozers and souvenir seekers.) The eastern side of the wall, however, was lined with a wide 'death strip' of mines, tank traps and barbed wire. Guards with vicious dogs patrolled the length of the wall, while others kept watch from tall towers, machine guns at the ready to shoot anyone who tried to cross. The wall itself was painted white to throw escapees' silhouettes into sharp relief.

At the western end of Leipziger Straße is Potsdamer Platz, once the busiest square in Europe, lined with hotels and cafés. Potsdamer Platz was flattened during the war, and then became a desolate stretch of no-man's land behind the Wall. Today traffic thunders around the circus again, but the surrounding landscape is still bleak. Daimler-Benz bought up most of the land soon after the wall came down, but the company's plans to build a new customer services division there are meeting strong local opposition. Most Berliners would prefer something of the old spirit of Potsdamer Platz to be revived.

From Leipziger Straße you can also see the big neon letters spelling Axel Springer Verlag on top of a concrete skyscraper. The late Axel Springer—the powerful right-wing founder of the publishing empire responsible for Germany's most sensationalist rag, the *Bild*—intentionally built his headquarters right up against the Wall. In Cold War days the lights also flashed the message *Berlin bleibt frei* (Berlin remains free) across to the hapless Ossis.

Axel Springer

 The late Axel Springer (he died in 1985) was the creator of *Bild Zeitung*, commonly referred to as just *Bild*, a sensationalist right-wing newspaper, which became Europe's biggest-selling tabloid with a circulation of 4.5 million. Springer was one of the editors permitted by the Allies to publish after the Second World War. Starting with a radio programme guide, then a Hamburg evening paper, he moved on, in 1952, to launch the *Bild Zeitung*, eventually building up the largest publishing empire in Europe. He was fiercely anti-communist and carried out a vendetta against Willi Brandt because of Brandt's liberal Ostpolitik. The *Bild* never ceased reminding its readers that the Chancellor was born illegitimate and had returned to Germany after the war in an Allied uniform. During the 1968 riots the *Bild* urged respectable Germans to take the law into their own hands. It was a *Bild* reader who shot the student leader Rudi Dutschke. The *Bild* still thrives on a diet of outrageous stories and opinions that pander to popular prejudice. But in the liberal segment of German society Springer's death goes largely unlamented.

South of Leipziger Straße, where Friedrichstaße crosses Zimmerstraße, you come to the site of **Checkpoint Charlie**—the main border crossing point for foreigners in and out of the

DDR. (The border post gets its name from the military alphabet. Checkpoints Alpha and Bravo were on the outskirts of Berlin). Checkpoint Charlie was a prefabricated observation hut that was erected in the middle of Friedrichstraße in October 1961. A dispute over the Western Allies' rights to move freely through the divided city had broken out. Both sides moved tanks to the border on Friedrichstraße, and for three tense weeks the world teetered on the brink of another war. The Eastern Bloc backed down, but Checkpoint Charlie remained, until a crane whisked the hut away in 1990. Nowadays all you can see is the top of a watchtower, more bits of the wall and the famous sign that warned in four languages: 'You are leaving the American sector'.

Far more interesting is the nearby **Haus am Checkpoint Charlie** at Friedrichstr. 44 *(daily 9am–10pm; adm DM7.50)*, a fascinating museum (with English texts) detailing the history of the Berlin Wall and various attempts at escape. You can see a homemade helicopter, tiny cars adapted for hiding escapees and also less subtle methods—such as a concrete-lined van that just barged through the border boom. Tunnelling was a popular method of getting out—until the DDR started planting deep mines. You can read stories of people who escaped along sewers, of a U-Bahn driver who took a trainful of his family and friends out along some disused track, and a group of septuagenarians who dug a tunnel big enough for their wives to walk upright in. Not all these tales had happy endings, however. At least 80 people died in their attempts to escape to the West.

From Checkpoint Charlie you can trace the line of the Wall westwards (down Zimmerstraße) to the **Topography of Terror** *(Tues–Sun 10–6; adm free)*, a patch of scrubby mounds and rubble which are all that remains of the headquarters of Hitler's SS (the Nazi militia) and the Gestapo (the secret police). Here people were interrogated and tortured, mail was intercepted, telephones were tapped and files were kept on anyone thought to be an enemy of the Third Reich. At one end, a prefabricated building has been built over the former Gestapo cellars. Accompanying this chilling memorial is a bland display of photographs and biographies of some Gestapo victims.

The grand building next door is the **Martin-Gropius-Bau** *(Tues–Sun 10–8; adm varies)*, named after its architect (not the Bauhaus Gropius, but his uncle). This is now Berlin's main venue for travelling art exhibitions. Whatever is on show, the magnificent tent-like **interior** is worth a visit in itself. On the first floor is the **Berlinische Galerie** *(Tues–Sun 10–8; adm DM4)*, an excellent permanent exhibition of paintings of the city by such residents as Lovis Corinth, Emil Nolde, Otto Dix and George Grosz.

Marx-Engels-Platz and the Cathedral

Unter den Linden comes to an end at the Schloßbrücke, a bridge designed by Schinkel which crosses onto an island formed by the River Spree. To the right of the bridge is Marx-Engels-Platz, once the site of the Kaiser's city palace. The communists blew up what remained of this symbol of Prussian militarism in the 1950s, and put up one of their own—the **Palast der Republik**, a giant, reflecting bronze glass box that contained the parliament chamber, bars, restaurants and a bowling alley—and mounds of asbestos insulation. Because of the latter the building is being demolished. At the time of writing controversy rages over what should replace it. A group of French artists (financed by private German money) have put up a full-size painted vinyl trompe l'oeil of the old Stadtschloß in a bid to convince Berliners that the old palace should be reconstructed. Most locals are not so sure.

The northern part of Marx-Engels-Platz, known as the Lustgarten (Pleasure Garden), is the forecourt to the grandiose **Berliner Dom**, a domed pile of a building in the style of the Italian High Renaissance. It took battalions of artists and craftspeople 11 years to build the cathedral (between 1894 and 1905), and a similar army to wrest it back from war damage and decades of neglect between 1990 and 1993. The gigantic Corinthian pillars, lavish gilded stucco and sheer scale of the interior combine with awesome effect. Visitors creep about between the pews, made painfully conscious of their lowly position on the Hierarchy of Being. From a separate entrance to the right of the main portal the **Imperial Stairway** would sweep the Kaiser up to a celestial gallery with a private view of the High Altar.

The Museum Island

The northernmost tip of this island in the Spree is known as the **Museum Insel** (Museum Island), a peninsula set aside by Friedrich Wilhelm IV in 1841 as 'a sanctuary of art and science'. The museum complex that grew up here is a rich architectural feast. Elegant Neoclassical buildings were linked by tree-lined streets and colonnades, with the Spree slipping quietly past on either side. Sadly, the DDR didn't look after the buildings very well, so for the moment you'll have to use your imagination as you pick your way to the exhibitions through a sprawling construction site. What is more, you are sure to find some museums closed and whole sections of others shut down for restoration. The glittering collections that were displayed here at the beginning of the century were stashed away in cellars and bunkers all over Berlin during the Second World War. Much of the booty stayed in the West when the Wall went up, and it is not yet clear what these museums will house when they are eventually renovated.

The first one you come to is the **Altes Museum**, which stretches across the top of the Lustgarten. This is perhaps Schinkel's finest achievement—87m wide, with a portico of 18 Ionic pillars and walls covered with Roman-inspired patterns, yet somehow preserving a temple-like harmony and calm. The Altes Museum is closed at the time of writing, and will probably house travelling exhibitions when it re-opens. The **Neues Museum**, just behind it, isn't scheduled to open again until the year 2000. The **Nationalgalerie** (Wed–Sun 9–5; adm DM2), next door to the Neues Museum, at present houses only 19th-century painting, with sparkling pieces by Lovis Corinth, Anselm Feuerbach and Max Liebermann, as well as surprise canvases by Cézanne, Degas and other French Impressionist painters.

Around the back of the National Galerie is the one museum on the island which shouldn't be missed—the **Pergamonmuseum** (Wed–Sun 9–5; adm DM4). When the Prussian adventurers plundered ancient lands they weren't content just with a few shards of broken pot, the odd marble torso or well-wrapped mummy. They brought back whole parts of cities. Star of the show, and the piece that gives the museum its name, is the **Pergamon Altar** in the antiquities section. The altar (the size of a respectable temple) was built in homage to Athena between 180 and 160 BC in the powerful eastern Aegean city-state of Pergamon. Archeologist Carl Humann excavated the altar towards the end of the 19th century and spent some 20 years reconstructing it in Germany. A broad staircase sweeps up to a row of Ionic columns way above your head, past a frieze that depicts a writhing wrestling match between the giants and the gods.

Also in the antiquities section, and scarcely less impressive, is the marble **Market Gate of the City of Miletus**, built by the Romans in Asia Minor in AD 120. Highlight of the Middle-East department is the **Ishtar Gate** (580 BC), from Nebuchadnezzar's Babylon—an enormous structure of blue-glazed tiles decorated with yellow horses, lions, bulls and dragon-like *sirrushes*. This was at the head of a processional way that led into the heart of Babylon and the city's ziggurat. In the Islamic section you can see a full 45m of the wall of the **Palace of Mshatta**, an 8th-century desert fort in what is now Jordan. And this is just for starters. The museum contains a wealth of other treasures: more arches, gates and reconstructed rooms and streets, as well as splendid mosaics, priceless Turkish carpets, and the more customary array of pots, statues and jewellery. If all the sections are open, the Pergamon museum can easily swallow up an entire afternoon, and even then you might want to come back for more.

The last museum on the island is the **Bodemuseum** *(Wed–Sun 9–5; adm DM2)*, a collection of antiquities rather overshadowed by the Pergamon next door. The best **Egyptian** exhibits ended up in Charlottenburg after the war (*see* p. 496), though the unique papyrus collection stayed behind. The museum's strongest point is the **Early Christian and Byzantine** section, which includes a 6th-century mosaic from St Michele in Ravenna and a collection of icons. There is also an uneventful array of 14th- to 18th-century European art.

The Nikolaiviertel

Behind the erstwhile Palast der Republik is the tiny Nikolaiviertel, one of the oldest parts of town, reached by following Rathausstraße off Marx-Engels-Platz. Actually, most of the Nikolaiviertel consists of buildings moved here from other spots around the city, or ersatz medieval houses put up in the 1980s. The quarter is a quiet, shady (if a little twee) corner of pubs and cafés, flash boutiques, jewellers—and even a Japanese delicatessen. At its heart is the **Nikolaikirche** *(Tues–Sun 10–6; adm DM2)*, one of the few genuine buildings still standing. The church goes back to the 13th century and is where Coelln and Berlin first decided to join forces in 1307 (*see* p. 470).

Also worth checking out are two inns, the **Knoblauchhaus** (genuine 18th-century) and **Zum Nußbaum** (Medieval pastiche—see **Eating and Drinking** below) and the **Handwerkenmuseum** at Mühlendamm 5 *(Tues–Sun 10–5; adm DM2)*, a small museum containing reconstructions of tradesmen's workshops and living quarters.

Around Alexanderplatz

Northeast of the Nikolaiviertel (still on Rathausstraße) is the **Rotes Rathaus** (Red Town Hall), so named for the colour of its bricks rather than its politics. It was built in the 19th century in imitation of an Italian Renaissance palace. A crimson carpet sweeps you up the stairway into vaulted foyers and high-ceilinged halls. No-one seems to mind if you wander in for a look. Since October 1991 this has been the seat of Berlin's Senate. Like Hamburg and Bremen, Berlin is an independent city-state within the Federal Republic.

Across a formally laid-out park is the **Marienkirche**, most of which dates back to the 18th century, though parts are 400 years older. Inside you can see an impressive 23m-long fresco of the Dance of Death, probably painted after the plague of 1484. Looming over the small church, in somewhat ridiculous contrast, is the 365m-tall **Television Tower**, topped with a giant revolving sphere. The sun, when reflected in the glass of this ball, forms a flaming cross which can be seen for miles around the city. (West Berliners used to call it the 'Pope's revenge'.) You can take a lift up to the revolving café or observation platform for a **view** that on clear days can extend as far as 40km *(May–Sept daily 8am–11pm, Oct–Apr 9–11; second and fourth Tues in month 1–11; adm DM5)*.

A few minutes' walk further along Rathausstraße brings you to the vast concreted expanse of **Alexanderplatz**, a barren, windswept square edged by ugly 1960s architecture. It was here that a million East-Berliners gathered on 4 November 1989 for the **demonstration** that led up to the opening of the borders. There is nothing, however, to remind you of *Berlin Alexanderplatz*, Alfred Döblin's evocative novel about the Weimar era. A few street traders liven up the scene a little, but otherwise the only object of any interest is the **Weltzeituhr** (World Time Clock) an odd 1960s contraption which tells the time in places all over the world (a fairly pointless exercise for East-Berliners, who used to use it as a rendezvous point, but who couldn't travel to the other end of their own city).

The Old Jewish Quarter

Monbijoustraße, the road that crosses the tip of the Museum Island, leads on to Oranienburger Straße, the main axis of what was Berlin's Jewish Quarter. Most of the city's large pre-war Jewish community was completely integrated into the population, but here, in the run-down **Scheunenviertel** (literally 'barn quarter') lived the new immigrants—poor families who had fled pogroms in eastern Europe and were still struggling to make a new life for themselves. Hitler used this area as a special scapegoat and it suffered badly on *Kristallnacht.* The death camps silenced the Scheunenviertel. The handful of Berlin's Jews that survived mostly went to live abroad.

But now, something of a revival is happening. The **Neue Synagog** (which was opened by the Kaiser himself in 1866, but bombed during the war) is being restored. The bright gilded domes are already finished, and soon the building will re-open as a Jewish community centre. You can buy salmon bagels around the corner, and there is already a kosher restaurant and an Israeli café. Oranienburger Straße is also becoming a trendy hotspot. It is best to visit at night when the street throngs with punks, fashion-victims, heavy-metal freaks and hookers. Nearby is the wildly popular **Chamäleon Varieté** (*see* **Entertainment and Nightlife** below). Up the top end of Oranienburger Straße is **Tacheles** (Yiddish for 'straight talk'—see **Entertainment and Nightlife** below), a deserted department store that has been occupied by artists, and is famous for its wild parties. During the day, if you don't look too conventional, and are not easily identifiable as a tourist, you can wander around for a look into the studios and galleries.

At the eastern end of Oranienburger Straße (turn left into Große Hamburger Straße) is the **Old Jewish Cemetery**, which was desecrated by the Nazis. Alongside is a Jewish Old Age Home, which dates back to the 17th century, and was the deportation point for over 55,000 of Berlin's Jewish community on the way to the concentration camps.

At the other end of Oranienburger Straße, after turning right into Chausseestraße, you will find the **Brecht-Haus** *(Tues, Wed and Fri 10–12, Thurs 10–12 and 5–7, Sat 9.30–11.30 and 12.30–2; adm free)*, the playwright's last home. Bertolt Brecht (1898–1956), best known for *The Threepenny Opera, Mother Courage and her Children* and *The Life and Times of Galileo*, revolutionized western dramatic theory and developed a sparse performing style that became much imitated in the latter part of this century. A committed communist, he came to live in this house in 1953, a few years after returning to East Germany from wartime exile in America. He died here just three years later. You can see the desk where he worked and the narrow bed on which he died, but the main point of interest is the **archive**, for aficionados only.

Around the Mitte

Just to the south of the Mitte, **Kreuzberg** was the stomping ground of West Berlin's anarchists and struggling artists, and home to its immigrant community of Turkish *Gastarbeiter*. Since the *Wende*, what was once an isolated patch of land in an odd corner made by the Wall is suddenly prime real estate. Kreuzberg seems to be losing its edge as the Turks, squatters, painters and punks head out to cheaper suburbs such as **Prenzlauer Berg**, north-east of the Mitte. For the moment, however, Kreuzberg is still the place to go for a taste of the other side of Berlin—the side that only begins ticking after dark.

Kreuzberg

Kreuzberg falls into two parts. The more comfortable, conventional **western quarter** (north of Platz der Luftbrücke U-Bahn station) is the home of woolly but affluent Greens, university staff and downwardly mobile advertising executives. Here the best parts to explore are the lush Victoria Park (with the hill and cross that give Kreuzberg its name), the sloping streets of gentrified 19th-century houses to the west of the park, and the cafés around Yorckstraße. The **eastern quarter** (around U-Bahn stations Kotbusser Tor and Schlesisches Tor) is the more wicked, wild and exciting half. Here the streets are filled with delightfully un-German cooking smells, the night spots are open till dawn, and, behind the doors of the squatters' houses, plots have been hatched from Baader-Meinhof terrorist attacks to the ritualized annual May Day riots. Oranienstraße, the main drag, is lined with cafés, galleries and alternative clothes shops, few of which show signs of life before noon.

The different sides of Kreuzberg were for years referred to locally by their respective postcodes (61 for the west and 36 for the east). By the time you read this book, however, the Federal bureaucracy will have 'simplified' Germany's postal code system. The old 5400 codes will have been replaced by 26,400 new ones. Some towns with just a handful of residents will have over 20 codes, single streets might have two or three—but suburbs or areas will have no general, easily identifiable code at all. What people will then call Kreuzberg 36, is not clear. But by that time everyone will probably have moved to Prenzlauer Berg to make way for offices and expensive apartments.

Museums in Kreuzberg

Although Kreuzberg only really comes alive at night, there are a few daytime sights to see. Top among these is the **Berlin-Museum** at Lindenstr. 14, near Mehringplatz *(Tues–Sun 11–6; adm DM4)*. This is an ideal rainy afternoon destination, cluttered with mementos of Berlin's history from a slab of the Wall to reminders of the Holocaust. Look out for the **Kaiserpanorama**, a giant stereoscope that surrounds you with 3-D pictures (usually of old Berlin), and the interesting collection of 19th- and early 20th-century toys. A little further west along the Landwehr Canal you come to the **Museum für Verkehr und Technik** (Museum of Transport and Technology) at Trebbiner Str. 9 *(Tues–Fri 9–5.30, Sat and Sun 10–6; adm DM4)*, a sprawling complex choc-a-bloc with Fokker triplanes, steam-cars, vintage limousines and ancient locomotives. The technology section, especially, is interestingly presented with plenty of hands-on opportunities to play with computers, work printing presses or experiment with the laws of physics.

Prenzlauer Berg

Like Kreuzberg, Prenzlauer Berg (commonly referred to as Prenzlberg) was once a crowded working-class suburb, but here the narrow, cobbled alleys of tall 19th-century tenements have survived. This crumbling, tumbledown quarter (watch out for plummeting balconies) became a magnet for dissidents under the old GDR regime. Today it is a vibrant, spontaneous, mercurial part of Berlin. The grey, rather forlorn streets are breaking out in cafés and night clubs. Attempts to squat houses here were quickly quashed by the police in 1990, but alternative Berlin, squeezed out of areas such as Kreuzberg, seems to be making Prenzlauer Berg its new home.

The most convenient places to arrive at are the Eberswalder Straße or Schönhauser Allee U-Bahn stations. Then wander along **Schönhauser Allee** or head for **Kollwitzplatz**, a few blocks east. Schönhauser Allee is the main shopping area in Prenzlauer Berg, and you'll find the best cafés and bars in the narrow streets to the east, and around Kollwitzplatz. South of Kollwitzplatz, at Kollwitzstr. 59 (formerly Weißenburger Str. 25), is the place where the artist Käthe Kollwitz lived (*see* p. 477). The house didn't survive the war, but the spot is marked by a sculpture, *Die Mutter*, based on one of her drawings. Also along Kollwitzstraße is a **Jewish Cemetery**, once the most prestigious in Berlin, but desecrated by the Nazis.

The smartly restored **Husemannstraße**, north of Kollwitzplatz, comes as a surprise. It was given the edge on its rundown neighbours in 1987, when East Berlin authorities tarted it up as part of Berlin's 750th birthday celebrations. The **Friseurmuseum** (Hairdressing Museum) *(Tues 10–12 and 1–5, Wed 10–12 and 1–6; adm DM4)* at No. 8 is a quirky collection of anything associated with hairdressing from ancient times to the present day, including some stylish period models and frightening contraptions for drying and curling hair. Nearby, at No. 12, the **Berliner Arbeiterleben um 1900** (Museum of Working Class Life around 1900) *(Tues, Thurs and Sat 11–6, Wed 10–8; adm DM2)* gives you a good idea of what life was like in these old tenements.

Charlottenburg and Dahlem

Some of Berlin's most dazzling museums are in Charlottenburg, just west of the centre, and in the southern suburb of Dahlem. Charlottenburg also offers a Schloß and fine gardens, but when the main picture gallery moves from Dahlem to the Kulturforum, the museums that remain may not be enough to lure you so far out of town.

Schloß Charlottenburg

Schloß Charlottenburg *(Tues–Fri 9–5, Sat and Sun 10–5; adm DM8, bus 109, 54, 74)* ranks as one of Berlin's most beautiful buildings. The Rococo palace was commissioned by the self-aggrandizing Elector Friedrich III (later King Friedrich I) in 1695, but it was his wife Queen Sophie Charlotte, a woman of taste, wit and intelligence, who kept a restraining hand on the design. The Schloß was named after the Queen following her death (from a throat infection) in 1705, but later Friedrich ran out of funds and couldn't complete it. When he died in 1713, the fresco painters and masons were laid off, and the garden was turned into a cabbage patch. In the 1740s Frederick the Great re-started work on the Schloß, but was soon diverted by his own project at Potsdam (*see* below). For another half a century successive artists and architects all did their bit, but their work went up in smoke during the Second World War. Today's Schloß is a skilful reconstruction.

The long, pale yellow building rises in the centre to a single modest cupola, crowned with a gold figure of Fortune—a gay 1950s version of the original, that swivels about like a weather vane. You can see the **interior** by guided tour only (in German, though you can get a written English text). The most remarkable sights here are the **Porcelain Cabinet** (where the walls are covered with mirrors and gold leaf and then lined from ceiling to floor with Chinese porcelain plates and vases); the more modest **White Room**, where sunlight floods in to pick out just the occasional spot of gilding; and the adjoining Concert Room, which has some superb work by the 18th-century Rococo painter **Antoine Watteau**.

In the wings of the palace you will find the **Galerie der Romantik** *(same times; adm DM4 or included in Schloß ticket price)*, an excellent collection of German Romantic painting ranging from Caspar David Friedrich's dreamy landscapes to the sharper, Pre-Raphaelite clarity of paintings by Carl Blechen and Friedrich Overbeck. Behind the Schloß, a formal French garden extends for some way before relaxing into the homely chaos of an English park. This is a favourite summer walking spot for Berliners (the gardens stay open until 9pm in the summer).

The Charlottenburg Museums

The twin-domed Neoclassical buildings on either side of the junction opposite the Schloß were originally an officers' mess, but now house museums. On the left is the **Ägyptisches Museum** (Egyptian Museum) *(Mon–Thurs 9–5, Sat and Sun 10–5; adm DM4)*, which landed the best of the Egyptian antiquities previously exhibited in the east. Absolute star of the show is the 3000-year-old **Bust of Nefertiti**, wife of the pharoah Akhenaton. Nefertiti's fine bone structure, high cheekbones and steady, melting gaze are quite bewitching. The bust was originally made as a model for other artists to work from (which explains why only one eye is drawn in—paintings would be done in profile). It was left abandoned on the studio floor in Amarna and found, buried under piles of sand, in 1912. The rest of the museum consists of a choice collection of statues, wooden models, painted mummy cases and sarcophagi. Each item is exhibited against a black wall and picked out by spotlight, making the overall effect almost magical. Look out especially for the **Berlin Green Head**, an astonishingly realistic carving of a chubby priest from the Ptolemaic period (*c.* 300 BC), and the gigantic sandstone **Temple Gate of Kalabsha** (20 BC).

The museum on the right hand side is the **Antikenmuseum** *(same times and prices)*, with a good collection of Greek and Roman artefacts (especially of Greek vases), but understandably a let-down after the Egyptian Museum. Next door is the **Bröhan-Museum** *(Tues–Sun 10–6; adm DM4)*, a fine collection of Jugendstil work that is especially strong on furniture (exhibited in reconstructed period rooms).

Beyond Charlottenburg

Around Charlottenburg are three sites with grim Nazi associations. None is especially worth the trek, unless you have a strong historical or personal interest in going. To the north is the **Plötzensee Memorial** *(daily 8–6, Bus 23 to Saatwinkler Damm)*, where the Nazis executed more than 2000 political detainees by hanging or guillotine. After a 1944 plot to assassinate Hitler, nearly 200 'conspirators' were executed—89 of them here at Plötzensee. The victims were slowly hanged with piano wire. Hitler had the deaths filmed so that he could watch them again and again. You can see hooks from which up to eight people could be hanged at a time, cards inviting Nazi officials to public executions and wreaths still left by the relatives of the dead.

To the west of Charlottenburg is Hitler's **Olympic Stadium** (Bus 218, U-Bahn Line 1), a prime example of self-important fascist architecture. It is cold and depressing when empty, and scarcely more cheerful when it fills up for a sports event or pop concert. Hitler's attempt to turn the 1936 Olympics into a showcase for Nazi Germany received a severe blow when black American runner Jesse Owens picked up four gold medals (Nazi doctrine viewed blacks as 'subhuman'). The Führer refused to shake hands with Owens, and in the end could gloat that Germany collected more medals than any other competing country.

Spandau (U-Bahn Line 7), some 6km further west, has a few restored medieval houses, but its most famous landmark—the prison where Hitler's one-time deputy, Rudolph Hess, was sole inmate for many years—has been demolished. The 93-year-old Hess was found hanging in his cell in 1987. The official verdict was suicide, but his family maintain that he was murdered, claiming that the old man was too weak to hang himself.

The Dahlem Museums

In the 1960s the West Berlin authorities established the Free University and built a new museum complex in the quiet suburb of Dahlem. The idea was to set up a rival to the East's Museum Island and Humboldt University. The Dahlem buildings are very much products of their time, but the collections (especially in the Picture Gallery) are almost impossible to beat. By the turn of this century Berlin had some of the best museums in Europe. The Prussians had garnered treasures from around the globe, and there were rich displays all over town. During the Second World War the pick of this booty was stored away for safekeeping in bunkers under Bahnhof Zoo and in disused salt mines in Thuringia. In 1945 the US Liberation Army sent many of the artworks back to the States. When the Cold War cut Berlin in two (and swallowed up most of Thuringia), the Americans sent their prizes back to the Western sector, and the East Berliners had to be content with much barer museums.

By far the best museum of the Dahlem complex is the **Gemäldegalerie** (Picture Gallery) at Arnimalee 23–27 *(Tues–Fri 9–5, Sat and Sun 10–5; adm DM4; take U-Bahn Line 2 to Dahlem-Dorf and follow the signs)*. The **Early German** section includes fine paintings by Konrad Witz, who introduced a subtle realism into previously crude German Gothic art; some dense, finicky Altdorfer landscapes; an excellent selection of Dürer including an astonishingly life-like *Portrait of Jakob Muffel* (1526); and an impressive array of work by the grandfather of wry eroticism, Lucas Cranach the Elder, including the *Fountain of Youth* (1546) in which naked old hags take a dip in the magic pool and emerge as prancing young belles. In the **Sculpture Court** adjoining the gallery is a good collection of German medieval carving, including work by the Masters Tilman Riemenschneider and Hans Multscher.

The **Dutch and Flemish** section contains text-book examples of work by Gerard ter Borch, Pieter Breughel, Jan van Eyck, Rogier van der Weyden and Pieter de Hooch. You can see Rembrandt self-portraits, and paintings of his successive wives (Saskia and Hendrickje) as well as the famous *Man with a Golden Helmet* (now thought to be by a pupil and not the Master himself). There are some gentle, rarely reproduced works by Vermeer, cruelly observed tavern scenes by Jan Steen, and warmly human portraits by Frans Hals (including the leering *Mad Babbe* 'as drunk as an owl').

The Italian collection is also stunning, with rare night scenes by Canaletto, poignant Raphael Madonnas, a large collection of Botticelli and some of Fra Filippo Lippi's best work. Look out, too, for Caravaggio's outrageously lewd *Cupid Victorius*.

Also in the complex are separate museums for **Indian**, **Islamic** and **East-Asian** art (included in ticket price), each stocked to the hilt with priceless statues, prints, textiles and precious objects. Your ticket also includes entrance to the **Museum für Volkerkunde** (Ethnological Museum), which specializes in the South Seas, but has exhibits from all five continents. This is a world of gruesome masks, richly coloured costumes, plumed head-dresses and mysterious carvings that appeals to everyone, especially children.

More Museums

Brücke-Museum, Bussardsteig 9, *(Wed–Mon 11–5; adm DM4; Bus 50 southwards from Spichernstraße U-Bahn station or northwards from Oskar-Helene-Heim, both on Line 2).* Fine collection of expressionist work on the edge of the Grunewald forest. You can feast your eyes on the gaudy canvases of Emil Nolde, Schmitt-Rottluff and Kirchner, then soothe your soul with a walk in the woods.

Gründerzeitmuseum, Hultschiner Damm 333, © 527 8329 *(Sunday tours at 11 and 12, or by appointment; S-Bahn Line 5 to Mahlsdorf).* Transvestite Charlotte von Mahlsdorff was persecuted for her homosexuality by the Nazis and narrowly escaped a firing squad. After the war she returned to the derelict and abandoned family home and (permanently assuming her new persona) set about restoring the mansion single-handedly, and filling it with antiques from the Wilhelmine period (in German *Gründerzeit*). East German authorities also gave her a hard time, and confiscated many of the exhibits, but the house is still well-stocked and makes a fascinating visit. On Sunday mornings Charlotte will show you around personally, and then entertain you to tea. She is also known to throw wild parties.

Nollendorfplatz *(U-Bahn Line 1).* Not a museum, but perhaps the object of pilgrimage for Christopher Isherwood fans. The writer of *Goodbye to Berlin* (on which the film *Cabaret* was based) lived at Nollendorfstraße 17, just south of the U-Bahn station. The house still stands and is marked with a plaque. In Isherwood's time Nollendorfplatz was, as it is now, the hub of Gay Berlin.

Around Berlin

West Berlin might have had an intimate, special atmosphere, but in the days before the *Wende* you could also feel very claustrophobic. You got to know the few accessible areas of greenery by heart, and would probably meet your neighbours if the weather was good. Potsdam and the surrounding countryside stood tantalizingly beyond the wall to the south-west. Now the barriers have dropped, suddenly opening up a hinterland of magnificent palaces, forests and romantic islands.

See also Directory entries for Brandenburg and Frankfurt an der Oder.

Potsdam

The Schloß

In 1744 Frederick the Great, tired of conquering people and leading armies, decided to build a Schloß *sans souci* ('without cares') where he could relax, escape Berlin and his wife (he had little time for either) and indulge his fantasies of being an erudite philosopher, man of letters, musician and speaker of French. A visit to the palace that he commissioned at Potsdam, with its gardens, follies and pavilions, can take a whole day, but is well worth the journey. (To get to Potsdam take the S-Bahn Line 3 to **Potsdamer-Stadt**. Any bus will then carry you over the bridge, past the vast dome of the **Nikolaikirche** (built by Schinkel in 1837–49 in imitation of London's St Paul's, but bare and dull inside) to the Platz der Einheid. From here Buses A1 and 695 leave for **Schloß Sanssouci** *(Apr–Sept 9–12.45 and 1.15–5; Feb, Mar and Oct closes 4pm; Nov–Jan closes 3pm; closed first Mon of the month; adm DM6).*

Frederick drew the first sketches for the Schloß himself, but it was his favourite architect, Georg von Knobelsdorff, who drew up the final plan. The single-story Rococo palace, with just one understated dome, rests gracefully atop a tier of terraced vines. (Frederick was desperate to appear tasteful, restrained and cultured.) Inside you can see the elliptical **Marmorsaal** (Marble Hall) where the King would conduct endless debates (in grating French) with the luminaries he had invited to court; the wildly Rococo **Konzert Zimmer** (Concert Room) where he gave recitals on the flute (even harder on the ears); and the **library** where he would compose French verse and formulate his literary opinions ('Shakespeare was a northern savage').

The royal bedroom is plastered with portraits of the king. Nearby are the more modest quarters of his most famous guest—the French philosopher and satirist Voltaire. Voltaire stayed at Sanssouci from 1750 to 1753—correcting Frederick's doggerel, flattering the monarch's ego and going slowly out of his head with frustration. The relationship ended with protracted public mud-slinging which went on long after Voltaire had stormed back to Paris.

Frederick had asked in his will to be buried on the terrace at Sanssouci. Instead he was interred alongside his father in the Garrison Church in Potsdam. Towards the end of the

Second World War the body was taken to a Hohenzollern family seat near Stuttgart, and it was only in 1991, after the end of the Cold War, that the body was returned (amidst much pomp and controversy), and Frederick's original wish fulfilled.

The Gardens

The Schloß **gardens** sprawl over 290 hectares (717 acres), with 75km of footpaths to wander about on. They were intended as an antidote to Prussian *Ordnung* ('order'). The best way to enjoy them is simply to follow your nose and be prepared for surprises. You will come across hidden gardens, temples and oriental follies. Here are some highlights.

From the palace, the terraces tumble down *à la Versailles* towards a tall fountain. Just to the east of the main building is the **Bildergalerie** *(mid-May–mid-Oct daily 9–12 and 12.45–5; adm DM4)*, containing a fairly mediocre collection of paintings which does, nevertheless, include work by Caravaggio, Rubens and Van Dyck. On a mound just behind the Schloß is a pile of fake classical ruins, the **Ruinenberg**, built to disguise the reservoir that feeds the park's fountains. To the north-west is the **Orangerie** *(mid-May–mid-Oct, 9–12 and 1–5; adm DM5)* which, with its high arches and elegant belvedere towers, rather upstages the Schloß. Inside is a gallery of Raphael copies, certainly not worth the entrance fee (though the view from the towers is good). South of the Orangerie, near the river which flows through the park, is a showy **Chinese Teahouse** with a good dollop of Rococo and some Japanese touches thrown in. The circular tea house is decorated with gilded figures and animals, one of which is an ape that bears Voltaire's features—an indication of the level on which Frederick was conducting their battle. At the far west end of the park (along Hauptallee, its central axis) is the **Neues Palais** *(Apr–Sept 9–12.45 and 1.15–5; Feb, Mar and Oct closes 4pm; Nov–Jan closes 3pm; closed every 2nd Monday; adm DM6)*—a heavy Neoclassical building which an embittered and increasingly lonely Frederick seldom used. His descendant, Kaiser Wilhelm II ('Kaiser Bill') took to its pomposity, and made it his summer residence. He fled during the upheavals of 1918 *(see* **History** p. 44), taking sixty railway carriages packed with the palace's contents—so there is little inside to warrant the entrance fee. At the southernmost tip of the park is the fetching **Schloß Charlottenhof** *(mid-May–mid-Oct daily 9–12.30 and 1–5; closed every 4th Mon; adm DM4)*, built by Schinkel in the style of a Greek Temple. Next door are some fake Roman Baths.

The Neuer Garten

Next to a lake on the other side of town is the **Neuer Garten** (Bus 695 from Schloß Sanssouci), laid out in the 19th century with its own quota of ruins, pyramids and marble palaces. The park is most famous as the location of **Schloß Cecilien**, a mock-Elizabethan mansion built by Kaiser Bill for his son, who had studied in England. This was the scene of the **Potsdam Conference**, where the Allies met in July 1945 to determine the fate of a defeated Germany. Franklin D. Roosevelt had died just six weeks earlier, and Winston Churchill was voted out of office halfway through proceedings—so Stalin had little difficulty in getting just what he wanted from new boys Clement Attlee and Harry S. Truman. You can still see the room with the big round table where the conference took place.

The Grunewald and the Havel Lakes

The thick pine forests and wide, clear lakes to the west of the city were one of the few country areas that West Berliners could escape to during the Cold War. Now that this idyllic countryside is no longer sliced in two by concrete and barbed wire, it makes an even more alluring alternative to the stench and racket of city life. If you visit over weekends it will seem that most of Berlin has had the same idea, but on weekdays it is possible to find a patch on the beach, and to wander through the woods in relative solitude. S-Bahn Line 3 brings you from the centre of town out to Grunewald and Wannsee. Local buses hop between sights, but walking or bicycling is a more rewarding way of getting about (you can hire bikes at Grunewald S-Bahnhof station). If you feel like taking to the water, *see* **Getting Around** p. 475 for details on boats and cruises.

Strandbad Wannsee (the largest inland beach in Europe, with a kilometre-long stretch of white sand) is the most popular place for sunbathing and a dip. You'll find quieter spots on the lakes that were behind the Iron Curtain, such as **Jungfernsee** (which borders on Potsdam). The best walks are in the **Grunewald**, just to the north of Wannsee, or south around **Babelsberg**. Here you can see **Schloß Babelsberg**, a romantic neo-Gothic castle in a park of beech and oak trees. Nearby is the cold, grey **Glienicke Bridge**, scene (in real life and countless spy-stories) of exchanges of secret agents who had been caught by the superpowers. In the middle of the Havel, between the Wannsee and the Glienicke Bridge is the **Pfaueninsel** (Peacock Island) *(daily Apr–Sept 8–6; May–Aug 8–8; Mar and Oct 9–5; Nov–Feb 10–4; ferry DM4.50)*. Friedrich Wilhelm II bought the island, and built a quaint **ruined castle** on it for secret rendezvous with his mistress. Cars, dogs, loud music and smoking are *verboten*, and the island is well stocked with peacocks and other exotic flora and fauna.

Shopping

Berlin's smartest shopping street is the **Kurfürstendamm**. Here, and in the surrounding side streets you will find a good, but by no means heart-stopping, array of fashion boutiques, art galleries and knick-knack shops. The Ku'damm leads into Breitscheidplatz, where there is a big shopping mall, the **Europa-Center**. The **KaDeWe** just across the road is Berlin's most upmarket department store, and has spawned an accompanying circle of trendy giftshops and designer houseware emporiums. In east Berlin **Friedrichstraße** is well on the way to becoming the main shopping drag.

Locals and other highstreet shoppers head for Karl-Marx-Straße in Neukölln or Wilmersdorfer Straße (both on U-Bahn Line 7). The **second-hand shops** for which Berlin is famous are mainly in Kreuzberg (Südstern and Gneisenaustraße) and in Prenzlauer Berg (Schönhauser Allee). Biggest of the lot is Garage (Ahornstr. 2), an underground car park where clothes are sold by the kilo. For **English books** try Marga Schoeller (Knesebeckstr. 33–34) or The Original Version (Sesenheimer Str. 17).

Be wary when buying **bits of the Berlin Wall** from street traders. Fakes abound. The real wall was made of a gritty concrete full of tiny pebbles and has a grimy feel—don't be fooled by so-called 'Certificates of Authenticity'. Traders on the eastern side of the Brandenburg Gate sell all manner of **Cold War memorablia**, from flags to complete Soviet military uniforms.

Berlin ✆ (030–) **Where to Stay**

After the Wall came down Berlin was glutted with visitors, and didn't have nearly enough hotel space for them. A frenzy of renovation and construction is beginning to put things right, but accommodation is pricey. It is still a good idea to book two to three weeks before arriving—a month or two in advance if you want much of a choice. If you are stuck without a room, the tourist information office (*see* p. 476) can help to find last-minute vacancies or private accomodation with families. If you are staying in Berlin for three or more days, it might be more economical to rent a holiday apartment. Cheaper hotels can be found in Kreuzberg and Schöneberg. Charlottenburg is an attractive quarter, convenient for the sights, and has hotels in all categories.

expensive

Bristol Hotel Kempinski, Kurfürstendamm 27, ✆ 884 340, fax 883 6075 (DM470–530). Traditionally Berlin's top address. Here you rub shoulders with visiting opera stars and the *crème de la crème* of Berlin society. One step out of the door and you're in the heart of the Ku'damm, inside you're in a hushed world of discreet luxury. Wallow in bed or sip cocktails next to the pool—and when it is all over you can check in your luggage (if you're flying Lufthansa) in the hotel foyer.

Grand Hotel, Friedrichstr. 158–164, ✆ 23270, fax 2327 3362 (DM480–580). Classic Grand Hotel just off Unter den Linden. Liveried bell-hops, antique furniture and a Bette Davis staircase. Such stuff that dreams are made on.

Berlin Hilton, Mohrenstr. 30, ✆ 23820, fax 2382 4269 (DM355–525). Smart, with elegant *Wintergarten* and a high standard of service. Make sure you get a room that looks out over the Gendarmenmarkt—one of the best views in Berlin.

Hotel Forum, Alexanderplatz, ✆ 23890, fax 2389 4305 (DM245–325). Towering 1960s hotel on Alexanderplatz, recently modernized and upgraded. A bit like living in an insurance company's headquarters, but the views out over Berlin are tremendous.

moderate

Sorat Art Hotel, Joachimstaler Str. 29, ✆ 884 470, fax 8844 7700 (DM265–285). Wacky 'designer' hotel with (extremely) individually decorated rooms. Choc-full of pieces by Wolf Vostell, the artist who buried two real cadillacs in concrete on nearby Rathenauplatz.

Queens Hotel, Guntzelstr. 14, ℂ 870 241, fax 861 9326 (DM220–260). Modern hotel in quite street just south of Kurfürstendamm. Charming staff, smart rooms and the bonus of plentiful free parking.

Hotel Charlottenhof, Charlottenstr. 52, ℂ 238 060, fax 2380 6100 (DM200–240). Friendly hotel just off the Gendarmenmarkt. Relaxed atmosphere and well-appointed rooms.

Askanischer Hof, Kurfürstendamm 53, ℂ 881 8033, fax 881 7206 (DM250–280). Small hotel right on the Ku'damm. Gargles and vocal hi-jinks from the theatre types that frequent it, but comfortable rooms in a posh part of town.

Riehmer's Hofgarten, Yorckstr. 83, ℂ 781 011, fax 786 6059 (DM240–270). Stately Jugendstil hotel at the tamer end of Kreuzberg. Pleasant old rooms with all mod cons.

Hotel-Pension Schönberg, Hauptstr. 135, ℂ 781 8830, fax 788 1020 (DM170–230). TV, mini-bar and all the trappings of more expensive places in a peaceful hotel just south of the centre. No restaurant.

Pension Güntzel, Guntzelstr. 62, ℂ 854 1350, fax 853 1108 (DM110–150). Comfortable, centrally situated family pension, with phones and TV in the rooms and ample parking. No restaurant.

Hotel Fischerinseln, Neue Roßstr. 11, ℂ 238 0770, fax 2380 7800 (DM160–180). Historic building in the Mitte near the Spree. Newly renovated and well-equipped.

Hotel Alpenland, Carmerstr. 8, ℂ 312 3970, fax 313 8444 (DM110–180). Good value Charlottenburg Hotel with helpful, friendly management. Just off Savignyplatz, a slightly seedy area of good eateries. No restaurant.

Hotelpension Hansablick, Flotowstr. 6, ℂ 391 4048, fax 392 6937 (DM170–190). Near the Tiergarten. Run by a collective, with a relaxed, alternative style. Generous breakfast buffet. No restaurant.

Hotel-Pension Dittberner, Wielandstr. 26, ℂ 881 6485, fax 885 4046 (DM110–180). Comfy, old-fashioned hotel in plum situation near the Ku'damm. One of the few hotels in the area to survive Allied bombs.

inexpensive

Pension Finck, Güntzelsstr. 54, ℂ 861 2940, fax 861 8158 (DM95–100). Not as smart as the Queens Hotel up the road, but half the price for a simple but perfectly adequate room near the Ku'damm. No restaurant.

Hotel Am Hermannplatz, Kottbusser Damm 24, ℂ 691 2002, fax 694 1036 (DM137). Seedy Berlin charm in one of the more hectic parts of Kreuzberg.

Hotel Transit, Hagelberger Str. 53–54, ℂ 785 5051, fax 785 9619 (DM95). Near Viktoriapark. Bustling with backpackers and 20-somethings in Berlin for a good time. No restaurant.

Hotel zur Reichspost, Urbanstr. 84, ℂ 691 1035, fax 693 7889 (DM80–125). Cheap and cheerful Kreuzberg guesthouse with parking facilities.

Youth Hostels: Jugendgästehaus am Zoo, Hardenbergstr. 9a, ℂ 312 9410; Jugendgästehaus Berlin, Kluckstr. 3, ℂ 261 1097; Studenthotel Berlin, Meiningerstr. 10, ℂ 784 6720. Advance booking recommended for Youth Hostels.

Private Rooms and Short-let Apartments

This is usually the cheapest (and often more interesting) option. The minimum stay is usually three days.

Erste Mitwohnzentrale, Sybelstr. 53, ℂ 324 3031. Rooms and apartments.

Mitwohnzentrale Ku'dammeck, Kurfürstendamm 227, ℂ 883 051. Best list of private rooms.

Mitwohnzentrale Kreuzberg, Mehringdamm 72, ℂ 786 6002. Good list of cheap rooms in Kreuzberg and eastern part of the city.

Agentur Wohnwitz, Holsteinische Str. 55, ℂ 861 8222. Rooms/flats all over town.

Berlin Homestays, 4 Nuffield Close, Bicester, Oxon OX6 7TL, UK, ℂ (0869) 242 011. British agency that can arrange rooms in east Berlin and tries to match visitors with like-minded hosts.

Eating and Drinking

Berlin's drink is **beer**. French Huguenots were responsible for introducing the local speciality, *Berliner Weiße*—a watery wheat beer that is traditionally served *mit Schuß* (with a dash of something added), either *mit grün* (with a shot of pungent woodruff liqueur) or *mit rot* (with a dollop of sickly raspberry syrup). Alternatively you can join the grumbly old men at the bar for a *Molle mit Korn* (light beer with a schnapps chaser).

Local **cuisine** in the windswept flats of working-class Berlin never amounted to much more than grudging variations on the theme of pork, cabbage and potatoes. The German penchant for referring to pickles and lumpy mushes of meat, tinned veg and mayonnaise as 'salads' (thankfully disappearing through much of the country) is still in evidence in the East, which got stuck in a culinary time-warp behind the Iron Curtain. The variety and quality of the restaurants in cosmopolitan West Berlin, however, was unequalled by any city in Germany. This is still the case, and establishments in the east of the city have perked up considerably in the last year or two. **Breakfast** is a Berlin speciality. Here it is a meal to linger over, served well into the afternoon in many cafés and comprising all manner of meats, cheeses, fruits, pickles, yoghurt and prodigious quantities of coffee or tea.

You'll find a cluster of good restaurants—from cheapo Chinese to chic French—in the streets around **Savignyplatz**, just north of the Ku'damm. Berlin abounds with atmospheric and idiosyncratic bars and cafés. Where you drink depends very much on your own preferences. Wherever you are staying you will be just a few minutes' totter from a neighbourhood *Kneipe*. Here you will find a drunken philosopher who will try to engage you in conversation, two blowsy *Hausfrauen* full of noisy, ribald humour, a quiet Turk in the corner and a handful of tired businessmen. The jukebox or the TV will be on (though nobody pays much attention) and the waggon-wheel chandelier casts a dim yellow light over the gold-framed pictures on the walls—three landscapes, a picture of a car, photographs of a local *Sportsverrein* and a print of Bismarck. The **Ku'damm** is full of tourists and locals with sunbed tans, white socks and BMWs. **Schönberg, Kreuzberg** and **Prenzlauer Berg** attract the weird, wild and wicked. (The strip between **Wittenbergplatz** and **Nollendorfplatz** is the place to begin a circuit of the gay bars.)

Here is but a sample of the thousands of restaurants, bars and cafés to chose from in Berlin, but enough to set you on your way to discovering what is possibly the most enjoyable aspect of the city.

Restaurants and Taverns

expensive

Bamberger Reiter, Regensburger Str. 7, ℂ 244 282 (U4 Viktoria-Luise-Platz) (DM100–130). Subdued atmosphere and Michelin-starred cuisine created by Franz Raneburger, himself a Berlin institution. Internationally influenced menu. The adjoining **Bistro** serves good food from the same kitchen at about half the price.

Rockendorf's Restaurant, Düsterhauptstr. 1, ℂ 402 3099 (S1 Waidmannslust) (DM175–200). Those in the know quietly let on that this is Berlin's best restaurant. French cuisine; subtle sauces, delicate meats and quirky surprises. Set menus only.

Alt-Luxemburg, Windscheidstr. 31, ℂ 323 8730 (U1 Sophie-Charlotten-Platz) (DM90–120). Charming Charlottenburg restaurant. Adventurous sauces and exotic flavour combinations are Patron Karl Wannemacher's speciality. Menu changes frequently.

moderate

Paris Bar, Kantstr. 152, ℂ 313 8052 (S3/6/9 Savignyplatz) (DM45–60). Classic French bistro. Good food and artsy clientele.

Florian (Grolmanstr. 52, ℂ 313 9184, S5/6/9 Savignyplatz; DM35–50). Starlets, TV presenters and gallery owners sip Sekt at the bar then nibble on colourful morsels of food.

Ermerlerhaus, Märkisches Ufer 10–12, ℂ 279 3617 (U2 Märkisches Museum) (DM30–70). One of east Berlin's gems. Sumptuous Rococo mansion on the Spree. *Gutbürgerlich* meats and stews downstairs (in Raabe Diele) and more delicate dishes upstairs (in the Weinrestaurant).

Borchardt, Französiche Str. 47, ✆ 229 3144 (U2 Stadtmitte) (DM40–60). High ceilings, Jugendstil mosaics and plush upholstery. The perfect place for a decadent Sunday brunch.

Zum Nußbaum, Am Nußbaum, ✆ 2431 3327 (U2 Klosterstraße) (DM25–35). Low-beamed 16th-century inn in the Nikolaiviertel. Rebuilt in the 1980s. Good-value meals—try the pickled herring dishes.

Restaurant Moskau, Karl-Marx-Allee 34, ✆ 279 1670 (U5 Schillingstraße) (DM35–45). Erstwhile East Berlin institution. Soulless 1960s building once patronized by Party big-wigs, now with a more relaxed atmosphere and good Russian and Ukranian cuisine. Find out what Chicken Kiev is *really* about.

Restauration 1900, Husemannstr. 1, ✆ 449 4052 (U2 Senefelder Platz) (DM25–45). One of the best in Prenzlauer Berg. Good wine list and superbly cooked German cuisine.

Ax Bax, Leibnizstr. 34, ✆ 313 8594 (U7 Wilhelmsdorfer Straße) (DM25–35). Good cold buffet and some idiosyncratic adventures with traditional German ingredients—pork, game and various fungi and berries.

Puvogels Medallion, Pestalozzistr. 8, ✆ 313 4364 (U7 Wilhelmsdorfer Straße) (DM35–50). Quietly elegant, tourist-free. Meaty menu that changes seasonally.

Auerbach, Köpenicker Str. 174, ✆ 611 5079 (U1 Schlesisches Tor) (DM20–30). Stained glass and candlelight, lighter new German cuisine and a *Szene* clientele.

Café Aroma, Hochkirchstr. 8, ✆ 782 5821 (U7, S1/2 Yorckstraße) (DM20–30). Rousing atmosphere, excellent Sunday breakfast (after 11am) and delicious Italian food. Meeting-place of the German-Italian Friendship Club. Say no more.

Franzmann, Golzstr. 32, ✆ 216 3514 (U7 Eisenacher Straße) (DM25–35). Good Schönberg restaurant in the new German style (lighter fare, influenced by French cuisine). Game and vegetarian specialities, and well-chosen Australian wines. Trendy clientele. Menu—and fashions—change twice-weekly.

Großbeerenkeller, Großbeerenstr. 90, ✆ 251 3064 (U1/7 Möckernbrücke) (DM25–35). Home-cooking, gargantuan breakfasts and customers who look as though they've been ensconced in their corners since the cavernous beer cellar first opened for business (in 1862).

Abendmahl, Muskauer Str. 9, ✆ 612 5170 (U1 Görlitzer Bahnhof) (DM35–45). Religious kitsch décor and some of the best value fish and vegetarian dishes in town. Also organic wine.

inexpensive

Gasthaus Dietrich Herz, Marheinekeplatz, in the markethall, ✆ 693 1173 (U7 Gneisenaustraße) (DM10–20). Flock wallpaper, hardly a soul under 60 and unbelievably cheap food—Schnitzels, pizzas and a daily special under DM10. Big breakfasts.

Lothar und Ich, Dominicusstr. 46, ✆ 784 4142 (U4 Rathaus Schöneberg) (DM10–25). Round-the-clock home-cooking, even managing venison and cranberry goulash for under DM15.

Einhorn, Mommsenstr. 2, ✆ 881 4241 and Wittenbergplatz 5, ✆ 218 6347 (U1/2/3) (DM8–15). Daytime vegetarian and wholefood snack-bar. Excellent salads and also tasty cakes. Packed at lunchtime.

La Culinaria, Pariser Str. 56, ✆ 883 3674 (U2/9 Spichernstraße) (DM20–30). Pastas with such curious departures from the norm as vodka sauce.

Baharat Falafel, Winterfeldtstr. 35 (U1/4 Nollendorfplatz) (DM5–10). Best falafel in town. Open till 2am for late-night munchies.

Ashoka, Grolmanstr. 51 (U1 Ernst-Reuter-Platz) (DM10–15). Good-value, basic Indian food just west of the Tiergarten. Open till 1am.

ethnic food

Lucky Strike Originals, Georgenstr. arches 177–180, ✆ 3084 8822 (S6/9 Hackescher Markt) (DM45–65). New Orleans jazz and spicy Cajun food in a cavern under the S-Bahn arches.

Tres Kilos, Marheinekeplatz 3, ✆ 693 6044 (U7 Gneisenaustraße) (DM35–45). Young crowd tank up on margaritas before tucking into delicious Mexican food.

Petit Chinois, Spandauerdamm 82, ✆ 322 5157 (U1 Kaiserdamm) (DM30–40). Informal café atmosphere and fresh, top-rate Chinese/Indonesian cooking.

Poony's, Burgermeister Str. 74, ✆ 751 5033 (U6 Kaiserin-Augusta-Straße) (DM25–40). Cut above the average Chinese—tasty food and tasteful décor.

Tabibito, Karl-Marx-Str. 56, ✆ 624 1345 (U7 Rathaus Neukölln) (DM20–30). Tasty, unflashy Japanese cuisine. Laid-back atmosphere as the young chef prepares your meal right before your eyes.

Thai Palace, Meierottostr. 1, ✆ 883 2823 (U2/9 Spichernstraße) (DM35–45). Popular restaurant offering the delicious Thai combination of curries and delicate spicy food.

Bombay Palace, Yorckstr. 60, ✆ 785 91 67 (U7, S1/2 Yorckstraße) (DM25-35). Homey rather than palatial, with friendly service (a treat in Berlin) and simple, tasty Indian food.

Merhaba, Hasenheide 39, ✆ 692 1713 (U7 Südstern) (DM30–40). Mouthwatering Turkish food in upmarket atmosphere. Popular with Kreuzberg *Szene*.

Bars and Cafés

Central

Café Kranzler, Kurfürstendamm 18 (U3/9 Kufürstendamm). Ku'damm classic for *Kaffee und Kuchen*.

Café Möhring, Kurfürstendamm 213 (U3/9 Uhlandstraße). The elderly ladies of Berlin sit with 'time dangling from their fingers', and eye each other up dauntingly.

Klo, Leibnizstr. 57, ✆ 324 2299 (U7 Adenauerplatz). Potty décor. Obsessed with things lavatorial. You even get your beer in a urine sample jar.

Café Savigny, Grolmanstr. 53–54 (S5/6/9 Savignyplatz). Artsy, academic and designer Berlin are At Home all day.

Schwarzes Café, Kantstr. 148 (S5/6/9 Savignyplatz). Round-the-clock breakfasts—though you would swear that it was exactly the same group of people sitting there 24 hours a day.

Opernpalais, Unter den Linden 5, ✆ 238 4016. Classy complex of restaurants and cafés on Unter den Linden. Ideal for a stylish lunch or gooey cream-cake when you're sight-seeing in the Mitte.

Café Silberstein, Oranienburger Str. 27 (S1/2 Oranienburger Straße). Awesome, but cripplingly uncomfortable sculpted metal chairs in the spot that is making a bid for the 'Trendiest Café' award in this fast up-and-coming area.

Café Oren, Oranienburger Str. 28. Jewish folk music and Israeli-inspired dishes (mainly fish and vegetarian, around DM20) in the old Jewish quarter.

Beth Café, Tucholskystr. 40 (S1/2 Oranienburger Straße). Jewish community meeting-place. Kosher food and good salmon bagels.

Veb Oz, Auguststr. 92 (U6 Oranienburger Tor). Another new trendy bar in the old Jewish Quarter. This one has a double-decker bar bus that will deliver you to the doorstep of surrounding nightclubs.

Café Berio, Maaßenstr. 7, ✆ 216 1946 (U1/4 Nollendorfplatz). Original 1930s café on Christopher Isherwood's beat. Good selection of cakes.

Café Einstein, Kurfürstenstr. 58, ✆ 261 5096 (U1/4 Nollendorfplatz). Tuxedo-clad waiters, divine Apfelstrudel, piles of newspapers and magazines, women who look like countesses and men who look like spies.

Kumpelnest 3000, Lützowstr. 23, ✆ 261 6918 (U1 Kurfürstenstraße). Much loved watering hole with a party atmosphere.

Turbine Rosenheim, Rosenheimer Str. 4 (U7 Eisenacher Straße). Erstwhile disco now pumps out opera and jazz. Would-be artists serve behind the bar, then graduate to the stools in front if they manage to sell any work.

Kreuzberg/Prenzlauer Berg/Schönberg

Café Übersee, Paul-Lincke-Ufer 44 (U1 Kottbusser Tor). Hardy Kreuzberg perennial on the Landwehr Canal. Breakfast until 4pm.

Café Bar Morena, Wiener Str. 60 (U1 Görlitzer Bahnhof). Famous Kreuzberg breakfast café—everything from bacon and eggs to quark (curd cheese) and pancakes served all day.

Bierhimmel, Oranienstr. 183, ✆ 615 3122 (U1/8 Kottbusser Tor). Through the swingdoors at the back of this ordinary Kreuzberg *Kneipe* is a genuine 1950s cocktail bar, complete with padded counter.

Madonna, Wiener Str. 22 (U1 Görlitzer Bahnhof). Dangerous, deafening and debauched.

Café Anfall, Gneisenaustr. 64, ✆ 693 6898 (U7 Südstern). Wacky décor that changes from time to time (at last count it was all bamboo huts and straw). Best of a line of popular Kreuzberg bars.

Babel, Käthe-Niederkirchner Str. 2 (U2 Senefelderplatz). Earthy colours and bare wooden tables, flower-shaped lampshades, sky-blue ceiling and a jolly mix of trendy Prenzlberg locals. Good-value breakfast. Open 24 hours.

Bla-Bla, Sredzkistr. 19a (U2 Eberswalder Straße). Eccentric Prenzlberg cocktail bar converted out of owner Heidi's front room. Sofa, piano and porcelain leopard still in place.

Galerie Café Eisenwerk, Sredzkistr. 33, ✆ 448 0961 (U2 Eberswalder Straße). New Prenzlauer Berg café-cum-gallery. The rusty iron décor is a little off-putting, but the mood is warm and friendly, and the art on the walls sometimes very good.

Café Lolott, Schönhauser Allee 56 (U2, S8/10 Schönhauser Allee). Down-to-earth coffee-house atmosphere that transforms into a disco as the evening wears on. Young Prenzlauer Berg crowd.

Beer Gardens

Alte Welt, Wissmannstr. 44 (U7/8 Hermannplatz). Wedged in between two old buildings in a cobbled backstreet. Long trestle tables where you sit elbow to elbow with students, stray yuppies and lads off the nearby building site.

Golgatha, Viktoria Park (U6/7 Mehringdamm). A Berlin summer's night institution. Hundreds crowd under the trees in Viktoria Park to quaff *Berliner Weiße* and munch sausages.

Brauhaus Joh. Albrecht 'Im Alten Fritz', Karolinenstr. 12 (U6 Alt-Tegel). Favoured watering hole of Frederick the Great and his horses. The Kupfer and Messing beers are reputed to be the best in Berlin.

Loretta's Biergarten, Lietzenburger Str. 89 (U3/4 Ku'damm). Pricey high-kitsch. Fairy lights and grottos just off the Ku'damm.

Kastanie, Schloßstr. 22 (U1 Sophie-Charlotten-Platz). Young, local Charlottenburg crowd under an enormous chestnut tree.

Potsdam and Wannsee

Grand Slam, Gottfried-von-Cramm-Weg 47–55, ✆ 825 3810 (S1/3 Wannsee) (DM150–175). English stately home atmosphere, with Berlin's poshest tennis club popping away outside. Fine Franco-German cooking.

Wirtshaus Halali, Königstr. 24, ✆ 805 3125 (S1/3 Wannsee) (DM25–45). Friendly restaurant on the edge of Potsdam. Fresh salads and German cooking with cheesy Alpine influences.

Minsk, Max-Planck-Str. 10, ✆ (0331) 23490 (DM20–30). Good Russian cuisine and views across the Havel to Potsdam.

Babelsberg Strandterrassen, Kleines Schloß, Park Babelsberg, ✆ (0331) 75156 (DM20–35). Lovely lakeside terrace restaurant serving passable German standards.

Drachenhaus, Maulbeerallee, Park Sanssouci, ✆ (0331) 21594. Pagoda-shaped café for *Kaffee und Kuchen* in the Sanssouci park.

Frochkasten, Kiezstr. 4, ✆ (0331) 21315 (DM15–25). Traditional *Kneipe* south of the town centre, near the Potsdam-Stadt station. Serves tasty meals.

Entertainment and Nightlife

Berlin's **listings magazines** are *Tip* and *Zitty*. They appear alternately at fortnightly intervals. Both can be bought at newsagents and in some cafés. *Zitty* is the better and more widely available of the two. Both are fairly easy to manage, even if your German is not up to much. Alternatively, you could pick up the excellent English-language freebie *Checkpoint* at venues around town.

Tickets can be hard to get for major concerts, opera and theatre. **Ticket agents** that can help include:

Theatre Kasse Centrum, Meinekestr. 25, ✆ 882 7611.

Kant-Kasse, Kantstr. 54, ✆ 313 4554.

Box-Office, Nollendorfplatz 7, ✆ 215 1954.

You can get **half-price tickets** for some shows from 4–8pm on the day of the performance from Hekticket, Rathausstr. 1, near Alexanderplatz, ✆ 242 6709.

Music

Berlin has one of the world's best orchestras, the **Berlin Philharmonic**, for years under the baton of the legendary Herbert von Karajan, now under the subtle guidance of Claudio Abbado. The orchestra's home is the **Philharmonie** (Box Office on Kemperplatz, ✆ 261 4883), but tickets generally have to be booked weeks in advance. The DDR's leading orchestra, the **Berlin Sinfonie Orchester** is also of an extremely high standard. They play in the **Schauspielhaus**, Gendarmenmarkt, ✆ 227 2129 (Large Hall), 227 2122 (Small Hall) or 227 2156 (returns). For mainstream **opera and ballet** head east to the **Deutsche Staatsoper**, Unter den Linden 7, ✆ 200 4762 (Box Office) or 208 2861 (information), which, under the directorship of Daniel Barenboim attracts the biggest stars. The **Deutsche Oper**, Bismarckstr. 35, ✆ 341 4449, is best known for its performances of Wagner's Ring Cycle. The **Komische Oper**, Behrenstr. 55–57, ✆ 229 2555, lives on a lighter diet of **operetta**, especially Offenbach and Johann Strauss.

Jazz fans congregate at Flöz, Nassauische Str. 37, ℭ 861 1000, to hear new bands and in the hope of catching a spontaneous jam session. Visiting big names usually play at Quasimodo, Kantstr. 12a, ℭ 312 8086. The Blues Café Berlin, Körnerstr. 11, ℭ 261 3698, is just what it says, and rather good. Big **rock bands** end up at a variety of venues such as the Olympic Stadium, the Waldbühne (in a natural amphitheatre nearby) and the Tempodrome (two tents in the Tiergarten). For other **live music** check out what is happening at the Metropol, Nollendorfplatz 5, ℭ 216 4122, or The Loft (same building, ℭ 216 1020). Both venues host new music and indie bands as well as smaller stars. Many pubs and nightclubs also feature live bands (Zitty and Checkpoint are the best sources for finding out what is going on).

Theatre

The theatre in Berlin doesn't come anywhere near its former glories in the days of Bertolt Brecht and Max Reinhardt. Brecht's old theatre, the **Berliner Ensemble**, Bertolt-Brecht-Platz, ℭ 282 3160, now churns out fairly mediocre versions of his work, interspersed with the odd Shakespeare or Dario Fo. The **Schaubühne am Lehniner Platz**, Ku'damm 153, ℭ 890 023, enjoys the best reputation for innovative productions of the classics, and the **Schiller-Theater**, Bismarckstr. 110, ℭ 319 5236, puts on good experimental work. Even deeper into the realms of the avant-garde is the **UFA-Circus**, Viktoriastr. 10–18, ℭ 755 030. For the really weird, keep your ears open for news of 'happenings' in Prenzlauer Berg or around Oranienburger Straße. There is little English-language theatre in town, although the **Hebbel Theater**, Stresemannstr. 29, ℭ 251 0144, sometimes plays host to visiting companies. For English-language **cinema** the best places to check out are Arsenal, Weiserstr. 25, ℭ 218 6848, and Babylon, Dresdener Str. 126, ℭ 614 6313, and Rosa-Luxemburg-Str. 30, ℭ 242 5076.

Be wary of places that offer traditional **Berlin Cabaret**. They are usually tourist traps trading off 1920s nostalgia. There was a strong political cabaret scene before the *Wende*, but the only venue to have kept its edge is **Die Distel**, Friedrichstr. 101, ℭ 200 4704—your German will have to be pretty good, though. The really exciting developments in live performance are in **varieté**, a heady mixture of performance art, whacky theatre, circus and political cabaret, similar to the New Variety scene in Britain. Best venues for this are **Chamäleon**, Rosenthaler Str. 40–41, ℭ 282 7118, near Oranienburger Straße, and **Bar Jeder Vernunft**, Schaperstr. 24, ℭ 883 1582.

Nightclubs

Berlin's club scene is a creature not easily pinned down to one spot. The best way to find out what is currently 'in' is to get talking in one of the trendier bars mentioned above, or to scour the listings mags. There are some trusty perennials, however. The **Metropol** (Nollendorfplatz 5) has a big dance floor, plays mainstream disco and hosts visiting bands. The massive defunct power plant **E-Werk**

(Wilhelmstraße opp. Treuhand) plays techno and is high on artificial colours and additives. You could also try the **Sophienclub** (Sophienstr. 6) in the old Jewish Quarter. There's a sweaty, writhing dance floor downstairs with a labyrinth of dimly lit rooms piled on top. In the same area is **Tacheles** (Oranienburger Str. 53–56), a vibrant artists co-operative in a previously derelict department store. Artists from all over the world live and work here and put on great parties, and sometimes live music and raves—though they don't always take kindly to tourists. For a taste of **gay** Berlin head to Motzstr. 19 where you'll find Pool (one of the city's best gay discos), Hafen (a relaxed bar with a friendly young crowd) and Tom's (a notorious old cruising bar full of notorious old men). Mann-O-Meter (Motzstr. 5, © 216 8008) has a quiet café and an information centre. Lipstick (Richard-Wagner-Platz 5, © 342 8126) has **women-only** nights on Mon, Wed, Fri and Sat.

The Spreewald

The River Spree enters Berlin in the south-eastern corner of the city. Here, as in the west of town, you'll find lakes crowded with sunbathers and windsurfers (**Müggelsee** is the most popular). A little way south, across flat open countryside, you come to the **Spreewald**, a natural forest where the river splits up into hundreds of streams and canals between the trees. The best base to explore the Spreewald from is Lübbenau (though the previously sleepy town is rapidly becoming touristy).

See also Directory entry for Cottbus.

Lübbenau

Lübbenau is under 100km from Berlin, so it is possible to treat an excursion here as a day trip, though the dreamy, slow pace of life on the water could easily tempt you to stay the night. Spreading out from the northern edge of town is an intricate network of canals—partly a wooded, watery suburbia, partly nature reserve. People get about on long flat-bottomed boats (*Kähne*) which are punted gondola-style from the back. Often you will see locals in traditional costume—the women in beautiful hand-stitched lace and wearing odd triangular head scarves (like old-fashioned nurses). Don't be surprised if the language sounds totally unfamiliar. The people here are **Sorbs**, a Slavic race who have preserved their customs and identity and who live quite happily as a minority group in this corner of Germany (*see* p. 465). Around town you'll see signs printed in both German and Sorb—starting with the name of the town itself: *Lubnjow*.

Getting Around

By car: Lübbenau is just off the A13, the main Berlin to Dresden road. Parking in town presents few problems, but there is no 24-hour petrol station, so it is advisable to fill up before you leave Berlin. There is a **petrol station** (open 7–6) on the way out of town at Boblitz on the Cottbus road.

By Train: The Bahnhof is in the middle of town. To get to the tourist office and the boats, walk straight up Poststraße. There is a train to Berlin Lichtenberg about every two hours (journey time 1hr 10min). Passengers can hire **bicycles** at the station.

By Boat: Most boats leave from the harbour on Dammstraße (*see* below). If you want to book a ride on a *Kahn* (with gondolier) in advance contact the Kahnfährgenossenschaft Lübbenau (Postf. 49 Dammstraße, ✆ (03542) 2225. Prices start at DM5 an hour for a bus-like boat, and rise steadily depending on the degree of privacy you desire. To hire a pedalo, canoe or *Kahn* of your own contact Bootsverleih Manfred Franke (Dammstr. 72, ✆ (03542) 2722). Prices start at around DM4 per hour.

Tourist Information

The **tourist information office**, Ehm-Welk-Str. 15, ✆ (03542) 3668, is on the Markt (which is on the northern edge of town, rather than at the centre). Here you can pick up brochures on Lübbenau and the Spreewald, and buy maps of the waterways (essential if you are going to head off in a boat on your own).

The Harbours

To get to the main 'harbour' (German: *Hafen*)—more a landing jetty—walk east from the market, along Ehm-Welk-Straße, then right into Dammstraße. This is the tourist hub of Lubbenau, and can get very busy. Coachloads of daytrippers pour in, crowd onto the *Kähne*, and are shunted off into the forest. When they return they mill around the stalls on the shoreline loading up with souvenirs and local specialities (honey, pottery, painted eggs, lace and bottles of pickled gherkins) or munch their way through mounds of fried forest mushrooms.

Yet there is another landing bay, just a few minutes away, that offers a different experience entirely. If, instead of walking down Ehm-Welk-Straße, you leave the Markt down Spreestraße (opposite the church), you come to a single wooden platform where just one or two *Kähne* are moored. Here the gondoliers (identifiable by their green waiscoats) chalk their names up on a blackboard, together with the time they intend to leave and the number of spaces left in the boat—or they sip coffee in the café under the trees waiting for private commissions. You can slip away on a *Kähne* for two (or four), with a checked cloth over a table between the seats, for a mobile picnic (which you bring along yourself). A little along the river to the left you can hire canoes. (If you really prefer to stay on dry land it is possible to follow footpaths along many of the waterways.) Here is a world of tiny arched footbridges, wooden cottages in the trees and glorious silence—just the trickling of the water, the odd plop of a frog and distant hammering as someone repairs a cabin. The forest is wet and dense (at times you feel as if you are paddling up a tributary of the Amazon) and is filled with musty smells and the tang of creosote, without which the houses and bridges would rot away. You can paddle about for hours and quite easily (though thoroughly enjoyably) get completely lost.

The Markt and the Schloß

There is not much else in Lübbenau to detain you, other than a simple Baroque **church** on the Markt and a sturdy Neoclassical **Schloß** (now a hotel) just north of the harbour. The Orangerie of the Schloß has been converted into a small **museum** *(May–Oct, Tues–Sun 9–5; adm DM3)* where you can see samples of Sorb traditional dress, embroidery and handicrafts. In an adjoining outhouse is an ancient steam locomotive.

Lübbenau ✆ (03542–)   ***Where to Stay***

Hotel Schloß Lübbenau, Schloßbezirk 6, ✆ 8126, fax 3327 (DM126–236). Big 19th-century converted Schloß with a gloomy Agatha Christie foyer. A touch seedy behind the scenes.

Pension Ebusch, Topfmarkt 4, ✆ 3670 (DM100–160). Best in town. Pretty pension on the Markt, with friendly owners and a beer garden.

Pension 'Zur Alten Feuerwehr', Schulstr. 2, ✆ 2366 (DM70–100). Comfortable rooms in converted fire station. Near the landing jetties.

Comfortable, inexpensive accommodation (around DM50) can be found in private rooms all over town. The tourist information office can help here, or you could try Brunnhilde Kuhn (Am Wasser 5, ✆ 63543) or Harry Filko (An der Quodda 2, ✆ 2944), both of whom have houses on the waterways.

Eating and Drinking

Spreewald-Idyll, Spreestr. 13, ✆ 2251 (DM15–35). New *Gaststätte* popular with the locals. Serves Spreewald specialities such as Quark (curd cheese) with linseed oil, onions, butter and potatoes.

Restaurant Strubels, Apothekengasse—off Dammstraße (DM15–30). Bald on atmosphere, but good cooking. Eel dishes a speciality.

Spreewaldhof Wotschofska, Lehdergraben, ✆ (03546) 7601 (DM20–50). Atmospheric old *Gaststätte* in the middle of the forest. Big shady beer garden. Local specialities and game dishes. Accessible by water only (a gondolier will point it out on your map).

Gasthaus Oppott, An der Quodda 1, ✆ 2844 (DM20–50). Small forest tavern, less subject to invasions by big *Kähne*. Mooring space for paddleboats and smaller *Kähne*. Good fish dishes.

Hanseatic Towns, the Coasts and Islands

Hanseatic Towns
the Coasts and Islands

The north of Germany is an enticing ragbag of moods. Here you find the old towns of the powerful medieval Hanseatic League, with their characteristic brick-gabled buildings, fierce sense of independence and grimy edge of seaport tack. Grandest of these is Hamburg, Germany's second largest city—lively, smart and culturally vibrant. Its arch-rival, Bremen, has a more youthful, alternative air. Along the Baltic coast the towns have the shabby-genteel charm of fading turn-of-the-century seaside resorts. The elegant old buildings are being spruced up, and the vast Trades Union 'Holiday Centres' built under the DDR are slipping a little uneasily into their new role of more upmarket hotels.

Further north, in Schleswig-Holstein, architecture and temperament become decidedly Nordic. Across the sea and mudflats to the west you can take your pick of island life—from lonely nature reserves where motor traffic is banned, to one of the chicest resorts in Germany, where the village shops stock Cartier and Chanel.

The countryside is mostly flat and wet, yet oddly beautiful with misty marshes, heather-covered heaths, fields bright with poppies or yellow rapeseed, and patchworks of lakes and forest. The various tribes that populate the north are traditionally supposed to be distant and taciturn. The Frieslanders in the west have their own language, knock back gallons of sweet black tea, look after their black-and-white cows and are closer to kinsmen across the Dutch border than to other Germans. The shepherds on the lonely Lüneburg Heath south of Hamburg were once believed to have magical healing powers. The people who live in the low-lying polders of Schleswig-Holstein, where the winters are long and dark, show the highest rates of alcoholism, suicide and incest in Germany and, to top it, are said to be downright pig-headed. '*Hupen zwecklos. Fahrer ist Dithmarscher*' reads the bumper-sticker—'No use in hooting. The driver is from Dithmarschen' (a region of Schleswig-Holstein). The stereotypes are, of course, exaggerated, but you certainly won't find spontaneous Bavarian-style sing-a-longs or backslapping Rhineland bonhomie here. Life is quieter, more restrained—but perfectly friendly and perhaps a little more sincere.

History: the Hanseatic League

Lübeck, Hamburg and Bremen were among the first cities in Germany to shoulder their way out of feudal control and organize their own systems of administration and justice, each becoming a wealthy, independent Free Imperial City of the Holy Roman Empire. In 1243 Lübeck and Hamburg signed a trade agreement. Gradually this alliance expanded to include nearly all the ports along the Baltic, and even some inland towns such as Cologne and Brunswick. This **Hanseatic League** was originally formed to fend off pirates and put an end to destructive bickering between the towns, but soon it became a powerful cartel, monopolizing Baltic trade and even opening trading centres abroad (the most important one was in London).

However, in the 16th century the herring shoals that were so vital to the local economy mysteriously took off to the North Sea. The Dutch, who had found a new way to preserve the fish, and had faster ships, began to crack the League's hold on Baltic trade. They also made better use of new trade routes to the Americas and the East. The Hanseatic League went into decline, and was finally killed off by the Thirty Years' War; the last nine members met in Lübeck in 1669. Hamburg, Lübeck and Bremen have survived as strong trading cities. Bremen and Hamburg kept their Free Imperial City status, and today are passionately proud that they are *Lände* in their own right.

Hamburg

Fynes Moryson, travelling through Germany in the early 17th century, decided to give Hamburg a miss because 'the people after dinner, warmed with drinke, are apt to wrong any stranger, and hardly endure an English-man in the morning when they are sober'. Today things could scarcely be more different. 'English gentleman's manners' are held in higher esteem than *savoir vivre*; fashion and style is remarkably English, and there is even a healthy local cricket club. '*Wenn es in London regnet, spannen die Hamburger die Schirme auf*' ('When it rains in London, Hamburgers put up their umbrellas'), locals say wrily.

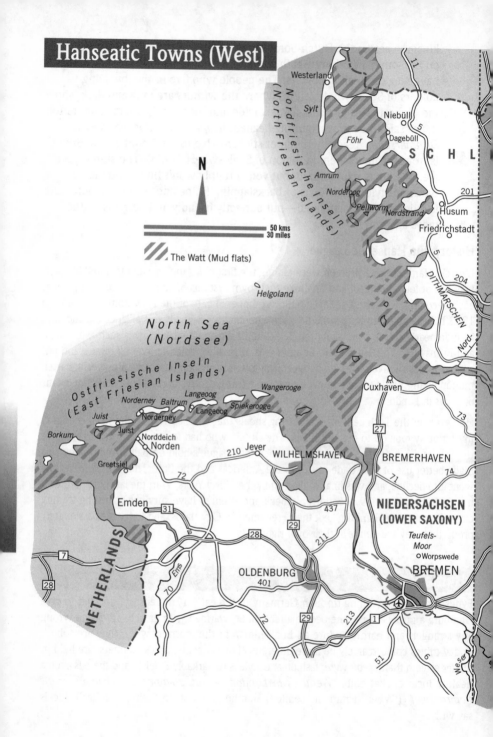

Hanseatic Towns (West)

N

50 kms
30 miles

The Watt (Mud flats)

Westerland

Nordfriesische Inseln
(North Friesian Islands)

Sylt

Niebüll

Föhr

Dagebüll

5

S C H L

Amrum

Norderoog

Pellworm

Nordstrand

Husum

201

Friedrichstadt

DITHMARSCHEN

204

Nord-

Helgoland

North Sea
(Nordsee)

Ostfriesische Inseln
(East Friesian Islands)

Wangerooge

Cuxhaven

Langeoog

Norderney   Baltrum

Spiekerooge

73

Juist

Norderney

Langeoog

27

Borkum

Juist

Norddeich

Norden

Jever

WILHELMSHAVEN

BREMERHAVEN

Greetsiel

210

74

72

71

Emden

31

437

NIEDERSACHSEN
(LOWER SAXONY)

28

29

211

Teufels-
Moor

NETHERLANDS

7

Worpswede

BREMEN

28

70

Ems

OLDENBURG

401

28

72

29

213

1

51

6

Weser

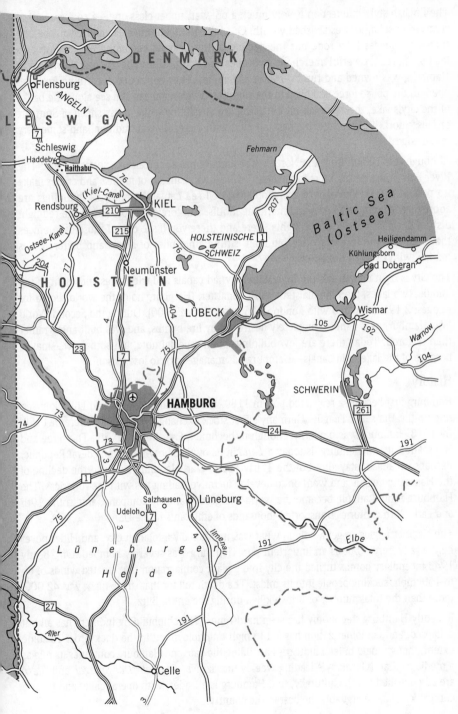

The English style in question is very much a pre-war, upper-class one—a cool grace that stems from solid, long-established wealth. Of all the Hanseatic cities Hamburg was the one that most successfully rode out the decline of the League, becoming one of Europe's leading ports. Powerful merchant dynasties grew up. Until the Second World War Hamburg was owned and run by 100 or so families. They controlled everything from the opera to the police force and lived in the sumptuous villas you can still see along the banks of the city's lake, the Außenalster. Yet Hamburg doesn't have the glossy sheen of Stuttgart or Düsseldorf. It is very much a harbour city, with a great liberal tradition, and some very rough edges.

Although it is 100km from the North Sea, Hamburg has all the air of a seafaring port. The River Elbe brings ocean liners to the heart of the town. Clusters of funnels and cranes make up part of the skyline. There are shops that sell sea captain's uniforms, buildings are adorned with sculpted boats and maritime motifs, and foreign sailors haunt the red-light district or pause to look at the sights. Here and there you'll see one of those little offices that seem unique to ports—one old man, sitting amid piles of boxes and battered files marked with exotic destinations.

The city is built on water—the River Elbe, myriad canals and tributaries and, right in the middle, two lakes, the Binnenalster and Außenalster. (Hamburg holds the world record for bridges: 2,195 compared with London's 850 and Venice's 400). During the Second World War Hamburg was almost completely destroyed by fire bombs, and was built anew rather than restored. Today there are few buildings of any special note, but somehow—maybe because of the lakes and canals—Hamburg has managed not to lose its soul.

History

Hamburg first became a registered port in 1189, and soon afterwards joined Lübeck in setting up the Hanseatic League. Germany's first stock exchange was founded here in 1558. By 1618 Hamburg was powerful enough to become a Free Imperial City. The 'Free and Hanseatic City of Hamburg' is today a *Land* in its own right within the Federal Republic. Perhaps because it stayed out of the Thirty Years' War, Hamburg survived the decline of the Hanseatic League and went on to develop lucrative trading ties with the Americas. The Hamburg-Amerika-Linie became the world's largest steamship company, and in the 19th and early 20th centuries transported thousands of emigrants to the USA.

The Nazis struggled to get a hold in what was traditionally a tolerant city, and Hitler never held a rally here—but as an important port Hamburg was severely bombed. On 28 July 1943 incendiary bombs turned the city into a giant conflagration that created winds of up to 160kmph, sucking people into its midst. The death toll for that single night was 42,000, more than the total number of British killed during the entire Blitz.

Recently Hamburg's economy has seen hard times. The shipbuilding industry has all but collapsed, and containerization has led to high unemployment in the dockyards. To some extent, though, new hi-tech industries are filling the gap, and Hamburg continues its role as a media capital. (Germany's leading weekly magazines, *Die Zeit*, *Der Spiegel*, and *Stern* are all published here). Culturally, too, Hamburg is a leader, with opera, ballet and theatre companies that are arguably the best in the country.

By Air

The **airport**, ✆ (040) 50750, is just 8km northeast of the centre. An Airport City Bus leaves from Kirchenallee in front of the Hauptbahnhof every 20 minutes (journey time 25min), or you can catch the underground to Ohlsdorf and then take the Airport Express bus. There are direct connections all over Germany and also to Paris, Amsterdam, London, Birmingham and Manchester.

By Car

Hamburg is on the A24, 274km from Berlin, and 100km from Bremen on the A1. Parking in the city centre can be difficult, so it is a better idea to leave your car in one of the parking garages around the outskirts and rely on the highly efficient public transport system.

Car hire: Avis, Drehbahn 15–25 ✆ (040) 341 651; airport ✆ (040) 50 75 2314); Herz, Kirchenallee 34 ✆ (040) 280 1201, airport ✆ (040) 50 75 2302).

Mitfahrzentrale: Citynetz, Gotenstr. 19, ✆ (040) 19 444.

By Train

The **Hauptbahnhof**, ✆ (040) 39180, is just to the east of the Altstadt. It is a busy station, served by IC and the high-speed ICE trains. There are connections all over Germany, including Bremen (54min), Berlin (3½hr), Frankfurt (3½–4½hr) and Munich (6hr).

By Boat

Travelling by boat up the Elbe is one of the best ways to arrive in Germany (*see* **Travel** p. 8). The main carrier to **England** (Harwich and Newcastle) is Scandinavian Seaways, Van-der-Smissen-Str. 4, ✆ (040) 389 030. For cruises to **Heligoland** try KG Seetouristik, Eppendorfer Weg 127, ✆ (040) 402 929. The best way to see the **harbour** is on a cruiseboat. These leave from the Landungsbrücke. An hour's cruise costs DM14. Trips around the Alster depart from Jungfernstieg every 45 mins from 10.45–6 (DM2.50 per landing stage); for information ✆ (040) 341 141. To rent a pedalo, yacht or 'kissing canoe' (equipped with a mattress) contact **Bobby Reich**, Fernsicht 2, ✆ (040) 487 824, or one of the companies opposite the Hotel Atlantic on the Außenalster.

Public Transport

A super-efficient network of buses, U-Bahn and S-Bahn trains and ferries gets you all over the city; for information ✆ (040) 322 911. Tickets are available from machines at the stops. As a visitor your best deal is to buy a **Hamburg-Card** which allows you free travel on all public transport, as well as free entry to the major museums and a host of other discounts. The price starts at DM9.50 for 24 hours, and the card is available from tourist information offices and some travel agents and hotels.

Taxis: ✆ (040) 686 868 or 611 122. Taxi for the **disabled**, ✆ (040) 410 5458.

Bicycle hire: The tourist information office in the Bieberhaus offers bicycles for hire at DM10 a day.

Tourist Information

Hamburg's five **tourist information offices** all stock maps and brochures. The staff can help with hotel bookings and city tours. **Bieberhaus**, Hachmannplatz *(Mon–Fri 9–6, Sat 9–3)*; **Hauptbahnhof**, main exit *(daily 7am–11pm)*; **Airport**, Terminal 3 *(daily 8am–11pm)*; **Hanse-Viertel**, Poststraße *(Mon–Fri 10–6.30, Thurs to 8.30, Sat 10–3, Sun 11–3)*; **Harbour**, St Pauli-Landungsbrücken between piers 4 and 5 *(daily 9–6; Nov–Feb daily 9–5)*.

Post office: There is a post office at the main exit of the Hauptbahnhof. The central post office, Hühnerposten 12, offers a **24-hour service**.

Bureaux de change: Deutsche Bank, airport *(daily 6.30am–10.30pm)*; Deutsche-Verkehrs-Kredit-Bank, Hauptbahnhof, south entrance *(daily 7.30–10)*.

Police: ✆ 110.

Medical emergencies: ✆ (040) 228 022.

Festivals

The **Hamburger Dom** dates back to the 10th century, when locals bullied the Archbishop into letting them have a winter fair inside the cathedral. The *Dom* itself has long since been demolished, but the name lives on in what is now North Germany's biggest funfair. Three times a year, the vast Heiligengeistenfeld (between St Michaelis and the TV tower, U-Bahn to St Pauli, Feldstraße or Messehallen) is crammed with show booths, roundabouts and hi-tech rides. Food stalls and beer tents do a roaring trade and on Friday nights there is a free fireworks display. The Spring Dom is usually from mid-March to mid-April, the Summer Dom from late July to late August and the Winter Dom from early November to early December.

There are two other city parties, both of which include open-air performances and other cultural events: the **Pert Birthday** festivities in May and the **Alster-vergnuugen**, a fair on the Binnenalster in August/September. The city's main cultural event (shared with other towns in the region) is the **Schleswig-Holstein Music Festival**, which attracts top-drawer artistes from around the world.

The Alster

In the heart of Hamburg is a 184-hectare lake, the Alster. A bridge divides it into two parts. The vast **Außenalster** (Outer Alster) is bordered by parkland and discreetly elegant villas, the much smaller **Binnenalster** (Inner Alster) is the best business address in town. To walk around the whole lake would take a good three hours, though a quick circuit of the Binnenalster takes just 20 minutes. Here the noble, weighty buildings are by law painted grey or white, or left in natural stone—no garish colours disturb the *gutbürgerliche* solemnity. Genteel old ladies, hooked together in pairs, parade slowly up the leafy Neuer Jungfernstieg on the way to marathon *kaffee und kuche* sessions. Pin-stripe-suited businessmen murmur quietly to each other as they head to expensive lunches. But along the southern edge of the lake, skateboards thunder over the concrete, and on the bridge that divides it from the Aussenalster the sleek ICE train shoots past towards the Hauptbahnhof.

The Außenalster is ideal for messing about in boats (*see* **Getting Around**, above), though in high summer so many people take to the idea that sailing begins to resemble water-born dodgems. Harvestehude (known as **Pöseldorf**, take the U-Bahn to Hallerstraße) on the west bank was where Hamburg's oldest and grandest families lived (many still do). To marry outside this tight circle, even into one of the families on the opposite bank (who were far too free with their money) was thought socially dangerous. 'The Alster is such a great divide', careworn mothers would sigh. Today you can wander the streets admiring the sumptuous villas (which the Allies tactfully neglected to bomb) or sip expensive drinks in a waterside café.

Around the Rathaus

Hamburg's lordly **Rathaus** dates back only to the 1840s. In 1842 a great fire destroyed most of the rather rickety medieval Altstadt, razing the old Rathaus to the ground. In its place the good burghers put up a neo-Renaissance pile, decked out with patron saints and maritime motifs. Step inside for a look at the imposing **lobby**, where people sit on low benches around the pillars—rather like menials awaiting an audience in some grandee's palace. You can see the rest of the interior—mainly dim, panelled rooms with heavy leather furniture—by taking a **guided tour** *(Mon–Thurs 10.15–3.15, Fri–Sun 10.15– 1.15, hourly in English; adm DM1).*

Backing onto the Rathaus is the Neoclassical **Stock Exchange** *(tours Mon–Thurs 11 am; adm free)*, built in the 1850s on the site of the 16th-century original. Past the Stock Exchange, over Adolphusbrücke, you come to Hamburg's chicest shopping district (*see* **Shopping** below). Arcades of expensive boutiques criss-cross the patch between the Gänsemarkt and the Rathausmarkt. Stylish cafés edge up to canals that flow between tastefully modern buildings. The atmosphere is subdued—you get the feeling that you're on the set of a *Vogue* fashion advert, just before the filming starts.

Back across Schleusenbrücke and over the Rathausmarkt you come to **Mönckebergstraße**, the realm of the big department stores and stamping ground of High Street shoppers (*see* **Shopping** below). **St Petri** pokes its steeple way above them all. With

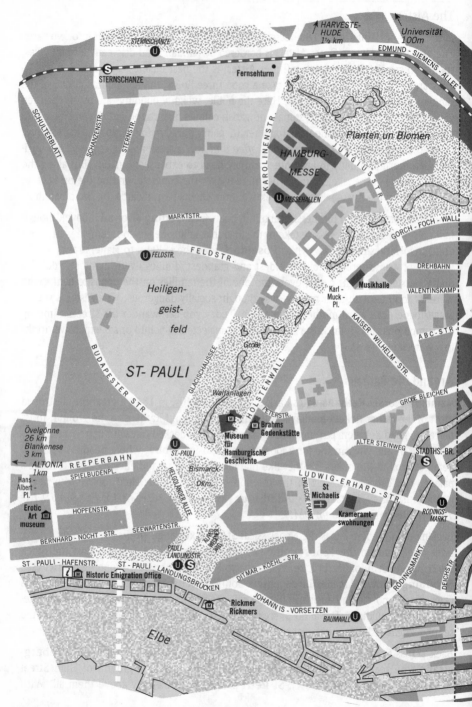

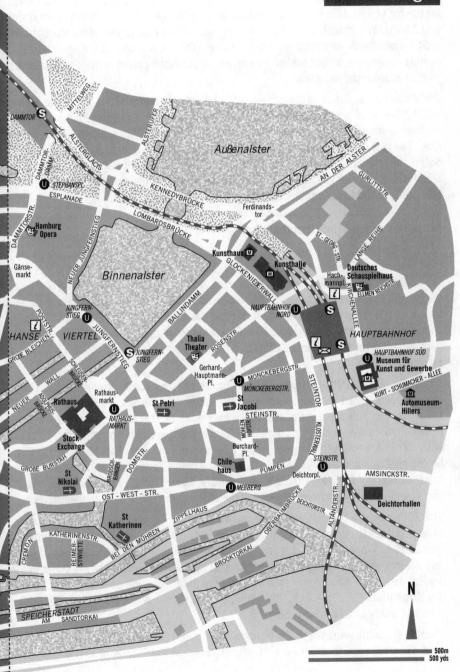

Außenalster

Binnenalster

DAMMTOR

MITTELWEG

ALSTERGLACIS

ALSTERUFER

AN DER ALSTER

GURLITTSTR.

STEPHANSPL.

DAMMTOR-DAMM

DAMMTORSTR.

ESPLANADE

KENNEDYBRÜCKE

Ferdinands-tor

ST-GEORG-STR.

LANGE REIHE

Hamburg
Opera

LOMBARDSBRÜCKE

NEUER JUNGFERNSTIEG

Gänse-markt

Kunsthaus

Kunsthalle

GLOCKENGIEßERWALL

Hach-mannpl.

Deutsches
Schauspielhaus

KIRCHENALLEE

ELLMENREICHSTR.

HANSE

POSTSTR.

JUNGFERN-STIEG

JUNGFERNSTIEG

VIERTEL

BALLINDAMM

HAUPTBAHNHOF
NORD

HAUPTBAHNHOF

GROßE BLEICHEN

JUNGFERN-STIEG

Thalia
Theater

ROSENSTR.

HAUPTBAHNHOF SÜD

SCHLEUSEN-BRÜCKE

WALL

Gerhard-Hauptmann-Pl.

MONCKEBERGSTR.

Museum für
Kunst und Gewerbe

KURT-SCHUMACHER-ALLEE

NEUER

ADOLPHS-BRÜCKE

Rathaus

Rathaus-markt

St Petri

MONCKEBERGSTR.

St
Jacobi

STEINSTR.

Automuseum-Hillers

RATHAUS-MARKT

STEINSTR.

Stock
Exchange

DOMSTR.

BROOSCH-RAVEN

MOHLEN HOFSTR.

Burchard-Pl.

STEINTOR

KLOSTERWALL

GROßE BURSTAH

Chile-haus

PUMPEN

STEINSTR.

AMSINCKSTR.

St
Nikolai

Deichtorpl.

NEUER

MEßBERG

OST-WEST-STR.

ZIPPELHAUS

Deichtorhallen

ALTÄNDERSTR.

DEICHTORSTR.

CREMON

St
Katherinen

KATHERINENSTR.

REIMER-STWIETE

BEI DEN MÜHREN

OBERBAUMBRÜCKE

BROOKTORKAI

SPEICHERSTADT

AM SANDTORKAI

N

500m
500 yds

records going back to the 11th century, St Petri claims to be Hamburg's oldest church, though most of the present structure was put up after the fires of 1842 and 1943, except for the big bronze door-knocker, which dates from the 14th century. Inside, portraits of proud burghers outnumber the religious paintings. Further east, just off Mönckebergstraße, is **St Jacobi**, with its distinctive copper tower. The church contains a precious 17th-century **organ** (one of the finest of the era), and an interesting panoramic view of Hamburg painted at about the same time.

A walk down Mohlenhofstraße and across Burchardplatz brings you to the **Chile Haus**, built in the 1920s by the expressionist architect Fritz Höger for a shipowner who had made his fortune from South American saltpetre. Höger shaped his brick building like an ocean liner. The best view is from Pumpen, where the walls come to a sharp point and you really do get the impression that you are standing beneath the bow of a ship. If this period of architecture interests you, have a look inside one or two of the entrance lobbies—all the original tiling and fixed furniture is still intact.

Museums around the Hauptbahnhof

Mönckerbergstraße leads east to the Hauptbahnhof. Nearby you'll find Hamburg's two most rewarding museums. The **Kunsthalle** *(Tues–Sun 10–5; adm DM3)*, just across from the north entrance, houses the city's main art collection. The most important early work is the winged altar done for St Petri by Master Bertram (1330–1414)—an impressive combination of gilded carving and 36 finely painted panels. Pride of the Dutch and Flemish collection is an early Rembrandt, *The Presentation at the Temple* (1627). Although Rembrandt was only 21 when he painted it, his subtle play of light and shadow is instantly recognizable.

The collection of **19th-century** German paintings is especially strong. Caspar David Friedrich gets a good showing; his famous *Wanderer over the Sea of Mist* (1815) is hung here. You can also see most of the works ever done by that painter of chubby babies, Philipp Otto Runge—including a portrait of his disagreeable-looking parents, their faces set with 'When are you going to get a proper job?' expressions. There are also fine paintings by the meticulous realist Wilhelm Leibl and by Anselm Feuerbach, arguably one of the finest painters of female portraits of the century. Lovis Corinth and Max Liebermann, Impressionists painting towards the end of the century, each get a room to themselves.

The **20th-century** collection includes good work by the German expressionists and some dreamy (rather than nightmarish) paintings by Edvard Munch, the Norwegian painter of *The Scream.* Work by the British artist David Hockney, and the usual collection of mud, felt, defunct electronic equipment and rotting fat by Joseph Beuys, brings you closer to the present day. If you want to see really up-to-the-minute art you will need to go next door to the **Kunsthaus** *(Ferdinandstor, Tues–Sun 10–6; adm free)*, which holds changing exhibitions of (mainly local) contemporary artists.

Outside the south entrance to the Hauptbahnhof you will find the **Museum für Kunst und Gewerbe** (Arts and Crafts Museum) *(Tues–Sun 10–5; adm DM3)*. This is a fascinating museum, with good collections of porcelain and medieval carving, some exquisitely worked musical instruments and even a full-size Japanese tea-house, where you can take part in a **tea ceremony** *(Sat 1 pm, 2 and 3, Sun 11, 1, 2 and 3; adm DM5)*. The collection of **Jugendstil furniture** is the best in Germany. Entire rooms are furnished with choice examples of the style, and you can even visit the complete 'Paris Room' from the 1900 World Exhibition. Surplus stock overflows into the museum's **restaurant**—a cluster of superbly done out small rooms. It is worth paying the museum entrance fee just for the chance to have coffee there.

A step or two further south, on Kurt-Schumacher-Allee, is the **Automuseum-Hillers** *(daily 10–5; adm DM5)*, with row upon row of shiny cars—from a 1934 Rolls Royce to a three-wheeler bubble car. There is also an arsenal of bicycles, scooters and motorbikes. Klosterwall leads off the end of Kurt-Schumacher-Allee to Deichtorplatz. From here, Deichtorstraße takes you to the **Deichtorhallen**, a vast former indoor vegetable market that now plays host to major visiting art exhibitions.

Along the Elbe: St Nikolai to St Michaelis

From Deichtorplatz, a walk west along Ost-West-Straße brings you to the gaunt, blackened spire of **St Nikolai**—all that remains of one of Germany's finest neo-Gothic churches. Today it is a memorial to victims of the Nazi regime, and to those killed by the same Allied bombs that destroyed the rest of the church. Across the hectically busy Ost-West-Straße you can see the more modest spire of **St Katharinen**. In the adjoining church hall there is an interesting audio-visual show on Hamburg's history *(German only, Mon–Fri 11 and 3, Sat and Sun 3; adm DM7)*. In the alleys west of the church, off Katherinenstraße, you can find small clusters of restored **17th- and 18th-century warehouses**, most of them now operating as restaurants. (The best ones are in Reinerstwilte, Cremon and Deichstraße).

If you take one of the bridges south across the Zollkanal, you find yourself in the **Speicherstadt** (literally: warehouse city)—an atmospheric island, criss-crossed by small working waterways and covered in tall, rather decorous 19th-century red-brick warehouses. The air is filled with the smell of coffee and spices. Persian carpets are stacked metres high in front of open upstairs windows, and stocky dockers still hump cargo about and hoist it to the upper floors with ropes and pulleys. Hamburg's main harbour (a little further west) is highly mechanized, and can unload a ship in a matter of hours, but here the pace is altogether more sedate. Apart from the odd small van puttering about, little would seem to have changed since the warehouses were built. Traditionally, companies can keep goods here tax free until the price is right—so you have to pass through a customs post to get onto the island. More oriental carpets are stored here, awaiting market fluctuations, than anywhere else in the world.

To the west (back along Ost-West-Straße and Ludwig-Erhard-Straße), you come to Hamburg's finest church, **St Michaelis**, known locally as *Michel*. Its distinctive Baroque spire is the most impressive part of Hamburg's skyline to travellers arriving up the Elbe, and has become the city's symbol. The 80m-high **viewing platform** *(May–Oct daily 9–5.30; Nov–Apr 10–4 except Wed, and Sun 11.30–4; lift; adm DM4)*, offers spectacular vistas across the harbour and the city. Every day at noon you can hear one of the three church **organs** in action. Through a small archway at Krayenkamp 10, at the foot of the Michel, is an alley of 17th-century almshouses, the **Krameramtswohnungen**. The shopkeepers' guild built these dinky cottages for members' widows, who were not allowed to carry on trading after their husbands' death. The houses were used up until the 1960s, but today most have been converted into shops. Hordes of tourists stomp about the quiet yard like a tribe of Gullivers and cramp into the one flat still in its original condition *(daily 10–5; adm DM2)*.

Along the Elbe: the Landungsbrücken, the Fischmarkt and the Reeperbahn

A narrow park leads down from St Michaelis to the Elbe, coming out just a short distance east of the **St-Pauli-Landungsbrücken**, once the port's main passenger terminal, now the boarding point for **harbour tours** (*see* **Getting Around**, above). The turn-of-the-century terminal buildings are worth a visit even if you are not catching a boat. From inside a solid-looking domed cube, four lifts take you 24m below the Elbe to a **tunnel** *(Mon–Fri 5.30am–8pm, Sat to 4.30; adm free)*, built betwen 1907 and 1911. A few minutes' eerie, echoing walk brings you up on the southern side of the river. Between Piers 4 and 5 of the Landungsbrücken, at the **Historic Emigration Office** *(daily 10–6, Nov–Feb 10–5)*, descendants of the 5 million passengers who passed through Hamburg on their way to the New World can find out on what boat their forefathers left. Moored at Pier 1 is **Rickmer Rickmers** *(daily 10–5.30; adm DM4)*, a restored East Indies windjammer, teeming with excited children, from the dark holds to the poop deck.

Hafenstraße leads west from the Landungsbrücke along the top of an embankment. The patrician mansions along its length were occupied by squatters in the 1980s, and police attempts to oust them led to many bloody battles. The authorities were only partially successful and many squatters still live in the graffiti-daubed palaces. The street has an unpleasantly aggressive edge. You'll have to brave it, though, if you want to visit the **Erotic Art Museum** *(daily 10am–midnight; adm DM4)*, a large collection of more unusual works by the likes of Lovis Corinth, Otto Dix, Jean Cocteau and many less reputable, but just as imaginative, artists.

Both the Hafenstraße and a less eventful dockside walkway lead west from the Landungsbrücke to the **Fischmarkt**. Here, on Sunday mornings between 6 and 10 (when an old law puts an end to trading before church services begin), you can buy not only fresh fish, but fruit, ethnic trinkets, plants and clothes. Its best to get there in the early hours when everything is touched with a misty dawn light. Bargain-hunting restaurateurs mingle with dewy-eyed lovers and fazed night-clubbers who have staggered straight off the dancefloor. Cafés do a roaring breakfast trade and jazz bands compete with the vendors' patter.

Running parallel to the Hafenstraße, but a little inland, is the **Reeperbahn**, main street of the St Pauli quarter and Europe's most infamous red-light district after the one in Amsterdam. The Reeperbahn, however, lacks the irony (and so also the charm) of Amsterdam's *walletjes*. Things only really get going after 10pm. Fast food, quick sex, gambling and peep-shows are the staple fare. Under the flashing neon lights persistent street-walkers tag along behind you, drunks and junkies lie about like human litter, and smarmy touts try to lure you into their dens, with an Ortonesque 'Naked ladies, sir, all alive'. Gone is any trace of the romance of a dockside brothel district, jolly sailors' taverns or the weary wink of a friendly Madame. Recently there have been some attempts to clean up the St Pauli quarter, and the main thoroughfares at least are slowly creeping upmarket. You will find one or two good restaurants, some trendy nightclubs and a couple of popular theatres, but on the whole the Reeperbahn remains sordid, exploitative and avoidable.

Northwest of the Centre

From the eastern end of the Reeperbahn, heading north in a curve reaching almost to the Außenalster is **Planten un Blomen**, a big and very popular botanical garden. At the beginning of the Holstenwall (which runs parallel to the gardens) is the **Museum für Hamburgische Geschichte** (History Museum) *(Tues–Sun 10–5; adm DM3)*. Here you'll find some rather good models of the city, cases of model boats and 250sq m of model railway *(demonstrated hourly on the half hour 10.30–3.30, not at 1.30 or on Sat afternoons)*. The museum also contains a well-preserved hall of a 17th-century Hansa merchant's house.

In Peterstraße (the first road to the right off Holstenwall) you can see some superbly restored 18th-century townhouses. The house at No. 39 is the **Brahms Gedenkstätte** (Brahms Memorial) *(Tues and Fri 12–1, Thurs 4–6, 1st Sat in month 10–2; adm DM2)*, an undynamic collection of memorabilia relating to the Hamburg-born Romantic composer.

Pick of the Suburbs

Altona, just west of St Pauli once belonged to the King of Denmark, and only became part of Hamburg in 1937. Hamburgers thought this rival trading town was *Al te na* (All too near)—and the name stuck. During the 19th-century boom, rows of grand villas were built in Altona, along the roads on the north bank of the Elbe, **Palmaille** and the **Elbchaussee**. (The best view of these mansions is from the river rather than the street.) Today Altona is a vibrant *Gastarbeiter* suburb with the liveliest spots in the area west of the Bahnhof, around Friedensallee and Friedens-Bahrenstraße.

At its north-eastern corner Altona blends with the **Univiertel** (University Quarter). The patch around Schulterblatt and Schanzenstraße is popular with students, but can seem a little rough. Things improve as you get closer to Harvesthude and the main campus, especially around Grindelhof and Rentzelstraße, where there are some good restaurants and cafés (see **Eating and Drinking**, below).

Carrying on west along the Elbchaussee you come to **Övelgönne** (bus 183), a pretty, but thoroughly gentrified, fishing village. The dreamy little harbour is crammed with carefully restored boats—from steam tugs to 19th-century fishing trawlers. All of them are privately owned and in working order, which means that you might arrive to find the harbour empty—but if you do bump into one of the enthusiasts they are usually only too happy to show you around. Further down the road is **Blankenese** (S-Bahn Line 1 or 11), traditionally a favourite with retired sea-captains, but now yuppy territory. Cottages, smart modern homes and elegant Jugendstil villas cluster tightly together on a steep hillside that slopes down to the Elbe.

Hamburg's swishest shopping district is in the corner formed by Jungfernstieg, the Neuer Wall and the Gänsemarkt. Smart new covered **arcades** wind through grand old buildings and stylish new ones. This is the place for designer fashions, gourmet treats and bankable jewellery. The Hanse Viertel, Galleria and Hamburgerhof are the pick of the arcades. Department stores and more conventional shops are to be found along **Mönckeberg-straße** (known as the *Mö*), and in the streets between the Mö and the Binnenalster. The best places for **antiques** are the 'Quartier Latin' on ABC-Straße near the Gänsemarkt and a spacious (rather cheaper) antique market at Klosterwall 9–21 (near the Deichtorhallen). The backstreets near the Landunsbrücke are the place to pick up maritime paraphernalia and naval uniforms, and the Markstraße in the Karolinenviertel (U-Bahn to Messehallen) is where you'll find more off-beat fashions and second-hand stores—though the laid-back proprietors usually don't open up shop until noon.

Hamburg © (040–) **Where to Stay**

expensive

Atlantic Hotel, An der Alster 72, © 28880, fax 247 129 (DM428–538). Pristine, glistening white Grand Hotel on the Außenalster, built in 1909 for passengers from luxury liners. Cool, airy elegance with soft colours and marble everywhere, and lofty ceilings even in the smaller rooms. The pricier suites look out over the lake, others open out onto a quiet inner courtyard. You can spend hours working your way through the breakfast buffet, staring out across the Außenalster.

Vier Jahreszeiten, Neuer Jungfernstieg, 9–14, © 34940, fax 349 4602 (DM465–545). Plush elegance, the epitome of Hamburg discrete wealth and favoured end-point of those old ladies on the Binnenalster intent on *Kaffee und Kuche*.

Renaissance Hotel, Große Bleichen, © 349 180, fax 349 18431 (DM325–455). Classy hotel in converted Fritz Höger (he of the Chile Haus) building. Attentive service. The rooms all have enormous beds and cool cotton sheets.

moderate

Hotel Hafen Hamburg, Seewartenstr. 9, © 311 130, fax 319 2736 (DM180–205). Cavernous old hotel overlooking the Landungsbrücke. Most rooms are spacious and individually furnished, and even non-residents come here for the breakfast. Sometimes subject to coach-party invasions.

Hotel am Holstenwall, Holstenwall 19, © 311 275, fax 316 264 (DM238–268). Personally managed hotel with a friendly atmosphere and an in-house theatre. Convenient for the city centre.

Hotel Fürst Bismarck, Kirchenallee 49, © 280 1091, fax 280 1096 (DM175). The most individual of the hotels near the Hauptbahnhof. A tall, narrow town-house—which means that some of the rooms are a little pokey. No restaurant.

Hotel Vorbach, Johnsallee 63–7, ✆ 441 820, fax 441 82888 (DM200–280). Converted Harvesthuder *Bürgerhaus*, run with appropriate style and solid Hamburger respectability by the same family for three generations. Tastefully modernized, and a step back from undignified city bustle.

Mellingburger Schleuse, Mellingburgredder 1, ✆ 602 4001, fax 602 7912 (DM225); U-Bahn to Poppenbüttel or Bus 276 to terminus. Restored 18th-century thatched farmhouse on the north-east edge of town. Cosy, piled high with rustic furniture and with genial, welcoming management.

Wedina, Gurlittstr. 23, ✆ 243 011, fax 280 3894 (DM145–195). Comfortable hotel with a garden and pool in quiet area near the Außenalster not far from the centre. Good value.

Eden, Ellmenreichstr. 20, ✆ 248 480, fax 241 521 (DM110–200). Modern, reliable, few-frills hotel near the station.

inexpensive

Hotel-Pension Riedinger, St-Georg-Str. 8, ✆ 247 463 (DM98–115 without private bathroom). Quiet *Pension* in the shadow of the mighty Hotel Atlantic. Well-managed and friendly. No restaurant.

Annenhof, Lange Reihe 23, ✆ 243 426 (DM90 without private bathroom). Bordering on a seedy area of town, but clean and comfortable. Helpful management. No restaurant.

Sarah Petersen, Lange Reihe 50, ✆ 249 826 (DM89 without private bathroom). Simple but comfortable *Pension* near station. No restaurant.

Youth Hostel: Jugendherberge Auf dem Stintfang, Alfred-Wegener-Weg 5, ✆ 313 488.

Eating and Drinking: Restaurants and Taverns

expensive

Atlantic Restaurant, Atlantic Hotel, An der Alster 72, ✆ 28880 (DM80–120). Genteel, sedate restaurant in the Biedermeier style where diners can enjoy unpretentious but good French-influenced cuisine. The menu changes seasonally, but comes up with such triumphs as cream of lobster soup with fresh basil and fillets of sole cooked in chablis.

L'Auberge Francaise, Rutschbahn 34, ✆ 410 2532 (DM90–150). A Hamburg institution. Impeccable service and classic French cuisine.

Le Canard, Elbchaussee 139, ✆ 880 5057 (DM80–150). Rival French cuisine from upstart chef Joseph Viehauser, in a flashy new building overlooking the Elbe. Excellent fish dishes.

Nikolaikeller, Cremon 36, ✆ 361 113 (DM50–60). In the cellar of a 19th-century waterside restaurant. Famed for its *Matjes* (marinated herring) —but good on other fish too. The crab soup is a must.

Cölln's Austern, Caviar und Hummerstuben, Brodschrangen 1–5, ✆ 326 059 (DM60–100). Classic oyster, caviar and lobster bar. Cool, elegant ambience. Also other fish dishes such as cod with Dijon mustard sauce and a herb parfait.

Schopenhauer, Riemerstwiete 20, ✆ 371 510 (DM20–30). Seventeenth-century inn near the *Speicherstadt*. Good lunchtime spot, with daily changing menu that includes delicacies such as cold duck breast and *Feldsalat*.

Zur Brandanfang, Deichstr. 25, ✆ 365 520 (DM30–40). Converted 17th-century half-timbered house liberally decorated with marine parphenalia. Good cold meat and cheese platters as well as heavier Hamburger fare.

Das Kontor, Deichstr. 32, ✆ 371 471. Popular with younger crowd. Serves *Matjes* and also fondue and raclette.

Alt-Hamburger Aalspeicher, Deichstr. 43, ✆ 362 990 (DM45–65). Eels. Roasted, grilled, smoked, or made into *Aalsuppe* (Hamburg's most famous speciality—a soup made with eels, vegetables and plums, tastier than it sounds).

Fischerhaus, St-Pauli-Fischmarkt 14, ✆ 314 053 (DM25–40). Good, plain fish dishes right on the Fischmarkt.

Kanzelmeyer, Englische Planke 8, ✆ 364 833 (DM30–45). Turn-of-the-century restaurant near St Michaelis. Touristy but with good, wholesome Hamburg cuisine.

Bistro Hof, Thadenstr. 78, ✆ 435 787 (DM45–65, reservation essential). The walls are covered in a vile yellow latex, and the tables are wonky, but the food is divine. Superb salads and fine meats with secret aromatic sauces. Good wine list.

Brouwer's, Dorotheenstr. 180, ✆ 480 7868 (DM20–30). Lovingly prepared and presented meals for small purses. The veal and chicken *en croûte* is delicious.

O Pescador, Ditmar Koehl Str. 17, ✆ 319 3000 (DM15–30). Excellent Portuguese fish restaurant in the lanes behind the Landungsbrücken. The swordfish is delicious and the DM12 set menu at lunchtime is always worth it.

Kajutte, Deichstr. 41 (DM10). *Imbiß* and *Stehcafé* among the posher converted warehouses in Deichstraße. Giant sausages, homemade *frikadellen*, daily fish specials.

Bars and Cafés

Central

M & M Bar, Hotel Reichshof, Kirchenallee 34/36, ✆ 248 330. Classic 1930s bar—about the only one left in Hamburg.

Galerie Stuben, Krayenkamp 10. Small café in the pretty Krameramtswohnungen courtyard. Unexpectedly quiet, as the tourists who flock to see the almshouses don't stay more than a few minutes.

Petit Delice, Große Bleichen 21, ℂ 343 470. At the end of the Galleria, one of Hamburg's smartest shopping arcades. Don your gladrags and Ray Bans for a coffee, salad or ice-cream at the water's edge.

Thämers, Großmarkt. The best of a number of good cafés with terraces on **Großmarkt**—a quiet, leafy square just north of St Michaeli. They also serve tasty snacks. A popular spot on summer evenings.

Schmidt's Theatre Bar, Spielbundenplatz 24, ℂ 314 804. Relaxed and pleasant adjunct to Hamburg's famous Variety theatre. An oasis in the Reeperbahn.

La Paloma, Gerhardstr. 2, ℂ 314 512. Just off the Reeperbahn. A 24-hour licence and a few original paintings on the walls give it the reputation of an arty hangout.

Mary Lou's, Hans-Albers-Platz. One of the less tacky bars in the red-light district. Noisy, friendly and popular with gay men.

Tiefenrausch, Hopfenstr. 34. Hyper-trendy cellar bar with slick young crowd and pulsating music.

Further Afield

Klein Fährhaus, Alsterpark. Elegant garden café on the west bank of the Alster near the Fährdamm boat stop.

Abaton, Grindelhof 14a; ℂ 45777. Big and cheery student drinking tavern near the university. Also serves steaks, pastas and vegetarian meals (DM20–30).

Erika's Eck, Sternstr. 98. Only opens for business at 2am. Quickly fills up with late-night drinkers and workers from the nearby abattoir who come in for big, meaty breakfasts.

Monsun, Friedensallee 36, ℂ 390 3148. Trendy theatre café in Altona, with quiet courtyard. Also does cheap, fresh meals (DM10–20).

Bolero, Bahrenfelder Str. 53, ℂ 390 7800. In Altona. Exotic beergarden with a Mexican touch and a lively young crowd.

Café Eisenstein, Friedensallee 9, ℂ 390 4606. Popular Sunday brunch spot in Altona. Cheeses, smoked salmon and heavenly coffee.

Schuldt's Café, Süllbergterrassen 34, ℂ 862 411. Peaceful beer-and-sausage café with a terrace high on the slopes of Blankenese, overlooking the Elbe.

Strandperle, Am Schulberg 2, ℂ 880 1112. In Övelgönne, right on the banks of the Elbe. Sip beer until midnight to a backdrop of harbour sounds.

Witthüs, Elbchaussee 449a, ℂ 860 173. *Kaffee und Kuchen* in the woods near Övelgönne. Difficult to find, but locals will show you the way.

Hamburg's chief **listings magazines**, available at newsagents, are *Szene*, *Oxmox* and *Prinz*. **Central booking agencies** for all events include CCH-Konzertkasse, Jungiusstr. 13, ✆ 342 025/6, and Theaterkasse Central, Gerhard-Hauptmann-Platz 48, ✆ 324 312. The Last-Minute-Kartenshop, Hanse-Viertel arcade, ✆ 353 565, acts as a normal booking agency and also sells **half-price tickets** between 3pm and 6.30pm on the day of the event.

Hamburg vies with Munich for the reputation of having the best **opera** company in Germany. The **ballet**, under the American John Neumeier, is undoubtedly in the top rank. Productions take place in the **Hamburg Opera**, Dammtorstr. 2, ✆ 351 721. Until recently the **Deutsches Schauspielhaus** (the State Theatre) was run by the legendary Peter Zadek—known not only for his shock treatment of the classics, but for acerbic one-liners such as 'We Germans are surely the only people on earth who enjoy a bad conscience more than a beautiful woman.' Briton Michael Bogdanov took over the reins until July 1993. Nowadays Frank Bambauer maintains the company's high standard. The two leading State Theatre venues are the **Deutsches Schauspielhaus**, Kirchenallee 39, ✆ 248 713, and **Thalia Theater**, Gerhard-Hauptmann-Platz, ✆ 322 666. The main concert hall is the **Musikhalle**, Karl-Muck-Platz, ✆ 346 920. There are three good local **symphony orchestras**, and Hamburg is also home to the renowned early music ensemble, the **Monteverdi-Chor**.

You can see exciting **experimental theatre** at Die Kammerspiele, Hartungstr. 9–11, ✆ 44 22 11, and in fringe theatres all over town. The intimate theatre-café Monsun, Friedensallee 36, ✆ 390 3148, plays host to new local and visiting **dance companies**. **English-language productions** can sometimes be caught at the St-Pauli-Theater, Spielbudenplatz 29, ✆ 314 344. The most famous spot for **varieté** (here a mixture of cabaret, striptease and drag) is **Schmidt** and **Schmidts Tivoli**, Spielbudenplatz 24 and 27, ✆ 311 231. The big names in **live music** play at the Markthalle, Klosterwall 49, ✆ 339 491. The **Fabrik**, Barnerstr. 36, ✆ 391 070, a converted factory in Altona with high ceilings and wooden galleries, stages excellent bands. The most popular mainstream **jazz** venue is the **Cotton Club**, Alter Steinweg 10, ✆ 343 878.

Madhouse, Valentinskamp 6 is the most enduringly popular mainstream **disco**. A more alternative crowd heads for spots around the station, such as Cocoon, Börsenbrücke 3 and Traxx, Altländerstr. 10. Porsches pull up outside the classier establishments along the west bank of the Alster, such as the Insel, Alsterufer 35. (*Szene* magazine is the best source of up-to-date information on 'in' clubs and discos). **Café Keese**, Reeperbahn 19, ✆ 310 805, is a Hamburg institution. Perfectly respectable, smartly dressed middle-aged couples dance cheek-to-cheek to a live band—but the ladies do the asking.

Bremen

Hamburg ist das Tor zur Welt, aber Bremen hat den Schlüssel ('Hamburg is the gateway to the world, but Bremen has the key') goes the local saying. On Bremen's coat of arms is an enormous key, a proud symbol of freedom. Like Hamburg, Bremen is city-state, a *Land* in its own right—Germany's smallest. Rivalry between the neighbouring 'Free Hanseatic Cities' has always been intense. Hamburg may be the bigger and more prosperous of the two, but Bremen has the edge when it comes to geniality. It is a quirky, rather folksy town with a fierce sense of tolerance and independence. In the market square you could meet a gruff old sailor with a face like a Toby jug, cheery knots of trendy youth—or even the prime minister out doing his shopping. The left-wing SDP city government has been in power continuously since the war, the university has a reputation for radical politics, and young people loyally stay put, rather than succumb to the lure of larger cities. All this gives Bremen a vitality, a mixture of local tradition and worldly-wise dissent that is quite special.

Bremen is a manageable, intimate city. It stretches some 30km along the river Weser, but is only a few kilometres wide (it claims to be the longest city in Europe). Neighbourhoods along the way have their distinctive charm and style, from the all-night buzz of *das Viertel* ('the Quarter') around **Steintor** to the sedate grace of 19th-century **Schwachhausen** mansions. The heady days of Hansa trading have left their mark—every second cup of coffee drunk in Germany passes through Bremen or is processed here, and the local brew, Beck's Beer, is shipped all over the world. Here the factories emit roasting coffee fumes and delicious yeasty odours, and on some days the city has the welcoming aroma of a good breakfast.

History

Legend has it that Bremen was founded by a mother hen, though nobody knows which came first, the story or the hen-and-chickens relief on one of the arches of the Rathaus arcade. A group of fishermen fleeing down the Weser saw the chicks scuttle under a bush after their mother, and decided that if the spot was safe enough for feeble fowl, it was safe enough for them. However the settlement began, by AD 780 it was important enough for Charlemagne to make it a bishopric. Fishing, boat-building, trading, and later brewing became the backbone of a strong economy. The local peasants and tradesmen were a stroppy lot, constantly doing battle with the archbishop and winning more rights and privileges. By 1358 Bremen's merchants wielded enough power to opt for civic independence and to join the Hanseatic League. After a century or two of prosperity, Bremen followed other members of the League into decline—though it did form a special alliance with Lübeck and Hamburg. After the Thirty Years' War the city was occupied by the Swedish, and later by the French, but was again granted Free City status in 1646.

Bremen enjoyed a boom in the late 19th century, and because the Weser was silting up established a new port at **Bremerhaven**, 65km away on the North Sea coast. (Bremerhaven is still part of the *Land* of Bremen, though the countryside in between belongs to Lower Saxony.) The Weser has now been dredged, so ocean-going ships can once again sail up as far as the harbour on the western edge of the Bremen.

City politics are traditionally liberal. Citizens gave Kaiser Bill the cold shoulder when he visited in 1913. When Hitler's stormtroopers shot into a group returning from an anti-fascist demonstration in 1933 the town responded, within a few days, with a 30,000-strong march. All opposition was later suppressed, but the Führer wisely avoided ever visiting Bremen. In 1949 Bremen's Free City status was renewed, and the SDP again took up the reins. Thirty years later the Greens made headlines when they won enough votes here to enter a regional parliament for the first time. Today the Green party governs together with the SDP—the first coalition since the war.

Financially, though, things are not so healthy. Local shipbuilding and steel industries have been dealt a fatal blow by changing economic trends, and the motor and aircraft-building industries are stricken by the European recession. A third of Bremen's jobs depend on the port, and brewing, tourism and new hi-tech ventures are gallantly keeping the state afloat.

Getting Around

By Air

Bremen's dinky airport is 20 minutes south of the city centre. You can even get there by tram (the No. 5 runs right into the Altstadt). There are daily flights to London, as well as flights to Amsterdam, Paris, Brussels and all main German airports.

By Car

Bremen is on the A1, about 100km from Hamburg. The A27 takes you up to Bremerhaven (65km). The centre of the city has been pedestrianized, and it is better to visit the sights on foot. Signposts on all approaches to the city direct you to parking garages around town.

Car hire: Avis, Airport, ✆ (0421) 558 055; Sixt Budget, Hastedter Heerstr. 32, ✆ (0421) 498 228.

Mitfahrzentrale: Citynetz, Horner Str. 63, ✆ (0421) 19444.

By Train

The **Hauptbahnhof** is a few minutes' walk north of the city centre. There are mainline (including ICE) connections all over Germany. Trains to Hamburg run at least hourly and take just over an hour.

Public Transport

Most sights are within walking distance of each other, but if you want to make use of the comprehensive network of buses and trams, your best bet is to buy a **Bremer Kartchen** (DM6, available from newsagents and drivers) which allows you unlimited travel on all buses and trams for 2 days. Over weekends one *Bremer Kartchen* is valid for two adults and two children.

Taxi: ✆ 14014.

Bicycle hire: Fahrrad Station, just outside Hauptbahnhof, ✆ (0421) 302 114 (from DM10.50 a day).

The main **tourist information office** is opposite the entrance to the Haupt-bahnhof, ✆ (0421) 308 000 *(Mon–Wed and Fri 9.30–6.30, Thurs 9.30–8.30, Sat 9.30–2—to 5 on the first Saturday of the month—Sun 9.30–3.30)*. There is another information kiosk in the Liebfrauenkirchhof (same times and number). Friendly and efficient staff can help with hotel reservations and booking tickets. They also offer all manner of maps and leaflets and informative city tours.

Post office: Bahnhofsplatz 25 (alongside Hauptbahnhof).

Banks: Branches of most main German banks are around Am Markt- and Am Dom. There is a Bureau de Change at the airport *(Mon–Fri 8–8 and Sat 9–2)*.

Medical emergencies and police: ✆ 110.

Markets: There is a daily flower market around the Liebfrauenkirche and a fruit and vegetable market behind the Rathaus and alongside the cathedral. Most locals head for a better-stocked market in the suburb of Findorff, north-west of the Hauptbahnhof (Tues, Thurs, Sat). The **Kajenmarkt** (Weser Promenade, Apr–Oct Saturdays) sells fish and all sorts of tasty goodies as well as arts and crafts—and there are usually live bands, too. There are two **fleamarkets** a respectable one on the Weser Promenade over the weekend and a delightfully tacky one on Sunday mornings in front of the Stadthalle (though the authorities are trying to put an end to this one). The **Weihnachtsmarkt** (Christmas Market; 30 Nov–23 Dec) on the squares around the Rathaus is one of the prettiest and most atmospheric in north Germany.

Festivals and Events

On 6 January the **Eiswette** (ice wager) takes place on the banks of the Weser, perpetuating a bet some 19th-century gallants had that the river would be frozen over by that date (a 50-50 chance at the time). The test was to be that a tailor weighing 99 pounds, carrying a hot iron, could cross the river at Punkerdeich. The losers had to foot the bill for a celebratory banquet. Today the ceremony takes place at Osterdeich and involves not only a tailor and a notary (as referee), but also the Three Wise Men (6 January is, after all, Epiphany). The odds are no longer equal, so people draw lots to decide who they should back—the losers still pay for a meal. The **Bremen Six Days** (an indoor bicycle endurance race at the end of January) has as much to do with cycling as the Ascot has with horseracing. Fleets of hapless cyclists pump their way round and round the track in Bremen's Stadthalle, virtually ignored by the crowds who drink, eat, parade and party on the outskirts. The biggest bash of all is the **Bremen Freimarkt** in the last two weeks of October. It began as a 'free Market' in 1035, but today involves a huge funfair (in front of the Stadthalle) with continuous merrymaking in the beer tent and in pubs and restaurants around town. Bremers (some with gingerbread hearts hanging around their necks) gorge

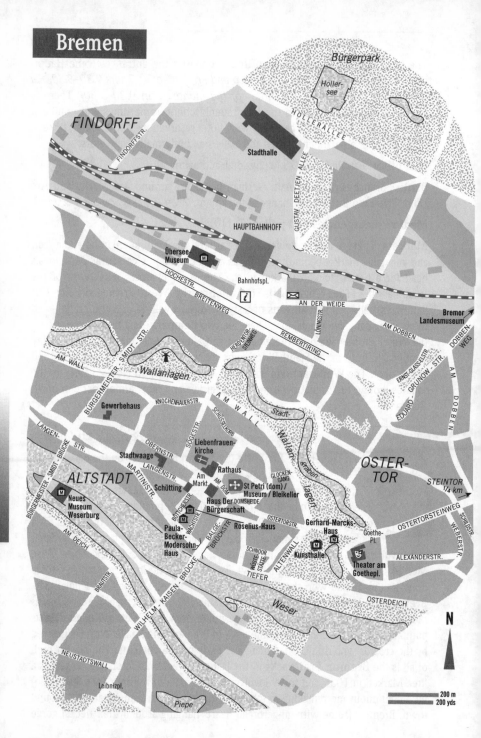

themselves on smoked eels, Bratwurst and all kinds of gooey sweets. Outrageous behaviour is excused with 'Ischa Freimaak'—local dialect for 'It's the *Freimarkt*', easy to articulate even when very drunk. On the second Saturday there is a parade of some 150 floats through the Altstadt—a spectacular show put on by local guilds and societies. Merrymakers in costume tag along distributing sweets and Schnapps with reckless abandon. The **Breminale** at the end of May is a little more sedate, with open-air theatre and music, shows and concerts all over town.

Around Am Markt

The main sights in Bremen are clustered around a patchwork of squares in the centre of the Altstadt, and this is the best place to begin your tour. **Am Markt** rates with the most elegant in Germany. Along the west side is a row of stately gabled buildings with little bits of gilding that flash in the sun. They are prime examples of the ornate **Weser Renaissance** style (*see* p. 59). If they look a little too good to be true, maybe it is because they are all reconstructions, moved here from their original positions along the Weser after the Second World War. Opposite is the **Haus der Bürgerschaft** (parliament building), a brave modern attempt to fit in with the surrounding architecture by reflecting it (literally, on long glass walls).

At the northern end of the square is Bremen's most famous building, the **Rathaus**, built in 1405. Good, straightforward Bremer logic determined its size. All the councillors were made to stand in a rectangle and a line was drawn around them. The dimensions of the central meeting room thus established, the Rathaus grew up apace. The façade (added in 1609), encrusted with decorative moulding, laden with statuary and topped by three elaborate gables, is a jewel of the Weser Renaissance. A tour of the **interior** *(Mon–Fri 10, 11, 12; Mar–Oct also Sat and Sun 11 and 12, 30 mins; adm DM4)* takes you through a sequence of splendid rooms. The most impressive of these is the **Obere Halle** (upper hall, sadly not always accessible) which runs along the entire front of the building. Enormous model sailing ships hang from the ceiling, four gorgeously decorated portals (from 15th–17th centuries) line up stiffly against one wall and a breathtakingly beautiful carved wooden stairway curves up to the mezzanine **Güldenkammer** (Treasure Room). On the second Friday in February every year the *Obere Halle* is the scene of a sumptuous banquet—the **Schaffermahlzeit**. Male-only and frostily exclusive (guests—mainly leading industrialists—can be invited just once), the *Schaffermahlzeit* marks the beginning of the shipping season and has been hosted by the city's merchants and sea captains every year since 1545. Beneath the Rathaus (and stretching way out under Am Markt) is an enormous vaulted **Ratskeller**. For a long time Bremen held the monopoly on Rhine wines, and today some 700 different varieties are stored here, the oldest being a 1653 Rüdesheimer (*see* **Eating and Drinking** below).

Outside the Rathaus, defiantly facing the cathedral, is the statue of **Roland**. Roland (a.k.a. Orlando) was one of Charlemagne's knights, who, for reasons long forgotten, came to be seen as the symbol of civic rights and privileges. The inscription on his shield, in local dialect, reads 'Freedom do I give you openly'. All over north Germany statues of Roland cock a snoot at the local cathedral—but Bremen had the first. The present statue is said to date back to 1404, but there are records of the archbishop's troops burning down a wooden one as early as 1366. In the middle ages, ever-practical Bremen housewives used the distance between Roland's pointy armoured kneecaps as a standard measure for cloth. Tucked away round the side of the Rathaus is a small statue of the **Bremen Town Musicians** by local sculptor Gerhard Marcks. The four heroes of the Grimm brothers' fairytale—a cock on the back of a cat on the back of a dog on the back of a donkey—never actually made it to Bremen but appear in every imaginable medium all over town. Holding both the donkey's forelegs supposedly brings you luck and puts money in your purse. Two bright bronze patches testify that the tradition is not dead.

Opposite the Rathaus is the **Schütting**, the Chamber of Commerce built in the 16th century, though much renovated in 1895. A little way down Langenstraße, which leads west off Am Markt, you can see the step-gabled **Stadtwaage** (Weighing House), built in 1586 and restored in the 1950s after bomb damage. A little further on (off Obernstraße) is the showy Weser Renaissance **Gewerbehaus** (1619), the trades guilds' headquarters.

St Petri (Dom)

Next to the Rathaus, facing onto a small square of its own, is Bremen's twin-towered **St Petri (Dom)**. Work began on the cathedral in 1070, and portals, towers and arches continued to be added up to the beginning of the Reformation. Bremen declared itself for Protestantism, but the cathedral itself passed back and forth between factions in a series of unseemly tussles, and was finally abandoned to fall into disrepair. One of the towers fell down and the other was struck by lightning. Half-hearted attempts were made to restore the church in the late 17th century, but it was only in 1894 that anyone really got down to it. Recent restorers have had the courage to revert to the original colour scheme. The brightly painted **interior**, with its striped arches and pretty motifs, is a refreshing change from safer universal whitewash given to other churches in the region. The cathedral's treasures were plundered during the Reformation, but in the small **museum** (Mon–Fri 10–5,

Sat 10–12, Sun 2–5; Nov–Apr Mon–Fri 1–5, Sat 10–12, Sun 2–5; adm DM2 or DM3 incl Bleikeller) you can see some medieval vestments and fine goldsmiths' work recently found in the bishops' graves. It is also worth popping down into the **crypts** which contain ancient carving, closer to German pagan traditions than to Christianity. In the east crypt you'll find a heavy **Romanesque font** resting on three gryphon-like legs.

Around the side of the church is the entrance to the **Bleikeller** (Lead Cellar) *(May–Sept Mon–Fri 10–5, Sat 10–12, same prices as museum).* In 1450 a workman repairing the cathedral roof fell to his death. As he came from outside Bremen he was put in one of the cellars used for storing lead—and forgotten. The corpse was found years later in a remarkable state of preservation. The local story goes that he was killed by the jealous lover of a local girl. The murderer told her that his rival had left Bremen, and later married her. But he got his comeuppance when she recognized the corpse some twenty years later. Nobody knows quite why this mummifying process happens, but a number of notables availed themselves of the facility, including the English Lady Stanhope. Today you can see quite a collection of bodies—teeth, hair, toe-nails and wrinkles intact—with expressions that range from utter indifference to fearful agony.

Over weekends and in the evenings you might see a woman polishing the cathedral door-knob, or a man in top hat and tails sweeping the steps. A small crowd looks on drinking beer and schnapps from a trolley, calling out encouragement and throwing down more rubbish. The diligent cleaners are men or women who have turned 30 without getting married. Friends put an advertisement in the local paper announcing the time of the ceremony and the errant 30-year-olds have to keep up their task until kissed by a virgin of the appropriate sex. (In these wicked times friends usually bring along a child to do the deed, just to be sure.) After a few minutes of cheery public humiliation everyone goes to a nearby pub.

Set in the paving stones near the cathedral's north portal is a stone etched with a cross. This marks the spot of Bremen's last public execution—that of serial killer **Gesche Gottfried**, who managed to despatch over 30 of her friends and family before being beheaded in 1831. It became the custom to spit on the stone whenever you passed by. One night in 1931 someone changed the cross into a swastika (the idea being that the citizens of Bremen should spit on it). The *Spuckstein* (spitting stone) stayed that way until 1936, when the Nazis changed it back to its original form. On this side of the cathedral you'll also find Bremen's main fruit and vegetable **market**. This spills round the back of the Rathaus to link up with a colourful **flowermarket** that spreads right around the **Liebfrauen-kirche**, filling the air with delicious fragrances. The Liebfrauenkirche itself, an elegant *Hallenkirche* with one Gothic and one Romanesque tower, is often the scene of good classical music concerts.

Gesche Gottfried

 Gesche Gottfried, who lived in Pelzerstraße in Bremen in the 1820s, had been dealt a few hard blows by life, her neighbours felt. She was pitied, and respected for the way she had so bravely borne her travails. Members of her family and close friends had

been dying about her in considerable numbers, yet she sailed though it all, with fortitude and composure. Her first marriage had been to a man named Miltenburg, an alcholic by whom she had three children. He died suddenly of a gall-bladder failure after eating his morning porridge. Luckily for the young widow, a friend of her husband, one Herr Gottfried, was waiting in the wings and wanted to marry her. At the last moment, though, Gottfried hesitated. He was, after all, taking on quite a responsibility as Gesche came complete with three children and two ageing parents. Fate, however, was on her side. Her mother died one afternoon after drinking lemonade, and her son fell ill and joined his grandma after eating too much cake at her funeral. Daughter and grandfather soon followed. Greta's brother came back from abroad to console her, but passed away suddenly himself not long after his welcome-home dinner. By this time Gesche was expecting Gottfried's child—but still he seemed reluctant to marry her. It was only on his deathbed, suffering from a sudden and mysterious illness, that he finally made the widow a respectable woman. The baby, however, was stillborn.

But all was not lost for Gesche. A wealthy widower named Zimmerman proposed to her, and even lent her a large sum of money—though he, too, died shortly afterwards. All in all some 30 of Gesche's friends and relatives died in odd circumstances. Perhaps this is why, in 1830, the young man who was sharing a house with her became suspicious of the white granules he saw on the meat that was to be his supper that night. Despite Gesche's assurance that this was only fat, he took a scraping to the local doctor, who had the grains analysed. They were grains of arsenic. Gesche was arrested, and admitted to having poisoned 'a few' people— though not all of those who had died over the preceding decade. She was beheaded outside the cathedral in 1831. It was to be Bremen's last public execution. Embedded in the cobbles on the spot you can still see a stone cross, called the *Spuckstein* (spitting stone), as it became the custom for locals to spit on it as they walked by.

Böttcherstraße and the Schnoor

In 1902 the coffee merchant **Ludwig Roselius**, the inventor of Café Hag (decaffeinated coffee) bought a 16th-century step-gabled house in Böttcherstraße, a run-down street just off the south end of Am Markt. Gradually Roselius bought up the whole street. He demolished most of the old houses and commissioned some of the best architects of the day to create an ensemble of red-brick architecture that ranges from traditional gabled façades to bold expressionist sculpted walls. Today most of the houses in Böttcherstraße are galleries, crafts workshops or restaurants, and throngs of tourists squeeze through for a look—but it is a corner of Bremen that shouldn't be missed. The **Roselius-Haus** at No. 6 is open as a **museum** *(Mon–Thurs 10–4, Sat and Sun 11–4; adm DM2.50)*. Here you can see Roselius' excellent collection of Dutch and German art as well as textiles, weapons and carving from the 12th–18th centuries. The prize of the museum is a priceless collection of medieval silver on loan from the *Kompagnie der Schwarzen Häupter zu Riga*, a wealthy merchants' guild. Next door to the Roselius-Haus is the **Paula Becker-Modersohn-Haus** (access through the museum) with paintings by the rather gloomy Worpswede painter (*see* **Around Bremen** below). Halfway down the street there is a dainty **glockenspiel** with Mießener porcelain bells. Inside the **Atlantis Haus** towards the end of the street is a spectacular spiral staircase, built in 1930.

Arrows on the pavement direct you from the end of Böttcherstraße across the busy Balgebrückstraße to the **Schnoor**, a medieval quarter of Bremen that largely escaped the bombs of the Second World War. It gets its name ('String') from the thin little houses that huddle together along the narrow alleys, rather like a thread of beads. The streams of tourists that have flowed down Böttcherstraße pour in here too, but somehow the Schnoor manages to keep its quaint, quiet charm. Cosy cafés and restaurants now occupy many of the houses, and in others you'll find crafts workshops, jewellers and diminutive gift shops stuffed to the brim.

The Kunsthalle and Beyond

Following Ostertorstraße (the main street leading east past the cathedral) you come to Am Wall, the road that traces the line of the old **city wall**. The fortifications themselves have disappeared and today the **Wallanlagen** is a shady park that follows the zigzag path of the old moat. Halfway along you can see one of Bremen's five remaining **windmills**.

At the point where Ostertorstraße joins Am Wall you'll find the **Kunsthalle** (Bremen Art Museum) *(Tue 10–9, Wed–Sun 10–5; adm DM6)*. The early Dutch and German sections have some big names including Rubens, Rembrandt, van Dyck and Cranach, although they are represented by relatively minor work. The museum's strength lies in the **19th- and early 20th-century** paintings. There is fine work by Lovis Corinth and a good collection of French Impressionists and German Expressionists, including two of Max Beckmann's most familiar works, *Self-portrait with a Saxophone* (1930) and the vibrant *Apache Dance* (1938). Painters from the nearby Worpswede colony (*see* p. 548), especially Paula Becker-Modersohn (1876–1907), feature strongly, too. The museum's **graphics collection** is particularly good. A group of superb watercolours by **Dürer** and drawings by Old Masters was thought to have been destroyed in the war, but recently surfaced in St Petersburg. Whether Bremen is to enter an Elgin Marbles style dispute with the Russians remains to be seen.

Next door to the Kunsthalle, in the old city gatehouse, is the **Gerhard-Marcks-Haus** *(Tues–Sun 10–6; adm DM4)*, a small museum devoted to one of the most significant of 20th-century German sculptors. Exhibitions change, but there is always an interesting selection of Marcks' sculptures and graphics on show. Beyond the museums, along Ostertorsteinweg, you come to Ostertor and Steintor, known to locals as **das Viertel**, the hub of the city's alternative scene and nightlife. Here you'll find delicatessens and fashion boutiques, trendy cafés and junkies (Bremen has a severe drugs problem). There are snack bars that dish out pizzas and kebabs until the early hours and some rather shady pubs that stay open all night. In the side streets you can see some of the finest examples of turn-of-the-century **Bremer Haüser**, noble homes akin to English Georgian architecture, but a touch more elaborate. The quietest time in *das Viertel* is around 5am, when there is a brief pause between revellers going home and others passing through on the way to work.

Outside the Altstadt

Just north of the Hauptbahnhof is the **Bürgerpark**, a stretch of green twice the size of London's Hyde Park. There are ponds, pavilions, wild patches and vast lawns. It is a superb place for a bracing autumn walk or a lazy summer picnic. Hidden in the trees you'll find a classy restaurant and a beer garden with a small open air stage, where on Sunday mornings you can listen to live jazz (*see* **Eating and Drinking** below). Along the west side, local artists have painted bright and witty murals on to sturdy wartime bunkers that proved impossible to blow up. (Mural painting has become a Bremen trademark. Blank walls and the ends of buildings all over town are decorated with delightful *trompe l'oeil* paintings). East of the Bürgerpark is the élite suburb of **Schwachhausen**, where you can see some really luxurious 19th-century villas. At the end of the main street, about 15 minutes' drive from the centre of town, is the **Bremer Landesmuseum** (Bremen State Museum), Schwachhauser Heerstr. 240 *(Tues–Sun 10–6; adm DM4, Bus 30, 31, 33 or 34)*, an interesting museum on Bremen's history, well worth the detour. There is a whole section devoted to seafaring, sumptuously carved patrician furniture and elaborate pieces of workmanship done by craftsman to qualify for the title 'Master'. In the grounds are a traditional farmhouse and barn. Back at the Hauptbahnhof you can visit the **Übersee-Museum** (Overseas Museum), Bahnhofsplatz 13 *(Tues–Sun 10–6; adm DM4)*, a good ethnological museum which draws from a large stash of booty donated by ship owners over the years.

Bremen's newest and most exciting museum, the **Neues Museum Weserburg Bremen** *(Tues–Fri 10–6, Sat and Sun 11–6; adm DM6)* is on a peninsula in the middle of the Weser (the entrance is on the Bürgermeister-Smidt-Brücke, ten minutes' walk from the Altstadt). Four old coffee warehouses have been converted into a museum of post-1960s art that covers five floors. The highly original idea of bringing together the collections of 11 private lenders under one roof means that Bremen can have a modern art gallery stocked beyond its wildest dreams. Each of the 11 lenders leaves a core of works with the museum for ten years, but also continually alters and adds to the collection on display. Works are not grouped chronologically, but according to each collector's preference (after long discussions with the curator). As you wander around the labyrinthine museum, you get a delightful sense of the quirks and personal tastes of the different contributors. One likes mainly American art, another only German painting. Some of the collections are tightly structured, others downright eccentric. Paintings by the same artist will crop up all over the building, each time giving you a slightly different angle on the work. The quality of the collections is top-rate, and the list of artists reads like a Who's Who of late-20th-century art: Beuys, A.R. Penck, Anselm Kiefer, Andy Warhol, Mario Merz and Richard Long to name just a few. Look out especially for excellent selections of work by Baselitz and Gerhard Richter, and for Kienholz's macabre installation, *Roxy*. Make sure also that you save enough energy to get up to the 5th floor, under the eaves. Here works have been especially chosen because they suit the loft-like atmosphere. Most intriguing of these are the various sound installations that you activate yourself by entering the room.

Bremen's main shopping area is in the glitzy modern pedestrian precinct around Obernstraße and Sögestraße. Here you'll find department stores, clothes shops, jewellers and alluring delicatessens. Sögestraße ('Sow Street') was once the road out to a pig-meadow. At one end is an irresistible statue of a swineherd and his charges, worn smooth by the bottoms of weary shoppers who succumb to the temptation to sit on the pigs. For bookshops, alternative fashions, ethnic jewellery and curious knick-knacks, head for the shops in Ostertor and Steintor.

Bremen ✆ (0421–) **Where to Stay**

expensive

Park Hotel Bremen, Im Bürgerpark, ✆ 34080, fax 340 8602 (DM420–490). Bremen's top address. Luxurious hotel overlooking a small lake in the Bürgerpark. Both staff and rooms pamper you to the limit.

Scandic Crown Hotel, Böttcherstr. 2, ✆ 36960, fax 369 6960 (DM315–355). Modern, efficient hotel off one of Bremen's most attractive streets. Some rooms look out over the Weser, others open up onto a quiet private courtyard.

moderate

Übersee Hotel, Wachtstr. 27–29, ✆ 36010, fax 360 1555 (DM170–240). Unspectacular, though centrally situated and well run. A good hotel to fall back on if others are full.

Hotel Bremer Haus, Löningstr. 16–20, ✆ 32940, fax 329 4411 (DM145–180). Smart, centrally located converted Bremer Haus. The service is attentive and the rooms comfortable..

Hotel Landhaus Louisenthal, Leher Heerstr. 105, ✆ 232 076, fax 236 716 (DM100–198). An 18th-century mansion, stylishly converted and run with personal flair. Set in a big garden in the north-eastern suburbs.

Gästehaus Roland, Glockengang 4, ✆ 325 453 (DM130). Down a murky alley behind the cathedral; the rooms are clean, the management helpful. No restaurant.

inexpensive

Hotel Weltevreden, Am Dobben 62, ✆ 78015, fax 704 091 (DM 80–110). Small hotel conveniently situated for Steintor nightlife. No restaurant.

Pension Haus Bremen, Verdener Str. 47, ✆ 498 7777, fax 498 7433 (DM90–110) A real bargain. Friendly, family-run converted Bremer Haus, not too far from the centre. No restaurant.

Hotel Enzensperger, Brautstr. 9, ✆ 503 224 (DM68–78). Simple guesthouse in pretty part of town, just across the Weser. No restaurant.

Youth Hostel: Kalkstr. 6, ✆ 171 369.

Bremen's main speciality is *Kohl und Pinkel*—mounds of curly kale served with smoked pork ribs, sausages, streaky bacon and *Pinkel* (a kind of groat sausage made, as one hostess discreetly put it, 'from the part of a bull which makes it not a cow'). *Kohl und Pinkel* is served only in winter after All Souls' Day, and is best approached after an invigorating walk. From November to February Bremers of all ages—groups of friends, work colleagues, members of sports associations—can be seen on a *Kohl-und-Pinkelfahrt*, a long walk to work up the appetite. Some may be wearing hats and carrying sticks decorated with cabbage leaves. Most will have a glass on a ribbon hanging around their necks. At every available opportunity along the way this is filled with Schnapps for a warming swig. Eventually they all pile into a restaurant (the destination is usually kept secret by the organizer) or somebody's house, and the feasting begins. Beer and Scnapps flow freely to wash it all down, and the most prodigious consumer at the end of the day is awarded a *Fressorden* (Guzzle Award).

Restaurants and Taverns

expensive

Meierei, Im Bürgerpark, ✆ 340 8619 (DM100–120). Stylish restaurant in the heart of the Bürgerpark. Excellent wine list and imaginative cuisine. Try the rabbit cooked with nettles and kohlrabi.

Das Kleine Lokal, Besselstr. 40, ✆ 71929 (DM90–110). Intimate restaurant furnished with old chairs and cut up bedsteads. Subtle, award-winning Franco-German cuisine. Menu changes according to what is in the market.

moderate

Médoc, Friesenstr. 103, ✆ 73550 (DM40–50). Academic types munch away at delicious home-cooking with a strong wholefood bias.

Ratskeller, Am Markt, ✆ 301 676 (DM30–50). Historic 15th-century vaults with carved wine vats and a list of over 700 German wines, some of which will set you back a few thousand DM. Along one wall are the *Priölken*, quaint 17th-century dining cubicles. Even today the doors are left open if a man and woman are dining inside alone. The fare ranges from subtle dishes such as medallions of pork in a creamy mustard sauce, to *Labskaus*, a seaman's favourite—corned beef cooked with potatoes, served with fried eggs and pickled cucumber.

Beck's in'n Snoor, Schnoor 34 (DM55–75). Popular but pricey tavern in the Schnoor. The generous seafood ragout is superb.

Spitzen Gebel, Hinter dem Schütting 1, ✆ 323 478 (DM25–30). Tiny red-brick house with a bar that also serves good food. The menu is simple and changes according to season, but the fish dishes are usually good.

Friesenhof, Hinter dem Schütting 12/13, © 337 6666 (DM40–60). Hearty Frisian cooking, with such winter-chill banishers as the *Bauernplatter* (farmer's platter) of medallions of pork, beef and turkey served with potatoes, vegetables, sauerkraut—and a fried egg on top.

Knurrhahn, Schüsselkorb 32, © 323 128 (DM25–25). Enduringly popular *gutbürgerliche* fish restaurant. Simply cooked favourites as well as exotica such as shark steak with paprika and onions.

Broccolli, Am Hulsberg 1, © 498 6600 (DM20–40). Just beyond Steintor. Sells mouthwatering *Auflauf* (vegetables, fish and meat baked with cheese in individual bowls—you can select your own fillings). Also enormous salads.

inexpensive

Kismet, Vor den Steintor, © 70775 (DM10–15). Best of a row of Turkish restaurants in Steintor. You choose from the day's dishes—bright with fresh vegetables—lined up in the window.

Tangente, Berliner Str. 41, © 75222 (DM15–20). Friendly Italian restaurant tucked away in a side street in Steintor. Mainly pizzas, though the calamari baked in tomato and garlic is heavenly.

Bars and Cafés

Ambiente, Osterdeich 69a. Pleasant café with a large *Wintergarten* overlooking the Weser. *The* place for a lingering Sunday breakfast.

Café Sand, Strandweg. Summer only. A tent across the river from Ambiente. Chairs and tables spill out onto the long sandy beach and arty types sit and sip beer well into the night.

Lagerhaus, Schildstr. 12. Large, trendy bar in an old warehouse in a sidestreet in the *Viertel*. Usually decked out with odd art.

Piano, Fehrfeld 64. Domain of Ostertor's chic new invaders.

St Pauli Eck, Alexanderstr. 1. Cosy, quiet nook, where regulars sit and bemoan the changes in Ostertor.

Wienerhof Café, Weberstr. 25. Relaxed, friendly *Viertel* pub with a slightly older crowd and an off-the-wall atmosphere.

Auf den Höfen. A leafy courtyard of pubs and restaurants off a street of the same name near Steintor. Most are worth a visit, but special recommendations are **De Stille**, a minute beer bar moved lock, stock and barrel from Berlin, and the very trendy new **Studio**. **Das Mas** serves tasty Spanish food and **Firlefanz** has good daily specials.

Schlachthof, Findorffstr. 51. Lively bar in an old slaughterhouse behind the Hauptbahnhof. The food is superb and cheap (DM8–DM12 for a main course). A good place for a slap-up Sunday breakfast (DM11) before visiting the fleamarket.

Rathstube Konditorei, Am Markt. Cosy cellar for *Kaffee und Kuchen*.

Café Stecker, Knochenhauerstr. 14, ✆ 12593. Chairs with pale pink upholstery, clientéle with mauve-rinsed hair and cakes that are all the colours of the rainbow.

Schnoor-Teestübchen, Wüstestätte 1, ✆ 326091. Old Schnoor house offering home made fruit crumbles and a long tea menu.

Entertainment and Nightlife

The free **listings magazine,** *Mix* gives a daily breakdown of music and film in Bremen. *Bremer Blatt* and *Prinz* (available from newsagents) include theatre and other events. **Opera, mainstream theatre** and **classical music concerts** are usually staged in the **Theater am Goetheplatz**, Goetheplatz, ✆ (0421) 365 3333, while visiting artistes usually end up in **Die Glocke**, Domsheide 6/7, ✆ (0421) 326690. Bremen enjoys an especially good reputation for **early and ancient music**. Concerts are held all over town, usually in churches; the tourist office runs a ticket reservation service. The **Bremer Shakespeare Company** has a nation-wide reputation for adventurous, imaginative productions, usually of Shakespeare in German. Their base is in the **Theater am Leibnizplatz**, Leibnizplatz, ✆ (0421) 500 333. **Concordia**, Schwachhauser-Heerstr. 17, ✆ (0421) 365 333, specializes in modern dance.

If you feel like dancing yourself, the best mainstream **discos** are **Woody's**, Rembertiring 19, during the week and **Modernes**, Neustadtwal 28, on a Saturday night. Super-trendies go to **Maxx**, Herdentorsteinweg 38, and at **Römer**, Fehrfeld 31, you can dance to music by some of Bremen's zanier bands. You can often also catch **live music** at the **Schlachthof**, Findorffstr. 51, ✆ (0421) 353 075, **Modernes**, Neustadtwall 28, ✆ (0421) 505 553, and **Kairo**, Reuterstr. 9–17, ✆ (0421) 392 772. There is good **jazz and blues** at **Wüstestätte**, Wüstestätte 11, ✆ (0421) 326 101.

Around Bremen

Bremerhaven (65km away on the A27, hourly trains from the Hauptbahnhof) is one of Europe's busiest container ports. It was heavily bombed during the Second World War, and is today mainly worth visiting for the **Deutsches Schiffahrtsmuseum** (German Maritime Museum) at Van-Ronzelen-Straße *(Tues–Sun 10–6; adm DM4)*. Star exhibit is a Hanseatic cog ship dating back to 1380 (though much of the time this is all but invisible in a tank of soupy water, intended to preserve it). The museum also contains countless models of old ships, reconstructions of cabins and all sorts of intrguing marine bric-a-brac. Seven real ships are moored outside, ranging from a wooden square rigger to a torpedo motor boat. You can poke around the crews' cabins, climb up onto the bridges and mess around in engine rooms. Children love it.

At the end of the 19th century a handful of artists set up a colony in the village of **Worpswede** (25km from Bremen of the A27, Bus 140 from the Hauptbahnhof) on the edge of a lonely peat bog, the **Teufelsmoor** (Devil's Moor). Most of them produced impressionistic landscapes, popular at the time, but with limited appeal today. **Paula Modersohn-Becker**, however, has shown more staying power with her wistful, rather depressing pictures. She painted mainly women and children, seemingly hard-pressed by a difficult life, in muddy, muted colours. Her work wasn't much appreciated during her short life, but the colony itself was a centre of 19th-century artistic life, and writers such as the poet Rainer Maria Rilke also spent time here.

Today artists and craftspeople still work in Worpswede which, although it gets very touristy over weekends, still has a quiet village air. As well as the many workshops and galleries you can see some beautiful old rustic houses, their steep thatched roofs coming almost to the ground and warm wooden interiors much the same as they have been for a hundred years.

Where to Stay

Hotel Naber, Theodor-Heuss-Platz 1, Bremerhaven, © (0471) 48770 (DM180–200). Centrally situated, modern hotel popular with business visitors.

Eichenhof, Ostendorfstr. 13, Worpswede, © (04792) 2676 (DM150). Cosy old country house with individually furnished rooms. No restaurant.

Deutsches Haus, Findorffstr. 3, © (04792) 1205 (DM120). Quiet, traditional family hotel.

Eating and Drinking

Natusch, Fischereihafen, © (0471) 71021 (DM50–80). Classy fish restaurant in the fishing port. Simple classic dishes and maritime decor.

Schampus, Schleusenstr. 33, © (0471) 45709. Friendly café patronized by Bremerhaven intellectuals.

Alt Bremerhaven, Prager Str. 47; © (0471) 46995. Bremerhaven's oldest pub, with a smoky, sleepy atmosphere.

Café Bahnhof, Alte Bahnhof, Worpswede. Comfy café filled with sofas and aspirant artists.

The North Sea Coast

A story tells of two East Frisian farmers sitting in their warm kitchen over glasses of *Korn* (the local firewater). '*Ja, ja*', sighs the one. A pause, and then again '*Ja, ja, ja*'. 'Johann', says the other, staring glumly into the embers, 'can't you, for one moment, stop discussing politics'. That sums up the mood of the North Sea Coast. Most of this lonely patch of Germany, dotted with isolated villages, is ignored by tourists. Yet there is something deeply alluring in the relentlessly flat countryside, the slow pace of life, and the solid, salt-of-the-earth lifestyle of many of the farming folk. Nothing is done without a bracing cup of sweet, dark *Ostfriesentee* (East Frisian tea). First you drop a *Kluntje*—a giant sugar crystal—into your cup. Then comes the potent brew and finally, over the back of a silver spoon so that it floats on the surface, thick delicious cream, fresh from one of the local black-and-white cows. You don't stir, just sip through the layers of taste, one at a time.

Further around this bottom corner of the North Sea, up towards the Danish border in North Friesia, life is much the same. North and East Frisians, and the West Frisians (who officially live in the Netherlands), have their own language and culture, and it seems that nothing will ever ruffle it. Off the coastline, across a large mudflat called the **Watt** are two strings of islands—a few of them sleepy backwaters, covered mostly by nature reserve, but others startlingly hectic, packed with families on seaside holidays, or *Schickie-Mickies* from all over Germany.

Klaus Störtebeker

The tiny ships that plied the North Sea and the Baltic during the golden years of the Hanseatic League were laden with grain, salt, furs and other riches, and were ripe for the picking. Bands of pirates formed, often with the backing of Frisian chieftains, and by the end of the 14th century were the terror of the northern trade routes, capturing even well-armed convoys of cargo ships.

The fearless exploits, cruelty and vast wealth of the pirate captains made them legendary figures. Foremost among them all was Klaus Störtebeker, a sort of seaborne Robin Hood whose bold raids and adventures were talked about with awe. He is supposed to have voyaged to the ends of the Earth, subjugated strange peoples and amassed a fabulous hoard of treasure. All we know for certain about him, however, is that he was a pirate king who controlled the North Sea coasts between 1370 and 1400, and that he was executed in Hamburg in 1401. Legend has it that he walked headless from the block and rescued 11 comrades.

After 1400, as a result of the vigorous efforts of Bremen and Hamburg, dangers from piracy diminished, but the Störtebeker legend lives on. Feasts are still held in his honour in villages along the Frisian coast, and a specially marked tourist road takes you to spots with Störtebeker associations.

Getting Around

By car: Local buses are erratic and train routes tend to radiate out of the big cities, so the best way to follow the coast is by car. For details of **ferry** connections to the islands *see* individual Directory entries. Larger roads also seem to head for the main towns, but there are plenty of local roads that meander along the shoreline. The **Green Coastal Road** is a 1230km scenic tourist route that runs from Bergen in Norway, through Denmark and Germany to Sneek in the Netherlands. You can get maps and information from the Bremen tourist office and in towns along the way.

By train: The main lines serving the region run from Bremen to Emden (2hr) with a connection to Norddeich (30min); from Bremen to Cuxhaven (1½–2hr) and from Hamburg to Westerland (3¼hr).

General information about the coastal route can be obtained from the Bremen tourist office (*see* above). For tourist offices along the way *see* the relevant Directory entries.

The East Frisian Coast and Islands

Emden, on the Dutch border 150km from Bremen, is a busy herring-fishing port. The **Ostfriesisches Landesmuseum** *(Mon–Fri 10–1 and 3–5, Sat and Sun 11–1, Oct–Apr closed Mon; adm DM3)* outlines the history of the region and offers a glimpse into local culture. It also has the largest collection of armour in Europe. There is (suprisingly for a small town) an excellent **Museum für Moderne Kunst** (Modern Art Museum) at Hinter dem Rahmen 13 *(Tues 10–8, Wed–Fri 10–5, Sat and Sun 11–5; adm DM3)* with a good collection of Expressionists. Twenty kilometres north-west of Emden is **Greetsiel**, a quaint fishing village with cobbled streets, dinky cottages, windmills and coachloads of tourists.

Norddeich, another few kilometres along the coast, is the main ferry embarkation point for the East Frisian islands. Norddeich hardly merits a glance, but neighbouring **Norden** warrants a quick stopover. In the small, early Gothic **Ludgerikirche** is an organ built in the 1680s by the famous Hamburg master, Arp Schnitger, and there are some attractive Renaissance façades in the streets around the market place. Inland, 65 km from Emden, is **Jever** (known to most north-Germans for its beer, a bitter Pils popular in the trendier cafés). In the dirty pink **Schloß** *(March–Dec, Tues–Sat 10–1 and 3–5, Sun 11–1 and 3–5; adm DM2)*, with its stubby Renaissance tower, you can see a truly magnificent **carved oak ceiling**, by the Antwerp artist Cornelis Floris in 1564.

The **East Frisian Islands** are flat, windswept flecks in the sea, famed for their sandy beaches and birdlife. **Norderney** is the most popular and in season becomes crowded and unbearably touristy. The scrabble for shekels has meant that lots of ugly modern building spoils what must have been a rather elegant resort at the turn of the century. A far better bet is **Langeoog**, where cars are banned. You get about by bike, horse-cart or in a little electric train. Most of the island is taken up by a nature reserve that attracts ornithologists from all over the world. **Juist** also bans motor traffic. The island is 17km long, and just a few hundred yards wide. The northern side is one long dune-ribbed beach and most of the island is a nature reserve, so although Juist is also popular with tourists, it is quite easy to be a solitary figure in the quiet, greyish landscape. Most people don't move far from the single village halfway along the island.

Some distance north of the archipelago is **Heligoland** (German *Helgoland*), a jagged outcrop of reddish rocks owned by the British until 1890, when it was swapped with the Germans for Zanzibar. It was a major German naval base during the First World War and the site of an important naval action.

Fynes Moryson, a British traveller passing through in the 17th century, noted that the inhabitants of Heligoland were so poor that they could 'yield no other tribute than stones for the Duke's building'. The rugged red cliffs would still seem to be the backbone of the local economy—for there is precious little else to explain why so many thousands of tourists should bother to make the three-hour ferry journey to see the island (apart, perhaps, from an opportunity to shop duty-free).

For practical information see Directory entries for Emden, Norden/Norddeich, Norderney, Langeoog, Juist, Oldenburg and Wilhelmshaven.

The North Frisian Coast and Islands

The North Frisian coast, battered by storms, is not a favourite with swimmers, and is pretty difficult for farmers, too. Hardy sheep munch away on the *Köge* (low flat polders, reclaimed from the sea), and you can travel for miles without seeing anything of note at all. The jewel of this hinterland is **Friedrichstadt**, just off the B5 about 120km from Hamburg. A group of Dutch Protestant refugees settled here in 1621, and the town they built—complete with canals, Dutch step-gables and little bridges—is still pretty much intact. A few kilometres further north is the hub of the region, **Husum**—a small fishing port famed for its catches of small, brown shrimps. These *Husumer Krabben* can be eaten boiled, but also make a delicious soup. Husum's most famous son, the 19th-century poet **Theodor Storm**, dubbed his hometown *die graue Stadt am Meer* ('the grey town by the sea'), and the name has stuck. This is a bit hard on Husum, which is made up mostly of rather elegant 18th- and 19th-century buildings. **Niebüll**, 40km further north, is the point where you catch the shuttle train to the island of Sylt. Just outside the town is the **Nolde Museum** *(March–Oct Tues–Sun 10–6; Nov 10–5; adm DM5)*, a superb collection of works by the expressionist **Emil Nolde** (*see* **The Arts and Culture** p. 64) displayed in the house he lived in for many years. As well as his characteristic harsh, vibrant canvases you can also see the watercolours he painted in secret after the Nazis had banned his work.

Sylt is the most famous of the North Frisian Islands. A narrow sliver of land connected to the mainland by a causeway, it is the favoured holiday destination of Germany's jet-set. Most come to their own or to rented villas, and accommodation for anyone else can be hard to come by. During the day they sunbathe stark naked on **Buhne 16** (a sheltered beach on the eastern shore between the villages of List and Kampen). At night, or on rainy days, they don fragments of designer clothing and hang about the expensive bars, gourmet restaurants and classy boutiques near Buhne 16 and in the main town, Westerland. Neighbouring islands don't rate a gossip-columnist's second glance, and so are far less expensive and not as overcrowded. Pick of the others are **Amrum** which has a couple of sleepy villages and a nature reserve, and **Norderoog** which has only one resident family—that of the warden of the island's **bird sanctuary** (and even they leave in the winter).

For further practical information see Directory entries for Husum, Niebüll and Sylt.

The Baltic Coast

The Baltic (German: *Ostsee*) coastline is better protected from the howling winds that chill the bones of holidaymakers huddling on North Sea beaches. Here you will find long, white, sandy shores (not always choked with *Strandkörbe*), chalky cliffs and quiet coves where the forests come right up to the dunes. There are plenty of gentle, sunny days in the summer, and pretty towns to visit when the weather isn't so hot. The most unspoiled spots are along the stretch of the coast that was once in the DDR. Inland are the Mecklenburg Lakes, at present a *Geheimtip* (insider tip), but fast becoming *the* spot for walking and watersports holidays.

Getting Around

By car/bicycle: This is very much an area to explore by **car** or **bicycle**. The A7 links Hamburg to Rendsburg (85km), Schleswig (110km) and Flensburg (140km). You can hire bikes at most main railway stations.

By train: Train connections to main towns are fairly good. There are two trains an hour from Hamburg to Flensburg (2¼hr) and to Schleswig (1hr 50min).

For practical information see Directory entries for Flensburg, Schleswig and Kiel.

From Flensburg to Lübeck

The eastern coast of Schleswig-Holstein is thick with campsites and busy resorts. The rich, rolling countryside is so pleasantly uneventful that locals quite unabashedly call the little inlets that lap their way inland 'fjords', and the collection of hills in the south (the highest of which pushes up to 168m) 'Holstein Switzerland'.

Flensburg, in the north, was once one of Denmark's richest cities, growing fat on the Caribbean sugar trade. Today it belongs to Germany, but still produces barrels of rum, has a vociferous Danish minority and feels more Scandinavian than German. It is a busy town—wide roads destroy its quiet atmosphere—but attractive nonetheless, with recently renovated merchants' houses and warehouses that date back to Hansa times.

Flensburg has the dubious distinction of having been the capital of the Third Reich under Grand-Admiral Dönitz for a week at the beginning of May 1945, after Berlin had fallen to the Red Army.

Thirty kilometres south along Autobahn 7 you come to **Schleswig**, once a major Viking trading settlement and later capital of Denmark. This is one town in the region that really is worth a visit. Even though it is a good 20km inland, it is at the end of a sailboat-bobbing 'fjord', and has a dreamy seaside atmosphere. The Altstadt huddles obediently around an imposing red-brick Gothic **cathedral**. Inside is the region's most prized artwork, the **Bordesholm Altar** (1514–21), an astounding piece of carving, 12m high and seething with over 400 perfectly detailed figures. The story goes that the duke who commissioned it had the artist, Hans Brüggeman, blinded so that he could never again carve anything so beautiful. On an island in the west of town is **Schloß Gottorf** *(Apr–Oct daily 9–5, Nov–March Tues–Sun 9.30–4; adm DM4, also valid for Viking Museum)*, a spritely white castle built in the 16th and 17th centuries. Inside there is a good collection of German medieval and expressionist art, and in an adjoining building you can see the **Nydam boat**, an extraordinarily well-preserved 21m-long oak rowing boat dating from AD 350. It was found in nearby marshes in 1863. Also rescued from the bogs (about 2000 years too late) are the mummified corpses of people who were tied up and left out to die. They're just as well preserved as the boat—some apparently peacefully resigned to their fate, others with faces twisted in screams of anguish. Just south of the town, at **Haithabu** on the B76, is an excellent **Viking Museum** *(Apr–Oct daily 9–6, Nov–Mar Tues–Fri 9–5, Sat and Sun 10–6; adm DM4)* on the site of the original 8th-century settlement. You can get there in 20 minutes by boat from the Stadthafen, or by taking buses heading for Kiel, getting off at Haddeby. Star exhibit is a Viking longship, only recently fully excavated, and still in the process of being constructed. Guided tours of the archaeological sites can also be arranged *(© (04621) 813 300)*.

If you take the **coastal road** from Flensburg to Schleswig (100km), you pass through **Angeln**, the region that was once home to the Angles, who colonized England in the 5th and 6th centuries and gave the country its name. The slightly hilly countryside dotted with half-timbered and thatched cottages is oddly reminiscent of Surrey or Kent.

Just off Autobahn 7, about 20km south of Schleswig is **Rendsburg**, an old trading town with an attractive Altstadt, but now most famous for three spectacular feats of engineering—the **Kiel Canal**, which connects the Baltic and the North Sea, the railway bridge over it, and the tunnel beneath it. Enormous ocean-going ships ply the canal, giving the odd impression out in the flat countryside that they're sailing over land. It was opened in 1895, and today takes more than 50,000 ships a year, more than either the Suez or Panama canals. The railway bridge was built at a great height to allow ships to pass underneath, and the track has to double back in an a wide loop to bring trains back to ground level at a station just a few kilometres across the canal. Next to the tunnel, which plunges four lanes of traffic deep into the earth, is an escalator for pedestrians—the longest in Europe at 1,278m.

At the end of another 'fjord', 40km east of Rendsburg is **Kiel** itself. As Germany's main naval base it was bombed to bits during the Second World War. Today's Kiel is an ugly town of 1950s utility building, but the students from the local university (north Germany's oldest) add a bit of verve. Just outside town is the **Schleswig-Holsteinisches Freilichtmuseum** (Open-air museum) *(July–mid-Sept, daily; Apr–mid Nov Tues–Sun; mid-Nov–Mar Sun and hols; adm DM5; Route B4 or buses to Molfsee)*, a curious mixture of historical accuracy and kitsch contrivance. You can see 30 carefully reconstructed local buildings (dating from the 16th–19th centuries) including a vicarage from 1569, a working watermill and cottages with box beds that the whole family used to squash into for warmth. Potters, carvers, bakers and other craftspeople beaver away using the old methods, and sell their wares.

The B76, which heads east out of Kiel takes you through **Holsteinische Schweiz** (Holstein Switzerland)—hardly Alpine, but scattered with over 140 lakes and popular with watersports enthusiasts and grannies taking the *Kur*. The B76 links up with the A1, which whips you south to Lübeck.

In the 13th and 14th centuries Lübeck was the spearhead of the Hanseatic League, the richest city in Germany and one of Europe's leading ports. The 'Queen of the Hansa' became a Free Imperial City in 1226, and the town council's **Statutes of Lübeck** became the basis of city government throughout the Baltic region. Its local decorative brickwork and shapely gables became a feature of city architecture along the entire North European coast; today Lübeck has more of the atmosphere of Amsterdam than of any southern German town. Powerful merchant dynasties grew up, and the inhabitants lived in style: Fynes Moryson, a 16th-century English traveller marvelled at the pipes that carried fresh water to the citizens' houses, each with an 'iron cock, which being turned, the water falls into their vessels'.

Lübeck weathered the decline of the Hanseatic League better than most members, and though later eclipsed by Hamburg and Bremen, was still a prosperous trading town at the beginnning of the 19th century. In the latter part of the century, at a time when Lübeck was already losing ground, two great German men of letters, the brothers Heinrich and Thomas Mann, were born into a local merchant family. Thomas Mann's epic novel *Buddenbrooks* chronicles the decline of one such Lübeck dynasty, and evokes the wealthy, rather stifling atmosphere of the town superbly.

Today Lübeck is the most resplendent of the Baltic towns, with a lively mix of cultures. Some 100,000 refugees fled here from Eastern Europe after the last war, and Turkish *Gastarbeiter* have also made their mark. Allied bombs destroyed about a quarter of the Altstadt, but romantic pockets have survived and rebuilding has been sensitive, extensive—and low-rise. You can still find cobbled alleys and squares lined with quaint red-brick houses; impressive mansions stand shoulder-to-shoulder along the grander streets, and the skyline of spindly steeples appears much as it would have done to a medieval visitor.

Getting Around

By car: Lübeck is on the A1, 96km from Hamburg and 200km from Bremen. Traffic is not allowed in the city centre on Saturdays and Sundays. The most convenient parking lot for the Altstadt is on Obertrave, near the Holsentor.

Mitfahrzentrale: Fischergrube 45, ℭ (0451) 71074.

By train: The **Hauptbahnhof** is a few minutes' walk west of the Altsadt, past the Holsentor, and on a main line to Hamburg (two trains an hour, journey time 40–50min).

By bicycle: You can hire bicycles from the shop at Schwartauer Allee 39, ℭ (0451) 42660. Surprisingly, Lübeck isn't as well laid out with cycle paths as most German cities—it is easier to walk between the sights.

Tourist Information

There are two **tourist offices**, one at the Hauptbahnhof, ℭ (0451) 72300 *(Mon–Sat 9–1 and 3–7)* and one on the Markt, ℭ (0451) 122 8106 *(Mon–Fri 9.30–6, Sat and Sun 10–2)*.

Post office: Main post offices can also be found on the Markt and across from the Hauptbahnhof.

Banks: Branches of most German banks are along Breite Straße or Königstraße. The bureau de change at the Hauptbahnhof is open on Saturday mornings, but not on Sundays or holidays.

Festivals

The main event of the year is a traditional fair in May—the **Markt Anno Dazumal**. The **Christmas Market** is particularly good, with a crafts market in the Heiligen-Geist Hospital and displays on fairytale themes outside the Marienkirche.

The Altstadt: the Holsentor to St-Petri-Kirche

Lübeck's Altstadt is on a compact, oval-shaped island ringed by the River Trave and an artificial moat. The western entrance was guarded by the **Holsentor** (1477), a madly eccentric gateway with two pixie-cap towers, once familiar to all Germans as the picture on the old DM50 note. It leans precariously in every conceivable direction, subsiding into the soft soil like a melting ice-cream cake. The gay red and black brickwork (a Lübeck speciality), moulded terracotta friezes and rows of arches and windows could be the design of an imaginative confectioner. Inside is a **museum** *(Apr–Sept Mon–Sat 10–5, Oct–Mar 10–4; adm DM4)* which gives you a ready introduction to Lübeck's history, with impressive models of old sailing ships and sobering depictions of Second World War bomb damage. To the right of the Holsentor is the **Salzspeichergrüppe** (row of salt warehouses)—attractive red-brick, gabled buildings built between the 16th and 18th centuries to store Lübeck's most precious trade commodity, en route from Lüneberg to Scandanavia.

More old warehouses and merchants' houses line **An der Obertrave** across the water. From here the narrow, cobbled Kleine Petersgrube winds up to the **Museum für Figurentheater** (Puppetry Museum) *(Tues–Sun 9.30–6.30; adm DM4)*. On the ground floor is a small display of German marionettes, but up a spiral staircase is a far more impressive selection of puppets from around the world, including some magnificent Thai and Javanese shadow puppets, awesome African creations and a finely carved Chinese glove-puppet theatre. In the adjoining **Marionetten-Theater** *(Im Kolk 20–22, © (0451) 70060)* there are puppet shows for children *(Tues–Sun 3.30pm; adm DM7)* and adults *(Fri and Sat, 7.30pm; adm DM12–15)*. On a mound above the museum stands the Gothic **St-Petri-Kirche**, a *Hallenkirche* built mainly between the 13th and 14th centuries, completely bombed out in 1942 but restored in the 1960s. Here and there in the whitewashed interior you can see patches of old frescoes, but the church is really only worth visiting if you are interested in one of the temporary exhibitions usually on show.

The Markt and the Rathaus

To the north of the St-Petri-Kirche, across Kohlmarkt, you come to the **Markt**, a large square that plays host to a daily flower market and a tiny fruit market, which is housed in a pavilion just a few yards long. There is a colourful full-scale market on Mondays and Thursdays. The Markt is flanked on two sides by dull post-war buildings, but is dominated by the spires and fancy brickwork of the Gothic **Rathaus**, the oldest town hall still in use in Germany. From the Markt your main view is of the plain rear façade of black, glazed bricks and a startlingly contrasting white-sandstone Rennaissance loggia, covered in carving. If you walk through one of the arches under the Rathaus to Breite Straße, you can see the front façade and get a better idea of how the building developed. The *Hauptbau* (Main Building, the northern wing) which dates from the 13th century has a decorative turretted wall stretching high above the roof line. Two big holes (cut to lessen wind resistance) give the wall a fragile, airy appearance. The *Neue Gemach*, an extension begun in 1440, has two rows of delicate pinnacles, each one topped off with a cheerful gold pennant. Here you can see the characteristic red-and-black Lübeck brickwork at its best—though the effect is somewhat spoiled by an over-elaborate Renaissance stairway tacked onto the façade. The exterior of the Rathaus is the most impressive part, but you can go on a **guided tour** of the interior *(Mon–Fri 11, 12, 3; adm DM3)*, where the highlight is a Baroque *Audienzsaal* with modest stucco ceilings and heavy chandeliers.

Opposite the Rathaus, across Breite Straße, is the **Café-Konditorei Niederegger**, a business with a longer history than its bland modern building suggests. In 1806 Herr Niederegger perfected the recipe for **marzipan**, which was first made in the middle ages in Lübeck, using imported Italian almonds. Since then the café's marzipan (which comes in all shapes and sizes—from pink piggies to enormous models of the city) has become world famous.

The Marienkirche and Buddenbrookhaus

Off the northern end of the Hauptgebau stretches the **Kanzleigebäde** (Chancellery), begun in the 15th century, but constantly rebuilt and extended up to the 19th century. Immediately behind the Kanzleigebäde is the **Marienkirche**, built in the French Gothic style (though in brick rather than stone) between the 13th and 14th centuries. This noble church with 185m-high twin towers and the highest brick nave in the world, right in the centre of town, was as bold a statement as any of the pride and power of the wealthy merchants who worshipped there. It brazenly outshines the bishops' cathedral, which is tucked away on lower ground on the southern edge of the Altstadt. Much of the fine carving and woodwork that filled the church was destroyed by Allied bombs, but restoration work after the war brought to light the original Gothic **frescoes**—dainty patterns in terracotta, green and grey. Art treasures that did survive include the densely carved 15th-century **high altar** (in which, curiously, one of the figures appears to be wearing sunglasses), a finely made gilded tabernacle and reliefs by the skilled Münster mason, Heinrich Brabender. Behind the high altar is the sensitively carved *Marienaltar* done in Antwerp in 1518. (Fynes Moryson, who saw it just 50 years after it was made, was unimpressed, remarking that the Madonna was dressed in buffin, like a burgher *hausfrau*.) There's also a modern stained-glass window showing the medieval Dance of Death, and an astronomical clock built in the 1960s. At the southern end of the church you can see the shattered remnants of two enormous bells, half sunk in the floor, lying just as they did after plummeting from the bell tower when the church was bombed. Today they are the focal point of a small memorial chapel.

Mengstraße runs down the northern side of the Marienkirche. **Heinrich and Thomas Mann** were born in the Baroque mansion at No. 4 to a wealthy city senator and grain-dealer. The younger brother, Thomas (1875–1955), is perhaps best known for his short story *Death in Venice* (1913, later made into a film with Dirk Bogarde), though his best works are the novels *The Magic Mountain* (1924), a complex allegory of the sickness of early 20th-century Europe, set in a sanatorium in Switzerland, and the splendid *Buddenbrooks* (1901), with which he made his name. *Buddenbrooks* is based very much on the writer's own family, and the city took a long time to forgive Mann the book's thinly veiled portraits of local notables and criticism of Lübeck society. Although he won the Nobel Prize for literature in 1929, Lübeck only honoured him with the 'Freedom of the City' just before he died in 1955.

Heinrich (1871–1950) is best known for *Professor Unrat* (1905), a searing attack on the stuffy German educational system. The book formed the basis of the film *The Blue Angel*, which shot its leading actress, Marlene Dietrich, to fame. Both brothers left the country in the early 1930s to live in exile in Switzerland, in France and finally just a few minutes drive from each other in California. Today the **Buddenbrookhaus** is a small **museum** *(daily 10–5, Thurs 10–7; adm DM4)*, with a few interesting photographs and details of the connections between real people and the fictional characters in Thomas Mann's novels, but none of the atmosphere of an old patrician mansion. The explanatory texts are in German only, so all but devotees are likely to smart at the entrance fee.

The Jakobikirche, Burgtor and Heilig-Geist-Hospital

Mengstraße leads back into Breite Straße. A few minutes' walk north along Breite Straße brings you to the **Jakobikirche**, a cosy church that was used by seamen, today most noted for the **Brömse Altar**, with carving by Heinrich Brabender, and the dark, sumptuous wooden **organ lofts**. From the church, Große Burgstraße leads down to the **Burgtor**, a more upright, modest affair than the other city gate.

Doubling back up Große Burgstraße towards the Altstadt, you come to the **Heilig-Geist-Hospital**, a hospice for the elderly founded in 1227. The **chapel** (today's entrance hall) has a splendid vaulted roof, freshly restored 14th and 15th century frescoes and a rood screen showing scenes from the life of St Elizabeth. Beyond this is the enormous **Langhaus**, a communal dormitory nearly 100m long. In the 19th century the Langhaus was divided up into little wooden cells, each with just enough room for a bed and small cupboard. These 'cabins' were used up until the 1970s. One has been kept fitted out, and you can peer in through the window for a look.

Königstraße

Große Burgstraße leads into Königstraße, where you can see more grand Baroque mansions. Two of them, the Drägerhaus (No. 9) and the Behnhaus (No. 11) have been combined into the **Museum für Kunst und Kulturgesichte** *(Apr–Sept Tues–Sun 10–5, Oct–Mar 10–4; DM4)*. Here, in the Drägerhaus especially, you really do get a glimpse of the sumptuous style of Lübeck patrician life. The greatest surprise is just how big these houses were. The front façades—which were subject to a tax—were kept narrow, but the houses stretch way back into large gardens. The Drägerhaus contains rooms furnished in the styles of the 18th and early 19th centuries. The interior of the Behnhaus has been modernized and converted into a gallery of mostly 19th-century art. There is a room devoted to the local painter **Johann Friedrich Overbeck** (1789–1869), founder of the Nazarene Movement *(see* **Art** p. 62), and also a number of paintings by the Norwegian painter **Edvard Munch** (1863–1944), including *Die Kinde des Dr. Linde*, familiar to many as the cover picture of the Penguin edition of *Buddenbrooks*.

Further along Königstraße you come to the **Katherinenkirche** *(Apr–Sept Tues–Sun 10–1 and 2–5; adm free)*, erstwhile Franciscan convent church, and now a museum. In niches on the outside wall you can see three sculptures by the Expressionist **Ernst Barlach**. He had just completed *Woman in the Wind, The Beggar* and *The Singer* in 1932 when the Nazis banned his work. After the war the sculptor **Gerhard Marcks** filled the remaining six niches to complete the sequence. Inside the church, tucked away beside the entrance is *The Raising of Lazarus* by Tintoretto. Also near the door is a dramatic carving of St George despatching the dragon, a copy of a work done by Bernt Notke in 1499. Notke was the most famous sculptor in the region around the 15th and 16th centuries, and his lively, imaginative work is spread throughout northern Germany, Denmark and Sweden.

The streets leading off Königstraße (such as Glockengiesser, down the side of the Katherinenkirche) are lined with cafés and bistros, Turkish food stores, junk shops and ethnic galleries. Through arches, and behind double doors in the walls are the hidden gardens and quiet courtyards of old almshouses (similar to the *Hofjes* dotted about Amsterdam). They are still lived in, but if you are discreet and don't go beyond any *Kein Eintritt* (No Entry) signs, are very much worth a peep. (Look out for names with 'Hof' or 'Gang' in them, such as Füchtings-Hof at Glockengeisser 23 and Glandorps-Gang at No. 39).

The Southern Altstadt

Aegidienstraße (the last street to lead off Königstraße) takes you down to the **Aegidien-kirche**, the church of craftspeople and less affluent merchants, renowned in its time for the quality of its music. Inside is a good Baroque organ (still used for recitals) and an eye-catching Renaissance **choir gallery**, gorgeously carved and suspended like a bridge over the nave. Around the corner from the church is the **St-Annen-Museum** *(Apr–Sept Tues–Sun 10–5, Oct–Mar Tues–Sun 10–4; adm DM4)*. Housed in what remains of a Gothic convent, the museum contains some good 13th–18th century religious art, including a superb *Passion Altar* (1491) painted for the cathedral by the Flemish artist **Hans Memling.** In the Paramentenkamer are rich vestments dating from the 14th century.

Across Mühlenstraße and down Fegefeuer you come finally to the **cathedral**, at the very edge of the Altstadt. The heavy, predominantly Romanesque, brick church was finished in 1230—with some Gothic bits (such as the porch on the south side) being added later in the century. Inside you'll find decorative Baroque side-chapels, and an enormous **Triumphal Cross** by Bernt Notke. On the **rood screen**, also carved by Notke, hangs a 17th-century clock which creaks and grinds and sends out the figure of Death to strike the hour.

Lübeck ✆ (0451–)

Where to Stay

expensive

Kaiserhof, Kronsdorfer Allee 13, ✆ 791 011 (DM175–275). Sumptuously furnished, luxurious converted patrician villa. No restaurant.

moderate

Hotel Charlie Rivel's Sohn, Glockengießerstr. 91/95, ✆ 76990, fax 78828 (from DM100). Zanily decorated individual apartments attatched to Valentino Rivel's restaurant (*see* below).

Hotel Jensen, An der Obertrave 4–5, ✆ 71646, fax 73386 (DM150–190). Converted waterside merchant's house. Dimly atmospheric and friendly.

Hotel Stadt-Lübeck, Am Bahnhof 21, ✆ 864 194, fax 863 221 (DM98–160). Best of the hotels around the station. Newly renovated with a keenly attentive management team. No restaurant.

Park Hotel, Lindenplatz 2, ✆ 84644 (DM140–175). Comfy Jugendstil villa between the Altstadt and Hauptbahnhof. Stuccoed ceilings, leaded windows and hotel furniture. No restaurant.

Hotel am Dom, Dankwartsgrube 43, ✆ 702 0251, fax 78886 (DM140–50). Recently converted, family-run hotel in quiet street near the cathedral.

inexpensive

Pension am Park, Hüxtertorallee 57, ✆ 797 598 (DM75 without private facilities–DM90). family-run Pension in a graceful turn-of-the-century house by a park.

Rucksack Hotel Backpackers, Kanalstr. 70, ✆ 74807 (DM19-24 per person without breakfast, in dormitory room (4–8 beds)). The name says it all—but there are private rooms as well as dorms.

Youth hostel: Gertruden Kirchhof 4, ✆ 33433—though a better bet is the YMCA, Grosse Petersgrube 11, ✆ 78982, in a renovated house in the Altstadt.

Eating and Drinking: Restaurants

Charlie Rivel's Sohn, Glockengießerstr. 91–95, ✆ 76990. Eccentric restaurant in a converted 17th-century house, run by Valentino Rivel, son of one of Germany's most famous clowns. The walls are smothered with photographs, and the building stacked with memorabilia of father and son's globe-trotting. Valentino and his wife Tanmara cook dishes from all over the world. Wild duck and venison dishes are specialities. You say what you are willing to pay, and they'll suggest a menu.

Schabbelhaus, Mengstr. 48 and 50, ✆ 72011 (DM100–150). Famous restaurant in old merchant house, crammed with heavy wooden furniture and serving gourmet food. More daring palates might appreciate the sirloin poached in wine with semolina dumplings and confit of shallots.

Restaurant Barin, Fischergrube 18, ✆ 77311 (DM60–80). Converted 15th-century house scattered with old pews, madonnas and other fragments plundered from churches. The food is good—with traditional duck, rabbit and meat dishes, and also a changing seasonal menu. Small courtyard garden.

moderate/inexpensive

Lübecker Hanse, Kolk 3–7, ✆ 78054 (DM40–80). French and regional cooking in an old house on one of Lübeck's narrowest streets. A local favourite, with scrumptious fish dishes.

Schiffergesellschaft, Breitestr. 2, ✆ 76 776 (DM40–60). Another renowned restaurant, in a 16th-century house built for seamen. Good wine list, but fairly unimaginative menu (dominated by standards such as roast beef and veal dishes) and stuffy waiters. Subject to invasions by visiting dignitaries and coach parties.

Hospiz Weinkellers, Am Koberg 6–8, ✆ 76234 (DM10–80). Three atmospheric cellars beneath the Heilig-Geist-Hospital. The cheapest and jolliest serves mainly baked potatoes. There is also a wine bar where you can get traditional snacks such as Blut und Leberwurst (black pudding and liver paté) and a classier restaurant which comes up with dishes such as sole baked with cheese, parsley and spinach.

Aubergine, Hüxstr. 57, ✆ 77 212 (DM25–60). Good salad bar, imaginative pasta dishes, and more complicated fare such as guinea fowl in a creamy thyme sauce.

Kontor, Mengestr. 52, ✆ 72 0111 (DM20–30). Next door to the Schabbelhaus, but considerably cheaper, and with excellent food. The menu changes seasonally, and includes such delights as cod with a mustard sauce with a dill salad.

Bars and Cafés

Prian's, Große Burgstr. 13. Peculiar café where the decor is inspired by Monty Python's *Life of Brian*. There's often good recorded jazz playing, but the management also has a policy of airing local bands' demo tapes in the hope of snaring a passing producer. Be warned. Breakfasts and light snacks are a bargain.

Amadeus, Königstr. 26. Trendy young crowd, fabric draped from the ceiling and fairy-lights in the aspidistras.

Marionette, Kolk 14–16, ✆ 706 0293. Friendly little wine bar in a 16th-century house, decked out with spare puppets from the museum next door.

Brauberger, Alfstr. 36. House brewery with big copper vats, tasty brew and the usual accompanying hunks of roast meat.

From Lübeck, once right up against the East German border, the B105 takes you along the Baltic coastline to the island of Rügen. This stretch of the coast is one of the fastest-changing regions of the old DDR. The big Trades Union 'Holiday Centres' now accommodate streams of tourists from the west of the country, and in places the beaches are becoming as crowded as in Schleswig-Holstein. But with a little rootling around you can still find beautiful, lonely spots, or step through a time warp into seaside resorts full of faded, peeling, but still rather elegant old buildings—for this was where the rich Hansa merchants would retire in the summer. Thankfully, recent development seems to favour restoring old buildings over putting up too many flash new ones, and the *Strandkörbe*—the hooded wicker chairs that protect their occupants from the wind—still line up on the beach as they have done for decades.

See also Directory entries for Schwerin, Wismar, Usedom, Greifswald, Hiddensee and Güstrow.

Getting Around

By car: The B105 goes along the coast from Lübeck to Rostock (120km) and Stralsund (190km) from where you drive over a bridge to Rügen. There is also a direct Autobahn connection from Berlin to Rostock (200km on the A24 and A19).

By train: Travelling east of Lübeck can be a slow process. There are trains every two hours from Lübeck to Rostock (1¾hr) and Stralsund (2¾hr).

Tourist Information

Rostock: Speicher, Schnickmannstr. 13–14, ✆ (0381) 25260. There is also a branch of the tourist information office at the Hauptbahnhof, ✆ (0381) 454 026.

Warnemünde: Passagierkai, ✆ (0381) 51248.

Stralsund: Rathaus, Alter Markt, ✆ (03831) 252 251.

Rügen: Markt 11, Bergen, ✆ (03838) 21129.

Rostock

In 1992 Rostock, the first main stop along the route and biggest town in the region, was catapulted ignominiously into world headlines by racist riots. Twenty-eight people were killed, young thugs set light to hostels and older residents stood by and applauded. It is, however, generally a calm and pretty place, with a curious mix of medieval and good modern architecture. Not everything is in pristine condition—Rostock has the romantic tang of an old seafaring town. Cats dart about the sidestreets near the port, old women stare suspiciously from their balconies and men's voices echo from dark drinking holes.

The best place to begin your look around is on the **Neuer Markt**, lined on one side by a neat row of gabled burgher houses, and on the other by the 700-year-old **Rathaus**. Seven

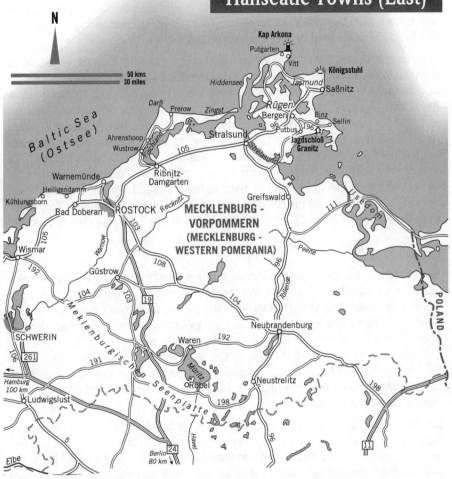

Gothic towers poke up behind a façade added in the 18th century. Steinstraße leads south off Neuer Markt to **Steintor**, a dumpy town gate with a rather menacing spire. From here you can follow a fragment of the old city wall past the **Lagebuschturm**, a 16th-century prison and ammunition store, to the **Kuhtor** ('Cow Gate', 1262), wide enough to drive herds of cattle through to market. The run-down streets and alleys north of the Kuhtor are the most evocative of the old working Hansa port. Here you'll find the 13th-century **Nikolaikirche**, Rostock's oldest church, half-converted into apartments, and the **Petrikirche** which until the Second World War had a 117m-high spire that guided sailors into port. Both churches are in a fairly miserable condition and are undergoing restoration.

Just off the northern corner of Neuer Markt is the **Marienkirche** *(Tues–Sat 10–12 and 3–5, Sun 11.15–12)* a late-Gothic brick church. It was intended to rival the Marienkirche in Lübeck—but such hopes were dashed when the nave collapsed, leaving an oddly truncated interior. Inside, the main attractions are an enormous Baroque **organ**, complete with its own salon-like gallery, a 13th-century **font** and an astronomical clock, which was built in 1472 and has been running continuously since 1643.

Kröpeliner Straße leads west from Neuer Markt, along a showily modernized pedestrian precinct dotted with medieval gables, to **Universitätsplatz**. Here you'll find a quirky modern fountain that lures passers-by to splash about on hot days, and the heavy yellow **Baroksaal** (Baroque Hall), sometimes opened up for concerts. Off the south-western corner of the square, in a quiet, leafy courtyard, is the **Kloster zum Heiligen Kreuz**, a Cistercian convent founded in 1270. Today it houses the **Kulturhistorisches Museum** (Museum of Cultural History) *(Tues–Sun 10–7; adm DM3)* where the star attraction is the 15th-century *Dreikönigsaltar* (Altar of the Magi), painted by an unknown local master. On one of the panels the kings travel by boat, and appear decidedly the worse for wear. Beyond Universitätslatz, at the end of Kröpeliner Straße, is the **Kröpeliner Tor**, a towering city gate begun in the 13th century and topped off with a Gothic gallery in 1400.

Around Rostock

Like so many of the main Hansa towns, Rostock lies slightly inland, up a navigable river. The town's closest Baltic Sea resort, **Warnemünde**, now really a suburb, is very much worth a visit (take the S-bahn from the Hauptbahnhof or travel north along An der Stadt Autobahn). Warnemüde led a double life as fishing village and wealthy merchant's holiday retreat. Today the promenade is lined with pretty cottages, many of them decked out with nets, anchors and colourful flotsam, as well as genteely crumbling 19th-century villas. Brightly painted boats bob in the tiny harbour, and retired sailors sit about and grumble. In the summer the town swarms with ice cream-licking holidaymakers and takes on something of the air of a seaside village in an Enid Blyton book.

Bad Doberan (15km west of Rostock on the B105) is famed for its splendid **Münster**, a statuesque red-brick Gothic church that sweeps up strongly out of the middle of a meadow on the outskirts of town. The church was finished in 1368 as part of a Cistercian Abbey and has been restored to pristine condition. Artworks inside include a 13th-century Madonna Lantern and a number of side altars dating from the 14th-century onwards. The town's other attraction is *Molli*, a narrow-gauge **steam train** *(information © (038203) 2154)* that puffs you out from the Bahnhof to **Heiligendamm** (once one of the Baltic's grandest resorts) and on to seething, touristy **Kühlungsborn**.

Just north-west of Rostock a spindly peninsula strays out to sea and vaguely follows the coastline east. (To get there take the B105 as far as Ribnitz-Damgarten, then follow the small road out of town in the direction of Wustrow and Prerow, or take the train to Ribnitz-Damgarten and catch Bus 210). Most of the outcrop has been declared a National Park, and though it can get quite busy in the summer, far fewer people wander out here than anywhere else alomg the coast. The main body of the peninsula links up to the mainland through **Fischland**, an isthmus in places barely a kilometre wide. The beaches are wild and windswept, with craggy dunes and isolated coves. At the turn of the century the scenery attracted droves of artists, who set up a colony in the village of **Ahrenshoop**. A handful of hopeful painters still exhibit their wares. **Darß**, the central section of the peninsula, is covered in thick forests, which stretch down to long white beaches and occasionally break open into small marshy patches that twitter with birdlife. There are more birds and exotic plants in **Zingst**, the tip of the peninsula—though this is also where you'll find the best swimming beaches and consequently the most tourists.

Where to Stay

Hotel Warnow, Lange Straße 40, ✆ (0381) 37381, fax 34728 (DM310–355). Rostock's leap into the luxury hotel market with smart new rooms, four state-of-the-art restaurants, and even Sunday brunch accompanied by a live Dixie band.

Hotel Warnemünde, Kirchenplatz 6, Warnemünde, ✆ (0381) 51216 (DM145–160). Cheerful, well-run new hotel set back from the promenade's bustle.

Hotel Gastmahl des Meeres, August-Bebel-Straße 111, ✆ (0381) 22301 (DM145–155). Small, friendly hotel on the edge of the Altstadt.

Haus Sonne, Neuer Markt 35, ✆ (0381) 37101, fax 458 2188 (DM95 without private bath). Good, clean, cheaper option in the middle of town.

Hotel Stolteraa, Strandweg 17, Warnemünde, ✆ (0381) 5321 (DM80 without private bathroom–DM180). Converted villa—pleasant rooms and friendly service.

Hotel am Alten Strom, Am Strom 63, ✆ (0381) 52581 (DM70–80 without private bath). Serviceable *pension*. The front rooms have a good view out over the fishing harbour.

Eating and Drinking

Fish, especially smoked fish and eel is a speciality all along the coast.

Gastmahl des Meeres, August-Bebel-Str. 111, ✆ (0381) 22301 (DM20–40). Serves big helpings of simple fish dishes.

Ratskeller, Rathaus, Neuer Markt, ✆ (0381) 23577 (DM20–40). Good food, especially the fish soups and stews, but keep a clear head and check your bill.

Krahnstövers, Große Wasserstr. 30. In a side-street near the Rathaus. Cavernous, atmospheric wine bar and pub, with a good selection of drinks and tasty light meals.

Zur Kogge, Wokrenterstr. 27, ✆ (0381) 34493. Jolly, touristy maritime tavern. Mainly for drinking, but with daily fishy snacks, too.

Café zur Traube, Theodor-Körner-Str. 72, Warnemünde, ✆ (0381) 52013 (DM20–30). Homemade fish specialities (daily changing menu).

Blumencafé, cnr Alexandrinen and Georginenstraße, Warnemünde. Fragrant florist-cum-café.

Stralsund (70km further along the B105) is smaller than Rostock, but has a rougher edge and less of a provincial atmosphere, though like so many east German towns, it dies at night. However, within an outer layer of ugly modern concrete suburbs is the choicest Altstadt on the coast. Street upon street of gabled Hansa houses criss-cross a small island hemmed in by the Strelasund (Strela Sound) and two narrow natural lakes—the Frankteich and the Knieperteich. Much of the Altstadt is in a sorry state of disrepair, but a manic restoration programme promises to transform Stralsund into a gem of Gothic, Renaissance and Baroque domestic architecture. This is a town that invites aimless wandering, and constantly offers little surprises (look out especially for the beautifully carved front doors).

Just north of the centre of the island is the **Alter Markt**, with Stralsund's showpiece, the Gothic **Rathaus**. The sheer ornamental façade, with seven spires, fancy brickwork and rows of decorative openings outdoes even the one in Lübeck. Integrated into the Rathaus complex is the **Nikolaikirche**, one of its two Gothic towers topped off with a Baroque spire. Pick of the artworks inside are a finely worked high altar and a 5m-high crucifix.

Fährstraße and **Schillstraße** to the east of the Alter Markt are lined with attractive gabled houses. Schillstraße leads to the **Johanniskloster** *(Tues–Sat 10–6; adm DM2)*, a former Franciscan monastery. Inside you can see fading 14th-century murals, pretty Gothic cloisters and courtyards, and (high under the roof) the **Raücherboden**, rooms where meat was once smoked, and which still have a musty, smoky aroma. Nearby is the **Kniepertor**, one of the old city gates.

The most impressive Hansa houses are in Mühlenstraße, which runs west off the Alter Markt. At the end of Mühlenstraße you can see another city gate, the Kütertor, then down Bielkenhagen you come to the **Meeresmuseum** (Museum of the Sea) *(May–Oct daily 10–5, Nov–Apr Wed–Sun 10–5; adm DM3)*. This has a reasonably good aquarium as well as various stuffed fauna from the Baltic region and odd bits of fishing equipment. Next door is the **Kulturhistorisches Museum** *(Tues–Sun 10–5; adm DM3)* where the highlights are a collection of 18th- and 19th-century toys, 10th-century treasures dug up on the island of Hiddensee, and an exhibition devoted to Ferdinand von Schill, the town's swashbuckling hero who (literally) lost his head warding off Napoleon's armies in 1809. Mönchstraße takes you from the museum to **Neuer Markt** in the south of the Altstadt. Dominating the square is the red-brick Gothic **Marienkirche** (built in 1360). The church is famed for its **organ**, built by the Lübeck master Friedrich Stellwagen between 1653 and 1659. The **tower** *(Mon–Fri 10–5, Sat 10.30–12.30 and 2.30–5, Sun 2.30–5; adm DM1)* offers a fine view over the whole Altstadt and across the sound to the island of Rügen.

Where to Stay

Good Morning Hotel, Fährbrücke 1, ℂ (03831) 297 093 (DM150). Converted cruiser moored near the Altstadt. Rooms are small and simply furnished, but smart and spotless. Service is brisk.

Norddeutscher Hof, Neuer Markt 22, ℂ (03831) 293161 (DM180–320). In the shadow of the Marienkirche. Comfortable but ordinary rooms at big prices.

Hotel Süß, Hainholzstr. 42, ℂ (03831) 390 124, fax 390 125 (DM160–180). New hotel with eager mangagement, well-appointed rooms and a sun terrace. They also hire out bicycles.

Youth Hostel: Am Kütertor 1, ℂ (03831) 292 160.

Private Rooms

As is so often the case in the East, these are the best value. The tourist office can book one for you. Pick of the bunch is Heide Weidemann, Voigdehagen 3, as yet no telephone (DM80), in a small farm on the edge of town. She's renowned for her slap-up breakfasts.

Eating and Drinking

Artus-Hof-Café, Alter Markt 8, ℂ (03831) 62219. Old-style upstairs café, overlooking the bustle of the Alter Markt, and popular with locals for coffee and cake.

Külpstube, Külpstraße, just off the Alter Markt. Simple pub offering good, cheap grub (daily changing menu).

Ben Gunn, Fährestr. 27. Watering-hole for Stralsund's trendies.

Scheele-haus, Fährstr. 23–4, ℂ (03831) 292987 (DM20–50). Beautifully restored old building. Stralsund's most elegant restaurant, and a good menu too—with local fish dishes, steaks and schnitzels.

Romantica, Alter Markt, ℂ (03831) 293 607 (DM15–40). Delightfully OTT Italian restaurant, draped with vines and scattered with the trunks of classical statues. Good pasta and pizzas.

Rügen

From Stralsund a causeway sweeps across the Strelasund to Rügen, Germany's largest island. Bus A417 will take you to Bergen in the middle of the island. Local buses and a narrow-gauge railway chug between resorts. Rügen's varied landscape and the battered grandeur of its resorts are a magnet to summer visitors, yet even then it doesn't lose its charm, though the main town, **Bergen**, and the ferry port of **Saßnitz** are eminently missable the whole year round.

The southern part of the island is covered by rolling grassland, freckled with woods and copses and is renowned for its beaches. **Putbus** (8km south of Bergen, Bus 406) is an eerily empty town of pompous whitewashed and greying Neoclassical buildings—though it does have a big, lush **Schloßpark**. Fourteen kilometres east (on the B196 or by narrowgauge railway to *Haltepunkt Jagdschloß*) is **Jagdschloß Granitz** *(daily 9–5; adm DM4)*, a pink granite 19th-century hunting lodge, built with grandiloquent lack of style by Prince Wilhelm Malte, the founder of Putbus. The lodge's main attraction is a wrought-iron spiral stairway up which you can make a dizzy ascent to the top of the central tower from which you get a magnificent view over the island. A kilometre or so further down the road you come to **Binz**, a lively resort with a long promenade, complete with band pavilion and rows of white benches occupied by biddies in open-toe shoes who stare dreamily out to sea. **Sellin**, 10km further down the coast, is a rather melancholic turn-of-the-century resort full of solid villas with peeling wooden balconies. Beyond Sellin lies a crooked peninsula offering some of Rügen's most sheltered (and most popular) beaches.

Jasmund, in the east, is so tenuously connected to the rest of Rügen that it is almost an island in itself. Here the land is hilly and thickly wooded. Crowds pour across to **Stubbenkammer** (Bus 408 or 419) where the forests end abruptly in a series of jagged white cliffs immortalized by the Romantic painter Caspar David Friedrich. The most dramatic of these, the **Königsstuhl** (King's Seat) stands alone, 117m high. Legend has it that anyone who scaled the face could become King of Rügen. These days people take an easier option and go up the back way via a footbridge, then queue for a look at the view (which is breathtaking, when you get there).

To the north the scenery becomes more rugged and the beaches stony and windswept. At **Kap Arkona**, the northernmost tip of the island, you can see an elegant **lighthouse** by the famed 19th-century Berlin architect Karl-Friedrich **Schinkel**—a romantic lone turret with what looks like a mini conservatory on top. Next to it is a startling, efficient, black and orange striped modern version. You can get a good view of both lighthouses from the nearby village of **Putgarten**, then wander down to **Vitt** a dinky fishing village of thatched cottages, hidden in the trees. Cars are *verboten* in Vitt—you can walk from Kap Arkona, or go in a horse-drawn carriage *(DM4 return)* from Putgarten. Vitt seems hardly to have changed in a hundred years and has long been a haven to artists and writers—though more and more tourists are beginning to discover it. (Vitt also has an excellent inn—*see* **Eating and Drinking** below.)

Where to Stay

In Summer private rooms and hotels on Rügen book out early.

Hotel am Strand, Strandpromenade 17–18, Binz, ℭ (038393) 2387 (DM55 without private bathroom–DM160). Modern hotel, complete with sauna, solarium and gym, on a quiet, leafy extension of the Binz promenade.

Kurhaus Binz, Strandpromenade 27, Binz, ℭ (038393) 5131, fax 2393 (DM55 without private bath–DM95). Cavernous old *Kurhaus* overlooking the sea. Simply furnished, but good value for the area.

Pension Ingeborg, Wilhelm-Pieck-Str. 18, Sellin, ℭ (038303) 291 (DM70–80). Big 19th-century house. The rooms can be a little gloomy—but the ones in the front have vast, private wooden balconies.

Eating and Drinking

Rosencafé, Schloßpark, Putbus (DM10–20). Surly service, but a long verandah overlooking the rose garden. Icecream, cakes and light meals.

Eiscafé Frank Nitschke, Strandpromenade, Binz (DM20–30). Ice-cream parlour that also serves the best home-cooked fish in town; the menu changes according to what is caught.

Zum Goldenen Anker, Vitt (DM15–40). Welcoming, cosy tavern famed for its eel—but with excellent other dishes, too.

The Mecklenburg Lake District and Lüneburg

Just inland from the coast (in the area between Güstrow, Neubrandenburg, Neustrelitz and Schwerin) is the Mecklenburg Lake District (German: *Mecklenburgischen Seenplatte*). At the moment this is one of the most unspoiled parts of Germany. Over 600 lakes make a patchwork with natural forests, rolling meadows and reedy marshland. Sleepy market towns and forgotten villages are dotted about in between. Nature enthusiasts wax eloquent about the rare species of plant, animal and birdlife you can find here, and are set to do battle with developers who want to turn the area into one giant watersports resort. Around the biggest lake, the **Müritz See** the land has already been declared a nature reserve, but in other places developers are winning. Apart from Lüneburg itself, the towns of **Waren** and **Röbel** are the most worth seeking out.

For practical information, see Directory entries for Neubrandenburg and Ludwigslust.

Getting Around

Public transport around the Lake District is dire, and a car (or bicycle) is the best way to get about. The region is about 150km across.

By car: Routes B192 and B198 are the most scenic. You can drive through to Lüneburg from the B198 via the B191 and B5 (another 100 or so kilometres from the edge of the Lake District), or pop down on the B4 from Hamburg, 50km away.

By train: The Berlin–Rostock train stops off in Neustrelitz, on the edge of the Lake District. There is one every 2 hours (time to Rostock 1½hr, to Berlin 1hr 20min). There are frequent trains from Hamburg to Lüneburg (journey time around 40 min). The Heide-Express, a **narrow-gauge railway train** meanders around the Lüneburg Heath (information ✆ (04131) 58136).

By bicycle: The countryside around the Mecklenburg Lakes and the Lüneburg Heath, south of Lüneburg, are ideal cycling territory. Many main railway stations hire out bicycles at low rates. You can also get bikes from the hire shop at Strelitzer Str. 46 in Neustrelitz or from Laden 25, Am Werder 25, Lüneburg ✆ (04131) 37960.

Tourist Information

Mecklenburg Lakes: Tourist office Waren/Müritz, Neuer Narkt 19, Waren/Müritz, ✆ (03991) 4172.

Lüneburg: Rathaus, ✆ (04131) 309 593.

For centuries, the foundation of Lüneburg's wealth was salt. The story goes that a Saxon hunter noticed a white crust on the skin of a boar he had killed, tasted it and found that it was salt—an immensely valuable commodity in those days. He found out where the boar had been wallowing, and so discovered the salt pan. (You can see some bones, said to be those of the boar, in the Lüneburg Rathaus). The salt spring, the **Ilmenau**, also provided a navigable connection with the River Elbe, so Lüneburg burgeoned as a trading centre too, eventually becoming an important member of the Hanseatic League. The city flourished from the 10th to the 16th centuries, but the Thirty Years' War and squabbles with the local Duke sent it into a decline. Apart from a short boom in the 18th century, Lüneberg remained a backwater, though salt continued to be mined here until 1980. Even the Allied bombers passed it by, so today it has the most intact Altstadt in the region.

The best place to begin a walk around is the **Markt**, where the Wednesday and Saturday markets are replete with produce from the surrounding farmland, and delicious honey from Lüneburg Heath. Rising grandly from one end of the square is the pale yellow Baroque façade of the **Rathaus** *(guided tours Tues–Fri 10am, 11, 12, 2 and 3; Sat and Sun 10, 11, 2 and 3; adm DM5)*. The façade was added in 1720, but the core of the building is much older, dating back to 1230. The **interior** is stunning—the biggest and best-preserved medieval Rathaus in the country. The guided tour takes you through the cosy *Körkammer* (1491) where councillors met to elect the mayor; the *Fürstensaal*, a dance-hall hung with elaborate candelabra made from stags antlers; the *Große Ratstube* (Council Chamber, 1564–82), one of Germany's most prized Renaissance interiors, thick with rich carving by Albert von Soest; and an earlier council chamber, the *Große Ratsaal* (1330), with 15th-century stained-glass windows and its gently arched ceiling covered in 16th century painting.

Across the square from the Rathaus is a Renaissance town house where the poet **Heinrich Heine** spent some time on a visit to his parents (and wrote the famous *Loreley*), and a Baroque **Schloß**, now a court. If you head east along Ochsenmarkt, and then south down Bäckerstraße you come to **Am Sande**, an elongated square, lined with an historical spectrum of gabled houses from the 15th to the 18th centuries (though these days rows of buses spoil the view). Finest of the all is the **Schwarzes Haus** (Black House) at the top of the square. Once a tavern and inn, it now has a more sober role as home to the local Chamber of Commerce. Way down at the other end of the square is the church of **St Johannis**, a brick *Hallenkirche* built between the 13th and 15th centuries. The church contains one of the oldest **organs** in the country, the bulk of it dating back to the 16th century (though what you see is a majestic Baroque case). In its day the instrument was considered a triumph of technical innovation. It is played briefly every Friday at 5.30pm, and in the summer there are recitals on Thursday nights. Look out also for the superb, sensitive painting by local artist Hinrik Funhof on the reverse side of the **high altar** (1483). Beyond the church (down Bei der Ratsmühle and across the Ilmenau) is the **Museum für**

das Fürstentum Lüneburg (Museum of the Duchy of Lüneburg) *(Tues–Fri 10–4, Sat and Sun 11–5; adm DM3)*. A good collection of folksy knick-knacks and rich merchants' furniture gives you a glimpse of life in Lüneburg in its heydey. The real strength of the museum, however, is an excellent medieval collection, including an attractively painted extendable table from 1330.

From the west end of Am Sande, Rote Straße leads down to Ritterstraße, where you'll find the **Ostpreußiches Landesmuseum** (Regional Museum of East Prussia) *(Tues–Sun 10–5; adm DM2)*, with exhibits on the history and art of the region that produced philospher Immanuel Kant, writer E.T.A. Hoffman and the artists Lovis Corinth and Käthe Kollwitz. At the end of the Second World War East Prussia was divided between Poland and Russia. Thousands of refugees fled to Lüneburg, and local bitterness at what is seen as Russian annexation is still strong. Next door is the **Brauereimuseum** *(daily 10–12 and 3–5; adm free)*, a jollier place full of copper vats, decorative mugs and all the sieves, vats and spoons needed to make beer. After soaking up the history of beer making, you can sample local brew in the adjoining beergarden.

A walk back north off Am Sande (along Am Berge and down Rosenstraße) brings you to the diminutive old port, the **Wasserviertel**. It is a quiet spot with water tumbling over a long weir, quaint bridges, willows trailing their leaves in the water, and houses and warehouses coming right up to the river's edge. Here you can see a 16th-century mill and the **Alte Krane** (old crane), re-built in 1792 (the original one dated back to the 14th century).

Southwest of the city centre is the **Salzmuseum** (Salt Museum), Sülfmeisterstr. 1 *(Mon–Fri 9–5, Sat and Sun 10–5; adm DM3)*, which tells you all you ever wanted to know, and more, about the 'white gold'. The museum is on the site of Lüneburg's last remaining salt lake, and in the summer between 11am and 3pm you can watch the whole process of panning and boiling. You can splash about in the salt springs a little further south in **SaLü**, a new complex of pools eqiupped with a waterchute and wave machine to liven things up. On the main road out to Hamburg, north-east of the centre is **Kloster Lüne** *(Apr–mid-Oct Mon–Sat 9–11.30 and 2.30–5.30, Sun 11.30–12.30 and 2–5; adm DM4)*, a rambling former Benedictine convent mostly dating from around 1400. Today it is an old age home, and access is restricted, but if you're here in the last week of August it is very much worth a visit as this is the only time you can see the precious collection of 13th–16th-century embroidery.

The Lüneburg Heath

South of Lüneburg, stretching as far as Celle near Hannover, is the scrubby, mysterious Lüneburg Heath (German: Lüneburger Heide). It is a lonely place, a blaze of purple when the heather comes out in August, shrouded in mists in autumn, and stark and frozen in the winter. Great barn-like farmhouses with thatched roofs reaching almost to the ground are dotted about the landscape. The heath is populated mainly by odd wind-swept sheep with straggly long hair and curly horns (cousins of the Corsican *mouflon*). The shepherds who tend them still often dress in traditional green *Tracht.*

Along the road stalls sell woolly fleeces, delicious local honey and top-rate potatoes. Here and there you'll also find British Army shooting ranges—an incongruous and insistent reminder that this is where Field Marshal Montgomery received the unconditional German surrender on 4 May 1945. Traffic is banned from most of the heath, large areas of which have been declared nature reserve, but there are numerous cycle and footpaths. The village of **Undeloh** in the heart of the Lüneburg heath nature reserve is accessible by road (head out of Lüneburg via Reppenstedt and Salzhausen), and makes a useful base.

Where to Stay

Lüneburg

Bergström, Bei der Lüner Mühle, ℰ (04131) 3080, fax 308 499 (DM206–216). Modern hotel with charming view out onto the *Wasserviertel*. Luxury rooms and an in-house sauna and solarium.

Hotel Bremer Hof, Lüner Str. 12–13, ℰ (04131) 36077 (DM120–198). Pretty, restored merchant's house that has been run as a hotel by the same family since 1889. Some rooms open out onto a quiet half-timbered courtyard.

Zum Heidkrug, Am Berge 5, ℰ (04131) 31249 (DM145). Late-Gothic town house, beautifully renovated. The rooms are individually furnished with period furniture and the staff are lively, friendly and efficient.

Alt Lüneburger Kutscher-Stube, Heiligengeiststr. 44, ℰ (04131) 44113 (DM100). Cosy old inn with a restaurant that serves good, plain food (DM20–30).

Hotel Stadt Hamburg, Am Sande 25, ℰ (04131) 44438 (DM65–80). Pretty basic, but centrally situated and cheap.

Lüneburg Heath

Accommodation in private rooms is abundant, and often a better idea than in hotels. Look out for cottages and farmhouses displaying *Fremdenzimmer* signs.

Pension Forellenhof, Heimbucher Str. 36, ℰ (04189) 593 (DM56–76). Comfortable, friendly pension in the village of Undelsh.

Hermann Marquardt, Zur Dorfeiche 3, ℰ (04189) 232 (DM40–50). Farmhouse with comfortable beds and a slap-up breakfast.

Eating and Drinking

Restaurant Zum Heidkrug, Am Berge 5, Lüneburg, ℰ (04131) 31249. Gothic town house converted in the 1930s. Good, imaginative cooking with seasonally changing menu that might include such dishes as turbot cooked with aniseed.

Ratskeller, Rathaus, Lüneburg, ℰ (04131) 31757 (DM20–40). Vaulted gothic cellar with solid *gutbürgerliche* cuisine.

Kronen-Brauhaus, Heiligengeiststr. 39–41, Lüneburg, ℰ (04131) 713 200. Beer hall with something of the atmosphere of a medieval banqueting room. Serves Lüneburg's own brew and hearty meaty dishes.

Hannover and the Harz Region

Märchenstraße-Fairytale Road

N

30 km
20 miles

↑ Bremen
90 km

HANNOVER

BRAUNSCHWEIG
(BRUNSWICK)

N I E D E R S A C H S E N

Hameln
(Hamelin)

Hildesheim

H E S S E N

(L O W E R   S A X O N Y)

Goslar
Bad Harzburg

Brocken
1142m▲

H
a
r
z

GÖTTINGEN

Hann.
Münden

KASSEL

T H Ü R I N G E N

Hanau
161km↓

Weser

Weser

Leine

Werra

Fulda

Aller

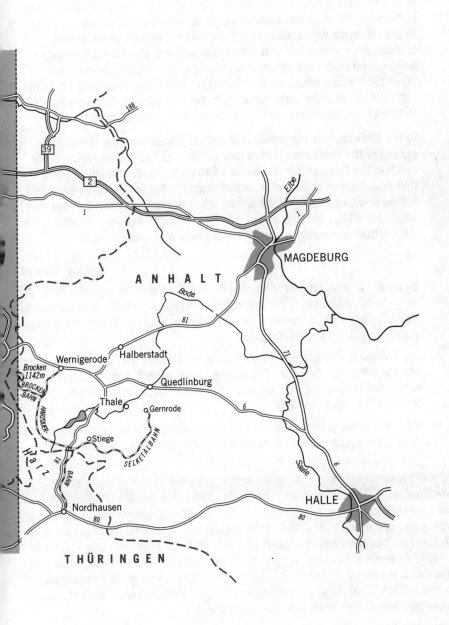

Before reunification the barbed wire, land-mines and shrapnel guns of the DDR's fortified border cut through the middle of the wooded hills of the Harz range. West German school children were bussed to look-out points to peer through field glasses at the guards (no ordinary East German citizens were allowed within 5km of the border). Neighbouring villages were cut off from each other, and local economies fell on lean times. Since the *Wende*, towns such as Götingen, Kassel and Hannover are in the centre of the country again. Roads have been re-opened, high-speed trains thunder in all directions, and sleepy towns have been startled into life.

In the 19th century the woods and market places were the stamping ground of the **Brothers Grimm** (*see* p. 208), and today the region forms much of the German Tourist Board's **Fairytale Road**. Though you will find pretty towns crammed with half-timbered houses, forests where Red Riding Hood's granny might have breathed her last, and silver mines that would have kept the Seven Dwarves 'heigh-hoing' well into the night, the main attractions along the route are the excellent **museums**.

Getting Around

By road: Two major **motorways** cross the region. Most of the important towns lie along the A7, which runs from Bremen and Hamburg south to the Austrian border. The A2 (Germany's major west-east artery) runs from the Ruhrgebiet through Hannover to Berlin and into Poland.

The **Fairytale Road** stretches from Hanau, the Grimms' birthplace on the River Main to Bremen in the north. The route is clearly marked, and you can get maps and further information from Deutsche Märchenstraße, Postfach 102660, Kassel, © (0561) 787 8001, fax 78787.

By train: Major rail routes criss-cross the region, with Hannover and Kassel now hubs of the united German rail network (*see* separate entries below for details).

Hannover

Hannover really only began to flower in the late 17th century, when a branch of the Welf dynasty (*see* pp. 581–2) built a palace here. Architecturally, the city had its heyday in the 19th century, but Allied bombs destroyed 80 per cent of the centre and little was rebuilt. Today Hannover is a sharp-edged, modern city famed for its trade fairs and for the pure, clear dialect spoken by the inhabitants (reputedly the 'best' German). It is already gearing up to host EXPO 2000. In lieu of sumptuous buildings, Hannover offers acres of splendid palace **gardens**. There are also some first-rate museums.

British visitors may enjoy rootling out information on the Royal House of Hanover. For some Americans there are connections too—thousands of locals emigrated to the New World (there are over 65 different 'Hanovers' in the US).

History: the House of Hanover

In the mid-17th century the north-German rulers of the house of Welf built a new summer palace at Herrenhausen, on the edge of the tiny Hanseatic brewing town of Hannover. Soon Hannover became the capital of a new Welf Duchy, and during the reign of **Ernst August** (1679–98) shone with one of the leading courts in Germany, with the philosopher **Gottfried Wilhelm Leibnitz** as ducal librarian and historian. Ernst August's wife Sophie was the daughter of Elizabeth Stuart (the 'Winter Queen', *see* **Heidelberg** p. 239). To ensure continuation of a Protestant line, the British parliament had appointed her as successor to Queen Anne. Sophie died just before Queen Anne, in 1714, and her son Georg Ludwig became George I of Britain. George I never learned to speak English (he was the first to pronounce Thames with a hard 't', the rest of the nation dutifully following suit). His court composer, **Georg Friedrich Händel** joined his employer across the channel, dropped his *Umlaut* and decided to stay. Like his successors George I divided his time between the two territories, though later Hanoverian monarchs began to learn the language and spend most of their time in England. In 1837 William IV died childless. **Victoria** ascended the British throne, but an ancient Salic law precluded women from succeeding in Hannover, so her uncle (another Ernst August) became King. It was he who employed the Neoclassical architect **Georg Ludwig Friedrich Laves** to give Hannover a stylish new look. Then in 1866, after the **Seven Weeks' War**, Hannover was one of the territories annexed by Prussia, and remained part of Prussia until 1946.

Getting Around

By Air

Hannover's airport, ✆ (0511) 977 1223, just north of the centre, offers connections all over Germany and direct flights to other European capitals as well as to London, Birmingham and Manchester. An express bus makes the journey between the airport and the Hauptbahnhof in 20 minutes (leaving approx. every 20min).

By Rail

The **Hauptbahnof** is right in the centre of town. There are daily connections (including many on the ICE) all over Germany including trains to Göttingen (1hr), Hildesheim (25min), Brunswick (2hr 50min), Goslar (1hr 20min), Hamburg (1½hr) and Frankfurt (2½hr ICE).

By Car

Hannover is 145km from Hamburg on the A7, and 275km from Berlin on the A2. These motorways are also major arteries south and west.

Mitfahrzentrale: Citynetz, Weißekreuzstr. 18, ✆ (0511) 19 444.

Public Transport

A network of buses, trams and underground trains covers the city. Most sites are within walking distance of each other, though the Herrenhausen gardens are a bit of a trek from the centre. A **24-Stunden-Karte** (24-hour pass) costs just DM7 and gives you unlimited travel throughout the network.

Boat Hire

Canoes, pedaloes and yachts can be hired at the north-east corner of the Maschsee, off Kurt-Schwitters-Platz.

Walking

A great stripe of red paint slapped down on the pavement leads you on a walk to all the major sights. An accompanying explanatory booklet—**The Red Thread**—is on sale at the tourist office (DM3).

Tourist Information

The Hannover **tourist information office** is opposite the Hauptbahnhof, ✆ (0511) 301 421, Ernst-August-Platz 2 *(Mon–Fri 8.30–6, Sat 8.30–2)*. Staff can offer information, maps and brochures and also run a room reservation service and ticket booking agency.

Post office: The main post office is next door to the Hauptbahnhof on Ernst-August-Platz.

Banks: Branches of the leading German banks can be found on Georgsplatz and along Rathenaustraße. Deutsche Bank has a branch at the Hauptbahnhof *(Sat 8–5 and Sun 10–2)*.

Police: ✆ 110.

Medical emergencies: ✆ 314 044.

Market days: There is a daily fruit and veg market on Am Markt, and a Saturday morning fleamarket on Hohen Ufer.

Festivals

Hannover's most famous festival, the **Schützenfest** (Marksmen's Fair) in early July, dates back to 1602. This is the biggest of many similar events in the region, and today has far more to do with beer-drinking than shooting. Over 2 million people come to Hannover to whirl about the funfair and consume prodigious quantities of food and *Lüttje Lage* (*see* **Eating and Drinking** below). Some even find time to watch the shooting competitions. On the first Sunday of the fair there is an interminable procession through the centre of town—involving around 10,000 marksmen in their traditional *Schützenverrein* (Marksmen's Society) dress, and hundreds of brass bands. (Recently international shooting clubs have joined the throng.) You can squeeze in with the crowds for free, or get tickets for grandstand seats from the tourist office (DM20).

Once a month, during the summer and early autumn, in the Herrenhausen gardens, you can see various countries' entries for the **International Baroque Fireworks Competition** (adm DM15 from tourist office). Whooshes, pops and bangs are largely dispensed with, as the pyrotechnics are accompanied by live classical music.

Of the many famous **trade fairs** held in Hannover, the **Pferd und Jagd Messe** (equestrian sports and hunting) in November is one of the most popular, attracting huntin', shootin' and fishin' enthusiasts from all over the world. The **Hannover Messe** in April is the biggest industrial fair in existence.

Around the Hauptbahnhof

A long, modern, pedestrianized **shopping precinct** stretches south from the Hauptbahnhof. At ground level, high-street shops sell bargain jewellery, designer kitchenware and stone-washed jeans. Below that is a gaudy, cacophonic tunnel of stores, crammed with trashy plastic bric-a-brac, pungent teas and spices, and refugee produce from Oriental bazaars. The surface level walkways converge on **Kröpcke**, Hannover's pavement *Treffpunkt* ('meeting place')—a gathering point for shifty youth, smart locals and weary shoppers. To the east, on Rathenaustraße is Laves' grand, colonnaded **Opera House** (1845–52). On Sophienstraße (off Rathenaustraße) is a quirkier 19th-century building, the red-and-yellow-brick **Kunstlerhaus** (art centre, *see also* Friesenkeller p. 584). Further along Rathenaustraße is the peculiar mock-Tudor **Börse** (Stock Exchange) built in 1845. A far more rewarding architectural experience is to be had west of Kröpcke, on Steintor, where you can see the **Anzeigerhochhaus**, a 1920s skyscraper built by Fritz Höger (architect of the Chile Haus in Hamburg, *see* p. 526). Its copper dome and streamlined brick walls are still an impresssive sight. (Steintor is the beginning of Hannover's red-light district, and can be a little seedy).

Around the Neues Rathaus

A walk south from Kröpcke, down the more upmarket Georgstraße and along Georgswall, brings you to the **Aegidean-Kirche**. After the Second World War the bombed-out church was deliberately not rebuilt, but kept as a peace memorial. Parts of the vine-covered ruins date back to the 12th century.

Georgswall leads onto the hectic Friedrichswall, one of the main circular roads around the city. Lording it over the traffic is Hannover's enormous **Neues Rathaus**, a gargantuan, ostentatiously decorated building with a dome, spires, spikes and fancy gables. Over 6000 underground pillars prevent it from sinking gracelessly into its boggy foundations. Inside you can see four **models** of Hannover—one up-to-date, one from 1689, one done just before the Second World War, and one showing the bomb damage in 1945. You can also wander around the palatial **interior** for a look at the black and gold mosaics of grape-bearing cherubs that adorn the walls and arches. A **lift** which travels diagonally rather than vertically *(Apr–Oct, Mon–Fri 9.30–12 and 2–5; adm DM 2)* hauls you up to the top of the dome for one of the best **views** over Hannover.

Next door to the Rathaus is the **Kestner Museum** *(Tues–Fri 10–4, Wed 10–8, Sat and Sun 10–6; adm free)*. An ugly glass and concrete box surrounds the original 19th-century building which was bequeathed to the city, together with the collection, by the nephew of August Kestner. A Hannoverian diplomat, Kestner was the son of Charlotte Buff, Goethe's model for his heroine in *The Sorrows of Young Werther*. Museums that expose the caprices and foibles of one person's taste are usually the most enticing—and this one is no exception. Starting upstairs you'll find a fine collection of Greek, Roman and Egyptian artefacts, including the supremely elegant **bust of the Pharoah Akhenaten** (*c.* 1358 BC), and a slender, beautiful *Woman Bearing Gifts* from the 11th Dynasty (*c.* 2050 BC). Downstairs you'll find original Tiffany lamps, mildly erotic statuettes and other excellent *Art Nouveau* pieces, as well as first-rate medieval booty gathered from churches around Lower Saxony. Look out especially for the ancient fabrics, treasure from the *Goldene Altar* of St Michael in Lüneberg, and an intricately wrought 14th-century bishop's crozier. The museum also has a **coin collection** of world renown.

On the other side of Friedrichswall, opposite the museum, are two elegant, rather restrained Neoclassical mansions by **Laves** (now housing offices).

The Maschsee and Museums

The **Maschsee**, Hannover's version of Hamburg's famous Alster lake, stretches for 78 hectares behind the Rathaus. In good weather the locals flock to promenade along the banks, have a flutter in the casino or mess about in boats.

Between the Rathaus and the Maschsee is the small **Maschpark** (which contains a diminutive lake—oddly mirroring Hamburg's Binnenalster). On the eastern edge of the park you'll find the **Landesmuseum** *(Tues–Sun 10–5, Thurs 10–7; adm free)*. Downstairs is a modest aquarium and a natural history museum, complete with fossils, skeletons and model dinosaurs. There is a good ethnology department focussing mainly on Peru and Mexico, and a prehistory section which includes a ghastly, blackened, but eerily well-preserved Iron-Age **bog-man**. The main attraction of the museum, however, is the **Landesgalerie** upstairs. Here you'll find a healthy stock of German Masters, featuring a good Cranach *Venus et Amore*, Holbein the Younger's superb *Portrait of Philip Melanchton* and a bizarre, contorted *Crucifixion* by Baldung. Look out also for woodcarver Tilman Riemenschneider's gently expressive *Madonna with SS Cyriacus and Johannes*, resplendent in its original colours. A vast Dutch and Flemish collection includes notable work by Rubens, Van Dyck and Rembrandt, and there is also a large (but less impressive) collection of Italian painting. Caspar David Friedrich's *Times of Day* (a series of small, misty landscapes) is a favourite in the German 19th-century rooms, but pride of place must go to Anslem Feuerbach's *Kindersländchen*—a wickedly witty send-up (populated entirely by chubby babies) of paintings of reclining nudes.

On Kurt-Schwitters-Platz, in the north-east corner of the lake, is the **Sprengel Museum** *(Tues 10–10, Wed–Sun 10–6; adm free)*, a superb museum of modern and contemporary art. Up-to-the-minute exhibitions by renowned living artists fill the ground floor. In the bewildering warren of the basement you'll find classic 20th-century art. There are one or two recognisable Picassos, but a much more arresting array of works by the French cubist **Fernand Léger**. German expressionists get a good showing, and there is an exceptional collection of **Max Beckmann**. The highlight downstairs is the display of collages and early paintings by Hannover Dadaist **Kurt Schwitters** (*see* **The Arts and Culture** p. 66), as well as a reconstruction of his original *Merz Building*. The **graphics collection** includes works by Picasso, Chagall and the major expressionists, as well as, oddly, one of Joseph Beuys' felt suits. Nooks at the end of many of the main rooms have been plastered with blown-up photographs of the artists and their studios, giving a twist of human interest to the exhibitions.

The Altstadt

You'll find Hannover's last remaining corner of Altstadt north-west of Friedrichswall, up Karmarschstraße. The mellow red-brick Gothic **Altes Rathaus** is very much in the Hanseatic tradition—pretty, but not a patch on the ones in Lübeck or Stralsund. Behind the Rathaus is the **Marktkirche**, a 14th-century *Hallenkirche* with fragments of the original stained glass preserved in the windows. Down Kramerstraße, a lane lined with restored half-timbered buildings, you come to the Holzmarkt and the **Leibnitzhaus**—a reconstruction of the elegant Renaissance façade of the house that belonged to court historian and philosopher **Gottfried Wilhelm Leibnitz**. Leibnitz is best known as a mathematician. He devised differential calculus independently of Newton, but at around the same time.

Next door is the **Historischesmuseum** *(Tues 10–8, Wed–Fri 10–4, Sat and Sun 10–6; adm free)*—a modern building that incorporates the **Beginenturm**, part of the medieval city wall. The museum contains some fine coaches belonging to the Hannover royal family—including a sporty 18th-century phaeton, and a gilded state coach which was used at the openings of the British Houses of Parliament. There are portraits of various familiar family members, and some extraordinarily well-preserved outfits that once belonged to a portly 17th-century duke. Upstairs, displays of photographs trace the city's history to the present day, and you can see models of the dinky **Hanomag**, a Noddy-car-like vehicle designed in the 1920s, and a forerunner to the Volkswagen.

Across the road, in Ballhof Straße, is the large, half-timbered **Ballhof**—a 17th-century sportshall now used as a theatre. From here an alley leads to the **Kreuzkirche** (built 1333), where there is an altarpiece by Cranach. The rest of the church is stark and plain, except for a side chapel which has been bedecked with icons by the local Serbian community who worship there.

Herrenhausen

It was the Welf Duke Georg von Calenburg who, in 1638, first had the idea of tarting up the patch of farmland he owned near the village of Höringehusen, just outside of

Hannover. By the middle of the century the Welfs had a summer palace there, and successive garden designers were each making their mark. Electress Sophie, wife of the great Duke Ernst August, called the gardens 'my life' and, before quietly dying in them on her daily walk one day in July 1714, had created (with her gardener Martin Charbonnier) one of the most spectacular Baroque sculpted landscapes in Europe. Despite being bombed and turned over to vegetables during the Second World War, the gardens—in what is now known as Herrenhausen—survive pretty much unaltered. The best bit, the Grosser Garten, is 3km from the city centre, so it is probably a good idea to catch tram 4 or 5 to Herrenhäuser Garten and then, if you have the energy after exploring the Grosser Garten, to walk back towards town through the lesser parks.

The **Grosser Garten** *(daily 8am–dusk; fountains Good Friday–Oct Mon–Fri 11–12.30 and 3–5.30, Sat and Sun 11–1 and 3–6; illuminations May–Sept daily at dusk for one hour; adm DM4 including admission to illuminations and special events)* is Hannover's showpiece. Almost from the outset the Grosser Garten was open to the public. A plaque at the gate (dating from 1720) permits commoners to disport themselves in the garden, providing that they don't throw anything at the swans, entrap the nightingales or resort to the benches when people of higher rank have needs of them. Just in front of the entrance is the **Grand Parterre**—a series of ornamental patterned gardens with enormous Baroque statues at each corner, centering on a 166-jet illuminated bell fountain. To one side is an octagonal maze designed in 1674, and on the other a **Baroque hedge theatre** designed between 1689 and 1692. Hornbeam hedges provide the scenery and dressing rooms, and the stage is decorated with gilded figures. Beyond this lie swan lakes, lime groves, small plots laid out recently to illustrate the history of landscape gardening, and the intriguing **Boskettgärten**, where courtiers used the nooks and corners formed by the hedges to conceal diplomatic intrigues and romantic trysts. In the rear part of the garden tree-lined avenues converge on the **Grosse Fontäne**, which squirts water at 140 km per hour through a 4mm-wide slit up to a height of 82 metres, making it the highest garden fountain in Europe.

The **Berggarten** *(same times; adm free)* across the road is a large botanical garden famed for its **orchid houses** *(adm DM2)*. Leibnitz carried out experiments on tobacco plants and mulberry trees here, supplying leaves for the Royal Silkworms at Hamelin. At the gate is the domed, yellow **Bibliothekpavilion**, designed by a young, light-hearted Laves. His stolid Neoclassical **Mausoleum** at the far end of the garden, built 30 years later for the Hanovers, is the work of a more established, sombre man. This is the last resting place of George I of England, the only English king not to be buried in Blighty. To the west of the Berggarten, on Alte Herrenhäuser Straße, is the **Fürstenhaus** *(Apr–Sept daily 10–6, Oct–May 10–5; adm DM4.50)*, erstwhile satellite palais of the main summer residence (which was destroyed by Allied bombs), now a museum containing a missable collection of old furniture, portraits of past rulers of Hannover and royal memorabilia.

Heading back towards town you pass through the **Georgengarten** (unlimited access), a large English-style park developed in the 19th-century as a contrast ot the formal Grosser Garten. Here the main feature is the 1.8km-long **Herrenhausen Allee**, a four-lane avenue lined with over 1000 lime trees. In the middle of the park is the **Wilhelm-Busch-Museum** *(Tues–Sun 10–5, Nov–Feb 10–4; adm DM3)*, with a permanent display of work by Wilhelm Busch (1832–1908)—an innovative cartoonist who first found a way to show movement in comic strips. Other satirical caricaturists feature in temporary exhibitions.

Hannover ✆ (0511–) | **Where to Stay**

Accommodation in Hannover is pricey, and seldom out of the ordinary. Tarifs given here are not valid during trade fairs. Then you can expect outrageous mark-ups—mostly around 50 per cent.

expensive

Kastens Hotel Luisenhof, Luisenstr. 1–3, ✆ 30440, fax 304 4807 (DM248–558). Hannover's classiest address attracts visiting celebrities to its tasteful, wood-panelled foyers, antique-lined corridors and sumptuous rooms—but is a touch stuffy.

Hotel Mercure, Am Maschpark 3, ✆ 800 80, fax 809 3704 (DM269–435). Modernized 19th-century building on the edge of the Maschpark. Quiet, plain but with touches of Gallic flair.

Romantik Hotel Georgenhof, Herrenhäuser Kirchweg 20, ✆ 702 244, fax 708 559 (DM215–265). Vine-draped, elegantly converted country house near the Herrenhausen gardens, family-run. Beats all other hotels in Hannover hands down when it comes to atmosphere—though the staff can be a little prickly. Excellent restaurant (*see* Stern's Restaurant below).

moderate

Hotel Körner, Körnerstr. 24–25, ✆ 16360, fax 18048 (DM160–210). Relaxed, modern hotel near the Herrenhausen park. You can laze about on the garden terrace, or swim against the current in the indoor pool.

CVJM-City-Hotel, Limburgstr. 3, ✆ 326 681, fax 363 2656 (DM172). Converted from the old YMCA building. Conveniently situated in the city centre, and perfectly clean and comfortable, despite its spartan origins.

Hotel Alpha Tirol, Lange Laube 20, ✆ 131 066, fax 341 535 (DM190–238). Small, modern hotel on the way out to Herrenhausen. Unexciting, but an adequate back-up if all else fails.

inexpensive

Hospiz am Bahnhof, Joachimstr. 2, ✆ 324 297 (DM92–106). Best bargain in the lower price range. Simple and centrally situated near the Hauptbahnhof.

Hotel Haus Tanneneck, Brehmstr. 80, ✆ 818 650, fax 283 4548 (DM90). In leafy suburbs 3km south-east off the centre (bus 21, 25 or 39 to Brehmstraße). Small but comfortable rooms.

Student Corps Saxonia, Wilhelm-Busch-Str. 13, © 702 605. The Student Corps club building sometimes lets out rooms. Quite fun, if you don't mind a gloomy Oxbridge atmosphere and earnest, conservative young men in funny caps. Prices vary, but are usually not that much more than youth hostel level.

Youth Hostel: Ferdinand-Wilhelm-Fricke-Weg 1, © 131 7674.

Eating and Drinking

Hannover's many trade fairs mean an abundance of restaurants, many with international menus—which is just as well for some visitors, as local *gutbürgerliche* cuisine is very much of the north-German meat-and-cabbage variety. The city is most known for its beer. The local Lindener Gilde brewery dates back to 1546 and its prize beer is *Broyhan-Alt*, a fine *Weißbier*. The local trick is to drink this as a **Lüttjen Lage**—holding a small glass of *Weißbier* between the thumb and forefinger and a glass of Schnapps curled in the middle finger. The knack is to drink the two simultaneously by pouring the Schnapps slowly onto the surface of the beer. This takes a steady hand and considerable skill. Frequent practice tends to be self-defeating.

Restaurants and Taverns

expensive

Stern's Restaurant, Herrenhäuser Kirchweg 20, © 702 244 (DM120–200). Shockingly pricey, but achingly delicious food. Imaginative variations on a more subtle Lower Saxon cuisine—such as roebuck simmered in cassis and dished up with wild mushrooms. In summer you can sit out on the softly lit garden terrace.

moderate

Brauhaus Ernst August, Schmiedstr. 13 (DM25–45). Huge new Hausbrauerei on the original site of the Leibniz Haus. They serve an unfiltered 'wholefood' beer, grills and good, hearty meals. There is live music most of the week. A sign forbids dancing on the tables, but you can jump about on the benches 'at your own risk'.

Altstadt, Knochenhauerstr. 42, © 328 732 (DM20–30). Best of the Altstadt taverns. Superb stews and tasty dishes such as venison cooked with peaches and forest berries and served with wild mushrooms and a cream sauce.

Friesenkeller, Künstlerhaus, Sophienstraße, © 322 700 (DM30–50). In the cellar of an attractive 19th-century yellow and red brick building (originally a museum, now an arts centre). Frisian specialities such as thick potato soup and salmon baked with spinach, cheese and mushrooms.

Altedeutsche Bierstube, Lärchenstr. 4, © 344 921 (DM30–40). Friendly, traditional tavern where you're most likely to see nifty Lüttjen Lage technique.

Entenfang, Eilersweg 1, ✆ 794 939 (DM20–35). Big leafy beer garden in Herrenhausen that serves up great hunks of pork and Grünkohl to blot up the beer.

Bars and Cafés

Tee Stübchen, Am Ballhof 10, ✆ 363 1682. Cosy wooden interior, a few tables out under the trees, a wide-ranging menu of teas and alcoholic drinks and excellent home-made cakes (the strawberry tart is heavenly).

Café Casa Nova, Am Markt 12, ✆ 321 797. Bearded men reading _El País_, smart businesswomen taking a quick lunch and arty boys showing off their haircuts. Salads and pastas as well as the usual _Kaffee und Kuchen_.

Markthalle, Karmarschstraße. Colourful indoor market that is mostly given over to Italian and Turkish fare, with stalls where you can stand and eat delicious salads and pastas. At Fleischerei Horst Nagel a bevy of pallid, unhelpful women (eventually) serve you heavy but tasty local food—dumplings, big joints of meat and mounds of sauerkraut, all for under DM10. Try _Oma's Eintopf_—mushy soup as granny made it.

Hameln (Hamelin)

Hameln (in German Hameln), 50km southwest of Hannover, still suffers from a plague of rats—chocolate ones, bread ones with straw whiskers, baskets of wooden ones on café counters, rats shaped into corkscrews or carved out as umbrella handles. But the city has far more to offer than Pied Piper bric-a-brac. It survived the Second World War relatively unscathed and has some of the finest examples of Weser Renaissance architecture to be found. Though the crush of tourists make you wish the motley flautist could return to thin out the streets a little, Hameln is certainly worth a day trip from Hannover, or a few hours stopover as you pass by.

See also Directory entries for Hann. Münden and Göttingen.

The Pied Piper—the True Story

In 1284, 130 people disappeared from Hamelin. No-one quite knows why. They might not even have been children (Old German often referred to citizens as 'children' of a city). Some say that they were young people who had danced themselves into a state of ecstacy and then wandered off into a bog; others believe that they were children who were lured away on a pilgrimage or crusade, or burghers who died of the plague. The most plausible explanation is that they were people taken off to colonize underpopulated areas such as Silesia and Pomerania to the east; the local Count of Schaumburg was known to have whisked people off to work on his plantation in Moravia, and there are villages in Transylvania that claim descent from the children of Hamelin. It is also certain that as a corn-trading and milling town alongside a river, Hameln would have had a serious rat problem. Just how these two facts

became wound up together in the Pied Piper legend is unclear. It was in the 16th century that the story first appeared of a stranger dressed in motley, who magicked away local children because he hadn't been paid for leading the town's rats into the River Weser (*see* p. 587). Later the Brothers Grimm published it as part of their collection of local folktales and today the tale has been translated into at least 30 languages. Visitors flock in and Hamelin profits very nicely indeed. At noon every Sunday from May to September someone dons pointy shoes and bright colours, scores of children dress up as rats, and the whole story is **re-enacted** in front of the Hochzeithaus.

Getting Around

By car: Hamelin is 47km south-west of Hannover on the B217. Most of the Altstadt is pedestrianized, but there is ample parking around the outskirts.

By train: The Hauptbahnhof is to the east of the town along Bahnhofstraße and Deisterallee. There are connections to Hannover (every 2 hours; ¾hr) and to Hildesheim (hourly; 50min).

Tourist Information

The **tourist information office**, © (05151) 202 617–9 *(May–Sept Mon–Fri 9–1 and 2–6, Sat 9.30–12.30 and 3–5, Sun 9.30–12.30; Oct–Apr Mon–Fri 9–1 and 2–5)* is in Deisterallee, on the edge of the Bürgergarten.

Osterstraße and the Markt

Entering Hamelin through what was the east gate (just past the tourist office on Deisterallee) you immediately step onto **Osterstraße**—the town's finest street, lined with the pick of its **Weser Renaissance architecture** (*see* p. 59). On the left is the **Rattenfängerhaus** (Ratcatcher's House), built for a city councillor in 1602; its only connection with ratcatching is a plaque on the wall relating the Pied Piper tale. The eccentric stonework, bumps and balls, spikes, scrolls and lavish carvings that adorn the façade are typical of the late Weser Renaissance style. Grotesque *Neidköpfe* ('jealous neighbours' heads', a type of domestic gargoyle) leer down at you. Inside there is now a restaurant (*see* below). Across the street is the **Garnisonkirche**, a solid Baroque building that served as church and social hall to the Hanoverian garrison in the 18th century. Since 1929 it has housed a bank.

Further up the street, on the right, is the **Leisthaus** (1585–89), built in delicate pink brick, the gables decorated in a lighter, earlier Weser Renaissance manner, and with an elegant two-storey bay window (another typical feature of the style). The statue of Lucretia in the gable above the window is a symbol of secular virtue, in contrast to the seven Christian Virtues on the frieze below (a common juxtaposition in German Renaissance architecture). The **Stiftsherrenhaus** (1556–8) next door is a solid, much less fancy half-timbered building, though the humanistic combination of biblical figures and classical deities carved on the consoles place it firmly in the Renaissance tradition. Behind the façades both houses are joined together to accommodate the **Museum Hameln** *(Tues–Fri 10–4.30, Sat and Sun 10–12.30, May–Sept also Sun 10–4.30; adm DM2)*. Here you'll find old books giving various versions of the Pied Piper story, statues of the Ratcatcher and a collection of ingenious mousetraps. In a more serious vein are a number of fine statues and a beautifully illustrated **missal** from the local Münster. At the end of the street is a festival hall, the **Hochzeitthaus** (Wedding House, 1610–17), a large, plain building, topped with typical Renaissance voluted gables. On the first floor on the Markt side is a **Glockenspiel** *(daily, 1.05pm, 3.35 and 5.35)*, predictably depicting the Pied Piper legend. A goose-stepping piper leads away the rats, then returns cloaked and hooded to dispatch the children. Alongside is the patchily rebuilt **Marktkirche** (one of the few Second World War casualties). Opposite is a pink-painted Renaissance confection, the **Dempterhaus**, built in 1607 for the local Burgomaster.

Bäckerstraße and the Münster

The other part of town worth exploring lies along Bäckerstraße (which leads south off the Markt) and the alleys that lead off it. Prettily painted half-timbered houses pop up along streets that lead down to the Weser, which thunders over a weir at this point. At Bäckerstraße 16 is the **Rattenkrug**, once a burgomaster's house, but for centuries an inn. Along Altemarktstraße (down the side of the Rattenkrug) is the imposing **Kurie Jerusalem** (*c.* 1500), a four-storey half-timbered building, originally a warehouse but now a play centre and music school. Just off the end of Bäckerstraße is the **Münster**, a rather heavy mixture of Romanesque and Gothic architecture, that is impressive to look at, but bare and disappointing inside.

Hameln ℰ (05151–)   ***Where to Stay***

Dorint Hotel Hameln, 164er Ring 3, ℰ 7920, fax 792 191 (DM150–350 without breakfast). Large, modern hotel overlooking the Bürgerpark. Comfortable rooms with vast plate-glass windows. Jazz sessions over breakfast.

Christenhof, Altemarktstr. 18, ℰ 95080, fax 43611 (DM155–175). Flawlessly converted 17th-century house. Understated furnishing, effervescent management, and there's even a sauna and swimming pool under the low stone arches of the cellar. No restaurant.

Hotel zur Post, Am Posthof 6, ℰ 7630, fax 7641 (DM129–149). New, central hotel. The rooms are small, but the service brisk and friendly.

Hotel Altstadtwiege, Neue Marktstr. 10, ℂ 27854, fax 27215 (DM85–120). Folksy hotel in an attractive part of the Altstadt.

Youth Hostel: Fischbecker Str. 33, ℂ 61157.

Eating and Drinking

Rattenfängerhaus, Osterstr. 28, ℂ 3888 (DM25–35). Atmospheric 17th-century house with a good kitchen. No rats on the menu, but you can get wild hare with forest mushrooms and a cream sauce.

Pfortmühle, Sudetenstr. 1, ℂ 29390 (DM20–30). Huge old mill on the banks of the Weser, with a riverside terrace. Tasty, basic food such as turkey steaks and roast pork.

Museums-Café, Osterstr. 8, ℂ 21553 (DM15–25). The café in the Stiftsherren-haus has a laid-back, alternative atmosphere, 14 varieties of tea, and good cheap food. The menu changes daily, but keep an eye open for the meaty home-made *Gulaschsuppe*.

Pfannekuchen, Hummenstr. 12, ℂ 41378 (DM10–20). Pot-bellied, half-timbered house in the heart of the Altstadt where you can get delicious sweet and savoury pancakes.

Hildesheim

The small town of Hildesheim, 30km south-east of Hannover, was all but flattened in the last days of the war, yet it can boast one of the most architecturally important churches in Germany, some beautiful half-timbered houses and two top-ranking museums. The painstakingly restored monuments are set in acres of bland post-war architecture, so Hildesheim is unlikely to detain you for more than a few hours, but the town does make a very worthwhile day trip from Hannover, or stopover on your way through to the Harz Mountains (*see* below).

Getting Around

By car: Hildesheim is 30km southeast of Hannover on the B6. You can also take Autobahn 7, which runs roughly parallel, but is less scenic.

Mitfahrzentrale: Annenstr. 15, ℂ (05121) 39051.

By train: The **Hauptbahnhof** is in the midst of the concrete sprawl in the north of the city (along Bernwardstraße, Almstraße and Hoher Weg). There are hourly connections to Hannover (35min) and Goslar (¾hr).

Tourist Information

The **tourist information office**, ℂ (05121) 15995, is a bit difficult to find—it is tucked away off a square behind the Rathaus at Am Ratsbauhof 1c (*Mon–Fri 9–6,*

Sat 9–1). Here you can buy a copy of the Hildesheimer Rosenroute (DM2), which sets you on a trail of white roses painted on the pavement, leading you to all the important sites.

The Markt

Hildesheim's Markt has a circus parade of different façades, from eccentric *fachwerk* to Rococo. An early Gothic **Rathaus** divides the square into two, thrusting up a cluster of pointed and stubby square gables. Next to it, on the south side of the square is the quirky **Tempelhaus**, a 15th-century building with turrets, fragile arches and mini-spires, perhaps the product of an earlier crusader's tale of buildings in the Holy Land. This is the only original building on the square which somehow survived the Allied bombs. Opposite, a luxury hotel lurks behind the façades of the **Stadtschänke**, a 17th-century inn, the appropriately named **Rokokohaus** and a voluminous 16th-century **Wollenwerbegildehaus** (Wool Weavers' Guildhall). Opposite the Rathaus is the **Knochenhaueramthaus** (Butchers' Guildhall), a massive half-timbered house resplendent with bright carvings of religious and humanistic figures. The tourist brochures, rather too confidently, call it 'the most beautiful half-timbered building in the world'. Upstairs is a mildly interesting **Stadtgeschichtliches Museum** (Museum of City History) *(Tues–Sun 10–6, Wed 10–9; DM3)*.

The Dom

You reach the heavily rebuilt cathedral down Rathausstraße, left along Hoheweg and right along Scuhstraße. Modern restoration has been aimed at reconstructing the church to the original Romanesque plan, which had been overwhelmed by Baroque embellishments. The Dom nestles quietly in its own close and contains **fittings** and **treasures** important enough for UNESCO to list the building as one of the world monuments to be protected at all costs.

The **bronze doors**, cast in a single piece in 1015, were originally made for St Michael's (*see* below), and were very probably the work of **Bishop Bernward** himself. Luckily, they survived the Allied bombs. Bernward ruled at Hildesheim from 993 to 1022, well-travelled, a skilled politician, erudite scholar, art-lover and (according to a contemporary biographer) an expert craftsman and brass-founder, he made Hildesheim a centre of art and learning. Most sculpture during the earlier Carolingian period had been small-scale work in ivory and bronze. In 1001 Bernward returned from a visit to his friend and erstwhile pupil, Emperor Otto III, in Rome, enthused by the scale of what he had seen there. He set up the bronze foundry which cast the doors—the first of their kind since ancient Rome, and precursors of the return of large-scale sculpture in the Romanesque period. The left hand door tells the story of Adam and Eve, the right-hand one the story of Christ. The tiny figures swell with emotional import. As God accuses the couple after their fall from grace, he jabs his finger at them with an energy that seems to surge up from his toes. The cowering humans deflect the blame—Adam backwards to Eve, Eve downwards to the serpent. It is a flat and simple scene, yet done with such skill that rage, accusation, guilt and fear hang there weightily.

Even more obviously inspired by Roman monuments is the towering bronze **triumphal column** (c. 1018) in the south transept, depicting scenes from the lives of Christ and John the Baptist. Just in front of the high altar hangs an enormous wheel-shaped **chandelier** (c. 1065), a representation of the heavenly Jerusalem, with towers and portals around its circumference. A heavy bronze **font** (1220) rests on kneeling personifications of four holy rivers and is encrusted with biblical figures.

In the quiet **cloister** *(Apr–Oct Mon–Sat 9.30–5, Sun 12–5; adm 50 pfennig)* you can see what is reputed to be a **1000-year-old rosebush**. According to the legend Louis the Pious, son of Charlemagne, hung some relics of the Virgin on the bush while he rested near 'Hildwins Heim' (Hildwin's homestead). When he got up to leave he couldn't get the relics off the rosetree and (as was the wont in those times) saw this as a divine instruction to stay put and build a church on the spot. Today the bush (if it is indeed the same one) is a scraggly creeper, but earned itself even greater kudos after the Second World War when, despite being almost razed to the ground, it suddenly burst into flower for the first time in years. In the middle of the cloister garden is the **St-Annen-Kapelle**, a greatly scaled-down version of a Gothic cathedral.

In the **Diözesanmuseum** *(Tues–Sat 10–5, Wed 10–7, Sun 12–5; DM4)* adjacent to the museum is a glittering collection of treasures, including two crucifixes and a pair of graceful candlesticks attributed to St Bernward, a stunning Ottonian **Golden Madonna**, carved in wood and layered with gold leaf, and numerous jewels and showpieces from the 12th century.

The Roemer-Pelizaeus Museum

Through an archway on the north side of the close, you come to a rather unpreposessing building which houses the Roemer-Pelizaeus Museum *(Tues–Sun 10–4.30; adm DM3)*, home to one of the best collections of **Egyptian antiquities** in the country. The written commentary is in German, but for DM3 you can hire an English **cassette tape** which explains the major exhibits. Highlights include the limestone funerary monument of Hemiuni (dating from 2530 BC), a walk-in 5th Dynasty cultroom of a minor official, rare wooden statues, an exquisite head of King Chephren and statues of more podgy-faced workers, some retaining their original colouring. Temporary exhibitions show off exceptional pieces from the vast collection of Egyptian jewellery and funerary models. The **Peruvian collection** in the museum's other wing is not quite as mind-blowing, but does include some impressive carving and fabrics.

St Michael

A walk north up Burgstraße brings you to Hildesheim's most important monument (also protected by UNESCO), the monastery church of St Michael, built 1001–31. The dumpy building with six solid towers occupies its own mound above the city in a brave attempt to reflect the heavenly Jerusalem. This was Bishop Bernward's pride and joy, and is perhaps Europe's prime piece of Ottonian architecture. Typically, the walls are blank and massive and the nave merely a hall that connects the two main points of focus of the church—the east and west units. The arches in the nave—rhythmically alternating thick supports with two decorative pillars, and painted in red and white stripes—were to become a standard feature of later Romanesque architecture. Later, after Bishop Bernward had been canonized in 1192, more elaborate additions were made to the church, which houses his relics. These include a finely carved **choir screen** (called the *Engelchorschranke* after the angels that decorate one side) and a magnificent painted **Romanesque wooden ceiling**—one of only two to have survived. Nearly 75 per cent of its 1300 oak panels depicting biblical scenes are original. The ceiling was removed during the Second World War, survived the bombing and is now back in place with unbelievably bright, newly restored colours.

The Southern Altstadt

If you follow Brühl or Hinterer Brühl south, you'll find some of the lanes—lined with pretty half-timbered houses and still mainly residential—that survived the war. Hinterer Brühl, Gelber Stern and Keßler Straße are the most attractive, and largely off the tourist track. At the end of Brühl is **St Godehard**, a Benedictine monastery built soon after St Michael, and already showing the influence that church had on later ecclesiastical architecture.

Hildesheim ☎ (05121–)   ***Where to Stay***

expensive

Hotel Forte Crest Hildesheim, Markt 4, ☎ 3000, fax 300 444 (DM275–395). Sumptuous conversion of three historic buildings into a world of panelled, padded luxury, including saunas, a gym and indoor pool.

Hotel Bürgermeisterkapelle, Rathausstr. 8, ☎ 14021, fax 38813 (DM140–170). Modern hotel behind the Rathaus which justifiably prides itself on its friendly service.

Hotel Zum Hagentor, Kardinal-Bertram-Str. 15, ☎ 35566, fax 14823 (DM110–130). Simple, central guesthouse run by helpful young couple. Modestly furnished, but comfortable rooms.

inexpensive

Kurth, Küsthardtstr. 4, ☎ 32817 (DM80–110). Cheap and cheerful option not too far from the sites.

Youth Hostel, Schirrmannweg 4, ☎ 42717.

Eating and Drinking

Ratskeller, Markt 1 (DM30–50). Better than usual Ratskeller with good selection of fish dishes as well as the expected steaks and schnitzels.

Kehr Wieder Stübchen, Keßlerstr. 75 (DM25–30). Cosy neighbourhood atmosphere in an old building on one of the prettiest streets in town. Schnitzels, steaks and salads.

Café Hindenberg, Hindenbergplatz (DM15–25). Popular, good-value eaterie with a wide-ranging daily menu of fish, meat and salads, and breakfast till late.

Café Brasil, Friesenstr. 15. Hildesheim's trendiest spot, in the southern part of the Altstadt.

Café Beste am Markt, Osterstr. 11, © 38929. A clutter of antiques, a dinky garden, good coffee and pancakes with such exotic fillings as gorgonzola and kirsch.

Braunschweig (Brunswick)

Henry the Lion (1129–95), founder of Munich (*see* p. 340), had initially patched up the feud between his family, the Welfs (Guelphs), and the ruling Hohenstaufens by befriending the Emperor Frederick Barbarossa. He regained the Duchies of Saxony and Bavaria that had been lost by his father. Later, though, he began to get a little too big for his boots, refusing to help pay for Frederick's campaigns and demanding control over the Free Imperial City of Goslar and its silver mines. Frederick stripped him of his titles once more, and sent him north to his homeland.

Holed up in Brunswick (German: Braunschweig) Henry set about building a city to rival anything that Frederick could boast. Brunswick became a powerful trading centre with connections that extended to Russia and England, and for centuries poured its money into art and grand buildings. Unfortunately, as Brunswick was—as it still is—in Lower Saxony's industrial heartland, it was catastrophically bombed in the Second World War. The buildings that went up after the war range from the unimaginative to the perfectly horrible, but enough of the impressive old monuments remain, or have been reconstructed, to warrant a few hours of your time. Brunswick also has the best **art collection** in the region.

Getting Around

By car: Brunswick is 50km east of Hannover on the A2 and 44 km north-east of Hildesheim on the B1.

Mitfahrzentrale: Bohlweg 42–3, © (0531) 14041.

By train: The Hauptbahnhof is to the southeast of the centre in one of the most dismal parts of town. Tram 1 or 5 will take you quickly to cheerier surrounds. There are rail connections to Hannover (at least hourly; 35min), Goslar (1¼hr) and Kassel (1¼hr).

Tourist Information

There are two **tourist information offices**, one at the Hauptbahnhof, © (0531) 79237 *(Mon–Fri 8–6, Sat 9–12)* and one in a pavilion on Bohlweg, near the Schloßgarten, © (0531) 46419 *(Mon–Fri 8.30–6, Sat 9–12)*.

The Burgplatz

Brunswick's most august buildings are grouped around the central square, the Burgplatz. In the middle of the square is the **Burglöwe**, an elegant if somewhat effete bronze statue of a lion (1166)—Henry's symbol, and the first free-standing monumental sculpture to be made since Roman times. The *Burglöwe*, which originally was gilded, looks across to **Burg Dankwarderode** *(Tues–Sun 10–5; adm free)*, a good 19th-century reconstruction of Henry's palace. Inside is a museum where, among medieval religious art, you'll find the original *Burglöwe* (the one in the square is the third replacement). Upstairs is a magnificently restored **Romanesque festival hall** complete with bright wall-paintings and gilded chandeliers.

Opposite Burg Dankwarderode is a sturdy Neoclassical building which now houses a well laid out **Landesmuseum** *(Tues–Sun 10–5, Thurs 10–8; adm free)*, featuring original statues from the cathedral, the second *Burglöwe*, local products and memorabilia, and a pictorial history of 20th-century Brunswick (including records of the few months in 1918–19 when the city was declared the capital of a socialist republic).

Across the south side of the square is a formidable Romanesque **cathedral** *(daily 10–1 and 3–5)*, begun in Henry's time. The hefty outward appearance—intended as a symbol of Welf power—and the later addition of a lighter Gothic bell-gable between the towers, was copied in other churches around the city. Inside you can see well-preserved Romanesque **frescoes** dating from 1220; an enormous seven-stemmed **candelabrum**, 4.8m high and 4m wide (12th century; the elongated, superbly carved wooden **Immervard crucifix** (1150); and the **tomb of Henry the Lion** and his English wife Mathilda, daughter of Henry II of England.

Elsewhere in the Altstadt

Another visitable bit of the Altstadt is the **Altstadtmarkt**, west of the Burgplatz (along Schuhstraße and Poststraße). Here you'll find a delicate Gothic **Rathaus** with open upper arcades and fashionably dressed statues of Welf rulers, highlighted with licks of gilding. In the middle of the square is a playful 15th-century fountain, the **Marienbrunnen**, while opposite stands the four-square **Gewandhaus** (linen hall) with its Dutch-influenced gable. **St Martini** *(Tues–Fri 10.30–12.30, Sat 9–12)*, modelled on the cathedral, is at the end of the square. Inside are 14th-century statues of the Wise and Foolish Virgins and a monumental canopied pulpit.

To the south of the Burgplatz down Bohlweg is the Gothic **St Aegidien** with an impressive carved pulpit by local sculptor Hans Witten, a contemporary—and some say equal—of the famous Tilmann Riemenschneider. In the adjacent monastery buildings is a small

Jüdisches Museum (Jewish Museum) *(Tues–Sun 10–5; adm free)* where the main attraction is a reassembled wooden Baroque synagogue that lay derelict for years, until it was dismantled and moved here in the 1920s.

North of the Burgplatz, also along Bohlweg, you'll find a crescent of parish churches— **St Katharinen**, **St Andreas** and **St Petri**—all modelled on the cathedral. Near St Petri, on Bäckerklimt, is the bronze **Eulenspiegelbrunnen** celebrating the semi-historical prankster **Till Eulenspiegel**. As an apprentice baker in Brunswick he moulded his dough into owl and monkey shapes (hence the creatures adorning the fountain), and later became legendary as an anarchic wit—punning, playing practical jokes and continuously cocking a snoot at authority. Anecdotes about him abound, the first book of Eulenspiegel stories came out in the 16th century and he has become an essential part of German folk culture; the German word for tomfoolery is *Eulenspiegelei*. He is most familiar to non-Germans as the subject of a symphonic poem by Richard Strauss, and an epic by the Nobel Prize-winning writer Gerhart Hauptmann. Since 1950 a 'Circle of Friends of Till Eulenspiegel' has made an annual award for wit; the first recipient was the post-war chancellor, Konrad Adenauer.

The Herzog-Anton-Ulrich-Museum

East of the Burgplatz, across the Schloßgarten, is the Herzog-Anton-Ulrich-Museum *(Tues–Sun 10–5, Thurs 10–8; adm free)*, an excellent regional museum named after the 17th-century duke whose collection forms its core. The museum was opened to the public in 1754, making it the first in Germany. The selection of **Dutch and Flemish painting** is by far the best in the region, with superb works by **Rembrandt**, including one of his last and most adventurous works, the *Family Group*, and a luminous *Christ Appearing to Mary Magdalene*. There's a rare work by **Vermeer**, a characteristically raucous *Marriage of Tobias and Sara* by Jan Steen, and fine works by **Rubens** and **Van Dyck**. The collection of **German Masters** has a good array of Cranach, and in the smaller **Italian** section you'll find notable paintings by Tintoretto, Giorgione and Palma il Vecchio.

Upstairs, in the **applied arts** department are extensive collections of porcelain from all over the world (especially Italy), Baroque bronze statues and antique furniture. Look out for the early 17th-century **ball-bearing clock**. A metal ball running down the layers of a pagoda-like Tower of Babylon gathers enough momentum to work the clock and set off a mechanism which transports another ball up to the top. On the hour a turbaned Turk beats his miniature tympanum.

Braunschweig ✆ (0531–)   ***Where to Stay***

Mövenpick-Hotel, Welfenhof, ✆ 48170 (DM190–250). Central, slick member of a chain of hotels noted for uniform high quality.

Frühlingshotel, Bankplatz 7, ✆ 49317 (DM136). Grand old 19th-century building. Decor hovers on the edge of high kitsch, and sometimes falls splendidly over. Service earnest.

Gästehaus am Kohlmarkt, Kohlmarkt 2, ✆ 242 010 (from DM90). Short story material. Up a wooden stairway, in an ornate turn-of-the-century building, Frau Asmer welcomes you with icy courtesy to her well-scrubbed rooms. No restaurant.

Pension Wienecke, Kuhstr. 14, ✆ 48170 (DM70–100). Convenient, down-to-earth, clean and quiet. No restaurant.

Youth Hostel, Salzdalumer Str. 170, ✆ 62268.

Eating and Drinking

Braunschweiger Hof, Ziegenmarkt 1 (DM20–30). Atmospheric restaurant set around a courtyard with an ancient well. Simple tasty food: spaghetti bolognese and veal with cream of mushroom sauce.

Mutter Habernicht, Papenstieg 5 (DM20–35). Dim, poky tavern that has survived since 1870 on a menu of *Gulasch* and cabbage, Kassler ribs and *Sauerkraut*.

Restaurant Friedrich, Am Magnitor 5 (DM25–35). Restaurant with garden in old half-timbered building in one of the few areas of town to escape war damage. Snacks and traditional meals such as potatoes with lumps of bacon.

Gewandhauskeller, Altstadtmarkt 1, ✆ 44441 (DM35–55). Cosy restaurant in the historic guildhall. Local specialities include *Mumme,* a rich sauce made from malt beer.

To the north of Brunswick are **Wolfsburg**, original home of the Volkswagen Beetle, and **Celle**, a must for fans of *fachwerk* architecture (*see* Directory). To the south are the hills and pristine villages of the Harz.

The Harz

The Harz Mountains stretch from Goslar in the west towards Halle in the east. Nowhere very dramatic, the mountains are highest in the western and central parts of the region, where they are stubby and forested, with sudden steep inclines. The highest peak, the Brocken (1142m), is supposedly the gathering place for witches on *Walpurgisnacht*, the 'Witches Sabbath', 30 April). Mostly the area is rolling grassland criss-crossed by streams, with knots of forest and pockets of small hills. It is ideal walking country, and though it snows in winter, the skiing is very much for beginners; younger Germans rather disdainfully refer to the Harz as *Rentnergebirge*, 'pensioners' mountains'.

The region was sliced in two by the old DDR border. Now that Germany is reunited, the *Wessies* are rediscovering the delights of narrow-gauge steam trains, and quiet, traditional villages unscathed by tourism—attractions that had disappeared from the over-commercialized western areas.

Goslar and **Quedlinburg** are good bases if you want to explore the region, but there are plenty of attractive towns along the way.

See Directory entries for Magdeburg, Halberstadt, Thale, Wernigerode.

By Car

You can best reach the Harz via Hannover and Brunswick along the A395, or alternatively along the A9 from Berlin, and then the B80. The new B6 (west–east) and the B81 (north–south) are the best main roads through the region, though the latter has a few sudden 14 per cent gradients. Until recently most roads stopped dead at the border, which means that for most west–east journeys you have to rely on smaller country roads.

By Train

Rail lines are similarly truncated, with lines from the west converging on Bad Harzburg, and Halberstadt being the most convenient location for connections eastward to Leipzig and Berlin.

One of the greatest attractions of the Harz is the old **narrow-gauge steam railway system**. The **Selketalbahn** runs for 35km between Gernrode, near Quedlinburg, and Stiege, with a connection onwards to Elsfelder Talmühle, where you can transfer to the Harzquerbahn. At 6.30pm every day you can see three steam trains waiting here for each other here, before they head off in different directions, a sight now unique. There are seven trains a day on the Selketalbahn, though not all go the whole way. The full journey takes 2 hours, and along the route you puff up steep hills, trundle through lonely woods and past secluded lakes. One of the locomotives, a *Mallet*, has been making the trip since 1897, and is the oldest functioning train in Germany (though the Selketalbahn is a normal railway service and sometimes you end up with a diesel locomotive and linked up to freight carriages).

The **Harzquerbahn** follows an even more impressive route, between Wernigerode and Nordhausen (in Thuringia). At one point you are heaved up a 1 in 30 gradient to Drei Annen Hohne, from where you can take the **Brockenbahn** to the summit of the mountain (¾hr). The Harzquerbahn offers roughly one train hourly between 6am and 5pm. The full journey time is 3 hours, but there are numerous possible stops along the way. As with a normal rail service, ticket prices vary according to your destination.

Tourist Information

General information on the region, as well as maps and details of marked walking trails, can be obtained from the **Harzer Verkehrsverband**, Marktstr. 45, Goslar, © (05321) 20031.

Goslar, 50km south of Brunswick on the edge of the Harz range, was once the 'treasure chest of the Holy Roman Empire', filling its coffers—and the pockets of many an emperor—with the proceeds of nearby silver, and later lead and zinc mines. It had the coveted status of a Free Imperial City, and was a favourite imperial seat. Silver mining is a relatively clean business, and Goslar, nestling in forests up against the mountains, is far from a grubby industrial town. Instead, you'll find street after street of pristine half-timbered houses, over 1500 in all; the entire town has been declared a monument. Even the public lavatories waft odours of potpourri into the air. To some tastes it is all a bit too twee, yet Goslar is not a museum town like Rothenburg in Bavaria. People live in the centre, rock music rattles the medieval windows and there are plenty of empty streets to get lost in—though the disproportionate number of junkies and alcoholics huddling in some corners of town would suggest that all is not as well as it seems.

Getting Around

By car: Goslar is just off the A395, about 50km from Brunswick. There is also a link to the A7, which takes you up to Hannover 70km away. Much of the centre is pedestrianized, but distances are manageable, so it is best to park on the outskirts of town and explore on foot.

By train: The **Bahnhof** is 15 minutes' walk north of the Markt (along Rosentor-straße). There are hourly connections to Hannover (1½hr), Hildesheim (1hr) and Brunswick (1hr).

Tourist Information

The **tourist information office** is at Marktplatz 7, © (05321) 2846 *(May–Oct, Mon–Fri 9–6, Sat 9–2; Nov–Apr Mon–Fri 9–1 and 2–5, Sat 9–2).*

Market Days: Tuesdays and Fridays, 7–1.

The Marktplatz

Goslar's Marktplatz has a subtle palette. Houses with grey slate roofs and walls set off the occasional patch of terracotta, cream or yellow ochre. On market mornings the square fills with bright canopies and barrows of local produce and fish, but the best view is to be had when everyone has packed up and gone home. Then you can clearly see the golden **Reichsadler** (Imperial Eagle), looking more like a bedraggled rooster, on his perch in the middle of the square. The carving is a copy (the 13th-century original is in the Rathaus).

On the western side of the square is the arcaded **Rathaus**, known for its **Huldigungssaal** *(guided tours only, Apr–Oct 10–5, Nov–Mar 10–4; adm DM3)*, a splendid medieval council chamber covered from floor to ceiling with 16th-century frescoes. In niches in the walls you can see city treasures such as the **Bergkanne** (1477), a gold and silver beer mug lavishly decorated with hunting scenes, and a facsimile of the **Goslar Evangelier** (1230), a gospel illustrated with intense Byzantine-influenced miniatures.

Across from the Rathaus is a **Glockenspiel** *(9am, 12, 3 and 6)* showing the history of Goslar. First you see the horse that pawed the ground and uncovered silver deposits, then Otto I to symbolize the sudden imperial interest in the city, and finally a succession of miners from various periods. (It would be more appropriate to end with a procession of tourists, as the last mine closed in 1988, and today it is visitors who keep Goslar's purses fat.) All the while the bells strike out merry German folk tunes, which coachloads of smiling biddies in the square below sing along to.

The **Hotel Kaiserworth**, on the southern side of the square, built in the 15th century as a guildhall for the cloth cutters was later embellished across the front by the addition of a row of German emperors. On one corner is a carving of a naked man who, tongue out with pleasure, excretes a gold coin—an odd variant on the goose that laid the golden egg, perhaps a symbol of Goslar's right to mint coins. Behind the Rathaus is the **Marktkirche** which contains a bronze **font** (1573) densely populated by Biblical figures. Just to the north of the church is the **Schuhhof**, an attractive shopping square edged with large 17th-century half-timbered houses.

South of the Marktplatz

Following Hoher Weg south from the Marktplatz, you come almost immediately to the 16th-century **Brusttuch**, a house covered in carvings on a favourite Renaissance theme, that of the the the unbridled sexuality of the *Wilde Mann* (Natural Man). Naked figures pop out of the woodwork, ladies cavort about on goats and a milkmaid manages simultaneously to churn butter and squeeze her buttocks. Further down the street is the more sombre **Grosses-Heiliges-Kreuz**, a barn-like half-timbered hospice built in 1254. The patients' cells have been converted into tiny crafts shops.

East of here, down Klapperhagen and Abzuchtstraße, a stream bounces through one of the quainter areas of town, occasionally passing an old mill. At the beginning of Abzuchtstraße is the **Goslarer Museum** *(daily Apr–Oct 10–5, Nov–Mar 10–4; adm DM3.50)*, a history museum that is saved from complete tediousness by some impressive treasures from the cathedral.

West of the Grosses-Heiliges-Kreuz (down Worthsatenwinkel, Bergstraße and Peterstraße) you'll find more richly carved half-timbered houses. At the end of Peterstraße is the peaceful Romanesque **Frankenberger Kirche**, once a favourite with local miners for their weddings. The Baroque **pulpit** inside is covered with busy cherubs carrying ropes, ladders, picks and hammers. There is also a bizarre **Triumphal Cross** on which the figure of Christ wears a wig made of the artist's hair, a custom in the Harz area.

At the end of Hoher Weg is the **Dom Vorhalle** (entrance hall), a top-heavy structure that is all that remains of the 11th-century cathedral. On the hill above is the **Kaiserpfalz** *(daily Apr–Oct 10–5, Nov–Mar 10–4; adm DM3.50)*. Although billed as the largest surviving Romanesque palace in Europe, it is mostly a 19th-century reconstruction; as Goslar fell from favour as an imperial residence during the 14th century, the original building fell into disrepair. Inside you can see the **Reichsaal** (Imperial Hall), propped up by heavy wooden pillars and covered in even heavier 19th-century Romantic murals. The **Ulrichskapelle** is more authentic, with a cross-shaped ground-plan that resolves itself into a Byzantine dome. Beyond the Kaiserpfalz you can follow the **city ramparts** east around to the **Zwinger** *(daily 9–5)*, a sturdy 16th-century defence tower where today you'll find a Turkish restaurant and a small display of medieval weapons.

North of the Marktplatz

From the Schuhhof, Münzstraße, one of Goslar's most attractive streets, leads up to the **Jakobikirche** where you can see a touchingly realistic **Pietà** by the Brunswick Gothic sculptor Hans Witten. An aged, heavy-eyed Mary cradles a body of Christ twisted with rigor mortis. There is more top-quality art to be found just along Jakobistraße in the **Mönchehaus-Museum** *(Tues–Sat 10–1 and 3–5, Sun 10–1; adm DM3)*. For some years Goslar has offered a prestigious international art prize, and the result is an exceptionally well-stocked museum for a small provincial town, with works by the likes of Max Ernst, Joseph Beuys, Georg Baselitz, Gerhard Richter and Anselm Kiefer.

North of the Jakobikirche, near the Bahnhof, is the **Neuwerkirche** which dates back to the 12th and 13th centuries. There is some fine Romanesque carving on the apse, while on the pillars in the nave you can see some curiously carved handles, symbols of the soul's flight from wickedness up to heaven.

Goslar ✆ (05321–)   ***Where to Stay***

Hotel Kaiserworth, Markt 3, ✆ 21111, fax 21114 (from DM160). Goslar's most prominent address. Converted from a 15th-century guildhall, with atmospheric vaulted restaurant and bar, but unimaginatively furnished rooms.

Das Brusttuch, Hoher Weg 1, ✆ 21081, fax 18297 (DM175–240). Small, friendly hotel in historic old house. The rooms are far from spacious, but comfortable—and there is a swimming pool under the roof. Good restaurant (*see* below).

Zur Börse, Bergstr. 53, ✆ 22775 (DM130). Friendly, privately run hotel in beautiful 18th-century half-timbered house. Good, traditional restaurant downstairs.

Gästehaus Noack, Rosenburg 26, ✆ 22585 (from DM85). Peaceful, clean well-run guesthouse just south of the Altstadt.

Youth Hostel, Rammelsberger Str. 25, ✆ 22240.

Eating and Drinking

Café Museum, Hoher Weg 5. Pleasant café with tea garden, near the Markt.

Café Die Butterhahne, Marktplatz (DM20–50). Good value despite its deeply touristy appearance and location. Scrumptious cakes and tasty, solid meals.

Das Brusttuch, Hoher Weg 1, ✆ 21081 (DM20–50). Busy tavern in 16th-century house. Wooden partitions, traditional murals and the odd chandelier dangling from the distant ceiling. Tasty food too—try the ragout with forest mushrooms and dumplings, or something from the seasonal menu.

Weisser Schwan, Münzstr. 11, © 25737 (DM25–25). 17th-century coaching inn, now serves Yugoslavian food, mainly grills. In summer there is a romantic beer garden in the old courtyard.

Brauhaus Goslar, Marstallstr. 1 (DM20–35). Big, noisy *Hausbrauerei* which opens onto a courtyard lined with bars. Meaty fare and its own unfiltered Pils.

Quedlinburg

Quedlinburg is the hottest *Geheimtip* (insider tip) since the *Wende*. For decades it has nestled in the north-eastern reaches of the Harz, on the whole carefully looked after by the DDR government but entirely unravaged by tourism. Over 1600 of Quedlinburg's buildings are listed as historical monuments, and UNESCO has declared the entire town a World Heritage Site. Street after street of bright, decorative half-timbered houses—spanning five centuries—stretch out below an old mountain Schloß. The town still has its medieval layout, with a canal from the River Bode dividing the merchants' quarter (the Altstadt) from what were once the smallholders' plots in the Neustadt.

Quedlinburg is beginning to wake up to its tourist potential, and word is spreading fast, but for the moment at least, even in high season, it is simply a stunningly beautiful residential town. There are no souvenir stalls, outcrops of ice-cream kiosks or coach loads of daytrippers. Instead local children play in the streets, family arguments echo from upstairs rooms and cooking smells fill the alleys. After a visit you'll be torn between wanting to tell everyone you see about it, and keeping very quiet indeed in the desperate hope that Quedlinburg will stay as it is.

Getting Around

By car: One of the secrets of Quedlinburg's timelessness has been its inaccessibility, but a new regional road, the B6, is rapidly being ploughed through the countryside connecting Quedlinburg to Wernigerode (about 30km away) and then to the A395 near Goslar (60km). Cars are discouraged in the Altstadt, but there is plenty of parking space around the outskirts. There are **24-hour petrol stations** on Harzweg and Gernröder Weg.

By train: The Bahnhof is just east of the city centre (along Bahnhofstraße). There is about one train an hour to Halberstadt (25min) from where you can get trains to Magdeburg (1hr) and back onto the main network.

Tourist Information

The **tourist information office**, ©/fax (03946) 2866, is on the Markt, next door to the Rathaus *(Apr–Oct Mon–Fri 9–5, Sat and Sun 10–4; Nov–Mar Mon–Fri 9–5)*.

Around the Markt

At the northern end of the long, triangular Markt stands a grey, rather plain **Rathaus** with a fancy Renaissance portal. To the right of the doorway is a **statue of Roland** (see **Bremen** p. 540) which the burghers put up as a symbol of defiance against church authority when Quedlinburg was a member of the Hanseatic League. A mere flat-faced stripling, this Roland was soon despatched when local abbesses regained the upper hand, and today stands meekly up against the Rathaus wall. Next to the Rathaus is a quaint, free-standing Hansel-and-Gretel-like half-timbered inn dating from the 16th century. Ranged around the Markt are more half-timbered guildhalls, a Baroque palace (now a music school) and a Neoclassical hotel, *Zum Bär*, which is undergoing indefinite 'renovations' while it shakes off the mantle of being a favourite *Stasi* holiday destination.

The **Marktkirche St Benedikti**, a so-called 'transitional' church (between Romanesque and early Gothic), is in a quiet close of 15th–17th-century houses behind the Rathaus. Quedlinburg's churches didn't fare quite so well under the DDR, and many are closed for a lengthy process of much-needed restoration. At St Benedikti it is already possible to visit the Baroque burial chamber of the Gebhardt family, which has a separate entrance at the side of the church.

Some of Quedlinburg's most evocative streets lie just off the Markt. Follow the narrow alley (no wider than a doorway) marked *Burgerhäuser* on the eastern side of the square, just past the tourist office. This will lead you to a tiny garden court of half-timbered houses, the Schuhhof, and on to the equally pretty residential lanes of Höle and Stieg. Half-timbered houses line both sides of the cobbled streets. Protruding upper stories loom over your head, and many of the houses are richly carved with the palmettoes, flowers and sunsigns that are characteristic of the Harz. Just east of here, across a trickling canal, is the **Neustadt**. Here the streets—with mainly 18th- and 19th-century buildings—are not as atmospheric as in the older part of town, but the Gothic parish church of **St Nikolai** *(Tues–Sat 10–1 and 1–3.30)* is worth a visit, mainly for its setting—a cosy oval close of half-timbered houses.

Off the northern end of the Markt a more important thoroughfare, Breite Straße (Broad Street), is the address of some of the town's grander Gothic and Renaissance buildings (Nos. 33 and 39 are especially worth a look).

South of the Markt

On Wordgasse, off the southern tip of the Markt, you'll find Quedlinburg's oldest building, an early 14th-century half-timbered house. It is the earliest surviving timber-frame house in Germany and one of the few remaining examples of a structure built using the simple, square-framed *Ständerbau* technique. Today it houses an interesting **Fachwerkmuseum** *(May–Sept daily except Thurs 10–5; adm DM2.50)* with displays on the development of *fachwerk* architecture. Almost next-door is the **St Blasiikirche**, a Baroque church tacked onto a fortress-like Romanesque tower. It has lain derelict for years and restoration is likely to take quite some time.

A walk down Blasiistraße and along Hoheweg will bring you to the foot of the **Schloßberg**, the hill topped by Quedlinberg's main church and castle. At Schloßberg 12, on the street below the hill, you'll find the **Klopstockhaus** *(Tues–Sun May–Sept 10–6, Oct–Apr 9–4; adm DM2.50)*, birthplace of the poet Friedrich Gottlieb Klopstock (1724–1803), whose epic *The Messiah* formed the basis of Handel's oratorio and whose verses also inspired Mahler's *Resurrection Symphony*. The house contains a museum of memorabilia really only of interest to fans. There are also momentoes of two other local personalities for good measure—**Dorothea Christiana Erxleben**, who in 1754 became the first German woman doctor, and **Johann Christoph GuthsMuths**, founding father of school PT. Just behind the Klopstockhaus is a museum *(same times and prices)* devoted to the life of **Lionel Feininger**, a German-American Cubist who was closely associated with Bauhaus *(see* **The Arts and Culture** p. 64). The gallery contains a good selection of his graphics and also a few oils.

The Schloß

The castle atop the hill was begun in AD 919, the same year that the local bird-loving Duke of Saxony, Heinrich der Vogler (Henry the Fowler), was elected King of Germany. For the next two decades Quedlinburg was an important centre of German political life. When Heinrich died in 936 his widow, Mathilde, founded a collegiate church for the daughters of the German nobility. The local abbesses were answerable only to the Holy Roman Emperor, and on religious matters directly to the Pope. They ruled over Quedlinburg and the surrounding countryside for the next 900 years. In the 15th century they successfully quashed the burghers' attempts at independence when the burghers joined the Hanseatic League (thus ensuring that Quedlinburg stayed small and unimportant), and succumbing in the end only to Napoleon.

You enter the complex through a medieval **gateway**. On the left the half-timbered houses of various court officials have now been converted into a restaurant and café. The **Schloßgarten** which stretches out in front (on top of the original heavy fortifications) gives you a splendid view out over the town. The other main secular buildings date back mainly to the Renaissance. The L-shaped **Wohntrakt** (dormitories) are at the time of writing undergoing renovation, but the Abbesses **Residenzbau**, with its elegant light reception hall is now the **Schloßmuseum** *(Tues–Sun May–Sept 10–6, Oct–Apr 9–4; adm DM2.50)*. The collection itself (of fossils, torture instruments, *Tracht* and furniture) is not especially interesting, but a visit does enable you to see the simple but elegant **interior** of the Residenz.

Opposite is the **Stiftskirche St Servatius** *(guided tours only, usually half-hourly 11–5, but check the board outside; adm DM2)*. Apart from a few Gothic touches, and the heavy handed 19th-century towers, the church is one of the finest examples of Romanesque architecture in the region. The columns in the nave, with splendidly carved capitals, mirror the pattern first developed at St Michael in Hildesheim *(see* p. 590). In the crypt are the tombs of Heinrich and Mathilde and in the northern transept is a rich treasury (many of the items only recently returned from Texas, where they had been taken in 1945 by an

American lieutenant). Look out especially for the jewel-encrusted cover of the **Adelheidevangelier** (a 12th-century Gospel), a similarly old and ornate casket containing the relics of St Servatius, and (if you're lucky and it is on display) a tapestry that dates back to 1200.

Where to Stay

moderate

Hotel am Brühl, Billungstr. 11, ✆ 395 152, fax 3952 (DM160). Spacious 1920s building just south of the Altstadt, for some years a distillery. Reclaimed by the Schmidt family after the *Wende* and run with pride and flair as an hotel. Individually decorated rooms and a first-rate breakfast. No restaurant.

Hotel zur Goldene Sonne, Steinweg 11, ✆ 2318 (DM140–160). Large half-timbered residence hall, built in 1671 and converted into a comfortable hotel. Very friendly and helpful staff.

Pension Theophano, Markt13–14, ✆/fax 2521 (DM140–180). Right on the Markt. Converted out of a 16th-century guildhall. Efficient service. No restaurant.

Hotel zum Schloß, Mühlenstr. 22, ✆ 3333 (DM140). Small, cosy half-timbered hotel in the shadow of the the the Schloß.

inexpensive

For cheaper options by far the best bet is to seek out a private room. Frau Klindt (Hohe Str. 19, no telephone) has a beautiful old timbered house in the Altstadt, and her neighbours also let out rooms. Otherwise the tourist office can help.

Eating and Drinking

Café am Finkenherd, Scloßberg 15, ✆ 3841. Good stop-off for *Kaffee und Kuchen* before the final climb up to the Schloß.

Schloßkrug, Schloßberg 1, ✆ 2838 (DM15–30). Historic castle outhouses converted into restaurant with a shady terrace. Food is simple (roast pork, chicken, chips and salad) but well-prepared and served in generous portions.

Zur Goldene Sonne, Steinweg 11, ✆ 2318 (DM25–45). Good restaurant in the 17th-century hotel. Various German dishes such as game stews and *Schweinhaxe* (leg of pork).

Quedlinburger Brauhaus, Blasiistraße, ✆ 3251 (DM20–30). Gleaming copper vats, tasty house brew and good, hearty meat-cabbage-and-potatoes cuisine.

Zum Schloß, Mühlenstr. 22, ✆ 3333 (DM30–60). Hotel restaurant popular with locals. Juicy venison steaks and other fresh fare.

Altenahr

Pretty, but very touristy, town in the magnificent Ahr valley, west of the Rhine near Andernach. Ascend beyond the half-timbered souvenir shops to **Burg Ahr**—the ruined 12th-century castle high above the town—for a sweeping view of the valley.
Tourist office: Bahnhof, ℗ (02643) 8848.

Annaberg

30km south of Chemnitz. Transport hub of the Erzgebirge and scene of the region's biggest festival, the *Rät*, which begins on the Saturday after Trinity Sunday (May/June).

Annweiler

Small village about 45km west of Speyer. Departure point for buses to **Burg Trifels** *(Apr–Sept daily 9–1 and 2–6; Oct, Nov and Jan–Mar Wed–Sun 9–1 and 2–6; adm DM3.50)*, a rebuilt 12th-century castle clinging to a jagged crag. Richard the Lionheart was imprisoned here in 1193.

Aschaffenburg

Dormitory town 40km east of Frankfurt am Main. It has an attractive *fachwerk* Altstadt; a pink palace, **Schloß Johannisburg** *(Apr–Sept daily 9–12 and 1–5; Oct–Mar daily 10–12 and 1–4; adm DM3.50)*, once residence to the Archbishops of Mainz, now a picture gallery; and a **Stiftskirche** which is a hotchpotch of Romanesque, Gothic and Baroque architecture and houses a superb painting by Grünewald.
Tourist office: Dalbergstr. 6, (06021) 30426.
Hotels/Eating out: The Hotel Post (Goldbacherstr. 198, ℗ 21 333; rooms from DM160) is an attractive old inn with a good restaurant. Good taverns and pubs are on the Rossmarkt.

Bad Ems

Elegant spa town in the Lahn valley, near Koblenz. It was a favourite cure resort of King-Wilhelm I of Prussia. The king's insulting dismissal of the French ambassador, who had come to Bad Ems in 1870 to get assurance that the Hohenzollerns would never again lay claim to the Spanish throne, precipitated the Franco-Prussian War.

Bad Honnef-Rhöndorf

Dormitory spa town just outside Bonn. Once home to Konrad Adenauer, first Chancellor of the Federal Republic of Germany. His old house at Konrad-Adenauer-Str. 8c is now a small memorial **museum** *(Tues–Sun 10–4.30; adm free)*.

Directory

Bad Münstereifel

Spa town in the valley of the River Erft 40km southwest of Bonn. Characterful town with its 13th-century city wall still in one piece. There is also an austere Romanesque church and a 12th-century building that locals claim is the oldest intact house in Germany.
Tourist office: Langenhecke 2, ℗ (02253) 505 182.

Bad Neuenahr-Ahrweiler

Double town in the Ahr valley 30km south of Bonn. Bad Neuenahr is a modern town with curing waters and a big casino. Ahrweiler is crammed full of half-timbered houses and has most of its medieval city wall intact.

Tourist office: Hauptstr. 60, ✆ (02641) 2278.

Hotels/Eating out: Giffels Goldener Anker (Mittelstr. 14, ✆ 2325; DM160) is a rather sleepy hotel near the Kurhaus. The Alte Post on Ahrweiler's Marktplatz has good food (DM25–45).

Bad Reichenhall

Old salt-producing town on Germany's southeast border, just 19km from Salzburg. You can visit the **Alte Saline** (Old Saltworks) *(Apr–Oct daily 10–11.30 and 2–4; adm DM6)*, which date back to the 16th century—though the present works are 19th-century mock medieval.

Tourist office: Wittelsbacher Str. 15, ✆ (08651) 3003.

Benndorf

Village just west of Koblenz. The main attraction is the delightful **Garten der Schmetterlinge** (Butterfly Garden) *(daily 10–5; adm DM4)* a large, covered hot-house that flaps and flutters with butterflies of all sizes. Looming on a hill nearby are the ruins of the 12th-century castle, Burg Sayn (not really worth the climb).

Bielefeld

Industrial town 35km north of Paderborn, a major British Army base during the Cold War. Little of note bar the **Kunsthalle** *(Tues, Wed, Fri and Sun 11–6, Thurs 11–9, Sat 10–6; adm DM2.50)* which has a good collection of German Expressionists and European and American abstract painting.

Tourist office: Hauptbahnhof, ✆ (0521) 178 844.

Blaubeuren

Village just west of Ulm. The main attractions are the **Blautopf**, a mysterious 20m-deep pool and the Gothic **Kloster** where there is a superb high altar with work by the Ulm masters Michel Erhart and Bartholomäus Zeitblom.

Bochum

Ruhrgebiet, midway between Dortmund and Essen. Modern industrial town that one could happily ignore were it not for two excellent museums. The **Deutsches Bergbaumuseum** (German Mining Museum) *(Tues–Fri 8.30–5.30, Sat and Sun 9–1; adm DM5)*; and the **Eisenbahn Museum** (Railway Museum) *(Wed and Fri 10–5, Sun 10–1; adm DM4)*. Both are leaders in their field with riveting displays. Bochum's Schauspielhaus is home to one of the best theatre companies in the country.

Tourist office: Hauptbahnhof, ✆ (0234) 13 031.

Hotels/Eating out: Arcade (Universitätsstr. 3, ✆ 33 311; from DM150) is a large hotel near the station. Stammhaus Fiege (Bongardstr. 23, DM25–45) serves beer brewed in-house and delicious food.

Brandenburg

Industrial town 30km west of Potsdam. Devastated in turn by the Allies, the Red Army, Stalinist architects and industrial pollution, yet beautifully situated on three islands in the river Havel. On the smallest and most atmospheric of the islands stands the cathedral—a mixture of Romanesque and Gothic, containing some fine carving. Treasures include the Brandenburg Evangelistary, a sumptuously illustrated Romanesque gospel book.
Tourist office: Plauer Str. 4, ✆ (03381) 237 734.
Hotels/Eating out: Zum Bären (Steinstr. 60, ✆ 24179) is a new hotel with enthusiastic owners. Ratskeller (Altstädisches Rathaus; DM25–45) serves good, reliable German cuisine.

Calw

(pronounced *kulf*). An exceptionally beautiful *fachwerk* town on the River Nagold, west of Stuttgart. It was the birthplace of Herman Hesse, and there's a Hesse Museum. Nearby are the evocative ruins of **Kloster Hirsau**, dating from the 9th to the 16th centuries.
Tourist office: Aureliusplatz, ✆ (07051) 5671.
Hotels/Eating out: Gasthof zum Rössle (Hermann-Hesse-Platz 2, ✆ 30 052; DM120); Hotel Ratstube (Marktplatz 12, ✆ 1864; fax 20 311; DM165). Both hotels serve good food.

Celle

40km northeast of Hannover. Small town with over 480 restored half-timbered buildings and a large Renaissance Schloß *(guided tours daily on the hour 9–4; adm DM2)*. The highlight of the Schloß tour is a visit to the Schloßkapelle adorned with a bright mannerist painting cycle.
Tourist office: Schloßplatz, ✆ (05141) 1212.
Hotels/Eating out: Fürstenhof (Hannoversche Str. 55, ✆ 2010; from DM200) is an elegant converted 17th-century palace; its Kutscherstube restaurant serves good food (DM35–60). Nordwall (Nordwall 4, ✆ 29077; from DM100) is a comfortable, centrally located hotel.

Chemnitz

80km west of Dresden. Known under the DDR as Karl-Marx-Stadt and famed for the enormous 40-ton bronze head of Karl Marx in the city centre. Chemnitz doesn't deserve its reputation as a dull industrial town. It has shady parks and quaint corners of beautiful old buildings. In the Schloßkirche on the hill above town are two superb carvings by medieval sculptor Hans Witten.
Tourist office: Straße der Nationen 3, ✆ (0371) 62 051.
Hotels/Eating out: Hotel Europa (Straße der Nationen 56, ✆ 6840; DM240) is a smart modern hotel in the centre of town. Hotel Sächsischer Hof (Brühl 26, ✆ 414 383; DM160–180) is a pleasant hotel in older part of town centre. Zum Türmer (Am Markt 19, ✆ 446 368; DM35–45) serves good local cuisine on the market square. Restaurant Miramar (Schloßberg 16, ✆ 31 521; DM25–45) has a large shady beergarden overlooking the town.

Cloppenburg

40km south of Oldenburg. Site of an excellent **Freilichtmuseum** (Open Air Museum) *(Mar–Oct Mon–Sat 8–6, Sun 9–6; Nov–Feb Mon–Sat 9–5, Sun 10–5; adm DM6)* with reconstructed rural buildings from all over Lower Saxony.

Coburg

90km northwest of Bayreuth. Seat of the Saxe-Coburg-Gotha family who provided spouses for royal families all over Europe (including Queen Victoria's consort, Albert). Star attraction is the massive **Veste Coburg** a fortress dating, in the main, back to the 16th century and home to the Saxe-Coburg-Gothas until 1945. Today it is a **museum** *(Apr–Oct Tues–Sun 9.30–1 and 2–5; Nov–Mar Tues–Sun 2–5; adm DM2.50)* with a vast and important collection of graphics (including works by Rembrandt, Cranach and Dürer). When the dukes were not in the Veste on the hill they lived in **Schloß Ehrenburg** *(guided tours Tues–Sun 10, 11, 1.30, 2.30 and 3.30; adm DM2.50)*, a sumptuous palace in the middle of town.

Tourist office: Herrngasse 4, ℂ (09561) 95 071.

Hotels/Eating out: Hotel Stadt Coburg (Lossaustr. 12, ℂ 7781; DM150) is a plain but comfortable hotel near the station. Goldener Anker (Rosengasse 14, ℂ 95 027; from DM90) is a central hotel with friendly management and a good restaurant (DM35–45).

Cottbus

120km southeast of Berlin. Unattractive main town of the Spreewald region. In the midst of the industrial sprawl and collapsing Stalinist architecture is a modest Altstadt. The altar in the Gothic Oberkirche is a Renaissance extravaganza of wood, marble, alabaster and sandstone featuring Jonah and the whale.

Tourist office: Altmarkt 29, ℂ (0355) 24 254.

Daun

Market town near Mayen in the heart of the Vulkaneifel (Volcanic Eifel). Uninteresting in itself, but a good base for exploring this region of crater lakes and volcanic outcrops.

Tourist office: Kurzentrum, Leopoldstr. 14, ℂ (06592) 71477.

Hotels/Eating out: Manderscheid (Wirichstr. 23, ℂ 2210; DM80) is a simple but pleasant *Pension* near the centre of town. Schloß-Hotel Kurfürstliches Amsthaus (Burgberg, ℂ 3031; DM180–250) is a sumptuously converted 18th-century Schloß with views over the valley.

Dessau

55km southeast of Magdeburg. Drab town with little to recommend it except that it was headquarters for the Bauhaus movement (*see* p. 64). Gropius' famous building for the school still stands and houses an extensive **museum** *(Wed–Fri 10–5, Sat and Sun 10–12.30 and 2–5; adm DM4)* of Bauhaus work.

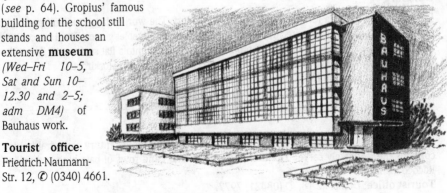

Tourist office: Friedrich-Naumann-Str. 12, ℂ (0340) 4661.

Dinkelsbühl

Attractive medieval town on the Romantic Road, 40km south of Rothenburg. The city wall survives almost intact. St Georg on the Weinmarkt is an elegant Gothic *Hallenkirche*. Dinkesbühl's **Kinderzeche**, a ten-day-long festival held around the third Monday in July, is one of the most popular in the region. Citizens re-enact an event from the Thirty Years' War in which children successfully plead with the conquering Swedish commander not to ransack their town. This is followed by much feasting and drinking.

Tourist office: Marktplatz, © (09851) 90240.

Hotels/Eating out: Deutsches Haus (Weinmarkt 3, © 2346; DM120–180) is a converted 15th-century mansion with comfortable rooms and an excellent restaurant (meals DM35–50). Roter Hahn (Lange Gasse 16, © 2225; DM90) is an atmospheric hotel with good restaurant attached (DM25–40).

Donaueschingen

50km northwest of Lake Constance. Source of the River Danube—a spring in the grounds of the local Schloß. The Scloß library possesses one of the three original manuscripts of the *Nibelungenlied*, but it is not on show to the general public.

Dortmund

Beer-brewing town in the Ruhrgebiet, home to six leading German breweries: Kronen, Union, Ritter, Thier, Stifts and Actien (DAB). The city was badly bombed in the Second World War and there is little apart from the beer to attract a casual visitor, though the four carefully restored city churches house some important Gothic art treasures (most notably work by Conrad van Soest, which can be found in the Marienkirche). There is also a good museum of modern art, the Museum am Ostwall *(Tues–Sun 10–6; adm free)* with a strong collection of Expressionists.

Tourist office: Südwall 6, © (0231) 25 666.

Hotels/Eating out: Drees (Hohestr. 107, © 103 821; DM150) is a modern, efficiently run hotel near the city park. Hotel Carlton (Lütge Brückstr. 5–7, © 528 030; DM100) is clean and fairly central. Wenker's (on the Markt) is a lively local beerhouse, as is the Krone establishment next door, but the pick of local brewery taverns is the Hövels Hausbrauerei (Hoher Wall 5, © 141 044; DM30–50) which has a large beer garden and sells excellent food.

Duisburg

Ruhrgebiet town, just a few kilometres from Düsseldorf. The world's largest inland port and, parks and the odd pedestrian precinct aside, the epitome of Ruhrgebiet gloom. The 16th-century cartographer Gerhard Mercator (whose projection of the globe onto a flat surface still forms the basis of modern maps) lived here for 42 years and is buried in the Salvatorkirche.

Tourist office: Königstraße, © (0203) 283 205.

Hotels: Haus Reinhard (Fuldastr. 31, © 331 316; DM150–200).

Eichstätt

30km northwest of Ingolstadt. Beautiful episcopal city with a 14th-century cathedral (which contains the intricately carved Gothic *Pappenheim altar*) and rows of pale blue and yellow Rococo mansions.

Tourist office: Domplatz 18, © (08421) 7977.

Emden

Charmless principal town of East Friesland. almost on the Dutch Border. It is saved from being utterly unremarkable by a good **Museum für Moderne Kunst** *(Tues 10–8, Wed–Fri 10–5, Sat and Sun 11–5; adm free)* which has a good collection of Expressionists, and the **Ostfriesisches Landesmuseum** *(Mon–Fri 10–1 and 3–5, Sat and Sun 11–5; closed Mon Apr–Oct; adm free)* which boasts one of the largest collections of armour in Europe.
Tourist office: Feuerschiff im Ratsdelft, ✆ (04921) 32 528.

Esslingen

A pleasant surprise in Stuttgart's suburban sprawl. The medieval town centre is almost entirely intact, large lengths of the old city wall remain, and vineyards reach almost to the market square. Especially worth seeing are the 15th-century **Rathaus** with its astronomical clock and the 14th-century bridge, the **Innerebrücke**, which has a chapel built into it.
Tourist office: Marktplatz 16, ✆ (0711) 351 2441.
Eating out: The shady Hafenmarkt is a good area for lunchtime restaurants. Gambrinus in Strohstraße serves good salads and local cuisine (DM25–40).

Flensburg

Northern harbour town at the head of a fjord on the Danish border. Many of the old merchant's houses have recently been restored and there are some attractive 17th-century covered shopping arcades. The town is famed for its rum distilleries (nearly 60 different varieties are produced here).
Tourist office: Nordertor 6, ✆ (0461) 25901.
Hotels/Eating out: Am Stadtpark (Nordergraben 70, ✆ 24 900; DM90–120) is a quiet hotel overlooking the fjord. Das Kleine Restaurant (Grosse Str. 3; DM20–35) serves simple meals and good salads.

Frankfurt an der Oder

Dull town on the Polish border, 80km east of Berlin. Largely rebuilt after the second World war and notable mainly as the birthplace of writer Heinrich von Kleist. Pretty dismal tourist facilities.
Tourist office: Karl-Marx-Str. 8a, ✆ 325 216.

Freudenstadt

60km south of Baden-Baden. The hub of the Northern Black Forest transport system and a tea-break spot for coach tourism. The market square is the largest in Germany (though its impact is spoiled by a highway trundling right through the middle). There is an odd L-shaped 17th-century **Stadtkirche** (constructed not only to segregate the sexes, but to make even the slightest glimpse impossible—all you can see from each wing is the pulpit).
Tourist office: Promenadeplatz 1, ✆ (07441) 8640.
Hotels/Eating out: Hotel/Weinstuben Bären (Langestr. 33, ✆ 2729; fax 2887; DM130–160), run by the same family for over a century, has a superb kitchen and comfortable rooms. The modern Hotel Schwanen (Forstraße 6, ✆ 2267; DM110–124) is a good second choice.

Friedrichshafen

Industrial town with a touristy promenade on Lake Constance, 20km west of Lindau. Once the home of the Zeppelin airship factory and the Dornier flying boat works. You can see some original aircraft and archive interesting film in the aviation section of the **Zeppelin- und Bodensee-Museum** *(May–Oct daily 10–5; Nov–Apr 10–12 and 2–5; adm DM3)*.
Tourist office: Stadtbahnhof, © (07541) 203 291.

Fulda

Attractive Baroque town 80km northeast of Frankfurt. Until 1989 the site of the 'Fulda gap'—the weak point in NATO's defence line where it was thought the enemy tanks would come trundling into western Europe. The town grew up around an abbey founded by St Boniface (a monk sent from England to convert the Germans to Christianity—his relics are in the cathedral). Local abbots became powerful secular princes in the late 17th and 18th centuries, and are responsible for Fulda's splendid Baroque centre, notably the cathedral and sprawling Stadtschloß. **Schloß Fasanerie** *(Apr–Oct Tues–Sun 10–12 and 1–4; adm DM4)*, 6km southwest of the centre is one of the finest Baroque palaces in Hessen.
Tourist office: Schloßstr. 1, © (0661) 102 345.
Hotels/Eating out: Zum Kurfürsten (Schloßstr. 2, © 70 001; DM120–160) is an 18th-century palace that once accommodated the likes of Queen Victoria, now a solid *bürgerlich* hotel. Gasthof Grüne Au (Abtstor 35, © 74 283; from DM90) is a small guesthouse next door to the cathedral. Felsenkeller (Leipzigerstr. 12, © 72 784; DM25–40) is a large pub with beergarden and good, hearty helpings of food. Dachsbau Bistro (Pfandhausstr. 7–9; DM30–50) has a more upmarket atmosphere and subtler cuisine.

Füssen

Alpine town on the Austrian border that marks the end of the Romantic Road. Pretty setting, but not much of interest to see except an odd 17th-century *Dance of Death* painting in a chapel attatched to the parish church of St Mang.
Tourist office: Augsburger Torplatz 1, © (08362) 7077.

Gera

Large Thuringian town, 45km east of Jena. Little in the way of sights, though there are a number of Baroque and Jugendstil mansions. The town is famed for its musical instrument makers, and has a friendly, lively atmosphere.
Tourist Information: Zentraler Platz, © 26432.

Görlitz

Germany's easternmost town, 45km east of Bautzen. At the moment it is a drab and depressing spread of crumbling buildings blackened by pollution. But Görlitz largely escaped Second World War bombing, and restoration work is revealing rows of splendid Renaissance and Baroque houses with interesting courtyards and arcades. Görlitz really was a forgotten corner of the DDR: attitudes towards visitors are still surly, and there are few facilities for tourists.
Tourist office: Obermarkt 29, © (03581) 5391.

Göttingen

Famous university town 45km northeast of Kassel. It lacks the lively student atmosphere of Marburg or Heidelberg, and has little else to recommend it save a small, mainly 14th-century Altsatdt and the **Gänseliesel**, a bronze statue of a goose-girl erected early this century which, according to tradition, students kiss after they pass their finals.

Tourist office: Altes Rathaus, ℂ (0551) 54000.

Hotels/Eating out: Hotel Zur Sonne (Pauliner Str. 10, ℂ 56 738; DM90–120) is a pleasant central hotel. Junkerschänke (Barfüsserstr. 5, ℂ 57320; DM45–60) is a 14th century tavern with superb German cuisine. Zum Schwarzen Bären (Kurzestr. 12, ℂ 58 284; DM30–40) is a16th-century tavern serving good food.

Griefswald

University town on the east Baltic coast; birthplace of the Romantic painter Caspar David Friedrich. The town is undergoing a massive restoration process which should transform its largely 14th-century Altstadt into one of the most impressive in the area. On the eastern out-skirts of town, in the village of Edena, you can see the haunting ruins of a 12th-century monastery that features in many of Friedrich's paintings.

Tourist office: Lange Str. 126, ℂ (03834) 3260.

Güstrow

60km northeast of Schwerin. Birthplace of Germany's foremost modern sculptor, Ernst Barlach. One of his most famous works, the *Flying Angel* can be seen in the cathedral, and there is an extensive exhibition of his work in his former lakeside studio, the **Barlach Atelierhaus** *(Tues–Thurs and Sun 9-12 and 1–5; adm free)*.

Tourist office: Markt 23.

Haigerloch

Small town perched above the River Eyach, 30km south of Tübingen. **St Anna's** church has a superb Rococo interior. In the Evangelischekirche, there's a painstaking full-size reproduction of the **Last Supper**. Tunnelled into the mountain is the **Atom-Keller Museum** *(May–Sept daily 10–12 and 2–5; Mar, Apr, Oct and Nov Sat and Sun same times; closed Dec–Feb; adm DM3)* where German scientists very nearly invented the atom bomb before 1945. There are remnants of a once strong **Jewish quarter** and a Jewish cemetery.

Hotels/Eating out: Café Charlotte on the high street has superb views and serves light meals. Gasthof Römer nearby offers more substantial dishes (DM35–45). Hotel Krone (Oberstadtstr. 47, ℂ (07474) 411; DM65) is a plain friendly hotel, with superb views from the upstairs rooms.

Halberstadt

This ancient town in the Harz foothills 55km southwest of Magdeburg, is at present undergoing a substantial facelift. The chief attraction is the noble Gothic cathedral, which has a particularly rich treasury.

Tourist office: Düsterngraben, ℂ (03941) 58316.

Halle

Grimy city 40km northwest of Leipzig. Birthplace of the composer George Frederic Handel: there is a **museum** *(Tues–Sun 9.30–5.30; adm DM1.50)* stuffed with memorabilia in the Baroque mansion where he was born. In the Altstadt you'll find a Gothic *Hallenkirche*, and rows of pollution-blackened Baroque and Renaissance mansions.

Tourist office: Marktplatz, ✆ (05201) 23340.

Hann. Münden

Small town at the meeting point of the rivers Fulda and Weser, 35km from Göttingen. Its odd name is an abbreviation of Hannoversch Münden (it was once part of the Kingdom of Hannover). The Altstadt is thick with half-timbered and Weser Renaissance houses, but there is little else to detain you.

Tourist office: Rathaus, ✆ (05541) 75313.

Heilbronn

A commercial town and wine centre in the Neckar valley, mostly rebuilt since the war. The Gothic **St Kilian's** church has a Renaissance tower. The real reason for a visit is *Heilbronner Herbst*, a lively wine festival lasting a fortnight following the first Saturday in September.

Tourist office: Rathaus, ✆ (07131) 562 270.

Hotels/Eating out: Insel-Hotel (Friedr.-Ebert-Brücke, ✆ 63 00; fax 62 60 60; from DM188). The Ratskeller (under the Rathaus) serves good Swabian specialities.

Hiddensee

Car-free island in the Baltic, off the western coast of Rügen. It was a popular artists' colony early this century (especially around the village of Kloster). A scenic day trip from Rügen.

Husum

Atmospheric grey-stone fishing port on the North Sea, 30km west of Schleswig. Home for many years to the 19th-century novelist Theodor Storm. There is a small, but not especially interesting **museum** *(Tues–Sat 10–4; adm DM1.50)* in his honour.

Tourist office: Rathaus, ✆ (04841) 666 133.

Idar Oberstein

Centre of the semi-precious stone industry in the Hunsrück mountains. Visit a traditional stone-cutting workshop, **Weiherschleife** *(Mon–Fri 10–12 and 2-5, Sun 10–12; adm free)* and a **Edelsteinmuseum** (Precious Stone Museum) *(May–Sept daily 9–6, Oct–Apr 9–5; adm DM5)*.

Tourist office: Oberstein, ✆ (06781) 27 025.

Ingolstadt

Wealthy town 60km north of Munich. The pristine Altstadt is encircled by a medieval city wall and a Neoclassical fortification. The **Liebfrauenmünster** has intricate vaulting, and the **Maria-de-Victoria-Kirche** is the work of star Baroque designers, the Asam brothers.

Tourist office: Hallstr. 5, ✆ (0841) 305 415.

Hotels/Eating out: Zum Anker (Tränktorstr. 1, ✆ 32091; from DM90) is a comfortable hotel in the Altstadt, with good restaurant (DM25–45).

Inn-Salzachgau

Name given to the triangle of fertile Alpine farming country bound by the River Inn and the Austrian border, southeast of Munich. Fine area for walking.

Jena

University town 20km southeast of Weimar; also the original home of the famous optical instruments firm founded by Carl Zeiss. The **Zeiss Planetarium**, built in 1925, was the first in the world (showing times vary), and there is an interesting **Optisches Museum** *(Tues–Fri 9–5.30, Sat 9–4; DM3)* in the west of town. The city itself did not come through the Second World War very lightly, but has a lively student and social life.
Tourist office: Löbderstr. 9, ✆ (03641) 24671.
Hotels/Eating out: Pension Kerzel (Lutherstr. 38, ✆ 25760; from DM90) is a plain but comfortable *Pension*. Hotel International (Ernst-Thälmann-Ring, ✆ 8880; from DM150) is stark and modern. Roter Hirsch (Holzmarkt 10; DM20–30) serves solid, inexpensive German food.

Juist

Tiny, quiet island in the East Frisian archipelago.
Tourist office: Rathaus, ✆ (04935) 809 222.

Kaub

Village on the Rhine, a few kilometres south of the Lorelei Rock. Nearby, on an island in the middle of the river, is **Pfalzgrafenstein** *(Apr–Oct daily 9–12 and 1.30–5.15; adm DM1.50)*, a fetching 19th-century remake of a 13th-century castle that features prominently in tourist brochures, but which has a disappointing interior.

Kiel

Capital of Schleswig-Holstein and home to North Germany's oldest university, but today an ugly town of scant interest bar the odd student tavern.
Tourist office: Auguste-Viktoria-Str. 16, ✆ (0431) 62230.
Hotels/Eating out: Kieler Kaufmann (Niemannsweg 102, ✆ 85011; from DM150) is a hotel set in a quiet old building near the sea. Ratskeller (Rathaus, ✆ 95494; DM35–45) offers plain cooking, and is popular with locals.

Kulmbach

Beer-brewing town 25km northwest of Bayreuth, famed for the ominously named *Kulminator 28*, supposedly the strongest beer in the world. The **Plassenburg**, a fortified castle above the town as an impressively ornate Renaissance courtyard and houses a collection of some 300,000 tin soldiers and other figurines.

Landshut

On the River Isar, 70km northeast of Munich. Wittelsbach capital from the 13th to the early 16th century (when Bavaria became united under Munich). The Altstadt is crammed with splendid medieval buildings, including the 133m-high tower of the church of **St Martin**—the highest brick structure in the world. Landshut is most renowned as the scene of Germany's largest costume pageant, the **Landshut Wedding**, which is held every four years (next one June/July 1997) re-enacting the marriage, in 1475, of the Duke of Lower Bavaria and a Princess of Poland.

Tourist office: Altstadt 315, ℂ (0871) 23031.

Hotels/Eating out: Pension Sandner (Freyung 627, ℂ 22379; DM90) is clean and conveniently situated. Hoferbräu (Neustadt 444; DM25–45) is a cheery tavern with reasonable tasty German fare.

Langeoog

Low-key, but attractive East Frisian island. The village is dull but the nature reserve on the eastern shore is famed for its seabird colonies.

Lemgo

Extraordinarily beautiful little town 12km north of Detmold. It was a thriving Hanseatic trade centre in the 1th-century and has inherited street upon street of elegant gabled houses, a rambling Rathaus and some fine old churches. The **Hexenbürgermeisterhaus** *(Tues–Fri and Sun 10–12.30 and 1.30–5, Sat 10–1; adm DM1.50)* is a supreme example of Weser Renaissance. It gets its name from a 17th-century witch-hunting mayor.

Tourist office: Haus Wipperman, Kramerstraße, ℂ (05261) 213 347.

Hotels/Eating out: Bahnhofswaage (Am Bahnhof, ℂ 3525; DM90) is a simple hotel near the train station. Zum Landsknecht (Herforder Str. 177, ℂ 68264; rooms from DM80, meals DM30–40) is a comfortable guesthouse with good restaurant.

Limburg

Small town in the Lahn valley 50km north of Wiesbaden; famed for its cheese. The medieval Altstadt survives largely intact, and an odd orange and white cathedral sticks up above the town.

Tourist office: Hospitalstr. 2, ℂ (06431) 203 222.

Ludwigslust

Small town 35km south of Schwerin with an enormous Baroque **Schloß** *(guided tours Tues–Sun 11, 1 and 2; adm DM3)* and extensive Schloßpark.

Tourist office: Schloßstr, 6, ℂ (03874) 2355.

Magdeburg

Capital of Saxony-Anhalt. The Gothic cathedral is truly impressive. Inside is a superb array of sculpture—from Romanesque to work by the 20th-century artist, Ernst Barlach. The **Kulturhistorisches Museum** *(Tues–Sun 10–6; adm DM1)* houses the Magdeburg Rider, a 13th-century equestrian statue, thought to be of Otto the Great. The city was badly bombed during the war, and the Altstadt has been poorly rebuilt.

Tourist office: Alter Markt 9, ℂ (0391) 35 352.

Hotels/Eating out: Hotel International (Otto-van-Guericke-Str. 87, ℂ 3840; DM180–200) is modern and functional. Grüner Baum (Wilhelm-Pieck-Allee 38–40, ℂ 32 166; DM90) is a clean, central guesthouse. Savarin (Breiter Weg 226; DM25–35) offers tasty German cuisine. Gastmahl des Meeres (Jacobstr. 20) is a good seafood restaurant.

Mannheim

One of Europe's largest river ports, at the confluence of the Rhine and the Neckar, 80km from Frankfurt. The centre of the city follows a grid plan (laid out in the 18th century), which divides it into 144 squares, each assigned a letter and number (hence the odd addresses). Tourist sights are few and far between, though the Baroque **Residenzschloß** has an impressive chapel *(daily 9–5; adm free)* and reception rooms *(Apr–Oct Tues–Sun 10–12 and 3–5; Nov–Mar Sat and Sun 10–12 and 3–5; adm DM1.50)*, all heavily restored after Second World War bomb damage. The **Kunsthalle** in Moltkestraße *(Tues–Sun 10–5; adm free)* has a good collection of Impressionists and other 19th- and early 20th-century art.
Tourist office: Kaiserring 10, ✆ (0621) 101 011.
Hotels/Eating out: Arabella (M2 12, ✆ 23050; DM110) is a comfortable little hotel near the Residenzschloß. Augusta (Augusta-Anlage 43, ✆ 418 001; from DM180) is smart and fairly central. Elsässer (N7 8; DM25–45) is a pleasant restaurant with a reputation for good food.

Marbach

Cosy *fachwerk* town north of Stuttgart, birthplace of **Friedrich Schiller**. You can visit his house *(daily 9–5; adm DM1)* at Niklastorstraße 20 and on the hill overlooking the Neckar there's a large **Schiller Museum**.
Eating out: The café at the Rathaus, next to the museum serves good food and has magnificent views. In Glocke (Marktstr. 48) you sit surrounded by hundreds of clocks, eating *Maultaschen*. Schiller himself used to frequent the Goldener Löwe, an inn in Niklastorstraße.

Mayen

Bland little town, 30km west of Andernach and transport hub of the surrounding Eifel region.
Tourist office: Altes Rathaus, ✆ (02651) 88 260.

Mönchengladbach

Headquarters of the British Army on the Rhine, 30km west of Düsseldorf. Little to see (unless you're visiting a soldier) except **Museum Abteiberg** *(Tues–Sun 10–6; adm DM3)*, a first-rate museum of late 20th-century art.
Tourist office: Bismarckstr. 23–7, ✆ (02161) 22 001.

Mosbach

Pretty *fachwerk* town on the Neckar. The **Gutleutkapel** has well preserved late-Gothic murals.
Tourist office: Rathaus, ✆ (06261) 8 22 36.
Hotel: Zum Lamm (Hauptstr. 59, ✆ 8 90 20, fax 89 02 91; DM100).

Mummelsee

Deep-blue lake on the Black Forest High Road, haunted by the hapless King Ulmon, condemned by a sorceress to live for 1000 years. He dutifully makes his appearance each summer in a white wig and rubber seaweed.
Hotels/Eating out: The only hotel/restaurant on the lake is the Berghotel Mummelsee (✆ (07842) 10 88, fax 30 266; DM110); ordinary and very touristy, adequate for a quick lunch.

Münden *see* Hann. Münden

Neubrandenburg

Largest town in the Mecklenburg lake region, 130km north of Berlin. Ugly and modern, though the medieval ramparts survive. There is a woeful lack of tourist facilities.
Tourist office: Ernst-Thälmann-Str. 35, ✆ (0395) 6187.

Niebüll

60km north of Husum. Small North Frisian village with one big claim to fame. Just outside was the home and studio of expressionist painter Emil Nolde—nowadays a **museum** of his work *(Mar–Oct Tues–Sun 10–6; Nov 10–5; Dec–Feb closed; adm DM4)*.

Norden/Nordeneich

Main departure point for trips to the East Frisian Islands. Ferries for the main islands of Juist and Nordeney leave directly from Nordeich (10min by bus from Norden Marktplatz; Juist, 3 daily, 1hr 20min; Nordeney 9–13 daily, 50min). Buses leave from Norden Bahnhof to various ferry embarkation points (Baltrum: bus to Nessmersiel, 3 crossings daily; Langeoog: bus to Benseriel, 3–5 crossings daily; Spiekeroog: bus to Neuharlingsersiel, 2–4 crossings daily; Wangerooge: bus to Harlesiel, 1–3 crossings daily). Norden tourist office can give you details of departure times.
Tourist office: Marktplatz, ✆ (04931) 17202.

Nordeney

Most popular of the East Frisian Islands. Touristy with long, sandy, but crowded beaches. Gently fading Neoclassical spa complex in the main town; most of the island covered by scrubby dunes.
Tourist office: Bülow Allee 5, ✆ (04932) 502.
Hotels: Georgshöhe (Kaiserstr. 24, ✆ 8980; from DM200) with pool and sauna, near beach.

Nördlingen

70km north of Augsburg. Least attractive and most modernized of the Romantic Road trio of walled medieval towns. (The others are Rothenburg and Dinkelsbühl.)
Tourist office: Marktplatz 2, ✆ (09801) 4380.
Hotels/Eating out: Zum Engel (Wembingerstr. 4, ✆ 3176; rooms from DM80, meals DM20–30) is a pleasant converted brewery near city wall.

Oldenburg

60km west of Bremen. Medium-sized town whose main role seems to be as a shopping centre for surrounding farmers. It has a small, moated Altstadt (criss-crossed with modern shopping malls) and a Gothic town church with a pristine 18th-century interior. In the 18th-century **Schloß** *(Tues–Fri 9–5, Sat and Sun 9–1; adm free)* you can see notable paintings by Tischbein.
Tourist office: Langestr. 3, ✆ (0441) 15744.
Hotels/Eating out: Hotel Heide (Melkbrink 49, ✆ 8040; from DM120) is a quiet, suburban hotel with good restaurant (DM35–45). Kartoffelkiste (Artillerieweg 56; DM10–25) concentrates on potatoes. Laterne (Heiligengeiststr. 19; DM25–35) serves pastas and traditional dishes.

Pommersfelden

Small town 20km south of Bamberg and site of **Schloß Weißenstein** *(guided tours Apr–Oct 9–12 and 2–5; adm DM5)*, a splendid Baroque Palace built by Prince Bishop Lothar von Schönborn at the same time as the Würzburg Residenz and the Neue Residenz in Bamberg.

Prüm

Winter sports resort north of Trier. The Baroque Salvatoribasilica keeps a relic of Christ's sandal.
Tourist office: Hahnplatz, © (06551) 505.

Rastatt

14km north of Baden-Baden. Margrave Ludwig moved the family seat from Baden-Baden to the red sandstone **Schloß** in 1705. Today it is a **Military Museum** *(Tues–Sun 9.30–5; adm free)*.
Eating out: Hofbräu Hatz on Poststraße produces one of the region's best beers, and serves *gutbürgerliche* food.

Remagen

On the Rhine, near Andernach. Scene of the one bridge that remained over the Rhine in 1945, and first crossing point of the Allied troops. The bridge no longer exists (it collapsed during the Allied crossing, due to overloading), but the towers on the Remagen side of the river are now a **museum** *(Mar–Nov, daily 10–5, DM2)* which tells the story.

Rolandseck

On the northern outskirts of Remagen. Worth a quick stopover for a look at the **Künstlerbahnhof** *(daily 10–5; adm DM2.50)*, the old railway station converted into a museum devoted largely to the works of Hans Arp.

Rudesheim

Celebrated, but utterly avoidable tourist trap on the Rhine. Known for its wines, but even more so for the **Drosselgasse**, a horrid street lined entirely by pubs and seething with tourists happy to be ripped off.
Tourist office: Rheinstr. 16, © (06722) 2962.
Hotels/Eating out: Hotel Rheinstein (Rheinsteinstr. 20, © 2004; from DM100) if you must: it has views over the Rhine and a reasonable restaurant (DM25–45).

Saarbrücken

Industrial town, capital of the tiny *Land* of Saarland, up against the French border. The town is mainly modern, with a 13th-century church of St Arnual and a run-down Schloß.
Tourist office: Trierer Str. 2, © (0681) 309 8222.
Hotels/Eating out: Novotel (Zinzingerstr. 9, © 58630; DM150) belongs to the modern, French-owned chain hotel. Brasserie Fröschengasse (Fröschengasse; DM35–55) is a trendy but pricey brasserie with good food. Zum Stiefel (Am Stiefel 2; DM25–45) is an attractive old inn with beer garden and serves tasty local specialities.

St Goarhausen

Rhine town closest to the famous Lorelei rock (*see* p. 163). You can get to the rock on Bus 6147. Above the town is the 14th-century Burg Katz (Cat Castle). It is only partially reconstructed (you need permission from the tourist office to visit the ruins). A few kilometres downstream is the much smaller Burg Maus (Mouse Castle), built for the Bishops of Trier but today an eagle and falcon station *(displays daily at 11am, 2.30pm and 4.30pm)*.
Tourist office: Bahnhofstr. 8, © (06771) 427.

Schleswig

Sleepy administrative town in Schleswig-Holstein.
Tourist office: Flensburger Str. 7, ✆ (04621) 87363.
Hotels/Eating out: Hotel Strandhalle (Strandweg 2, ✆ 22 021; DM150) is an attractive nautical hotel near a marina. Senatorkroog (Rathausmarkt; DM35–55) serves good fish dishes.

Schneeberg

Old silver-mining town in the Erzgebirge, 20km southeast of Zwickau. Known especially for its lively, traditional Christmas fairs. In the Stadtkirche there is a huge Passion altar by Cranach.
Tourist office: Rathaus, ✆ (03772) 2251.
Hotels/Eating out: Karlsbader Haus (Karlsbader Str. 56, ✆ 8734) is a comfortable hotel, fairly central. Ratskeller (Rathaus, DM25–45) offers hearty local cuisine.

Schwäbisch Gmünd

45km east of Stuttgart, until 1991 an important American army base. The magnificent Gothic cathedral, the Heiligkreuzmünster, is the work of Heinrich Parler and his son Peter (who was later to become famous as the architect of the cathedral in Prague).
Tourist office: Prediger, ✆ (07171) 603 415.

Schwäbisch Hall

65km northeast of Stuttgart. Pretty town of half-timbered houses on the slopes beside the River Kocher. The impressive, sloping Marktplatz is used during the summer as an open-air theatre.
Tourist office: Am Markt, ✆ (0791) 751 246.
Hotels/Eating out: Ratskeller (Am Markt 12, ✆ 6181; rooms from DM100, meals DM30–40) is a well-modernized medieval house with comfortable rooms and good cuisine.

Schwerin

65km southwest of Rostock. Founded in 1160, though the Altstadt comprises mainly 17th- and 18th-century buildings. Centrepiece of the town is a splendidly over-the-top neo-Gothic castle that soars up out of an island in a lake in the middle of town.
Tourist office: Markt 11, ✆ (0385) 83830.
Hotels/Eating out: Stadt Schwerin (Grunthalplatz 5, ✆ 812 498; DM100) is a simple clean hotel, near the station. Gastmahl des Meeres (Grosser Moor; DM25–45) serves well-prepared seafood dishes. Weinhaus Uhle (Schusterstr. 13, ✆ 864 455; DM35–55) is a good wine tavern.

Schwetzingen

Small town 12km west of Heidelberg. The nondescript pink 18th-century palace is surrounded by one of the most imaginative Schloß parks in Germany. Not only are there formal gardens, but also a wilder Romantic section with mock ruins, temples and even a mini mosque.
Tourist office: Schloßplatz, ✆ (06202) 49 33.
Eating out: Asparagus (season Apr–June) has been grown locally for centuries. Restaurants around the Schloßplatz serve it *au naturel* or smothered in odd sauces.

Sigmaringen

80km southwest of Ulm. Sigmaringen is dominated by its castle (largely a 19th-century rebuilt hotchpotch), seat of the Catholic branch of the Hohenzollerns, with over 3000 suits of armour and a coach museum. The castle would be the only real reason for a visit.
Tourist office: Rathaus, ✆ (07571) 106 223.
Hotels/Eating out: Hotel Traube (Fürst-Wilhelmstr. 19, ✆ 1 22 27; DM80) is a pleasant half-timbered hotel near the centre. Also Hotel Bären (Burgstr. 2, ✆ 1 28 62; DM80–130). Fidelio on the steps up to the Schloß is a chic café, and a good place for a coffee or a snack.

Straubing

Market town on the Danube 30km east of Regensburg. Bavaria's second largest fair (after the Oktoberfest) packs the town out in August. In the **Gäubodenmuseum** *(Tues–Sun 10–4, DM2)* there is an exceptional collection of Roman finds, including suits of armour and masks.
Tourist office: Rathaus, ✆ (09421) 16307.

Sylt

North Frisian island, known as the St Tropez of the North. Once the haunt of Thomas Mann and Marlene Dietrich, it still attracts Germany's jetset and aspirant *Schickeria*. Smartest village on the island is Kampen, but Keitum has pretty thatched cottages and a handful of galleries. Prices everywhere are high. A causeway connects Sylt with the mainland (train only, though you can load your car on the back—for a price).
Tourist office: no tourist office, but there is an accommodation agency, ✆ (04651) 19412.
Hotels/Eating out: Hinchley Wood (Kirchenstieg, Kampen, ✆ 41546; DM100) is a private hotel run by ex-RAF officer. Hotel Benen-Diken-Hof (Süderstraße, Keitum, ✆ 31 035; from DM250) is a luxurious Frisian-style hotel. Gogärtchen (Strönwai, Kampen, ✆ 41242; DM55–85) is a chic bar and restaurant on a street nicknamed 'Whiskystraße'. Dorfkrug Rotes Kliff (Alte Dorfstr. 1, Kampen, ✆ 43500; DM25–45) is a traditional thatched Frisian house serving hearty local food.

Thale

Small village 10km southwest of Quedlinburg. In itself not much to look at, but a convenient base for hiking in the surrounding hills and valleys. Numerous marked trails and spectacular scenery .
Tourist office: Bahnhof, ✆ (03947) 2597.
Hotels/Eating out: Brauner Hirsch (Rosstrappenstr. 1, ✆ 2504; from DM90) is an old half-timbered building, with pleasant management and a good restaurant.

Titisee

Pretty, but very commercialized southern Black Forest lake resort. Popular with the middle-class, middle-aged and pensioners. Mini-golf, pedaloes and amateur choirs.
Tourist office: Kurhaus, Seestraße; ✆ (07651) 81 01/2/3/4.
Hotels/Eating out: Hotel Seehof am See (Seestr 47., ✆ 83 14; DM140) is a cosy waterside hotel. The attractive Hotel Alemannenhof (Postfach 6 Titisee-Neustadt, ✆ (07652) 745; fax (07651) 8 81 42; DM240) is also on the lake and is known for its good restaurant.

Überlingen

Attractive old town on the Bodensee. The 15th-century **Münster** is particularly worth a visit for the superbly carved high altar (Jörg Zürn, 1618). There is more fine woodcarving in the Gothic council chamber of the old **Rathaus**.
Tourist office: Kurverwaltung, Landungsplatz 7, © (07551) 40 41.
Hotels/Eating out: Hotel/Weinstube Hecht (Münsterstr. 8, © (07551) 6 33 33; fax 33 10; rooms from DM160).

Usedom

Baltic island, south of Rügen. Not nearly as attractive as Rügen, and decidely more downmarket. The eastern tip of the island is in Poland, and vast stretches of the rest are out of bounds as a military zone. This is where Werner von Braun researched and developed the V2. At Peememünde, in the northwest of the island, you can visit a small **museum** *(Tues–Sun 9–5; adm DM3)* which heralds the research centre as the 'Birthplace of Space-Travel' and rather skirts around what the V2 was actually designed to do. The east coast is lined with resort towns, and here you can see some of the graceful, white-painted architecture that adorns the region.

Vogtsbauernhof

Popular open-air museum near Gutach in the Black Forest *(Apr–Oct daily 8.30–6; adm DM4)* with Black Forest farmhouses, workshops, and a chapel dating from the 16th century.

Weilburg

Pretty town on the Lahn, dominated by an elegant 16th-century **Schloß** *(Mar–Oct 10–12 and 1–4; Nov–Feb 10–12 and 1–3; adm DM3)* with a large Schloßgarten and fine Baroque church.
Tourist office: Mauerstr. 8, © (06471) 31424.

Wernigerode

Colourful town of brightly painted and richly decorated half-timbered houses in the Harz.
Tourist office: Breite Str. 12, © (03943) 3035.
Hotels/Eating out: Hotel Weißer Hirsch (Markt 5, © 32434; prices under review) also has a good restaurant (DM25–40).

Wiesbaden

Capital of the *Land* of Hesse, though it has long been outstripped in size and importance by neighbouring Frankfurt. A well-to-do spa town, it is still full of grand Wilhelmine architecture from its heyday at the turn of the century.

Tourist office: Hauptbahnhof, ✆ (0611) 172 9781.

Hotels/Eating out: Schwarzer Bock (Kranzplatz 12, ✆ 1550; from DM200) is a 15th-century inn, remodelled at the turn of this century and now a smart hotel. Central (Bahnhofstr. 65, ✆ 372 001; DM100) is a reliable hotel near the station. Domizil (Moritzstr. 52) is a bar which serves inexpensive meals.

Wilhelmshaven

Large, ugly port on the North Sea. Built in the 19th century, rebuilt after the Second World War.

Tourist office: Börsenstr. 55b, ✆ (04421) 25281.

Wismar

Baltic coastal town 30km north of Schwerin. A little run-down, though renovation is underway. Good examples of Hanseatic red-brick architecture and an enormous market square.

Tourist office: Bohrstr. 5a, ✆ (03841) 2958.

Hotels/Eating out: Stadt Wismar (Breite Str. 10, ✆ 2498; DM120) is a functional, central hotel. Alter Schwede (Am Markt 22; DM30–40) is a pleasant tavern with varied menu.

Wittenberg

35km east of Dessau. The town made famous by Martin Luther when he nailed his 95 Theses to the church door and set off the Reformation (*see* p. 41). Inevitably, the monastery where Luther lived (later dissolved and given to him as a home) is now a **museum** *(Tues–Sun 9–5; adm DM4)*. Inside, as well as comprehensive documentation of the reformer's life and work, is an interesting exhibition devoted to the life of Lucas Cranach the Elder (a friend of Luther). Almost next door is the **Melanchthonhaus** *(Mon–Thurs 9–5, Sat and Sun 10–12 and 2–5; adm DM1)* with a display that commemorates the brilliant Melanchthon (Latinized name of Philipp Schwarzend), Luther's closest friend and side-kick, and the true architect of the Augsburg Confession (*see* p. 329). Other sights in town include the Stadtkirche St Marien where Luther was married and where he often preached, and the Schloßkirche where he nailed his Theses to the door (the original doors were destroyed during the Seven Years' War).

Tourist office: Collegienstr. 8, ✆ (038852) 2239.

Hotels/Eating out: Goldener Adler (Markt 7, ☎ 2053; from DM90) is a busy, central hotel. Schloßkeller (☎ 2327; DM30–50) is a good restaurant located in Schloß vaults. Haus des Handwerks (Collegienstr. 53a; DM25–40) offers tasty *gutbürgerliche* cuisine.

Wolfsburg

50km northeast of Brunswick. The original home of Volkswagen. You can tour the factory at Wachla 17, ☎ (04921) 886 2390 *(weekdays at 1.30, registration at 12.30; adm free)*, but there is little else to do in town.

Wolfenbüttel

Small town, a few kilometres south of Brunswick (Braunschweig), with over 600 half-timbered houses. The **Herzog-Augustus-Bibliothek** *(daily 10–5; adm DM5)* is built up around a 130,000-strong collection of books assembled in the 17th-century by the local Welf duke. The collection includes the Gospel Book of Henry the Lion, sold by the Welf family after the Second World War, but bought back in 1983 by the Lower Saxony government for £10 million, making it the world's most expensive book. At present, however, only facsimile pages are on display.
Tourist office: Stadtmarkt 8, ☎ (05331).

Worms

20km north of Mannheim, on the Rhine. Seat of the Imperial Diet which in 1521 issued the Edict of Worms condemning Luther; favourite royal residence (both Charlemagne and Frederick Barbarossa were married here); featuring prominently in the *Nibelungenlied* (this is where Siegfried came to the Burgundian court and where Hagen pitched the Nibelungen treasure into the Rhine); boasting one of the most magnificent **Romanesque cathedrals** along the Rhine. Other sights include a 12th-century synagogue (restored) and the Gothic Liebfrauenkirche which has given its name to the wine produced in the surrounding vineyards (*Liebfraumilch*). Despite an august history Worms is a dreary town of bland shopping malls and small factories.
Tourist office: Neumarkt 14, ☎ (06241) 25 045.
Hotels: Weinhaus Weis (Färbergasse 19, ☎ 23500; from DM90) a small hotel near the cathedral; Wormse Eck (Klosterstr. 80, ☎ 6671; from DM90), south of the centre, plain but comfortable.

Wuppertal

Ruhrgebiet. Home to the famous dance company run by Pina Bausch, and birthplace of Friedrich Engels. There is a small, uninteresting, Engels museum *(Tues–Sun 10–1 and 3–5; adm free)*. The **Von der Heyt Museum** *(Tues 10–9, Wed–Sun 10–5; adm free)* is a better bet with good works by major French Impressionists. The town has a unique overhead railway, built in 1900.
Tourist office: Elberfeld Bahnhof, ☎ (0202) 563 2270.

Zwickau

90km south of Leipzig. Attractive medieval Altstadt. The main church, the Marienkirche, is full of excellent late-Gothic carving. Erstwhile home of the spluttering DDR car, the Trabant. Production ceased in 1990 but the Trabbi and its ancestors are celebrated in the **Automobil-museum** *(Tues and Wed 9–4, Thurs 9–6, Fri 9–2, Sat and Sun 10–2; adm DM1)*. The composer Robert Schumann was born here (though he lived most of his life in Leipzig and Bonn), and you can see displays on his life in an interesting commemorative **museum** *(Tues–Fri 10–5, Sat and Sun 10–12; adm DM2)*.

1000 BC–100 BC	Tribes collectively called the *Germani* settle in the area between the Rhine, the Oder, the Baltic Sea and the Danube, previously inhabited by Celtic tribes.
60 BC–20 BC	Roman invasions. Forts built at Trier, Cologne and Mainz.
9 BC–AD 9	Roman armies extend the empire eastwards to the Elbe, but by AD 9 rebellious local tribes have forced them back to the Rhine.
314	Emperor Constantine introduces Christianity and sets up bishopric at Trier.
4th–5th century	Roman Empire collapses under onslaught of Huns, Vandals and Goths.
481–511	Clovis, King of the Franks, establishes the Frankish Empire under the Merovingian dynasty, after conquering the other German tribes.
From 768	Charlemagne expands the Frankish Empire to include most of Western Europe, and establishes a capital at Aachen. The Carolingian Period.
800	Charlemagne crowned emperor in Rome by the Pope.
814	Death of Charlemagne. The empire is divided among his grandsons. The eastern kingdom—the basis of the future German state—goes to Louis the German.
936–973	Reign of Otto the Great—the Ottonian Period.
1152–1190	Reign of the Hohenstaufen Emperor Frederick Barbarossa—a time of commercial and agricultural prosperity. First use of the term Holy Roman Empire to denote the Germanic realms.
1241	Formation of the Hanseatic League, a trading association of some 200 north German towns—but elsewhere the country is racked by feuds, with little chance of unity.
1356	College of Electors established to elect subsequent Holy Roman Emperors. In practice the crown usually goes to a member of the Hapsburg dynasty, ruling from Vienna.
1386	First German university founded in Heidelberg.
1440	Gutenberg invents the movable-type printing press in Mainz.
Early 16th century	German Renaissance centering on painters such as Dürer, Cranach, Holbein and Grünewald.
1517	Martin Luther nails his 95 Theses to the church door in Wittenberg, and sets off the Reformation.
1524	The Peasants Revolt (fired by Luther's teaching) erupts and is bloodily suppressed.
1555	The Peace of Augsburg establishes religious equality for the Protestant and Roman Catholic faith—but subjects have to assume the faith of their rulers.
1618–48	The Thirty Years' War devastates the country and reduces the population by over one third. The Peace of Westphalia parcels Germany into more than 300 separate states.
1701	Frederick III, Elector of the powerful state of Brandenburg, has himself crowned King Frederick I, and renames his country the Kingdom of Prussia.
1740	Frederick the Great succeeds to the Prussian throne. His 46-year reign is a time of expansion and cultural progress. Berlin becomes a major European capital.
1756	Prussia emerges as a great European power after the Seven Years' War (Prussians and British against Saxons. Austrians, French and Russians).

Chronology

1803	Beginning of Napoleonic Wars. Many Germans initially see Napoleon as a liberator, but later resent French domination.
1807	The French defeat the Prussians.
1815	The Prussians drive out the French. At the Congress of Vienna a loose federation of 39 German states is formed.

1834	Formation of the *Zollverrein* (Customs Union) creating a unified German market.
1835	First railway opens. Germany is becoming increasingly industrialized and a labour movement emerges.
1848	Popular uprisings lead to formation of a National Parliament in Frankfurt, but its powers are hollow.
1862	Bismarck becomes Prime Minister of Prussia.
1866–67	Seven Weeks' War. Prussia defeats Austria, and Bismarck unites the German states (excluding Austria) under the German Confederation.
1867	Karl Marx publishes *Das Kapital* in Hamburg.
1870–71	France declares war on Prussia, but is defeated. The Prussian King Wilhelm I is proclaimed Kaiser (Emperor) of a united Germany. Bismarck is the Chancellor.
1885	Karl Benz in Mannheim and Gottlieb Daimler in Stuttgart simultaneously invent the petrol-powered motor car.
1888	Kaiser Wilhelm II comes to the throne and dismisses Bismarck two years later.
1897	Rudolf Diesel patents his diesel engine in Augsburg.
1914	Assassination of Archduke Franz Ferdinand sparks off the First World War.
1918	Germany defeated. The Kaiser abdicates and the Weimar Republic is declared.
1919	The Treaty of Versailles exacts crippling reparations and reduces German territory by nearly 14 per cent.
1923	Failure of Hitler's Munich *Putsch*.
1929–1933	Unemployment reaches six million (a third of the potential workforce).
1933	Hitler appointed Chancellor. He blames the communists for the Reichstag fire, and suspends democratic and civil rights.
1936	German troops re-occupy the demilitarized Rhineland.
1938	Hitler annexes Austria. At the Munich Agreement Britain, France and Italy agree to German occupation of the Sudetenland in Czechoslovakia.
1939	Germany invades Poland thus starting the Second World War.
1945	Germany is defeated and divided among the Allies into four zones of occupation. Berlin (in the Soviet zone) is similarily divided.
1948–9	The Soviets blockade all land and water routes to Berlin. For 10 months the Western Allies supply their zones by airlifts.
1949	Federal Republic of West Germany and German Democratic Republic of East Germany created. Konrad Adenauer becomes the first Chancellor of West Germany.
1953	Rebellion against Soviets in East Germany is crushed by Russian tanks.
1955	The Federal Republic joins NATO; the GDR becomes a member of the Warsaw Pact.
1957	West Germany signs Treaty of Rome, establishing the European Economic Community.
1961	Erection of the Berlin Wall.
1969	Willi Brandt becomes Chancellor and begins policy of Ostpolitik, easing relations with the GDR.
1971	Erich Honecker succeeds Walter Ulbricht as First Secretary of the Communist Party in the GDR.
1972	Munich Olympic Games. Eleven Israeli athletes are killed by Palestinian guerilas.
1974	Willi Brandt resigns after a spy scandal and is succeeded by Helmut Schmidt.
1983	Helmut Kohl becomes Chancellor. The Greens emerge as a national political force.
1989	Mounting exodus of East Germans to the West after Hungary opens its borders with Austria. The GDR government falls and the Berlin Wall is opened.
1990	Germany officially reunited.

Abtei	abbey
Altstadt	old town—usually the medieval part of the city
Bad	spa town (precedes the name of the town, e.g. Bad Godesberg)
Bahnhof	railway station
Berg	mountain
BRD	German initials for Federal Republic of Germany (West Germany)
Brücke	bridge
Brunnen	fountain, spring, well
Bundes-	federal, hence Bundestag (Federal Parliament)
Burg	castle
Burgermeister	Mayor
DDR	German initials for German Democratic Republic (ex-East Germany)
Denkmal	monument, memorial
Dom	cathedral
Dorf	village
Evangelisch	Protestant
Fachwerk	half-timbered
Fasching, Fastnet	alternative names for Carnival in Bavaria and Swabia
Feiertag	holiday
Feierabend	hometime, used by shop assistants to refuse service 10 minutes before closing.
Festung	fortress
Flughafen	airport
Fluß	river
Funk	radio—hence Funktaxi and Funktelefon are not what might be expected.
Fürst	prince
Gasse	alley
Gastarbeiter	foreign labourers (literally, 'guest worker'). Some have been in Germany for decades, yet even their children are denied citizenship.
Gasthaus/hof	inn, guest house
Graf	count
Hafen	harbour
Hauptbahnhof	main railway station
Hauptstraße	main street
Heide	heath
Heimat	homeland, hometown—capable of releasing waves of sentiment and loyalty
Herzog	duke
Höhle	cave
Hof	court (e.g. of a prince); also courtyard or mansion
Insel	island
Jagdschloß	hunting lodge
Jugendherberge	youth hostel
Jugendstil	German version of *Art Nouveau*, later tending towards Expressionism
Junker	Prussian landed gentry
Kaiser	Emperor
Kammer	room, chamber

Glossary of German Terms

Kapelle	chapel
Karneval	Carnival
Kaufhaus	department store
Kino	cinema

Kirche	church
Kloster	monastery, convent
König	king
Kunst	art
Kurhaus	central clinic of a spa town or health resort
Kurort	health resort
Land	state in the Federal Republic (pl. *Länder*)
Landgrave	count (in charge of an important province)
Margrave	count in charge of a March (frontier district)
Markt	market, market square
Meer	sea
Münster	minster, often used of any large church
Naturpark	protected natural area
Ostpolitik	Willy Brandt's policy of detente with the GDR
Palas/Palast	residential part of a castle
Pfarrkirche	parish church
Platz	square
Prinz	prince, but since 1918 used as a general aristocratic title
Rathaus	town/city hall
Ratskeller	restaurant in cellar below the Rathaus
Reich	empire
Reisebüro	travel agency
Residenz	palace
Ritter	knight
Saal	hall
Sammlung	collection
Schatzkammer	treasury (e.g. of a cathedral)
Schickie-Mickie	yuppie (often shortened to *Schickie*), collectively the *Schickeria*
Schloß	palace, castle
See	lake
Stadt	town, city
Stadthalle	not the city hall (Rathaus), but communal sports/conference hall
Stammtisch	table in a pub or tavern reserved for regulars; invade at your peril
Stift	collegiate church
Strand	beach
Straßenbahn	tram
Tal	valley
Tankstelle	filling station
Tor	gate (usually once part of a medieval wall)
Tracht	traditional costume
Turm	tower, ditto
Verkehrsamt	tourist office; also *Verkehrsverein* or *Fremdenverkehrsamt*
Viertel	quarter, district
Volk	people, folk—soured by Hitler's abuse of the word, but still a powerful concept
Wald	forest
Waldsterben	disease (caused by pollution) which is killing German forests
Wallfahrt	pilgrimage
Wasserburg	castle surrounded by water (usually more than just a moat)
Wende	(literally: 'the turn' or 'the change')—the term describes the 1989 revolution and subsequent reunification of Germany
Zeughaus	arsenal
Zimmer	room

German has never enjoyed a particularly good press. Holy Roman Emperor Charles V considered it as fit only for speaking to his horse. Mark Twain sends it up wickedly in his essay *On the Awful German Language*, and the narrator of Anthony Burgess's novel *Earthly Powers* calls it 'a glottal fishboneclearing soulful sobbing sausagemachine of a language'.

It is a language of devilish complexity. There are three, rather than two, genders; nouns *and* adjectives decline; it is full of irregular verbs and deceptive conjugations; and the syntax is ornate, and often littered with parentheses that lead the inexperienced astray. The verb often comes only at the *end* of one of these arduous syntactical journeys. *Punch* once carried a cartoon of 'The Man who Died of Boredom while Waiting for a German Verb to Arrive'. More recently, simultaneous interpreters at an international conference were struck dumb during one long, impassioned outburst by a German delegate, as they too awaited the elusive particle. (All one section of the audience heard through their headphones was 'I missed the bloody verb').

But there are some advantages. Nouns are capitalized and easy to spot. This helps you to make some sense of written passages, even if your knowledge of German is scanty. Spelling is phonetical, so once you have grasped the basics of pronunciation there are few surprises. German is a precise language. Numbers of words can be combined into a single new one that hits the nail right on the head (such as *Mitbürger*—literally 'with-citizen'—a foreign permanent resident). Sometimes, though, this gets out of hand. 'These things are not words,' lamented Mark Twain, 'they are alphabetical processions'.

Pronunciation

Consonants: Most are the same as in English. There are no silent letters. *g*s are hard, as in English 'good', but *ch* is a guttural sound, as in the Scottish 'loch'—though *sch* is said as 'sh'. *s* is also pronounced 'sh', when it appears before a consonant (especially at the beginning of a word), as in *stein*, pronounced 'shtine'. Otherwise the sound is closer to 'z'. *z* is pronounced 'ts' and *d* at the end of the word becomes 't'. *r*s are rolled at the back of the throat, as in French. *v* is pronounced somewhere between the English 'f' and 'v', and *w* is said as the English 'v'.

Vowels: *a* can be long (as in 'father') or short, like the 'u' in 'hut'. Similarly *u* can be short, as in 'put', or long, as in 'boot'. *e* is pronounced at the end of words, and is slightly longer than in English. Say *er* as in 'hair' and *ee* as in 'hay'. Say *ai* as in 'pie'; *au* as in 'house'; *ie* as in 'glee'; *ei* like 'eye' and *eu* as in 'oil'. An **umlaut** (¨) changes the pronunciation of a word. Say *ä* like the 'e' in 'bet', or like the 'a' in 'label'. Say *ö* like the vowel sound in 'fur'. *ü* is a very short version of the vowel sound in 'true'. Sometimes an umlaut is replaced by an *e* after the vowel. The printed symbol *ß* is sometimes written *ss*, and is pronounced as a double 's'.

Here are some practice sentences:

Verstehen Sie Deutsch?	*fairshtayen zee doitch?*	(Do you understand German?)
Nein, ich verstehe kein Wort.	*nine, ich fairshtay kine vort*	(No, I don't understand a word)
Haben Sie Zimmer frei?	*haben zee tsimmer fry?*	(Do you have any rooms free?)

Language

The standard of English in West Germany is pretty good—though restaurants off the tourist track seldom have an English menu. Before reunification the second language in East Germany was Russian. English is rapidly filling the gap, but you are advised to go armed with essential German phrases.

Useful Words and Phrases

yes/no/maybe		*ja/nein/vielleicht*
excuse me		*Entschuldigung, bitte*
it doesn't matter		*es macht nichts*
I am sorry		*es tut mir leid*
please		*bitte*
thank you	(very much)	*danke(schön)*
it's a pleasure		*bitte(schön)*
hello		*guten Tag; hallo*
hello (in Bavaria)		*grüß Gott*
goodbye/bye		*auf Wiedersehen; tschüss*
good morning/evening		*guten Morgen/Abend*
good night		*guten Nacht*
how are you?	(formal)	*wie geht es Ihnen?*
	(informal)	*wie geht es Dir?* or *wie geht's?*
I'm very well		*mir geht's gut*
I don't speak German		*ich spreche kein Deutsch*
do you speak English?		*sprechen Sie Englisch?*
I don't know		*ich weiß nicht*
I don't understand		*ich verstehe nicht*
how do you say...		*wie sagt man...*
my name is...		*mein Name ist... ; ich heisse...*
I am...	English (man)	*ich bin Engländer*
I am...	English (woman)	*ich bin Engländerin*
	American	*Amerikaner(in)*
	Australian	*Australier(in)*
	Canadian	*Kanadier(in)*
	a New Zealander	*Neuseeländer(in)*
I come from...	England	*ich komme aus England*
	Scotland	*Schottland*
	Ireland	*Irland*
	Wales	*Wales*
	the United States	*den Vereinigten Staaten*
	Canada	*Kanada*
	Australia	*Australien*
	New Zealand	*Neuseeland*
leave me alone		*lass mich in Ruhe*
with/without		*mit/ohne*
and/but		*und/aber*
is this table free?		*ist der Tisch frei?*
the menu please		*die Speisekarte bitte*
the bill please		*die Rechnung bitte*
I would like...		*ich möchte...*
how much does this cost?		*wieviel kostet es?*
cheap/expensive		*billig/teuer*
where is/are...?		*wo ist/sind...?*
who		*wer*
what		*was*
why		*warum*
when		*wann*

how do I get to...	(town)		*wie komme ich nach...*
	(building or place)		*wie komme ich zur/zum...*
how far is it to...			*wie weit ist es nach...*
how long does it take?			*wie lange dauert es?*
near/far			*nah/weit*
left/right/straight on			*links/rechts/gerade aus*
help!			*hilfe!*
can you help me?			*konnen Sie mir bitte helfen?*
I am ill			*ich bin krank*
I am lost			*ich weiß nicht, wo ich bin*
I am hungry			*ich habe Hunger*
I am thirsty			*ich habe Durst*
I am hot			*mir ist warm*
I am cold			*mir ist kalt*

Notices and Signs

open/closed	*geöffnet/*	hospital	*Krankenhaus*
	geschlossen	pharmacy	*Apotheke*
closed (literally: rest day)	*Ruhetag*	post office	*Post*
no entry	*eingang verboten*	airport	*Flughafen*
(emergency) exit	*(Not) ausgang*	customs	*Zoll*
entrance	*Eingang*	railway station	*Bahnhof*
toilet	*Toilette*	train	*Zug*
Ladies/Gents	*Damen/Herren*	platform	*Gleis*
bathroom	*Badezimmer*	reserved	*besetzt*
push/pull	*drücken/ziehen*	rooms to let	*Fremdenzimmer*
bank	*Bank*	pedestrian zone	*Fußgängerzone*
bureau de change	*Wechselstube*	picnic area	*Rastplatz*
police	*Polizei*	way round/circuit	*Rundgang*

Days and Months

Monday	*Montag*	March	*März*
Tuesday	*Dienstag*	April	*April*
Wednesday	*Mittwoch*	May	*Mai*
Thursday	*Donnerstag*	June	*Juni*
Friday	*Freitag*	July	*Juli*
Saturday	*Samstag*	August	*August*
(northern Germany)	*Sonnabend*	September	*September*
Sunday	*Sonntag*	October	*Oktober*
January	*Januar*	November	*November*
February	*Februar*	December	*Dezember*

Numbers

one	*eins*	seven	*sieben*
two	*zwei*	eight	*acht*
three	*drei*	nine	*neun*
four	*vier*	ten	*zehn*
five	*fünf*	eleven	*elf*
six	*sechs*	twelve	*zwölf*

thirteen	*dreizehn*	ninety	*neunzig*
fourteen	*vierzehn*	hundred	*hundert*
seventeen	*siebzehn*	hundred and one	*hunderteins*
twenty	*zwanzig*	hundred and forty-two	*hundertzweiundvierzig*
twenty-one	*einundzwanzig*	two hundred	*zweihundert*
twenty-two	*zweiundzwanzig*	thousand	*tausend*
thirty	*dreissig*	three thousand	*dreitausend*
forty	*vierzig*	million	*eine Million*
fifty	*fünfzig*	billion (thousand million)	*eine Milliarde*
sixty	*sechszig*	billion (million million)	*eine Billion*
seventy	*siebzig*	1994	*neunzehnhundert-*
eighty	*achtzig*		*vierundneunzig*

Time

watch/clock/hour	*Uhr*	month	*Monat*
alarm clock	*Wecker*	year	*Jahr*
what is the time?	*wie spät ist es?*	season	*Jahreszeit*
one/two o'clock	*eine/zwei Uhr*	spring	*Frühling*
quarter-past two	*Viertel nach zwei*	summer	*Sommer*
half-past two	*halbdrei*	autumn	*Herbst*
half-past three	*halbvier*	winter	*Winter*
quarter to three	*Viertel vor drei*	century	*Jahrhundert*
morning	*Morgen; Vormittag*	today/yesterday/	*heute/gestern/*
afternoon	*Nachmittag*	tomorrow	*morgen*
evening	*Abend*	this/last/next week	*diese/letzte/nächste*
night	*Nacht*		*Woche*
week	*Woche*		

Driving

car hire	*Autovermietung*	parking place	*Parkplatz*
filling station	*Tankstelle*	no parking	*Parken verboten*
petrol/diesel	*Benzin/Diesel*	driver's licence	*Führerschein*
leaded/unleaded	*verbleit/bleifrei*	insurance	*Versicherung*
my car has	*mein Auto hat*	one-way street	*Einbahnstaße*
broken down	*Panne*	except	*außer*
accident	*Autounfall*	(on no-entry signs)	
garage (for repairs)	*Autowerkstatt*	get in correct lane	*einordnen*

Food and Drink

breakfast	*Frühstuck*	glass	*Glas*
lunch	*Mittagessen*	bottle	*Flasche*
dinner	*Abendessen*	salt/pepper	*Salz/Pfeffer*
supper	*Abendbrot*	milk/sugar	*Milch/Zucker*
menu	*Speisekarte*	bread/butter	*Brot/Butter*
bon appétit	*guten Appetit*	filled roll	*belegtes Brotchen*
cup	*Tasse*	mustard	*Senf*
pot (e.g. of coffee)	*Kännchen*	home-made	*hausgemacht*

à la	*Art*	prawns	*Garnalen*
fresh	*frisch*	mussels	*Muscheln*
boiled	*gekocht*	clams	*Venusmuscheln*
steamed	*gedämpft*	squid	*Tintenfisch*
baked	*gebacken*	eel	*Aal*
roasted	*gebraten*	vegetables	*Gemüse*
smoked	*geräuchert*	salad	*Salat*
stuffed	*gefüllt*	tomatoes	*Tomaten*
stew/casserole	*Topf; Eintopf*	cucumber	*Gurke*
starters	*Vorspeise*	peppers/capsicums	*Paprika*
soup	*Suppe*	onions	*Zwiebeln*
main course	*Hauptgericht*	garlic	*Knoblauch*
meat	*Fleisch*	chives	*Schnittlauch*
sausage	*Wurst*	herbs	*Kraute*
ham	*Schinken*	jacket potatoes	*Pellkartoffeln*
cold cuts	*Aufschnitt*	mashed potatoes	*Kartoffelbrei*
pork	*Schweinefleisch*	chips	*Pommes frites*
knuckle of pork	*Schweinehaxe*	boiled potatoes	*Salzkartoffeln*
bacon	*Speck*	rice	*Reis*
beef	*Rindfleisch*	beans	*Bohnen*
lamb	*Lammfleisch*	(red) cabbage	*(Rot) kohl*
veal	*Kalbfleisch*	mushrooms	*Pilze, Champignons*
oxtail	*Ochsenschwanz*	maize	*Mais*
hare	*Hase*	peas	*Erbsen*
rabbit	*Kanninchen*	cauliflower	*Blumenkohl*
liver	*Leber*	spinach	*Spinat*
game	*Wild*	leeks	*Lauch*
venison	*Hirsch, Reh*	lentils	*Linsen*
ham	*Schinken*	chickpeas	*Kichererbsen*
mincemeat	*Hackfleisch*	dumplings	*Knödel; Klösse*
steak	*steak*	asparagus	*Spargel*
meatball	*Boulette*	aubergine	*Aubergine*
chop	*Kottolett, Schnitzel*	dessert	*Nachtisch*
poultry	*Geflügel*	tart/cake	*Torte/Kuchen*
chicken	*Huhn; Hähnchen*	ice-cream	*Eis*
duck	*Ente*	(whipped) cream	*(Schlag) sahne*
turkey	*Truthahn; Puter*	nuts	*Nüße*
goose	*Gans*	almonds	*Mandeln*
fish	*Fische*	chocolate	*Schokolade*
trout	*Forelle*	cheese	*Käse*
carp	*Karpfen*	fruit	*Obst*
salmon	*Lachs*	apple	*Apfel*
haddock	*Schellfisch*	orange	*Apfelsine; Orange*
perch	*Zander*	lemon	*Zitrone*
pike	*Hecht*	grapefruit	*Pampelmuse*
cod	*Kabeljau*	banana	*Banane*
sole	*Seezunge*	pineapple	*Ananas*
flounder	*Butt*	pear	*Birne*
plaice	*Scholle*	cherry	*Kirsche*
herring	*Hering, Matjes*	peach	*Pfirsich*
tuna	*Thunfisch*	plum	*Pflaume*
lobster	*Hummer*	grapes	*Trauben*

raisins	*Rosinen*	(mineral) water	*(Mineral) wasser*
raspberry	*Himbeer*	fruit juice	*Saft*
strawberry	*Erdbeer*	beer	*Bier*
redcurrant	*Johannisbeer*	red/white wine	*Rotwein/Weißwein*
drinks	*Getränke*	brandy	*Brandwein*

Menu Reader

Aal	Eel—popular in the north. Served smoked or *grün*, cooked in creamy herb sauce
Aalsuppe	Soup made with eel, plums and vegetables (Hamburg)
Bauernfrühstück	Literally 'peasant breakfast'—ham, egg and potatoes—or any large, hot breakfast
Bohnensuppe	Thick bean soup
Brägenwurst	Sausage made with brains
Braunkohl	Kale
Bratwurst	Grilled sausage (usually pork)
Eisbein	Boiled knuckle of pork
Eintopf/Topf	Stew, casserole or thick soup
Festessen	Ham, sauerkraut and pease pudding (Hunsrück)
Flädlesuppe	Soup with strips of pancake cut into it
Forelle	Trout
Gaisburger Marsch	Thick beef soup with noodles and potatoes
Grünkohl	Cabbage
Gulaschsuppe	Thick, peppery beef soup
Halbes Hähnchen	Half a chicken (grilled)
Halver Hahn	Cheese and rye sandwich (Cologne)
Handkäse	Hand-pressed curd cheese (Hessen)
Himmel und Erde	Blood sausage, potatoes and apple purée (Rhineland)
Heidschnukenbraten	Roast lamb from the Lüneburg Heath
Kasseler Rippchen	Pickled loin of pork (named after a Berlin butcher called Kassel, not the town)
Kohl und Pinkel	Cabbage and various pork cuts (*see* p. 546)—northern winter favourite
Labskaus	Corned beef, herring, beetroot, potato and a fried egg (North Germany)
Leberknödel	Doughy bake of minced meat and smoked bacon
Leberknödel	Liver dumplings
Maultaschen	Giant ravioli, stuffed with meat and usually spinach too (Baden)
Mettwurst	Pork and beef sausages
Mehlpüt	Pear and butter sauce dessert
Pfefferpotthast	Spicy boiled beef
Pumpernickel	Dark rye bread
Puffbohnen mit Speck	Broad beans and bacon (Saxony)
Reibekuchen	Potato cakes
Sauerkraut	Pickled cabbage
Sauerbraten	Braised pickled beef (Rhineland)
Schlachtplatte	Platter of various meats, usually including blood sausage and offal
Schweinshaxe	Roast knuckle of pork
Schweinepfeffer	Jugged pork
Semmelknödeln	Bread dumplings
Spargel	Asparagus
Spätzle	Noodles
Speckkuchen	Substantial bacon quiche
Weißwurst	Veal and pork sausage, sometimes with brain (Bavaria)
Zünger	Pig's tongue (Bavaria)
Zwiebelbraten	Beef in brown onion sauce

History/General

Fulbrook, Mary, *A Concise History of Germany* (C.U.P 1990). By far the most compact and accessible account of German history—from murky beginnings to the 1989 revolution.

Mann, Golo, *The History of Germany since 1789* (Penguin). Hefty tome, but a good read. Insider's account of the paradoxes of the nation—in history, philosophy and art—ending just after the Second World War.

Tacitus, *The Germania* (Penguin). Amusing, perceptive and at times delightfully personal account of the Germanic tribes knocking about in Roman times.

Einhard and Notker the Stammerer, *Two Lives of Charlemagne* (Penguin). Einhard was a courtier of the great Charlemagne, and Notker was tutor to one of the emperor's descendants a century later. Both biographies are full of anecdote and revealing personal detail.

Chadwick, Owen, *The Reformation* (Pelican). Solid standard work on one of the most important events in European history.

Bainton, Ronald, *Here I Stand* (Lion). Biography of Martin Luther—a livelier introduction to the Reformation than Chadwick's book.

Wedgwood, C.V., *The Thirty Years War* (Methuen). Account of the devastating 17th-century conflict.

Duffy, Christopher, *Frederick the Great: A Military Life* (RKP). Good biography of another of the nation's great movers and shakers.

Taylor, A.J.P., *Bismarck: The Man and the Statesman* (Hamish Hamilton 1955). Characteristically controversial portrait of the 19th-century architect of German unification.

Blunt, Wilfred, *The Dream King* (Hamish Hamilton 1970). Thorough, if pompous, biography of Ludwig II, builder of fairytale castles and patron of Richard Wagner.

Willet, John, *The Weimar Republic* (Unwin & Hyman) and *The New Sobriety* (Thames & Hudson). Meticulously researched and well-written studies of the art and politics of the ill-fated republic.

Bullock, Alan, *Hitler: A Study in Tyranny* (Pelican). Classic biography of the *Führer.*

Shirer, William, *The Rise and Fall of the Third Reich.* Massive; a good complement to Bullock's biography.

Bielenberg, Christabel, *The Past is Myself* (Corgi). Moving personal account of Nazi Germany before and during the war by the British wife of a German lawyer and resistance fighter.

Ardagh, John, *Germany and the Germans* (Penguin). Detailed, unbiased and up-to-date view.

Craig, Gordon, *The Germans* (Penguin). Another excellent introduction to a complex people.

Wallraff, Günther, *Lowest of the Low* (Methuen). Wallraff disguised himself as a *Gastarbeiter* for two years, and the mistreatment he uncovered caused a scandal—but he was later accused of fabricating evidence.

Art and Architecture

Good books on specific periods to dip into are:

Albrecht Dürer: The Complete Woodcuts and *The Complete Etchings, Engravings and Drypoints* (Dover). Excellent record of the work of one of the world's greatest graphic artists.

Baxendall, Michael, *The Limewood Sculptors of Renaissance Germany,* (Yale University Press). Superb study of Tilman Riemenschneider, Veit Stoss and their ilk.

Vaughan, William, *German Romantic Painting* (Yale University Press 1980). Good introduction to the country's most popular art movement.

Dube, Wolf-Dieter, *The Expressionists* (Thames & Hudson). Thorough introduction to the 20th-century school of German art that made most impact on the rest of Europe.

Whiteford, Frank, *Bauhaus* (Thames & Hudson). History of the influential school of architecture and design.

Further Reading

Travel Books and Guides

Russell, John, *A Tour in Germany* (1825). Ironic and hilarious, packed with prejudiced diatribes.

Twain, Mark, *A Tramp Abroad* (Century Hutchinson). Wicked, witty account of a west German tour.

Baedecker, Karl, *The Rhineland, Northern Germany, Southern Germany* and *Berlin*. These learned early 20th-century guides (not their present-day descendents) are classics of their kind, and are still worth a read.

Heine, Heinrich, *A Winter's Tale* (Angel). Narrative poem of the writer's journey from Paris to Hamburg in the mid-19th century. Evocative, with acerbic comments on contemporary German life.

Leigh Fermor, Patrick, *A Time of Gifts* (Penguin). Written 40 years after the author's walk, in 1933/4, from Rotterdam to Constantinople. Luscious prose; combines youthful adventure and retrospective analysis.

Gumbel, Andrew, *Berlin*, (Cadogan Books). Cadogan's indispensable companion for a longer stay in Berlin.

Fiction in English

Jerome, Jerome K., *Three Men on the Bummel* (Penguin). Story of a cycling trip through Germany at the turn of the century. Not quite as successful as its forerunner, *Three Men in a Boat*.

Mansfield, Katherine, *In a German Pension* (Penguin). Funny, sometimes cruel, early stories.

Isherwood, Christopher, *Goodbye to Berlin* (Methuen). The short stories about Weimar Berlin that later became the play *I am a Camera* and the musical *Cabaret*.

Walker, Ian, *Zoo Station* (Abacus). Perceptive view of life in 1980s Berlin.

German Literary Landmarks

Grimmelhausen, Johann Jacob Christoffel von, *Simplicius Simplicissimus* (Dedalus). Epic novel written and set in the early 17th century, and one of the most important German works of its time.

Goethe, Johann Wolfgang von, *The Sorrows of Young Werther* (Penguin). Novella that was the first to deal directly with suicide. *Selected Verse* (Penguin). *Faust Part One, Faust Part Two* (Penguin). Goethe's life work, and arguably the supreme achievement of German literature. In this version, the essentially good Faust strays into a pact with the devil because he is impatient with the limitations of traditional learning.

Hoffmann, Ernst Theodor Amadeus, *Tales of Hoffmann* (Penguin). Nightmarish and bizarre tales by a sad, schizophrenic writer of fantasy.

Kleist, Heinrich von, *The Marquise of O and Other Stories* (Penguin). Tales from Germany's other great master of the short story.

Heine, Heinrich, *Complete Poems* (OUP). Energetic, critical poems that have been well translated.

Hölderlin, Friedrich, *Selected Verse* (Anvil). Vivid, formal verse that trails a wake of defeated translators.

Schiller, Friedrich, *The Robbers, Wallenstein* and *William Tell* (Penguin). Core works of Germany's most respected dramatist after Goethe.

Büchner, Georg, *Complete Plays* (Methuen). The author died at the age of 23, but *Danton's Death* and the unfinished *Woyzeck* alone have established Büchner's position on the world literary stage.

Fontane, Theodor, *Before the Storm* (OUP). Set in Prussia during the Napoleonic Wars, and regarded by many as the greatest novel to emerge from the 19th century.

Mann, Thomas, *Buddenbrooks* (Penguin). Charts the decline of a merchant dynasty in the author's native Lübeck. *The Magic Mountain* (Penguin). An allegory of European society, set in a Swiss sanatorium.

Hesse, Hermann, *Narziss and Goldmund* (Penguin). Picaresque, some say homo-erotic, novel set in a medieval monastery. *The Glass Bead Game* (Picador). Difficult but rewarding novel about an élite group which develops a game that creates order out of the world's conflicts.

Remarque, Erich Maria, *All Quiet on the Western Front* (Picador). Classic novel of the First World War.

Brecht, Bertolt, *Poems* and *Plays* (Eyre Methuen). The influential 20th-century dramatist also wrote fine poetry, which has been sensitively translated.

Grass, Günther, *The Tin Drum* (Picador). Gripping and fantastical novel about the curious Oskar, whose scream can shatter glass. A candid examination of German guilt and responsibility for Nazism.

Böll, Heinrich, *The Lost Honour of Katharina Blum* (Penguin). A young woman's life is destroyed by the tabloid press and her accidental involvement with a terrorist. Top-seller from popular post-war novelist.

Notes
Italicised page numbers indicate maps; places mentioned on only two or three pages do not generally have all buildings listed; there are no sub-entries for history and travel (at the beginning of entry for each place) or accommodation, eating out and entertainment (at the end of each section).

648   *Index*